Daughters and Fathers

John Singer Sargent, *The Sitwell Family Portrait* (1900)

Daughters and Fathers

EDITED BY

Lynda E. Boose

AND

Betty S. Flowers

THE JOHNS HOPKINS
UNIVERSITY PRESS

BALTIMORE AND
LONDON

© 1989 The Johns Hopkins University Press

All rights reserved
Printed in the United States of America

The Johns Hopkins University Press, 701 West 40th Street,
Baltimore, Maryland 21211
The Johns Hopkins Press Ltd., London

The paper used in this publication meets the minimum requirements
of American National Standard for Information Sciences—Permanence
of Paper for Printed Library Materials, ANSI Z39.48-1984.

The frontispiece is reproduced from *The Sitwell Family Portrait,* by John Singer Sargent
and is used by permission of the Trustee of Mr. S. Reresby Sitwell's Settlement and the
Royal Academy of Arts, London.
The epigraph beginning Part 2 is from Louise Glück, *Dedication to Hunger,* and is used
with the permission of the author. The epigraph beginning Part 3 is from *Inanna,* by
Diane Wolkstein and Samuel Noah Kramer. Copyright © 1983 by Diane Wolkstein and
Samuel Noah Kramer. Reprinted by permission of Harper & Row Publishers, Inc.

LIBRARY OF CONGRESS CATALOGING-IN-PUBLICATION DATA
Daughters and fathers.
1. Fathers and daughters.   I. Boose, Lynda E., 1943–   .   II. Flowers, Betty S.
HQ755.85.D38 1988   306.8′742   88-45407
ISBN 0-8018-3665-4 (alk. paper)
ISBN 0-8018-3666-2 (pbk.: alk. paper)

Contents

CONTENTS

III. *In Nomine Filiae:* The Artist as Her Father's Daughter

Acknowledgments

WITH GREAT APPRECIATION we wish to acknowledge the following individuals and institutions. Keith Byerman, Carol Christ, Julie Crittenden, Marianne Hirsch, Kathy Jackson, David Kastan, Jane Marcus, Ned Perrin, Donald Reiman, Peter Saccior, Claire Sprague, Pam Weinburger, and Melissa Zeiger made numerous contributions to the ideas within this book and to the idea of the book, from its inception. The National Museum of Women in the Arts and especially Krystyna Wasserman, Librarian of the National Museum of Women in the Arts, Liana Cheney of Lowell Art Institute, Carol Zemel, Department of Art History, SUNY Buffalo, Barbara E. Reed and staff at the Sherman Art Library, Dartmouth College, David Smith, Department of Art History, University of New Hampshire, Dan Larsen, the Embassy of Denmark, Washington, D.C., and Walter Liedtke, Curator of European Art, Metropolitan Museum of Art, New York, gave suggestions and assistance in locating the various paintings included. Joanne Allen, Sara Jackson, Sarah Lyons, and Karen McCormick labored diligently on the bibliography, mechanics, and format of this book. Dartmouth College and the University of Texas Research Institute supplied faculty research grants that made completion of the project possible.

Daughters and Fathers

Introduction

THE REVELATION of something that in retrospect seems obvious impels the question, Why, *until* now, has so self-evident a phenomenon escaped collective comment? Behind our decision to produce this collection lies just such a question about a cultural phenomenon that, once articulated, seems just that obvious: the silence that historically has enveloped the subject foregrounded by *Daughters and Fathers*. Yet while the territory of daughter and father is a discourse that stands virtually unmapped, it is hardly a space that could be called unmarked. The relatively dark discursive terrain that this family relationship occupies has been written all over by tacit injunctions that have forbidden its charting.

Quite literally, the impetus for the anthology grew out of the interest expressed by the volume of mail received after the May 1982 *PMLA* publication of Lynda E. Boose's "The Father and the Bride in Shakespeare." The letters came almost equally from women and men, those from men often including the personal notation that the writer was himself the father of a daughter. Almost universally, the letters commented, often wistfully, on how rare it was to see any analytical discussion of fathers and daughters. But there were two letters in particular— one implicitly and the other overtly hostile—to which the genesis of this book is, ironically, probably most indebted. To read these two letters was like suddenly confronting the invisible commandments that demarcate the father-daughter territory and prohibit discursive entrance into it. One, sent by a woman scholar, though polite in tone, was written to insist that Cordelia's eventual return to King Lear dramatized a daughter's proper loyalties, and her death, a condign punishment for having initially given "nothing" to a request that Cordelia recognizes as a thinly veiled paternal commandment "to love her father all." The other, from a male academic, though strikingly unacademic in tone, was, by self-description, a "first strike aggression" against a "member of the henhouse" who should have dared to interrogate the demands made of daughters by such Shakespearean fathers as Lear, Capulet, Brabantio, and others. That a woman critic should even be writing on Shakespeare, let alone on Shakespearean fathers, suggested to this writer some kind of frightening displacement of patriarchal hegemony within the academy that was equivalent to the one that Regan and Goneril enact when they

1

push both of the play's fathers out of doors, unaccommodated, to face the unkind elements. The first of these letters had read the clash between daughter and father in *King Lear* strictly in domestic, familial terms. The other had read that contestation as an implicit anagram of the relationship between women and the outer world of cultural power.

If *culture* is taken in Clifford Geertz's sense to mean the structures of meaning through which people give shape to their experience (*Culture* 312), and if those structures are themselves understood as an assemblage of texts, or "imaginative works built out of social materials" (449), then the erasure of a topic that is transparent in such texts hints at an ambivalence about or threat attached to what has been left out. Attempting to "read" that absence, to illuminate what is *not* included in the cultural text, becomes a crucial way of understanding what the culture has mapped by its very attempts to circumnavigate. Furthermore, it becomes a way of demystifying the scripts that we ourselves, as cultural actors, unwittingly reproduce.

It says something telling for example, that of the possible structural permutations of parent-child relationships inscribed in our literary, mythic, historical, and psychoanalytic texts, the father and son are the first pair most frequently in focus, and the mother and son the second. It says perhaps even more that within these priorities, only in the mother-son narrative has there been a repeated emphasis on the question of good parenting. As journalist Eileen Fairweather comments, "Our culture is top-heavy with images . . . about what constitutes good *mothering;* our concept of good fathering is almost nonexistent"(201). Of all of the binary sets through which we familiarly consider family relationships, the mother-daughter and father-daughter pairs have received the least attention, a heirarchy of value that isolates the daughter as the most absent member within the discourse of the family institution. In the 1970s, as the feminist movement began to reposition women as subjects, the ongoing search to reclaim a lost heritage of personal and cultural models concurrently thrust the mother-daughter relationship into new discursive prominence. The narrative of father and daughter, however, remained wrapped in its tacitly agreed-upon invisibility until a very few years ago, when all at once it began to surface in formats as various as scholarly journals, sociological and psychoanalytic studies, women's magazines, popular fiction, autobiographical essays, and commercial television—a phenomenon of sudden emergence that makes it equally relevant to consider not only what accounts for the historic erasure of a subject but also what cultural signals suddenly authorize its articulation.

Before the daughter-father relationship can be isolated as a separate subject, it first needs to be positioned as a part of the massive intellectual debate that Western humanities and social sciences scholarship has been engaged in since approximately the early 1970s over the structure, history, and literary/visual representations as well as the psychosocial, philosophical, religious, and political implications of "the family"—an ideal that has, in the wake of this debate, been deconstructively placed into question to such an extent that by now the term itself probably calls for quotation marks. Protected by an ideology that had culturally positioned it as a divinely ordained feature of human sociobiology, the family had enjoyed a relatively unproblematized intellectual history in the West, disturbed early in the twentieth century only by such voices as those of Freud and Engels. Then suddenly, over the past decade and a half, its structural dynamics, its psychodynamics, and, eventually, its political construction have been subjected to a series of revisionist studies that have turned the family into perhaps the primary subject at risk in Western scholarship. Rather than a natural, essential, transhistorical entity, the family has been recharacterized as a thoroughly cultural production, an entity whose capacity for biological reproduction has masked recognition of its monumental historical importance as a site for ideological reproduction. When we think about the family, what we have is never anything that can rightly be identified as "the family" so much as a *discourse about* such a construction. In examining the family, therefore, although we may recognize the modeled norm as being less an empirical description than an ideological prescription, so coercive is the ideology that is everywhere present in the culture's dominant discourse that despite what "real" families look like or act like, the ideological prescription determines the expectations against which the society descriptively measures its real families and readers measure literary representations of them.

Therefore, since this collection is focused on the literature produced by the British-American tradition of Western culture, the majority of essays in *Daughters and Fathers* have assumed and foregrounded that one construction that singularly defines the family within Anglo-American dominant discourse: the so-called nuclear group. Although precisely when this model achieved its absolute status is still the subject of intense debate among European historians, the nuclear group first appears in the Hebrew bible and is thus embedded in the religious as well as the political history of the West. In Europe, by the sixteenth or seventeenth century, if not earlier, the nuclear family had clearly emerged to dominate the wider kinship (clan) arrangement in which it had previously been contained (see Ariès; Flandrin; Hanawalt; and Stone). Eventually, the paradigm comes to dominate Western thought so pervasively as almost to preempt even imagining any arrangement other than its familiar, four-cornered configuration. The ideology upon which this model is predicated—and which it, in turn, structurally ensures in the culture as a

3

whole by reproducing it inside the family unit—is closed, hierarchical, patronymic, and patriarchal.

While the recent explosion of family scholarship has been invaluable in probing the political implications behind early modern Europe's empowerment of a centralized, absolute monarchy through its ideological promotion of the patriarchal nuclear family, the work has often unconsciously tended to reflect the same patriarchal bias of the historical institution in question. Effectively, scholarship reproduces the model it critiques when it contains, for instance, such unrecognized assumptions as that which assumes that children somehow all belong to the same (i.e., male) sex and are socially constructed by the same (i.e., masculine) impositions of gender. That women still tend to get pushed to the margins of the investigation is, most especially at this particular historical moment, doubly ironic. Not only does such a marginalization repeat the politics of the history it investigates but it does so despite the fact that contemporary commitment to family issues probably owes more to the feminist challenge to family constitution than to any other factor. Nonetheless, even in the late 1970s, when historian Christopher Hill noticed the sudden prominence of family scholarship in historical studies and intuitively recognized that its initiating impetus lay outside the academic center, his comment that "the family as an institution rather suddenly became fashionable, perhaps as a by-product of the women's liberation movement" ("Sex, Marriage, and the Family" 450), is couched in wording so dismissive as effectively to trivialize even his own insight. Perhaps the key ingredient that revisioning the inherited family discourse depended upon was the acquisition of a metadiscourse capable of recognizing and anatomizing the gender system upon which the ideology of family had been constituted. Rather than being "perhaps . . . a by-product," the discursive impetus that enabled the current reexamination of family should be accurately positioned as a fully conscious, political product of feminist academic scholarship.

While the feminist challenge is undoubtedly the most significant determinant in the late twentieth century's questioning of its inherited family mythology, obviously there are other important factors. In America, much of this research seems to have been, whether consciously or not, itself a progressively political response to a topic whose thoroughly political nature became increasingly recognized. The current American initiative to query the nuclear configuration arguably goes back to the social experiments of the 1960s, reemerging into the scholarship of the seventies and eighties as both a product of and a reaction to a national political scene in which perceived threat to the so-called traditional family had prompted a conservative reaction that had made "Saving the Family" the most heatedly political, undisguisedly ideological of publicly debated topics. It was, in any case, within the milieu of sociopolitical contestation outside the academy that scholars within it began asking new questions and pressing for a newly demystified discourse of the history of this institution. This new discourse shifted attention away from the aesthetics of representation and refocused it to include the politics: it compelled the recognition that representations of the family, perhaps especially literary ones, are ideological vehicles. And they are so because they re-present and thus reproduce a model that, in the act of transmission, is either being reified or reformulated, affirmed or challenged—yet a model that, through formulation, is nonetheless being tacitly assumed. Nor can the literary critic imagine herself or himself to stand outside of such political considerations; for it is not only the author but also the critic who re-presents, and thus participates in the politics of literary representation. Incipiently, by choosing to foreground the daughter-father material and read a given text through those dynamics, the contributors to *Daughters and Fathers* have themselves ineluctably entered into the representing of the problematic and culturally suppressed topic that this collection places into scrutiny.

Taken collectively, the essays in this book inscribe the same contradictory assumptions about the nature of family that mark the debate within the wider scholarly discourse. Sometimes the family and the relationships within it are essentialized and appear as transhistorical, psychological verities; at other times family relationships and psychoanalytical definitions of them are historicized and occur as products of historically specific modes of social production. In short, the jury is still out, and as yet there is no consensus on precisely how this entity, the nuclear family, should be understood. If there are no answers, there are nonetheless underlying questions, the more important of which involve the extent to which nature or nurture is seen as shaping the constitution of gender, the internal relationships, and the positional distributions of power within the family; and the extent to which the historical and mythic paradigms of the family are seen as having ever undergone—or being themselves even capable of accommodating—anything like the self-transformation that repeatedly emerges, in this collection and elsewhere, as the implicit desire energizing so much of the contemporary dialogue on the family. These questions infuse current scholarship with a subtext of implied convictions that lie beneath and suggest a personal bedrock from which the critical arguments are shaped. For when the subject is the family in English language texts, each of us who grew up within those national and linguistic boundaries unavoidably brings to such texts two of the same weighty pieces of culture-specific baggage that their authors likewise packed along, even if stamped by a different era: in one hand we unconsciously carry the cultural propaganda of our idealized version of the closed nuclear family; but in the other we carry what may in fact contradict or seem at odds with that ideal. In the second hand we carry our individual-specific histories of socialization inside of some literal family that may or may not have looked remotely like the idealized version but that nonetheless itself existed within the measuring framework of its containing ideology.

When the discourse that transmits and historically guarantees a particular institution seems to veer around rather than authorize investigation of one of its available relational configurations, the avoidance becomes integral to any study of the relationship itself: the gaps suggest threat. Implicitly, the essays in *Daughters and Fathers* undertake to subvert a historical silence and thus also the protective taboo that has been transmitted by the disembodied voice of patriarchal culture—the voice that is amorphous, unlocatable, and hence reverberates everywhere. The extent to which that silent prohibition does still speak seemed implicit, for instance, in the otherwise curious admission we received from several well-known (male) psychoanalytic critics who awkwardly confessed that they had never really considered daughter and father as a paired topic— despite the facts that both scholars were professionally invested in studying family dynamics and that both were themselves the fathers of daughters. Moreover, the injunction "Thou shalt not speak" apparently exerts as pervasive an effect on daughters as it does on fathers. As British novelist Michele Roberts says in the opening lines of her essay written for the recently published *Fathers: Reflections by Daughters*: "Break the silence, I tell myself, break the taboo. I'm struggling against feelings of betrayal and disloyalty involved in attempting to write an article in which my father, and my feeling for him, will appear, however invented, however transformed or veiled" (89); or as Cora Kaplan acknowledges in the analytical piece that appears in that same volume, "I started out by thinking I could integrate my own experience as a daughter with that of Elizabeth Barrett Browning. . . . But after writing a page or two about myself and my father, I realised how deeply—and irrationally—I felt such a public exposure of our embattled but loving history to be an attack, a betrayal. . . . there are quite ordinary areas of my personal history which I can not yet transform into public prose"(116). Before venturing into this territory it thus seems pertinent to acknowledge that for the editors, the process of collecting, reading, editing, contributing to, and overseeing this volume has similarly proved to be an intensely personal way of reconsidering our own relations to fathers, both familial and cultural. Quite possibly, the subject may likewise have elicited such introspection not only from all the women/daughters who contributed to *Daughters and Fathers* but from the male contributors as well, all of whom are themselves fathers of daughters.

Beyond asking why it has taken until now for father-and-daughter to become an authorized subject in the discourse of family, there is a counterpart question that also needs asking: Why is this topic emerging now at all? When viewed as a paradigm of women's relations to male culture, the father-daughter engagement has a clear and timely significance for major feminist concerns. But in terms of the literal, familial model, that the focus on father and daughter should occur precisely at this moment in Western history is either quite illogical or profoundly paradoxical. For behind the intensity of the massive interrogation of the nuclear, father-headed family, the ironic truth of the matter is that—especially in America—the discussion is taking place after the fact. It is occurring when the idealized nuclear model is fast becoming more a myth of the past than a statistical norm of the present, taking place within a society where the single-parented—almost invariably mother parented—family has been steadily emerging as a blatant contradiction to the nuclear image that nonetheless still defines the normative ideal. The U.S. Census indicates that the number of single, mother-headed families jumped almost 200 percent between 1970 and 1981—from 956,000 to 2.7 million—and the figure is likely to be significantly higher by the end of the current decade. Conversely, during that same period, the number of single-parent, male-headed families actually declined. So while the daughter has traditionally been the figure most absent from family representations that enshrined the father's authoritative presence, inside of literal domestic space it has been the father who has been—and is rapidly becoming even more so—the family's most absent member.

Therefore, between the contradictory contexts of paterfamilial ideology and the growing social reality of essentially fatherless families, how are we to read the sudden new interest in the patriarchal nuclear family, in the mythology of fathers, and, ultimately, in the drive to exhume the culturally suppressed narrative of father and daughter? Why is the daughter-father subject emerging into analytical focus apparently only after its reality within the family has been sufficiently jeopardized to make it actually a threatened species? Does this sudden articulation imply a newly felt freedom from that bond? or an attempt to reclaim it? Is the relationship something that can now be exhumed from its problematic past because it is no longer felt to exist in and threaten the present? Or does the desire for exhumation tacitly participate in the desire for resurrection? As the daughter-father representations are re-presented in the following essays, though the reader will no doubt hear an anger that speaks out, perhaps especially in the voices of women critics, beneath even the anger what is the desire that speaks? The question that readers must finally address to the individual essays within this collection is whether the representations of father and daughter argue for foreclosure or whether they reflect a perhaps even unconscious attempt to recreate a reformulated, though more benevolent model of essentially the same ideology that the investigation of daughter and father is, at the same time, subjecting to challenge: the closed, hierarchical, and patriarchal nuclear bond. Essentially, where does the ideology about family, and the family itself, go from here? By considering such questions, the reader engages with the same underlying problematic that the contributors to *Daughters and Fathers* have been willing to explore. To deconstruct the inherited family model by anatomizing it is to put at risk the companion myth that enshrines the family as the individual's sole refuge in an uncaring world; to question the culture's most potent political myth is to query its most personally invested one. To make the nuclear family the object of investigation is, unavoidably, to place into question each scholar's own socialization process—and likewise each reader's.

IN THE FACE of an unwritten taboo, turning any proscribed object into the subject of written discourse is necessarily an act of deliberate subversion. Therefore, in the spirit of such subversion, *Daughters and Fathers* (en)titles itself by inverting, and hence renegotiating, the expected linguistic formula of its syntax. In this title, it is the daughter who precedes the father into their joint articulation as subjects, leading him into it by the equalizing conjunction whose syntactical position is immovable and whose assertion of connection is the element necessary to create relational sense out of the two nouns. Similarly, the titles to the book's three sections reflect this principle of deliberate subversion, calling attention to the act of naming and thus, inferentially, to the particular break in the family enclosure that—within a system predicated on family transmission through paternal surname—occurs precisely at the conjunction of daughter and father.

The parameters of *Daughters and Fathers* can be broadly defined by describing its focus as essentially literary and its examination concentrated on the narratives produced generally within the confines of Western culture. Otherwise, however, this collection is, by design, pluralistic rather than homogeneous in circumscription: it includes essays that span a number of different historical eras, reflect a variety of authorial perspectives and methodologies, and probe into a number of questions about the daughter-father relationship. Every voice within these bindings was not, by virtue of inclusion, bound methodologically nor ideologically to sing the same note. By its use of a wide-angle lens, *Daughters and Fathers* positions itself as a text that draws upon the principle of difference in order to propose a vantage point inclusive enough to encompass the complexities of a subject that is, through this study, being foregrounded as a topic and placed into the unaccustomed light of collective scholarly inquiry. Ultimately, such heterogeneity is intended to solicit the reader to think beyond even the collection itself—to evoke the reader's own thoughts about the numerous potential essays, literary, historical, or even autobiographical, that are not—but might have been—included in *Daughters and Fathers*.

CULTURAL FILIALOGY

As the neologism that names the first section of the book implies, the six essays that initiate *Daughters and Fathers* are each in some way concerned with origins—with scrutinizing the theoretical ideas through which the daughter-father relationship has been culturally understood and transmitted. Thus, although references to psychoanalytic and structuralist theory appear in essays scattered throughout the collection, it is in this section that Lévi-Strauss's anthropological thesis of social bonding through daughter exchange, Freud's psychoanalytic work on daughter-father relationships, and Jacques Lacan's repositioning of Freud's terminology and assumptions are placed into the foreground and explored/critiqued in terms of their theoretical implications. Also included in this theoretically concentrated section are two essays that, because they originate in ethnic considerations outside of the Anglo-American ideology that contains them, incipiently provide a space for looking at the daughter-father relationship in ways that intervene with any fixed understanding of its construction.

In an opening structural overview of Western culture's central daughter-father texts, Lynda E. Boose's "The Father's House and the Daughter in It" connects the general absence of daughters in cultural discourse to the way that daughters problematize the story of patriarchal exchange—whether in *Beowulf*, the *Oedipus* trilogy, or the Hebrew bible—by exposing its tacit authorization for the father's retentive, implicitly incestuous impulse. Masked beneath the authorized father-son narration of Genesis lies Judeo-Christianity's founding paradigm of its suppressed daughter-father myth: the story of a daughter enacting a delegitimated rebellion against the Father, who acknowledges neither relationship to her nor participation in the desire that is then ejected from the garden space only to reemerge in the stories of Lot and of Jacob—to reemerge, in other words, whenever daughters are written into the father's text. In "*Filia Oedipi*," David Willbern next provides a study that is apparently the first comprehensive attempt to chart the chronological complexities and fluctuations in Freud's theorizing about father and daughter, including a discussion of the issue that later essays will problematize: Freud's discounting of the seduction theory and his strangely unprofessional alteration of several case testimonies in which the father had been identified as the incestuous seducer of his daughter. Willbern's essay is followed by one that, though widely known, is being here reprinted in revised format as an integral part of the psychoanalytic dialogue on daughter and father: Jane Gallop's Irigarayan challenge to Freudian theory and the practice of psychoanalysis, "The Father's Seduction," from her book, *The Daughter's Seduction*. Continuing the dialogue but shifting its point of view, Christine Froula's "The Daughter's Seduction: Sexual Violence and Literary History" brings together psychoanalysis and history to analyze the repressive effects of a long history of literal and literary sexual violence that has dictated the "hysterical script" of women's silence in order to protect the father's power. Arguing that the metaphysical abuse and seduction suffered by women readers of male literary culture are continuous with physical sexual violence, Froula traces the fate of women's words from Homer's silenced Helen and Freud's discredited hysterics forward to Virginia Woolf, Maya Angelou, and Alice Walker—who, by writing women's stories of sexual violence into literary history, undo the patriarchal cultural script and reclaim the daughter's voice. In Raymund A. Paredes's following essay, the daughter-father dynamic is approached from the perspective of an ethnic model that lies slightly outside of the dominant ideology that historically colonized it. In "The Evolution of Daughter-Father Relationships in Mexican-American Culture," Paredes looks at the myths that are central to the ideal of family imagined by America's most rapidly growing ethnic minority culture. To follow an evolutionary pattern that accounts for the diverse cultural influences that make up the Mexican-American tradition, Paredes examines the implicit ideology embedded in such patriarchal legends as those about Malinche, *la llorona*, the Virgin of Guadalupe, and the strangely haunting *romance*, "La Delgadina." The section concludes with an essay that, in its title, likewise locates the daughter-father relationship as something that has undergone evolution. In Hortense Spillers's essay, "'The Permanent Obliquity of an In[pha]llibly Straight': In the Time of the Daughters and the Fathers," even the social roles of daughter and father and hence also any basis for their relationship are located in a historical problematic that dates back to the Atlantic slave trade. Working with the fictions of black writers and focusing on the theme of incest in Ralph Ellison's *The Invisible Man* and Alice Walker's "The Child Who Favored Daughter," Spillers redefines incest as being not a tacit reinforcement of paternal authority but an inverted castration of it. In Spillers's essay, incest becomes, not just a monstrously patriarchal act perpetrated against daughters, but the act that unwittingly inverts the law of the father by invalidating the differentiation necessary even to posit father and daughter as roles of social formation. And thus Spillers concludes the section on cultural theory by speaking into it from a perspective outside it, challenging the constitution of the patriarchal family by bringing incestuous desire into its discourse in such a way as to show it as destroying the discourse itself.

IN NOMINE PATRIS: THE DAUGHTER IN HER FATHER'S HOUSE

The second section of *Daughters and Fathers* is defined by a title that, while it encloses the daughter, privileges the father and invokes echoes of two powerful sources of paternal authority: the legal system of patronymic surname and the religious one inscribing partriarchal authority within the invocation of an omnipotent model. The essays in this section are grouped beneath this heading because of the control the patriarch, literary or familial, exerts over the daughter inside the family representations that the various included essays investigate. In the pieces subsumed by "the name of the father," the daughter's authority is seen as being still contained within or unsevered from the authority of the father. The section begins with a focus on male novelists and their relations to family roles, to their own authorship, and to specific novels they produced. In the Foucauldian essay that opens this section, "Engendering the Exemplary Daughter: The Deployment of Sexuality in Richardson's *Clarissa*," Janice Haney-Peritz explores the sociosexual semiotic that underwrites Richardson's novel construction of an exemplary female subject, a subject whose cultural authority depends not only on her position as the father's daughter but also on her power to effect the (re) production of a certain class and gender ideology. In Evan Carton's "'A Daughter of the Puritans' and Her Old Master: Hawthorne, Una, and the Sexuality of Romance," the focus is placed on the deeply personal, highly gendered way that Hawthorne imagined his act of writing novels. In Carton's analysis, the act of authorial engendering is seen not so much as a site for social reproduction as the locus of Hawthorne's own guilty rebellion against the obligations of masculine identity—as an escape from the father and the patriarchal province through an act that Hawthorne ambivalently associated with the sphere of the daughter. The following three essays then move into a space in which, although daughters progressively emerge as the writers in focus, daughterhood is clearly not yet self-authoring enough to produce texts that confirm independent separation from the father's authority. The first of these pieces balances a father's and a daughter's poetic texts. Drawing upon the lives, letters, and works of a poet/father and a poet/daughter who apparently felt a definable "anxiety of influence" in relation to him, Elizabeth Butler Cullingford's "A Father's Prayer, A Daughter's Anger" examines the literal and literary formations that construct an ambivalent dialogue between the two most famous poetic meditations on the father daughter relationship: W. B. Yeats's "A Prayer for My Daughter" and Sylvia

11

Plath's "Daddy." The next essay in this group, and the first in it to give exclusive focus to the daughter/writer, looks at the problem of literary heritage in a new way. Moving from the nineteenth century and George Eliot's *Silas Marner* to the twentieth century and Edith Wharton's *Summer*, in "Life's Empty Pack: Notes toward a Literary Daughteronomy," Sandra M. Gilbert characterizes women's authorship as a riddle of daughterhood bequested with an empty pack of disinheritance transmitted by powerful literary mothers whose fictions proclaim allegiance to the law of the Father—the law that the literary mothers, by being authors themselves, have themselves violated. In Betty S. Flowers's following analysis, "Christina Rossetti: Dialogue with the Father God," the focus turns to the daughter/poet's strategic search for a voice within a religious tradition that denies her a place not only in its Holy Trinity but even in its Holy Family. In the resolution that Rossetti is seen as having found, through use of the religious dialogue format, the poet/daughter/soul strategically inscribes herself within an orthodoxy that allows her both to create the Father and subsequently to engage Him in a dialogue that repeatedly confirms her worth. And yet, in Rossetti's solution the daughter's subject, for both her text and her life, is still the father—how she may please him and whether she may please him enough to merit the only confirmation she has imagined: the withheld paternal acknowledgment.

IN NOMINE FILIAE: THE ARTIST AS HER FATHER'S DAUGHTER

The title of the final section is a subversion, not of syntax, but of the logic of patronymics. To find a space in which language would authorize the daughter, the title steps outside orthodox usage and appropriates the authoritative signifier for a series of essays focused on daughters whose careers were marked by a conscious struggle to find authority outside their fathers and in themselves. The placement of essays into this rather than the previous section does not necessarily imply that these daughters transcended the problem of self-authority more fully than did those placed earlier. Rather, it indicates that the writers of these essays have chosen to give greater weight to the daughter's struggle and its potential for success. In the opening essay, "The Clergyman's Daughters: Anne Bronte, Elizabeth Gaskell, and George Eliot," Dianne F. Sadoff links psychoanalytic confession and narrative fictionalizing as an analogy that enables us to read the unconscious strategies of desire for the rejecting father that recur within the fictions of these three Victorian "good girl" novelists; by transferring desire for or repressed humiliation at the hands of fathers onto substitutes for him, the novelists attempt a daughterly cure within the acceptably womanly scene of writing. In the following essay, "Murderous Poetics: Dickinson, the Father, and the Text," Joanne Feit Diehl argues that Emily Dickinson found the freedom to exercise the active will and the internal authority to write, not by resolving the patriarchal conflict through fictionalized surrogates, but by overtly conceiving of her chief adversary as the Father and repeatedly, aggressively confronting him inside the battleground of her poetry. In an essay from which we have borrowed the subtitle of this section, "Cam the Wicked: Woolf's Portrait of the Artist as Her Father's Daughter," Elizabeth Abel focuses on Cam, the silent daughter of *To the Lighthouse,* as a means of exploring the competing claims of maternal and paternal genealogies. If Lily Briscoe is Woolf's vehicle for thinking back through her mother, Cam is the figure who enables the author to dramatize the narrative dilemma of the daughter who thinks back through her father. Positioned next to this essay is Katherine C. Hill-Miller's analysis of Virginia Woolf's paternal aunt, Anne Thackeray Ritchie. Drawing upon the correspondence, diaries, external comments about, and fictions written by Anne and her father, William Makepeace Thackeray, Hill-Miller's essay, "'The Skies and Trees of the Past,'" assesses how Anne Thackeray's bifocal vision of herself as her father's son as well as his daughter created the conditions for her prodigious output yet simultaneously set in motion the very factors that would lead her father as she turned sixteen, to forbid her from wasting any more time "scribbling." If Anne Thackeray's literary heritage proved a weighty burden, the daughter's power to reject her heritage is the focus of Judith Kegan Gardiner's essay on contemporary Australian writer Christina Stead, "Male Narcissism, Capitalism, and the Daughter of *The Man Who Loved Children.*" Through Stead, we suddenly confront a perspective that is slightly outside the American family and its reproduction through—and of—American politics. In Gardiner's analysis of Stead, fatherhood functions as a psychopolitical as well as familial territory, and the daughter's expression of confrontational creativity becomes a psychologically and politically necessary rebellion against the directions formulated by the family patriarch, the avuncularly narcissistic American capitalism represented by Louie's engulfing father, Sam. For its concluding essay, *Daughters and Fathers* turns from the twentieth century back to the sixteenth, to an essay called "Erasing the Stigma of Daughterhood: Mary I, Elizabeth I, and Henry VIII," in which Leah S. Marcus takes up the task of presenting history's most famous model of the politics of the father-daughter relationship. Through her historical analysis of Mary and Elizabeth Tudor and the strategies by which each daughter/ruler individually wrestled with acquiring legitimacy and self-authority as well as power, Leah Marcus brings the essays in this collection to a formal conclusion with the model of Elizabeth I, who moved from the status of a daughter declared illegiti-

13

mate to becoming England's most famous monarch, the monarch who eventually defined Tudor history, not by extending it, but by ending it in herself.

FOLLOWING the Marcus essay is an afterword by Carolyn G. Heilbrun, whose own feminist scholarship has long recognized and validated the personal and political significance of focusing attention on—and perhaps even reinventing—the cultural sentences that define a daughter's relationship to the father.

Son. Intrinsic val. . . . Emotional val. plus 100% times nil plus val. crop.
Emotional val. 100% times increase yearly for each child plus intrinsic val. plus
liquid assets plus working acquired credit. . . . Daughter and you could maybe
even have seen the question mark after it and the other words even: *daughter?*
daughter? daughter? trailing off not because thinking trailed off, but on
the contrary, thinking stopping right still then, backing up a little
and spreading like when you lay a stick across a trickle of water, spreading
and rising slow around him in whatever place it was that he could lock the
door and sit quiet. . . .
   —William Faulkner, *Absalom, Absalom!*

Sofonisba Anguisciola, *Father Amilcare and His Children* (c. 1558–59)
Source: Nivaagaard Art Collectiion, Nivå, Denmark. Used by permission.

I
Cultural Filialogy

LYNDA E. BOOSE

The Father's House and the Daughter in It:
The Structures of Western Culture's
Daughter-Father Relationship

THE STRUCTURES that define Western culture's ideology of the family interact with its literal drama much as the *Six Characters* of Pirandello's play interact with the play itself: they intrude into its action and imperceptibly construct its script. In Western culture's family drama, the roles of daughter and father are kinship statuses that, for a variety of reasons, are peculiarly shaped by such controlling models. Lévi-Strauss's well-known analysis of kinship systems argues that the most significant rule governing any kinship structure is the ubiquitous existence of the incest taboo as a mechanism that imposes the social aim of exogamy and alliance upon the biological events of sex and procreation. While models do exist in which socially defined statuses take precedence over biology—among the Nuer, for example, "fatherhood" belongs to the person (male or female) in whose name cattle bridewealth is given for the mother (Rubin 169)—for the majority of the Western world *father* historically denotes a biologically fixed male status of structural authority within the nuclear group. Even when fatherhood is not biological, the institution retains the same hierarchy. Marriage to a child's mother grants a man the status of stepfather; legal adoption of a child socially obscures any distinction and, in American law, places the adopted child inside the patronym and thus within the boundaries of "legitimacy."

In the anthropological narration of family, the father is the figure who controls the exogamous exchange of women. The woman most practically available to be exchanged is clearly not the mother, who sexually belongs to the father, nor the sister, who comes under the bestowal rights of her own father. The exchangeable figure is the daughter. Thus, if the prohibition of incest is essentially a mechanism to control internal family sexuality so that outward exchanges can take place, then the incest taboo would seem to have a special applicability to one particular pair. And if it is true, as anthropology asserts, that the origins of culture are synonymous with the evolution of kinship, then culture has

19

essentially been built upon the relationship it has seemed least eager to discuss—that between father and daughter.

THE ABSENT DAUGHTER

Given the relevance of the daughter as the figure upon whose mobility the whole kinship structure rests, one might expect to find her occupying a central focus in anthropological studies. Instead, what one finds here and elsewhere is a certain bland indifference to her presence that betrays the work of cultural normalization.[1] When, for instance, anthropologist Fredrik Barth sets up a theoretical model of "an elementary kinship situation in Western society" in order to analyze "how individual experience feeds back on cultural standardization," his paradigm unwittingly reflects precisely the kind of gender-status assumptions that do indeed model the process of "cultural standardization." We quickly learn that the "status set of husband/father, wife/mother, and child," which will "serve as a basis for [the child's] interaction in a variety of activities," is like the Holy Family in that it, too, really means father-mother-son: "In every community little boys go out every day and try to mobilize this basic kinship triad for new purposes. . . . [But] obviously, the father-mother-child set is no good for organizing a group of boys for an egalitarian operation; for such tasks one must invent or borrow another organizational framework. But where the activity is one that can be adequately handled with the kinship statuses, I would expect them to be mobilized" (9). By inference, it would seem as if ignoring daughters were so natural as to be unremarkable.

The relative absence of father-daughter discussion has something to do with a cultural metrics that assigns value almost by literal poundage. In the four-cornered nuclear enclosure that is at once the source for and product of Western ideologies about the family, the father weighs most and the daughter least. To consider the daughter and father in relationship means juxtaposing the two figures most asymmetrically proportioned in terms of gender, age, authority, and cultural privilege. Each of these asymmetries is controlled by the idiom of presence, which defines the father, or absence, which identifies the daughter. Furthermore, since the father traditionally has occupied outside cultural space and been absent from the inner family sphere, while the daughter has been restricted to the inner one, even their literal spatial locations construct polarities defined by these terms. All such dichotomies work to create a gap. They also work, however, to elicit the myriad tensions that tend to flow into such gaps.

Inscribed within patriarchal narrative is something more specific than just a general erasure of woman. What is specifically absent is the *daughter*. For however much history has suppressed the feminine, for a society's metaphysical or political hierarch to be imagined as a father and for its text to engender a father-to-son transmission that will guarantee paternal authority, the third member of the family, the mother, must be invoked into language and implicitly placed, in fact, prior to the son. Because she is the necessary mediator between the synonymous masculine pair, the empty vessel through whom, in psychoanalytic terms, the father's phallus and sign of the father's authority is passed to the son, the mother obtrudes into cultural narration as surely as her pregnant body, sign of herself, asserts its visual disruption into the ordered maleness of things. The son receives the externally evident sign of the father and becomes synonymous with him at birth. By parallel, what the daughter receives from the mother is not the sign *of* maternity but the hidden receptacle *for* it, the so-called empty space. Not only does she not receive the phallus from the father—which Freudian and Lacanian symbology has made much of—but neither does she receive pregnancy from her mother. Daughterhood is, in fact, inseparable from absence in the psychoanalytic definition of social development, for it is the daughter's recognition of her "castration," her renunciation of the active, phallic state, and her acquiescence to passivity that, in Freud's assessment, constitutes the prerequisite step backward that sets her on the pathway to "normal femininity."[2]

In both Freudian and Lacanian theory, the psychosocial dynamics of the family resemble something akin to an all-determining game of who's-got-the-phallus. By these terms, the daughter is clearly the one person who *does not*. To become an official player, the daughter must eradicate the one kinship status that is contained within, yet liminal to, the family institution. She enters the cultural story, we might say, only by relinquishing her structural isolation/independence from its male-authored script and becoming an agent to ensure its duplication. Yet, as psychoanalytic theory makes clear, what allows her even this entree is the receipt of a signal passed on to her not *from* the mother but from the phallus that is the sign of the father. Even this, however, is a signal that she may acquire not from the males of her natal family but beyond its boundaries, outside its house. In a peculiar way, the daughter inherits nothing from either father or mother. She essentially lacks parentage and is almost by definition illegitimate. Unlike the son, she is the temporary sojourner within her family, destined to seek legitimation and name outside its boundaries.

That the father and son are structurally homologous needs little illustration. It is the central presumption upon which the Greek, Hebrew, and Christian foundation myths depend and the central metaphor in which psychoanalytic theory is grounded. Furthermore, in most of the Western world it constitutes the basis for nomenclature from which kinship through patriliny is derived, the legal foundation upon which economic inheritance and all that is generally subsumed by the term "history" has been constructed. Even when kinship structures are bilateral and property and descent through daughters is at least as significant as that which is passed through sons—which is the case in England, for example—cultural ideologies about patrilineage "associated with inherited patronymics (surnames, etc.)" distort the system, so "that it is made to appear 'as if' it were a patrilineal structure" (Leach, "Complementary Filiation" 56). Since daughters are subsumed as mothers and their independent contributions are obscured by their loss of name, the end result is that the society *imagines* itself through a "chain-male linkage," and the relevance of daughters is obliterated from cultural consciousness. But while father and son constitute one, mother and daughter are a dyad of separable opposites marked, respectively, by (received) presence and absence. Together they constitute an ambiguity in kinship structures that, as Edmund Leach points out, is most evident "in the case of patrilineal descent associated with lineage exogamy. Every married woman first joins the local lineage group as an alien. She is intrinsically evil; a foreign object, a sexual object, dirty. But in due course she becomes the mother of new members of the lineage. In the second capacity she is intrinsically good, the very criterion of virtue and cleanliness, the antithesis of a sexual object" (*Culture and Communication* 74–75). While yet within her father's house, a daughter is set apart from the other three members as the only one who does not participate in extending its integrity into history. When her patronymic identity as daughter is exchanged for one that marks her as wife, she is still the alien until she has once again changed her sign to "mother of new members of the lineage"—which by implication means mother to a son.

WHAT IS IN A NAME?

Of the myriad factors that construct the seeming irrelevance of daughters, unquestionably, a determining one is the patrilineal transmission of name. When Bill Cosby, American television's most positive image of fatherhood in the 1980s, reflects on why he wanted children, he admits that he "did ask God to give me a son because I wanted someone to carry on the family name" (15). The father-to-be asking the divine father to give him a son so that he may transmit his own father's name is a narration in miniature of the cultural reproduction that has historically marginalized daughters. And within the narrated model, the position of daughter means something even more problematic than irrelevance: it means family betrayal. That Juliet's marriage to Romeo will constitute negation of her father, while Romeo's will confirm, not betray, his paternal line, is the painful knowledge that motivates Juliet's famous first

22

balcony soliloquy. Within the stark alternatives forced upon the daughter but not upon the son, Juliet is the play's fully tragic figure compelled to choose between absolute imperatives:

> O Romeo, Romeo, wherefore art thou Romeo?
> Deny thy father and refuse thy name!
> Or, if thou wilt not, be but sworn my love,
> And I'll no longer be a Capulet.　　*(Romeo and Juliet* 2.2.33–36)

Trying to discover a logic by which becoming a Montague can be re-imagined outside of the dichotomy she has just articulated, Juliet attempts to rationalize a structure that both she and her audience already know is impervious to external logic:

> 'Tis but thy name that is my enemy;
> Thou art thyself, though not a Montague.
> What's Montague? It is not hand, nor foot,
> Nor arm, nor face, nor any other part
> Belonging to a man. O, be some other name!
> What's in a name? That which we call a rose
> By any other name would smell as sweet.　　(2.2.38–44)

Though Romeo, as a son, remains comically oblivious to the profound question that Juliet has posed about surname transmission and seems to imagine that he can erase the problem by swearing to "be new baptiz'd; / Henceforth I never will be Romeo" (2.2.51–52), Juliet's query, "What's in a name?" is not only the most famous line of this play but might well be the subtitle of it. Within a story about two warring houses, the presuppositions about kinship make the question at once merely rhetorical yet simultaneously the reason why it is Old Capulet, but not Montague, who must necessarily play out the role of tragic nemesis. In marrying Romeo, Juliet becomes a Montague lady, a traitor to her father's project, whose change of name guarantees the extension of the enemy line and the simultaneous extinction of the Capulets. The chronological arrangement of the narrative merely recapitulates the deepest logic of kinship structures: in the interim between Romeo's marriage to Juliet and the consummation of it inside the Capulet house, Romeo kills Tybalt, the last surviving Capulet male. The marriage and the murder are structural analogues. Within a world where daughters belong to either their father's house or their husband's, there is no neutral space, and dramatic equity is possible only by killing Romeo and Juliet and entombing this Montague pair inside the Capulet family crypt. What is in a name, indeed!

Within patronymic signification, "history" itself—a written record of genealogy through name—actually stops with a daughter (see Rackin

336; and Spiegel). Most of European royal history could actually be defined as a series of negotiations around daughters, including the fourteenth-century French invocation of Salic law prohibiting inheritance of the crown through daughters (Saccio 79). As wives in classical Greece or the hapless English queens Catherine of Aragon and Anne Boleyn some twenty centuries later realized, only the birth of a son contributes to and therefore confirms the mother's role in the patrilineal project. For while in England a crowned daughter does transmit her royal father's throne and thus ensures the royal succession as effectively as would a son, with her ascendancy die the father's hopes of dynastic self-perpetuation. When Elizabeth Tudor took the throne, "Tudor history" died—and would have died even if she had produced sons. It seems fair to say that Elizabeth was, by consequence, the most desirable woman in all of English history, for through marriage to her, not only could a man have appropriated the de facto power of rule but, through her production of sons, he could have seized history itself and marked it with his own name, regardless of the fact that such sons would have inherited the throne through the name that marriage inevitably erases—the name of the mother's father. Henry VIII's determination to have both Mary and Elizabeth Tudor declared illegitimate even before another legitimate heir existed illustrates that for Henry, a wife's production of daughters did not signify her contribution of at least possible or even backup heirs for the Tudor line; rather, it signified her refusal to carry out the Tudor project.[3] The logic that two legitimate daughters in hand were worth one son in the imagination was not a point that Henry's insulted ego was prepared to concede.

Nor does the modern biological recognition that sex is determined by the father make any real difference. For lurking beneath modern scientific data is the stubbornly powerful association that links masculinity to the production of sons—an association that marks the production of daughters as a psychic threat that can be rationalized only through defensive projection. When a son is born, the cultural psyche traditionally credits the determination of sex to the father's masculinity; but when the child is a daughter, her sex is somehow reimagined as the mother's fault. In modern India, for example, where amniocentesis has been turned into a weapon for determining the sex of a fetus so that female children can be aborted, "even though the father is the determining factor in the sex of a child, women are blamed for not having sons. . . . a woman bearing female children invites the wrath of her husband and in-laws." According to a January 1986 report of a study of eight thousand abortions done in Bombay hospitals, "all but one involved female fetuses" ("Amniocentesis"). Extreme as this situation may seem, it nonetheless illustrates the deepest of assumptions about a mother's role within family structures reproduced through patrilineal ideology: her role is that which in the West is modeled by the mother Mary—to be the vessel through which the father reproduces himself.

EXOGAMOUS EXCHANGE; OR, THE DEPLOYMENT OF DAUGHTERS

As psychology tells us, inside the nuclear family the mother's role is first to enable the reproductive linkage between father and son and afterwards to mediate it. As anthropology tells us, inside kinship systems the daughter's role between two male groups is analogous. In Lévi-Strauss's terms, the exchange of women between male exchangers constitutes the "supreme rule of the gift."[4] According to this theory, giving one's daughter not only sets up a reciprocal system of gift transactions, it connects the male exchange partners as affines, which thus superimposes a network of relations that ideally will take precedence over intergroup hostilities. Gayle Rubin has done a stunning feminist critique of the notion that the origins of culture should be prescriptively invested in this "traffic in women." For Rubin, what such a system might lead us to infer is not the origins of culture, but the ultimate locus of women's oppression. "If women are the gifts, then it is men who are the exchange partners. And it is the partners, not the presents, upon whom reciprocal exchange confers its quasi-mystical power of social linkage. The relations of such a system are such that women are in no position to realize the benefits of their own circulation. As long as the relations specify that men exchange women, it is men who are the beneficiaries of the product of such exchanges—social organization" (174). Rubin's point is clearly apt as an analysis of the *effects* of such a system. But a work that was written down in approximately the tenth century and dates back even farther as an oral text casts an equally skeptical light on even the *effectiveness* of a system of exchange that seems remarkably similar to the model from which anthropology has inferred the origins of culture. Lévi-Strauss's first critic is the Anglo-Saxon epic hero Beowulf.

In *Beowulf*—as in the elementary kinship systems just described—kings marry their daughters to enemy tribes in the hope that the affinity created through such alliances will preclude the otherwise compulsory hostilities that underlie the masculine revenge code of the world of this poem. Although peace among these Germanic brother tribes rests almost entirely upon such exchanges, the daughters and the daughter-wives themselves make only the most fleeting of appearances inside the narration, suddenly entering the mead hall at the height of celebration to distribute the captured golden treasure and pass the mead cup among the warriors, bringing with them the signifying idea of the gift itself and, through representation, defining the mediating ideal of "splendid bestowals" that bond the "good king" with his "chosen retainers [who will] stand by him . . . serve him when war comes" (lines 22–24). Whenever these elusive female figures appear, their appearance is always synonymous with the same culture-asserting emblems: the mead hall, the golden cup, the gifts, and the comitatus bond between the king and his warriors. Overtly, both the emblematic woman who bears the "vessels of mead . . . the gem-studded cup" (2020, 2023) and the gold she distributes are positive mediators. But from the poem's opening description of the construction of Heorot, King Hrothgar's mead hall, both the daughter and the treasure/gift have problematically also objectified the desires that will eventually destroy that same structure. The mead hall has been built by "many peoples throughout middle-earth" (75); within its civilizing enclosure, the scop labors to preserve the tribe inside the poetic construction of its heroic deeds. But from the proleptic opening of the poem, what threatens these two enclosures is not the external monsters—the "outlaws"—whom Beowulf comes to conquer. As the poet cryptically reminds us before even beginning the narration of the hero, both the hall space and the cultures whose deeds are woven together within it will be annihilated—because they already have been—not by the outlaws but by the in-laws, by "the war-flames, malicious burning . . . the sharp-edged hate" between son-in-law and father-in-law that awaken "in murderous rage" (82–85). The absent referent who mediates this doom is the daughter. Like the poet, she can do nothing but attempt to weave together the violent past; like the poet, in reconnecting it she can do nothing but reconstitute it.

Although daughters are as nearly absent from the action of *Beowulf* as is the ideal of peaceful alliance from the culture, stories about daughter exchanges serve as one of the poem's major structural devices, acting as one of the few bridges to weave together its crumbling narration. Simultaneously, however, these same stories repeatedly determine the ongoing cultural erosion they exist to prevent. For the daughter stories inevitably occur either through flashback to a war of the past or through prediction of some equally ominous event of the future, both of which are inextricably woven into the poet's attempt to inscribe the present glory into the tribe's record of past victory. Just as a daughter story is told, the daughter past suddenly enters the hall in the person of the king's wife, the "peace pledge" acquired through an earlier transaction. As she distributes the signs of victory, simultaneously the boasts of the warriors enclose the future in the revenge code that has dictated the past; the juxtaposed daughter story then allusively connects the presence of this queen to that inevitability. The most striking example of such an unannounced, seemingly unrelated switch from present celebration to past disaster occurs amidst Heorot's first celebration of Beowulf's victory over Grendel. The suddenly inserted history of Hildeburh's marriage to Finn both usurps the celebration and sets up the paradigm that henceforth predetermines all future stories about daughter exchanges. After peace was presumably cemented by Hildeburh's marriage to the enemy king, the arrival of her brother and his thanes reinvokes a deadly triangulation that implicitly sets off—and does not placate—the old hatreds. In the ensuing blood-shed, the daughter/wife eventually loses all her male kin and becomes, emblematically, the guiltless agent of all such losses, the figure fated to dramatize, as mourner for both sides, the contradictions inherent in the code she exists to ensure. In characteristically cryptic understatement the poet comments: "Not without cause did Hoc's daughter mourn / the web's short measure that fated morning / when she saw their bodies, her murdered kinsmen" (1076–78). The poet can return to the Beowulf story line only after narrating the erasure of this exchange—after recounting the murder of Hildeburh's husband and the Danes' reappropriation of their lost treasure. Of "every good heirloom they found in [Finn's] house," the most important reacquisition is Hildeburh; and thus the scop narrates that the remaining warriors carried "the queen back to the Danes, / brought her to her people" (1155–58). Although Hildeburh is Finn's wife, the mother of Finn's son, and can be called "queen" only because of that kin-group identity, the seeming contradiction of the poet's emphatic identification of "her people" as her natal tribe tells us quite clearly that there is a countersystem of possession at work within the culture that is a force equal to, if not perhaps subliminally more powerful than, that of exogamous exchange.

This "Frisian episode" in *Beowulf* is not merely a story of the past; like all such stories, it is simultaneously an allusive history of the present and the future. In Heorot, as the ominous song of Finn's wife concludes and the celebration of Beowulf's victory resumes, "then Wealhtheow [Hrothgar's wife] came forth / glistening in gold" (1162–63) to hand Beowulf the gold cup with which the daughter/wife is repeatedly associ-ated. It will be, of course, the "treasure cup . . . the immense legacy of a noble race" (2231–33), that is taken from the dragon's hoard and handed to Beowulf as a peace pledge that will unearth the final doom for the Geats in the second part of the poem.

When the narrative shifts from Hrothgar's Scylding (Danish) ter-ritory to Hygelac's Geat kingdom, the only linkage that weaves the two sections together is a series of daughter stories that at first seem focused on the Geat queen, Hygd. While Hygelac's wife, "the daughter of Haereth, went down the hall / pouring mead-cups, . . . bore the strong drink to the warriors' hands" (1981–83), Beowulf suddenly invokes the companion scene at Heorot in which both Hrothgar's wife and daughter, Wealhtheow and Freawaru, "passed to those heroes the gem-studded cup" (2023). As our former picture of the bonding between king and his thanes is suddenly expanded to include Hrothgar's daughter, we also learn in retrospect that "she has been promised, young, gold-laden" (2024), to the Danes' primary enemy, Ingeld, the Heatho-Bard. And—in a highly unusual moment in the epic—we hear Beowulf himself criticize Hrothgar for believing "that with the young woman he'll settle his share / of the killings and feud. But seldom anywhere, / after a slaying, will the death-spear rest . . . though the bride be good" (2028–31).

What makes the nearly absent daughter/wife so central in this otherwise emphatically masculine epic is the way she both determines and exposes the dangerously paradoxical linkage between the culture's two defining systems of value: its idealization of male blood kinship and the possession of treasure. Within this world, treasure signifies nothing short of all aesthetic, existential, spiritual, and generative values. It is the transactional sign that culturally reproduces the inviolable father-son bond between king and thane; it exists to be acquired, accumulated, and hoarded so that it may both create and regenerate the group bond by being circulated within it. At the same time that Beowulf is showered with treasure and given Hrothgar's sword, he is officially adopted into the group as Hrothgar's son who is committed to protect Hrothgar's heir. The problem arises when treasure is circulated outward—or, in terms of daughters, when it is circulated exogamously. The culture places its only overt value on the blood bond between father and son. Likewise, the most valued treasure is the sword that is passed from father to son. Inevitably, it is the sight of this sword in the possession of an enemy that reinstigates warfare. Repeatedly, however, this discovery takes place in narrative connection with and as a consequence of the exchange of the "peace-weaver" daughter to the enemy tribe. For through marriage, the exchanged daughter/new wife—queen becomes the instrument by which both the enemy king's male lineage and his comitatus bond are produced and confirmed. In thus providing all the bonds necessary for the enemy's survival, it is symbolically the daughter/wife who catalyzes the emasculating vision of the tribal/familial treasure being worn by the enemy. As the mother to enemy sons, it is she who is symbolically reinvoked in the unexpected attack on Heorot by Grendel's mother that follows the ominous Hildeburh story, an attack that is labeled "No good, exchange / that those on both sides had to pay with the lives / of kinsmen and friends" (1304–6). Furthermore, as the narrative transfers from Hrothgar's hall to Grendel's, it is within the mother's underwater lair that Beowulf's own sword fails, and he saves himself only by seizing the ancient sword he discovers hanging within this "hostile hall" alongside the body of the son, Grendel. As the means of production for all the bonds within either her father's or the enemy's group, the daughter is every tribe's central treasure. She is herself both the pledge cup and that which generates the sword. As potentially multiple mediator of bonds inside, outside, or between oppositions, she defines the poem's emblematic nexus of conflicting desires. In the third and last monster narrative of the poem, the attempt to create peace by exchanging the cup is finally imagined as an outright theft of the old dragon's treasure: "The hoard had been pilfered, / its treasure lessened" (2283–84). When transferred from the dragon's hall to Beowulf's, the cup awakens the same "war flames, malicious burning" and a "time for the sharp-edged hate" that followed the exchange of Hrothgar's daughter—the proleptic event in the poetic structure that always already foredooms these tribes even before the oral narration of their history begins. As an understatement, one might say that in these elementary kinship structures, daughter exchanges do not work in Lévi-Strauss's model way to create benign relationship through affinity. From the historical material that is fused with the mythic text of *Beowulf*, it seems apparent that for the Germanic groups that the epic celebrates, the exchange system engendered intertribal annihilation that was, to say the least, socially noncontributive.

Now, while *Beowulf* is hardly an argument for removing the right of bestowal from the father and giving it to the daughter, it is, in both form and content, a surprisingly astute commentary on the impossibility of unifying the social or literary text by placing highly treasured yet essentially powerless mediators between powerful oppositions. The problem with the bestowed daughter being the conjunction between antithetical male subjects should be obvious from the male-female-male syntax that constructs it. The pattern signifies an inherently violent text of desire and competition, not one of mutual cooperation. Repeatedly in *Beowulf*, the daughter stories evoked to mediate the textual, chronological, and kinship affinities work instead to erode them. The text itself begins to crumble from within. Its narratives of past daughter deployments cannot unify it any more than they can cement past enmities. The daughter is linked by binding loyalties to two kin groups and to the past and future between them. Having been bestowed rather than having bestowed herself, she lacks the power signified by that right and thus essentially remains locked into the liminal state of transition, neither fully separated from her former house nor aggregated into her new one. In the New Guinea highlands Hagen groups, in fact, wives are often referred to as "women in between." Their connections to their natal family make their relationships to a husband's group not wholly trusted, and local lore is full of threatening stories about wives who secretly poison their spouses over an insult directed at members of their original kin (Marilyn Strathern).

In *Beowulf*, what seems to thwart the effectiveness of the daughter

29

exchanges is some kind of half-articulated perception that the putatively exchangeable object, the daughter, is simultaneously not really exchangeable at all. The positive economics of the intent—to acquire power, alliance, prestige, and material benefit—seem to be in unacknowledged collision with a negative economics dictated by the avoidance of loss. If the exchange of daughters for social benefits seems an inadequate explanation of the forces that construct the father-daughter axis of family, the problem may lie in the way that its explanation of social economics circumvents other factors of possession and loss—factors that are not only personal but institutional, and factors that would seem crucial to an institution as defensively constructed and as invested in the symbolics of blood as is the family. By giving too little weight to what we might call an "emotional economics," the anthropological construction of family ends up producing a narrative of disinterested fathers that is quite at odds with the picture drawn by most Western myth and literature, where the father most frequently appears as a blocking figure bent on retaining, not exchanging, his daughter. Furthermore, the exchange argument, which is the product of an attempt to explain the universal existence of the incest taboo, begins its theorizing from the implicit presumption that the incest taboo works. Besides providing little or no explanation to account for the strikingly high incidence of father-daughter incest that research of the late 1970s and 1980s has made us aware of, the exchange theory itself, by the very way it dismisses the issue, inadvertently constitutes one more collusive factor in maintaining the cover on what Florence Rush has called society's "best kept secret."[5]

Perhaps because I cannot help but think that the cultural script, whether historical or contemporary, contains something more fraught with ambivalence than a narration of disinterested fathers who callously traded off their daughters in exchange for social benefit, I also think it possible to read this traffic in daughters in a more paradoxical way. Admittedly, paternal behavior more callous than mere disinterest was apparently routine in classical Greece, where fathers were legally permitted to cast female infants out on hills to die, or in twentieth-century China, where female infanticide is reportedly still practiced.[6] There are, however, texts that use a symbolic perspective to provide alternative insights into such apparent lack of paternal concern. In Shakespeare's *The Winter's Tale*, Leontes wants his infant Perdita thrown into the fire and is only with difficulty persuaded to cast her to the mercy of the elements instead; in *Pericles*, the father leaves his infant Marina with a king and queen unrelated to him and returns to see her only years later. Underlying both narrations of daughter abandonment, however, is a text of unconscious incestuous desire, one that is born to the father along with his daughter and one that is structurally reflected in the emblematically conjunctive death of the mother. Avoidance, abandonment, and discarding of the daughter function in these plays as inverted mirrors that reflect the father's flight from incest. Taken collectively, even the variants of the Cinderella story reflect this peculiar duality. Although the daughter-stepmother-stepsister narrative remains relatively similar in the majority of versions, the father's position in the Cinderella story changes frequently enough from variant to variant to suggest that his relationship to the daughter's plight is the problem that necessitates manipulation to shift the textual focus away from the latent father-daughter material and deflect it into a mother-daughter conflict. In some European versions the father is inexplicably absent; in others, he passively (but blamelessly) allows his only blood child to be treated as a drudge. In yet others, however, the daughter's menial status in a home not her own is the consequence not of her father's indifference but of incestuous demands from which she has fled into hiding. In all the above symbolic accounts, paternal neglect serves as a suggestive hieroglyph that masks the seemingly opposite impetus of transgressive desire.

Instead of measuring what the daughter does not materially contribute to the family, we might alternatively consider just what she threatens to subtract from it. If she is classified as the family's most expendable member, it may be because within the system constructed by patriarchy she is actually its least retainable. To an institution that fears loss, the daughter's presence by definition constitutes a threat to its maintenance of closed boundaries. In multiple ways, she signifies all that the father desires and simultaneously cannot have. As even Polonius has the wit to recognize about Ophelia, "I have a daughter—have while she is mine" (*Hamlet* 2.2.106). For despite the obvious kinship benefits potentially available to the Polonius family through the fruition of Hamlet's courtship of Ophelia, Shakespeare shows Polonius and Laertes spending all their time avoiding loss, not pursuing gain, devoting their energies to blocking the courtship, apparently preferring to retain Ophelia's "fair and unpolluted flesh" (5.1.239) as an unusable family commodity rather than yield it to the "unmast'red importunity" (1.3.32) of even a princely bridegroom.

For fathers compelled by cultural dictates to lose their daughters, the rationale of "gift giving" in order to acquire kin-group benefits might better be understood as being not necessarily the *cause* for such an exchange but an invaluable psychic defense *against* its necessity. Such a rationale would serve as a powerful way by which the loss of a daughter through marriage could be psychologically reconstrued as an investment. For losing one's daughter through a transaction that the father controls circumvents her ability ever to choose another man over him, thus allowing him to retain vestiges of his primary claim. And patriarchal

31

history may have hung on to father bestowal so stubbornly not only because it reified society's male dominance, as Rubin's analysis demonstrates, but also because giving daughters such as Ophelia primary rights in themselves would threaten a psychic defense valuable to the father. The bestowal design places the daughter's departure from the father's house and her sexual union with another male into a text defined by obedience to her father—not preference for an outside male. So long as the strategy operates, the loss of a daughter can be psychologically mitigated, and defeat by a rival male constructed into public rituals that redefine this transfer as the father's magnanimous gift. Within this fiction, daughters do not abandon or displace their father, nor do fathers reexperience the Oedipal defeat once felt at the hands of their own fathers. Daughters leave their father's house because their fathers decree and then enact this severance by giving them away. It may even be that paternal bestowal psychologically functions in a way analogous to the Big Man gift systems of highland New Guinea, in which the father can imaginatively humiliate his rival and expose his inferiority by giving him something too valuable ever *to be* reciprocated (Rubin 172).

MYTHIC AND LITERARY MODELS

The conflict between separation and retention dominates and spatializes Western culture's father-daughter texts. Essentially, the literary dialectic repeats the exogamy-incest opposition of kinship structures. We seldom find sons locked inside their fathers' castles, because retention and separation are not the defining stress lines of the father-son narrative. In the archetypal father-son structure, the son's departure is authorized inside a circular pattern that predicts both his inevitable return and the concurrent threat of displacement/usurpation that he will pose. Myths such as that of the Prodigal Son, King Herod, the Ouranos-Kronos-Zeus story, Freud's theory of the primal horde, the *Oedipus* trilogy, *Hamlet,* and the *Henry IV* dramas exemplify a pattern that is implicit anyway in patrilineal families or in a theology in which the son is synonymous with the father. The father-son relationship is repeatedly mythologized as a potentially patricidal struggle for authority that is spatially located in the open terrain of outside cultural space. The structural dynamics are triangular in the sense that they are mediated by mutual desire for the father's prerogative. If the narrative includes a third person, it is a woman (usually the mother), who objectifies this mutual desire. Her presence, however, essentially only intensifies, and does not prevent or redraw, the collision-course formula.[7]

By contrast, a literal triangulation defined by an again male-female-male syntax is the crucial construction necessary to make father-daughter texts dynamic. Whereas the structural correspondence between father and son by itself guarantees narrative action and change, the asymmetries of gender and power that control the father-daughter bond would, without the addition of the external male rival, produce a static narrative. The daughter's struggle with her father is one of separation, not displacement. Its psychological dynamics thus locate the conflict inside inner family space. Father-daughter stories are full of literal houses, castles, or gardens in which fathers such as Danae's or Rapunzel's, or Brabantio or Shylock, lock up their daughters in the futile attempt to prevent some rival male from stealing them. The motif also occurs through riddles of enclosure such as the casket riddles in *The Merchant of Venice* or those in the Apollonius of Tyre story (in John Gower's *Confessio Amantis,* reused in Shakespeare's *Pericles*), which enclose the daughter in the father's verbal labyrinth and lure her suitors to compete with and lose to the preemptive paternal bond.

These same psychodynamics of the father-daughter bond likewise spatialize texts such as Faulkner's *Absalom, Absalom!* and "A Rose for Emily," Hawthorne's "Rappaccini's Daughter," *Romeo and Juliet,* and biblical stories such as those of Jepthah's or Jacob's daughter. Within the spatial image, the daughter—the liminal or "threshold" person in family space—symbolically stands at the boundary/door, blocked from departure by the figure of the father (and/or the son or other male heir to the father's position). For the narrative to progress—for the daughter to leave the father's enclosure—the outside rival male must arrive and create a magnetic pull on the daughter, who otherwise remains within, in psychological bondage to her filial bonds. Only when the retention structures disappear is the necessity for this external male obviated. And by implication, the retention structures disappear only when the patriarchal nuclear model is also absent. The triangle is absent, for example, from the Sumerian myth of *Inanna, Goddess of Heaven and Earth* (Wolkstein and Kramer). So, however, are the structures that suggest the Oedipal nuclear family: the enclosure of the father's house and the configuration of male kin as blocking agents who barricade it. This myth, unlike the legends of the Greek daughter-goddess figures, narrates a journey of the daughter's development and growth that is actively enabled at various stages by her brother and father. Unlike the intervening male kin in Faulkner's novels or those in the Dinah and Shechem story of Genesis 34, those in Inanna's family intercede only when she turns to them for help. When they do, they act to remove rather than erect structures that block her progress forward. In perhaps the most unusual fiction of a daughter's desire for the father's authentication, Inanna acquires the *me,* or all the powers possible, by defeating Enki, her sky-god father of wisdom, in a beer-drinking contest. In this myth, it is through the familiar father-son contest pattern that the daughter establishes her right to both paternal validation and separate equality.[8]

In Western narrative, the text of a daughter outside her father's house rarely, however, follows the Inanna pattern of a quest for independent identity. Perhaps especially in nineteenth-century women's fictions, the quest of a daughter displaced from the house most often inscribes her disguised search to reenter it. By making her at last the idealized and chosen love object of a (usually older) male authority figure, such as an employer, godfather, or clergyman, the fiction not only allows the heroine to remain a good girl loyal to her father, it satisfies the daughter's fantasies of perpetual childhood security through union with the father masked by her status as wife.[9] In patriarchal myths, the daughter out of her correct locale sets up the threat of territorial invasion and usurpation of the father's cultural space. When the threat of insurrection comes from the son, it fits into the authorized structure of patriarchy. When it comes from the detached daughter, it engenders a vision of social inversion that must be vehemently quashed within the fiction, if allowed to enter the cultural canon at all. When the narrative does occur, it does so through myths about anomalous female creatures such as the infamous Amazons, whose challenge to the patriarchy is synonymous with their status as unassigned, masculinized females who roam unstructured out in open (male) cultural terrain. Nonetheless, despite the structural independence of such daughters, their function in the Greek mythological canon was apparently to serve rather than challenge patriarchal ideology. In Wm. Blake Tyrrell's analysis, even "the Amazon belongs to a social dialogue concerning the marriage system. The myth portrays one version of the consequences of the daughter's refusal to leave her mother upon her father's request that she be married" (xviii).

Though all margins are considered dangerous, bodily margins are thought to be especially so because they mirror the points of vulnerability to the body politic. Menstruating women thus pose a particular threat of pollution to the male houses and societies they occupy. The sexual maturity of a son signifies full entry into both family and patriarchal community; since it is simultaneously defined as an accession to wisdom and political authority, it is often accompanied by ceremonies of social incorporation. The daughter's sexual maturation means something else entirely, something defined restrictedly as her entrance into a sexual status. It is recognized by marks of exclusion that aggregate her into the always marginal status of women, not into the community as a whole. In Western families, a daughter's first menstruation is typically treated with an embarrassed silence that marks it as a "woman's secret" to be communicated in whispers that carry the double message of family pride/family shame. Her adolescence seems, in fact, to crystallize the paradox of her place within the family. On the one hand, since she is its one female who is a full blood member, the loss of family blood that marks the threshold of her maturity symbolically asserts the subtraction she signifies and physically defines her as the breach in the wall of family enclosure. To circumvent this symbolic loss, a Siane daughter in the New Guinea eastern highlands must have her first menstruation on natal clan territory so that the "paternal spirit" she is thought to give birth to may be captured and retained before she is sent away in marriage to another clan (Andrew Strathern 30–31). At the same time, however, since menstruation marks the daughter's entrance into the margins of desire, her presence likewise threatens to invite incestuous desire and hence pollution within the family boundaries. In orthodox Brahmin groups, the requirement that daughters marry before their first menstruation is explained by Mary Douglas as a way the group ensures the purity of its women (145). It also suggests, however, a way that the group defrays another underlying fear that makes the mature daughter's sexual presence a threat to pollute the internal dynamics within the family space.

By religious and historical tradition, the daughter acquires maturity by acquiring "the curse" by which the Father marked a woman's fallen status with expulsion. Likewise, the rituals that frequently accompany a daughter's passage spatially define her at a new distance from her father. Often, she is isolated into a space such as a special hut that symbolically marks her existence beyond and outside the family house. For the father, the daughter's adolescence signifies a contradictory mélange of threats: loss, desire, and betrayal. According to contemporary research, "seductive fathers who were not habitually violent became violent during their daughters' adolescence. Others, perhaps in order to avoid becoming violent and paranoid, completely withdrew from their daughters. They reacted to their daughters' emerging sexuality either with an attempt to establish total control or with total rejection" (Herman 117). Narratives authored by daughters show a rather sad familiarity with these polarized reactions: "Certainly puberty was the point at which he cut off from us, and when my elder sister married he blurted out to me, on the way to her wedding, that he had long felt jealous of our boyfriends," writes Eileen Fairweather in a personal account of what she describes as her "futile struggle to win my father's love" (201). For novelist George Eliot, what accounts for Mr. Tulliver's sudden and bitter withdrawal of affection from the daughter who had formerly been "the desire of his eyes" is the fact that Maggie's "father was bitterly preoccupied with the thought that the girl was growing up—was shooting up into a woman."[10] For the daughter, the moment is a confusing one that sets her emerging sexuality into a scene connected with her father's inexplicable rejection and thus

35

with emblematic rejection by the male world. For the father, whose unbidden desires no longer hide themselves in an infant's unconscious repression, the assertion of new emotional and physical distance from the daughter serves as a defense against conscious recognition. In trying not to be the incestuous father, he instead becomes the rejecting one who turns away from his daughter precisely at the moment in her psychological maturation when she will begin turning more actively towards him. The proxemics that seem to characterize this crucial point in a daughter-father relationship might be described as an ironically constructed dialectic defined by "too close" or "too distant" polarities. Yet from the implications of recent studies, the resolution to the father's incestuous attraction may lie not in the seeming logic of distance but in the paradox of greater closeness. For the fathers who seemed least inclined to become incestuous were those whose relations with their daughters had been from birth defined by active participation in a physical and maternally nurturing role.

No doubt because the daughter's sexuality does signify a dual threat, the sexualized daughter often appears in mythic narrations as the rebellious and unfavored one. Furthermore, her appearance is frequently connected to myths of paternal castration. The "good" daughters of Western religious myth are the obdurately virginal, armor-clad Athena, the mental extension of her father's thoughts who acts out the patriarchal dictates to abjure men and subjugate rebellious women, and the virgin mother Mary, whose dual status promises perpetual loyalty to both the Father and the Son. The "bad" daughters are the hoydens such as Eve, whose sexual union with Adam follows her rebellion against the Father, and Aphrodite, the personified icon of sexuality who is engendered as a consequence of Kronos's castration and symbolically married to a cripple. When Shakespearean fathers such as Brabantio and Shylock lose the daughter they have so concertedly locked up, neither father wishes ever again to see the treacherous emblem of his own sexuality who, in passing herself over to his enemy, has dispossessed and hence castrated him. As Shylock says, "[M]y daughter is my flesh and my blood. . . . You take my house when you do take the prop / That doth sustain my house" (*Merchant of Venice* 3.1.35; 4.1.373–74). As sexual traitor to her father, Desdemona becomes the symbolic traitor to patriarchy, the adulteress who "has deceive'd her father, and may thee" (*Othello* 1.3.293). Nevertheless, while stealing herself out of her father's house may pragmatically resolve a daughter's otherwise insoluble problems, the solution paradoxically creates new structural ones. For by consequence of the design of the Oedipal nuclear family, to establish a new family bond, such a daughter betrays the old one; to enter a new family house, she violates the literal structure on which the patriarchal family as an institution is symbolically built.

Admittedly, what unbalances any analysis of mythic and literary father-daughter patterns is the distressing scarcity of models of benevolent fatherhood. Tyrannical paternity seems to mar the father-daughter text even more conspicuously than that of father and son. But the very pervasiveness of the model may suggest what historian Christopher Hill has analyzed, in another context, as the sign of a vigorous form of cultural propaganda invoked to enforce "attitudes [that] were by no means so universally accepted" as might have been wished ("Sex, Marriage, and the Family" 461). If, as Wm. Tyrrell has asserted, the Amazon myth drew a frightening picture of the consequences to patriarchy were daughters allowed to remain unmarried and roam free outside their fathers' homes, then the myth may also suggest that individual fathers behaved in unpatriarchal ways frequently enough to generate the need for such cultural retraining. Patriarchal ideology has always imagined that women—and especially the unstructured daughter—pose the ultimate threat to its power. But women may not be the real threat to patriarchy; it may instead be the fathers themselves. To quell the menace of paternal behavior deviating from the authoritarian ideal, the cultural mythmaking apparatus seems continually to have needed to reproduce patterns of dictatorial, resolutely unsentimental fatherhood modeled into father-gods and god-the-fathers. By insinuation, the model is divinely sanctioned. The greatest menace to patriarchy would be the threat of fathers rebelling against the archetypes they inherited; the most dangerous myth would have been the unwritten one in which Zeus killed Kronos but did not then reincarnate him.

As a genre, tragedy has a special way of laying bare the problematics behind a cultural code, of simultaneously dramatizing and disassembling the mythic prescriptions of its own cultural propaganda. In Shakespearean comedy, fathers have been either banished from the stage or depotentiated within the drama in order that Jack may have Jill and all may go well. In tragedy, the father assumes a particular prominence. Yet even the tyrannical fatherhood modeled for us by any number of Shakespearean patriarchs is often the quintessentially human expression of the authoritarian extremities of a father's possessive love and overwhelming fear of loss. Whether the numerous father-daughter archetypes in Shakespeare's plays reflect anything biographical is obviously unknowable, since so little historical evidence remains. What does remain, however, is the will in which virtually everything was deeded to Susanna and her already well-to-do husband, while only a dowry portion was left to the second daughter, Judith.[11] Like the will, the texts of Shakespeare's plays seem to have room for the father's relation to only one daughter. When more than one is included, the result is *King Lear*. In the pattern that emerges from both the Lear and the Gloucester plots of this play, the internal family lines are drawn by the father's exclusionary preference for one of his same-sex children. Rebecca West, using resonances from *Lear*, narrates the same pattern in *The Fountain Overflows:* "Children were like their father's family or their mother's, and Cordelia had taken her inheritance from Papa. That gave her some advantages, it did indeed. . . . Mary and I were not pleased about this. It made us feel that Cordelia was not only closer to Papa than we were, owing to an unfair decision of Nature, but that she was also an object on which he had worked to bring her up to the standards of his taste. He had not done that to us."[12] In most accounts, the paternal preference is for the older daughter. Studies of successful women indicate that the significant majority are first daughters who benefited from a strongly enabling relationship with their fathers (Heilbrun 49–50); studies of incest-abused daughters likewise indicate that the first daughter was the one "chosen" by her father (Herman 67–125). And although it may be equally true that mothers favor one daughter (or one son) over the other, the father's position as chief authorizing figure and primary model for the daughter's later male relationships makes the father's differential behavior more significant in terms of the daughter's relationship to the world beyond her father's house. The situation Rebecca West describes—that children are coded as being "like their father's family or their mother's"—is probably typical in families. But for a daughter—whose relationship to the patronymic identity of her family is tenuous at best and usually temporary—not being "like [the] father's family" reconfirms her amorphously illegitimate status.

   Although myth and literature provide a veritable index for every type of family homicide, stories in which daughters kill fathers occur almost as infrequently in mythology as they do statistically in society. Wives murder husbands, mothers kill sons, and sisters occasionally slay brothers; like Medea, women seem capable of killing almost any male within the family except the father. Goneril and Regan are castrating daughters who take sadistic delight in cutting off the symbolic potency of Lear's train of knights and thrusting him out of gates, but even they stop short of patricide and deflect their energies into sororicidal competition over Edmund. By inference, there seems to be some particularly strong taboo that exists at the boundary of a daughter's violence against the father, a boundary that Lady Macbeth discovers when she is unable to kill Duncan because he "resembled / My father as he slept" (*Macbeth* 2.2.12–13). When a daughter does kill a father, the event is certain to receive an almost mythic notoriety that carries with it the overtones of cultural anxiety. The (unproven) story of the infamous Lizzie Borden has even made its way into jump-rope rhymes. And when the *Reader's Encyclopedia* describes the murder of Francesco Cenci, for instance, the entry attributes the murder to Beatrice Cenci, the "beautiful parricide," who "with her brothers" is said to have plotted it. We are then told that "she was executed in 1599, and at the trial her counsel, with the view of still further gaining popular sympathy for his client, accused the father probably without foundation, of having attempted to commit incest with her" ("Cenci, Beatrice"). On the matter of the father's guilt, the *Encyclopedia* speaks with the same dismissive voice as did Freud.

Roman legend does record Tullia's patricide of King Servius Tullius; and in a Samson-Delilah castration archetype that occurs also in a Welsh and an Irish tale, the Greek daughter Scylla murders King Nisus by cutting off his life-giving purple lock in order to aid Minos, the enemy who is besieging the gates of her father's city (Graves 1: 91.*c*–91.3). When daughters murder fathers, the event almost inevitably occurs inside this triangular structure in which the daughter is positioned between father and lover; in some versions it is literally the daughter, and in others it is the lover she aids who kills her father. But as Edmund Leach points out in his comments on the structure of myth, whenever "a father or the father's double is killed by his enemy because of the treachery of the daughter, who loves the enemy, . . . the victorious enemy then punishes the daughter by desertion or murder" (*Lévi-Strauss* 81). When the authorized narration of patriarchal exchange is usurped by the story of a daughter who kills the father and takes over her own circulation, the narrative itself reacts against that threat, forcefully coopting it through the agency of the victorious lover, the son figure who has—because of the daughter's help, ironically enough—become the new surety for patriarchal myth. Nonetheless, as a mythic motif, daughters killing fathers is comparatively rare. The daughter's need for paternal approval and her residual awe of the godlike father seem to override the violent impulses of revenge or competition. On the literal level of the patricidal story, daughters would thus appear to have an admirably moral record. But since patricidal myths are symbolic expressions of competitive political success, and since the daughter's cultural fathers include her literary predecessors and political or corporate superiors, her psychological inability to overcome the father—which is rooted back in family dynamics but produced by and then reproduced into cultural ones—may pose a myth as problematic as it is benign. By contrast, in addition to a social history that is routine enough to be unspectacular, there are a number of well-known myths and tales in which fathers murder daughters. They generally do so, however, within structures of sacrifice that mask desire behind the impersonal facade of priestlike detachment. Rather than being infamous, the best-known

39

daughter murder narratives are famous. And the most famous such stories seem to follow one of three sacrificial patterns.

MYTHS OF DAUGHTER SACRIFICE

In the Agamemnon-Iphiginia and Jepthah–his daughter model, the father sacrifices his daughter to the perceived demands of the patriarchy and thus affirms his membership in it. By sacrificing the virginal blood of his family to the divine will, he ensures the success of the cultural project. Or to restate the paradigm in Lévi-Strauss's terms, he "exchanges" his daughter for a socially beneficial alliance. But through the father's participation in his daughter's blood, the exogamous model leads back to the incestuous one in which it is anyway implicit. The sacrificial structure of the Appius-and-Virginia story (a Roman legend reused by Chaucer as "The Physician's Tale") is, by contrast, a retention model. In it, to "save" his daughter from the lustful demands of some superior father (usually a judge or king), the father kills her (or, alternatively, his grief persuades her to kill herself) inside a text that disguises possessive annihilation as paternal protection. This murderous retention story shares its structure with a third, seemingly quite different narrative, a model that occurs infrequently in myth, quite probably because it lacks deflecting devices and brings incest and murder into too close a proximity. In the "Many Furs" Cinderella story the father threatens to kill his daughter, and in the Saint Dympna folk tale of Christian martyrology he does kill her for refusing to marry him.[13] In this variant of the daughter-sacrifice construction, the defense of a literal sacrifice has been stripped away along with the presence of superior fathers whose demands compel it. In this model, the daughter's body is the undisguised locus for blood sacrifice to her father's incestuous desire. Despite the seeming differences in the above three story types, all three depend upon a symbolics of blood that embeds the father's violence in the narration of virgin sacrifice. And all three expose the subliminal extent to which a daughter's virginity is perceived to "belong to" the blood of—and therefore to—the father.

Of all the plot constructions of daughter sacrifice, perhaps the most seductive is the one that masks itself in texts unmarked by the revealing sign of violent possession. It is also the model that relocates the child-parent dynamics inside a complex circular design of family romance and points to a mother-son structure lurking beneath that of daughter-father. Like the "Many Furs" tale, this paradigm seems to require the absence of a mother; it is one we might call the Antigone model or even the Oedipus-Antigone complex. From what we now know about the way Freud's Oedipal theories of infant sexuality were used by the psychoanalytic institution as a formidable weapon in culture's mass conspiracy to suppress the daughter's story and avoid acknowledging the father's guilt, perhaps it is worth speculating about how incest might have been understood had Freud granted the last two plays of the Sophoclean trilogy the same weight he granted *Oedipus Rex*. Perhaps, had he done so, instead of essentially dropping the seduction theory in favor of infant sexual fantasy as the model he saw supplanting it, Freud might have recognized the way that *Oedipus at Colonus* dramatizes the father's seduction of his daughter as embedded within the attempt to reconstruct his lost union with the mother, an adult reversion to infantile dependency and a state of helplessness to which women—and, in particular, daughters—are expected to respond. By playing the son, the father impels his daughter into the role of mother; and where a daughter stands for the mother, there is no superior father to make the son give up his (surrogate) mother. For the father, the regressive design is clearly a high-probability strategy that promises to undo the defeat that as an infant he suffered from his own father. The only threat comes from son figures (his own or other men's), who lack both his authority over and his bond with the daughter. Had Freud made the final two plays a model for theorizing, he might also have perceived the seductive appeal that the father's/brother's cry for love exerts on the daughter. His failure to consider such models is all the more fascinating when placed alongside the revelation that what Freud called his own daughter Anna was, amazingly enough, "Antigone" (Peters 15–21)

The Antigone model, which Elizabeth Abel deftly identifies in her analysis of *To the Lighthouse*,[14] narrates the full story of a daughter's self-sacrificing complicity with the father's needs and inscribes the father's desire back into a pattern of sexual and textual regression. When eventually we hear Oedipus angrily tell Polynices that the two daughters were "born to nurse me" (Sophocles, trans. Fagles 1545), the *Oedipus at Colonus* text has returned to repeat the underlying struggle of *Oedipus Rex*: the father-son competition for the mother. But the pattern of textual/sexual regression has actually been on stage since the play's opening scene, in which we learned that the father, having lost his mother when he lost his wife, has turned his daughter/sister into his maternal nurturer. When Oedipus appeals to Antigone through the claims of pity, "sit me down, watch over the blind man," she responds, "No need to teach me that, not after all these years" (24–25). When the forlorn old man calls to her, "Come to your father! / Let me embrace you," the daughter responds, "All you want, all will be done— / I long for it father, just as much as you" (1251–54). While the two daughters are busy sacrificing themselves to nurture their father (Antigone clearly favored over the nearly ignored, younger Ismene), the two sons are back in Thebes repeating the Laius-Oedipus combat in busy competition for the father's prerogative and throne. And as Oedipus bitterly recognizes, his sons "love the crown more than their own father" (466). But since Oedipus's daughters are also his sisters, the expectation that daughters and sisters must be mothers to their fathers and brothers structurally anticipates the conflicting claims that will, in the final play—and in such texts as Faulkner's *Absalom, Absalom!*—nullify the daughter's marriage and convert her separation from family into a sacrificial reenclosure in it. In retaining his daughter, Oedipus defies the exogamous demands of the culture, a point that Creon (albeit for self-serving motives) makes clear by telling Oedipus that Antigone is a poor child whose only existence is "Always tending you, / crushed by the gloom and poverty of your life, / And at her ripe age unmarried" (851–53).

As Antigone is repeatedly led or dragged in different forms of literal and psychological bondage back and forth across the stage, her body progressively becomes the emblematic territory for various competitive forms of patriarchal possession, political and familial. Even in the loving benediction through which the dying father finally releases his daughters, his claims perpetuate the primacy of his bond:

> All that I was on earth is gone:
> no longer will you bear the heavy burden
> of caring for your father. It was hard, I know,
> my children, but one word alone repays you
> for the labor of your lives—love, my children.
> You had love from me as from no other man alive,
> And now you must live without me all your days to come.
>
> (1828–34)

The loving possessiveness of this speech makes it perhaps the father's archetypal expression. The ambivalence that marks Antigone's lament perhaps likewise makes hers the paradigmatic daughter's response. Having spent twenty years bound to her filial duty, Antigone admits that although her life has been bitter, "you can really yearn for sorrows past to come again! / What wrenched my heart was love, love after all / as long as I held my father in my arms!" (1923–25). Yet nonetheless, when Oedipus is dying—and dying without male heirs, having disowned his two ungrateful sons—the story denies us the logic of its own self-enclosed family structure. For rather than pass his power to the daughters who surely have earned this patrimony, Oedipus instead selects a surrogate son in Theseus. To the clearly disappointed daughters he says only, "[N]ever ask to see what law forbids . . . / Now go—quickly. Only the appointed one, / Theseus, let him stand beside me: / he alone must see this mystery" (1861, 1863–65). Antigone and Ismene are excluded from their father's death and from even knowing the location of his tomb. To Theseus alone, "the appointed one," does Oedipus confer the special knowledge that his words mystify into a potently exclusive male preserve. And thus the patriarchal transmission of cultural authority is preserved intact. If the desires of the family seem to have been privileged over and against the culture's exogamous dictates by Oedipus's retention of his daughters, the cultural status quo has been resecured by his ultimate reversion to the same father-to-son transmission of authority that replicates the initiating pattern behind the tragic events of this trilogy. Oedipus establishes his full right to become the root and source, the engendering father of Greek legend, precisely through the exclusion of his daughters from the inheritance of power.

Left with nothing but desire to join her father in death, Antigone can find no substitute direction other than further repetition and return. As the concluding play of the trilogy narrates, in transferring her sacrificial maternalism from father to brothers she moves once again into the mother's position, where mediation between competing claims is once again dramatized as literal annihilation. In the last play, just as she is led off to death, Antigone acknowledges, "O dear brother, doomed / in your marriage—your marriage murders mine, / your dying drags me down to death" (956–58). Indeed, her marriage has been murdered by a brother's marriage—by the marriage of son to mother that has made brother simultaneous with father. But even more, it has been destroyed by the father's regression back to son, the psychological maneuver that has propelled the daughter back into the middle to repeat the role of the "doomstruck mother." When Antigone identifies her fate as bound up with her mother's—"the coiling horrors . . . / you with your own son, my father—doomstruck mother" (952–53)—the structure of the trilogy insists that we read her reference through the regression, the coiling in upon itself, that the concluding two plays encode. Within the teleology of the absolutely closed family that these three plays dramatize, what entombs the daughter's future is not so much the original sin of the mother and son that pre-existed her but the regression back to it that the daughter and father have played out. The full truth of the Oedipal drama includes an important narration of how the father-daughter bond is made invincible through the progressive restatement of its asymmetries of age and authority accompanied by their simultaneous inversion. It is the truth not only of Oedipus's assertion that his two daughters were "born to nurse me" but of Lear's desire to make his daughters his mothers and "to set my rest / On [Cordelia's] kind nursery" (*King Lear* I.i.123–24). Nonetheless, the lurking presence of the father's infantility is a truth so bitter that Lear threatens to whip the Fool for speaking it.

WHILE IT IS not surprising that the origin myths most familiar to Western civilization depict creation anthropomorphically in terms of definable family structures, what is surprising is that those structures are incomplete: they lack daughters. And while the (patriarchal) nature of the cultures in which these myths originated makes their dominant father-son focus and their usual inclusion of a subordinate mother seem likewise predictable, such logic is not really adequate to explain away the repeated extrusion of the fourth member of family. Without her, the creation story itself is incompletely created. Furthermore, her absence wrecks the explanatory potential that in part impels such paradigmatic myths. In the most important Egyptian myth of origins, three of a woman's four nuclear family roles are collapsed together, so that Isis may be mother, consort/wife, and sister to Osiris—but not daughter. In the Greek Ouranos-Kronos-Zeus narrative, the preoccupation with father/son usurpation suppresses even the myth of male-female relationship, and the earth mothers Gaia-Rhea-Metis occur only as named wombs within the text. When the first real daughters finally appear, they force their way into the narrative through accidental forms of paternal parthogenesis that in themselves suggest threat and repression. Aphrodite, engendered by the sperm from Kronos's severed penis which Zeus hurls into the foam, emerges from the depths of the sea inscribed within a myth of father castration. Even Athena, who leaps fully armed from Zeus's aching forehead after he has swallowed her mother to prevent the birth of sons, is born in almost an allegory of emerging repression.

My purpose in exploring this general absence of daughters is not to generate a repetitious catalog of exclusions. The following exploration—which focuses on an exegetical reading of the family structures inscribed within the Judeo-Christian creation story—assumes, along with Freud, that disturbances of the expected and normal potentially lend greater insight into the normal than can direct study. The daughter's presence is normal to the biological realities of family; her absence is therefore loaded with significance. When viewed structurally, these narratives are marked by fossil traces suggesting that the daughter's presence has been suppressed by transformation into other, less problematic designs. If we recognize religious texts as "myth" in the sense used by anthropologist Edmund R. Leach—as "the expression of unobservable realities in terms of observable phenomena" ("Genesis" 1)—and if we then use structural concepts of kinship as a lens through which to look at the encoded family narrations, what emerges into shadowy form from beneath the creation story of Genesis is the special license masked by that same mytho-logic that structurally authorizes it.

The reading of the Old Testament that follows is not concentrated on its historical implications. To analyze what we can know about the literal history of a daughter's life inside the ancient Hebrew world—and there is no reason to suppose that it differed significantly in surrounding cultures—would be an entirely different enterprise. As a brief summary, it seems obvious from references in the bible and legal codifications in Talmudic law and the Mishnah that even skeletal notions of consent or child abuse were conceptually nonexistent. Daughters were sexual property belonging exclusively to the father; like Laban's daughters, Leah and Rachel, they existed to be bartered for economic profit. As the Genesis narrative of Jacob's daughter Dinah makes likewise clear, rape was not considered a violation of the daughter so much as a theft of property that deprived her father and necessitated compensation to him (according to Deuteronomy 22, the price the rapist of an unbetrothed virgin owed the father was fifty shekels). Although the Talmud recommended against marrying off daughters until they were between twelve and twelve and a half years of age, fathers were allowed to sell them into either marriage or concubinage well before that age. Perhaps most shocking of all is the fact that so long as paternal permission was involved, daughters were considered available for sexual use after the age of three years and one day. As incredible as this authorization may sound to modern readers, the point that a female child of "three years and one day could be betrothed by sexual intercourse" is reaffirmed even by the sophisticated twelfth-century Talmudist Moses Maimonides in his monumental clarification of Talmudic law, *The Mishnah Torah*.[15] There is some recorded controversy over this statute, but the controversy involves haggles over the "one day" clause.

As the above synopsis shows, the evidence from legal documents argues only an estranged and bleakly inhumane history of daughter-father relationship. Yet I personally feel ill at ease in accepting such a history as the whole story of the daughter-father bond, be it that in the biblical era or otherwise. Because a daughter was the least economically useful member of a patrilineal and primogenitural institution, social historians tracing evidence such as this have perhaps been overhasty to infer that she was likewise the least cherished. Drawing on a number of historical documents from sixteenth-century England, historian Lawrence Stone has argued, for example, that the Elizabethan family was a unit organized exclusively around goals of patriarchy, patrilineage, and primogeniture, that it virtually lacked emotional bonds, and that daughters "were often unwanted and might be regarded as no more than a tiresome drain on the economic resources."[16] Such histories are invaluable for their representation of the legal and economic truths that constructed the family. But their inferences are clearly inadequate to account for the emotional and psychological truths, the problematic bonds of love and possession that define, for instance, the families of Shakespeare's sixteenth-century dramas. They are equally unable to account for the enormous importance that the official creation myth of Judeo-Christianity vests in Eve, who is, despite the refusal to name her as such, its first daughter figure.

While the family is a historical institution, it nonetheless differs significantly from other institutions. It is first of all unique in having women as indispensable components. Furthermore, it is a private as well as public unit that, Janus-like, faces inward as well as outward. The face that looks outward into the masculine and public world is unlikely to expose emotional ambivalences written on its other side. These other truths get written not in its official documents but inside the masking devices of what we might call the archetypal histories of family—its literary and mythic texts. Acknowledging the history of women as patriarchal property has been both descriptively and diagnostically important, for only this exhumation has enabled contemporary social research to recognize the powerful psychic residues of that history in such modern problems as rape, child abuse, wife battering, and incest. But the economic text subsumes its repressed opposite: material possession constructs and is constructed by a politics of sex at work inside the closures of kinship. For although the daughter was clearly regarded as legal property inside the family, she has never been a commodity to be bartered in the same way as an ox or an ass. She is explicitly a *sexual* property acquired not by economic transaction but from the father's sexual expenditure and his own family bloodline—which makes the father's loss of her a distinctively personal loss of himself. Furthermore, since her worth as property is synonymous with her sexuality, retaining her is problematically invested in that same value. The relationship between father and daughter may well have taken so long for the culture to articulate because it is locked into a conflicted text of desire and sanction that is complicated in ways that even the mother-son dynamic is not. The same asymmetries of age, authority, and gender privilege that work to separate mother and son exist by mirrored opposite in the father-daughter relationship and consequently recomplicate rather than resolve it. The very fact that culture has *needed* to impose a taboo to ensure an exogamous exchange of its daughters and the fact that it has evolved a ritual of husband-wife marriage that is primarily a father-daughter separation rite both suggest that the father-daughter relationship has no effective internal mechanisms for negotiating its dissolution. The tangent at which the father and daughter meet is the line that potentially threatens almost every enclosing structure of the family unit. That boundary, moreover, is a double one: one of its markers defines the father's control over inner family space; the other, his authority in the space of the outside, cultural world. And the daughter's movement to cross that threshold and move out of the father's house, whether into the house of another man or into the world of paternal institution, threatens the father, familial or cultural, with loss.

In the following proverb from Ecclesiasticus, the different family spaces occupied by a son and daughter are reflected by the different syntaxes into which they are placed. The patriarch places the son—even a "badly brought-up" one whose behavior is a "disgrace"—into legitimate recognition as a child he "fathered." The daughter, however, is dissociated from direct acknowledgment of his paternity and relegated to the implicitly maternal sphere of "birth," where she is defined, for no specific fault, as being simply a "loss." But whether we read "loss" as referring primarily to a family's economic and patrilineal goals or whether we understand it as pointing to a more complex locus of unstated emotional investments, the ambiguity in the word itself perhaps best sums up the liminal space historically occupied by daughters within their father's house:

> It is a disgrace to have fathered a badly brought-up son,
> And the birth of a daughter is a loss.   (Si. 22:3)[17]

THE CONSTRUCTION OF FAMILY IN THE
BIBLICAL CREATION MYTH

It testifies to the process of cultural reproduction that most readers raised in the Judeo-Christian tradition were trained to read right over the first description of creation in Genesis 1:26 and assimilate only the familiar rib version of chapters 2 and 3, in which the fall is already embedded. Feminist biblical scholars such as Phyllis Trible have found in Genesis 1 a mitigating authorization for women's equality, a suppressed "feminist" content that in turn would reconcile feminism with biblical tradition and allow contemporary daughters a way back to the Father. Yet, as John A. Phillips recognizes in his analysis of the idea of Eve, it is vain to try to reconcile the Genesis text by imagining that the woman's position changes from that of an equal in chapter 1 to that of a subordinate in chapter 3 only as a result of being blamed for the fall. For "the position of Eve is always the same. It is her situation at the time the Yahwist is writing" (115). It is equally impossible to segregate sections of the bible away from the exegetical process of reading it backward that defines its authority in Western culture. For readers, there is never a beginning, only an *"in the beginning."* When we begin even a first reading of the first verse of Genesis, we are already inside a narrative that was written backward, transmitted in time through further readings backward, and is thus always already inseparable from the process that has culturally reproduced it. It is a process that Mieke Bal's study of biblical passages about the female body, the transgression, and its consequences discusses as a "*collocation*" involving the "retrospective fallacy," which consists of "the projection of an accomplished . . . character-image on previous textual elements which *lead* to the construction of that character" (23). Because it contributes, if destructively, to the production of myths, the process is a necessary consideration in any attempt to account for the nature of and the "problematization of the represented ideology" (22).

Genesis 1, the so-called Priestly version, effectively problematizes the represented ideology by contradicting the preferred story line of chapters 2 and 3. Although it was apparently written later than the Yahwist version, in the narrative organization it has been placed so as to precede the familiar creation-fall story. In light of the way that almost every authorization of Genesis 1 is subsequently erased by chapters 2 and 3, the positional relationship of the two narratives plus commentaries outside the official text showing how the contradiction was rationalized are invaluable for what they say about the shadowed family constructions masked beneath such transformations. As the Genesis text wrestles to reconstitute the family into an arrangement that will produce its desired model, the story repeatedly shows the marks of backward erasure, extrusion, and transformation. Modeling the family by circumventing the norms of its empirical realities not only defines the operation at work in the book of Genesis, however. As Clifford Geertz puts it, religious beliefs "do not merely interpret social and psychological processes in cosmic terms—in which case they would be philosophical, not religious—but they shape them. In [these beliefs] is embedded also a recommended attitude toward life" (*Interpretation* 124). In the paradigm that the religious texts of Judeo-Christianity set up, father and son are made first analogous and then, in Christianity, synonymous. By the time the creation-fall narrative in the Hebrew text concludes, the story will have accomplished its father-to-son transmission, and Adam, the acknowledged son, will have graduated to the role of father. At this point the absent mother also will appear, emerging into designation out of the unnamed and unassigned female transgressor of the Father's garden. Within this narrative, what is conspicuously absent is the figure that lurks beneath the text, the figure who is also the one repeatedly subjected to erasure, extrusion, and transformation.

Throughout the book of Genesis the role of the woman is under constant negotiation. Until her position in the family is finally fixed as the "Mother of All the Living"—which occurs only after the fall—she is the crucial character, whose centrality is made the more obvious by the repeated ways she is shifted from margin to margin, the figure who always occupies an anomalous relationship to the story she has clearly been brought in to dynamize. In short, until she has played out her role and been kicked out of the Father's garden into motherhood, Eve is a problem. And "the story of Eve is . . . at the heart of the concept of Woman in Western civilization. . . . she is also Everywoman, the prototypical woman, all of her sex who are yet to come" (John A. Phillips xiii).

In the Jerusalem Bible, the story in Genesis 1 reads:

> God said, "Let us make man in our own image, in the likeness of ourselves, and let them be masters of the [creatures already created]."
> God created man in the image of himself,
> in the image of God he created him,
> male and female he created them.
> God blessed them, saying to them, "Be fruitful, multiply, fill the earth and conquer it. . . . See, I give you . . . all the trees with seed-bearing fruit; this shall be your food." (Gn. 1:26–29)

Here, the syntactical parallelism in the middle three lines implies that man and woman are created simultaneously and equally, both formed in the image of the divine parent whose masculine *He* must, by inference, be simultaneously cogendered. In this version, human sexual union is blessed, and there is no taboo distinguishing the antinomies of life and death that Genesis 2 will subsequently associate with abstinence from versus indulgence in the knowledge of good and evil. Here, the common parentage of man and woman constructs them as son and daughter and makes God overtly a father (if covertly a mother) who authorizes their implicitly incestuous union.

Confronted with a canonical text irreconcilable with the one privileged by all theological traditions that subscribe it, scriptural apologists usually interpreted the contradiction by superimposing a creation-fall story backward upon Genesis 1; with uncanny perception, the fiction inserted in the gap actually expresses the deepest logic of the official story it justifies. In the various exegetical readings, only the daughter figure is extruded from the garden, and the family is thus returned by erasure to a world of only fathers and sons. In the most popular such legend, the woman is Lilith, who creates dissension by continually reminding Adam of her equality until she is finally removed from the garden when she refuses Adam's demand that the sexual act be performed with him on top.[18] The patriarchal exegesis is on one hand clearly political and seems designed to necessitate and hence justify the creation of a second—and this time clearly subordinate—mate for Adam. But when Lilith's place inside this fossil family legend is considered structurally, the Father's action to remove her from the garden suggests another, unacknowledged story of possession embedded in that of expulsion. The rationale for expulsion is actually one in which the father removes his daughter from sexual experience; the price of her removal is the simultaneous eradication of license for the son's sexuality and denial of the opportunity the legend offers to define women's subordination by letting Adam enact it. For according to the legend, when Adam tries to rape the unsubmissive Lilith, she calls upon the Father, whereupon she is removed from the danger that threatens her purity. Because she can neither return nor die, legend leaves her to wander around the Red Sea, an immortal emblem of sexual desire who continues throughout history to haunt the unbidden fantasies of mankind. The legend is noncanonical and exists at the margins of the official construction. Likewise, Lilith, the sexualized daughter demanding equality, does haunt—and does get extruded from—the mythic histories of the patriarchal family.

On one side, the Adam-and-Eve narration is bracketed by a creation myth constructed by a son and an expelled daughter. On the other side, in Genesis 6:18, is a fossil myth of the fall brought about by the "daughters of men." In this odd (and for that reason, obscure) fragment, the "sons of God," or the "Watcher angels," are seduced down to earth by desire for the "daughters of men"; since the Noah story follows this section, the corrupt but heroic offspring produced from this union are used by the Yahwist as the motive for God's decision to destroy humanity by the flood. As Phillips points out, in the Old Testament Apocrypha, the union is said to defile not the hapless daughters but the immortal sons; and from such elaborations of the Watcher story begins a backward reading that attributes the origin of evil to Eve and fuses that evil with her sexual seduction of the son (John A. Phillips 46–47). Here, as in Genesis 1, the problem revolves around a woman positionally coded as "daughter."

When the Yahwist version of chapter 2 creates man and woman all over again, it erases both the synchronism and the parallelism of the chapter 1 creation by dissociating God from the parentage of the woman, simultaneously erasing the incestuous implications of the son-daughter union by eliminating the chapter 1 license for the human children to be fruitful and eat unrestrictedly of all the "trees with seed bearing fruit." In this version, the woman who will later be called Eve is reasoned into being neither as God's daughter nor as Adam's copartner in fruitful multiplication but as the anomalous member of the "helpmeets" created to solace Adam's aloneness, a group that includes birds, cattle, beasts, and woman (Leach, "Genesis" 7). Adam's maternal parent is implicitly present in the earth from which he is shaped. But Eve, who is born from Adam's body through Yahweh God's appropriation of Adam's rib and subsequent cloaking of it in flesh, ends up with a nebulous parentage lost in ambiguities. No matter how her parentage is read, what does seem clear is that the text has tried to detach her genealogy from the Father and place it with Adam in the form of a subtraction from his body. By making Adam the donor, the myth enables sexual union to be imagined as a form of male re-union with male flesh rather than with flesh that is totally separate, radically other, and conspicuously not-male. When the Christian text writes a new version of the creation story, it manages to suppress sexual congress altogether by avoiding the necessity for either father or son to procreate. When the divine Son, the "second Adam," emerges in the New Testament, a literal but virginal mother enters the drama of procreation and replaces the clay of maternal earth. But rather than the son designated to be the father of man, what is created is the Son of God and Son of man who cannot displace—because he simultaneously *is*—the Father. The Christian revision ingeniously manages to avoid the necessity for a partner-sibling for its son and thus obviates the problematic sexual presence of that untitled and unentitled woman in the Father's garden. Once the human mother has emerged in the Christian drama and has become part of a trio that can (dis)inclusively be called the Holy Family, if not the Holy Trinity, even the structural presence of the unacknowledged, shadowy daughter of the garden trio disappears, subsumed beneath and obviated by—because reformed into—the mother.

As historical investigations attest, behind the Hebrew construction of family lies the suppressed Babylonian and Canaanite mythology of the dethroned mother Goddess, the powerful serpent/dragon-mother who threatens to swallow up creation until she is eventually overcome in battle by Marduk, the son-warrior.[19] The terrifying serpent-mother-goddess does indeed cast a long shadow across the Hebrew text—across its insistence on a single male deity who is One and likewise across the character of the recreated mother, Eve. But suppress her as the tradition might, it eventually does—because it must—authorize the mother's re-entry. What the tradition will not allow to be overtly included is its daughter. Both the Judaic and the Christian myths of family genesis insistently refuse the nuclear family logic of four and just as repeatedly insist, through various transformations, that the three authorized roles within the family are father, son, and mother. The omission, however, creates a flaw in the structure that calls attention to itself. Every mythological system depends upon a persistent sequence of binary opposition that discriminates categories in the form "x is what not-x is not" (Leach, "Genesis" 3). But although we might expect that such an opposition would disparage the female (the not-x) in order to privilege the male (the x), the very terms for binarism are actually broken down by the way the paradigm in Genesis 2 eliminates even the common base of filial relationship necessary for comparing the category "son." By suppressing the matching category, the text creates a myth through which the Father denies his paternity of the daughter and leaves the woman who occupies that role in a strangely illegitimate relationship to the narrative. She is placed in the garden because she is predestined to emerge out of its enclosure as mother; yet, since Yahweh has revoked the license in chapter 1 for fruitfulness immediately before the woman is created, even her ability to emerge into that identity has been denied before she enters the story. Behind the official ideology of the transgression-expulsion story, the sequence of family roles works like a code for reading what is subliminally scripted as the father's story of the peculiar sins of the daughter. Decoded, the accusations might read: *because of* the daughter's sin against the father, sons must henceforth leave their father's control—"This is why a man leaves his father" (Gn. 2:24)[20]—and displace their father by acquiring that status themselves; *because of* the daughter's disobedience, daughters likewise leave the protective enclosure and turn into the maternal figure that the patriarchal narrative had earlier, and with great difficulty, at least temporarily suppressed.

Despite the resistance the text offers to its daughter figure's sexuality, for Genesis to chronicle the tribe's founding fathers, sexuality must occur, and Eve must cohabit with Adam so the sons of Israel may come into being. But because it is the action the text refuses to authorize, it must be accomplished through a mediation that disclaims and hence masks its authorization. At the deepest layer of the sacred myth of paternal generation, the (unacknowledged) daughter is the structural catalyst that enables both the myth and its masking. By consequence, however, she is also the figure who problematizes it and hence gets erased from it.

Whenever Genesis tries to cover up the threat that is posed by its daughter, inevitably it ends up only reconstituting it. When the Yahweh creation erased the Father's parentage of the woman and reneged on its preceding authorization for son-daughter union, the resolution only reconstructed a new family romance in which Eve's position is, ironically, once again that of a daughter. Since the overt phallocentricity of this book of begettings leaves little conceptual space for recognizing hermaphroditic implications that would blur its preemptive category of maleness, the maternal construction of Adam's role gets subordinated. Through the emphasis the myth places on Eve's derivation from Adam's rib, understanding is weighted towards reading the borrowed male part as symbolically phallic. But through Adam's implied paternity, the narrative unavoidably ends up recoding the paradigm of human procreation into a tacitly condoned but overtly disclaimed act between father and daughter, beneath which still lurks the outline of the uneradicated son-and-daughter original. On one hand, the text acknowledges no authorization for incest; at the same time, it tacitly allows for what it then projects onto the unacknowledged daughter it violates. To circumvent all this, the creation myth would have had to do what it refuses to do: go outside itself and import (as it later does to provide wives for Cain and Abel) a woman whose genesis is separate from either the Father's *or* his fathering son's creation.

In Edmund Leach's explanation of Lévi-Strauss's work, the imperative that defines any given system of kinship is one of binary opposition: "Every human society has rules of incest and exogamy. Though the rules vary they always have the implication that for any particular male individual all women are divided by at least one binary distinction, there are women of *our kind* with whom sex relations would be incestuous and there are women of the *other kind* with whom sex relations are allowed" ("Genesis" 4). This polarity creates a dilemma that necessitates mediation. To procreate with one of "our kind" violates a taboo and is thus undesirable. But although marriage ritual does what it can to erase the "otherness" of the daughter/bride/wife by such acts as changing her name and carrying her over the threshold into the enclosure of her new kinship house, she remains an import who is not of "our" bloodline. And to procreate with the "other kind" threatens the whole concept of closed structure upon which distinction depends. The dilemma thus set up is one the Yahweh creation story resolves by having it both ways. By being excluded from God's paternity, Eve becomes an outsider, the "other kind," with whom Adam's procreation is lawful. But if she really were this "other kind," she would of course have a father elsewhere, which would threaten not only the closures of family but all the mythic exclusions upon which the theology depends. Furthermore, it would wreck the exclusively patriarchal ideology of the myth by providing humanity with an original genealogy of separate matrilineage. What happens is a solution by which Eve is thrown out of the Father's house and then simultaneously reinscribed into it. Encoded into an archetypal liminality, she is relocated outside the family because she is inside it, inside the family because she is its outsider.

Perhaps nowhere are the implications of Eve's dual relationship as (unacknowledged) daughter/outsider more evident than in her use as mediator of the symbolic fruit, the knowledge of good and evil which precipitates the fall. All myths have several crucial stories (Lévi-Strauss's "mythemes") that they must narrate to establish a beginning that justifies patriarchal organization: rebellion against the father, acquisition of knowledge, the intrusion of evil, and the origins of procreation, plus gender roles and privileges. While pantheistic structures such as Greek mythology split these stories, a monotheistic design such as the Hebrew text compresses all such myths into one. The fall is such a multivocal narrative: it tells and subsequently masks all of its important narrations. While almost all interpretations of the fall have been forced to acknowledge its sexual subtext, patriarchal exegesis has inevitably privileged not the myth that has been masked but the myth that covers it. The masking myth—"Adam's Fall"—narrates the familiar story of the son's rebellion against the father. But the narrative structure actually sets up a sexualized daughter-father text in which the Adam material appears merely as a renarration. Behind its masking story, the Judeo-Christian creation myth is one of a daughter's rebellion. Human history is initiated by the (unacknowledged) daughter's appropriation of the forbidden fruit from the sign of the Father that stands erected at the center of the enclosed garden. But when the text is confronted with a daughter's desires that have no legitimate place in its symbolic order, it (and the church fathers who provided its gloss) mutes them by denial. By reassigning the fall to Adam and reasserting the primacy of the father-son relationship, the story represses the more threatening material of its father-daughter text. To effect all this, however, it must subject itself to a labyrinth of self-exposing transformations.

To enable its myth of human history, the text first needs an outsider to suggest evil into Paradise and a marginal resident to instigate rebellion against its Father/Creator—roles that the serpent and the unacknowledged daughter neatly fulfill. In making Eve the active figure, however, the narrative unavoidably reconstructs the Promethean myth of heroic choice, wherein Eve's theft of forbidden knowledge becomes dangerously analogous to the heroic act of humanity's first culture-bearer. Denied the eminence of tragic heroism, Eve's rebellion is mythologized into a formula of disobedience and punishment that contains within it three essential paradigms of the family: its origins, its patriarchal construction, and the hidden threats that, like the serpent, lurk seductively within it.

The existence of the nuclear family as an institution is possible only through a daughter's transgression against and departure from the closure of her father's house. On one level, Eve's appropriation of the forbidden fruit—which, like the serpent, has exegetically been understood as being a representation of Eve herself (John A. Phillips 41)—mythologizes the daughter's rebellion into sexual maturity through the seizure of her own fruitfulness and her choice to give it to another male. At this stratum of the myth, the fall anthologizes the daughter's dispossession of her father, her separation from him, the reason why a son likewise "leaves his father . . . and joins himself to his wife" (Gn. 2:24), and their joint departure from the natal boundaries. Eve's choice and Adam's subsequent one are clearly necessary. Yet the act is nonetheless a violation that not only is cursed by the Father but results in his erecting a permanent barrier of psychic separation between himself and the children who, at the daughter's instigation, have chosen their own precarious freedom over the perpetual security offered them.

Embedded in this one text of transgression through separation is its complementary opposite of violation through appropriation. In it, the "seed bearing fruit" on the Father's tree signifies the Father's phallic self—the "Father's phallus" in both its Lacanian meaning as symbol of paternal authority and its Freudian significance as the physical sign of "presence" and biological superiority. The taboo on plucking/ingesting this knowledge of good and evil forbids the daughter from appropriating/castrating/incestuously partaking of the Father's potency and privilege. These symbolic meanings become even clearer if we follow the time-honored pattern of reading the bible backward. In Leviticus, the taboo on fruit reappears, and with it, its phallic significance. The fruit taboo resurfaces just before the children of Israel are to enter the Promised Land, a space that recapitulates the Father's original garden (Frye 72). Like Paradise, it has rules defining the right of occupation. Before Yahweh allows his wandering children to enter this second refuge, he enjoins them: "Once you have entered this land and planted a fruit tree of any sort, you are to regard its fruits as its foreskin. For three years it shall be a thing uncircumcised, and you must not eat it" (Lv. 19:23).

From this symbolic perspective, the structures of this narrative create a many-textured myth indeed. Placed into a psychoanalytic context, it narrates the daughter's desire to acquire the father's knowledge/power through acquiring the (phallic) sign that has been denied her. In taking it for herself, Eve dramatizes the amorphous threat to patriarchal construction inherent in the daughter's independent, unassigned status. By asserting her desire for the sign that confers exclusive rights to the male, she symbolically challenges every privilege of the sex/gender system that the father's phallus signifies. In then giving it to Adam, however, Eve enters the psychoanalytic narration in which woman becomes the (empty) medium through which male authority is passed from father to son, her aggressive right to possess it converted into the passive right to transmit it. And indeed, once she has transferred the fruit to Adam's possession, she transfers also her narrative centrality and subsequently disappears into the margins of the Genesis story. The terms of the father's punishment codify and legitimize the system that her seizure threatened—the system that is, of course, already in place at the time the Genesis myth is being written. Eve is ordered out of the unassigned daughter's position and into the role of mother. Furthermore, her denied desires are perpetuated into a frustrated "yearning" for all that the father authenticates only in his son and sole heir: "Your yearning shall be for your husband, / yet he will lord it over you" (3:16). Read psychoanalytically, the iconographical moments of the garden and the fall sequentially recapitulate the story of the pre-Oedipal state of ignorance and the daughter's fall into the knowledge of what her "castration" culturally signifies. In its language of "longing," the myth even recognizes what Freud would have called penis envy, or the daughter's recognition of absence. It is likewise a recognition of what Freud's feminist interpreters have defined as being another kind of knowledge—the knowledge of a cultural form of evil instituted by the way that "cultural stereotypes have been mapped onto the genitals" (Rubin 195).

At the same time that the myth transmits the Freudian psychoanalytic narrative of the "catastrophe" that leaves "the path to the development of femininity . . . open to the girl," it also transmits the dangerous potential inherent in the daughter's subsequent "transition to the father object" ("Some Psychical Consequences," *SE* 19:241). In this construction, Eve's seizure of the Father's seed is mythically analogous to an act of daughter-father incest. At the spatial center of his family enclosure, the Father has planted the invitation to transgress accompanied by a prohibition against doing so. The ambivalence of the Father's part in the fall—which has even provoked its share of theological controversy—is extremely valuable for a reading of the family text this myth inscribes. The father desires and forbids desiring; he simultaneously wants but does not want the transgression he has provoked but will deny and punish. The ambivalence is, furthermore, textually masked by perhaps its most psychologically accurate defense. The seduction is split away from the Father and enclosed inside a narrative that denies paternal complicity by transmitting the seduction from the serpent to Eve and from Eve to Adam. In the first projection, the seduction is assigned to the (phallic) serpent introduced within the text not as Satan (an identification that occurs only later in the bible) but as "the most subtle of wild beasts that Yahweh God had made" (3:1).[21] The chain of biblical deflections that always protects fathers begins here. It was thus not the Father but the serpent who seduced the daughter. By the time the Adam story is over, it will be the daughter who seduced her father.

Read through its family structures, the text describes the father's (unacknowledged) seduction of his daughter and the daughter's punished reach for love and union with the all-powerful and distant parent. Once she has transgressed, she is simultaneously rewarded and punished, authorized and subordinated, acknowledged by his first address to her and rejected/ejected from his spatial enclosure. The unsignified daughter who has hitherto lacked any acknowledged family relationship is ordered into signification by being severed from the father but authorized to enter the official family design as wife/mother. As she does so, and as the biblical narrative moves out of myth and into history, the daughter-father story that has been problematically asserting its potency is congruently repressed and remains visible only in the structure of Adam's paternal authority over the wife/mother, whose new status will alone guarantee him the title of patriarch. Now that the original sanction to be fruitful and multiply has been transformed into structures of taboo, transgression, and punishment, the human family and history may begin. Adam is ordered into history only as a laborer in the workaday world, his absence from the domestic domain thus guaranteed. It is Eve who is ordered exclusively into the creation of family and thus into enabling the design of the story from which her presence as daughter has been and will continue to be excluded. It will be some time before a father and his daughter are officially allowed to enter the story. When they do appear, they do so within the incestuous tale of Lot and his daughters. By then, however, the cultural paradigm to rationalize father-daughter incest has already been fixed into orthodoxy. Lot will be blamelessly seduced by his daughters, just as Adam was unwittingly seduced by the woman he fathered, "the woman you put with me; she gave me the fruit, and I ate it" (3:12). From a modern perspective, Adam's self-exonerating voice comes perilously close to anticipating the syntax through which, until quite recently, the father-daughter incest story has been rationalized. The family as a historical institution, its tradition of gender-exclusive roles, and the relationship that threatens it from within are thus mediated into being by means of a complex myth that simultaneously depends upon the daughter's disobedience to and erasure from its construction.

From now on, with the exception of the anomalous story of Ibzan (Jg. 12:9), Old Testament fathers studiously avoid ever giving daughters away. In fact, the narrative avoids daughters almost altogether, and we usually hear about them only when they are coming into the "us" group as new wives. Concurrently, however, as Julian Pitt-Rivers points out, the rest of Genesis constitutes nearly a meditation on the question where wives for the patriarchy should come from, how closely they should be related to "us" or how "other" they should be (165, 128). Buried beneath these narratives in which Yahweh makes his divine disapproval of foreign wives amply clear runs the progression that implicitly answers the suppressed daughter question. In its explicit focus, the story sequence proposes a variety of possible alternatives to the question whether a brother should marry his sister (or patrilineal cousin) or give her away for political alliance; its progression is interrupted by the incestuous tale of Lot and his daughters, which suddenly proposes an alternative to the brother-sister conjunctions. In the structurally similar Abram-Sarai, Abraham-Sarah, and Isaac-Rebekkah narrations, where husbands duplicitously offer their sister-wives to the local ruler, the outcome is always the same: husbands are not punished (in fact, they usually profit), but Yahweh nonetheless exerts pressure on the foreigner to return the exchanged woman to her brother-husband. The women cycled outward are thus repeatedly returned to the patrilineal enclosure. In a choice between (His) sons' making even profitable alliances and losing (His) daughters, Yahweh seems tacitly to prefer the Adam-and-Eve resolution, which keeps daughters within the father's patriline but blurs the retention by renaming them wives/mothers.

Between the Abram-Sarai story in Genesis 12 and its renarration as Abraham and Sarah in Chapter 20, the story of Lot intervenes to present an exemplum of the perils of daughter exogamy. Up until Lot, no father has begotten a first-born daughter, and none of the really important patriarchs (Adam, Noah, Abraham) are recorded as having begotten any daughters at all. Having detached himself from the nomadic family and settled in the city of Sodom, Lot destroys this impressive record by becoming the first father to produce no sons. Although Lot has cooperatively married his two daughters to the locals in Sodom (and has even generously offered them to the mob of men outside his door), the Sodomite men prefer homosexuality; the sons-in-law choose to stay in the condemned city rather than leave with their wives, and Lot's foreign wife is so loathe to depart that she turns back for a (very) final look. The message seems clear: cities lead to various forms of demasculinization (production of daughters and homosexuality); foreign marriages leave one's daughters frustrated and sterile; and marriages so thoroughly exogamous as those that Lot has effected contribute no sons to the patrilineal project. Having been depleted by going too far towards exogamy, fertility can now be recovered only by going too far in the other direction. But the text needs a mediator, an available Eve to pluck the fruit from/offer it to her father. And the available mediator is once again the daughter(s), to whose desire for "a man on earth to come in to us after the manner of all the earth" (RSV, 19:31) the incestuous act is attributed. Inside the furtive space of a cave, Lot's desire is hidden beneath that of his daughters, who give him wine rather than an apple and seduce him into impregnating them with his sons. The narrative makes it emphatically clear, however, that the father did not volitionally participate in this incestuous act. Like Cinyras in Ovid's tale, who was tricked by his daughter Myrrha, Lot was unwittingly seduced after being made drunk by his daughters.[22] Although it is unclear just who he thought had stopped by the cave on the two sequential nights of his seduction, on both occasions Lot himself "was unaware of her coming to bed or of her leaving" (19:33, 35).

Now, while this union is not a wrong solution (it goes unpunished and without further comment), it is not an altogether ideal one (the sons that are born go on to father the Moabites and the Ammonites). A better answer implicitly was Abraham's, which was to marry the woman who "is my sister, she is the daughter of my father, but not the daughter of my mother" (20:11). But although Abraham and his patrilineal half sister Sarah did produce the one son Isaac, since this son came when the infertile Sarah was nearly one hundred years old, and then only by Yahweh's intervention, this marriage apparently is not yet the ideal combination for reproducing the patriarchy.

The defining move in the right direction is Isaac's marriage to Rebekkah, who is his father's brother's daughter (or patrilineal parallel cousin). In fact, modern ethnologists document that marriage to the father's brother's son is still the preferred arrangement for daughters in Middle Eastern kinship patterns (Barth 11; Pitt-Rivers 162). Not only does the Isaac Rebekkah union produce Jacob and Esau but the wife who already comes from within the family has the good sense to despise Esau for marrying two foreign Hittite women and to ensure that the birthright preference goes to the second son, Jacob, who marries two of his own kin. By head count, Jacob's production clearly wins the ram: he sires twelve sons and only one daughter, and by the time he goes to Egypt he has accumulated sixty-six bloodline descendents, sixty-four of them male. Jacob's success is ensured four times over by the structure of his marriage: not only does he acquire two wives but he acquires sisters who constitute a lineal double of each other; what is more important, Laban's daughters, Leah and Rachel, are both products twice over of Jacob's own patriline. As Pitt-Rivers shows by tracing this genealogy, Jacob marries two of his own father Isaac's father's brother's son's son's daughters, who are simultaneously Rebekkah's brother's daughters and thus again connected back to the father Abraham through Rebekkah's derivation from him (155). Through daughters such as Rebekkah marrying their patrilineal parallel (or "first") cousins, independent matrilineage (such as Sarah's) and even the "otherness" of a wife's separate surname eventually become indistinguishable from the father's line. In leaving their father's house through marriage, in-marrying daughters only reenter it through the collateral door. By repeatedly providing a woman directly related to the father's brother as the answer to where wives should be found for the sons, the narrative is indirectly answering the question it has not approached about what to do with one's daughters: it is to marry daughters to males related as closely as possible to the father's structural parallel, his brother, while avoiding marriage to any one of the father's three direct competitors, his own father, his brother, or his son. The evaded daughter issue then explosively emerges in the Genesis 34 story of Jacob's one daughter, Dinah.

What makes this story of particular interest is that although it culminates the brother-sister sequence and involves the same structural triangle among brother(s), sister, and prospective foreign husband, Dinah is not a sister-wife but an unmarried daughter. In this story, the text is not wrestling with its former preoccupation concerning where to get wives for the sons of the tribe. Here, the suppressed counterpart question what should be done with one's daughters usurps the narrative focus. And as the daughter issue emerges, so does a newly violent text of sexual possession. Based on his study of Mediterranean kinship systems, Pitt-Rivers presents a compelling explanation of this biblical incident. In his analysis, the tale marks the historical emergence of a new kind of complex (rather than elementary) kinship structure based on a new honor code—a code that was clearly not in operation during the earlier sister-wife stories of Genesis, where men quite happily offered their wives to the local rulers in order to procure protective and profitable alliances. But "from the moment that the notion of honour is attached to female purity kinship loses its basis of reciprocity and becomes political and ego centered, a competition in which the winners are those who keep their daughters and take the women of other groups in addition" (166). In other words, at the point that the male-honor/female-shame code evolves, culture can no longer even pretend to be arbitrated by the deployment of daughters and the traffic in women.

Once the external integrity of family becomes invested in withholding its most marginal and least retainable figure, the iconographic spatializations of kinship clearly require redefinition. But the norm that now emerges into centrality is not, I would argue, anything truly *new* to family structure, as Pitt-Rivers implies. The potent impulse of paternal retention/possession has always been the defining and problematic nucleus within the exchange patterns that have struggled to contain it. It is, in fact, precisely that tension that energizes the narratives of such elementary kinship cultures as those from which *Beowulf,* the Abraham-Sarah story, and the biblical creation myth itself all arise. Not only is this impulse inextricable from the myth of paternal creation in which it resides, it is psychologically and politically coimplicit in the collected history of indictment that patriarchal ideology has accumulated backward and reinscribed forward into its texts of the "Father's righteous anger" against Eve, the proto-woman and proto-daughter. Disassembling the misogynistic polemics of Judeo-Christian history involves rethinking the creation myth through the family dynamics already at work inside this mythologized father's house. The patristic fathers of early Christianity could debate for centuries whether God had authorized sex in the garden or whether it was by definition a fallen act precisely because, despite the fact that the garden story is a genesis myth designed to mythologize the origins of the Jews, in the book of Genesis the Father *gives* no clear license for sexuality, and the taboo he establishes immediately before creating Eve implies that he acts to ban it right before he authorizes the woman/daughter to enter the text. The taboo is an admonition he gives to Adam, the other male in this space. When Eve is thereupon created, the biblical language authorizes her *not* as Adam's wife but as his (asexual) helpmate. The Father's Paradise was never an exogamous space, nor does the Father who created the woman ever give her as a sexual gift to Adam in prelapsarian Eden. It is Eve herself who sexualizes this enclosure, Eve who sexually gives herself away from the Father, and Eve who compels the proto-exogamy of the movement away from family domain. Like every daughter within her father's house, Eve as daughter is the inevitable traitor within, the breach in enclosure. Though patriarchal history obviously depends on daughters enacting this very role, Eve does not earn patriarchal affirmation for playing her part. Her part dispossesses the father; and thus, for performing it, she becomes the unacknowledged locus for a patriarchal history of women's "disobedience."

The Jacob-and-Dinah story, where the retention impulse finally erupts, narrates the arrival of Jacob's clan into the Shechem area. Dinah goes out alone one day from her father's house and is promptly seduced or raped by the local prince, Shechem. Shechem, however, loves Dinah; and if we read the Elohim version, where the incident is described as a seduction, the desire is apparently mutual. Shechem's desire for Dinah is so great that he and his father go to Jacob, request Dinah as Shechem's wife, offer a covenant of mutual exchange of wives between the groups, and even agree that all the Shechemite men will have themselves circumcised in order to comply with Israelite laws. Over an emotional matter— because Shechem "was deeply in love with Jacob's daughter" (34:19)— the Shechemites have essentially agreed to cut away part of their body/self and eradicate the boundaries of cultural difference in order that exogamous exchange can take place—and take place, not within their own laws, but within the codes of the interloping group. All in all, for Jacob's group, the offer would seem to be a rather good deal. But Dinah's brothers, Simeon and Levi, are suddenly obsessed with a sense of outraged personal honor that is new to the Genesis text: "Is our sister to be treated like a whore?" (34:31). After deceptively agreeing to the pact, they wait until the third day after the circumcision, when the Shechemite men are sorely incapacitated, then pillage the town, kill all the males, rape and carry off all the wives and children, seize Dinah back from Shechem's house, and depart. The act does not go entirely unpunished: Jacob is upset with the sons who broke the covenant and subsequently demotes them from his inheritance, thus clearing the way for Judah (from whose line David will eventually emerge). But in relation to the marriage question that the Genesis narratives are focused on, the text has resolved its submerged daughter issue and done so in a way that deflects blame away from the father. The mistake of inferring that marriage necessarily involves the *exchange* of women is an error that Pitt-Rivers dubs " 'Shechem's fallacy' in honour of its first perpetrator" (166).

Within a world of family strategies based on overt accumulation, it is still essential that sons marry and reproduce the tribe. And while it is not wholly unimportant that daughters marry (and if so, within the patriline), the fact of their marriage is less important than their position as signifiers of family honor. Whether they marry or not, the answer to what one does with daughters is clear: keep them. As formal legal codes begin to emerge into the Old Testament narration, what the culture has sanctioned is obviously not the daughter's rights; but neither has it privileged the exogamous needs of the group as a whole. What has been privileged at the expense of all else is the paternal prerogative to retain daughters: "If a man seduces a virgin who is not betrothed and sleeps with her, he must pay her price [to her father] and make her his wife. If her father absolutely refuses to let him have her, the seducer must pay a sum of money equal to the price fixed for a virgin" (Ex. 22:15). Implicitly, while seducing a betrothed virgin would deprive her espoused husband of the sexual right of possessive use, seducing an unbetrothed daughter deprives the father of the perilously similar sexual right of possessive retention.

Through the displacement of exchange codes by uncodified but unprohibited retention privileges, the daughter who has been excluded from the patrilineal and patronymic significance of the family house finally earns a legitimate place within it by becoming its imprisoned signifier. When daughters such as Dinah in Genesis 34 or Jephthah's daughter in Judges 11 cross over the threshold of the father's house unaccompanied by a male who would signify ownership, they cross into a tacitly forbidden zone where the daughter's presence impugns the family honor and signifies random sexual availability. Her revised relationship to both family and society therefore proposes a whole new sexual economics. Daughters are no longer valuable for their imagined worth as property to be traded; their value now resides in being possessions to be retained, the ultimate extension of which would be the system of female purity that Mary Douglas describes in South India and Ceylon (Sri Lanka). Here, "the purity of women is protected as the gate of entry to the castes. . . . As for their unfortunate womenfolk, strict seclusion is their lot. Few of them marry at all until on their deathbed. . . . If they go out of their houses, their bodies are completely enveloped in clothing and umbrellas hide their faces. When one of their brothers is married they can watch the celebration through chinks in the walls" (144–45).

The male-honor/female-shame code, though it may be more particular to the Middle East, imposes a set of values familiar enough even in the West. Under the operating rules of the code, the daughter's presence in cultural space no longer serves as the sign of an available transaction that presumably will reduce male violence by reconstructing opposed groups into kinship affines. Her body signifies the social/political juncture where competing desires meet. Within such a sexualized economy, the perceived worth of the family appreciates in direct proportion to the daughter's absence from outside space coincident with communal knowledge of her *un*available presence within. And a newly eroticized literary game dependent on virginal daughters immured behind walls, doors, gates, and mansions is made possible. Its watchword is that which Iago shouts at Brabantio: "Look to your house, your daughter, and your bags" (*Othello* 1.1.80)—a warning that seems doubly relevant since *bags* here also means testicles. The greater the proportion of nobility the literary text wishes to assign its families, the more elaborate must be its construction of symbolic edifices such as Faulknerian mansions with daughters locked inside. And because barriers function to increase rather than reduce desire, it is less the presence than the strategic absence of the daughter that eroticizes the literary or social text.

Eventually, the literary and literal interplay of cause and effect becomes too circular to disentangle. Since the code of masculine honor depends upon sexual conquest, and since an unenclosed daughter culturally signifies a "loose" commodity available for competitive male possession, even the father who is conscientiously trying to give his daughter the same spatial freedom that sons have always enjoyed is faced with a genuine dilemma; for eventually, the system that evolved out of measuring male prestige by the accumulation and enclosure of women encloses even its fathers within it. Out of legitimate fear for his daughter, even the most liberating of fathers may find himself being inexorably pushed by culture back into the patriarchal model of possessive fatherhood that he is trying to revise and undo. For in the world routinely reflected in today's daily news—a world in which eroticized violence against women has reached truly staggering statistics—new lines to contain *paternal* behavior have been drawn, ironically enough, in the outside space of male authority. The lines are ones that progressively redefine outside terrain as a space of jeopardy for one's daughters, not, as a father once might have imagined, a space where his authorization might enable her enfranchisement. Inevitably, the violence is enacted upon the body of the daughter. But it actually works as perhaps the most effective way that culture threatens potentially dissident fathers and redraws the hierarchies of gender and power upon which the authority of its own ideology depends.

Since retaining the daughter involves a figuratively if not literally incestuous choice that implicitly threatens to pollute the internal family space, even a daughter's presence within the safety of family is not unambivalent. Inevitably, the enclosure of the daughter resexualizes the space inside the family and compels the necessity for a detailed taboo to define illicit congress within it. When the codified taboo emerges in Leviticus 18, it places almost every conceivable family female—mother, sister, aunt, cousin, sister-in-law, niece, daughter-in-law, granddaughter, and so on—off-limits. Conspicuously, the only one not included is the daughter. As Judith Herman comments, "The wording of the law makes it clear that . . . what is prohibited is the sexual use of those women who, in one manner or another, already belong to other relatives. Every man is thus expressly forbidden to take the daughters of his kinsmen, but only by implication is he forbidden to take his own daughters. The patriarchal God sees fit to pass over father-daughter incest in silence" (61). Nonetheless, the unstated taboo is implicit. Though it "forbids [the father] to make sexual use of his daughter, no particular man's rights are offended, should the father choose to disregard this rule. As long as he ultimately gives his daughter in marriage, he has fulfilled the social purpose of the rule of the gift. *Until such time* as he chooses to give her away, he has uncontested power to do with her as he wishes. Hence, of all possible forms of incest, that between father and daughter is the most easily overlooked" (60; my italics).

The incest prohibitions in Leviticus constitute the supreme rule not so much of the gift, as Lévi-Strauss would describe it, as of the *deed* established to demarcate male territory. First and foremost of its concerns, however, are its transparent attempts to avoid curtailing the desires of the father. Those rights that privilege the father at the expense of the son occur first in the list; those that privilege sons, uncles, or other male kin are structurally subordinate. And in terms of preventing proprietary conflict, these contractual allocations that omit proscribing the daughter would presumably work quite well—that is, if patriarchal organization did not depend upon daughters' getting married and if the legislation that tacitly allows for father-daughter sexual liaison had not concurrently set up a system dependent on men possessing exclusive rights in women. Because the purity of a wife is a law of first priority within the symbolics of blood upon which patrilineal ethics depend, it is at the juncture of a daughter's marriage and the transfer of proprietary rights from father to son-in-law that the system threatens to break down. The breakdown menaces the society with exactly the kind of male violence that the incest laws were instituted to prevent. Furthermore, the conflict threatens to point a finger directly at the figure whom the code was designed to privilege, the one status role that the Hebrew testament repeatedly goes out of its way to exempt from blame of any sort. It is therefore precisely at this juncture—where the father's unofficial privilege conflicts with the exogamous laws that guarantee patriarchal rule—that another law is called for to negotiate three problems: deflect blame away from the privileged patriarch; reharmonize the social text by projecting any father–son-in-law hostilities onto the powerless daughter, who cannot reciprocate; and yet do so through a ritual resolution designed to inhibit further instances of this unproscribed violation by marshaling moral disapproval against the unnamed, but tacitly implicated, father.

It is in this context that the elaborately detailed punishment for the accused bride in Deuteronomy 22:13–21 makes particular sense. All of the numerous proscriptions codified in Deuteronomy are essentially purification laws to "banish evil from Israel." This one, however, is unique in both its detail and its ritual implications. Unlike other crimes that the code indicts, the violation this statute wishes to eradicate is one that seems to require prescripted, communal enactment. It is further unique in thrusting the father to the very center of the drama, making him a special actor protected by a formulaic dialogue yet tacitly placed into a communal arraignment in the role of defendent against the son-in-law's charges of the daughter's impurity. In the three sex laws that follow this one in Deuteronomy 22 the father is either unmentioned or minimally important. If, for instance, a man forcibly seizes an *unbetrothed* virgin and "is caught in the act," he must pay her father fifty shekels and (if her father consents) marry her (22:28–29). If a man lies with a *betrothed* virgin *inside the city,* the two offenders are to be taken *outside the gate* of the town and stoned to death—she because she "did not cry for help" and he because "he violated the wife of his fellow." The father is not involved here, but the male violator (as well as the female property that is now soiled) must die because he has violated the *future rights* of another man; executing him *outside* the gate will thus preclude conflict from erupting *within* the community (22:23–25). A particular spatial logic controls each of these two purifications. In the first instance, although an impurity took place through the shedding of virgin blood outside of marriage, no one had a prior marriage claim on this virgin, so no threat of communal violence is involved. The matter can consequently be resolved by retroactively placing the fornication inside of marriage. *Where* the act took place is not even mentioned, since the impurity, a form of community "dirt," will not be dirt anymore once it has been relocated within the "inner" space of sanction.[23] There is, by consequence, no "evil" to have to banish outward. In the second situation, however, space becomes all-important: to purify what happened *inside* the town and annul the threat of violence attached to a betrothed virgin, the daughter who stepped *outside* her home and the man with whom she stepped *outside* the marriage sanction must be extruded in order to thrust out the impurity they brought within. They are thus to be executed *outside* the gates, which "banishes evil from the midst." No mention is made that the whole community must take part in this execution.

The spatialization that resolves the indictment of the accused bride differs significantly in all its implications. Here, when a husband publicly defames his bride by saying she was not a virgin, suddenly the father is thrust forward as the defendent in front of a jury of elders. He is to take his daughter to the city gate and, in a prescribed dialogue, produce the cloth that contains the blood-stained evidence of her virginity. It is not the husband who must establish guilt but the father who must demonstrate innocence. If the evidence of virginity is there, the groom is to be flogged and must pay the father 100 shekels "for publicly defaming a virgin of Israel." Since the payment is made to the father, we should here read "for publicly defaming a virgin's father." And since the price is double what the fornicator owed the father, and since in this case the husband is to be publicly flogged, this crime—defaming the father—is significantly more serious than the implicitly condoned rape of the unassigned virgin, for verbal defamation is a form of status pollution and is thus a major offense inside patriarchal honor codes. Implicitly, the husband has accused the man who gave him this woman of having taken the husband's property (her virginity) in advance. If the father produces the cloth marked with his daughter's blood, punishment of her husband by public letting of his blood constitutes a public purification of the father's name.

If, however, the bride's virginity cannot be substantiated, "they shall take her to the door of her father's house and her fellow citizens shall stone her to death for having committed an infamy in Israel by disgracing her father's House." This crime is not merely "an evil" to be "banished from the midst"; it is "an infamy in Israel" that is said to disgrace the father's house, the place from which the punishment implies it emanated. The trial had been situated at the margins of the town, at the gates that mark the boundary between inside and outside. The punishment, however, is relocated inside. Rather than follow the design of the second punishment, which locates the impurity as something *outside* the community and family, this one instead splatters the daughter's blood onto— and thus pollutes—the boundary of the father's house. The proposition that because there was no hymeneal blood shed in her husband's house the daughter's blood is to be shed on her father's door tacitly accuses the father but then masks the father's guilt behind its transposition of cause and effect. The punishment, however, exposes the underlying syntax: it marks the house, the inner location where, by inference, the pollution occurred. As opposed to the unmarked, unimplicated father of the betrothed virgin who, along with the man who violated her, was stoned to death outside the town, in this ritual the father is left marked and polluted with the implicating sign of violent desire that is here, in the punishment as it was in the crime, deflected onto the body of the daughter. To uphold the moral code of the group, the law has substituted pollution beliefs for the legal sanctions that the community does not wish to enact. The situation resembles Mary Douglas's description of the Nuer tribe's way of upholding ideals that the community validates but frequently honors more in the breach than in the observance. In Douglas's words, pollution beliefs work to "buttress a simplified moral code." They mark forbidden sexual contacts with signs of danger and transgression. But they do so without taking the violations into the legal zone, where matters of principle would involve consequence and hence interfere with the personal desires of those whose superior status must remain unquestioned in order for the community to work (129–39).

Daughters seem particularly problematic because they so thoroughly embody the ambiguous attributes of what Victor Turner has defined as "liminal *personae* ('threshold people')," who "slip through the network of classifications that normally locate states and positions in cultural space. . . . they are betwixt and between the positions assigned and arrayed by law." Typically, such figures "may be represented as possessing nothing. . . . Their behavior is normally passive or humble; they must obey their instructors implicitly, and accept arbitrary punishment without complaint." Liminal roles are inherently dual ones. They are "often regarded as dangerous, inauspicious, or polluting"; simultaneously, however, they are viewed as mysteriously sacred, peculiarly independent, and personifying the special power of the weak. They seem both dangerous and indispensable to the community because they embody its potential for something other than "the normative system of bounded, structured, particularistic groups." In "structured societies, it is the marginal or 'inferior' person or the 'outsider' who often comes to symbolize . . . the sentiment for humanity." Particularly in Shakespeare's final four tragicomic "romances," daughters embody this special potential for such symbolic redemption. Once daughters have been incorporated into the socially legitimized role of wife/mother, however, their threat to the social text is absorbed into the closed structure; "the impetus soon becomes exhausted . . . and becomes itself an institution among other institutions" (94–130, passim).

The signs that potentially portend outer communal violence and inner family violation come together in the daughter's menstrual blood and make her sexualized body the intersection of multiple threats to both family and community. Inside patriarchal construction, community and family can be rescued from their own potential violence only when daughters become wives—when the liminal danger of virginal menstruation shed within the paternal house is countered by the antidote of hymeneal blood shed inside the husband's. It is therefore not the daughter's passage to adolescence that receives the ritual of community sanction. The ritual that legitimates the daughter is the same one that eradicates her daughterhood and relocates her dangerous fertility inside the authorized status of wife/mother. Yet what the wedding ceremony is really all about is not the union of bride and groom (which comes during the wedding night) but the separation of daughter from father. From the structural dynamics of the ceremonial script, it seems clear that Western tradition has always recognized the peculiar force of the daughter-father bond and the need to invoke special powers to sever it. Even while the ceremony is busy separating the bride and transferring her to her husband, however, it unavoidably memorializes and thus paradoxically reasserts all of the tensions that define the conjunction of daughter and father.

The church service of Western tradition (which evolved around the thirteenth century and remains only nominally changed in the twentieth) is a performative script that visually narrates and spatially resolves the problems of retention and separation. It begins by visually bringing the groom and the emblematic father/priest into the space occupied by the congregation, thus placing the groom's claim into a shared context with the religious and social demands of the community. The ceremony then pauses to await—and exerts a coercive pull upon—the father's delayed arrival and his symbolically prolonged consent to come into harmony with the community by delivering up his daughter. When at last they enter, even the position of the bride on the right arm of her father visualizes the replacement dynamics being dramatized, for she enters the church in the same structural relationship to father as she will leave it with husband. By the spatial configurations it dictates, the script tacitly acknowledges and works to control the father's potential to block the performance. When father and bride at last reach the altar, the text ensures the segregation of the father and his rival. Decked in the symbols of virginity, the daughter stands in paradigmatic tableau as mediator between father and husband, pulled as it were between the name, the house, and her symbolic choice of allegiance between the two important males in her life. This problematic father-daughter-(other) son triangulation, in which the father's sign is inherently the dominant one, is not allowed to control the drama at the altar, however. It is instead controlled by the superimposition of a more powerful geometry constructed around a rival father spatially located on what is literally and figuratively a higher plane. By standing directly above the bride, the representative of the divine Father creates the dominant triangle that visually defeats the earthly one. At the moment of severance, when the priest asks, "Who giveth this woman to be married unto this man?" the father is denied any verbal response whatsoever in the traditional service of the 1559 English Book of Common Prayer; in modernized versions, he is authorized only the proverbial "I do," which affirms and anticipates the vows that will unite his daughter to another man.[24] When this innocently coercive question is asked, it is to the figure of the emblematic Father, not to the actual rival, that the father must yield by relinquishing physical possession of his daughter's hand. By making the father stand at the altar as witness that he knows of no impediments to his daughter's lawful union and by then forcing him to watch the priest place her hand into that of her husband, not only does the ceremony reaffirm the taboo against incest but it levels the full weight of that taboo on the relationship between father and daughter.

The groom's family and the bride's mother are irrelevant to these archetypal dynamics. Only the father must act out, must dramatize his loss before the community. And by virtue of a figurative truth, it is furthermore he who must "pay" for his daughter's wedding. Though it might be argued that the church service ritualizes no more than the transfer of a passive female object from one male to another, in reality it ritualizes the community's coercion, not of the bride, but of her father. By playing out his ceremonial role, the father implicitly gives the blessing that licenses the daughter's deliverance from bonds that would otherwise become bondage. And while contemporary daughters frequently represent their changed relationship to husbands by eliminating the wife's traditional vows of matrimonial obedience, they seem to feel something either psychologically unchangeable or as yet unchanged in their relationship to fathers. For the majority of today's most independent daughters still choose to be "delivered" to the altar and "given away" by their fathers. Once a father has performed his prescribed role, it is he who becomes the displaced and dispossessed actor of the script. And—like every father of every bride—he must leave the sanctified space alone. Having performed the loss of his daughter within a dialogue that masks loss under gift, having played out the structural drama of his own defeat, the father is required to retire from the scene and, from his seat in the congregation, watch his child discard his name and pledge henceforth to forsake all others—the "others" that now include him.

Fathers in the Hebrew testament seldom if ever acknowledge their daughters by direct address; they speak only to their sons. But if structures can tell us anything, the design of Ecclesiasticus, one of the banished books of the bible, provides an appropriate gloss on all that the absence of daughter-father discussion within the culture has subsumed.

Having lectured his son with his few (hundred) brief precepts about the problems of life, the morose narrator of Ecclesiasticus saves for his penultimate warning a list of "the cares of a father over his daughter," every one of which reflects anxieties about his own relationship to his daughter's sexuality:

> Unknown to her, a daughter keeps her father awake,
>> the worry she gives him drives away his sleep:
> in her youth, in case she never marries,
>> married, in case she should be disliked,
> as a virgin, in case she should be defamed
>> and found with child in her father's house,
> having a husband, in case she goes astray,
>> married, in case she should be barren.
> Your daughter is headstrong? Keep a sharp look-out
>> that she does not make you the laughing stock of your
>>> enemies,
> the talk of the town, the object of common gossip,
>> and put you to public shame.   (Si. 42:9–11)

Notes

1. I am indebted to Wick Wadlington for his comment about the bland indifference that makes ignoring the daughter seem "the most natural and unremarkable thing in the world. This is to me the most significant kind of abnormality, betraying the *work* of cultural normalization."

2. "Femininity," *SE* 22:128. For a detailed account of Freud's changing perspectives on the father-daughter relationship see David Willbern's essay in this volume, "*Filia Oedipi*: Father and Daughter in Freudian Theory."

3. Leah Marcus's essay in this volume, "Erasing the Stigma of Daughterhood: Mary I, Elizabeth I, and Henry VIII," discusses Henry's reactions to having fathered a daughter.

4. In his famous "Essai sur le don," Marcel Mauss originally articulated the theory of gift giving and reciprocity as the basis for social exchange in primitive cultures. Building on Mauss's work, Claude Lévi-Strauss, in *The Elementary Structures of Kinship,* defined women as the most valuable gift to be given, marriage as the most basic form of exchange, and the incest taboo as a mechanism to ensure such exchanges.

5. Judith Herman's 1981 analysis of case studies and Diana E. H. Russell's 1986 statistical research on father-daughter incest have been two of the most widely read works to force the actualities of this issue into social consciousness. But Russell locates 1978 as marking the "beginning of a new look at incest from a more victim-oriented perspective. In that year Sandra Butler's *Conspiracy of Silence* and Louise Armstrong's *Kiss Daddy Goodnight* gave us the first feminist

analyses of incest ever published in book form—building on feminist author Florence Rush's earlier groundbreaking work" (3). She likewise points out that while "incestuous abuse has been increasing over the past few decades," it is not a new phenomenon by any means. And "while it is reasonable to expect that clinicians . . . would have been the ones to break the silence . . . it appears that the higher the status of the mental health professionals, the more unwilling they have been to question their old assumptions about the rarity of incestuous abuse and about their favorite scapegoats—the seductive child and the collusive mother" (4).

But if the late 1970s marked the beginning of a greater cultural awareness about incest, the late 1980s may mark the emergence of a disturbing counterreaction, a massive cultural denial that rationalizes itself, as does the denial of rape, by grossly exaggerating the number of false or mistaken allegations. Through media deployment of such distorting generalizations, the society's outrage and its judicial concern become displaced from the victim and focused back onto ensuring the rights of the privileged. In terms of the way the society manages incest, the only real distinction between the 1980s and the previous decade, when incest was still a suppressed subject, may simply be that the subject has changed venues and now rests in the hands of a new and more powerful set of cultural fathers: in the 1980s the mental health professional has been replaced by the probate judge. In 1987, after a six-year study conducted by doctors from Harvard Medical School and Massachusetts General Hospital, headed by Harvard psychiatrist Muriel Sugarman, a new phenomenon termed "divorce incest" was identified, in which the children typically were not abused *until* the divorce or separation took place. Having followed a group of "19 children age 6 or younger whom the researchers believed had been sexually abused by their biological father during visits after separation or divorce," the study reported that at the court level, in spite of substantial documentation of incest by social-service agencies, "allegations were disbelieved in 73.7 percent of the cases," and not one of the men accused was prosecuted. In fact, the judicial system seemed so loathe to side against the privileges of the father that "in nearly 60 percent of the cases, the children were forced to have [continued] visits with their fathers."

In the psychoanalytic narrative that rationalized incest, the daughter stood accused of fabricating the story, and the mother of collusion with the crime through her failure to recognize the signs, confront the father, and take appropriate steps to protect the child. In the emerging legal narration the child's testimony is still discounted, but the mother now stands accused for taking precisely the actions that she was earlier condemned for not taking. When a mother takes divorce incest to court, the court manages to disregard the child's allegations by attributing them to the presumed vindictiveness of the divorcing mother, never considering, as Sugarman notes, that "divorcing fathers might be vindictive or vengeful enough to abuse a child in order to hurt the mother" ("Study: Abused Children"). Confronted with the legal system's refusal to terminate the father's access to the child or take steps to protect the child from further assault, mothers have begun to go outside the system of patriarchally instituted law, turning to an underground railroad that has developed to hide abused children in safe-houses

71

across the country, away from the privileges of the father that the courts, by inaction, have tacitly protected. But by thus removing her child from physical jeopardy, the mother places herself into a new legal jeopardy, as was illustrated by the widely publicized 1987 Massachusetts custody case over eight-year-old Nicole LaLonde, in which the mother, defying a court order and attempting to prevent her daughter from being handed back over to the father's unsupervised visitation rights, spent six months in jail for contempt of court for refusing to reveal the daughter's whereabouts. Yet as Daniel Golden's *Boston Globe Magazine* report makes clear, the LaLonde case is by no means an isolated incident.

6. That it was considered "perfectly acceptable, even at Athens, for a healthy female infant to be exposed . . . by placing it in a clay vessel and leaving it in a temple or in the wilderness. . . . if the father willed it" is discussed by Philip Slater (29 n. 7). According to a 1985 analysis in the *Los Angeles Times,* in modern-day China the increase of female infanticide has been coincident with the one-child limit placed on family reproduction ("China").

7. For the idea of triangulation and mediation of desire see Girard.

8. The potential for the father to act as the primary enabling figure in his daughter's life is discussed by Carolyn G. Heilbrun in *Reinventing Womanhood.* In studies on the rarity of great women artists, Barnett and Baruch found "that no woman embarked upon a career as an artist without a male mentor, most often her father, to give her support . . . and access to the 'gatekeepers' of the profession" (32). Speaking from her extensive background in lobbying for feminist causes on the national political scene, Marjorie Bell Chambers comments that one of the most important political lessons she has learned is that the men she can finally count on to support women's projects are not only men who have mothers whom they love and wives whom they respect as equals but "men who have only or mostly daughters" (235–36). So long as a man has sons or mostly sons, he almost automatically imagines himself projected through his sons and consequently remains much less aware of or concerned over the subtle but powerful forces that would prevent daughters from equal access to the same successes.

9. In particular, see two essays in this volume: Dianne Sadoff's "The Clergyman's Daughters: Anne Bronte, Elizabeth Gaskell, and George Eliot" and Sandra Gilbert's "Life's Empty Pack: Notes toward a Literary Daughteronomy."

10. *The Mill on the Floss,* qtd. in Owen 175.

11. All biographies of Shakespeare discuss the oddities of his last will and testament; Schoenbaum's is the most recent and most detailed. In the fictionalized version of Shakespeare's final days dramatized by Edmund Bond's play *Bingo* the contents of the will and Judith's marginal relationship to her father are central to the plot. For an extensive treatment of Shakespeare's father-daughter plays see my 1982 *PMLA* article plus the books by Diane Dreher and Peter Erickson.

12. Qtd. in Owen 134.

13. Marianne Hirsch sets before us the two recent and strikingly different readings of the Grimm's fairy tale *Allerleirauh* ("Many Furs"). In the introduction to her *Father-Daughter Incest,* Judith Herman discusses the parallel *Allerleirauh* and Saint Dympna stories and dedicates her book to the many unknown, incestuously abused daughters whom the two stories represent.

Herman's reading of the tale centers on the daughter: the thematic point of this Cinderella version is to "warn young girls that it is dangerous to be left alone with a widowed father. . . . In some variants of the tale, the daughter suffers because the father replaces her mother with a cruel stepmother. In others, the daughter suffers because the father wishes to marry her himself" (1). By contrast, Peter Brooks's psychoanalytically based narratological analysis, *Reading for the Plot: Design and Intention in Narrative*, sees *Allerleirauh* as a story that "works through the problem of desire gone wrong and brings it to its cure" (9). As Hirsch points out, for Brooks, the protagonist of the tale is the father, whose desire must be redirected, while Allerleirauh functions as only an overly eroticized object in the story that is named for her. Thus, "from Brooks's perspective . . . woman's role in narrative is to be the object who waits to be exchanged and passed on at the right moment" (166).

14. See Abel's "Cam the Wicked: Woolf's Portrait of the Artist as Her Father's Daughter" in this volume.

15. Maimonides, *The Book of Women*, bk. 4, qtd. in Rush 16–29.

16. 112. Steven Ozment contends with Stone's analysis and illustrates a much more benevolent model of sixteenth-century family relations. By failing to take up the issue of differential valuation of sons and daughters within families, however, Ozment's analysis leads us to infer an ungendered kind of equality that the documents used by Stone, for instance, quite thoroughly repudiate.

17. Unless otherwise noted, all biblical citations in this essay are from the Jerusalem Bible.

18. In particular, see John A. Phillips 38–40 and 180 nn. 3–6, where a listing of Jewish legends containing the Lilith story is provided. Although her intriguing story has stayed alive inside cultural rumor, except in one remaining reference (Isa. 34:14–15), Lilith has been completely exorcised from the canonical Scriptures.

19. In his opening chapter (3–15), Phillips provides a concise description of the universal way that all ancient Near Eastern creation stories contain a mythologized struggle for patriarchal societies to overcome their mother-goddesses. Though he notes that not all Old Testament scholars agree that a theogony and struggle among the gods underlie the book of Genesis, Phillips finds vestigial linguistic evidence connecting the Hebrew *tohu-wa-bohu* to Tiamat, the great dragon-mother of the Mesopotamian creation saga, who was vanquished by her son Marduk and then split into earth and sky, thus making her carcass become the primordial matter of the universe. In "Tiamat and Her Children" Kittye Delle Robbins discusses both the disappearance of the mythic Mesopotamian mother and its psychic implications. For a fascinating reading of the way the denied maternal occupies various interstices of the garden story see Froula, "When Eve Reads Milton."

20. In *The Great Code: The Bible and Literature*, Northrop Frye comments that "the chief point made about the creation of Eve is that henceforth man is to leave his parents and become united with his wife. The parent is the primary image . . . that . . . has to give way to the image of the sexual union of bride-groom and bride" (107).

21. Like the fruit, which is the other mediating object of the transgression

sequence, the serpent carries a richly ambivalent symbolism that allows it to be read (as it has been) as either an emblematically male or female sign. The fact that interpreters have imagined the Satan-Eve dynamics in terms of Eve's "seduction" suggests the serpent's symbolically male identity, as does the projection of Satan, a male, back into the serpent. Furthermore, since the patriarchal mentality of the writer(s) of Genesis almost automatically presumes maleness unless otherwise noted, the mere fact that it is *not* identified as female argues for viewing it as male. The ultimate indicator I see for its phallic symbolism is based less on Freud's association than on the way the serpent functions inside this myth as a disclaimed part of/agent of the Father. Indeed, its description in Genesis as "the most subtle of wild beasts that Yahweh God had made" almost anticipates—and seems embedded in—Augustine's famous use of the fall to explain the frustrating unruliness of the male sexual body. Accordingly, though all parts of the male body worked by direction of the will in the prelapsarian state, as a punishment for man's having rebelled against God, his head, God left men with one rebellious and unruly body member which would remind them of the fall by likewise rebelling against the control of their own heads.

22. The genealogy in Ovid's tale is interesting. From the union of Pygmalion and the perfect female he designs, the daughter Paphos is born. She has a son named Cinyras, whose daughter Myrrha seduces him. From this incestuous union is born the son most famous both for his beauty and for his avoidance of women, Adonis. Like the Lot story in Genesis, Ovid's incest narrative goes out of its way to exculpate the father; in fact, when Cinyras calls for light and discovers his daughter in his bed, he tries to kill her, but she is instead turned into a Myrrha tree, in which guise she is said to weep out her name perpetually in self-confessing tears (*Metamorphoses* 10.298–518). Patricia Joplin does a particularly good job of articulating how violence and daughter exchange are repeatedly coimplicit in classical mythology and how elaboration of the erotic theme of incest in such myths as Ovid's account of Philomela signifies precisely the kind of mimetic desire that betrays the existence of a political rivalry hiding beneath the text that rationalizes it. Female chastity and a woman's body are sacred, Joplin points out, not out of respect for the integrity of the woman as a person but out of respect for violence. "Because her sexual body is the ground of the culture's system of differences, the woman's hymen is also the ground of contention. The virgin's hymen must not be ruptured except in some manner that reflects and ensures the health of the existing political hierarchy. The father king regulates both the literal and metaphorical 'gates' to the city's power: the actual gates in the city's wall or the hymen as the gateway to his daughter's body" (38).

23. In Mary Douglas's chapter "Internal Lines" she examines the connections between social pollution and cultural ideas of "dirt."

24. The question dates in English tradition back to the York manual and remains in effect in the 1559 Book of Common Prayer (408). See my essay "The Father and the Bride" for an analysis of the marriage ritual substructure underlying a number of Shakespeare's father-daughter plays.

DAVID WILLBERN

Filia Oedipi: Father and Daughter in Freudian Theory

Oedipus Come to me, child. Let me embrace the body I never thought to touch again.
Antigone. You shall. It is what I long for too.
                    —Sophocles, *Oedipus at Colonus*

IN THE LATE 1890s a young Viennese woman, daughter of a physician, suffered from somatic symptoms with no apparent cause. Her father subjected her to standard medical treatments, to no avail. Then a friend suggested she visit an innovative practitioner who was gaining local repute in treating hysteria. The young woman, however, had heard of this doctor, and replied, "What good would that be? I know he'd say to me: Have you ever had the idea of having sexual intercourse with your father?" (Freud, *SE* 11:236–37).

A century later, questions raised by Freud's ideas about the shifting erotic valences of the father-daughter relationship are manifold. The topic turns towards several cruces in psychoanalytic theory, including hysteria, the seduction theory, female sexuality, the Oedipus complex, clinical transference, and even the death instinct. In order to review these related issues, I shall retrace some familiar ground. Freud has provided conceptual maps, but there remain shadows and unknown regions in this dark continent of psychoanalytic theory.

My goal is to design a fair formulation from what are in Freud only partial plans. Unlike other core theoretical issues—the Oedipus complex, the dream work, narcissism—the tangled web of father-daughter ties is not clearly explicated in one text or three; instead, this issue is typically subordinated to developmental and Oedipal theory. Yet throughout the Freudian corpus resonate echoes of this most passionate propinquity. A full characterization of Freud's thinking and feeling on the matter requires a careful survey of all his writings. Further, my focus is on *Freud's* thinking and feeling about the father-daughter relationship. Such a focus will therefore be one-sided, viewed through paternal eyes—the patriarchal perspective. Freud sometimes characterized the daughter's perspective, but he was naturally more familiar with the father's. It is difficult, if not impossible, to be in two places at the same time. Fathers have always been sons as well, but never daughters.

The general question may be best encountered through a pathological turn of intrafamilial love: the seduction theory of the neuroses. Though Freud's views have recently been subject to controversy, the general line of his thought is clear. Briefly stated, Freud never abandoned nor rejected the thesis that actual sexual trauma in childhood ("a passive sexual experience before puberty") could form the core of a hysterical or neurotic condition. He did stop insisting on its ubiquity in the aetiology of such pathology. While it remained certain that some hysterics were abused in childhood, not all were. Seduction was not a necessary precondition for neurosis. Freud's error was one of emphasis: as he listened to his patients, he overvalued reality and undervalued fantasy. He also erred by analogy. Thinking that prepubertal sexual contact with adults was analogous to contracting the tubercle bacillus, he could write that all hysterics must have been "infected" by seduction (*SE* 3:209, 204n). Correcting this error made possible his discovery of the varieties of infantile sexuality, the Oedipus complex, and the potent interplay of fantasy and reality, desire and occasion. To imagine the path of childhood seduction as a one-way street is merely to abandon basic ideas of psychoanalysis: it is simplistic, retrograde, and mistaken.[1]

Freud's theoretical position on the question of childhood seduction is clear and understandable. The thoughts and emotions he encountered while developing his theory, however, are more complex. They deserve attention especially as they involve the father-daughter relationship, for in more than one case Freud was reluctant to point his finger at the offending father. In 1892 he encountered a young woman whose acute "virginal anxiety" presaged his later famous "Dora." This adolescent girl, named "Katharina ———" for Freud's case history, found herself, like Dora, pressured by the incestuous demands of the adult world immediately around her. Freud at first wrote that the source of pressure was her drunken uncle; in 1925 he admitted (in an additional footnote to the case) that it was her father. He made a similar distortion in another case in *Studies on Hysteria* ("Elisabeth von R.") and repeated the same instance in an 1896 essay on hysteria (*SE* 2:134n, 170n, 164n, 208n). In April 1897 he wrote to his friend Fliess about a young woman whose father, grandfather, and male cousin had made regular advances to her and to her sister when they were children. Freud commented that this was "a quite ordinary case of hysteria" (*SE* 1:246–47). In December of the same year he recounted a terrible tale of a girl of two "brutally deflowered" by her father (*Complete Letters* 288). Yet he wrote in 1897, "I myself am still in doubts about matters concerning fathers" (*SE* 1:246; *Letters* 237). During the summer of that year he suffered writer's block, stopped his obsessive work on *The Interpretation of Dreams*, and confessed to Fliess his feelings of "bottomless laziness, intellectual stagnation, summer dreariness, vegetative well being." "My reluctance to write," he continued, "is downright pathological." The remark refers initially to his reluctance to answer Fleiss's correspondence, but surely it resonates personally. At the conclusion of the letter Freud remarked of "this period of intellectual paralysis": "Every line is torture. . . . I am dull-witted. . . . I believe I am in a cocoon, and God knows what sort of beast will crawl out." Troubled by "grave doubts" about the thesis of paternal aetiology, he finally settled on a theory of mutual seduction that enabled the further development of psychoanalysis. Still, in December 1897 he wrote to Fliess, "My confidence in paternal aetiology has risen greatly" (*Letters* 252–55, 261, 264–66, 286).

The rise and fall of the seductive father in Freud's thought can be and has been speculatively attributed to manifold motives. I shall only note that in the 1890s Freud was engaged on the project of self-analysis that was to produce two major culminations: the dream book and the theory of the Oedipus complex. He was in his late thirties, the father of four. He was writing in a social context where bald statements of paternal incest may have seemed indecorous even to him (his 1924 footnotes to *Studies on Hysteria* are self-rebukes on just this point). From an analytic perspective, Freud's disguise of paternal seducers in the early hysteria cases may have indicated his own denial of incestuous desire: in 1892 his first-born child, Mathilde, was five. "Incest is no uncommon event," he wrote in 1913, "even in our present-day society" (*SE* 13:122). In 1917 he acknowledged the actuality of childhood seductions in some cases but noted that the regular appearance of the father as the seducer in girls' accounts indicated Oedipal fantasy (*SE* 16:370). As late as 1938, almost his final year, he still relied on the occasion of childhood seduction or sexual abuse by adults as a potential traumatic source of neurosis. But of greater significance, he continued, were the mutual wishes of the Oedipus complex (*SE* 23:187). As his theories developed and deepened, he restored the father to a place in *both* reality and fantasy and showed how the interplay of these two modes permeated the sexual dynamic of the Oedipal family.

To examine this dynamic it will be useful to sketch a history of Freud's concepts of female sexuality. In his early *Three Essays on the Theory of Sexuality* (1905), female sexual development was explicitly subordinated to male and subsumed by the latter theoretical structure. "We might lay it down," wrote Freud, "that the sexuality of little girls is of a wholly masculine character," that is, active, focused on the phallic organ (the clitoris). This fundamentally masculine, active character of female sexuality is normally repressed during puberty, when the clitoris becomes an erotic catalyst for vaginal arousal and passive receptivity in the emerging woman (*SE* 7:219, 9:217–18).

The hinge that opens female sexuality from childhood into femininity is the critical discovery of genital difference. In Freud's view, the little girl's revelation is quick and decisive: "She makes her judgment and her decision in a flash. She has seen it and knows that she is without it and wants to have it" (*SE* 19:252). Her developing "penis envy" is a "wound to her narcissism, . . . like a scar." She feels inferior and projects that feeling into a generalized contempt for all women, her mother in particular, thus beginning a gradual process of turning towards her father as a love-object. Redirecting her erotic energies has an unconscious motive: to recover the penis lost, removed, or denied. "The girl's libido," wrote Freud, "slips into a new position along the line—there is no other way of putting it—of the equation 'penis-child.'" She now wishes for a child by her father; "the little girl has turned into a little woman" (*SE* 19:253–56).

As Freud began to consider this question of specific genital difference, rather than the early "phallic" period of undifferentiated sexuality, he realized that his theory managed only male experience. In a 1923 essay on infantile sexuality he wrote about the primacy of the phallus: "Unfortunately we can describe this state of things only as it affects the male child; the corresponding processes in the little girl are not known to us" (*SE* 19:142). A year later, explaining the normal "dissolution" of the Oedipus complex, he wrote: "The process . . . refers . . . to male children only. How does the corresponding development take place in little girls? At this point our material—for some incomprehensible reason—becomes far more obscure and full of gaps" (*SE* 19:177). Freud was not at a theoretical loss for long. Confronting his ignorance, he theorized a more complicated female sexual development, involving two major shifts of focus. In his revised theory, the little girl gradually shifts her primary erotogenic zone from clitoris (the penile homologue) to vagina (whose existence had been "virtually a mystery"), *and* she shifts her desired love-object from mother to father. Female sexual development is thus doubly biphasic. From being a little girl who is sexually a "little man" with a little clitoris-penis, the young woman becomes a "castrated" female with a newly discovered vagina who wants a penis for herself— and a baby from her father. That is, her wish for a penis becomes normally the wish for a baby, and if she later bears a child (especially a son), its unconscious significance reverses the prior symbolic equation, so that the baby represents a penis and not merely an Oedipal "gift" from the father (*SE* 21:221–45, 20:36–37). Such a psychic project is hard work. At the end of his 1933 essay "Femininity" Freud suggested that the difficult biphasic development of women takes more out of them than the less complex male sexual progress requires of men. He imagined a woman of thirty, whose "libido has taken up final positions. . . . There are no paths open to further development." It is as though the task of normal female sexual development "exhausts" a woman (*SE* 22:134–35). It is in such comments that Elizabeth Janeway hears a tone of sympathy in Freud's writing about women: "There is always a note of sadness in it, a sense that women's condition sentences them to an unfulfilled life" (75).[2]

Disappointed by her mother and her sex, wishing unconsciously for a penis, the young woman of Freudian theory enters the Oedipus complex "as though into a haven of refuge" (*SE* 22:128–29). In a sense, she never really leaves it, nor does she ever really leave behind her earlier erotic attachment. She turns to her father (Lacan called this move *père-version*) but in the shadow of her mother. "Every step of the way, as the analysts describe it," writes Nancy Chodorow, "a girl develops her relationship to her father while looking back at her mother" (126). Freud regularly characterized a daughter growing up under the watchful eyes of her mother, whose duty it was to protect her child from pernicious sexual knowledge, to guard her emerging adolescent sexuality, and to inhibit her sexual activity. "It is the daughter's business," wrote Freud, "to emancipate herself from this influence and to decide for herself on broad and rational grounds what her share of enjoyment or denial of sexual pleasure shall be" (*SE* 7:229–30, 14:267). Freud was often liberal in his attitude towards sexual convention, but this praise of rationality and emancipation from parental influence implies a sunny social view that is clouded by his psychological theory, which posits an omnipresent and deeply ambivalent pre-Oedipal relationship at the core of female sexual identity.

Freud had long noted that the earliest object-relation for all infants, male and female alike, was the mother—specifically, her breast (*SE* 7:222–23). His later considerations of female sexuality led him to the momentous discovery he characterized in 1931:

> We have, after all, long given up any expectation of a neat parallelism between male and female sexual development.
>
> Our insight into this early, pre-Oedipus, phase in girls comes to us as a surprise, like the discovery, in another field, of the Minoan-Mycenean civilization behind the civilization of Greece.
>
> Everything in the sphere of this first attachment to the mother seemed to me so difficult to grasp in analysis—so grey with age and shadowy and almost impossible to revivify—that it was as if it had succumbed to an especially inexorable repression. (*SE* 21:226)

Behind Freud's evocative imagery must hover the shadow of his own mother, Amalie, who had died in 1930 at the age of ninety-five. Perhaps the final loosening of his own maternal bond enabled him to reconsider his major theories of sexuality and of death. An understanding of the pre-Oedipal phase now became essential to the study of female psychology. The mother reassumed her primary role as caretaker, seducer, and even source of the knowledge of castration; "by her care of the child's body she becomes its first seducer" (*SE* 21:233, 23:188–89).

The structure of Oedipal wishes in later Freudian theory was thus complicated by the discovery of early infant-mother relationships that prefigure the father-daughter bond. No longer could Freud simply assume a symmetrical pattern of cross-sexual unconscious erotic attraction tion—son to mother, daughter to father. Instead, he began to see that the girl's primal bond to her mother adumbrated her later attachment to her father. So those early seduction stories of his first female patients were not simply fantasies of paternal love or penis envy but wishes of restoring a lost maternal union. Ultimately, before the figure of the seductive father stood the original seducer, the original erotic manipulator of the infant—the mother. "The fact that the mother thus unavoidably initiates the child into the phallic phase is, I think, the reason why, in phantasies of later years, the father so regularly appears as the sexual seducer. When the girl turns away from her mother, she also makes over to her father her introduction into sexual life" (*SE* 21:238).

At these late points in the evolution of Freud's thought the father has become displaced as the agent responsible for childhood seduction, or castration threats, and has become a secondary, substitute love-object. For the girl's pre-Oedipal identification with her mother forms the bedrock of her sexuality (Chodorow 57–170). Yet it is just this identification that ultimately enables a woman's heterosexuality to emerge, since a man unconsciously searches for a sexual object that answers to his Oedipal wish. Once he has potentially found her, in marriage, he may find that the wish is satisfied only indirectly, through the paradoxical recirculations of Oedipal patterns. "How often it happens," Freud exclaimed, "that it is only his son who obtains what he himself aspired to! One gets an impression that a man's love and a woman's are a phase apart psychologically." Thus, through the traditional Oedipal arrangements that marriage provides, a daughter may ultimately come to represent her husband's mother. Further to deepen the matrix of unconscious relations, her husband also becomes not only a father figure but "her mother's heir as well" (*SE* 22:133–34).

The dense intricacies of intrafamilial erotic life detailed by psychoanalytic theory are vividly evoked in a poem by W. B. Yeats, published in the same year as Freud's essay on "Female Sexuality" (1933). Both texts explore the same topic: Yeats's poem could be a demonstration and elaboration of Freud's ideas. "A Woman Young and Old" is a rich, remarkable evocation of female sexual development within a family, in terms easily translatable into psychoanalytic theory. I quote part 1, "Father and Child," and the first stanza of part 2, "Before the World Was Made":

(I)
She hears me strike the board and say
That she is under ban
Of all good men and women,
Being mentioned with a man
That has the worst of all bad names;
And thereupon replies
That his hair is beautiful,
Cold as the March wind his eyes.

(II)
If I make the lashes dark
And the eyes more bright
And the lips more scarlet,
Or ask if all be right
From mirror after mirror,
No vanity's displayed:
I'm looking for the face I had
Before the world was made.   (*Collected Poems* 308)

The shift in perspective between stanzas is as abrupt as a cinematic "shot / reverse shot." From speaking in the father's loud, public voice the poem cuts to the daughter's quiet, private musings, which apparently ignore the paternal challenge. A psychoanalytic view of the father's anger could see a defense, an attempt to suppress his own incestuous desire. Conversely, the stark confrontation between anxious paternal authority and cool sensual attraction, focused on the issue of name, latently suggests that the daughter's eroticism may be devoted to a man whose cold, windy eyes reflect (in a certain light) the father's. With the tones of paternal ire ringing in her ears (Freud initially conceived of the superego as the father's voice—as Lacan put it, *le non du père*), the daughter is rapt in reflection. In reality and in fantasy, however, she is looking for another, earlier face, which she mirrors in makeup both cosmetic and psychic: the pre-Oedipal, pre-patriarchal, maternal face, the face she had before she encountered the world. "The precursor of the mirror," wrote Winnicott, reflecting Lacan, "is the mother's face" (Lacan, *Écrits* 1–7; Winnicott 111–18).

As she matures, Yeats's woman still hears the patriarchal command,

and she continues to ignore its precepts. In part 5, "Consolation," she says,

> O but there is wisdom
> In what the sages said;
> But stretch that body for a while
> And lay down that head
> Till I have told the sages
> Where man is comforted.
>
> How could passion run so deep
> Had I never thought
> That the crime of being born
> Blackens all our lot?
> But where the crime's committed
> The crime can be forgot. (310)

Woman's carnal knowledge subdues traditional sagacity, yet the sexual embrace poses a seminal question (such as Yeats's Lady Jane, echoing Eve, might ask). Paradoxically, wisdom intensifies passion by introducing the concept of original sin, whose crime can be enacted and allayed through repetition. Bliss erases blame, but only temporarily. Neither the energies of sexuality nor the voice of poetry can stave off the eventual solitude of death. Here are the final lines of "A Woman Old and Young" (from part 11, "From the 'Antigone'"):

> Pray I will and sing I must,
> And yet I weep—Oedipus' child
> Descends into the loveless dust. (315)

Before this final moment, Yeats's woman romanced, matured, and died. She was a child, a father's daughter. A version of her character appeared in one of Yeats's earlier poems, "A Prayer for My Daughter" (1919). In the poem, violent storms threaten an infant's sleep, while her father imagines her future. At the ebb of World War I his concerns are social and political, to be sure, but he himself is perturbed,

> Imagining in excited reverie
> That the future years had come,
> Dancing to a frenzied drum
> Out of the murderous innocence of the sea. (*Collected Poems* 212)

His reveries run to images of her beautiful face, to Helen of Troy, and to Venus, goddess of love, "that great Queen, that rose out of the spray, / Being fatherless could have her way"—as though a father might impede or intercept her way. In Yeats's volume, "A Prayer for My Daughter" immediately succeeded "The Second Coming," which specifically imagines paternal rape and monstrous, miraculous birth. Both Helen and Venus chose oddly in love, leading the father to muse,

> It's certain that fine women eat
> A crazy salad with their meat
> Whereby the Horn of Plenty is undone. (212)

Finally he weathers his psychic storm of desire by sublimating and transmuting an unconsciously incestuous father-daughter relationship into licit marriage.

> And may her bridegroom bring her to a house
> Where all's accustomed, ceremonious;
> For arrogance and hatred are the wares
> Peddled in the thoroughfares.
> How but in custom and in ceremony
> Are innocence and beauty born?
> Ceremony's a name for the rich horn,
> And custom for the spreading laurel tree. (214)

By denying cheap carnal commerce and renaming verdant eroticism in the proper terms of culture (*custom* and *ceremony*), the father can regain his daughter's innocence, while still imagining its proper loss and symbolic restoration in procreation (*rich horn* and *spreading tree*).

A daughter's sexuality is not always so well managed. In his *Jokes* book Freud recounted the story of a father who leaves his adolescent daughter with a family friend while he goes on a long trip, charging the friend with protecting the girl's virtue. Upon his return he discovers his daughter pregnant. When questioned, the friend admits that she slept in the same room with his son but that there was a screen between the two beds. The angry father retorts, "But he could have simply walked around the screen!" "Yes," muses the friend. "There is that. It could have happened like that" (*SE* 8:57–58). The incestuous displacements of this anecdote are obvious. Moreover, it indicates the place of a daughter as a risky commodity in the family economy and a father's ambivalent failure to maintain that commodity's value by placing it at Oedipal risk.

The artificial innocence of Freud's joke can be juxtaposed to the more genuinely innocent knowledge of a four-year-old girl whose mother (an American) wrote a letter to Freud that he found worth recording. The child had produced a series of associations around the grand mystery of procreation: (1) marriage produces babies, (2) trees grow in the ground, and (3) God made the world (*SE* 18:266). Freud quickly interpreted the conventional symbolism of mother earth and God the Father, though unaccountably he missed the phallic potential of trees. The little girl's displacement of paternity to divinity is typical, reinforced by cultural custom. It is the final move in a process of idealization begun early, in response to the father's typically absent, mysterious, and powerful function in the family. Such idealization can eventually suffer from reality, as Freud suggested when he considered the fate of the Oedipus complex in a girl. Though unlike the corresponding structure in a boy, it may never be "dissolved," noted Freud, it can suffer "the experience of painful disappointments. . . . The little girl likes to regard herself as what her father loves above all else; but the time comes when she has to endure a harsh punishment from him and she is cast out of her fool's paradise" (*SE* 19:173). Freud's Old Testament allusion implicitly makes the little Eve not merely the victim of punishment but the source of illicit desire as well.

Daughters lie at the genesis of psychoanalysis. It was a young woman obsessed with her father's fatal illness who first demonstrated the benefits and hazards of hypnosis to Breuer and then (by report) to Freud. This first recorded case of psychoanalysis involves "Fraulein Anna O.," who in 1881–82 underwent with Breuer what she termed the "talking cure" or "chimney sweeping" (*SE* 2:22 ff.). Freud's later summary and analysis of the case formed the first of his public lectures on psychoanalysis: he chose Anna O. to introduce his theories (*SE* 11:9–20). The woman's "profoundly melancholy phantasies" started from "the position of a girl at her father's sick-bed," and her symptoms recapitulated, through a process of identification and denial, her experience of nursing her terminally tubercular father. Her symptoms, wrote Freud, were "mnemic signs of [her father's] illness." They also expressed her own unconscious wishes and fears, erotic affections and aggressions (Hunter 94–95). Those unconscious motivations found apt expression in a therapeutic situation that mirrored her position as a daughter at her father's sickbed. Breuer devoted himself to treating the bedridden woman, listening to her curious polyglot linguistic inventions, implicitly encouraging her talk. When she not surprisingly acted out her filial position by experiencing hysterical pregnancy and imagining the birth of "Doctor Breuer's child," she made manifest an unconscious father-daughter relationship at the origins of psychoanalysis. But Breuer retreated from this advent of analysis: after hypnotizing his patient into silence, he "fled the house," according to Ernest Jones, "in a cold sweat" (Jones 1:223–26). The perturbed physician then kept silent for years, although Freud surmised the situation through the veil of Breuer's sudden resistance to psychoanalysis. Later he recounted details of the incident, remarking that "at this moment [Breuer] held in his hand the key that would have opened 'The Doors to the Mothers,' but he let it drop" (*Letters* 408–9).[3] Like most of Freud's imagery, the allusion to Goethe merges uncanny insight with sexual symbolism and points towards later theoretical developments: the discovery of pre-Oedipal infant-mother relationships. Dilating the image places Breuer in the position of paternal seducer and phallic discoverer, Anna O. in the position of virginal daughter and procreative mother, while their phantom child, produced through the analytic intercourse of their therapy, becomes the prototheory of psychoanalysis itself (Hunter 100). Breuer may have wished to abort this birth or to expose it only on a mountainside, but like a mythic hero (or heroine), it survived and thrived. Freud adopted it, named it, and raised it with attentive care, eventually legitimizing a once-bastard issue.

Another daughter brought forcibly to Freud's attention was the famous "Dora," whose commanding, tubercular, syphilitic father took her to Freud for psychological repair. The young girl suffered from various hysterical symptoms and was enmeshed in a web of adult sexual machinations unusual even in late-nineteenth-century Vienna. Her adulterous father conspired with his lecherous friend ("Herr K.") to trade Dora for "Frau K." (whom Dora had served as babysitter) so that the affair between Frau K. and Dora's father could continue. Both Freud and Dora were well aware of this implicit arrangement (7:1–122, esp. 34).

The case has recently been reviewed through various prismatic lenses: revisionist psychoanalysis, feminism, sociology, and narratology (Bernheimer and Kahane). I will focus briefly on the place of Dora as an emblem of the father-daughter relationship at the origins of psychoanalysis. Once again a young girl possessed secret knowledge that her father(s) wanted both to reveal and to repress. She communicated this knowledge through hysterical symptoms and improper speech. What disrupted her psychic virginity was a blight of sexual knowledge inflicted on her from without and aroused from within by her own wishful curiosity. Dora seemed an innocent repository of sexual secrets, whom Freud took care to keep innocent, though he found himself discussing sexual arousal and various perversions with her. It was through Dora that Freud, like Breuer with Anna O., confronted analytic transference. Unlike Breuer, he did not retreat from the discovery, though he took several years to develop a theory and never fully explored (at least publicly) his own countertransference. For Freud pressed his analytic attentions on Dora with the same ardor in which he imagined Herr K. pressing his body against hers in the crucial scene by the lake. His reading of that scene correlated adult seduction with the child's unconscious fantasy, in a mutuality of attractions translated by repression into symptom. The father's acts were real, *and* so were the daughter's wishes.

Freud's experience with Dora—not entirely a happy one—granted him insight into the world of *fin de siècle* Viennese sexual customs. A continuing parade of women recounted similar stories in his consulting room, until in 1908, in a remarkable essay on current cultural convention, Freud sketched a dismal picture of Viennese marriage: a groom eager to express his sexuality takes a bride rigorously kept ignorant of how she might help and share. Since a daughter's psychic attachments are fast-bound to her parents until wedlock, and even after, she "enters marriage uncertain of her own feelings." Retarded in love, she can only disappoint her husband. She is typically frigid ("anaesthetic"), and by the time she thaws out, "at the climax of her life as a woman," the marriage is ruined. Freud continued to plot a bleak trajectory: "And, as a reward for her previous docility, she is left with the choice between unappeased desire, unfaithfulness, or a neurosis." After next considering typical male sexual anxieties, Freud concluded that modern morality conspired to unite a frigid woman and an impotent man in the confining bonds of matrimony (SE 9:177–203, 197–98).

Not only was the sexual function of many women thus "crippled" by such ethical artifices, but their enforced sexual ignorance restricted all curiosity. Women are thus "scared away from *any* form of thinking," wrote Freud, "and knowledge loses its value for them." Freud continued to speculate that feminine "intellectual inferiority" was rooted in social sexual suppression, which inhibits thought (SE 9:198–99).

As if to demonstrate the psychosociological thesis thus propounded, for his 1917 public lectures Freud invented an elaborate narrative of two young women and their parallel sexual development. In this story, one girl is the daughter of a rich landlord, the other the daughter of his lower-class caretaker. The bourgeois and proletariat girls, living upstairs and down in the same house, engage in mutual masturbation instigated by the carnally wise lower-class child. Later they indulge individually, though the lower-class girl gives up masturbation at puberty, later marries, and will likely, so the story goes, have a child. She may, elaborated Freud, become an actress or even an aristocrat. And she will be neurosis-free. The upper-class girl, on the other hand, will feel guilty for her masturbation, perhaps giving up the act but not the guilt. She will become disgusted with the fuller sexual knowledge she eventually obtains but will also become aroused and wish to masturbate, thereby feeling guiltier. She will eventually become neurotic, "cheated of marriage and her hopes in life"—another victim of the repression enforced by "civilized" education. Here is Freud's synopsis of this Viennese "upstairs-downstairs" fiction.

> Sexual activity seemed to the caretaker's daughter just as natural and harmless in her later life as it had in childhood. The landlord's daughter came under the influence of education and accepted its demands. From the suggestions offered to it, her ego constructed

ideals of feminine purity and abstinence which are incompatible with sexual activity; her intellectual education reduced her interest in the feminine part which she was destined to play. (*SE* 16:352–54)

The whole episode reads like a Viennese Victorian novel, unlaced. Since Freud evidently had no easy recourse to case history, he constructed this two-story house of fiction from the psychic and social timber of his times. The story is remarkable for its interplay of social institutions, cultural repression, and the force of personal pleasure, along with its awareness of the implausibility and theatricality of conventional feminine behavior. It is also a psychodrama: a narrative of intrapsychic architecture in which the two interactive levels of consciousness and unconsciousness are represented as above and below, culture and carnality. Freud's narrative posits the daughter as subject and object of sexual knowledge and repression and the father as agent of permission and restriction.[4]

One of Freud's most dramatic actual cases involved a daughter whose father's angry glance literally drove her—in a female version of Kafka's "The Judgment"—to jump over a wall onto the train tracks below. Freud interpreted her suicide attempt as a highly overdetermined act, representing not only a submission to her father's will but a rejection of him and revenge on him for begetting a rival child. The daughter unconsciously punished her parents and herself through the act and furthermore enacted her wish to have a child by her father (Freud's interpretation here relies on puns in the German narrative). "It was remarkable, too," Freud continued, "that both parents behaved as if they understood their daughter's secret psychology" (*SE* 18:148–62, 160). The mother was tolerant, since she appreciated her rival's retirement from the field, and the father was furious, since his love was rejected.

Though not all so dramatic, each of Freud's accounts of Oedipal dramas discloses explicitly or implicitly the two-way paths of Oedipal desire. A child's wishes may be spontaneous and developmental, but they also coincide with and are urged by the parents' unconscious desires and preferences (father for daughter, mother for son). The mutuality of childhood seduction is reenacted later, when the maturing daughter stimulates a resurgence of her father's Oedipal wishes. Father and daughter then reconstitute a cautious choreography of mutual eroticism and ambivalence, a dance of mermaid—the seductive daughter/mother—and minotaur—the Oedipal father/son (Dinnerstein).

The romance of Jocasta and Oedipus delineates the *locus classicus* of one style of this dynamic; Freud placed their myth at the center of his theory. Though he regularly resisted the analogous term "Electra complex," for the little girl's part in the Oedipal story, Freud did describe one case whose Oedipal geometry is similar to that of the classic myth. Like *Oedipus Rex,* the case comes from dramatic literature: Ibsen's *Rosmersholm.* Freud's reading, an acute piece of literary criticism, demonstrates how Rebecca West has replicated her original incestuous circumstance by taking her mistress's place at Rosmersholm. She cannot then allow herself to marry a "legitimate" father figure even though she is apparently free to do so, since she has committed incest (unknowingly, as the manifest level must have it) with her "illegitimate" father (*SE* 14:324–31).

To avoid the pitfalls dramatized in these tragic narratives, a father in an erotically charged Oedipal relationship to a daughter must find some middle ground. Ideally managed, father-daughter love can simultaneously allow symbolic expression of incestuous wishes while sustaining unconscious repression of incestuous desire. For both daughter and father, the other can be available in fantasy but not in actuality (Marjorie Leonard). This unconscious configuration is analogous to the "transference love" of psychoanalytic treatment, and the father's proper position is similar to the one Freud prescribed to analysts (*SE* 12:159–71). Recent feminist revisions of psychoanalysis press the analogy into emblematics, so that the father's "seduction" of the daughter becomes replicated in the male analyst's "seduction" of the female patient (typically hysteric) through hypnosis, suggestion, transference, and insistently sexual interpretations (Gallop 56–79; Irigaray, "Psychoanalytic Theory").

Freud was initially surprised by the power of the transference. He reported that it was a sudden embrace by a hypnotized female patient, interrupted by the timely entrance of a servant, that convinced him to abandon hypnosis in order to search for "the mysterious element that was at work behind hypnosis"—that is, repression, and ultimately the transference (*SE* 20:27). Unlike Breuer, his colleague in hysteria, Freud did not run from his discovery; he was, however, sometimes at a loss how to deal with it. When he realized that the transference of a female homosexual patient involved a "sweeping repudiation of men," he terminated her treatment and recommended (to her parents) a female doctor (*SE* 18:164). Freud's awareness of Dora's transference seems to have ignored his own identification with Herr K., whom Freud knew and who discussed the girl's case with Freud and Dora's father. However accurately Freud's interpretation of the scene by the lake revealed unconscious motives, his reconstruction of Herr K.'s erection very likely manifested his own wish, if not physical sensation. When he concluded that Dora would like a kiss from him just as she wanted one from Herr K., he implicitly acknowledged the other side of transference, where paternal passion meets filial fantasy. In the final pages of the case history, describing how Dora rejected his treatment, Freud wondered whether he should have pressed further his therapeutic suit by showing "a warm personal interest." What if Herr K. had similarly ignored the girl's ambivalent denials and persisted (*SE* 7:74, 109–19)? His question discloses the potential rapist in the therapist.

Transference love, like every other kind, is a repetition of infantile love. Initially, as in the Dora case, Freud characterized the transference as daughter-to-father. In a later essay on technique he was careful to describe it as infant-to-parent (ultimately infant-to-mother). Warning analysts against the hazards of succumbing to the temptations that the transference love of young women offered to a male analyst, Freud wrote: "He must not stage the scene of a dog-race in which the prize was to be a garland of sausages but which some humorist spoilt by throwing a single sausage on to the track" (*SE* 12:169). This coarse, juicy image entices interpretation. It places the analyst in directorial control of a theatrical scene that abruptly becomes an animal contest, in which symbols of rampant carnality pursue primitive goals. Only through the momentary renunciation of instinctual gratification—that is, by obeying the central code of culture—can the greater good of analytic success be achieved. At any point in the contest, the urges of appetite can change the progress into a chaotic mixture of flesh—dogs devouring a sausage. Behind the crude genital symbolism ("a single sausage on the track") lies the primitive object of oral desire, the original source of food: the maternal breast. To translate the fable into theory: acting out one style of transference love (daughter-father) prevents the discovery of another, earlier scene—the reenactment of original satisfaction. The joker in the pack, that "humorist" who spoils the game by introducing instant gratification, is literally *diabolic*: he thwarts analysis by *throwing across* its path the tempting obstacle (*dia,* "across" + *ballein,* "to throw"). He is the agent of both resistance and sexual desire, residing in the analytic conspiracy of doctor and patient. The analyst thus comes to occupy every position in this fantasy-fabliau. He is both stage director and heckler, trying to maintain conscious technique, while his unconscious imp of the perverse seeks to thwart him. He joins the racing dogs in pursuit of the garland of victory, while he also symbolizes the source(s) of that victory. What the patient seeks is in him, but he cannot give it to her. Indeed, to throw the sausage on the track, to offer the penis to the patient's envious desire, would only spoil the game, since it is for her always an impossible desire, however symbolically fulfilled. Only by refusing this unconscious request and resisting the unconscious temptation on his part can the analyst arrive with his analysand at the finish line, where he sits symbolically in the depersonalized guise of the mother, bearing the "garland" of gratification.

"Transference love" is a benevolent term for a highly ambivalent set of unconscious emotions. Its darkest side transmutes an implicit master-slave relationship into sheer submission to paternal power: its perverse turn is masochism. Conventionally, the daughter's way is finally to submit to the patriarchy in order to derive the pleasures of security and protection. This conventional submission may be seen as a type of masochism. A daughter's culturally normal situation is pathologically intensified by sadomasochistic fantasies such as Freud analyzed in his essay "'A Child Is Being Beaten'" (1919). Even the syntax of this phrase, quoted by a female patient, indicates the passivity of the scene, and the malleability of subject and object. Through a series of linguistic transformations, Freud arrived at a standard interpretation of such fantasies (or memories):

1. "My father is beating the child [whom I hate]."
2. "I am being beaten by my father."
3. "A child is being beaten [(male), while I (female) look on]."

$(SE$ 17:184–86)

The first statement combines an actual familial scene, available to memory, with an accompanying affect (sibling rivalry). The second statement expresses the critical *wish,* or set of wishes, merging incestuous desire with masochism and self-punishment. This statement delineates the scene of unconscious fantasy, discoverable only through analysis. The third statement is the conscious translation, the edited version spoken by the patient. Freud was not yet satisfied with these layers of interpretation. He continued to note that such fantasies in a woman fulfill the unconscious wish to be a man, since the "whipping boys" are usually male and stand in for the woman. Another reading, using current sexual slang, indicated a masturbation fantasy at work: the child represents the clitoris $(SE$ 19:254).

The questions of feminine passivity and masochism that Freud addressed in this essay opened up much larger issues, which he considered in another 1919 paper on masochism. In it he equated, or deeply analogized, the "death instinct" with "primal sadism" and termed its intra-organic operations "erotogenic masochism." He then took the further step of linking the nature of woman to this implicit equation, so that masochism, woman, and the death instinct merged in the metaphoric vortex of theory $(SE$ 19:161–65).

At this point the topic of the father-daughter relationship risks becoming lost in theoretical abstraction, as the seductions of Freudian mythology overwhelm the more straightforward design of theory. Yet just this symbolic linkage of woman and death empowers a crucial essay of Freud's, written explicitly about the father-daughter relationship. In 1913 he set himself what he called a "little problem" in the interpretation of myth and literature. The resulting essay, "The Theme of the Three Caskets," quickly opened onto the larger questions of life and death (*SE* 12.289–301). Starting with Shakespeare's *Merchant of Venice* and the contest in Belmont for Portia's hand, Freud read the three caskets as symbols of woman, or of woman in her three mythic guises: mother, wife/lover, and death (the three Fates, "three forms of the figure of the mother"). Freud's reconstruction of time as a series of incestuous relationships was occasioned by Shakespeare's dramas of father and daughter, which Freud translated into symbolic dramas of son and mother. He thus read the last scene of *King Lear* as one in which the old king symbolically encounters death in the guise of his daughter, who represents his mother ("mother earth"). In the final sentence, he wrote: "But it is in vain that an old man yearns for the love of woman as he had it first from his mother; the third of the Fates alone, the silent Goddess of Death, will take him into her arms." The image offers a compelling blend of frustration and satisfaction, infantile and adult sexuality. Death thus eroticized bears uncanny connotations. It seems a comfortable conclusion: a blend of the erotic and fatal, infantile and adult, life and death. It represents theory yearning after mythology. Much of the essay's significance likely pertains, moreover, to perturbations relating directly to Freud's life at the time. Such personal material is only barely hidden, and drives the essay from within.

Like Lear, Freud had three daughters. In the months preceding this 1913 essay, at age fifty-seven, he was dealing with his twenty-year-old daughter Sophie's sudden engagement to Max Halberstadt. The couple undertook the engagement without asking parental permission. He was thus forced to face the sexual life of his daughter as a secret event. His letters to the couple during this period are subtle, complex, charming expressions of paternal affection and annoyance. He wrote that he felt "superfluous" and that his blessing must be a mere formality. He would of course grant it, but first Mr. Halberstadt should travel to Karlsbad to visit his prospective in-laws. To Sophie, who was apparently dissatisfied with her parents' lack of sheer joy over her action, Freud suggested that her distress was a symptom of her guilty conscience. Another letter to Halberstadt announced simply: "It is very strange to watch one's little daughter suddenly turn into a loving woman" (read: "a woman who loves another man"). In his next letter to his prospective son-in-law he labeled Sophie (jokingly, one assumes) "the little shrew" and wished Max a good marriage (*Letters* 296–300).

Themes of paternal intimacy and filial betrayal were thus close to Freud's own personal history as he analyzed these Shakespearean plays about daughters leaving fathers for husbands. There remain further connections. Always acutely aware of his own mortality, Freud was especially concerned during the decade 1910–20. His intestinal trouble was severe during 1912–13 (as he reported in letters to his wife, Martha), and he admitted to feeling depressed (*Letters* 301). He seems to have had an early fear of cancer (though the actual pathology was not yet diagnosed). For some time, probably under the influence of Fliess's numerology, he believed he would die before 1918 (Ernest Jones 2:392). His identification with Lear is especially notable in the "Three Caskets" essay. In April 1912 he wrote to Ludwig Binswanger: "An old man like me . . . shouldn't complain (and had decided not to complain) if his life comes to an end in a few years" (*Letters* 295).

A more revealing letter is to Sandor Ferenczi, in July 1913. In it Freud wrote that he intended to spend several happy weeks in Marienbad, "free of analysis." "My closest companion will be my little daughter [Anna, seventeen], who is developing very well at the moment (you will long ago have guessed the subjective condition for the 'Theme of the Three Caskets')" (*Letters* 307). The "Three Caskets" essay is thus framed by the daughter-mother pair (Freud's mother was seventy-eight at the time). In terms both theoretical and biographical, the latent incestuous bond reaches historically towards the mother (the past) and projectively towards the daughter (the present and future). In fact, Anna Freud was the youngest daughter, who nursed her father during the sixteen years of his lingering cancer, who spoke for him in public (she read his seminal paper on sexual difference at the 1925 Homburg International Psycho-Analytical Congress), who helped him to die, and who carried his project forward. She never married and remained in her father's house, devoted to only two personal relationships—with Freud and with Dorothy Burlingham, her longtime companion and colleague. "Anna will never marry," her mother Martha once said, "until she finds a man exactly like her father" (Freeman and Strean 82).

Freud's relations with his own daughters may therefore most vividly illustrate his theories about that complicated bond. An early reference (1897) concerns a dream of "over-affectionate feelings towards Mathilde," his first-born. She was then eleven, a myth enthusiast like her father. Interpreting the dream in a letter to Fliess, Freud wrote that "the dream of course shows the fulfillment of my wish to catch a *Pater* as the originator of neurosis, and so to put an end to my doubts about this which still persist" (*Complete Letters* 249).[5] This is a neat evasion of an incestuous wish by intellectual sublimation into theory, as Charles Bernheimer has noted (Bernheimer and Kahane 14). By a generic interpretation involving *the* Father, Freud both subsumes and avoids his own specific significance as *a* father.

No such cerebral subterfuge was available in the winter of 1920, when Freud's favorite daughter, Sophie, died in the postwar influenza epidemic. For Amalie, his mother, he played the Stoic role:

Dear Mother,

I have some sad news for you today. Yesterday morning our dear lovely Sophie died from galloping influenza and pneumonia. [Here he adds three sentences about travel details.] I hope you will take it calmly: tragedy after all has to be accepted. But to mourn this splendid vital girl who was so happy with her husband and children, is of course permissible.

I greet you fondly.

Yours,

Sigmund   (*Letters* 332)

After thus demonstrating the attitude he wished for his mother, and for himself in relation to her, he wrote the next day to Oscar Pfister. In a long letter describing Sophie's vitality and his sorrowful surprise at her death, he remarked, "Tomorrow she is to be cremated, our poor Sunday child!" He continued: "I work as much as I can, and am thankful for the diversion. The loss of a child seems to be a serious, narcissistic injury; what is known as mourning will probably follow, only later" (333). To Ferenczi, one week after the death, Freud wrote:

Please don't worry about me. Apart from feeling rather more tired, I am the same. The death, painful as it is, does not affect my attitude towards life. [He quotes Goethe: *Daseins susse Gewohnheit* ("the dear lovely habit of living").] Deep down I sense a bitter, irreparable narcissistic injury. My wife and Annerl [Anna] are profoundly affected in a more human way. (334)

Grief and mourning, those "more human" emotions, were left to the women: mother, wife, daughter. As a man, Freud stoically endured the pain of an injury to himself: "Blunt necessity; mute submission" (Ernest Jones 3:19; Schur 330–31). Now the Freudian prototype of the "narcissistic wound" is castration. Freud expressed in terms of theory the profundity of his own unconscious response to the loss of a child. It is not only the father who symbolizes a penis for the daughter but the daughter who, like a son, symbolizes the father's generative extension into the future and remains in reality and in fantasy his flesh.

Freud's most intense personal relation to his daughters, or to any of his children, was to Anna, his youngest. Before she was fourteen he had begun regular conversations with her about psychoanalysis, often on long walks along Lake Garda in northern Italy (Peters 18). He acknowledged in a letter her significance to the "Three Caskets" essay. It was Freud's uniquely unorthodox decision to psychoanalyze his own daughter, however, that signified—but hardly revealed—the complexities of this particular case. Steven Marcus remarks, "Freud was not beyond good and evil, but in this instance he gave it a good try" (*Freud* 216).

Freud's favorite nickname for Anna was Antigone, the name of the heroine who witnessed her father Oedipus in his blindness and insight, became his caretaker and confessor, spoke on his behalf, guided him to Colonus, and was with him when he died (Peters 15–21). After his passing, she remained to enact a final episode in the continuing family drama of Oedipus. She was not only her father's daughter—"true daughter of an immortal sire," as Ernest Jones termed her in his dedication to *The Life and Works*—but his son (Freeman and Strean 74; Sophocles, *Oedipus at Colonus,* trans. Watling, lines 1364–66). She embodied the final answer to the riddle of the Sphinx, by becoming the "third leg" that helped support her sightless sire. Analogously, Freud's theory of the father-daughter relationship became a late support for the aging Oedipal project. The daughter, herself missing a penis, ironically becomes the missing element that potentiates and completes psychoanalytic theory. She symbolically restores the absence she embodies. Lacan's rereading of Freudian theory makes a similar point. "Paradoxical as this formulation may seem," wrote Lacan, "it is in order to be the phallus, that is to say, the signifier of the desire of the Other, that a woman will reject an essential part of her femininity, namely all her attributes in the masquerade. *It is for that which she is not that she wishes to be desired as well as loved.* But she finds the signifier of her own desire in the body of him to whom she addresses her demand for love" (*Ecrits* 289–90).

It is on just this point, of course—the primacy of the phallus—that Freud's daughters of theory most vigorously diverged. Helene Deutsch, Karen Horney, Marie Bonaparte, Joan Riviere, Melanie Klein, Anna Freud, and other contemporary women enacted a historic struggle of "Freudian" siblings over the explanatory potency of the phallus. The debate continues. My goal here is not to engage the theoretical issues but to characterize Freud's relationship to the fact, idea, and image of woman as daughter. One event, albeit anecdotal, emblematically encapsulates that relationship: H.D.'s story of Freud's bronze statue of Athena.

Hilda Doolittle underwent two brief analyses with Freud in Vienna, in 1933 and 1934. She was forty-seven and Freud was seventy-seven. Their encounter was a curious blend of directed therapy, training analysis, aesthetic discussion, and mutual appreciation (Holland, "Freud and H.D."). She imagined him as a powerful father, and he in turn (so she believed) found in her a representation of his lost Sophie (Doolittle, Letter to Bryher; *Tribute*).[6] After Freud's death in 1939, she wrote a long essay about her experience, *Tribute to Freud*. In it, she described a moment when Freud escorted her into his study, separate from the consulting room, and displayed several specimens from his collection of ancient artifacts. Holding a small bronze statue of Pallas Athena, he said, "*This* is my favorite. . . . She is perfect, *only she has lost her spear*" (74; her italics). In recollecting this stunning moment of iconographic interpretation, H.D. responds with associations to another face of Athena, "Winged Victory"—thereby substituting power for privation and answering the Freudian concept of penis envy with an emblem of female strength (DuPlessis and Friedman).[7] The anecdote may or may not be a reliable account of Freud's behavior, but it testifies at least to the enduring acuity of his insight and to his valuation of the image of woman, perfect in her loss. Athena, who sprang fully grown and fully armed from the forehead of her father, Zeus, moreover represents a mythology of the patriarchal genesis of wisdom (philosophy, psychology) in the guise of a motherless daughter. The Freud-H.D.-Athena encounter is a brief moment, but it can be placed momentarily against that other primal myth of origin that structures psychoanalysis—the Oedipal.

Another poem, by a modern woman, offers humorous and affectionate insight into this poignant, profound relationship of father and daughter.

One day lying on my stomach in the afternoon trying to sleep
    I suffered penis envy (much
            to my surprise
And with no belief in Freud for years
         in fact extreme
antipathy) What could I do but turn around
and close my eyes and dream of summer
        in those days I
        was a boy
whistled at the gate
    for Tom

Then I woke up
Then I slept
and dreamed another dream
In my drowned father's empty pocket
there were nine dollars and the salty sea
he said   I know you   my darling girl
you're the one that's me.   (Paley 239)

Passively musing in the inner oneirotic space of the feminine, the woman dreams herself at play in the masculine world. To "turn around," as the daughter in her *père-version* finally must, means to imagine herself as both her own and her father's, both girl and (tom)boy, whistling like Huck Finn for a missing friend (or a missing organ) "at the gate." Her fantasy is disrupted by the reality of absence, or rather it is replaced by a new dream of reality. Though fathers die, their pockets are never empty. They contain a seminal gift: the recognition of difference *and* mirroring. Father and daughter reconstitute a special dual unity that integrates Oedipal and pre-Oedipal relations. Together yet apart, their ambivalent bond blends conflict and comfort, rejection and identification, seduction and betrayal. It persists indelibly in memory, dream, theory, and practice.

Notes

1. This street is traveled doggedly by Jeffrey Masson in his recent polemic, *The Assault on Truth*. Yet some of the questions it raises—and the energy it has aroused—are worth review.

2. A succinct summary of Freud's changing views on female sexual development and the Oedipus complex is provided by Strachey's introduction ("Editor's Note") to "Some Psychical Consequences of the Anatomical Distinction between the Sexes," *SE* 19:243–47. For recent representative neo-Freudian reviews and critiques of Freud's ideas see Mitchell 1–131; and Irigaray, "Psychoanalytic Theory."

3. Freud's reference to "The Doors to the Mothers" alludes to an intense and obscure episode in Goethe's *Faust,* bk. 2, act 2.

4. This narrative is uncannily buttressed by a reminiscence of Freud's son, Martin. He recalls that as children, his sisters refused to play with a neighboring "ranger's daughter" after they discovered (while swinging) that she wore no underpants (Freeman and Strean 67).

5. *"Pater"* is editor Masson's reading; the *Standard Edition* has "father" (*vater*).

6. I thank Susan Stanford Friedman for the reference to this unpublished letter in the Beinecke Library.

7. The DuPlessis-Friedman essay is preceded by a previously unpublished poem by H.D., "The Master." Written in 1934 (one year after Yeats's "A Woman Young and Old" and Freud's "Female Sexuality"), the poem blends admiration, affection, and anger in lines that attest to the imaginative power of H.D.'s relationship (transference) to Freud, though the work is not among her best. She did not want it published.

JANE GALLOP

The Father's Seduction

LUCE IRIGARAY is a French psychoanalyst whose feminist readings of Freud and the philosophers—published in *Speculum de l'autre femme*—caused her to be expelled from the Lacanian department of psycho-analysis at Vincennes. The first third of *Speculum de l'autre femme* is called "The Blind Spot of an Old Dream of Symmetry." It is a close reading of "Femininity," one of Freud's *New Introductory Lectures on Psycho-Analysis* (1933). This encounter between Irigaray's feminist critique and Freud's final text on woman is an important training ground for a new kind of battle, a feminine seduction/disarming/unsettling of the positions of phallocratic ideology. Irigaray's tactic is a kind of reading: a close reading that separates the text into fragments of varying size, quotes it, and then comments with various questions and associations. She never sums up the meaning of Freud's text, nor does she bind all her commentaries, questions, and associations into a unified representation, a coherent interpretation. Her commentaries are full of loose ends and unanswered questions. As a result, the reader does not so easily lose sight of the incoherency and inconsistency of the text.

That could be seen as a victory for feminism. The Man's order is disturbed by the woman with the impertinent questions and the incisive comments. But as with all seductions, the question of complicity poses itself. The dichotomy active/passive is always equivocal in seduction; that is what distinguishes it from rape. So Freud might have been encouraging Irigaray all along, "asking for it." "By exhibiting this 'symptom,' this crisis point in metaphysics where the sexual 'indifference' that assured metaphysics its coherence and 'closure' finally exposes itself, Freud proposes it to analysis: his text asking to be heard, to be read" (*Speculum* 29.)[1]

Freud might have seduced Irigaray. It might be psychoanalysis that has won over feminism. The very strategy of reading with which Irigaray works Freud over is presented by Freud himself earlier in these *New Introductory Lectures,* where he writes, "We ask the dreamer, too, to free himself from the impression of the manifest dream, to divert his attention from the dream as a whole on to the separate portions of its content and to report to us in succession everything that occurs to him in relation to each of these portions—what associations present themselves to him if he focuses on each of them separately" (*SE* 22:10–11).

Freud's text asks for analysis. Not just any analysis, but the peculiar technique developed in psychoanalysis for dealing with dreams and other "symptoms." Freud proposed the model of the rebus for understanding dreams. According to the dictionary, a rebus is "a riddle composed of words or syllables depicted by symbols or pictures that suggest the sound of the words or syllables they represent." As a total picture, a unified representation, the rebus makes no sense. It is only by separating the picture into its elements, dealing with them one at a time, making all possible associations, that one can get anywhere. So psychoanalysis in its technique if not its theory offers an alternative to coherent, unified representation.

The rebus-text shatters the manifest unity so as to produce a wealth of associations that must necessarily be reduced if the goal of interpretation is to reach a final, definitive meaning, the "latent dream-thoughts." The unconscious is reappropriated to the model of consciousness—a circumscription analogous to the reappropriation of otherness, femininity to sameness, masculinity. Whereas Freud proposes the rebus as merely a path to the "latent thoughts," Irigaray radicalizes Freud's rebus. Irigaray's dream analysis ("The Blind Spot of an Old *Dream* of Symmetry") does not offer a final latent thought; it merely presents the abundance of associations, not editing those that "lead nowhere."

Yet Irigaray's encounter with Freud is not a psychoanalysis. Freud is not there to associate. Irigaray both asks questions (the analyst's role) and supplies associations (the dreamer's role). And since many questions go unanswered, they appear directed to the reader, who thus becomes the dreamer. She aims, not to decipher Freud's peculiar psyche, but rather to unravel "an old dream," everyone's dream, even Irigaray's dream. The dream is everyone's inasmuch as everyone is within "the metaphysical closure," inasmuch as any reader is a "subject," which is to say inasmuch as any reader has been philosophically reduced to a unified, stable, sexually indifferent subject, trapped in the old dream of symmetry.

(*Symmetry* from the Greek *summetros*, "of like measure"; from *sun*, "like, same" and *metron*, "measure." Symmetry is appropriating two things to like measure, measure by the same standard, for example, the feminine judged by masculine standards. Judged by masculine measures, woman is inadequate, castrated.)

Irigaray impertinently asks a few questions. And in her questions a certain desire comes through, not a desire for a "simple answer," but a desire for an encounter, a heterosexual dialogue. Not in the customary way we think of heterosexual—the dream of symmetry, two opposite sexes complementing each other. In that dream the woman ends up functioning as mirror, giving back a coherent, framed representation to the appropriately masculine subject. There is no real sexuality of the *heteros.* "Will there ever be any relation between the sexes?" asks Irigaray (*Speculum* 33).

Irigaray's reading of Freud seeks that "relation between the sexes." Her aggression is not merely some man-hating, penis-envying urge to destroy the phallocentric oppressor. She lays fiery siege to the Phallus, out of a yearning to get beyond its prohibitiveness and touch some masculine body. It is the rule of the Phallus as standard for any sexuality that denigrates women and makes any relation between the sexes impossible, any relation between two modalities of desire, between two desires, unthinkable. The rule of the Phallus is the reign of the One, of Unicity. In the "phallic phase," according to Freud, "only one kind of genital organ comes to account—the male" ("Infantile Genital Organization," *SE* 19:142). Freud, man, is arrested in the phallic phase, caught in the reign of the One, obsessively trying to tame otherness in a mirror-image of sameness.

In her next book, *Ce Sexe qui n'en est pas un,* Irigaray says: "What I desire and what I am waiting for, is what men will do and say if their sexuality gets loose from the empire of phallocratism" (133–34). The masculine exists no more than does the feminine. The specificity of both is suppressed by the reign of the Idea, the Phallus. Freud is not without a certain awareness of this. Something like the trace of a nonphallic masculinity can be read in a footnote that appears a few sentences after his statement about "one kind of genital organ": "It is remarkable, by the way, what a small degree of interest the other part of the male genitals, the little sac with its contents, arouses in the child. From all one hears in analyses one could not guess that the male genitals consist of anything more than the penis" (*SE* 19:42). "By the way," in a remark marginal to the central thrust of his argument can be found that which must be left aside by phallocentrism. Yet it is precisely because of the anatomical discrepancies in "all one hears in analysis" that analysis can be the place where the untenable reductions that constitute the reign of the Phallus are most noticeable.

The difference, of course, between the phallic suppression of masculinity and the phallic suppression of femininity is that the phallic represents (even if inaccurately) the masculine and not the feminine. By giving up their bodies, men gain power—the power to theorize, to represent themselves, to exchange women, to reproduce themselves and mark their offspring with their name. All these activities ignore bodily pleasure in pursuit of representation, reproduction, production. "In this 'phallocratic' power, man is not without loss; notably in regard to the enjoyment of his body" (Irigaray, *Ce Sexe* 140).

Irigaray's reading of Freud's theory continually discovers an ignoring of pleasure. The theory of sexuality is a theory of the sexual function (ultimately the reproductive function), and questions of pleasure are excluded, because they have no place in an economy of production. Commenting on Freud's discussion of breast-feeding, Irigaray remarks: "Every consideration of pleasure in nursing appears here to be excluded, unrecognized, prohibited. That, certainly, would introduce some nuances in such statements" (*Speculum* 13). A consideration of pleasure would introduce a few nuances into the theory (*nuance* from *nue*, "cloud"). A consideration of pleasure might cloud the theory, cloud the view, reduce its ability to penetrate with clarity, to appropriate. The distinction of active and passive roles becomes more ambiguous when it is a question of pleasure. And it is the distinction active/passive that is in question in Freud's discussion of nursing.

Freud writes: "A mother is active in every sense towards the child; the act of nursing itself may equally be described as the mother suckling the baby or as her being sucked by it" (*SE* 22:115). The sentence seems contradictory. If a mother is so clearly "active in every sense," why is the only example chosen so easily interpretable as either active or passive? The difficulty is symptomatic of one of the most insistent problems for Freud—the relationship of the dichotomies active/passive and masculine/feminine. According to Freud, the opposition active/passive characterizes the anal phase, whereas masculine/feminine is the logic of adult sexuality. In this discussion of the mother Freud is trying to show how improper it is to identify feminine with passive, masculine with active, since a mother is clearly feminine and clearly active. Again and again in different books and articles over a span of twenty years, Freud will try to differentiate and articulate the anal dichotomy and the adult sexual opposition—without much success.[2]

Irigaray suggests that Freud's model of sexuality has a strong anal erotic bias. The faeces become other products (a baby, a penis, a representation, a theory),[3] but the emphasis is on the product. Why else would the ambiguous nursing (describable in either active or passive terms) be so clearly an "activity"? Indeed nursing constitutes the model of the Freudian oral phase, which is defined as prior to the opposition active/passive. Freud's anal logic thus even intrudes into the very state defined as pre-anal. In this case, the inconsistency cannot be explained as a legacy in a later stage from the earlier, anal period; we are faced with the anal fixation of the theory itself.

An accusation of contradiction could be leveled at this point. Earlier in the present text Freud has been deemed "arrested in the phallic phase." Now he is judged "arrested" in the anal phase. It is not a question of resolving this contradiction, of fixing the diagnosis of Freud's personal pathology. Freud himself acknowledged that the stages of development are not clearly separate and distinct. The attempt to isolate each stage could be considered an effect to reduce sexuality to only one modality at any given moment, symptomatic of the rule of the One.

The investment in unicity, in one sexuality, shows itself in Freud's description of the little girl "in the phallic phase." Freud insists that in the phallic phase little girls only get pleasure from their clitoris and are unfamiliar with the rest of their genitalia. (Remember, the phallic phase is characterized as recognizing only one kind of sexual organ.) Yet others have found girls at this stage aware of vaginal sensations, and Freud dismisses this peremptorily as well as somewhat contradictorily: "It is true that there are a few isolated reports of early vaginal sensations as well, but it could not be easy to distinguish these from sensations in the anus or vestibulum; *in any case they cannot play a great part. We are entitled to keep our view* that in the phallic phase of girls the clitoris is the leading erotogenic zone" (*SE* 22:118; my italics). Why it is that "they cannot play a great part"? Because then "we" would not be "entitled to keep our *view*," keep our *theoria* (from *theoros*, "spectator," from *thea*, "a viewing"). Entitled by what or whom? The blind spot is obvious: what must be protected is "our view," appropriate to the masculine.

Freud insists on reducing the little girl's genitalia to her clitoris because that organ fits "our view," is phallomorphic, can be measured by the same standard (*summetros*). "We are now obliged to recognize that the little girl is a little man," declares Freud (*SE* 22:118), making the phallocentric economy clear. The girl is assimilated to a male model, male history, and "naturally" is found lacking. The condition of that assimilation is the reduction of any possible complexity, plural sexuality, to the one, the simple, in this case to the phallomorphic clitoris.

Once reduced to phallomorphic measures, woman is defined as "really castrated," by Freud/man. As such she is the guarantee against man's castration anxiety. She has no desires that do not complement his, so she can mirror him, provide him with a representation of himself which calms his fears and phobias about (his own potential) otherness and difference, about some "other view" that might not support his narcissistic overinvestment in his penis. "As for woman, *on peut se demander* ["one could wonder, ask oneself"] why she submits so easily . . . to the counterphobic projects, projections, productions of man relative to his desire" (Irigaray, *Speculum* 61).

The expression for wondering, for speculation, that Irigaray uses above is the reflexive verb *se demander,* literally "to ask oneself." Most of the "impertinent questions" in *Speculum* seem to be addressed to Freud, or men, or the reader. But this question of woman's easy submission she must ask herself. And the answer is not so obvious. A little later she

101

attempts to continue this line of questioning: "And why does she lend herself to it so easily? Because she's suggestible? Hysterical? But one can catch sight of the vicious circle" (*Speculum* 69). This question of the complicity, the suggestibility, of the hysteric who "finally says in analysis [what is not] foreign to what she is expected to say there" (*Speculum* 64) leads us to the contemplation of another vicious circle—the (hysterical) daughter's relationship to the father (of psychoanalysis).

The daughter's desire for her father is desperate: "the only redemption of her value as a girl would be to seduce the father, to draw from him the mark if not the admission of some interest" (*Speculum* 106). If the phallus is the standard of value, then the father, possessor of the phallus, must desire the daughter in order to give her value. But the father is a man (a little boy in the anal, the phallic, phase) and cannot afford to desire otherness, an other sex, because that opens up his castration anxiety. The father's refusal to seduce the daughter, to be seduced by her (seduction wreaking havoc with anal logic and its active/passive distribution), gain him another kind of seduction (this one more one-sided, more like violation), a veiled seduction in the form of the law. The daughter submits to the father's rule, which prohibits the father's desire, the father's penis, out of the desire to seduce the father by doing his bidding and thus pleasing him.

That is the vicious circle. The daughter desires a heterosexual encounter with the father and is rebuffed by the rule of the homological, raising the homo over the hetero, the logical over the sexual, decreeing neither the hetero nor the sexual worthy of the father. Irigaray would like really to respond to Freud, to provoke him into a real dialogue. But the only way to seduce the father, to avoid scaring him away, is to please him, and to please him one must submit to his law, which proscribes any sexual relation.

Patriarchal law, the law of the father, decrees that the "product" of sexual union, the child, shall belong exclusively to the father, be marked with his name. Also that the womb that bears that child should be a passive receptacle with no claims on the product, the womb "itself possessed as a means of (re)production" (*Speculum* 16). Irigaray understands woman's exclusion from production via a reading of Marx and Engels, which she brings in as a long association near the end of her reading of Freud's dream. That exclusion of the woman is inscribed in her relationship to the father. Any feminist upheaval, which would change woman's definition, identity, name, as well as the foundations of her economic status, must undo the vicious circle by which the desire for the father's desire (for his penis) causes her to submit to the father's law, which denies his desire/penis but operates in its place and, according to Irigaray, even procures for him a surplus of pleasure.

The question why woman complies must be asked. To ask that question is to ask what woman must not do anymore, what feminist strategy ought to be. We cannot wait for an answer, deferring the struggle against phallocentrism until a definitive explanation is found. In lieu of that "answer," I would like slowly to trace a reading of a section of *Speculum* that concerns the father of psychoanalysis and his hysterics but also the father of psychoanalytic theory and his daughter Irigaray.

Irigaray reads in Freud an account of an episode from the beginnings of psychoanalysis that "*caused* [*him*] *many distressing hours*" (Irigaray's italics): "In the period in which the main interest was directed to discovering infantile sexual traumas, almost all my woman patients told me that they had been seduced by their father. I was driven to recognize in the end, that these reports were untrue and so came to understand that hysterical symptoms are derived from phantasies and not from real occurrences" (Freud, *SE* 22:120; Irigaray, *Speculum* 40). Irigaray suggests that the reader "imagine that x, of the masculine gender, of a ripe age, uses the following language, how would you interpret it: 'it caused me many distressing hours,' 'almost all *my* woman patients told *me* that they had been seduced by their *father*.'" Irigaray invites her reader to interpret Freud. She does not offer a definitive reading, closing the text, making it her property, but only notes those phrases that seem interpretable, drawing the rebus but not giving the solution, so as to induce her reader to play analyst.

"And let us leave the interpretation to the discretion of each analyst, be she/he improvised for the occasion. It would even be desirable if she/he were, otherwise he/she would risk having already been seduced, whatever her/his sex, or her/his gender, by the *father* of psychoanalysis" (*Speculum* 40–41; Irigaray's italics). The reader is considered an analyst and capable of his or her own interpretation. But Irigaray recognizes that "the analyst" in question may not "really" be a psychoanalyst, but rather the recipient of a sort of battlefield promotion, prepared only by the experience of reading Freud with Irigaray. *Speculum* becomes a "training analysis," the reading of it preparing the readers to make their own interpretations. And the analyst trained by *Speculum* is likely to be a better analyst of Freud than a proper psychoanalyst, for any analyst— male or female, masculine or feminine, *Irigaray herself*—is likely to have been seduced by Freud, seduced by his theory.

There is a contrast here between two different kinds of analysts. The one privileged by Irigaray is an amateur, a "wild analyst,"[4] not "entitled" to analyze but simply a reader, who can catch symptoms and make her or his own interpretations. The other sort of analyst is a professional, which is to say, he or she has investments in analysis as an identity and an economically productive system and a transference onto Freud, that is, a belief in Freud's theory, having been seduced into sharing "our view," giving a predictable "Freudian" interpretation, one that always hears according to the same standards, returning every text to preexistent Freudian models. Irigaray as an analyst is perhaps not as likely to give an attentive, specific interpretation as is her reader. We thus find suggested here an overthrow of a certain hierarchy between theoretical writer as distributor of knowledge and reader as passive, lacking consumer.

But certain questions pose themselves to this reader at this point. Can Irigaray really overthrow that hierarchy, or is this merely a ruse to flatter the reader into less resistance, a ploy to seduce her reader? For she *does* go on to interpret, having simply deferred it for a few sentences. As in an artificial, Socratic dialogue, if she asks the reader to think for him- or herself, that reader will produce an answer that the teacher expected all along, the right answer. Irigaray is fantasizing a reader, one who would make the same associations as she does, one created in her own image.

It is thus interesting that at this point Irigaray is reasoning by analogy—Freud : hysteric ∷ father : daughter ∷ Freud : any other psychoanalyst. Analogy, as Irigaray has said, is one of the "eternal operations which support the defining of difference in function of the a priori of the same" (*Speculum* 28). The analogy of analyst to father is the analytical analogy *par excellence,* the fact of transference. Transference is the repetition of infantile prototype relations, of unconscious desires in the analytical relationship. Without transference, psychoanalysis is simply literary criticism by an unimplicated, discriminating reader, lacking either affect or effect.

The example of *the* analytical analogy suggests a way of overturning the phallocentric effects of analogy. Analogy cannot simply be avoided: it is radically tempting. Transference occurs everywhere, not just in psychoanalysis but in any relationship where the other is "presumed to know"—relationships with teachers, loved ones, doctors. But psychoanalysis provides the opportunity to analyze the transference, to take cognizance of it as such and work it through. Similarly, Irigaray's use of analogy in a context where analogy has been analyzed provides a way of making the economic function of analogy evident. The phallocentric effect of analogy would be explicit and thus less powerful.

Her use of analogy as well as her projection of a reader in her own image, a narcissistic mirror, means she has acceded to a certain economy of the homo——and the auto——, the economy that men have and that excludes women. Irigaray uncovers a sublimated male homosexuality structuring all our institutions: pedagogy, marriage, commerce, even Freud's theory of heterosexuality. Those structures necessarily exclude women, but they are unquestioned because sublimated—raised from suspect homo*sexuality* to secure homo*logy*, to the sexually indifferent *logos,* science, logic. Of course, the "answer" is not to set up another homosexual economy, but that may be necessary as one step to some heterosexuality. "Of course, it is not a question, in the final analysis, of demanding the *same* attributions. Still it is necessary that women arrive at the same so that consideration be made, be imposed of the differences that they would elicit there" (*Speculum* 148–49). Women need to reach "the same"; that is, they need to be "like men," able to represent themselves. But they also need to reach "the same," "the homo": their own homosexual economy, a female homosexuality that ratifies and glorifies female standards. The two "same"s are inextricably linked. Female homosexuality, when raised to an ideology, tends to be either masculine (women that are "like men") or essentialistic (based on some ascertainable female identity). The latter is as phallic as the former, for it reduces heterogeneity to a unified, rigid representation. But without a female homosexual economy, a female narcissistic ego, a way to represent herself, a woman in a heterosexual encounter will always be engulfed by the male homosexual economy, will not be able to represent her difference. Woman must demand "the same," "the homo," and then not settle for it, not fall into the trap of thinking a female "homo" is necessarily any closer to a representation of otherness, an opening for the other.

Yet having posed these questions of Irigaray's own imaginary economy, I might also say that she was right about her reader. Her fantasized reader would be the impertinent questioner she is. I am asking Irigaray Irigarayan questions, reopening the interrogation when Luce becomes too tight, when she seems to settle on an answer. I have been seduced into a transference onto her, into following her suggestion, into saying "what is not foreign to what I am expected to say," into playing "wild analysis."

"This seduction," she continues, "is covered of course, in practice or theory, by a normative statement, by a *law,* which denies it." A new element is introduced by Irigaray and emphasized: the law. This term, foreign to the Freud passage she is reading, not suggested by him, is Irigaray's own association, her remaining in excess of the Freudian seduction. *Law* is a political term referring to patriarchy, the law of the father, and here it will refer to Freud's legislative control of his theory, his normative prescriptions.

Her text continues with another sentence from Freud: "It was only later that I was able to recognize in the phantasy of being seduced by the father *the expression of the typical Oedipus complex* in women" (*SE* 22:120; Irigaray, *Speculum* 41, Irigaray's italics). The seduction by the father is not only a mere fantasy but the manifestation of a typical complex, one that is supposed to be universal and therefore a law of Freudian theory. Given Irigaray's introduction to this passage, we read that the Oedipus complex, the incest taboo, the law forbidding intercourse between father and daughter, covers over a seduction, masks it so that it goes unrecognized. Also covered over is a seduction in the theory, whereby psychoanalysts through their transference onto Freud (their unfulfillable desire for his love and approval) accept his immutable theoretical laws.

"It would be too risky, it seems, to admit that the father could be a seducer, and even eventually that he desires to have a daughter *in order to* seduce her. That he wishes to become an analyst in order to exercise by hypnosis, suggestion, transference, interpretation bearing on the sexual economy, on the proscribed, prohibited sexual representations, a *lasting seduction upon the hysteric*" (*Speculum* 41; Irigaray's italics). Freud as a father must deny the possibility of being seductive. Patriarchy is grounded in the uprightness of the father. If he were devious and unreliable, he could not have the power to legislate. The law is supposed to be just, that is, impartial, indifferent, free from desire.

"It is necessary to endure the law that exculpates the operation. But, of course, if under cover of the law the seduction can now be practised at leisure, it appears just as urgent to interrogate *the seductive function of the law itself*" (*Speculum* 41; Irigaray's italics). For example, the law that prohibits sexual intercourse between analyst and patient actually makes the seduction last forever. The sexually actualized seduction would be complicitous, nuanced, impossible to delineate into active and passive roles, into the anal logic so necessary for a traditional distribution of wealth and power. But the "lasting seduction" of the law is never consummated and as such maintains the power of the prohibited analyst. The seduction that the daughter desires would give her contact with the father as masculine sexed body. The seduction that the father of psychoanalysis exercises refuses her his body, his penis, and asks her to embrace his law, his indifference, his phallic uprightness.

Psychoanalysis works because of the transference, which is to say, because the hysteric transfers her desire to seduce her father, to be seduced by him, onto her analyst. But since the fantasy of seducing the father is produced in analysis, it is produced for the analyst—in order to please him, in order to seduce him, in order to give him what he wants. The installation of the law in psychoanalysis, the prohibition of the analyst's penis by the doctor in a position to validate the hysteric, to announce her as healthy, sets up the desperate situation outlined by Irigaray: "the only redemption of her value as a girl would be to seduce the father" (*Speculum* 106).

"Thus is it not simply true, nor on the other hand completely false, to claim that the little girl fantasizes being seduced by her father, because it is just as pertinent to admit that *the father seduces his daughter* but that refusing to recognize and realize his desire—not always it is true, *he legislates to defend himself from it*" (*Speculum* 41; Irigaray's italics). The father's law is a counterphobic mechanism. He must protect himself from his desire for the daughter. His desire for the feminine threatens his narcissistic overvaluation of his penis. It is so necessary to deny his attraction for the little girl that Freud denies her existence: "We must admit that the little girl is a little man." If the father were to desire his daughter, he could no longer exchange her, no longer possess her in the economy by which true, masterful possession is the right to exchange. If you cannot give something up for something of like value, if you consider it nonsubstitutable, then you do not possess it any more than it possesses you. So the father must not desire the daughter, for that threatens to remove him from the homosexual commerce in which women are exchanged between men, in the service of power relations and community for the men.

Also, if the father desires his daughter as daughter, he will be outside his Oedipal desire for his mother, which is to say also beyond "the phallic phase." So the law of the father protects him and patriarchy from the potential havoc of the daughter's desirability. Were she recognized as desirable in her specificity as daughter, not as son ("little man") nor as mother, there would be a second sexual economy besides the one between "phallic little boy" and "phallic mother." An economy in which the stake might not be a reflection of the phallus, the phallus's desire for itself.

"Refusing to recognize and realize his desire—not always it is true—, he legislates to defend himself from it." Irigaray's interjection—"not always it is true"—briefly gestures in the direction of the question of real, actualized father-daughter incest, currently quite a burning question. The recent emphasis on real incest threatens to deny important psychoanalytic insights in the same gesture that it perhaps correctly accuses Freud of a blind spot.[5] Irigaray's more complex accusations—"not simply true . . . nor completely false"—about father Freud's defensiveness are finally more useful to a feminist understanding of the binds of the father-daughter relationship. Briefly, the veiled seduction, the rule of patriarchal law over the daughter, denying her worth and trapping her in an insatiable desire to please the father, is finally more powerfully and broadly damaging than actualized seduction. As surprisingly widespread as incest may be, the veiled seduction traps all women in its vicious circle.

"In place of the desire for the sexed body of the father there thus comes *to be proposed, to be imposed, his law,* that is to say an institutionalizing and institutionalized discourse. In part, defensive (Think of those 'distressing hours' . . .)" (*Speculum* 41–42; Irigaray's italics). The father gives his daughter his law and protects himself from her desire for his body, protects himself from his body. For it is only the law—and not the body—that constitutes him as patriarch. Paternity is corporeally uncertain, without evidence. But patriarchy compensates for that with the law that marks each child with the father's name as his exclusive property.

"That is not to say that the father *should* make love with his daughter—from time to time it is better to state things precisely—but that it would be good to call into question this mantle of the law with which he drapes his desire, and his sex (organ)" (*Speculum* 42; Irigaray's italics). The strategic difference between a prescriptive *should* and a suggestive *it would be good* is emphasized by this sentence. But suggestion may have always been a more devious, more powerful mode of prescription.

"It would be good" to question the law's appearance of indifference, as Irigaray questions it, and find the phallic stake behind it. "It would be good" to lift "the mantle of the law" so that the father's desire and his penis are exposed. But that does not mean that the "answer" is for the father to make love to his daughter. Irigaray, above all, avoids giving an answer, a prescription such as "the father *should* make love with his daughter." Not that he might not, not that it might not be a way to lift the law and expose the sexed body. The *should* is underlined because that is what Irigaray will not say: she will not lay down a law about how to lift the law.

If she did lay down such a law—"the father should make love with his daughter"—it, like all laws, would mask and support a desire. The negated appearance of this law suggests the mechanism Freud called *Verneinung,* the "procedure whereby the subject, while formulating one of his wishes, thoughts or feelings which has been repressed hitherto, contrives, by disowning it, to continue to defend himself against it" (Laplanche and Pontalis, *Language* 201). What surfaces that Irigaray needs to disown is her desire to impose the law upon the father, her desire for a simple reversal rather than an overthrow of patriarchy.

This sentence is marked as symptomatic, asking for analysis, by the parenthetical remark that "from time to time it is better to state things precisely." "From time to time" pretends that this is a random moment; it just happens to fall that at this moment she will be precise. But this is the only such remark in all of her reading of Freud; this is the point where she is most afraid of a misunderstanding. Her desire to be precise is in direct contradiction to something she says later in *Speculum* about feminist strategies of language: "No clear nor univocal statement can, in fact, dissolve this mortgage, this obstacle, all of them being caught, trapped, in the same reign of credit. It is as yet better to speak only through equivocations, allusions, innuendos, parables. . . . Even if you are asked for some *précisions* [precise details]" (178). All clear statements are trapped in the same economy of values, in which clarity (oculocentrism) and univocity (the One) reign. Precision must be avoided if the economy of the One is to be unsettled. Equivocations, allusions, and so on, are all flirtatious: they induce the interlocutor to listen, to encounter, to interpret, but defer the moment of assimilation back into a familiar model. Even if someone asks for *précisions*, even if that someone is oneself, it is better for women to avoid stating things precisely.

Yet on one point Luce Irigaray tightens up, prefers to be precise, to return to an economy of clarity and univocity. The locus of her conservatism, her caution, her need to defend herself, is the question of making love with the father. It is terrifying to lift the mantle of the law and encounter the father's desire. What if in making love the father still remained the law and the daughter were just passive, denied? The father's law has so restructured the daughter and her desires that it is hard, well nigh impossible, to differentiate the Father (that is to say, the Law) from the male sexed body. What if making love with the father were merely a ruse to get the impertinent daughter to give up her resistance to the law?

Irigaray clutches for something stable, something precise, because she, too, is a "subject," with a stake in identity. And the law of the father gives her an identity, even if it is not her own, even if it blots out her feminine specificity. To give it up is not a "simple" matter; it must be done over and over.

Later she will say of her method in *Speculum*, "What was left for me to do was to *have an orgy with the philosophers*" (*Ce Sexe* 147; Irigaray's italics). Intercourse with the philosophers, the father of psychoanalysis included, is her method of insinuation into their system, of inducing them to reveal the phallocentrism, the desire cloaked in their sexual indifference. Perhaps these are merely two different moments in her inconsistency—a brave, new, loose moment ("have an orgy with the philosophers") and a defensive, cautious moment (refusal to make love with the father).

But perhaps these are not merely two moments. The two situations are *analogous, but not the same*. Some terms may be more frightening, more sensitive, than others. *Father* may be more threatening than *philosophers*. She writes in *Ce Sexe*: "As far as the family is concerned, *my answer will be simple* and clear: the family has always been the privileged locus of the exploitation of women. Thus, as far as familialism is concerned, there is no ambiguity!" (139–40; my italics). Yet earlier in the same text she says she cannot give a "simple answer." Also *faire l'amour* ("make love") may be more threatening than *faire la noce* ("have an orgy"). Maybe what frightens her is not seduction of the father or by the father but "making love." "Love" has always been sublimated, idealized desire, away from bodily specificity and towards dreams of complementarity, and the union of opposites, difference resolved into the One. "Love" is entangled with

109

the question of woman's complicity; it may be the bribe that has persuaded her to agree to her own exclusion. It may be historically necessary to be momentarily blind to father-love; it may be politically effective to defend—tightly, unlucidly—against its inducements in order for a "relation between the sexes," in order to rediscover some feminine desire, some desire for a masculine body that does not respect the Father's law.

Notes

This essay is an abridged version of chapter 5 of my book *The Daughter's Seduction: Feminism and Psychoanalysis,* copyright © Jane Gallop 1982, and used by permission of the publishers, Cornell University Press and The Macmillan Press Ltd. I would like to thank Roswitha Both for help with this abridgment.

1. Here and throughout this essay, I use my own version of the French original.

2. The most glaring of these symptomatic attempts to disengage the anal definitions from the genital can be found in a 1915 footnote to the third of Freud's *Three Essays on the Theory of Sexuality;* a footnote to chapter 4 of *Civilization and Its Discontents;* and here in "Femininity."

3. Freud provides the model for metaphorization of faeces in "On Transformations of Instinct as Exemplified in Anal Erotism."

4. The term is Freud's from his article "Wild Psycho-analysis."

5. See, e.g., Masson.

CHRISTINE FROULA

The Daughter's Seduction: Sexual Violence and Literary History

A still, small voice has warned me again to postpone the description of hysteria.
—Freud to Fliess, January 1, 1896

I felt sorry for mama. Trying to believe his story kilt her.
—Alice Walker's Celie in *The Color Purple*

IN HER SPEECH before the London/National Society for Women's Service on January 21, 1931, Virginia Woolf pictured the woman novelist as a fisherwoman who lets the hook of her imagination down into the depths "of the world that lies submerged in our unconscious being." Feeling a violent jerk, she pulls the line up short, and the "imagination comes to the top in a state of fury":

> Good heavens she cries—how dare you interfere with me. . . . And I—that is the reason—have to reply, "My dear you were going altogether too far. Men would be shocked." Calm yourself. . . . In fifty years I shall be able to use all this very queer knowledge that you are ready to bring me. But not now. You see I go on, trying to calm her, I cannot make use of what you tell me—about women's bodies for instance—their passions—and so on, because the conventions are still very strong. If I were to overcome the conventions I should need the courage of a hero, and I am not a hero. . . .
>
> Very well says the imagination, dressing herself up again in her petticoat and skirts. . . . We will wait another fifty years. But it seems to me a pity. (*Pargiters* xxxviii–xxxix)[1]

Woman's freedom to tell her stories—and indeed, as this fable shows, to know them fully herself—would come, Woolf went on to predict, once she is no longer the dependent daughter, wife, and servant. Given that condition, Woolf envisioned "a step upon the stair": "You will hear somebody coming. You will open the door. And then—this at least is my guess—there will take place between you and some one else the most interesting, exciting, and important conversation that has ever been heard" (xliv).

111

But that was to be "in fifty years." In 1931 Woolf still felt a silence even within all the writing by women that she knew—even, indeed, within her own. Woolf's fable of silences that go unheard within women's writing points to a violence that is all the more powerful for being nearly invisible, and it interprets women's silence in literary history as an effect of repression, not of absence. In this essay, I will explore the literary history implied by Woolf's fisherwoman image, reading it backward, through Homer and Freud, to elucidate the "conventions" that bound her imagination; and forward to contemporary works by women that fulfill Woolf's guess that women would soon break a very significant silence. Drawing upon feminist analyses of Freud's discovery and rejection of the seduction theory of hysteria, I will argue that the relations of literary daughters and fathers resemble in some important ways the model developed by Judith Herman and Lisa Hirschman to describe the family situations of incest victims: a dominating, authoritarian father; an absent, ill, or complicitous mother; and a daughter who, prohibited by her father from speaking about the abuse, is unable to sort out her contradictory feelings of love for her father and terror of him, of desire to end the abuse and fear that if she speaks she will destroy the family structure that is her only security (Herman, esp. chaps. 1, 4–7). By aligning a paradigmatic father-daughter dialogue in Homer's *Iliad* with Freud's dialogue with the hysterics, we can grasp the outline of what I will call the hysterical cultural script: the cultural text that dictates to males and females alike the necessity of silencing woman's speech when it threatens the father's power. This silencing ensures that the cultural daughter remains a daughter, her power suppressed and muted, while the father, his power protected, makes culture and history in his own image. Yet, as the hysterics' speech cured their symptoms,[2] so women, telling stories formerly repressed, have begun to realize the prediction of Woolf's fisherwoman. Maya Angelou's *I Know Why the Caged Bird Sings* (1969) and Alice Walker's *The Color Purple* (1982) exemplify the breaking of women's forbidden stories into literary history—an event that reverberates far beyond their heroes' individual histories to reshape our sense of our cultural past and its possible future directions.

CULTURAL FATHERS AND DAUGHTERS: SOME INTERESTING CONVERSATIONS

What is the fisherwoman's story—the one that got away? The answer I wish to pursue begins with the earliest conversation between man and woman in our literary tradition, that between Helen and Priam in book 3 of the *Iliad*. Although readers tend to remember the Helen of the *Iliad* as silent—beauty of body her only speech—the text reveals not Helen's silence but her silenc*ing*. As they stand upon the city wall gazing

down at the battlefield, the Trojan king and patriarch Priam asks Helen
to point out to him the Greek heroes whose famous names he knows.
Her answer exceeds Priam's request:

> "Revere you as I do,
> I dread you, too, dear father. Painful death
> would have been sweeter for me, on that day
> I joined your son, and left my bridal chamber,
> my brothers, my grown child, my childhood friends!
> But no death came, though I have pined and wept.
> Your question, now: yes, I can answer it:
> that man is Agamemnon, son of Atreus,
> lord of the plains of Argos, ever both
> a good king and a formidable soldier—
> brother to the husband of a wanton . . .
>   or was that life a dream?"   (Homer 73)

Helen begins by invoking her own fear of and reverence for Priam. But
this daughterly homage to her cultural father only frames her expression
of her longing for her former life and companions. Helen, however, is
powerless to escape the male war economy that requires her presence to
give meaning to its conflicts, and so she translates her desire for her old
life into a death wish that expresses at once culturally induced masochism
and the intensity of her resistance to her own entanglement in the warriors' plot.

Priam appears to reply only to the words that directly address his
query:

> The old man gazed and mused and softly cried:
> "O fortunate son of Atreus! Child of destiny,
> O happy soul! How many sons of Akhaia
> serve under you! In the old days once I went
> into the vineyard country of Phrygia
> and saw the Phrygian host on nimble ponies,
>
> . . . .
>
> And they allotted me as their ally
> my place among them when the Amazons
> came down, those women who were fighting men;
> but that host never equaled this,
> the army of the keen-eyed men of Akhaia."   (74)

Priam seems not to notice Helen's misery as he turns to imaginary
competition with the admired and envied Agamemnon. What links his
speech to Helen's, however, is the extraordinary fact that the occasion he
invokes as his most memorable experience of troops arrayed for battle is a

113

battle against the Amazons. That Amazons come to his mind suggests that, on some level, he *has* heard Helen's desires. Priam's speech recapitulates his conflict with Helen, and hers with Greek culture, as an archetypal conflict between male and female powers. Significantly, Priam does not say which of these forces triumphed. But in leaving the action suspended, he connects past with present, the Amazons' challenge with this moment's conflict between his desires and Helen's, who, merely in having desires that would interfere with her role as battle prize, becomes for Priam the Amazon.

What does it mean that Helen should become the Amazon in Priam's imagination? Page duBois and Wm. Blake Tyrrell analyze the Amazon myth as a representation of female power that has escaped the bounds within which Greek culture, specifically the marriage structure, strives to contain it. Marriage, writes duBois, "in Lévi-Strauss' sense, the exchange of women between men of the same kind, was culture for the Greeks" (41). In Tyrrell's analysis, the Amazon myth is about daughters, warriors, and marriage: it projects male fear that women will challenge their subordinate status in marriage and with it the rule of the father. In Varro's account of the mythology of Athens's origins, the female citizens of Athens were, under Cecrops, dispossessed of their social and political authority after they banded together to vote for Athena as their city's presiding deity and brought down Poseidon's jealous wrath: "they could no longer cast a vote, no new-born child would take the mother's name, and . . . they are no longer called Athenians but daughters of Athenians" (Tyrrell 29, citing Pembroke 26–27). From the Greek woman's lifelong role of daughter, her deprivation of political, economic, and social power, the Amazon myth emerges as "the specter of daughters who refuse their destiny and fail to make the accepted transition through marriage to wife and motherhood" (Tyrrell 65). Such unruly daughters threatened to be "rivals of men," "opposed or antithetical to the male as father" (Tyrrell 83). Becoming a rival in the male imagination, the daughter also becomes a warrior—as Helen does to Priam; as Clytemnestra does to Apollo when, in the *Eumenides,* he laments that Agamemnon was not cut down by an Amazon instead of by her; as Dido does to Aeneas in his premonitory conflation of her with Penthesilea in *Aeneid* 1. These allusions suggest that the Amazon figure, a figment of the male imagination, functioned to contain the threat of a female uprising within the arena of the battlefield—that is, to transform the invisible threat of female revolt into a clear and present danger that males might then band together to combat in the regulated violence of war. In linking Helen with the Amazons, Priam dramatizes the threat that female desire poses to the male war culture predicated on its subjugation. Their conversation replicates the larger design of Homer's epic, which, being "his" story, not hers, turns the tale of a woman's abduction and silencing into the story of a ten-year war between two male cultures. Priam's battle with the Amazons remains suspended in his speech because that battle has not ended. In this conversation, however, it is Priam, the cultural father, who triumphs, while Helen's story, by his refusal to hear it, becomes the repressed but discernible shadow of Priam's own.

Helen's exchange with Priam is one skirmish in her culture's war against the Amazons. A subsequent conversation between Helen and Aphrodite depicts another battle in the form of a cultural daughter's seduction. Here, Helen opposes Aphrodite's demand that she join Paris in bed while the battle rages outside: "'O immortal madness, / why do you have this craving to seduce me? / . . . / Go take your place beside Alexandros! / . . . Be / unhappy for him, shield him, till at last / he marries you—or, as he will, enslaves you. / I shall not join him there!'" Helen passionately and eloquently resists her cultural fate, but Homer's Olympian magic conquers her. Aphrodite silences Helen and enforces her role as object, not agent, of desire by threatening her: "Better not be so difficult. / . . . I can make hatred for you grow / amid both Trojans and Danaans, / and if I do, you'll come to a bad end" (82).[3] The male-authored goddess, embodying the sublimated social authority of Greek culture, forces Helen to relinquish control over her sexuality to the "higher" power of male culture and, like a complicitous mother, presses her to conform to its rule. Helen easily resists being "seduced," angrily thrusting back upon Aphrodite the role of compliant wife/slave that the goddess recommends to her. But this scene blurs the distinction between seduction and rape—between being "led astray" and being sexually violated—for Helen can resist sexual complicity only on pain of being cast out altogether from the social world, constructed as it is upon marriage. She can be a faithful wife or a "wanton," a "nightmare," a "whore"; she can be a dutiful daughter or an unruly one. But she cannot act out her own desire as Menelaus and Paris, Agamemnon and Akhilleus, Khryses and Hektor, can theirs. Indeed, if wanton in Troy and wife in the bridal chamber are the only choices her culture allows her, she cannot choose even from these: whereas Paris can propose to settle the dispute by single combat with Menelaus (69 ff.), or the Trojan elders, seeing Helen on the wall, murmur "let her go [back to Greece] in the ships / and take her scourge from us" (73), there is never a question of Helen's deciding the conflict by choosing between the two men.[4]

Although not literally silenced by Aphrodite's metaphysical violence, Helen, surrendering her sexuality, is simultaneously subdued to her culture's dominant text of male desire. "Brother dear," she tells Hektor,

> "dear to a whore, a nightmare of a woman!
> That day my mother gave me to the world
> I wish a hurricane blast had torn me away
> to wild mountains, or into tumbling sea
> to be washed under by a breaking wave,
> before these evil days could come! . . ." (152)

Helen's will to escape the warriors' marriage plot here turns against the only object her culture permits: herself. She names herself from its lexicon for wayward daughters and passionately imagines death as her only possible freedom. Using the names her culture provides her, weighted with its judgments, Helen loses power even to name herself, her speech confined between the narrow bounds of patriarchal culture and death. That she imagines her death as an entry into the wild turbulence of nature allegorizes the radical opposition of male culture to female nature that the Greek marriage plot enforces: Helen, the Greeks' most exalted image of woman, is also a powerfully expressive subject who must, precisely because her desire is so powerful, be violently driven back into nature.[5]

Death failing, Helen fulfills her prescribed role by participating in her culture's metaphysical violence against herself: "You [Hektor] are the one afflicted most / by harlotry in me and by his madness, / our portion, all of misery, given by Zeus / that we might live in song for men to come" (153). She sacrifices herself upon the altar of patriarchal art, a willing victim who not only suffers but justifies her culture's violence. (Men too suffer the violence of the Greek marriage plot—Helen's "we" includes Hektor—but whereas Hektor resists Andromakhe's pleas and follows his desire for honor into battle, Helen's and Andromakhe's desires are entirely ineffectual.) If the poem, like the war, seems to glorify Helen, in fact she and all the female characters serve primarily to structure the dynamics of male desire in a culture that makes women the pawns of men's bonds *with each other* and the scapegoats for their broken allegiances. The poem's opening scene portrays woman's role in Greek culture as the silent object of male desire, not the speaker of her own. While Agamemnon and Akhilleus rage eloquently over their battle prizes Khryseis and Briseis, the women themselves speak not at all. They are as interchangeable as their names make them sound, mere circulating tokens of male power and pride—as Akhilleus's apology to Agamemnon upon rejoining the battle confirms: "Agamemnon, was it better for us / in any way, when we were sore at heart, / to waste ourselves in strife over a girl? / If only Artemis had shot her down / among the ships on the day I made her mine, / after I took Lyrnessos!" (459).

The *Iliad* suggests that women's silence in culture is neither a natural nor an accidental phenomenon but a *cultural achievement*, indeed, a constitutive accomplishment of male culture.[6] In Helen's conversations, Homer writes the silencing of woman into epic history as deliberate, strategic, and necessary—a crucial aspect of the complex struggle that is the epic enterprise. In Helen, the *Iliad* represents the subjugation of female desire to male rule by means of a continuum of violence, from physical "abduction" to the metaphysical violence that Greek culture exerts against woman's words and wishes. To a greater extent than we have yet realized, Homer's epic is about marriage, daughters, and warriors; it is about the Amazon.

The *Iliad* is an ancient text, and we have moved very far from the world that produced it—a fact often invoked to distance readers from the violence against women in which the poem participates. But if we set Helen's conversations next to a powerful analogue of our century, Sigmund Freud's dialogue with hysterics and with the phenomenon of hysteria, the paradigmatic force of her "abduction" into the cultural father's script becomes apparent. As the *Iliad* tells the story of a woman's abduction as a male war story, so Freud turned the hysterics' stories of sexual abuse into a tale to soothe a father's ear. And just as Priam's repressed fears seep into his speech in his allusion to the Amazons, so Freud's repression of the daughter's story generates symptomatic moments that "chatter through the fingertips" ("Fragment," 7:77–78) of his psychoanalytic theory.

Freud's conversations with hysterical patients began in the 1880s. At first, Freud, unlike Priam, was able to hear his patients' stories, and he found that in every case analysis elicited an account of sexual abuse suffered in childhood at the hands of a member of the patient's own family—almost always the father, as he belatedly reported.[7] On this evidence, Freud developed his "seduction theory," the theory that hysterical symptoms have their origin in sexual abuse suffered in childhood, which is repressed and eventually assimilated to later sexual experience. Freud first formulated the seduction theory in a letter to his colleague and confidant Wilhelm Fliess in October 1895, and he presented it to the Vienna psychiatric establishment on April 21, 1896, in a paper titled "The Aetiology of Hysteria" (*SE* 3). The paper, Freud wrote to Fliess, "met with an icy reception" (Schur 104), summed up in Krafft-Ebing's dismissal of it as "a scientific fairytale" (*Origins* 167n). For a time Freud pursued the research by which he hoped to prove the seduction theory, writing to Fliess in December 1896: "My psychology of hysteria will be preceded by the proud words: '*Introite et hic dii sunt* [Enter, for here too are gods]'" (*Origins* 172). His pride in his discovery was short-lived, however, for within a year he would write again to confide "the great secret which has been slowly dawning on me in recent months. I no longer believe in my *neurotica*" (*Origins* 215). From this point, Freud went on to found psychoanalytic theory upon the Oedipus complex.

Historians of psychoanalysis consider Freud's turn from the seduction theory to the Oedipus complex crucial to the development of psychoanalysis. Anna Freud wrote that "keeping up the seduction theory would mean to abandon the Oedipus complex, and with it the whole importance of phantasy life. . . . In fact, I think there would have been no psychoanalysis afterwards" (Masson 113). This opinion has prevailed among psychoanalysts, but since Freud was already discovering the unconscious, infantile sexuality, and symbolic process in treating hysterics, it does not appear to be well-founded. A more critical reading of Freud's abandonment of his seduction theory has emerged from feminist scholarship over the last decade. Several critics have argued—Luce Irigaray from feminist theory, Alice Miller as well as Herman and Hirschman from clinical evidence, Marie Balmary from a psychoanalytic reading of the "text" of Freud's life and work, Florence Rush from historical evidence, among others—that Freud turned away from the seduction theory not because it lacked explanatory power but because he was unable to come to terms with what he was the first to discover: the crucial role played in neurosis by the abuse of paternal power.

For purposes of the present argument, the issue is best put in terms of credit or authority: the hysterics, Breuer's patients and his own, confronted Freud with the problem of whose story to believe, the father's or the daughter's. From the first, Freud identified with the hysterics strongly enough that he could hear what they told him. Yet, although he could trace the etiology of hysteria to sexual abuse suffered in childhood, Freud could not bring himself to draw the conclusion that his evidence presented to him: that the abuser was most often the father. The cases of Anna O., Lucy R., Katharina, Elisabeth von R., and Rosalia H. described in *Studies on Hysteria* all connect symptoms more or less closely with fathers or, in Lucy's case, with a father substitute. In two cases, however, Freud represented the father as an uncle, a misrepresentation that he corrected only in 1924; and his reluctance to implicate the father appears strikingly in a supplemental narrative of an unnamed patient, afflicted with a limp, whose physician-father accompanied her during her hypnotic sessions with Freud. When Freud challenged her to acknowledge that "something else had happened which she had not mentioned," she "gave way to the extent of letting fall a single significant phrase; but she had hardly said a word before she stopped, and her old father, who was sitting behind her, began to sob bitterly." Freud concludes: "Naturally I pressed my investigation no further; but I never saw the patient again" (*SE* 2:100–101n). Here Freud's sympathies divide: had the father not intruded, Freud undoubtedly would have heard her out as he had Katharina; but made aware of the father's anguish, he "naturally" cooperated with it even to the extent of repressing from his text the "single significant phrase" that may have held the key to her neurosis.

In larger terms, too, Freud's work on hysteria posed the dilemma whether to elicit and credit the daughter's story, with which rested, as other cases had shown, his hope of curing her limping walk, or to honor the father's sob, which corroborated even as it silenced the girl's significant word. The list of reasons Freud gave Fliess for abandoning the seduction theory is, as Balmary points out, not very compelling; indeed, it contradicts the evidence of *Studies on Hysteria*. Freud complains that he cannot terminate the analyses, even though several cases (notably Anna O./Bertha Pappenheim, who was Breuer's patient) are there described as terminating in a lasting cure. He complains of not being able to distinguish between truth and "emotionally charged fiction" in his patients, even though he had linked the vanishing of symptoms with the recovery of traumatic experience through memory—whether narrated with apparent fidelity to literal fact, as in Katharina's case, or in dream imagery, as by Anna O., whom, Breuer wrote, he always found to be "entirely truthful and trustworthy" (*Studies on Hysteria* 43). And Freud claims to have been frustrated in his attempt to recover the buried trauma, despite his success in some instances. Only one item on the list is upheld by the earlier cases: "the astonishing thing that in every case *my own not excluded,* blame was laid on perverse acts by the father, and realization of the unexpected frequency of hysteria, in every case of which the same thing applied, though it was hardly credible that perverted acts against children were so general" (*Origins* 215–16).[8]

Freud could not credit the daughters' stories for a number of reasons, the fact that the sobbing fathers, not the limping daughters, paid him his (at that time meager) living being only the most obvious. The problem was precisely that sexual abuse of children by fathers appeared "so general": not only was it uncovered in a high percentage of Freud's patients but it could not be contained within the bounds of the hysterics' private and individual histories. During the years between conceiving and abandoning the seduction theory, Freud was engaged in self-analysis, in which he discovered, through dreams, his own incestuous wishes towards his daughter Mathilde and, through symptoms exhibited by his siblings, the possibility that his father Jakob had abused his children. Jakob died on October 23, 1896, initiating in Freud an intricate process of mourning that ultimately strengthened his idealization of and identification with his father. Freud's dream of Irma's injection, which concerned a patient who shared his daughter Mathilde's name, created a fantasy version of a destructive father-daughter relationship between physician and patient. Recent research (Herman; Russell) has traced many continuities between the problem of father-daughter incest and the dominance of male/paternal authority in society as a whole; Freud, too, faced implications that would have changed the focus of his work from individual therapy to social criticism. The "icy reception" with which the professional community of *fin de siècle* Vienna greeted his 1896 lecture, which did not explicitly implicate fathers in hysteria, was indication enough that Freud, if he credited the daughters, would risk sharing their fate of being silenced and ignored. The stakes for Freud were very high, for the fathers who paid him also represented, as had Jakob, the privileged place in culture to which Freud, as a male, could aspire. Acceding, upon Jakob's death, to the place of the father, he acceded also to the father's text, which gave him small choice but to judge the daughters' stories "hardly credible."

Yet Freud could not easily call in the credit that he had already invested in the daughters' stories. As Jane Gallop notes, he continued to speak of "actual seduction" long after he had supposedly repudiated it, with the difference that he now deflected guilt from the father to, variously, the nurse, the mother, and, by way of the Oedipus complex, the child herself (144–45).[9] Balmary argues persuasively that Freud's own hysterical symptoms grew more pronounced as he undertook to deny what he was the first to discover, that "the secret of hysteria is the father's hidden fault"; and that the texts documenting his turn to the Oedipus complex betray that turn as a symptomatic effort to conceal the father's fault.[10] Seduced by the father's sob story, Freud took upon himself the burden his patients bore of concealing the father's fault in mute symptomology.

Hysterics, Freud wrote, suffer from reminiscence (*SE* 2:7). As Priam in his reply to Helen does not forget her words, so Freud in his later writings does not forget the daughter's story but rewrites it as the story of "femininity," attributing to mothers, nurses, and a female "Nature" the damage to female subjectivity and desire wrought by specific historical events.[11] Yet when Freud concludes in "Femininity" that woman has an inferior sense of justice and suggests that the "one technique" she has contributed to culture, the invention of plaiting and weaving, is designed to conceal the shame of her genital lack (*SE* 22:132–34), it is he who, like Priam, is ingeniously weaving a cultural text whose obscured but still legible design is to protect the *father* (conceived broadly as general and cultural) from suspicion of an insufficiently developed sense of justice. Like Priam, Freud makes subtle war on woman's desire and on the credibility of her language in order to avert its perceived threat to the father's cultural preeminence. If, in doing so, he produces a theory that Krafft-Ebing could have approved, he also composes a genuine "scientific fairytale."

It appears, then, that Freud undertook not to believe the hysterics not because the weight of scientific evidence was on the father's side but because so much was at stake in maintaining the father's credit: the "innocence" not only of particular fathers—Freud's, Freud himself, the hysterics'—but also of the cultural structure that credits male authority at the expense of female authority, reproducing a social and political hierarchy of metaphorical fathers and daughters. The history of the seduction theory shows Freud's genius, but it also shows his seduction by the hysterical cultural script that protects the father's credit and Freud's consequent inability, not unlike Helen's, the hysterics', or Woolf's fisherwoman's, to bring the story of sexual abuse and silencing to light. When Helen sublimely paints herself and Hektor as willing victims upon the altar of an art that serves the divine plan of Zeus, "father of gods and men," she speaks this cultural script—as Priam does in reminiscing about Amazons, as the hysterics with their bodily reminiscences and Freud with his theory of femininity did, and as Woolf's fisherwoman does, with her imagination gagged and petticoated in deference to the "conventions."

Women's literary history has important continuities with the actual and imaginative histories told by Homer, Freud, and Herman. Woman's cultural seduction is not merely analogous to the physical abuses that Freud's patients claimed to have suffered but *continuous* with them. Woolf's recurrent and autobiographical fisherwoman image is an apt figure for this continuity: arising from her buried experience of sexual abuse at the hands of her half brother George Duckworth as well as from the male "conventions" that deny women a voice to tell this story, it merges literal and literary sexual abuse. Herman shows that the abusive or seductive father does serious harm to the daughter's mind as well as to her body, damaging her sense of her own identity and depriving her voice of authority and strength. For the literary daughter—the woman reader/writer as daughter of her culture—the metaphysical violence against women inscribed in the literary tradition, although more subtle and no less difficult to acknowledge and understand, has serious consequences. Metaphysically, the woman reader of a literary tradition that inscribes violence against women is an abused daughter. Like physical abuse, literary violence against women works to privilege the cultural father's voice and story over those of women, the cultural daughters, and indeed to silence women's voices. If Freud had difficulty telling the difference between his patients' histories and their fantasies, the power of such cultural fantasies as Homer's and Freud's to shape their audiences' sense of the world is self-evident.[12]

But the Freud of 1892 understood the power of language to cure. Woolf, we remember, predicted a moment when women would break through the constraints of the cultural text and begin "the most interesting, exciting, and important conversation that has ever been heard." If the literary history of cultural fathers and daughters resembles the histories Freud elicited from his patients, we could expect the cultural daughter's telling of her story to work not only a "cure" of her silence in culture but, eventually, a more radical cure of the hysterical cultural text that entangles both women and men.[13] To explore these possibilities, I will turn to a daughter's text that breaks even as it represents the daughter's hysterical silence, crossing images of literal and literary sexual abuse: Angelou's autobiographical *I Know Why the Caged Bird Sings*.

THE DAUGHTER'S STORY AND THE FATHER'S LAW

Early in her memoir, Angelou presents a brief but rich *biographia literaria* in the form of a childhood romance:

> During these years in Stamps, I met and fell in love with William Shakespeare. He was my first white love. Although I enjoyed and respected Kipling, Poe, Butler, Thackeray and Henley, I saved my young and loyal passion for Paul Lawrence Dunbar, Langston Hughes, James Weldon Johnson and W.E.B. DuBois' "Litany at Atlanta." But it was Shakespeare who said, "When in disgrace with fortune and men's eyes." It was a state with which I felt myself most familiar. I pacified myself about his whiteness by saying that after all he had been dead so long it couldn't matter to anyone any more.
>
> Bailey and I decided to memorize a scene from *The Merchant of Venice,* but we realized that Momma would question us about the author and that we'd have to tell her that Shakespeare was white, and it wouldn't matter to her whether he was dead or not. So we chose "The Creation" by James Weldon Johnson instead. (11)

This passage, depicting the trials that attend those interracial affairs of the mind that Maya must keep hidden from her vigilant grandmother, also raises the question of what it means for a female reader and fledgling writer to carry on a love affair with Shakespeare, or with male authors in general. While the text overtly confronts and disarms the issue of race, the seduction issue is only glancingly acknowledged. But this literary father-daughter romance resonates quietly alongside Angelou's more disturbing account of the quasi-incestuous rape of the eight-year-old Maya by her mother's lover, Mr. Freeman—particularly by virtue of the line she finds so sympathetic in Shakespeare, "When in disgrace with fortune and men's eyes."

Mr. Freeman's abuse of Maya occurs in two episodes. In the first, after her mother rescues her from a nightmare by taking her into her own bed, Maya wakes to find her mother gone to work and Mr. Freeman grasping her tightly. The child feels, first, bewilderment and terror: "His right hand was moving so fast and his heart was beating so hard that I was afraid that he would die." When Mr. Freeman subsides, however, so does Maya's fright: "Finally he was quiet, and then came the nice part. He held me so softly that I wished he wouldn't ever let me go. . . . This was probably my real father and we had found each other at last" (61). After the abuse comes the silencing: Mr. Freeman enlists the child's complicity, informing her that he will kill her beloved brother Bailey if she tells anyone what "they" have done. For the child, this prohibition prevents not so much telling as asking, for, confused as she is by her conflicting feelings, she has no idea what has happened. One day, however, Mr. Freeman stops her as she is setting out for the library, and it is then that he commits actual rape, which the terrified child experiences as "a breaking and entering when even the senses are torn apart" (65). Again threatened with violence if she tells, Maya retreats to her bed in a silent delirium, but the story emerges when her mother discovers her stained drawers, and Mr. Freeman is duly arrested and brought to trial.

At the trial, the defense lawyer as usual attempts to blame the victim for her rape. When she cannot remember what Mr. Freeman was wearing, "he snickered as though I had raped Mr. Freeman" (70). His next question, whether Mr. Freeman had ever touched her prior to that Saturday, reduces her to confusion because her memory of her own pleasure in being held by him seems to her to implicate her in his crime: "I couldn't say yes and tell them how he had loved me once for a few minutes and how he had held me close. . . . My uncles would kill me and Grandmother Baxter would stop speaking. . . . And all those people in the court would stone me as they had stoned the harlot in the Bible. And mother, who thought I was such a good girl, would be so disappointed" (70–71). An adult can see that the daughter's need for a father's affection does not cancel his culpability for sexually abusing her. But the child cannot resolve the conflict between her desire to tell the truth, which means acknowledging the pleasure she felt when Mr. Freeman gently held her, and her awareness of the social condemnation that would greet this revelation. She knows the cultural script and its hermeneutic traditions, which hold all female pleasure guilty, all too well, and so she betrays her actual experience with a lie: "Everyone in the court knew that the answer had to be No. Everyone except Mr. Freeman and me. . . . I said No" (71). But she chokes on the lie and has to be taken down from the stand. Mr. Freeman is sentenced to a year and a day but somehow manages to be released that very afternoon; and not long thereafter, he is killed by her Baxter uncles. Hearing of Mr. Freeman's death, Maya is overwhelmed with terror and remorse: "a man was dead because I lied" (72). Taking his death as proof that her words have power to kill, she descends into a silence that lasts for a year. Like Helen's sacrificial speech, Maya's silence speaks the hysterical cultural script: it expresses guilt and anguish at her own aggression against the father and voluntarily sacrifices the cure of truthful words.

Maya's self-silencing recalls the link between sexual violation and silence in the archetypal rape myth of Philomela. Ovid's retelling of the Greek myth entwines rape with incest as Tereus, watching Philomela cajole her father into allowing her to go with Tereus to visit her sister Procne, puts himself in her father's place: "He would like to be / Her father at that moment, and if he were / He would be as wicked a father as he is a husband" (144–45). After the rape, in Ovid's story as in Angelou's, the victim's power of speech becomes a threat to the rapist and a further victim of his violence: "Tereus did not kill her. He seized her tongue / With pincers, though it cried against the outrage, / Babbled and made a sound like *Father*, / Till the sword cut it off." Like Priam's thoughts of Amazons, this scene projects a war between the father's desire, represented by the sword, and the daughter's, represented by a tongue with power to tell her story.[14] The tongue's ambiguous cry connects rape/incest with the ownership of daughters by fathers, sanctioned by the marriage structure, and it interprets Procne's symmetrical violation of killing her son Itys: she becomes a bad mother to her son, as Tereus has been a bad father to the daughter entrusted to him. In the suspension wrought by metamorphosis, Tereus becomes a war bird, and Procne and Philomela become nightingales whose unintelligible song resembles the hysterics' speech. In silencing herself, Maya—who knows why the caged bird sings—plays all the parts in this cultural drama. She suffers as victim, speaks the father's death, and cuts out her own tongue for fear of its crying "Father."

Maya breaks her silence when a woman befriends her by taking her home and reading aloud to her, then sending her off with a book of poems, one of which she is to recite on her next visit. We are not told which poem it was, but later we find that the pinnacle of her literary achievement at age twelve was to have learned by heart the whole of Shakespeare's *Rape of Lucrece*—nearly two thousand lines. Maya, it appears, emerges from her literal silence into a literary one. Fitting her voice to Shakespeare's words, she writes safe limits around the exclamations of her wounded tongue and in this way is able to reenter the cultural text that her words had formerly disrupted.

But if Shakespeare's poem redeems Maya from her hysterical silence, it is also a lover that she embraces at her peril. In Angelou's text, Shakespeare's Lucrece represents the violation of the spirit that Shakespeare's and other stories of sleeping beauties commit upon the female reader. Maya's feat of memory signals a double seduction—by the white culture that her grandmother wished her black child not to love, and by the male culture that imposes upon the rape victim, epitomized in Lucrece, the double silence of a beauty that serves male fantasy and a death that serves male honor.[15] The black child's identification with an exquisite rape fantasy of white male culture violates her own experience, her reality. Would not everyone be surprised, she muses, "when one day I woke out of my black ugly dream, and my real hair, which was long and blond, would take the place of the kinky mass that Momma wouldn't let me straighten? My light-blue eyes were going to hypnotize them. . . . Because I was really white and because a cruel fairy stepmother, who was understandably jealous of my beauty, had turned me into a too-big Negro girl, with nappy black hair, broad feet, and a space between her teeth that would hold a number two pencil" (2). Maya's fantasy bespeaks her cultural seduction, but Angelou's memoir recovers a truer history, rescuing the child's voice from its silences both literal and literary.

RECREATING THE UNIVERSE: FROM CULTURAL
DAUGHTER TO WOMANIST WRITER

If Angelou presents one woman's emergence from the hysterical cultural text, Alice Walker's *The Color Purple* deepens and elaborates its themes to work a more powerful cure. Published in 1982 (right on schedule with respect to Woolf's prediction), Walker's novel not only portrays a cure of one daughter's hysterical silence but rewrites from the ground up the cultural text that sanctions her violation and dictates her silence. Whereas the memoir form holds Angelou's story within the limits of history, Walker stages her cure in the imaginary spaces of fiction. Yet Walker conceived *The Color Purple* as a historical novel ("Writing" 356), and her transformation of the daughter's story into a fiction that lays claim to historical truth challenges the foundation of the conventions, social and cultural, that enforce women's silence. Walker retells the founding story of Western culture from a woman's point of view, and in an important sense her historical novel—already celebrated as a landmark in the traditions of black women's, black, and women's writing—also stands in the tradition inaugurated by Homer and Genesis. Her hero Celie is a woman reborn to desire and language; and Walker, while not one with Celie as Angelou is with Maya, is a woman writer whom Woolf might well have considered a hero.

The Color Purple tells the story of a daughter who is raped by her "Pa" at the age of fourteen. It begins in its own prohibition: its first words, inscribed like an epigraph over Celie's letters, are her "Pa"'s warning, "*You better not never tell nobody but God. It'd kill your mammy*" (11). Thus is Celie robbed, in the name of her mother, of her story and her voice. Later, her pa further discredits her when he hands Celie over to Mr. ____ (ironically reduced to generic cultural father), a widower in need of a wife/housekeeper/caretaker of his children, with the warning "She tell lies" (18). Isolated, ignorant, and confused, Celie follows her pa's prohibition literally, obediently silencing her speech but writing stumblingly of her bewilderment in letters to God: "Dear God, I am fourteen years old. I am I have always been a good girl. Maybe you can give me a sign letting me know what is happening to me" (11).[16] Celie's rape leaves her with guilt that blocks her words. But through her letter-writing she is able at once to follow the letter of the father's law and to tell her story, first to that imaginary listener, the God of her father's command, and later to the friend who saves her from silence, Shug Avery.

These ends are all the more powerful in that they emerge from Celie's seemingly hopeless beginnings. With the first of Celie's two pregnancies by her pa, he forces her to leave school: "He never care that I love it" (19). Celie keeps studying under her younger sister Nettie's tutelage, but the world recedes from her grasp. "Look like nothing she say can git in my brain and stay," Celie writes God. "She try to tell me something bout the ground not being flat. I just say, Yeah, like I know it. I never tell her how flat it look to me" (20). While this passage conveys the pathos of Celie's isolation, its comic cast foretells what will eventually prove the source of Celie's strength: her fidelity to the way things look to her. One important instance is her feeling for her mother, who is too weak and ill to intervene in the incest and who dies soon after Celie's second child is born. "Maybe cause my mama cuss me you think I kept mad at her," Celie tells God. "But I ain't. I felt sorry for mama. Trying to believe his story kilt her" (15).

As Celie never loses her identification with her mother, she is saved from her isolation by three other women who become her companions and examples and whose voices foil Celie's submissive silence. Sofia, who marries Mr. ____'s son Harpo, is at first a problem for Celie, who tells God: "I like Sofia, but she don't act like me at all. If she talking when Harpo and Mr. ____ come into the room, she keep right on. If they ast her where something at, she say she don't know. Keep talking" (42). When Harpo consults her about how to make Sofia mind, Celie advises: "Beat her," propounding the cultural script of violent male rule in marriage, the only one she knows (43). But when Sofia angrily confronts Celie, a friendship forms, and Celie begins to abandon her numb allegiance to the father's law. Shug Avery, a brilliant blues singer and Mr. ____'s longtime lover, enters Celie's life when Mr. ____ brings her home ill for Celie to nurse. Like Sofia, Shug talks: "she say whatever come to mind, forgit about polite" (73). Mary Agnes, Harpo's girlfriend after Sofia's departure, begins, like Celie, as a relatively weak and silent woman. But when she is elected to go ask help from the white warden for Sofia in prison, she returns from her mission battered and bruised, and only after some urging—"Yeah, say Shug, if you can't tell us, who you gon tell, God?" (95)—is she able to tell the others that the warden has raped her. Telling the story, she comes into her authority and takes back her name along with her voice: when Harpo says "I love you, Squeak," she replies, "My name Mary Agnes" (95).

Mary Agnes's example is important for Celie, who until now has buried her story in her letters. One night soon afterward, when their husbands are away, Shug comes into bed with Celie for warmth and company, and Celie tells her everything: "I cry and cry and cry. Seem like it all come back to me, laying there in Shug arms. . . . Nobody ever love me, I say. She say, I love you, Miss Celie. And then she haul off and kiss me on the mouth. *Um,* she say, like she surprise. . . . Then I feels something real soft and wet on my breast, feel like one of my little lost babies mouth. Way after while, I act like a little lost baby too" (108–9). To know all alone, Balmary writes, is to know as if one did not know. To know with another is conscious knowledge, social knowledge, *con-science* (159 ff.; cf. Herman 178 ff.). Celie's telling of her story is an act of knowing-with that breaks the father's law, his prohibition of conscience. Knowing her story with Shug begins to heal Celie's long-hidden wounds of body and voice.

The radical conscience of Walker's novel goes beyond restoring Celie's voice to break down the patriarchal marriage plot that sanctions violence against women. This dismantling begins with another wound when Shug and Celie find the letters from Nettie that Mr. ____ has spitefully hidden since the sisters' separation. From them, Celie learns her lost history: that their father had been lynched when they were babies for having a store that did too well; that their mother, then a wealthy widow, had lost her reason and married a stranger, the man Celie knew as her "Pa"; that he had given Celie's two children by him to Samuel and Corrine, the missionaries to whom Nettie had also fled; and that, Corrine having died, Samuel, Nettie, and Celie's children are returning to the United States from their African mission. Celie's first response when she finds the intercepted letters is a murderous fury towards fathers both physical and metaphysical. Shug has to disarm her of the razor she is about to use to kill Mr. ____, and the scales fall from her eyes with respect to the God to whom she has been writing: "Dear God, . . . My daddy lynch. My mama crazy. All my little half-brothers and sisters no kin to me. My children not my sister and brother. Pa not pa. You must be sleep" (163).

With Shug's help, Celie is able to translate her murderous rage into powerful speech and to meet Mr. ____ on the battlefield of language. Patriarchal family rule and patriarchal metaphysics break down simultaneously as Shug and Celie leave Mr. ____'s house for Shug's Memphis estate. Celie's self-assertion is met with scorn by Mr. ____: "Shug got talent, he say. She can sing. She got spunk, he say. She can talk to anybody. Shug got looks, he say. She can stand up and be notice. But what you got? You ugly. You skinny. You shape funny. You too scared to open your mouth to people" (186). But Celie's voice gains strength as she comes into knowledge of her history, and for the first time she finds words to resist Mr. ____:

> I curse you, I say.
> What that mean? he say.
> I say, Until you do right by me, everything you touch will crumble.
> He laugh. Who you think you is? he say. You can't curse nobody. . . . You black, you pore, you ugly, you a woman. . . .
> A dust devil flew up on the porch between us, fill my mouth with dirt. The dirt say, Anything you do to me, already done to you.
> Then I feel Shug shake me. Celie, she say. And I come to myself.
> I'm pore, I'm black, I may be ugly and can't cook, a voice say to everything listening. But I'm here.
> Amen, say Shug. Amen, amen. (187)

Celie's curse, enhanced with epic machinery, translates the physical violence that, in her rage, she wants to inflict upon Mr. ____ into the metaphysical violence of language; and in its effects, it asserts the real power of words to work changes in the world. Celie's curse does not kill Mr. ____, as her razor would have done. Rather, it signals the decline and fall of the father's law and creates temporary separate spheres for women and men from which both eventually emerge transformed, able to share the world in a different way. During her interlude with Shug in Memphis, Celie consolidates her newly won authority by achieving economic independence. Earlier, Shug had distracted Celie from her murderous rage by suggesting that the two of them sew her a pair of pants. "What I need pants for?" Celie objects. "I ain't no man" (136). In Memphis, while trying to think what she wants to do for a living, Celie "sit[s] in the dining room making pants after pants" (190) and soon recognizes her calling, founding "Folkpants, Unlimited." In this comic reversal, the garment that Celie at first associates strictly with men becomes the means, symbolic and material, of her economic independence and her self-possession.

Celie's emergence from poverty and silence has drawn criticism from Marxian theorists as a fable of good fortune that, like the lottery, plays to fantasies of economic liberation that defuse rather than mobilize resistance to oppression; and, indeed, the magical ease with which Celie emerges from poverty and silence classes Walker's "historical novel" with epic and romance. Walker's Shug has a power that is historically very rare, and Celie and Nettie's inheritance of their father's house, in particular, indulges in narrative magic that well exceeds the requirements of the plot. But Celie's utopian history allegorizes not only women's need to be economically independent of men but the daughter's accession to the symbolic estate of culture and language that such cultural fathers as Homer and Freud had long appropriated—to a position in language and culture from which she can speak her desires and, by the very act of giving them real, social existence, affect and change the world. As Celie's curse frees her from her old life, it also transforms Mr. ____, who falls into a hysterical depression when Celie leaves him. Mr. ____'s crisis acts out the death of the cultural father whom he had earlier embodied and his rebirth as Albert. In the role of cultural father, Mr. ____'s law had been unspoken, his ways immutable, and his words so close to the patriarchal script that he did not have to finish his sentences: "Harpo ast his daddy why he beat me. Mr. ____ say, Cause she my wife. Plus, she stubborn. All women good for—he don't finish. He just tuck his chin over the paper like he do. Remind me of Pa" (30). By the end of the novel, with the help of his son Harpo (201), Mr. ____ has abandoned that role to become Albert and to "enter into the creation" (181). By the novel's last scenes, Albert's life is scarcely differentiable from Celie's, and he tells her, "Celie, I'm satisfied this the first time I ever lived on Earth as a natural man" (230).

An important effect of Albert's transition from patriarch to natural man is the abandonment of that strictly literal stake in paternity that the marriage structure serves. As a "natural man," Albert, like the other characters, spends a lot of time concocting devious recipes to hide the taste of yams from Henrietta, who, Celie explains, has to eat yams to control her chronic blood disease, but "Just our luck she hate yams and she not too polite to let us know" (222). Henrietta, Sofia's youngest child, whose "little face always look like stormy weather" (196), is a crucial figure in the novel. Though Harpo tries to claim her as his sixth child, she is nobody's baby; only Sofia (if anyone) knows who her father is. Nonetheless, Harpo, Albert, and everyone else feel a special affection for "ole evil Henrietta" (247), and as they knock themselves out making yam peanut butter and yam tuna casserole, it becomes apparent that, in Walker's recreated universe, the care of children by men and women without respect to proprietary biological parenthood is an important means of undoing the exploitative hierarchy of gender roles (cf. Chodorow; and Dinnerstein). If Celie's discovery that "Pa not pa" liberates her from the law of the father that makes women and children its spiritual and sexual subjects, Albert, in learning to "wonder" and to "ast" (247) and to care for Henrietta, escapes the confines of the patriarchal role. As the functions of father and mother merge, the formerly rigid boundaries of the family become fluid: Celie, Shug, and Albert feel "right" sitting on the porch together; love partners change with desire; and most important, children circulate among many parents: Samuel, Corrine, and Nettie raise Celie's; Celie raises Mr. ____'s and Annie Julia's; Sofia, Odessa, and Mary Agnes exchange theirs; and the whole community, including the white Eleanor Jane, becomes involved with yams and Henrietta. Whereas in the patriarchal societies analyzed by Lévi-Strauss the exchange of women forges bonds between men that support male culture, in Walker's revised creation story children are the miracle and mystery that bond all her characters to the world, each other, and the future.

Walker's rewriting of the creation myth dismantles gender hierarchy and the patriarchal conception of God that supports it in Western tradition. The God to whom Celie writes her early letters loses credibility once she learns, through Nettie's letters, that nothing is as the law of the father proclaims it. When Shug hears her venting her wrath, she is shocked: "Miss Celie, You better hush. God might hear you." "Let 'im hear me, I say. If he ever listened to poor colored women the world would be a different place, I can tell you." Shug deconstructs Celie's theology: "You have to git man off your eyeball, before you can see anything a'tall," she explains. "He on your box of grits, in your head, and all over the radio. He try to make you think he everywhere. Soon as you think he everywhere, you think he God. But he ain't"; "God ain't a he or a she, but a It. . . . It ain't something you can look at apart from everything else, including yourself. I believe God is everything . . . that is or ever was or ever will be. And when you can feel that, and be happy to feel that, you've found It" (175–79). In Walker's cosmos, the monotheistic Western myth of origins gives way to one of multiple, indeed infinite, beginnings that her new myth of Celie's fall and redemption celebrates. Walker's is not a Creation finished in the first seven days of the world but on ongoing one that celebrates all creators. When, for example, Sofia, with what Harpo calls her "amazon sisters," insists on bearing her mother's casket, Harpo asks,

> Why you like this, huh? Why you always think you have to do things your own way? I ast your mama bout it one time, while you was in jail.
> What she say? ast Sofia.
> She say you think your way as good as anybody else's. Plus, it yours. (196)

Walker echoes this moment in her epigraph, which translates Harpo's "here come the amazons" (198) into: "Show me how to do like you. Show me how to do it" (i). She fills her historical novel with creators, authorities, beginnings, "others." Like all authors of epic, she collapses transcendence and history; but her history differs from that of earlier epics. Originating in a violation of the patriarchal law, it undoes the patriarchal cultural order and builds upon new ground. "Womanlike," Walker writes, "my 'history' starts not with the taking of lands, or the births, battles, and deaths of Great Men, but with one woman asking another for her underwear" ("Writing" 356).[17] Violating the "conventions" that daunted Woolf's fisherwoman, Walker breaks the father's law, writing into history a story long suppressed, and by that act she enlarges the terrain of history. Under a revised sign of transcendence, Celie's last letter—addressed to "Dear God. Dear stars, dear trees, dear sky, dear peoples. Dear Everything. Dear God"—records the expanded vision of history that informs Walker's novel:

> Why us always have family reunion on July 4th, say Henrietta, mouth poke out, full of complaint. It so hot.
> White people busy celebrating they independence from England July 4th, say Harpo, so most black folks don't have to work. Us can spend the day celebrating each other.
> Ah, Harpo, say Mary Agnes, sipping some lemonade. I didn't know you knowed history. (249–50)

Walker ends her novel with a beginning: "I feel a little peculiar round the children," Celie writes. "And I see they think [us] real old and don't know much what going on. But I don't think us feel old at all. . . . Matter of fact, I think this the youngest us ever felt" (251). As Celie's beginning could have been a silent end, so her ending continues the proliferating beginnings that the novel captures in its epistolary form, its characters' histories, and the daily revelations that Shug names God.

Walker's telling of the daughter's long-repressed story also marks an important beginning for literary history. In her hands, the forbidden story recreates the world. Restoring women's repressed experiences to cultural knowledge, she disrupts the patriarchal economy of desire that has dominated Western literature and laid down its laws and conventions. Against the heroine compliant with the male conventions, against the abused daughter blinded to her own history, Walker creates women who fight those conventions and in doing so become veterans of their own pasts. "What I love best about Shug," Celie tells Albert, "is what she been through. When you look in Shug's eyes, you know she been where she been, seen what she seen, did what she did. And now she know. . . . And if you don't git out the way, she'll tell you about it" (236). Walker's woman as hero gives voice to "all this very queer knowledge . . . about women's bodies for instance—their passions" that Woolf could not yet "make use of," and in doing so, she enters into that "most interesting, exciting, and important conversation" that Woolf forecast, fifty years before.

Notes

This essay is a revised version of "The Daughter's Seduction: Sexual Violence and Literary History," which appeared in *Signs* 11 (1986): 621–44, and is used by permission of the University of Chicago Press.

1. Cf. "Professions" 240–41; and *Room* 5–6. Woolf's fisherwoman image first surfaces in *Room*, where, intently following an idea tugging at her line, she is suddenly interrupted by an Oxbridge beadle who banishes her from the lawns across which she strides in heedless absorption and so frightens her fish into hiding. "Professions," the later essay version, tamed for publication, represses the passion along with much of the narrative of the speech.

2. Here I must clarify my analogy of a "cure" of women's silence in literary history, with respect to the hysterical repression of the story of sexual abuse in patriarchal culture, to the hysterics' "talking cure." Orthodox Freudians point out that Freud later found the talking cure to be only temporary: the hysterics had relapses, the symptoms returned. The fact remains, however, that telling their stories did "cure" or relieve the hysterics' symptomatic body language, translating that muted "speech" into shared, conscious knowledge. Even if this relief was only temporary, it still uncovers the structure of hysteria as a culturally induced repression of paternal sexual abuse. Nor is it surprising that the symptoms often returned, for, as Herman's history of the reception of sociological studies on father-daughter incest indicates, the immense cultural pressure to repress this story is only now beginning to diminish (9–21). The fact that all Freud's patients had to leave the analyst's office to return to a world that confirmed the abusers and not the abused suggests that relapses may more accurately be attributed to the pervasive cultural repression of father-daughter incest than to the ineffectuality of the "talking cure."

With respect to women's repression of the story of sexual abuse in literary history, my claim in this essay is that this silence is itself a culturally induced hysterical symptom which such works as Angelou's and Walker's translate into public, social discourse, thereby in some measure relieving the symptom of silence as well as furthering (though not of course completing) a wider cultural cure.

3. Cf. Shakespeare's use of magic to quell unruly female desire in *A Midsummer Night's Dream*, in which Amazon power, embodied in Hippolyta, whom Theseus wooed by his sword and won by doing her injuries, also symbolizes disruptions to marriage caused by female solidarity and independent female desire. Shakespeare resolves the conflict between Oberon and Titania (over the changeling her votaress left her) in favor of patriarchal rule by a figural violence: the *magic* flower upon which Oberon's power depends.

4. Ann L. T. Bergren analyzes Helen's ambiguous status in Greek culture as object of exchange and agent of her own desire. Gorgias, defending Helen, poses three readings of her flight with Paris—abduction by force, persuasion by speech, and capture by love—all of which represent her as compelled "not otherwise than if she had been raped" (83). But such a defense also denies Helen the agency of her own desire, circumscribing it within the male ethical scheme attendant upon the marriage structure. Priam's exoneration of Helen—"You are not to blame, / I hold the gods to blame" (73)—similarly circumscribes female desire within this male scheme, which asserts its preeminence in judging women "guilty" or "innocent."

5. Sherry B. Ortner argues that childbearing and attendant social responsibilities and psychic structures cause women to be more closely associated with nature than men. But as the *Iliad* suggests, the founding texts of Western culture manifest an active antagonism to female desire, social power, and language—in other words, to female culture-making. If, as de Beauvoir, Dinnerstein, and others have argued, it is *woman as nature* that male culture seeks to bring under control, the effect of men's and women's equal involvement in "projects of creativity and transcendence" (Ortner 87) would be not only to dissolve the male culture/female nature dichotomy but to transform the "nature" of culture.

6. For the encyclopedic function of Homeric epic see Havelock, chaps. 3–5. That the primacy of the male voice and story over the female cannot be achieved without struggle nor maintained without the elaborate reproduction of its motives and methods in its audience points to the need for feminist analyses of the didactic and encyclopedic functions of primary epic.

7. The editors of the *Standard Edition* trace (without critique) the vicissitudes of Freud's acknowledgment of sexual abuse on the part of fathers in a note to "Femininity" (22:120n).

8. Balmary supplies the italicized phrase, omitted in *Origins*, from the 1975 German edition of the Freud-Fliess correspondence.

9. I have found Gallop's treatment of father-daughter seduction provocative and enlightening. For her, however, *seduction* is a metaphor for persuasion, and actual incest does not enter the picture. The sociological and literary texts that I discuss emphasize the damaging effects of incest and seduction on the daughter, who is, by virtue of age, family position, and gender, far weaker than the father; and I argue further that the abuse and silencing of individual daughters is contin-

uous with the more general silencing (by circumscription of the daughter's speech within the bounds set by the father's law) of women in culture.

10. Balmary powerfully reinterprets the Oedipal myth, recovering aspects suppressed in Sophocles' and Freud's accounts that reveal Oedipus's crimes to be an unconscious repetition of his father's, as well as biographical materials, also suppressed, that uncover the sudden, unexplained disappearance of Jakob's second wife Rebecca and the likelihood that Freud was conceived before Jakob married Freud's mother Amalie, his third wife.

11. Denial of the reality and the power of female desire is pervasive in Freud's "Femininity"; for example, he equates libido with masculinity, so that "we are now obliged to recognize that the little girl is a little man" (*SE* 22:118), and he judges that "the suppression of women's aggressiveness which is prescribed for them constitutionally and imposed on them socially favors the development of powerful masochistic impulses" (*SE* 22:116). Similarly, Freud plays for power over Dora by castigating her for masturbating; and reading her dream of the *Bahnhof,* he can acknowledge Dora's desire only by placing her in the role of the masculine subject, the engineer. Feminist critiques of "Female Sexuality," "Femininity," and the Dora case engage the issue of Freud's preconceptions of femininity in his treatment of hysteria (see esp. Cixous and Clément, Moi, Jacqueline Rose, and the essays and further bibliography in Bernheimer and Kahane).

12. While many Freudians simply follow Freud in rejecting the seduction theory for the Oedipal theory, others have tried to explain and resolve these apparently contradictory moments in his theory. For example, Laplanche and Pontalis attempt to reconcile early and late Freudian theory, seduction as fact and as fantasy, by means of Freud's concepts of "psychic reality" and "primal fantasy." For them, the daughter's seduction story is such a fantasy, its reality "to be sought in an ever more remote and hypothetical past (of the individual or the species) which is postulated on the horizon of the imaginary and implied in the very structure of the fantasy" ("Fantasy" 17). Although this view does not entirely deny the possibility of actual seduction, actual seduction would only form the basis for fantasies that the daughter would otherwise have had to generate *ex nihilo,* in accordance with the innate workings of the human mind.

By contrast, the concept of a hysterical cultural script that I am proposing, exemplified in the juxtaposition of Homer and Freud, bridges the gap between the actual and the imaginary not by sacrificing history to the imaginary but by understanding history as the origin of the imaginary. That actual seduction is far more common than our culture has been willing to acknowledge, recent research (Herman; Russell) has proved beyond question; and physical abuse is continuous with the metaphysical abuse that women have experienced in patriarchal culture. The problem, then, is not to "decide" whether Freud's patients were telling him history or fantasy but to understand the continuum of physical and metaphysical abuse that connects Helen's rape/abduction by Paris, her silencing by Priam, and her seduction by Aphrodite. If psychic reality is to be found where the horizons of history and imagination cross, that is because *actual* abuse is to be found in both domains.

13. Sandra M. Gilbert, studying George Eliot, and Dianne F. Sadoff, study-

ing Eliot and Bronte, find that the dynamics of literary fathers and daughters as reflected in these nineteenth-century women writers' works induce a more complete and permanent circumscription of female desire and language than the twentieth-century women writers I am discussing show. Woolf, Angelou, and Walker hearteningly counter Gilbert's bleak conclusion that "even in more apparently rebellious works, the text discovers no viable alternative to filial resignation" ("Life's Empty Pack" 3/8). Herman's history of twentieth-century sociological scholarship on incest and its reception (9–21) makes visible the changes women's increasing cultural power has already made in the discourse about sexual abuse, and women's literature shows a comparable expansion.

14. The ambiguity of father figures in Ovid's retelling points to the fact that the father's ownership of his daughter gives him privileged sexual access to her, whether or not he avails himself of it. Herman notes that incest victims frequently report that men find their histories arousing, as though they too envy the place of the bad father (98). See also Brownmiller, who concludes that the cultural taboo against acknowledging the high incidence of father rape arises from the "patriarchal philosophy of sexual private property," of which children are an extension (311). For an excellent study of the inscription of cultural violence against women in the Philomela myth see Joplin.

15. Maya's identification with Lucrece conceals by revealing, exemplifying Freud's view of the hysterical symptom as "a compromise between two opposite affective and instinctual impulses," one trying to bring to light and the other trying to repress ("Hysterical Phantasies," *SE* 9:164). Freud posits a conflict between homosexual and heterosexual desire as the symptom's cause, but Maya's case suggests that the conflictual nature of the symptom is better explained by the social danger in which the victim finds herself. When Freud marks the desire to tell as masculine and the desire to conceal as feminine, he denies the daughter's real and *positive* desire to tell her story.

For an excellent discussion of *The Rape of Lucrece* and the earliest critique of the poem as a representation of rape see Kahn.

16. Cf. the incest victim in Herman's study who "wrote private letters to God" (99).

17. Cf. the title of Jacob's essay in Woolf's *Jacob's Room:* "Does History Consist of the Biographies of Great Men?" (39).

RAYMUND A. PAREDES

The Evolution of Daughter-Father
Relationships in Mexican-American Culture

IN CONSIDERING the nature of daughter-father relationships in Mexican-American culture, the scholar or imaginative writer must engage a complex of cultural traditions often described as among the most patriarchal in the world. Inevitably, directly or indirectly, the writer must come to terms with machismo, that distinctive Latin American code of masculinity so widely misunderstood in the United States. He or she must also confront the looming figures of Malinche and Guadalupe—Mexico's renderings of the wicked and virtuous female archetypes—as powerful and sometimes inadvertent influences on delineations of women characters. Of course, other factors originating from Mexican culture affect Mexican-American daughter-father relationships. The writer must not only weigh these but also take into account the highly variable impact of American culture on Mexican-American families.

A consideration of Mexican-American daughter-father relationships begins with an examination of this phenomenon in Mexican aboriginal and Spanish cultures, the earliest antecedents of Mexican-American traditions. These cultures, one American and pagan, the other European and Christian, differed widely and consequently did not blend easily. But on the issues of women's roles and, more specifically, daughter-father relationships, Indian and Spanish attitudes and practices resembled one another remarkably.

In the sixteenth century, when the conquest of Mexico was undertaken, the most powerful of Mexican peoples were the Aztecs; from their own accounts and those of various Spanish observers we have learned a good deal about their habits of child-rearing. Much more so than mothers, fathers were responsible for preparing daughters for their eventual obligations as wives and mothers (Mirandé and Enríquez 20). In a series of exhortations, fathers taught Aztec girls that these roles were ordained and consequently were to be fulfilled gracefully. Physical pain—particularly from childbirth and sheer hard work—was to be accepted without complaint. In loving and patient voices, fathers guided their "precious gems" and "beloved doves" towards lives of acquiescence before male authority. Among the Aztecs, only chastity—virginity before marriage, fidelity unto death thereafter—equaled submissiveness as a female virtue.

Throughout childhood, Aztec girls were taught the importance of their destiny as propagators of the race. Aztecs regarded the reproductive cycle itself as sacred and greeted births with lavish celebration. For women, the "fulfillment of [their] most essential biological function reaped [for them] the highest rewards the society could offer" (Mirandé and Enríquez 23).

Aztec girls learned that if their highest duty was motherhood, their most heroic act was to die in childbirth. Victims of childbirth were called *mocihuaquetzque*, "valiant women," and were as much esteemed as warriors who had given their lives in battle. These "valiant women" were allotted a special place in the afterlife alongside fallen warriors; a few were elevated to the status of *ciuatateo*, "goddesses." As Mirandé and Enríquez point out, "even in failure, [the Aztec mother] was sanctified" (23).

While Aztec girls were instructed gently, they were made aware of the harsh penalties imposed on women who deviated from acceptable behavior. Girls learned that even minor breaches of social convention such as immodesty of dress dishonored not only themselves but their parents and ancestors. Violations such as promiscuity and adultery were so shameful that fathers would themselves call for death as the appropriate punishment for their wayward daughters (Hellbom 247). In his chronicle of Aztec life, the Dominican priest Bartolomé de Las Casas describes how daughters of the nobility were rarely permitted to go out in public, and only with close supervision and on the condition that they keep their eyes to the ground. Las Casas also tells of a young nobleman who climbed a wall to speak with a daughter of the king of Texcoco. When the king learned of this adolescent mischief, he promptly ordered his daughter drowned; the boy, it should be noted, was not punished. Las Casas reports that the king of Texcoco had another daughter executed for adultery, even though her husband pleaded for her life (Mirandé and Enríquez 103–4). Las Casas was not the most disinterested of observers, and many of his stories must be regarded skeptically. But there exist other sixteenth-century reports of Aztec fathers inflicting hideous punishments on their daughters. Apparently, for some Aztec fathers at least, the loss of a daughter was less disagreeable than enduring a living reminder of their family's humilation.

From a broad historical and cultural perspective, the Aztecs' treatment of women was not exceptional: certainly Spanish culture was not perceptibly kinder. The Mexican poet Octavio Paz noted that the Spanish attitude towards women could be expressed "quite brutally and concisely in two sayings: 'A woman's place is in the home, with a broken leg' and 'Between a female saint and a male saint, a wall of mortared stone.'"

Paz continues that for the Spanish male, woman "is a domesticated wild animal, lecherous and sinful from birth, who must be subdued with a stick and guided by the reins of religion" (*Labyrinth* 36). There is doubtless some poetic license in Paz's claims, but available scholarship supports the view that Spanish culture has traditionally been heavily male-dominated.

Spanish sexism manifested itself in a tradition of patriarchy that resembled the Aztec variety, the major difference being the influence of Catholicism. Traditionally in Spanish culture, women have carried the primary responsibility of preserving and conveying church doctrine. And as loyal Catholics, they have also been expected to obey church fathers as diligently as they would their natural ones. The profoundly patriarchal structure and vocabulary of Catholicism instilled in Spanish women an intense reverence and humility before their various father figures. The church promoted patriarchy not only as a religious principle but as a social one, considering it to be the cornerstone of orderly community life (Griswold del Castillo 27). Spanish girls learned that being a good Christian and an obedient daughter were inseparable.

The Catholic clergy justified patriarchy with biblical citations, and the Spanish government enforced it with laws. The *siete partidos* of 1265, which serve as the foundation of Spanish legal principles, describe husbands and fathers as "lords" and "absolute monarchs" in the "nation" of the family (Griswold del Castillo 28). Several scholars have connected traditional Spanish patriarchy to a particular strain of nationalism, the notion of *limpieza de sangre,* "cleanliness of blood." A concern—verging on a national obsession—for maintaining purity not only of race but of religion and culture is understandable in a people fearful of extinction during eight hundred years of Moorish domination. Spanish men required, so they felt, great authority to protect their vulnerable daughters and wives from contamination, corruption, and, ultimately, damnation (Gutiérrez 33). Ostensibly for their own well-being, Spanish girls were taught to regard obedience as the highest virtue: they were to proceed in orderly fashion from the role of obedient daughter to that of obedient wife.[1]

Probably the most significant treatment of a daughter-father relationship in traditional Spanish culture is "La Delgadina," a *romance* dating from the seventeenth century that is known throughout the Spanish-speaking world and, as a dramatic example of cultural vitality and continuity, is still performed in Mexican-American communities.[2] The version presented here is Mexican, set in Morelia in the state of Michoacán and collected recently along the Texas-Mexican border (Paredes, *Cancionero* 7, 14–16).[3] With marvelous and agonizing simplicity, it vividly portrays the power of the Spanish, now Mexican, father:

Delgadina se paseaba
de la sala a la cocina,
con su manto hilo de oro
que su pecho le ilumina.

Delgadina se paseaba
en su gran sala cuadrada,
con su manto hilo de oro
que en su pecho le brillaba.

—Levántate, Delgadina,
ponte vestido de seda,
porque nos vamos a misa
a la ciudad de Morelia.—

Cuando salieron de misa
en su sala la abrazaba:
—Delgadina, hija mía,
yo te quiero para dama.—

—No permitas, madre mía,
ni la Virgen soberana,
que es ofensa para Dios
y la perdición de mi alma.—

—Júntense los once criados
y encierren a Delgadina,
échenle bien los candados—
dijo el rey con mucha muina.

—Remachen bien los candados
que no se oiga voz ladina,
si les pide de comer
no le den comida fina.

—Si les pide de beber
le darán agua salada,
porque la quiero obligar
a que sea mi prenda amada.

—Mariquita, hermana mía,
un favor te pediré,
regálame un vaso de agua
porque me muero de sed.—

—Ay, hermana de mi vida,
no te puedo dar el agua,
si lo sabe el rey mi padre
a las dos nos saca el alma.—

—Papacito de mi vida,
tu castigo estoy sufriendo,
regálame un vaso de agua
que de sed me estoy muriendo.—

—Júntense los once criados,
llévenle agua a Delgadina
en vaso sobredorado
y en jarros de losa china.—

Cuando le llevan el agua
Delgadina estaba muerta,
con sus ojitos cerrados
y con su boquita abierta.

La cama de Delgadina
de ángeles está rodeada,
la cama del rey su padre
de diablos está apretada.

Delgadina está en el cielo
dándole cuenta al Creador
y su padre en los infiernos
con el Demonio Mayor.

Y con ésta me despido
a la sombra de una lima,
aquí se acaba cantando
la historia de Delgadina.

Delgadina walked about from the hall to the kitchen,
in her cloth-of-gold mantle that illuminates her breast.

Delgadina walked about in her great square hall,
in her cloth-of-gold mantle that shone against her breast.

"Arise, Delgadina, put on a silken dress,
for we are going to mass in the city of Morelia."

When they came back from mass, he embraced her in the hall:
"Delgadina, daughter of mine, I want you to be my mistress."

"Don't let it happen, my mother, nor you, all-powerful Virgin,
for it is a sin against God and the perdition of my soul."

"Come together my eleven servants, and put Delgadina in prison;
see that she is well locked up," said the king in great anger.

"Fasten the padlocks securely so that no shrill voice is heard;
and if she wishes to eat, do not give her any fine food."

"If she wishes to drink, you will give her salty water,
because I want to force her to become my sweetheart."

"Mariquita, sister of mine, I will ask you a favor:
give me a glass of water, for I am dying of thirst."

"Oh, my beloved sister, I cannot give you the water,
for if the king my father knows it, he will tear out both our
        souls."

"My beloved father, I am suffering from your anger;
give me a glass of water for I am dying of thirst."

"Come together my eleven servants, take water to Delgadina
in a gilded glass and jars of fine china."

When they took her the water, Delgadina was dead,
with her little mouth open and her little eyes closed.

Delgadina's bed is surrounded by angels;
the bed of the king her father is crowded with demons.

Delgadina is in Heaven being judged by God;
her father is in Hell, with the Chief Devil.

Now with this I say farewell, under the shade of a lime tree;
here is the end of the singing of the story of Delgadina.

In "La Delgadina," the role of the Spanish father as lord and absolute monarch is literalized; the father here is actually a king whose authority is not to be challenged, certainly not by any woman, whether
Delgadina, her sister, or her mother. Remarkably, Delgadina, although
appalled by her father's demands, continues to answer him reverently
and lovingly ("Papacito de mi vida") even to the moment when she
weakens before his awesome sovereignty. Despite the father/king's wickedness, the ballad holds him accountable to no earthly authority; only in
death can he be judged by God and finally condemned.

Although the ballad printed here only hints at Delgadina's capitulation to her father's perversity, other versions recount how, abandoned by her mother and siblings, she decides quite unambiguously to submit to her father; of course she dies before the incest can occur. Other versions also depict the omnipotence of the father more elaborately. Sometimes not one but two or more siblings ignore Delgadina's pleas for water out of fear of their father's wrath. In still other versions, Delgadina not only is denied assistance by her family but is rebuked for resisting patriarchal authority. "We will give you nothing," says her mother in a New Mexican version, "because you didn't want to do as your father ordered" (Campa 32). In several versions Delgadina's disobedience is presented as a threat to family stability. The single constant in the Delgadina ballads is her death. She must die, trapped as she is in an impossible dilemma. She is pressed on one side by the cultural obligation to honor her father's demands, regardless of their fairness, and on the other by the equally compelling imperative to maintain her virginity until marriage. Delgadina is doomed because she cannot accomplish both. The cruelest irony of her plight is that until he himself was drawn to her beauty, her father was doubtless the most vigilant guardian of her chastity. Doubtless, too, if she had somehow lost it before he himself could possess it, of all the family members he would have been the most outraged.

Similar as they were, Indian and Spanish modes of patriarchy fused over nearly three centuries of colonialism into a rigid set of prescriptions for the behavior of Mexican women. The extremes of women's behavior came to be embodied in two legendary figures, Malinche and Guadalupe. Malinche (or Marina), a young Aztec woman of noble lineage who, through a series of misfortunes, was sold into slavery, became the conqueror Cortés's all too willing translator, informant, and mistress. In this last role, she bore a mestizo son and thus became one of the great symbolic mothers of Mexico. While Malinche remains obscure historically, she thrives in her legendary manifestations, invigorated regularly by a succession of journalists, scholars, creative writers, and even popular singers. Occasionally Malinche appears as a romantic and even heroic character, but more commonly she appears as a hopelessly naive and passive woman, a traitor and a whore. For Octavio Paz, Malinche is "La Chingada" (the violated mother), a woman "forcibly opened, violated, or deceived" (*Labyrinth* 79), and an enduring symbol of female physical and emotional vulnerability. As illegitimate "hijos de la Chingada" (children of the violated mother), Mexicans are easily persuaded of the tenuousness of female virtue. Malinche is the Mexican Eve, the fallen mother who bears her children under a cloud of shame and sin. Mexican men have been quick to connect Malinche to a Western tradition of female troublemakers. Ignacio Ramírez, a prominent nineteenth-century intellectual and political activist, in comparing "Cortés's concubine" directly with Eve, lamented that "it is one of the mysteries of fate that all nations owe their fall and ignominy to a woman" (Rachel Phillips 111).

Despite various attempts to rehabilitate Malinche's reputation, she has remained the dominant Mexican symbol not only of "damned femininity" but national inferiority as well.[4] Significantly, Malinche is accompanied in Mexican legendry by another powerful symbol of female depravity, *la llorona*. A mythic figure, *la llorona* seems related to Cihuacóatl, the Aztec goddess who wailed uncontrollably for women who died in childbirth. *La llorona* reportedly made her first appearance on the darkened streets of Mexico City about 1550, like Cihuacóatl dressed in white and weeping frantically. The sources of *la llorona*'s anguish vary from one version of the legend to another. In some accounts, she murders her children while grief-stricken after being abandoned by her lover. Afterward, mad with guilt, she roams about aimlessly calling after them. In other versions, she appears as a ghostly villain who, after being executed for murder, returns to her home region to avenge herself on unsuspecting men and children. A few versions identify *la llorona* explicitly as Malinche.[5] In these, after being discarded by Cortés, she kills her bastard son and consequently is condemned to an eternity of public grief, wailing in the night for all Mexicans to hear, guilty not only of murder but of the betrayal of her homeland.

Whatever versions of the legends of Malinche and *la llorona* one encounters, together they present an overwhelmingly negative image of women. Malinche's easy manipulation by a ruthless European invader has proved an indelible source of humiliation to successive generations of Mexicans. *La llorona* represents the extreme of woman's purported potentiality for irrational acts of violence and vindictiveness. Significantly, both legendary women have failed in fulfilling the conventional roles of wife and mother. Malinche never achieves marriage, and *la llorona*, in the few versions where she appears as a wife, is invariably abandoned by her husband. Malinche's primary legacy to her son is the gnawing awareness of her treason and his illegitimacy, while *la llorona* stands, quite simply, as the worst of imaginable mothers.

The remedy for the turmoil incited by the likes of Malinche and *la llorona* is, of course, greater male—and especially paternal—authority and vigilance; the legends surrounding these two women imply as much. Men must carefully instruct and supervise women to protect them from exploitation, corruption, and, as *la llorona* makes clear, violent criminality. The woeful examples of Malinche and *la llorona* both have influenced Mexican conventions of male behavior. For instance, although the origins of the Mexican macho have frequently been traced to the bravado of the Spanish *conquistadores*, surely his swaggering masculinity may be regarded, in part at least, as a response to the perceived vulnerability of women. As much as Cortés, Malinche illustrates to Mexican men the advantages—indeed the necessity—of toughness and aggressiveness. Furthermore, the model of the proud, stern, and aloof Mexican father, with a sizable brood as evidence of his masculinity, can be said to compensate for the deficiencies of mothers such as Malinche and *la llorona*. Where mothers are extraordinarily weak, fathers must be extraordinarily strong, lest the family and, finally, the social order collapse altogether. The corrupt father who exercises his authority irresponsibly, such as the one in "La Delgadina," is an aberration, the price that must be paid for the assurance of the strong paternal figure. Octavio Paz has observed that "admiration for the Father . . . expresses itself very clearly in a saying [Mexicans] use when [they] want to demonstrate [their] superiority: 'I am your father'" (*Labyrinth* 80). This expression, used commonly by Mexican-Americans as well, is the ultimate assertion of authority and, finally, domination.

Malinche and her mythic elaboration, *la llorona*, together symbolize one extreme of female behavior in Mexican culture; the other extreme, embodying the virtues associated with idealized womanhood, finds expression in the Virgin of Guadalupe, the patron saint of Mexico. As the supreme example of Spanish and Indian syncretism, the Virgin is "the central symbol of Mexican history" (Paredes, *Folktales* xvii). According to legend, she was first seen on December 9, 1531, by Juan Diego, an Indian recently converted to Christianity. Diego was walking to mass when a dark-skinned apparition called to him on a hill where a sanctuary commemorating Tonantzin, the Aztec goddess of fertility, had once been located.[6] The Virgin instructed the startled Diego to communicate to Fray Juan de Zumárraga, the recently appointed bishop of Mexico, her wish to have a church built on the hill. Diego complied, but Zumárraga dismissed his story. Diego saw the Virgin twice more and at last was provided some evidence of his unusual experiences. The Virgin told Diego to pick some roses for the bishop from the hilltop where only cactus normally grew. Diego wrapped the flowers in his cloak and hurried to tell his tale to Zumárraga once more. The bishop listened impatiently until Diego unrolled his cloak to reveal, not the roses, but a wondrous image of the Virgin on the fabric. At last convinced of the miracle, the bishop ordered the church built. In 1754 the Lady of Guadalupe was declared patroness of Mexico by Pope Benedict XIV.

News of the Virgin excited the Indians, who quickly accepted her as their own and flocked to Catholicism. Some cynics have dismissed Guadalupe as little more than a clever stratagem of the Spanish clergy to proselytize the Indians. Certainly, word of the apparition had this effect; but whatever the sources and intentions of the earliest legends about her,

Guadalupe's significance for Mexicans has grown far beyond the purely religious. Whereas Malinche represents woman as victim and betrayer, Guadalupe is the protective and reassuring mother.

The virgin as idealized woman is, of course, found in countries around the world; in Catholic countries the archetype is metamorphosed into variations of the Virgin Mary. Because Catholicism associates the highest religious values with celibacy, a commitment to virginity restores Catholic women to the state of innocence they enjoyed before the Fall (Marina Warner 73). In Latin America, where various countries have adopted versions of the Virgin Mother as national protectors (Lafaye 226), admiration for her has evolved into a secularized cult of femininity comparable in its extensiveness to machismo. This phenomenon, called marianismo, centers on a belief in feminine spiritual superiority and extols the virtues of humility, sacrifice, and submissiveness. In marianismo, the impractical virtue of virginity has been replaced by "post-nuptial frigidity" (Stevens 94–96). Decent Latin American women, according to the tenets of marianismo are not to enjoy sex but merely to endure it as a marital and biological obligation.

For Mexicans, Guadalupe represents the apotheosis of marianismo and, with Malinche, completes the madonna/whore dichotomy well known in patriarchal cultures. Guadalupe provides Mexicans an attractive alternative to Malinche as the national symbol of maternity. As Carlos Fuentes has written: "The image of the . . . virgin, Guadalupe, saves [Mexicans] from the fear of being sons-of-a-whore: we now see our mother as pure and enshrined" (qtd. in Paredes, *Folktales* xxvii). Guadalupe not only relieves Mexicans of the memory of Malinche but restores some of their lost dignity and confidence. Little wonder that Father Hidalgo, the leader of the Mexican war for independence in 1810, rallied his compatriots with the cry "Long Live Our Lady of Guadalupe!" and that a hundred years later the peasant Emiliano Zapata would carry her banner into combat against an oppressive government. December 12 is the day of Guadalupe in Mexico, the most festive time of year and "the central date in the emotional calendar of the Mexican people" (Paz, "The Flight of Quetzalcóatl" xix).

Like all nations, Mexico has been shaped by its myths and legends. The stories of Malinche (as well as her counterpart, *la llorona*) and Guadalupe have provided generations of Mexicans with paradigms of female behavior, the first to be repudiated and the second to be emulated. The modern Malinche frequently appears in films, television, and paperback novels as *la mala mujer*, "the bad woman," who rejects conventional roles and resists male authority. Guadalupe is equally conspicuous, seemingly battling with Malinche for control of the Mexican image of women. Mexican daughter-father relationships, historically and currently, exist in the context of these cultural phenomena.

In the northern Mexican territories that would be ceded to the United States in 1848, the cultural traditions that took root were essentially the same as those of the interior. To be sure, life in Greater Mexico had its special qualities, but the Mexicans there lived largely as their brethren to the south did.[7] The scholarship treating family relations among the northern Mexicans is not extensive, but it does support notions of cultural continuity. Ramón Gutiérrez, in his study of family life in New Mexico from 1660 to 1846, noted that the authority of the father resembled that of the traditional Spanish patriarch and was invoked to protect wives and daughters from corruption. Richard Griswold del Castillo investigated Mexican family life in the Southwest after the Mexican War (1846–48) and also found traditional patterns of patriarchy. In looking through some family papers from New Mexico, Griswold del Castillo discovered that children, through a series of lengthy instructions transmitted across generations, were taught to regard their fathers as family priests, "dispensing moral lessons and interpreting the word of God" (27). For Mexican fathers, religious authority was a cornerstone of their power. Patriarchy was so strong that fathers dominated their children even beyond marriage. In California it was not unusual for an aged father to whip a married son with children (28). Such treatment of a married woman was infrequent, but fathers felt free to rebuke their daughters of whatever age or circumstances for violations of social and ethical conventions.

In California, Arizona, New Mexico, and Texas, men of Mexican heritage justified their domination of women with familiar arguments. A *californio*, Ignacio Coronel, traced the perceived weakness of women to biblical sources. Writing in the 1860s, Coronel explained that "the first woman (Eve) did not have any rivals; nevertheless, she wanted to obtain the apple; and ever since then, in a spirit of imitation, women have not ceased to accuse one another of this desire. . . . Man born before woman is thus more noble than she" (Griswold del Castillo 29). Because women were considered so susceptible to temptation, fathers supervised their daughters closely and seldom allowed them away from home. Girls were taught to believe in their own inferiority and to "enjoy" the security and stability of male authority.

The cultural pressures on girls and young women of Greater Mexico to fulfill conventional roles was tremendous. As it did in Spain and in the Mexican interior, the Catholic church vigorously promoted patriarchy not only in its religious services but in its elementary and secondary schools. Spanish-language newspapers regularly published items advis-

145

ing girls to obey their parents (especially their fathers) and to accept happily their destiny as wives and mothers. Griswold del Castillo notes that traveling theater troupes often presented plays that promoted patriarchy and conventional roles for women (85–86).

Given the intensity of patriarchy in nineteenth-century Greater Mexico, women were not generally encouraged to record their experiences and feelings; even more than children generally, girls were taught to be seen and not heard. Consequently, as far as we currently know, until well into the twentieth century the body of literature of any type—novels, stories, poems, autobiographies—produced by women of Mexican heritage is disappointingly small. What is available, however, confirms what one might suspect. An anonymous teenage girl from San Antonio complained in her diary of her "almost cloistered life" and expressed resentment of the freedom allowed her brother. One of her entries, for January 12, 1889, reads: "Papa and Carl [her brother] went to the ranch to get wood. I wanted to take a ride today but they were too mean to me. I don't go anywhere" (Griswold del Castillo 75).

If we examine the folklore record of Greater Mexico, we find numerous examples of the same kinds of patriarchal material that pervaded Mexico from the beginning of the colonial period. Versions of "La Delgadina" were known throughout the region in the nineteenth century, as were legends about Malinche, *la llorona,* and the Virgin of Guadalupe. In addition to versions of traditional *romances* and legends, the region produced its own sizable body of folk narratives which reveal something of daughter-father relationships. For example, various folk tales focus on disputes caused by the traditional Mexican practice of fathers' determining (with assistance from mothers) whom their daughters would marry. In one, a king has a witch turn his daughter into stone when he fears she will elope with an unwanted suitor. In a well-known New Mexican legend, a girl commits suicide when her father rejects her suitor. One legendary narrative known in Texas and California, "La Condenada" (The Damned Girl), tells of a young woman who defies her parents and attends a dance and, later the same night, a saloon. The mother finds the daughter there and tries to take her home. But the daughter, encouraged by a male companion (the Devil in disguise), kills her mother with a dagger. The companion then offers the girl money if she will return home to murder her father as well. She stabs her father as he calls her "condenada" and "maldecida" (cursed girl). As he dies, he pronounces a curse on her, telling her that the earth around the home will swallow her up over a six-day period. Defiant still, the girl sneers: "I don't believe you, I'm the master of my own fate." But the girl begins to sink into the ground as soon as she leaves the house. Finally, the authorities, unable to help, block off the area and watch as the girl sinks slowly in accordance with her father's curse (Elaine K. Miller 170–72). Obviously, this narrative justifies the Mexican system of parental authority: it indicates that children, especially girls, get into trouble—even to the point of consorting with the Devil—when they are allowed to follow their own whims. Another important feature is the way the narrative treats differently the authority of the two parents. The daughter is clearly despised for killing her mother but seems to escape, at least for the moment, without any punishment. But when she kills her father, her punishment is immediate, gruesome, and fatal.

"La Condenada" is one of many narratives from Greater Mexico that depict the harsh penalities disobedient daughters must face. Other narratives emphasize, not punishment, but rather the sheer power fathers hold over their daughters. A New Mexican narrative popular among women features a poor Spaniard who sells his three beautiful daughters into marriage to magical princes disguised as lizards. The daughters, who have never been away from home, are, quite naturally, frightened when they encounter the lizards; after all, they have only their father's word that the reptiles are really handsome and wealthy princes. But when their father instructs them to close their eyes and walk away with the lizards, they dare not disobey; off they go to their uncertain fate (DeHuff 123–25). A narrative such as this is rich in symbolic information regarding daughter-father relationships. Clearly, this narrative conveys the fear Mexican girls felt when they were sent off by their fathers into arranged marriages with husbands they knew barely, if at all. Moreover, the representation of the prospective bridegrooms as lizards has obvious phallic connotations, figuring the dread of virginal, homebound, un sophisticated girls as they faced their future as wives and mothers.[8]

A large number of Greater Mexican narratives treat daughter-father relationships favorably but invariably within the boundaries of conventional roles. In some folk tales we find fathers trying desperately to find suitable husbands for their beautiful and dutiful daughters; others tell of fathers who risk their lives and even kill in defense of their daughters' honor. Occasionally, such naratives end with a wedding scene in which the radiant daughter, in customary Mexican fashion, approaches her father and pleads, "Papá, bless us." The bride and groom then kneel before the father, who touches the daughter's lips and gives the blessing. Engaging as they are, such happy endings are awarded only to daughters who have pleased their fathers with submissiveness to their authority.

These folk narratives generally date from the nineteenth century or earlier and represent a time when the Mexican-origin population of the Southwest was maintaining its cultural heritage virtually intact. Not until the twentieth century did Anglo-American culture begin to alter the lives of these people dramatically.* Mexican and, as the process of acculturation advanced, Mexican-American men watched this development anxiously. Anglo-American culture threatened to undermine not only the Mexican-Americans' language and collective identity—possible eventualities that Mexican-American women could also regard as tragic—but their system of patriarchy as well. Mexican-American men viewed this last prospect as tantamount to emasculation. Not surprisingly, then, over the course of the twentieth century Mexican-American men have defended no element of their traditional culture against Anglo influences more tenaciously then their hegemony over their wives and daughters.

Most recent scholarship on the Mexican-American family maintains that Mexican-American men have indeed preserved the traditional structure of patriarchy. William Madsen, who studied Mexican-American culture in south Texas during the 1950s, wrote:

> While the Mexican American male may be a second-class citizen in an Anglo-dominated world, he can be a king in his own home. He is entitled to unquestioning obedience from his wife and children. He is above criticism due to his "superior" male strength and intelligence. . . . To a large extent, the supremacy of the male compensates for the subservience he may have to demonstrate on the job or in the presence of a social superior. *En mi casa yo mando* (In my house I command) is the byword of the Mexican American husband no matter who gives the orders outside of his home. . . . [The] husband and father is seen as a direct image of God. He is aloof, absolute, and forceful in administering justice. (48)

In discussing the role of the woman, Madsen explains that the Virgin of Guadalupe is the "holy model for female behavior," possessing "all the most prized values of womanhood: purity, sanctity, tolerance, love, and sympathy" (48). Arthur J. Rubel, also writing about Mexican-Americans in Texas, explains that girls are prepared by both their parents for marriage and motherhood. They are taught to be "paragons of virtue" so that they might attract good husbands; bad behavior not only diminishes their desirability as prospective brides but casts shame on their families (77). These views of Mexican-American family life are obviously consistent with this recent assessment of Mexican family structure: "The Mexican family is founded upon two fundamental propositions: a) the

---

*I use "Anglo-American" (or simply "Anglo") as it is commonly applied in the Southwest: to refer to all non-Latin Caucasians.

unquestioned and absolute supremacy of the father and b) the necessary and absolute self-sacrifice of the mother" (Díaz-Guerrero 3).

Most scholarly observers of the contemporary Mexican-American family have tended to see it as a northern manifestation of the traditional Mexican variety; compared with the Anglo-American family, it appears to scholars to be static, oppressive, and even pathological, particularly in its treatment of women. According to this widespread view, the major culprit in the Mexican-American family is the notorious macho, who terrorizes his wife and daughters and leads a life of reckless promiscuity. In this sort of environment, Mexican-American girls, the conventional sociological wisdom maintains, suffer low self-esteem, lack competitive drive, and exhibit high levels of neurotic behavior.

Recently, a group of Mexican-American scholars has attempted to draw a more balanced portrait of the Mexican-American family, contending that over the past forty years or more it has demonstrated a very high adaptability to the cultural and social circumstances of the United States. In this view, the Mexican-American macho has evolved into a more sensitive figure who helps his wife to establish a loving and nurturing environment for their children. When contemporary Mexican-Americans refer to their fathers as macho, they wish to indicate respect and admiration. In this revisionist view, machismo "is not a pathological force or a tool for protecting male prerogatives, but a mechanism for upholding family pride and honor" (Mirandé 151). This reassessment of machismo and the family does not reject the conventional view that Mexican-American families are patriarchal; rather it simply depicts the mode of patriarchy more favorably. Despite his resistance to change, the Mexican-American father has loosened the bonds of patriarchy.

As Mexican-American scholars have argued that machismo has softened, they have also maintained that Mexican-American women have gained in influence and autonomy. Recent studies demonstrate that mothers have greater decision-making power than previously believed. Daughters now exercise greater freedom than in earlier generations; the practice of arranged marriages, for example, has all but disappeared. Although their fathers may still prefer conventional roles, Mexican-American daughters clearly have a wider range of career choices. These changes, of course, are relative: Mexican-American daughters today are still supervised more carefully than their brothers, and they still complain that their fathers are overprotective.

If we look beyond the scholarship to biographical and fictional treatments of Mexican-American family life, we find considerable evidence supporting the view that it has changed inexorably since the beginning of the century. In a recent collection of autobiographical statements, four generations of Mexican-American women from New Mexico talk about some of the changes. One *viejita,* "old woman," recalls that at town dances in the early years of the century girls were closely chaperoned and were not allowed to speak privately to men. Girls were sent off into marriage by their fathers, usually by age seventeen. The *viejita* recalls the fear of these girls as they were suddenly transformed from sheltered daughters into wives and mothers (Elsasser, Mackenzie, and Tixier y Vigil 9). The older women invariably remember their fathers as stern, punishing figures but with affection. Explains one: "My father was a very, very strict man. Now that I realize why he was, I'm happy that he was" (30). The younger women describe somewhat different relationships with their fathers. A middle-aged single mother of nine children who supports herself as a house painter recalls that her father taught her to work hard in case she "got herself a bum" (106). And a young and very modern woman speaks lovingly of her father's support of her political activities but also notes that when she left home to work in politics, he traveled with her to approve her living arrangements (128).

The changes that have come over Mexican-American families in the last several generations have not always been accepted gracefully, particularly by fathers who could hardly bear to see a part of their authority slip away. José Antonio Villarreal's *Pocho,* the first major Mexican-American novel written in English, treats the experience of Americanization as it affects a California family in the years just before World War II. The major character in the book is Richard Rubio, who records his father's steady deterioration in the face of American culture. Juan Rubio is one of the great old-fashioned machos of Mexican-American fiction, a violent man who fought in the Mexican Revolution and esteems women in inverse proportion to the annoyance they cause him. After the Revolution, Rubio labors in the agricultural fields of California but eventually installs his family in a home in Santa Clara. Early in the novel, Consuelo, Juan's wife, seems the perfect mate for him. As Richard explains, "She always followed rules and never asked the why of them" (62). But as the novel proceeds, Consuelo, influenced by "American ideas," awakens sexually and begins to question her husband's authority. These developments are difficult enough for Juan to accept, but he must also deal with the growing independence of his six daughters.[9] Villarreal makes clear that traditional Mexican patriarchy is untenable in the liberal environment of the United States. Juan, his sense of masculinity threatened on all sides, becomes more intractable and dreams of returning to Mexico. By the end of the novel, the Rubio household is in shambles. Luz, the oldest daughter, mocks her father and finally ignores his commands totally. His authority destroyed, Juan abandons his family to cohabit with a sixteen-year-old girl recently arrived from Mexico and thus, presumably, thoroughly trained in the art of submissiveness.

Villarreal tries to sympathize with the Rubio women's desire for greater personal freedom, but his heart is with Juan. Through Richard, Villarreal expresses his view that the Rubio family, thrust so suddenly into an alien culture, is bound to come apart under the weight of Americanization. Juan is faulted for his unwillingness to cede any of his authority, but the fact remains that the family indeed functions best when he is in full command. Consuelo and Luz are justified in their complaints but have no ability to lead the family. As Richard watches his family disintegrate, he realizes that "a family could not survive when the woman desired to command" (134). At the close of the novel, Richard is now mature and responsible, his heart set on becoming a writer; his sister Luz (the only daughter whose character is developed), without a father's authority, is still angry and confused, probably headed for trouble.

Other male Mexican-American writers have supported traditional patriarchy. In *Chicano,* Richard Vásquez traces the effects of Americanization through several generations of the Sandoval family. Most of the Sandoval men are exaggerated machos who abandon wives to marry other women and otherwise flaunt their masculinity. As the family settles in the United States, cracks in its patriarchal structure begin to appear almost immediately. Daughters talk back to their fathers, complain about strict supervision, and leave home without permission. When one daughter, Angelina, decides to leave her father's house, he replies: "I know this never would have happened in Mexico. It's because you see all the gringas, who have no sense of proper behavior. No one looks after the gringas to see that every man that happens by doesn't take advantage of them. It's because you've seen them in their loose way that you no longer want to have propriety" (82). The Sandoval women continue to drift away from their fathers and their traditional culture, ultimately with terrible consequences. The novel comes to focus on Mariana, an intelligent and sensitive young woman whose father, Pete, has allowed her an uncharacteristic amount of freedom as a "cultural concession." Mariana begins to date an Anglo college student who finds Mariana, her family, and her culture rather exotic. In an utterly predictable series of events, Mariana gets pregnant, is abandoned by her Anglo lover, and dies from a bungled abortion.

The argument implicit in Vásquez's novel follows a line of thought traceable to the medieval Spaniards and the pre-Columbian Aztecs. Although Mariana is decent enough, she is still a woman, vulnerable to male predators. Without strict paternal supervision, she will inevitably be corrupted. It is among the oldest of stories, updated to point out the dangers of American culture (in the person of Mariana's Anglo lover) to Mexican-Americans. Pete's "cultural concession" becomes a tragic mistake, and the reader is left with Vásquez's confirmation that daughters

151

and families survive only through the strict exercise of patriarchy.

If male Mexican-American writers have frequently defended patriarchal family structure, it is not surprising that a number of women writers have sought to dismantle it. One of the most promising developments in Mexican-American writing over the past fifteen years has been the emergence of various talented women writers, a phenomenon that itself suggests that Mexican-American family structure is changing to allow women broader educational and career opportunities. The appearance of women writers augers still more change, for to take up a career as a woman author is to make a commitment against the conventions of Mexican-American womanhood: humility, passivity, and, most of all, silence.

In Mexican-American literature by women, the father is conspicuous by his absence. Mexican-American women have written extensively about their mothers and grandmothers, sisters and brothers, girlfriends and boyfriends, but very little about their fathers. Apparently, the Mexican-American father remains for his daughters a remote, aloof, and ever shadowy figure who takes little interest in their routine affairs. His presence is felt indirectly, however, through a series of rigid family rules that daughters find oppressive and archaic. In the short story "Growing," Helena Maria Villamontes describes the feelings of Naomi, a fourteen-year-old who is chaperoned everywhere by her younger sister in accordance with her father's wishes. "America is different," Naomi argues, "here girls don't need chaperones." Hoping for support, Naomi turns to her mother, who only shrugs and says: "You have to talk to your father." When Naomi approaches her father to request relief from his harsh rules, he is unyielding: "Tú eres mujer [you are a woman] he thundered, and that was the end of any argument, any question, and the matter was closed because he said these three words as if they were a condemnation from heaven" (66). As the story ends, Naomi realizes that her father had lost trust in her when "her body began to bleed." In contrast, her father trusts the younger sister, Lucia, precisely because she has not reached puberty. In the final sentence of the story, Naomi whispers to Lucia: "Enjoy being a young girl because you will never enjoy being a woman" (73).

The tradition of suppressing female sexuality and the persistence of conventional machismo make for a high degree of sexual tension between fictional Mexican-American daughters and fathers. Several stories by Mexican-American writers, both female and male, treat the difficulty Mexican-American girls have in telling their fathers about the onset of menstruation. On the surface, girls feel simply that their fathers will not understand "female problems." But more deeply, this difficulty of communication points to certain sexual fears of both father and daughter.

152

The father does not want to confront the fact that his daughter is now physically a woman. He fears the emerging sexuality that normally accompanies menstruation; he fears most of all that he will be drawn to it. The daughter, having witnessed all her life male attempts to suppress women's sexuality, understands, as Naomi does in the Villamontes story, that her emerging womanhood raises the possibility of sexual longing for her father. In some ways, his very remoteness makes him more appealing.

The vexing issue of daughter-father sexuality is not usually treated explicitly by Mexican-American women writers, many of whom are restrained by traditional standards of politeness. In her poem "I Sing to Myself," Alma Villanueva only touches the issue but suggests nonetheless that whatever the potential dangers of sexual feelings between daughter and father, they are less painful than the absence of affection altogether:

> I could weep and rage
> against the man who never
> stroked my child fine hair
> who never felt the pride of
> my femininity grow in his loins
> never desired me in a secret father's way
> the man who
> > dropped his seed in my mother's
> > womb, then called it quits   (99).

One of the most skillful depictions of the daughter-father bond is Estela Portillo Trambley's "The Paris Gown," which focuses on a Mexican woman, Clotilde, who has settled in Paris as an art dealer. She is an elegant figure, much admired by her granddaughter, Theresa, who is visiting her. Theresa, coming from a traditional patriarchal family, is excited by her grandmother's independence and asks how she achieved it. Clotilde begins with a recollection of her father's misogyny, his belief that a man "must never allow a woman to outdo him" (5). The father resents Clotilde's talents, especially because they are greater than his son's. "I was just a daughter, an afterthought," Clotilde explains. When she speaks out against his unkindness, he accuses her of insanity and threatens to have her sent to a nunnery, that traditional dumping ground for willful women in Hispanic culture.

After more difficulty with her, Clotilde's father arranges a marriage to a wealthy old widower, pleased that he has accomplished a good business transaction as well as rid himself of a troublemaker. Initially stunned by the news, Clotilde recovers to plot her escape. She feigns interest in the upcoming engagement ball, and her father, happy that she is now "lost in her own frivolity," lavishes her with affection and even buys her a Paris wedding gown. At the engagement, the orchestra plays, and Clotilde waits in her bedroom, ready to make her descent down a long staircase. She hears her father call her name, and she appears. To the astonishment of everyone, she is not wearing her Paris gown but is "stark naked." For Clotilde, her action is perfectly symbolic, an expression not only of her defiance but of her abused innocence.

The displeasure Mexican-American women express over their relationships with their fathers is occasionally mitigated by the awareness that their fathers' lives are hard and their work generally unrewarding. Sandra Cisneros, in a humorous and poignant collection of fictional sketches entitled *The House on Mango Street,* presents a father who spends little time with his daughter, not out of indifference, but simply because he works such long hours to support his family. Cisneros creates a vivid image of the father, still tired from the previous day's work, dressing silently in the morning dark. For the daughter, the father's silence is a virtue, indicating his pride and endurance. At one point, the daughter hears of her grandfather's death in Mexico and wonders what she would do if her own father died. Cisneros has struck an important issue here: the economic exploitation of Mexican-Americans, both men and women. The perception is incompletely formed, but Cisneros's sympathetic daughter intuits that her father is himself a victim, overworked and underpaid, demoralized by his inability to pull his family out of the barrio.

The economic factor figures somewhat differently in Rita Gutiérrez-Christensen's "Eulogy for a Man from Jalostitlan," by any measure the most effusive literary treatment of a Mexican-American patriarch. In this poem, the father is a farm worker who has raised four daughters on his own, cooking and cleaning and nurturing his children before and after long days in the fields. He shares with his daughters a sense of triumphant struggle against long odds. The poet remembers the constant poverty and the family outings during which quail eggs are gathered for supper. Through the hardship, the father holds his dignity and gently directs his daughters towards a better life. When all his daughters eventually buy their family homes, he plants fruit trees against the possibility of misfortune.

In many ways, the "man from Jalostitlan" is a typical Mexican-American patriarch, autocratic, proud, and intimidating, but these qualities are balanced by the capacity for kindness and love. For the poet, there is no inherent incompatibility between machismo and tenderness. At the father's funeral, families of farm workers gather, not only to mourn his death but to celebrate the institution of fatherhood that he epitomized.

On the most fundamental level, these diverse biographical and literary depictions suggest that Mexican-American family structure is not as rigid as scholars have generally supposed. Degrees of acculturation and assimilation vary from family to family, making possible considerable variety in daughter-father relationships. The longstanding Mexican paradigm of the obedient, passive daughter and the powerful, unyielding father has begun to crack under the pressure of American principles of egalitarianism. This is not to say that Anglo-American culture is without inequities in its own daughter-father relationships, but they seem less severe than those long associated with Mexican-American family structure.

The frustration and impatience that Mexican-American women have expressed about their relations with tradition-minded fathers is, to some extent, the result of their American point of reference. Influenced by contemporary modes of feminism in this country, they tend to see, not how far Mexican-American family structure has evolved, but how much further it needs to change. The prevailing feeling is still one of considerable oppressiveness. Cherríe Moraga, a powerful and provocative writer who calls herself a "Chicana feminist lesbian," expressed her gratitude that while her mother was Mexican-American, her father was Anglo: "Had I been born of a Chicano father, I sometimes think I never would have been able to write a line or participate in a demonstration" (112–13). Moraga may not be a typical spokesperson for Mexican-American women, but her sense of the Mexican-American father as stifling is widely shared.[10]

Regarding the response of Mexican-American fathers to the views of their daughters, we can say little. The fathers hold to form: silent and seemingly remote from their daughters' daily affairs. In Mexican-American literature, very few daughter-father relationships are presented from the latter's point of view, and these invariably seem superficial or ephemeral. To be sure, one can make the same point about father-son relationships: they are almost always presented from the son's perspective.[11] Probably, this situation is largely the result of the fact that while Mexican-American literature has grown in volume and craftsmanship during the past twenty years, it has been created largely by relatively young people without long experience as parents. Allowing for this, however, there still seems to be at work something cultural, some enduring psychological quality of the Mexican-American father: he provides, he leads, he instructs, he oppresses; but he does not talk about it.

Notes

I want to acknowledge the inadvertent assistance of my daughter Sara in the preparation of this essay. Over the past thirteen years she has called my attention, lovingly and otherwise, to the issue of daughter-father relationships.

1. The woman who rejects vehemently the role of obedient daughter and wife—*la mujer esquiva*—and seems aloof, passionless, and indifferent to men appears regularly in Spanish Golden Age drama. Where these women appear, the action of the play usually focuses on inducing them towards conventional roles (see McKendrick). The modern Mexican equivalent of *la mujer esquiva* is *la mala mujer,* "the bad woman."

2. Luis Valdez's *Corridos,* a recent theatrical production built around a series of traditional Mexican and Mexican-American songs, features a performance of "La Delgadina." *Corridos* played in Los Angeles in December 1984.

3. This translation in English, by Américo Paredes, is provided solely for the reader's convenience. No attempt has been made to retain the meter and other poetic qualities of the original.

4. Various observers, most notably Samuel Ramos in his classic *Profile of Man and Culture in Mexico,* have detected a national inferiority complex in Mexico. As to the matter of Malinche's current reputation, here is a translation of a stanza from "La Maldición de Malinche" (The Curse of Malinche), a song recently popular in Mexico:

Oh, curse of Malinche!
Sickness of the present.
When will you leave my country?
When will you free my people?   (qtd. in Mirandé and Enríquez 247)

5. A recent work by a prominent Mexican-American writer, Rudolfo Anaya, entitled *The Legend of La Llorona,* also presents Malinche as the first crying woman. Anaya is sympathetic to Malinche and invests her with tragic but noble qualities.

6. Interestingly, some scholars have linked Tonantzin to Cihuacóatl, the weeping goddess from whom *la llorona* derives. So it may be that the greatest and most terrible of legendary Mexican women have a common origin.

7. "Greater Mexico" refers to the region of the present southwestern United States—Texas, New Mexico, Colorado, Arizona, and California—where large numbers of people of Mexican heritage live and preserve their cultural identity. All of this region, of course, was once owned by Mexico. Texas won its independence in 1836 and entered the Union a decade later. In 1848, as part of the settlement to end the Mexican War, the other territories were taken over by the United States. The term "Greater Mexico" comes from Américo Paredes.

8. The frequent appearance of lizards, snakes, and other reptiles in Mexican-American folklore has been thoughtfully analyzed by Rosan A. Jordan in her essay "The Vaginal Serpent."

9. Juan's fathering of so many daughters and only one son is ironic, since Mexican machos are said to greatly prefer sons over daughters.

10. Moraga is also notable for her attempt along with other Mexican-American women writers to revise the image and reputation of Malinche. See Moraga 98–101.

11. Not surprisingly, sons depict their relationships with their fathers much more positively than women do. Villarreal's *Pocho* is a case in point; Rudolfo Anaya's *Bless Me, Ultima* is another.

HORTENSE J. SPILLERS

"The Permanent Obliquity of an In[pha]llibly Straight": In the Time of the Daughters and the Fathers

THE TITLE'S REFERENCE to a passage from *Moby-Dick* is itself an obliquity in relationship to the theme of this essay. But I adopt it here as a kind of lookout on the subject as it concerns kinship and filiation among African-Americans cast as daughters and fathers. In short, the line of inheritance from a male parent to a female child is not straight. It is "oblique," since she, if everybody looks handsome, will one day shed his name, his law, and the effects of his household for another male's. In that regard, the patriarchal daughter remains suspended as a social positionality between already established territories. Bearing a name that she carries by courtesy of legal fiction and bound towards one that she must acquire in order "to have" her own children, "daughter" maintains status only insofar as she succeeds in disappearing, in deconstructing into "wife" and "mother" of *his* children. This is the familiar law of high patriarchist culture in a heterosexual synthesis as the little girl imbibes it, and from then on she is a more or less willing agent in the text of a cultural conspiracy. Among African-Americans in the midst of violent historical intervention that, for all intents and purposes, has *banished* the father, if not in fact *murdered* him, the father's law embodies still the guilt that hovers: one feels called upon to "explain," make excuses for, his "absence." But the African-American-father-gone is the partial invention of sociologists, as the African-American female-as-daughter is consumed in their thematics of the "Black Matriarchate" (Frazier; Rainwater and Yancey).

This lopsided textual sociometry which eats up female difference and identity in notions of the ahistoric Familius Aeternus essentially reconfigures in fiction by black American writers as a *puzzle*, not a *closure*. This articulated problematic comes nearer the "truth" because it plants ambiguity at the heart of an interpretation of the father's law. What secrets do these texts cover up? Maya Angelou's *I Know Why the Caged Bird Sings*, putative "autobiography"; Gayle Jones's *Corregidora*; James Baldwin's *Just Above My Head*; Ralph Ellison's *Invisible Man*; Alice Walker's "The Child Who Favored Daughter" (From *In Love and Trouble*) and *The Color Purple,* all embody fictions concerned in part with fathers and daughters and all posit an incestuous link between them. But of these selected texts, only Ellison's *Invisible Man* and Walker's "The Child Who Favored Daughter" project a sufficient symbolic apparatus that renders a sustained contemplation of the theme of father-daughter incest bearable. Indeed, it seems that certain ideas, like the face of the Divine, can only be approached with a very wide-angle lens; intimations of incest are among them.

It seems that parent-child incest, in its various ramifications, remains the preeminent dream-thought that not only evades interpretation (or dreaming) but is so layered itself in avoidance and censorship that an interpretive project regarding it appears ludicrous and useless. On one level of imagination incest simply *cannot* occur and never does (Roustang). Under the auspices of denial, incest becomes the measure of an absolute negativity, the paradigm of the outright assertion *against*—the resounding "no!" But on the level of the symbolic, at which point the "metaevent" is sovereign, incest translates into the unsayable, which is all the more sayable by the very virtue of one's muteness before it. The fictions of incest therefore repose in the involuted interfaces between ephemeral event and interpretive context, but more than that, these fictions materialize that "other" and alien life that we *cannot* recognize or acknowledge (and it's probably a good thing!) as being for consciousness. In that regard, fictions about incest provide an enclosure, a sort of confessional space for and between postures of the absolute, and in a very real sense it is only in fiction—from the psychoanalytic session to the fictive rendering—that incest as dramatic enactment and sexual economy can take place at all. Whether or not father-daughter incest actually happens, and with what frequency, is not a problem for *literary* interpretation. For good or ill, it belongs to the precincts of the local police department (and the "cat" should go to jail).

But before we attempt a reading of portions of Walker's and Ellison's work, we should make a handful of admissions that *are* permissible. I attempt this writing, in fact, as the trial of an interlocking interrogation that I am persuaded of by only 50 percent: Is the Freudian landscape an applicable text (say nothing of appropriate) to social and historical situations that do not replicate moments of its own cultural origins and involvements? The prestigious Oedipal dis-ease/complex, which apparently subsumes the Electra myth, embeds in the heterosexual "nuclear family," which disperses its fruits in vertical array. The father's law, the father's name, pass "down" in concentrated linearity and exclusion: not only "one man, one woman," but these two—this law—in a specific locus of economic and cultural means. But how does this model, or does this model, suffice for occupied or captive persons and communities in which the rites and rights of gender-function have been exploded *historically* into sexual neutralities?

The original captive status of African females and males in the context of American enslavement permitted none of the traditional rights of consanguinity. The laws of the North American Slave Code stipulated that the newborn would follow the status of its *mother* (Davis; Goodell)—the *partus sequitur ventrem*—but that stroke of legal genius, while it assured the hegemony of the dominant class, did nothing to establish maternal prerogative for the African female. The child, though flesh of her flesh, did not "belong" to her, just as the separation of mothers and children becomes a primary social motif of the Peculiar Institution. Exceptions to the gender rule intrude a note of the arbitrary, but this very arbitrariness, depending on individual instances of human kindness in slaveholders, throws in even bolder relief the subjugative arrangements of the "institution." For the African female, then, the various inflections of patriarchalized female gender—"mother," "daughter," "sister," "wife"—are not available in the historical instance.

If North American slavery in its laws outraged the classic status of motherhood in the African case, then it asymmetrically complicated notions of fatherhood. In effect, the African person was twice-fathered but *could not* be claimed by the one and *would not* be claimed by the other. The person, following the "condition" of the mother, very often bears only a first name—Niger I, Niger II, Phoebe, Cassius, Jane, Sue (Myers). While the suppression of the patronymic engenders a radically different social and political economy for African-Americans, it involves us, relatedly, in nested semiotic readings. Not only is the African name "lost" to cultural memory, but on that single ground the captive African is symbolically broken in two, ruptured along the fault of a "double consciousness" (DuBois) in which the break with an indigenous African situation is complete, but one's cultural membership in the American one remains inchoate. A social subject in abeyance, in an absolute deferral that becomes itself a new synthesis, is born: the African-American, whose last name, for all intents and purposes, becomes historically *X*, the mark of his or her borrowed culture's profound "illiteracy."

In this fatal play of literally misplaced/displaced names, the African father is figuratively banished; fatherhood, at best a cultural courtesy, since only the mother knows for sure, is not a social fiction into which he enters. Participation in the life of his children, indeed the rights of patriarchal privilege, are extended to him at someone else's behest. In this historic instance, the "unnatural" character of the reproductive process is rendered startlingly clear: reproduction is covered by culture, in culture, at every stage, so that "free" sexuality remains the scandalous secret in the father's house. Only by executive order and legislative edict does re-productive process gain cultural legitimacy for African-Americans as *freed* persons, which suggests the origins of the myth of parenting in sociopolitical consensus. In this calculus of motives, the "master" and his class—those subjects of an *alternative* fatherhood—cannot be said to be "fathers" of African-American children at all (without the benefit of quotation marks), since by their own law the newborn follows the "con-dition" of the mother. But in those instances where they were begetters of children, the puzzle of the father is fully elaborated. As "owners" of human "property," they offer impediment to the operations of kinship; by denial of kinship, they act out symbolically the ambiguous character of fatherhood itself, perpetuating it in this case as blank parody. In that regard, the notorious *X,* adopted by illiterate persons as the signatory mark and by quite literate black American Muslims in the twentieth-century United States as the slash mark against a first offensive, comes to stand for the blank drawn by father's "gun."

We situate ourselves, then, at the center of a "mess," altogether convoluted in its crosshatch of historic purposes. There is no simple way to state the case, but crudely put, we might ask, To what extent do the texts of a pyschoanalytic ahistoricism, out of which the *report,* the *trans-actions,* of incest arise, abrade or reveal against the historic scene and its subsequent drama? Does the Freudian text translate, in short (and here we would include the Freudian progeny, Lévi-Strauss and Lacan among them)? This question in its various guises provides the background against which the hermeneutical enterprise unfolds to the black schol-ar/critic. We are a long way from specific acts of texts, but every (black) reader shall be discomfitted. Let that be a law, inasmuch as one is at-tempting to read not only a given text—Foucault's "parallelepiped"—and the vortices of subtexts spinning around it but also this against and/or despite those pretexts that neither go away nor yield the secret.

The preeminent rule of incest is that everybody has one (Lévi-Strauss). This universal prohibition involves us in a democracy of an-cient scandal that must be related in some sense to the architectonics of domesticity. If possible, children have their own bed in their own room, as do adults, or the circumstance (at least in America) is identified as "poverty." By age six the child, mysteriously, has already acquired a sexual consciousness and loses her place in the parental bed *between* the lovers. The Lacanian "imaginary" has long ago dissipated into the "sym-bolic"—the realm of division, of father-sovereignty (Eagleton, *Literary Theory;* Lacan, *Ecrits* and *Language of the Self*). But how many layers of flesh, like so many blankets, are required to cover household carnality? The violation of this fundamental layering generates the drama of Ellison's Trueblood clan in *Invisible Man,* and Houston Baker's interpretation of the incest scene is solidly grounded in an economically determined reading. The latter, however, seeks perspective, with Baker's model of the black artist, grounded, in turn, in an American cultural situation. "Daughter," however, drops out of Baker's critical protocol into an elaboration of "family." But in the sexual confusion engendered by incest, "family" loses the delicate balance of sexual economy and hierarchization that makes "father" father, "daughter" daughter, and the entire household gender-distinctive. It would appear that the incest prohibition obtains to a symbolic function as well as an actual and historic one: in order to fix the male and female in specific cultural work, it is *male* sexuality that must be sealed off, impeded, by implication, in order to *found* female sexuality and its limits. It is not surprising, then, that the legends of incest are "male-identified," phallogocentrically determined.

But the excess inherent in the prohibitive nature of incest also leads us to suspect that it engages us (under wraps) with its opposite—the *failure* of potence as human possibility, which is the only way we could explain the unwritten father's law that surrounds and covers the nubile young female in his household (Walker, "The Child Who Favored Daughter" 35). Alice Walker inscribes her story "The Child Who Favored Daughter" with this epigram: "that my daughter should / fancy herself in love / with *any* man! / How can this be?" (my italics). Why does father need to pose to himself such an inquiry unless there is an element of too much protest? In other words, the drama of incest as it plays in fiction expresses the fatherly fear—on the level of the symbolic   that his "cargo" is hardly sufficient to bring under permanent rein the sexual impulses represented (in his own febrile imagination) by the silent and mighty sexuality of the females within his precincts. Why else would the father want to appropriate a lover's status (since, theoretically, *all other* women outside his "sphere of influence" are available to him) unless the very ground on which his sexuality is founded (the household) threatens to slide beneath him in the prohibitive mark itself? These counters of interdiction, then, do not ease the way to a phallic sovereignty but open to even greater exposure the principle upon which a threatened male sexuality is said to turn.

The entire tale of incest in *Invisible Man* is told by Trueblood, who is also a singer of the blues, "a good tenor." For all intents and purposes, the wife/mother Kate and the daughter/surrogate lover Matty Lou are deprived of speech, of tongue, since what they said and did and when are reported/translated through the medium of Trueblood. These silent figures, like materialized vectors in a field of force, are *interestingly* silent in the sense that incest fiction, even written by women, *never*, as far as I know, establishes the *agency* of the incestuous act inside the female character. This fiction in a fiction, central to the kind of symbolic content that the "I" must absorb in order to achieve the "biographical" uses of history, is articulated, appropriately, on the margins of the novel's "society." In the approach to the Trueblood cabin, the driver of the car that bears "Mr. Norton" must turn off the highway "down a road that seemed unfamiliar. There were no trees and the air was brilliant. Far down the road the sun glared cruelly against a tin sign nailed to a barn. A lone figure bending over a hoe on the hillside raised up wearily and waved, more a shadow against the skyline than a man" (31). Farther on, we are told that taking a hill, the occupants of the chauffeured car are "swept by a wave of scorching air and it was as though we were approaching a desert" (36). This abrupt fall into an alternative topographical center catches "invisible man" and his charge out on a radically different plain of human and symbolic activity wherein the play of signs between interlocutors focuses a mismatch of meanings and intentions. Because the road by which he is traveling is "unfamiliar" to "invisible man," he both knows it and does not, which would suggest that he has no idea where he is and every right to dread the undifferentiated and impulsive intimations hinted in the "crude, high, plaintively animal sounds Jim Trueblood made as he led [his] quartet" in song (36–37). "Out here," where time has ceased, attested in the parallelism and contrast between an ox team, sunlight on a tin sign, a lone figure bending over a hoe, and "a powerful motor purring" in the precise articulations of a *measurable* and oscillating "mph," we are prepared, without even knowing it, for a venture into the marginal state; the suspension of "rules"; the cultural vestibularity that transports us to the region of "danger and power" (Douglas). But "danger" and "power" for whom? In a traditional reading of this powerfully *intruded* narrative, Jim Trueblood emerges wealthier, healthier (because of "new wealth," we are led to suppose), and wise. But is it true?

In his marginality, Trueblood becomes a twice-marked figure: (1) by his literally peripheral status to the novel's college community from which he is set apart, as though "criminal" and contaminated (as he is, in fact, according to the rules of "civilization"); and (2) by the imaginably hideous, fly-swarmed ax mark that he will carry a fictional eternity, inflicted by his wife Kate, who sides with civilization and determines, according to Trueblood's imitation of her, that he "done fouled." This terrible scar that designates him (until his "change comes") a mesmerized, agonized precultural inscription suggests that no *man* crosses the boundary of undifferentiated sexuality, even in a dream, unless he is prepared to pay the cost of a crucifixion/castration. Even though the evidence tells us no such thing about Trueblood, since wife *and* daughter are simultaneously pregnant, as though the promise of a twin birth, we might imagine that Ellison's narrator suggests—between the lines, where the actual sex act has indeed occurred—that Trueblood not only has copulated his last "blow" but will live to tell his privation (equal to the silence of the pregnant female) over and over again in a stunning repetition crisis, in a riveting narrative obsession that resembles in every way the awful perambulatory nightmare of Coleridge's "ancient mariner." Trueblood tells his story because he cannot help himself, and he has no idea why "white" men in their exhibitionist urge need to *pay* him (somebody-anybody) to hear what they would love to perform. Trueblood becomes their whore/gal of "dangerous," "powerful" entertainment, appointed to maintain their notions of the "civilized" (by refocusing marginality as a living space) as well as provide them the "kicks" they need—substituting his *flesh* for their distanced and protected bodies—that orality renders. This *oral* tale is articulated in a *novel*, a *writing*, as Trueblood enters the chain of signifiers as an item of syntax, albeit a powerful one. But the tale is essentially absorbed as an aspect of elixir with which "invisible man" "returns" to the "world" as a "novelist," as one who has discarded rather more simplified narrative urges. Trueblood is the "man" "invisible man" must slay, then reencounter, and make articulate, if he will comprehend the coeval period of African-American consciousness. Trueblood is, as Baker contends, the "true blood," and that is precisely the problem.

The violation of the incest taboo entangles Trueblood, it seems, in his own blood lines, which merge inner and outer at the source of difference—the ahistoric, reified female. So trammeled, father/man, as such, disappears into an "endless" progression of enclosures that replicate the vaginal/uterine structure in which "he" has every right to fear that "he" will get "lost" and, quite correctly, fall bereft of his "penal" powers. I am not certain that this reading is right, but Ellison's narrator has so loaded the dream sequence—the major portion of the tale—with an invaginated symbolic plan that we seem justified in reading the breach of the incest taboo, as it is elaborated in this scene, as a symptom of an inverted castration complex. We could say, if this notion holds water, that the implanted fetus *is* the male loss, as the vaginal vault "swallows" the thrust towards it. Taking the relevant text apart at this point might be helpful.

As Trueblood explains to an anxious, greedy-for-adventure Norton, the family, on the particular night of cold, huddles together for warmth—"me on one side and the ole lady on the other and the gal in the middle" (42). The daughter's intermediary posture here is highly suggestive. Since Matty Lou is pubescent, we might say that she is made to effect a sexually competitive possibility between father and mother. In that sense, we are close to a marriage of three. From another point of view, the intervening child body poses as a "cock blocker," a strategy of contraception that is not necessarily recognized as such. In that sense, the male must "penetrate" layers of mediation in order to reach the "target," and as unhappy fathers "unbedded" by the presence of little-boy sons grudgingly admit, no man can get through all that. But the narrator plants a female body in this space for quite obviously practical narrative reasons. We might wonder to what extent, under the circumstances, "daughter," in this case, forms a collusive bond with "mother" in opposition to the wonted powers of the male organ. From this angle, the *doubled* female body becomes a frontier that offers resistance to assault: in order to "enter," Trueblood must first climb Brodnax Hill, as it were, and run the gauntlet of a scalding landscape before the awful climax of this tale can be reached.

Falling off to sleep in this "dark, plum black" atmosphere, Trueblood thinks his way back to Mobile and a particular young woman he knew then. Living in a two-story house on the river, Trueblood and his lover would listen to the sounds of the Mississippi and of boats moving along it. But sound modulates into visual synaesthesia, translating into "young juicy melons split wide open a layin all spread out and cool and sweet on top of all the striped green ones like it's waitin just for you, so you can see how red and ripe and juicy it is and all the shiny black seeds it's got and all" (43). These contiguous rhetorical properties that render sound visible suggest not only the loosening of coherence, as the liminal state between waking and dreaming induces, but also the lapse of distinctions that sustains the boundaries between parts of the family. Trueblood, at this point, transforms into the mercurial "boundary crosser," no longer conscious that it is his "daughter" sleeping beside him. But this loss of customary place that installs us on a frontier of danger and power has already been prepared for by the sort of sleeping arrangements that adhere and according to the absence of even a hint of light. As Trueblood tells it, the room is as "black as the middle of a bucket of tar" (42). Things turn elemental—"me, the old lady and the gal"—even though Trueblood discovers a plenitude of narrative turns to elaborate the event.

If the preceding sequence might be termed a narrative "preplay," then what follows equals a full-dress "opening night." Trueblood "recalls," in the inauguration of the dream proper, that he is looking for "fat meat," but appropriate to the charged insinuations of nearly every line of his narrative, "fat meat" is exactly what we think it is—a full-grown "watermelon." One thinks also of the "strickoline," or "fat *back*," of a southern diet that garnishes a vegetable platter or offers a bacon substitute with a cerealized rice dish, buttermilk biscuits, and sweetened coffee spiked with Old Grandad. Many a southern child remembers that bourbon in certain southern households is refrigerated! Trueblood, aptly, then, is looking for the "grail" of his environment, as it runs parallel to the symbolically inscribed female flesh. Because it is *basic* for him, it is "holy," as one must risk his life, his sex, in order to have it. Yes, the "watermelons" are lying in wait for Jim Trueblood, but he "mistakes" the reasons why.

Because we are not responsible, we are told, in any ethical sense for what we dream and cannot be held accountable for what we desire, Trueblood is, technically speaking, not blameworthy. In fact, he was not "there" when it happened, so that he has committed no mistake, even though his "innocence" (de facto, or is his a guilt de jure?) provokes in him the sense of unconscionable error and the terrible consequence of guilty ignorance. Trueblood has prestigious precedent in this regard, as "invisible man" recalls a fictitious English professor "Woodridge," who assigned his class readings from "Greek plays" (31). But the single impenetrable element of the puzzle of fatherhood as Trueblood enacts it has to do with the manifestations of the feminine that appear across the dreamscape. It is as though another layer of intrusion is intercalated between Trueblood and "his woman/women," which introduces an Ellisonian "boomerang" into this otherwise "straight" Freudian family drama with an Electra twist. Brodnax holds the key to "fat meat," as Trueblood *climbs* to his place, but not finding the "master" "home," Trueblood enters anyway, and we appear to mix signals, momentarily, with Richard Wright's Bigger Thomas and the pervasive "whiteness" that surrounds Mary Dalton. Trueblood enters a door into a "big white bedroom," as on occasion with his "Ma," Trueblood has gone to the "big house."

But is "Ma" in this instance a function of the gigolo between her boy and "Miss Thang," so that, *for him,* carnality comes to rest in a surrogate female, the other woman, who initiates the young male into the ceremonies of the throbbing flesh? (In Faulkner's *Absalom, Absalom!* we are led to surmise that sexual license arises always *in* the other woman.) In Ellison's case, it is a "white" woman who engenders Trueblood's entré on the terrain of interdiction. A "white lady" steps out of a grandfather's clock, and she is robed in "white silky stuff and nothin else" (45). Clearly, we are meant to understand a doubling of the prohibitive effect in this scene, as we already know, without Trueblood's having to tell us, that "she" is "holding" him and "he" is "scared to touch her cause she's white" (45). But this "she" is holding his *fantasies* as much as anything else his dream body brings to bear on the scene; we could even say that Trueblood's body "perambulates" and materializes his fantasies, so that the "real" world of scarcity to which Trueblood is fixed like an object in protective coloration has always historically translated into a potentially mutilated body. In that regard, this transactional scene ejects a body turned inside out, in which case the symbolic thrust of the passage does nothing to disguise or ameliorate the real situation of the dreaming body.

The power and the danger that this moment projects apparently claim it under the auspices of pleasure, but the end—of the dream and of the tale—brings on Trueblood the truth of a severe disjuncture—the torn flesh of his face—the *branding* that establishes his deep knowledge of the forbidden female.

Frantz Fanon projects a "white" woman in the "big house" at the center of the displaced African male's prerevolutionary consciousness, but in the Fanonian scheme the "woman" appears to be a familiar appurtenance of a politicocultural empowerment. We expect from her (at this angle) an implacable muteness, just as Ellison's female bodies speak only through the embodied vocality of Jim Trueblood. But is it possible to retrieve from this representational cul-de-sac a different reading? How did this "woman" get in Trueblood's dream and/or the other way around? In other words, what does this scene suggest about the "daughter" of this incestuous coupling, and does "she," on the "lower frequencies"—which is exactly where *this* daughter occurs spatially in the dream, "beneath" the "blond"—speak also for the "white" woman?

Because Matty Lou, the "ole lady," "Ma," and the "white" woman—essentially appropriating the same function of the feminine, melding into a gigantically sexualized repertoire—all occupy the same semantic/symbolic fold, we have no business telling them apart, except that the intrusive markers of "whiteness" (and they fix this scene in obsessive repetition) signal the difference that we cannot overlook. But we assume that we know already what the not overlooking means. This shrouding detail not only offers an obstruction and evasion of what *might* have occurred—"that woman just seemed to sink outta sight, that there bed was so soft"—but also covers the identity of "daughter" so completely that she configures as an obscured aspect of landscape, a "dark tunnel . . . like the power plant they got up to the school":

> It's burnin' hot as iffen the house was caught on fire, and I starts to runnin', tryin' to get out. I runs and runs til I should be tired but ain't tired but feelin' more rested as I runs, and runnin' so good it's like flyin' and I'm flyin' and sailin' and floatin' right up over the town. Only I'm still in the *tunnel*. Then way up ahead I sees a bright light like a jack-o-lantern over a graveyard. It gets brighter and brighter and I know I got to catch up with it or else. Then all at once I was right up with it and it burst like a great big electric light in my eyes and scalded me all over. Only it wasn't a scald, but like I was drownin' in a lake where the water was hot on the top and had cold numbin' currents down under it. Then all at once I'm through it and I'm relieved to be out and in the cool daylight agin. (45–46)

Since Trueblood's dream is "literary," we have nothing, we assume, to "discover" that the narrator does not deliberately point out. The symbol system of the dream apparatus appears to work, then, both transparently and symbolically as the consciously manipulated stuff of a waking intelligence, working through Trueblood as a mimetic device. We rightly assume that Matty Lou and Trueblood are already sexually entangled at this point and that the "scalding" stands for an ejaculation. When Trueblood wakes, he will try "to move without movin," or having "flown" in, now "walk out" (46). But these contradictory signals point, in a deeper sense, to an even greater paradox, which I do not think the narrator foresees: the "white" woman becomes the symptom of a sexual desire that locates expression in the "daughter," so that the former is the term that drops out of sight, as the latter loses both human and social identity. We could say by way of these subtilized displacements that *sexuality,* domesticated as a sacralized body and firmly inscribed within an enclosure that hides its "true" purposes in objects of evasion, escape, décor, can only be executed in the "underground" of *sex,* the actual confrontation between the genitalia. This basic situation, wherein subjectivity "thingifies," transposes into an unlocalized space that is neither here nor there. This "u-topic" suspension, brought on by a "burning" house, that mobilizes the droll and the dreadful (a "jack-o-lantern over a graveyard") is appropriately undifferentiated, as the "dark tunnel" and the pit-dark in which the dreaming bodies sleep have already signaled. In this order of things, "father" "runs," "sails," "floats," as though rescued from the immediate situation that moors him even to a dream context, and "daughter" becomes the instrument of his "release." In this "dark" of the "oceanic," there are no "fathers" and "daughters," but only "children," whose being finds the perfectly magical formula that abandons them to the situation of a not-human other.

The scene splits wide open not only between a pair of female legs but at the moment of juncture between "houses"—"civilization," "sexuality," and a feminine body identified as such—and the "lay of the land" (I borrow freely from the title of Kolodny's brilliant study)—tunnels, graveyards, and the open air. But each of these externalized interiorities that suggests freedom within a uterine enclosure translates marginality—the "tunnel" is nowhere yet, and the "graveyard" describes the largest future. We are here in passage, at the entrance to the forbidden currents of a "civilized sexuality" under the auspices of a "white" man-not-at-home. That a "woman" guards the inner sanctum of Brodnax's "big house" poses "blond" and "daughter" in the way of a furious combat that neither can "win" *as such*. But even before these faces of the feminine can be brought into contact, the *intervened* masculine must be moved aside as the teller of the tale. There is no simple leaping this breach, and moreover, this sexual drama essentially poses a male and only one of the two females; if that is so, then "sexuality" also eludes the house of the father (or the circumstance of the "true blood") as that boundary across which subject/subjectivity cannot go. The "white" woman in that regard is fixed as the "female body in the West" (Suleiman) in the first and last *frontier* of a "barred subject" (Wilden). "Daughter," the stuff of which "she" is made, is established, relatedly, as a "barred subject," both plus and minus. That "she" bears the pregnant body shadows forth a fundamental economy of female signification: a body integrates and "hides" those layers of the flesh that give it identity and differentiation. There is at work in the "white" woman a "different" and informing "femininity" for which we yet have no name, except to call it "not woman." In this place of incestuous linkage, there is also "not man." In the fictional enactment of incest, then, black is not a color; it is a circumstance wherein human becomes thing, and thing turns human, in an absolute lapse of a hierarchical movement.

We would go farther: wherever incest occurs as a fictional/symbolic motion, it takes place in the "dark, plum black . . . as the middle of a bucket of tar." The shape, the outline, melt down in an inexorable play of sameness, of identities misplaced and exchanged. One can no more find a "father" here than she can a "daughter," and the one thing we cannot account for is Trueblood's "presence" in the "big house" in the first place. The male body *between* female stuff, the forbidden presence on the run from the "burning" dream house, renders a fugitive and an outlaw; this "father," in the twice-theft of the prohibited "gift," forms an analogy with the band of the banished brothers. But it is not Trueblood's place to "kill" the fathers who have run him off but the task of "invisible man" in the making of a fictionalized social order that resurrects history and steps into "culture"/differentiation. Here the theme of a fictional incest allows us to see closer up the *failure* of phallic signification, not its fulfillment.

Even though Alice Walker's "father," by implication, in "The Child Who Favored Daughter" executes "the judge, the giver of life" (35), his doing so impels him towards madness. In fact, the closural passage of the narrative, in its fierce immobilization of human and natural subjects, poses a sculptural stasis as (and in the place of a) dramatic immediacy: "today" hardly registers a near presence of chronology, but refers to all the "now"s that possibly roll in upon the standing mastectomy inflicted on the "child, who favored Daughter," who is *his* "daughter." These embodied surrogate motions, in which this "father" replays *his* father and this "daughter" replays his sister called "Daughter," touch neither time nor "realism" but intrude themselves as an awful lyrical moment of eleven published pages between a "birth" (the tale's inauguration) and a "death" (its closure) in the subjunctive passivity of an aftermath, stylized by anaphora and the hint of a paradox of motion:

Today he is slumped in the same chair facing the road. The yellow school bus sends up clouds of red dust on its way. If he stirs it may be to Daughter shuffling lightly along the red dirt road, her dark hair down her back and her eyes looking intently at buttercups and stray black-eyed susans along the way. If he stirs it may be he will see his own child, a black-eyed Susan from the soil on which she walks. A slight, pretty flower that grows on any ground; and flowers pledge no allegiance to banners of any man. If he stirs he might see the *perfection of an ancient dream still whispered about, undefined.* If he stirs he might feel the energetic whirling of wasps about his head and think of ripe late summer days and time when scent makes a garden of the air. If he stirs he might wipe dust from the dirt daubers out of his jellied eyes. If he stirs he might take up the heavy empty shotgun and rock it back and forth on his knees, like a baby. (45–46; my italics)

It is as though the narrator has not told us a tale at all, but a shorthand of one, an idea that lights across the mind and is gone. In that regard, "The Child Who Favored Daughter" renders a "dream" that actualizes a "nightmare" that reflects a "might have happened." But does this dreamer awake to discover that it is not so? Trueblood lives to *talk;* the "father" of "daughter" never did, except that in an unguarded moment of self-reflection the deepest layers of his psyche find a "ventriloquist." This story does not read like a "case history," but seems to embody one.

The story has two beginnings, one seen through the lens of the character called "child" (35–36), the other, over the same objective terrain of a "given" nature, filtered through the eyes of the character called "he" (37 ff.). In the second segment the narrator sketches in relevant psychological detail concerning his past—a beautiful and beloved sister "impaled on one of the steel-spike fences near the house." (39). "Cut down" by a father dishonored and shamed by her liaison with "the lord of his own bondage," she has already "recurred" in the atavistic nightmare alluded to in the opening line: "She knows he has read the letter," whose contents will crucify the "child." In this deadlock grid of "original sin" (and incest is certainly a candidate for "it"), and on the terrain of the intramural and internecine that "stages" the "family" as a network of shared neuroses, fathers and sons link back to a common ancestry of "unnamable desire" that threatens all females alike. In these lines of poetry from the tale, "sisters" and "spouses" enjamb across run-on lines that do not stop:

Memories of Years
Unknowable women—

sisters
spouses
illusions of soul   (39 [twice]; my italics)

Because "he" has lost "Daughter" and is never the same, "the wom-
en in his life faced a sullen barrier of distrust and hateful mockery. . . .
His own wife, beaten into a cripple to prevent her from returning the
imaginary overtures of the white landlord, killed herself while she was
still young enough and strong enough to escape him" (40). But she
leaves "a child, a girl, a daughter." Seizing on an absolutely striking
narrative/descriptive detail that becomes a powerful lacuna in the Walker
text, Harryette Mullen points out that Walker's female characters are
often in search of *mothers*. Specifically addressing *The Color Purple* as a
critique of patriarchy in the West, Mullen observes: "The story presupposes two things: a powerful black husband/father with the financial
means to dominate his family; and a weak, dead, or otherwise absent or
estranged mother who is unable to protect herself or her children from
this man" (45). I would not necessarily agree with Mullen that this man is
"powerful," but in the case of *The Color Purple* he is certainly powerful
enough, and enough is as much as a feast.

But certainly the critical thematic of the missing/absent mother
(who is always assumed) throws a different light on fictionalized father-
daughter incest. We recall that the mother of James Baldwin's Julia Miller
is deceased in *Just Above My Head* when Joel turns his daughter into more
than his sporadic lover; the mother figure of Maya Angelou's *I Know
Why the Caged Bird Sings* (1971) has either just abandoned her bed, with
her daughter in it, beside Freeman, or just left the house, permitting him
just the space of isolation he needs to ostracize himself and the twice-
abandoned girl child still further. In the tale of Trueblood, Kate, who will
raise very hell when she "dead" awakens, is asleep when her mate commits the mistake of his life. In Walker's *Color Purple*, Celie apparently
takes on the function of a surrogate wife, as in "The Child Who Favored
Daughter," "Daughter" becomes proto-, or Ur-lover, who makes "wife"
a superfluity, if not an outright impossibility. In effect, there can be no
"daughter" without "wife/mother," as this story lives and breathes the
consequences of such absence. Appropriately, a girl child springs up over
a female's dead body, having none of the prerogatives extended
"daughter" in the hierarchic, father-centered household. Exposed, therefore, to a childman, locked in powerful infantile memory that lives on
into the moment, Walker's "child" reinscribes the surrogate motions of a
man who wishes to sleep with his sister. Failing that, he "invents" a
female body who essentially reinstitutes the sister's erotic reign that leads
instead to daughter-murder.

There is an immediate cause of war in this male character's soul that offers an element of intrusion comparable to Trueblood's "white" woman of his dream. "Daughter" of the story, like the "real" "Daughter," loves a "white" man; she has apparently written him a "love letter," which becomes, in propinquity to the gun across his knees, a major dramatic prop of the tale. Armed with his "evidence"—"white man's slut!" (would it have made a difference had the "white" man married her? I doubt it)—he is determined to beat this hell out of her and to force her to deny that she wrote the letter, in short, to deny the erotic signature, behind which she stands firmly ensconced, that fills him with a desire that agonizes. And kills. We could say that this occasion marks one of those rare fictional instances in which a woman's "scribbling" will bring on her literal castration. These marks on the page precisely time and measure the short distance between her life and death, and we nearly wish that she had not written it, or had not been discovered or betrayed, until we realize that this is not an avoidable tale of detection: It is Walker's version of an allegory in which race becomes the most pellucid, loud alibi for the male to act out a fundamental psychodrama. Having had a sister whom he could not love in an open, consummated way, this "father" never finds love at all. Carnality knocks him down, and his response to it is typically "penal," punitive; he flails and beats; his medium, his memory, are guns, "steel-spiked fences," and great big butcher knives. In short, he is a perfect Sadeian sadist with none of the ostensible "pleasures," so far as we can tell. I doubt that the sniff of "white" man's flesh makes a great deal of difference here, except that it "breaks" the law, and this male character knows only that—the heat, the rush, the dread, the domination of his enforced, ball-busting, back-breaking labor. He will use his "gun," not where it counts, but only against one who will whimper and drag her hair in the dirt ground before him. Because he will toss her castrated breasts to the dogs, yelping at his feet, we are led to suppose, he joins them, and no man can or should live as a dog (even though some of them have done remarkably well as cockroaches). The ambiguous closure in which the male figure is either dead or as dead as we need him reminds us, however, that imputing "blame" and coming up with a "moral" are to render the story realistically. The narrator, I think, means anything *but* that, as we are called upon to observe, to inquire into a configuration of psychic forces, of imaginative possibilities that may or may not be enacted, as fictionalized incest remains a negative drive in a field of force.

Inasmuch as incest in Walker's tale must be described between quotation marks, twice (in fiction and then not "really"), it probably goes even further than Trueblood's narrative to alert us to the familial economies of symbolic father-daughter incest. All the instruments of torture in this feminized space—"the shed"—are an unmistakable weaponry—a "harness from the stable" whose "buckles" draw blood, "curling into the dust of the floor" (42). They are wielded, unmistakably, in an attitude of maiming, but in the allegory it either is never clear or is conflatedly transparent exactly what the father wants to murder and pulverize. Clearly, "ambiguously," "he" "loves" her, as the lines from the letter, in his night-long vigil (it seems), refer both to her own writing and what runs through his mind in a wounding flash: "It is rainsoaked, but he can make out 'I love you' written in a firm hand across the blue face of the letter" (42). This is fairly remarkable, because we are almost persuaded that the one thing that rushes him out of his father's closet, so to speak, is this female's *writing*—even "rainsoaked," it is a firm hand "across the blue. . . ." Would she still have been a girl-child alive, riding on a "yellow school bus," except for that act of inscription that affirms beyond guess her powers of desire? to *choose*, to *say who* and *when* she wants? Her "crime" has been her desire. The "daughter" cannot *want*, and so far as this one is concerned, "no amount of churchgoing changed her ways" (43). It is a patent contradiction to the father's law that the young nubile female in his midst should *desire*. (The wishes of "wife," even an adulterous one, do not matter, since she has already been "had.") He is flummoxed, however, in the face of the daughter's vast and untried sexual possibilities, and we suspect why: "he," essentially, drew "his" woman out of another man's familial/sexual integrity, which move "kills" the father, if the "law" works, throughout all the generations, and I suppose we could say that not until a man marries—which, humorously, depends on a woman's consent—does he complete his Oedipal mission and gain, thusly, "brotherhood" in the status of a patrimonial destiny.

Does the incestuous instinct become, then, in the fictional text the fatherly plea that the young woman not "disgrace" her father, not "cut him loose" in the transfer of unspoken sexual allegiance? We are accustomed to think that men exchange women, as the fundamental reason of property behind the prohibition, but is it possible that the female figure, the woman, simply by looking at what she wants, fixing it at eye level, effects the point of transfer and transit that must be blocked off at all costs? Does this vast and fundamental negation, then, cover this muted place at which the father gains insight into his own limitations of body and flesh? Perhaps it is not by accident that the unwed daughter, especially in the house of a dead father, is viciously referred to in heterosexist language and tradition as the "old maid," the aged female "stuff" whom Father need not "marry"?

Because this daughter *writes* her wish, she assumes the proportions of a monstrosity (the narrator has also given her "school books," off whose sight the father's eyes glide down to the point of promise), as she becomes, exactly, "in the shed"—rain-soaked, hair-draggled, immured in the blood of her flesh. He sees her blouse, "wet and slippery from the rain," sliding off her shoulders, "and her high young breasts are bare":

> He gathers their fullness in his fingers and begins a slow twisting. The barking of the dogs creates a frenzy in his ears and he is suddenly burning with unnamable desire. In his agony he draws the girl away from him as one pulling off his own arm and with quick slashes of his knife leaves two bleeding craters the size of grapefruits on her bare bronze breast and flings what he finds in his hands to the yelping dogs. (45)

Any woman reader of this paragraph is convinced by now, if not by anything preceding it, that this swift, matter-of-fact, single, choreographed verbal gesture does *not* qualify as the imitation of any *conceivable* action. We must be somewhere else, in a region of imagined revenge. There is no apparent and immediate aftermath that the text records—no noise? no hysterical motion? no drowning? And no Divinity comes down here now? And how could a woman write this, without self (or other?) intervention? We read it again and decide that it is comparable with a female body "impaled on a steel-spiked fence *near the house*" (my italics). And it remains unbearable. No act of criticism that I could perform on the text at this point would retrieve the passage for me as a *usable text*, since it transgresses every sexual/sexually discursive aspect of a cultural code that I have received from father/mother (the most immediate and evident sexual "origin") as a plausible carnality and therefore a potential mimesis/representation of a sort. But that point at which my own readerly sensibilities switch off, at which my own aesthetic rules go in revolt, at which, in *this* case, I, in an empathetic gesture that has no business intruding itself between the "clean" text and me, may well demarcate precisely that moment at which I should hang on, inasmuch as it possibly signalizes the "quick slash marks" that divide "me"—violently—from the peace and "piece" of self-imputed w(hole)ness. Irigaray's "This sex which is not one" not only inscribes the symbolic outcome of the female's divided labial economy but offers this configuration as the groundwork of a different system of signification altogether. If this is so, then "Daughter" in Walker's text escapes not only the patriarchal household of this tale (by death?) but also, consequently, the unitary implications of the phallic by which she is adjudged an other.

If "Daughter" escapes patriarchy by mutilation and effacement only, then the "victory" is hardly worth the father's cost, since this fictionalized circuit of desire has "shorted out," as it were. If the incestuous impulse leads, by a *detour*, to a "more or less manifest endogamy," then the "realization of incest is not only possible, it is necessary, albeit through a third party, lest any form of relationship between human beings become exhausted" (Roustang 99). According to this theory, father-daughter incest must occur on the symbolic level, and therefore in its manifestations as the incest taboo, in order to bring about "differences in cases where identity threatens to block the functioning of some fixed culture" (102). Roustang goes so far as to contend that

> incestuous desire is operative for the individual only if it actually remains a possibility, but that possibility, to remain valid, must be the effective deviation, the actual derivation of incest. If incest is unrecognized, rejected, repressed, the individual will be left with nothing but the arid, closed field of some abandonment or deadly depression. If incest is overtly practiced and the individual has eyes, ears, and sex only for those closest to him or their surrogates, then he will always be on the verge of fragmentation and breakdown. (101).

The father of Walker's text cannot recognize the ground of his own "unnamable desire," or else he recognizes it all too well. Having "eyes, ears, and sex only for those closest to him"—in this instance, a ruse or surrogate for "daughter"—he actually carries out, on the level of an inverted dream, the motions of breakdown and falling apart that the text displaces through the daughter's dismemberment. We are left, I believe, with a stunning excision, pointing in two directions at once. The text both engenders and conceals these oppositional vectors by circumvention. The slumping figure that we encounter in the closural scene of the tale cradles a "heavy empty shotgun" that might be read as a deflated tumescence. But the essential stillness of the passage, as though time will not cease in an eternity of undifferentiated movement, also claims it for a death at the level of vegetal growth: the dirt daubers have seized this body, "jellied" its eyes, as the choreographed effects of the natural overwhelm names, identities, and genders in a democratic rage for sameness. This reduction to the fundamental, brought on by an oversupply of the domestic phallus (the one "near the house"), not only parodies a "return of the repressed" but also mocks the father's law as a basic castration fear.

But what might it mean for *this* daughter to "underwrite" *this* father? In other words, how is it that we know daughter only through father? Indeed, it seems that "he" marks the founding auspices of a female representation and that we have no way out. I would maintain, however, that the *loss of difference,* which occurs in an actualized fictitious outcome of incest, as in the tale of Trueblood, or in a surrogate fictitious outcome, as in "The Child Who Favored Daughter," abolishes those very sexual distinctions that hold the father-daughter relationship in a delicate balance. Its violation, in at least two contemporary fictional instances, brings about "castration," or its equivalent: in the case of Trueblood, the daughter's pregnancy and a sexual future from which Trueblood has been barred; in Walker's father's case, a future rolling backward and ahead towards unlocalized human origins. In either instance, sexual "life" or human-as-sexed-subject stalls at the moment of penetration, so that the penis, in this "speaking," actually lops itself off. If this is so, then the suspension of the taboo generates the deepest division, if to signify here is to break up into layers of fragmentation. A sort of magic pervades this economy. Fathers and daughters are called upon to divide without division, to acquire that difference that no one ever thought was other than difference in the first place; since this is true, "father" can save himself only in by-passing the daughter's sex, which is also anatomically inscribed, but it is the "difference within" that he must only guess. Have we, then, done nothing more than point out that even in fiction—especially in fiction—the incest taboo prevails, and prevails for very good reason?

It seems that we have arrived at the household of the African-American daughter and father by a kind of detour of our own. This arriving possibly demarcates a text running parallel to that of a Eurocentric psychomythology, and I would concede that by way of it we land also on the ground of pure (fictional?) speculation. The Freudian/Lacanian text of incest and phallic signification might apply to this community of texts—both fictional and historical—only by accident, which the writers sense more palpably than do the sociologists. The father and the daughter of this social configuration are "missing" historically because the laws and practices of enslavement did not recognize, as a rule, the *vertical* arrangements of their family. From this angle, fathers, daughters, mothers, sons, sisters, brothers, spread across the social terrain in horizontal display, which exactly occurred in the dispersal of the historical African-American domestic unit. In this movement outward from a nuclear centrality, family becomes an extension and inclusion—anyone who preserves life and its callings becomes a member of the family, whose patterns of kinship and resemblance fall into disguise. In other words, the "romance" of African-American fiction is a tale of origins that brings together once again children lost, stolen, or strayed from their mothers. We pursue this thematics in works by Frances E. W. Harper, Pauline Hopkins, and Charles W. Chesnutt, among others, late in the nineteenth century and early into the twentieth (Carby; Tate). Certainly, we also encounter the changeling, the orphaned, or lost child in other fictions, but I am not acquainted with any other cluster of fictional texts based in a historical experience that seems *designed* to sever the maternal bond, shrouding the paternal connection in redoubled uncertainty. On this basis, it is fair to say that one aspect of the liberationist urge for freed persons is not so much the right to achieve the "nuclear family" as it is the wish to rescue African-Americans from flight, to arrest their wandering away from . . . toward, essentially to bring the present into view rather than the past. We could go so far as to say that African-Americans in historic flight perfectly inscribe the "body in pain" (Scarry), on a contracted world ground, whose sole concern becomes the protection of the corporeal body, and it is the corporeal, carnal body that incest brings brazenly into relief precisely because it is prohibited.

If "family," on this historic occasion, describes, for all intents and purposes, a site of interdiction and denial, we could go so far as to say that the mark of incestuous desire and enactment—a concentrated carnality—speaks for its losses, confusions, and above all else its imposed abeyance of order and degree. We might tentatively look at the situation this way: moments of African-American fiction show father-daughter incest or its surrogate motions as an *absence,* not an overdetermination. *Something is wrong* precisely because fathers and daughters, in a cultural marginality, fictively inscribed, are impeded in their movement towards culture / difference / division. The urge here compels characters *to get out* of incest, out of the carnal body, whose only means of expression remains the flesh, as Trueblood's branding makes evident, into the "clean" blood. If this is true, then the prohibition must be embraced (in order to cancel out the other interdiction) not only in the father's interest but in order that the daughters might know the appropriate lover and the future. In this case, the origins of the incest taboo are not at all shrouded in mystery, nor are they longer-going than the history of the United States, for example: wherever human society wishes to move into an *articulation,* the father must discover and humbly observe his limit. In that regard and at least from the viewpoint of a couple of writers, father-daughter incestuous desire and taboo possesses no originary moment, but arises each day, as a precise diachronic unfolding, in a situation of blindness and overcoming.

Note

Though coming to my attention too late to inform this writing, W. Arens's book, *The Original Sin: Incest and Its Meaning,* promises to correct our notions concerning the historic origins of incest.

They cross the yard
and at the back door
the mother sees with pleasure
how alike they are, father and daughter—
I know something of that time.
The little girl purposefully
swinging her arms, laughing
her stark laugh.

It should be kept secret, that sound.
It means she's realized
that he never touches her.
She is a child: he could touch her
if he wanted to.
         —Louise Glück, from *Dedication to Hunger*

Edgar Degas, *The Bellilli Family* (1858–62)
Source: Musée d'Orsay, Paris. Used by permission.

II

In Nomine Patris: The Daughter
in Her Father's House

Engendering the Exemplary Daughter:
The Deployment of Sexuality in
Richardson's *Clarissa*

For how many women is it true that their whole energies seem spent in ever more complicated ways of pleasing him? How many have the feeling that their proudest moments of independence turn out to be a communication with their father? . . . Some fathers desire a devoted and obedient slave, others a suffragette. In reality most probably want both at the same time—a fatal contradiction which daughters can spend most of their lives and ingenuity trying to resolve.
 —Olivia Harris, "Heavenly Father"

IN HER ESSAY on the issue of "literary daughteronomy," Sandra Gilbert argues that "until recently . . . every powerful literary [and] every literal mother" seems to have presented the woman writer with "the conundrum of the empty pack"—"the riddle of daughterhood." Here is the riddle: when the female precursor "achieves her greatest strength, her power becomes self-subverting: in the moment of psychic transformation that is the moment of creativity, the literary mother, even more than the literal one, becomes the 'stern daughter of the voice of God' who paradoxically proclaims her 'allegiance to the law' she herself appears to have violated" ("Life's Empty Pack" 357). According to Gilbert, the law in this riddle is the "Law of the Father," a law that defines culture as "patriarchal and phallocentric" and in so doing ensures that what the literary mother passes on to her daughter is her own disinheritance: the name of the father as the sign of the mother's loss. In other words, what the woman writer inherits from her powerful precursors is the position of being the father's daughter.

  As Gilbert represents it, this position entails a specific paradigm of female sexuality, a paradigm theorized by Freud as the "female Oedipus complex." Having recognized the difference castration makes, the little girl undertakes the lengthy and difficult developmental process of "relinquish[ing] her earliest mother attachment and transfer[ring] her affection to her father." If all goes well for the girl, then the result will be what Freud represents as a positive development: the emergence of a "normal feminine attitude in which she takes her father as love-object" (372). According to Gilbert, George Eliot's *Silas Marner* recounts just such a "positive" development; moreover, it does so in a powerful way, in a voice that inspires Edith Wharton to repeat the process in *Summer*. However, in repeating the paradigm of female sexuality she inherited from her mother, Wharton reveals what Gilbert believes to have always been the dark underside of the "positive" female Oedipus: the father's incestuous desire for the daughter. In patriarchal society, the man is "absolutely forbid[den]" to desire his mother; in consequence, he turns to the daughter, for not only is she a "suitably diminished 'milk-giver'" but she is also a woman who "belongs to the father alone" (373).

As illuminating as Gilbert's analysis of "literary daughteronomy" is, it leaves at least one question still to be answered. From her literary mother the daughter inherits the position of being the father's daughter and with it, an incestuous paradigm of female sexuality. But where, one wonders, did the literary mother get this paradigm? Unlike Freud, who occasionally suggests that female nature is responsible for the emergence of the female Oedipus, Gilbert is unflinching in her insistence that daughterhood and the sexuality it entails are cultural constructs, the products of a "patriarchal order." However, by privileging Lévi-Strauss's and Freud's accounts of that "order," Gilbert may inadvertently reinforce their cultural fatalism, a fatalism that can be even more de-bilitating than a relatively easily discredited biological fatalism.[1] Both Freud and Lévi-Strauss identify culture as a product of the incest taboo, and both assign to kinship the essential function of (re)producing and then regulating incest. Yet in so doing, they efface the role ideology and history play in the production of the sexed subject—the subject of culture (de Lauretis; Silverman).

The Marxist theoretician Louis Althusser has argued that since the "Law of Culture" has very real consequences, we cannot do without the analytical tools Freud and Lévi-Strauss have given us for understanding that law; nor can we do without the insights Lacan has produced by putting Freud's and Lévi-Strauss's tools to use ("Freud"). However, if we want to dispel a potentially debilitating cultural fatalism, then we need something more than these tools and insights: we need "historical materialism," a frame of reference in which it is assumed that the func-tions served by kinship structures vary historically (217), as do the ideo-logical paradigms in which persons inscribed in real kinship structures "live their functions" (211). In short, "it is not enough to know that the Western family is patriarchal and exogamic"; in addition to this knowl-edge, we need a "mass of research" on the historically various functions and historically various ideologies of familiar relations (211).

Ironically, however, it is just such a "mass of research" that leads the social historian Lawrence Stone to argue that the Western family has not always been patriarchal. In *The Family, Sex, and Marriage in England, 1500–1800,* Stone describes the emergence amongst the eighteenth-century upper bourgeosie and squirarchy of the "closed domesticated nuclear family," a new kind of family "serving rather fewer practical needs but carrying a much greater load of emotional and sexual commitment" (413). Unlike the "restricted patriarchal nuclear family" of the seventeenth-century, this new kind of family was more sexually liberated than repressed, more openly equalitarian than hierarchically authoritarian, and more bound by affection and habit than by economic and political interests. Rather than dictate the choice of a spouse, parents now approved or vetoed choices made by their children—choices in which affection and compatibility were as important as property and status. Strict settlements—the practice of signing property over to children before they are born—became common, as did the practice of stipulating an allowance for the wife in the marriage contract. According to Stone, by giving the wife and children a legal right to property, these common practices effectively undercut patriarchal power. At the same time, the practice of swaddling babies declined, the incidence of maternal breast-feeding rose, the tendency to foster out the young decreased, and the material and emotional involvement of mothers in child-rearing increased. Instead of going off to school, many children were educated at home, where Lockean-based attempts to "create a liking" for learning replaced the physically coercive practice of flogging (280). Of course, children were still obliged to obey their parents; however, that obligation was now based on what Bishop Fleetwood identified as their "parents' love and care of them" rather than on the sovereign principle of submission to patriarchal authority (165).

According to Stone, this new type of family was the result of a liberal and liberating set of values, a set he calls "affective individualism." On the one hand, the belief that a person has a property right in himself led to the growth of individualism and with it, to the demand for privacy and autonomy. On the other hand, the "progressive reorientation of culture towards the pursuit of pleasure in this world" (159) engendered a new appreciation of and capacity for desire and feeling. In the development of both of these tendencies, Stone sees the effects of the contract theory of government, the Puritan emphasis on introspection, the libertinism of the Restoration, the proliferation of novels about sex, love, and marriage, and perhaps most fundamentally, the entrenchment of a market economy and the rise of a middle class. But even though Stone believes that a market economy and middle class are necessary conditions for the emergence of "affective individualism," he does not consider them sufficient; something more is needed: a "spirit" that is both hard to come by and easy to lose, since it "lacks any firm foundation in biological, anthropological, or sociological data" (425).

Although Stone contends that the changes he documents are real and concrete, he also recognizes that affective individualism is very much a matter of "verbal style" (89). Picking up on this recognition, Jean Hagstrum has identified a line of literary texts that "reflect" the emergence of "affective individualism" while "embod[ying] the social changes" that "*mentalité*" produced (2). Within this antiheroic tradition devoted to the ideal of "heterosexual friendship," Samuel Richardson's novels appear to be a "watershed," for as Hagstrum sees it, Richardson's "stunning originality" was to give us "not ideas but a world," not a sermon but novels in which "sexuality, love, and the desire for union in marriage serve as motives of action and as creators of the personal *Gestalt*" (190). Although Hagstrum finds *Pamela* and *Sir Charles Grandison* interesting, he, like most other critics, believes that *Clarissa* is Richardson's most powerful creation. Unlike some critics, however, Hagstrum argues that what makes *Clarissa* so great is its presentation of a "true heroine" (210), a woman of sensibility who is not only "the champion of downtrodden woman of her day and all days" (201) but also a "touchstone" of and for "humanity" (199).[2]

In citing Richardson's novels as key moments in the development of "affective individualism," both Stone (156) and Hagstrum verge on the recognition that novelistic discourse may be as important as the family in the production and reproduction of a certain kind of cultural subject. Althusser, however, helps us to understand why and how this is indeed the case. As I have already noted, Althusser not only maintains that the functions served by kinship structures vary historically but also insists that persons inscribed in kinship structures live their functions ideologically. In other words, ideological representations always mediate familiar relationships. Furthermore, they do so in a way that is potentially novelistic, for as Althusser defines it, ideology is "a 'Representation' of the Imaginary Relationship of Individuals to their Real Conditions of Existence" ("Ideology" 152). Although this definition owes something to Lacan's differentiation of the "imaginary" and the "symbolic" from the "real," Althusser gives the Lacanian terms a historical and material twist. No longer does the real signify some purely natural or organic realm of being; instead, it refers to historically specific relations of production as well as to other relations—such as familial relations—that derive from them. Likewise, the imaginary no longer designates some presymbolic mirror phase in which the child spontaneously identifies "himself" with and as an exemplary image; instead, it refers to a socially mediated process of identification, the never-ending process of becoming a subject of culture.

184

According to Althusser, ideology constitutes cultural subjects by means of various discursive practices. These practices address individuals, inviting them to identify with the subject of discourse and in so doing to place themselves in the structure of relations that produces the discursive subject at issue. Although a person may refuse to identify with a specific discursive subject, he or she cannot refuse all invitations for identification, for to do so would be to have no place in the symbolic order of culture, no relationship to the real conditions of human existence, no social relationships, no history, and no language. But even though it is inhuman to be nonideological, all ideologies are not equally humane. Discursive practices that invite identification while suppressing or encouraging us to ignore the real means and relations by which the subject is produced are suspect; so too are those practices that explicitly falsify the historical and material conditions of our existence. In producing subjects, these kinds of discursive practices also promote subjection; as Althusser puts it, they function as "transparent myths in which a society or an age can recognize itself (but not know itself)" ("'Piccolo Teatro'" 144).

It is precisely these kinds of discursive practices that most interest Foucault. In *The History of Sexuality* he argues that ever since the eighteenth century there has been a veritable explosion of discursive practices dealing with the issue of sex. Like Stone, who links the decline of the patriarchal family with the rise of the pleasure principle, Foucault links the demise of sovereignty with the birth of a new kind of interest in sex. However, unlike Stone, who thinks that "power is a zero-sum game" (426), Foucault believes that with the demise of sovereignty, the workings of power are neither so clearly nor so distinctly calculable. Hence he is less sanguine than Stone that the eighteenth-century interest in sex marks an authentic liberation. Indeed, Foucault suggests that what passes for liberation might be better considered as subjection. By positing the existence of sexuality, the discourse on sex invites individuals to identify some such thing as their most prized possession, the authentic reality of their inner being, their self.[3] Furthermore, since these discourses often lay claim to liberating the real truth of sex from the repressions mandated by some sort of sovereign power, they suppress the means by which sexuality is really produced: the powerful deployment of a discourse on sex and sexuality. But finally, what Foucault seems to find most troubling is the way these discourses falsify the material condition of our existence—the body. By subjecting individuals to the truth of their sexuality, the discourse on sex produces disembodied subjects, people who are out of touch, if not downright untouchable.

In Foucault's social history, the family plays a secondary role, for as he sees it, sexuality was initially deployed in novel rather than familiar sites. Having seduced confession out of the enclosures of religion and into the literary marketplace, the printing press transformed it from a discourse concerned with sin and salvation to a discourse intent on (re)producing the subject of desire—the sexual subject. Nevertheless, since both the family and sexuality are places where the public and private intersect, the two were bound to come together in a way that led to the "affective intensification" of family life, most especially of bourgeois family life (109). As an emerging historical force, the bourgeosie took up the deployment of sexuality in order to engender and identify itself as a class, as a body to be "cared for, protected, cultivated and preserved" (123). According to Foucault, it was this class body, as well as the sexuality that produced it, that generations subsequent to the eighteenth century inherited and, in one form or another, reproduced.

Although the ways of inheriting culture are multiple, the novel has long been an important means of producing cultural subjects. From its eighteenth-century beginnings, novelistic discourse has been concerned with representing the social, familial, and sexual relationships of individuals—a concern that underwrites its ideological power. The novel invites readers to identify with the characters, situations, and actions it represents; and readers usually oblige, if only because as individuals they need to represent their imaginary relationship to the real conditions of their existence. Of the eighteenth-century novelists, none was quite as good as Richardson at inducing the reader's identification. With the publication of *Pamela,* a new social vogue appeared: not only did people refer their feelings and actions to Pamela, talking about her as if she were real, but some women also began to talk and act like Pamela, so much so that *to Pamela* enjoyed a brief life as an English verb. Although all of this attention seems to have surprised Richardson, its effect was to make him a less naive writer. By the time he began *Clarissa,* he was well aware that his "new way of writing" was ideologically powerful. In consequence, his statement that Clarissa was designed to be an "Example to her Sex" (*Selected Letters* 90) should be taken quite seriously.

Besides indicating his interest in sex,[4] Richardson's statement records his awareness that women had become avid novel readers. As Ruth Perry explains, urbanization and the market economy changed the lives of many upper- and middle-class women. No longer were they directly involved in economic production or indirectly involved in the political affairs of the state. As women of "leisure," they now had time to wonder just what they were to do and to be in an urban society governed by the marketplace. Since what many of these women did was to read novels and write letters, *Clarissa* is at least in part addressed to them.

Compared with his contemporaries, Richardson seems to have been unusually sensitive to the question of what women should do and be.

However, in the following pages, I will argue that *Clarissa* deals with this novel question in a familiar way—a way that serves the interests of Richardson's class and, by way of that class, of his gender. As I see it, the eighteenth-century bourgeoisie sought to identify itself as a class by distinguishing its sexuality from that of others. In Richardson's *Clarissa*, this project engendered a novel subject of discourse, an exemplary woman whose position was nevertheless structured by familiar relations. More specifically, Richardson placed his exemplary subject in the position of being the father's daughter. However, since he did so in a way that is appealing not only to men but also to women, *Clarissa* has exerted a powerful influence over the development of novelistic discourse—so much so that even those who have never read *Clarissa* have probably been subject to its ideology.

ALL IN THE FAMILY

Women's approval, companionship, makes me feel happy, but it does not ever make me feel virtuous, safe or good. Men's approval, which does make me feel virtuous, does not make me feel happy, safe or good. And in this conflict between being happy and virtuous I am never at peace. Virtue, far from being its own reward, becomes tortuously its own punishment.
—Sara Maitland, "Two for the Price of One"

In Richardson's first novel the family is screened from view. As a servant to the gentry, Pamela is as good as an orphan. In his own way, Mr. B is also an orphan: both his father and mother are dead, and as the master of his household, he is in a position to ignore the advice of his married sister Lady Davers. It is in this relatively open space—the unfamiliar space of a "household"—that Richardson produces a series of blissfully satisfying and therefore utterly fantastic transformations: with comparative ease, Mr. B changes from a master to a father to a lover to a husband, while Pamela is made to follow suit, playing in turn the roles of servant, daughter, beloved, and wife.

In *Clarissa*, however, the nuclear family is not screened from view. Consequently, transformations become more difficult to effect, and the text turns complex, staging not one but three interlocked scenes: the family scene, the seduction-rape scene, and the death scene. Of these three scenes, the first appears to be the most novel, if only because it is there that the emergence of sexuality engenders conflict about the position of the daughter—about what she should do and be.

The novel begins with a letter to Clarissa from her close friend Anna Howe. In the opening line of that letter Anna refers to a "disturbance" in the Harlowe family, a disturbance made public by a wounding. Anna, however, is concerned not only with the actual wound that James has suffered but also with the wound that Clarissa's reputation may suffer if she does not explain and justify her role in the disturbance. In responding to Anna's demand for explanation and justification, Clarissa refers to a time before the present, a time when she enjoyed "everybody's love and good opinion" (1:4). Now, however, an "unhappy transaction" has "strangely discomposed" her family, thereby making her place a matter of serious concern.

At first glance, it would seem that the "unhappy transaction" to which Clarissa refers is nothing more nor less than Lovelace's wounding of James. It is this wounding that definitively sets the Harlowes against Lovelace, raises their interest in the question of Clarissa's loyalty, and eventually provokes their demand that Clarissa marry. But if it is easy to understand why the wounding confirms the Harlowes in their opposition to Lovelace, it is more difficult to figure out why it provokes so much anxiety about Clarissa's loyalty and marriageability. Since Clarissa never welcomed Lovelace's attentions, she supposes that the concern about her place is some mysterious perversion. However, the perversion may not be as mysterious as Clarissa thinks it is.

With James's wounding, a symbolics of blood comes into play, a symbolics that carries quite specific sociopolitical and familial implications when what is at issue is the power of a sovereign body. On the one hand, blood is precarious: "easily spilled, subject to drying up, too readily mixed, capable of being quickly corrupted" (Foucault 147). On the other hand, sovereign power entails "the right to decide life and death"—a right symbolized by the sword and legitimated in the seventeenth century by reference to "the ancient *patria potestas* that granted the father of the Roman family the right to 'dispose' of the life of his children and his slaves" (Foucault 135). As I read it, this legitimation effected a historical alliance between the sovereign and the patriarch, an alliance that made a preindustrial division of labor possible. By displaying the power of the sword—the power "to *take* life or *let* live"—the sovereign exerted control over the shedding of blood (Foucault 136). By dictating when and who his children married, the patriarch exerted control over the mixing of blood. Working in tandem, the sovereign and the patriarch produced the image of an inviolable body—a social body in which blood was no longer precarious.

If James's wounding reasserts the precariousness of the blood, it also makes visible the Harlowes' inability to wield the sword. Nevertheless, their power is not totally in jeopardy, for they have the ability to staunch the wound by asserting the father's control over the mixing of blood. To suture the wound that Clarissa's suitor has dealt the family, Mr. Harlowe declares that it is time for Clarissa to marry and that he has just the man for her.

Although this symbolics of blood accounts for Mr. Harlowe's insistence that Clarissa marry someone of his choosing, it does not account for the choice of Solmes. Behind this turn in the plot there is another "unhappy transaction," one that is first mentioned in the postscript to Anna's opening letter. In that postscript, Anna asks Clarissa to send her a "copy of the preamble to the clauses in your grandfather's will in your favor" (1:3). When we read that preamble, we discover that Clarissa's grandfather did something strange, something not "strictly conformable to law or to the forms thereof": he willed to Clarissa his "estate," the land that in accordance with accepted social practices should have gone either to his son or to his grandson, James (1:21–22). At this point the reader may begin to suspect that it is not only Lovelace's wounding of James that has so "strangely discomposed" the Harlowes but also the grandfather's will. Indeed, after her vague reference to an "unhappy transaction," Clarissa reflects on her grandfather's will before turning to her account of Lovelace's entry into the family scene. It seems, then, that the first sign of trouble is the grandfather's will. Like Lear's decision to divide his kingdom, this will gives *Clarissa* an opening that resembles a fairy tale; in the beginning, Clarissa had a fairy-grandfather who in willing her his estate "strangely discomposed" the family.

In the preamble to his will, the grandfather emphasizes the "delight of [his] old age" (1:21), a delight he not only attributes to his relationship with Clarissa but also attempts to prolong by means of his will. It is this attempt that necessitates changes in the terms of a will. Refusing to observe the "forms" of law, the grandfather couches his will in terms of need and desire. Since neither his sons nor James needs his estate, he wills it to Clarissa. Furthermore, he seeks to "enjoin" respect for his willful desire by appealing to the desire of others: if they "would wish their own last wills and desires to be fulfilled by their survivors," then the Harlowes must not dispute his will (1:21). The emphasis on delight, the interest in prolonging pleasure, and the references to need and desire, all mark the emergence of a new kind of will, a sexualized will that is intent on privileging the feminine—the "amiable," "kind," and "tender" Clarissa (1:22).

As the grandfather's will suggests, Stone may be right in arguing that the eighteenth century was more sexually equalitarian than the seventeenth century. However, as Susan Okin has pointed out, that equalitarianism was still quite limited. Although strict settlements were common, they were ruled by the principle of primogeniture; when a woman received property, it was usually personal rather than real property. Furthermore, the practice of strict settlements was offset by the common-law proviso that what belonged to the woman became the husband's when she married. And finally, even when the husband was not the legal trustee of a woman's property, he was the most decisive force in determining its disposition.

In willing Clarissa his estate, the grandfather transgresses the sovereign law of primogeniture, thereby obstructing the transmission of male dominance from father to son. Not wanting to disturb her family, Clarissa gives the disposition of her inherited estate to her father. But this is nothing more than a stopgap measure; implicitly, it puts Mr. Harlowe and James in Clarissa's debt, a debt that undercuts the very male dominance that Clarissa's deference might otherwise effect. A marriage between Clarissa and Solmes, however, promises to be more than a stopgap measure. Since Solmes seems willing to return the estate to the Harlowes, he provides James with a way to dig himself out of debt. In receiving Clarissa from the Harlowes, Solmes would incur a debt, a debt that would be settled when the grandfather's estate was returned to the family. That return would not only repair the damage caused by the grandfather's transgression of the law but also reinstitute the transmission of male dominance, although now the circuit would involve a man besides the father and son: the husband Solmes.

Although the Clarissa who refuses to marry Solmes may seem to be someone quite different from the grandfather's amiable, kind, and tender girl (Dussinger 85), such is not the case. What links the two is a sexualized will, a will that is not "strictly conformable to law or to the forms thereof" (1:22). This sexualized will rises to the surface of the text in Clarissa's account of her interview with Aunt Hervey, the family member who has been sent to present her with the marriage settlements:

> And then, to my great terror, out she drew some parchments from her handkerchief, which she had kept (unobserved by me) under her apron; and rising, put them in the opposite window. Had she produced a serpent I could not have been more frighted.
>
> Oh! my dearest aunt, turning away my face, and holding out my hands: hide from my eyes those horrid parchments! Let me conjure you to tell me—by all the tenderness of near relationship, and upon your honour, and by your love for me, say, are they absolutely resolved that, come what will, I must be that man's?
>
> My dear, you must have Mr. Solmes: indeed you must.
>
> Indeed I never will! This, as I have said over and over, is not originally my father's will. Indeed I never will—and that is all I will say! (1:428)

The description of where Aunt Hervey had hidden the letter of the law, the reference to the serpent, the terror at the sight of the text, and the appeals to the woman's love and honor, all betray the sexualization of Clarissa's will, a sexualization that is linked to the grandfather not only by the repetition of the word *will* but also by the affective intensification of what should have been a legal scene.

In their attempts to expose the hidden truth of *Clarissa*, some modern critics have uncovered what they presume to be the initial secret of Clarissa's sexuality: her unconscious desire for Lovelace (Price 281; Traugott 194; Watt 229). However, it seems to me that Clarissa's sexuality is neither unconscious nor hidden. It is explicit not only in her refusal to countenance Solmes—a refusal based on sexual repulsion—but also in her relationship with her mother. Desirous of her mother's approval and support, Clarissa divulges her heart to Mrs. Harlowe in a series of conversations that are punctuated with palpitations, kisses, sobs, and fainting spells. It is in these scenes that Clarissa makes clear her revulsion at the thought of marriage to Solmes, her anger at James and Arabella, her distrust of Lovelace, and her anxiety about heterosexual relations. But even though Mrs. Harlowe both recognizes and values Clarissa's passionate heart, she still insists that Mr. Harlowe be obeyed. This insistence confounds Clarissa, so much so that it provokes her not only to complain to Anna that her mother is too compliant but also to associate unquestioning compliance with the maternal heart and unquestioned strength with the paternal will. Unlike her mother, Clarissa would identify her heart with her will, thereby defining her self as the place where the maternal and the paternal converge. If at one level such an identification makes it impossible for Clarissa to consider marrying a man she finds sexually unattractive, then at another it leads her to argue that because marriage requires the wife to relinquish her will to her husband, a woman should only be "obliged" to marry a man "she can love" (1:153).

Both the grandfather's will and Clarissa's stand signal the emergence of sexual desire within the family scene. However, as James's strategic provocation of the family attests, desire is not solely the property of Clarissa and her grandfather. Although most of James's actions can be explained in terms of the role he must play as the son who is to preserve the house by inheriting dominance, there is one exception to this rule: his initiation of a sword fight with Lovelace. Since James's assigned role is to preserve the bloodline, and since the family has already agreed to defer to his wishes in regards to Lovelace's suit, the sword fight appears strangely unnecessary. In an effort to understand that bloody event, Clarissa produces a number of explanations for James's behavior. At one moment she attributes it to the hatred James feels towards Lovelace, a hatred rooted in the competition the two men engaged in at the university; at another moment she attributes it to a fault in James's character, to an imperiousness nurtured and indulged by the family. But ultimately, Clarissa traces the event back to James's ambition: by amassing property and wealth, James hopes to engender a new line of descendents, a noble

191

line. Since Lovelace's suit threatens this project, James takes up the sword, not only against Lovelace but also against Clarissa. In both instances, however, a curious sort of pleasure attends James's sword play; he revels in the blood that flows from the wound Lovelace gives him and delights in tormenting Clarissa with the wound her body must be made to suffer for the family. Such pleasure suggests that James has invested an old mode of power with a new desire: he wields the sword not in an attempt to preserve the ancestral house but in the interests of acquiring a bigger and better house.

In the Harlowe family, the father is the only one who appears to be without desire. Consequently, his character is something of an enigma. Of course, Mr. Harlowe does get caught up in James's struggle, but even so, he seems an unwitting accomplice, a man whose will is usurped and sexualized without his knowing or wanting it. Although Clarissa recognizes that her father is more or less an unwitting accomplice, his naiveté ultimately confounds her; he is both deaf to her pleas for understanding and unresponsive to her various attempts to appeal to his desire. The problem is that unlike the rest of the Harlowes, Mr. Harlowe knows nothing of desire. Standing apart from the fray, he can do little more than repeat the law of parental authority, the law that gives *him* the right to be obeyed.

One of the oddest things about Samuel Richardson was his reluctance to abrogate the law of parental authority. In letters to a number of his female friends, Richardson not only upheld the parent's right to decide what was "fit and reasonable" for the child but in one instance went so far as to argue that Clarissa should have deferred to her parents (*Selected Letters* 144–50). In a more roundabout way, Richardson also stands up for Mr. Harlowe in the text of *Clarissa*. Perhaps because he partially identified with this gout-ridden man, Richardson represents Mr. Harlowe as superannuated and irascible rather than as base and perverse. Indeed, Mr. Harlowe appears to be a figure from the past, the representative of a time when the father's display of authority was good for the house. In *Clarissa*, however, times have changed. Whether Mr. Harlowe realizes it or not, his family has been sexualized, and consequently the issue of alliance has been invested with desire.

If at one level Richardson can be said to represent this troubling situation, then at another he must be read as producing it. Indeed, what really disturbs the Harlowe family is Richardson's interest in sexuality, an interest figured in terms of a will, a beleaguered daughter, and an ambitious son. By so "strangely discompos[ing]" the Harlowe family, not only does Richardson engender a distinction between James's perverse sexualization of patriarchal power and Clarissa's novel feminization of sexuality but he also opts for the latter. He makes Clarissa the most valuable member of the Harlowe family as well as the exemplary subject of the novel. Nevertheless, it is important to remember that in choosing Clarissa over James, Richardson opts not for the daughter's rights but for her feminine sexuality—for Clarissa's willful heart.

Although Richardson's choice is clear, it leaves at least one issue unresolved: the social relationships of this feminine sexuality. By the end of the novel's family scene, all we know is what is not possible. In choosing Clarissa over James, Richardson makes a marriage between Clarissa and Solmes impossible. However, he also makes another social relationship impossible: a community of women. By dividing mother from daughter and by keeping Anna at a safe distance, Richardson isolates Clarissa in a way that allows him to distinguish her feminine sexuality from both Mrs. Harlowe's heart-felt maternalism and Anna's willful feminism. While both of these women receive letters from Clarissa, it is Anna who is chosen to play the role of receiver of Clarissa's message. In assigning Anna this role, Richardson not only formalizes his desire to keep her at a distance but also justifies the later scenes at which his enforcement of distance will strain the reader's credulity. That Richardson would prefer to strain credulity rather than bring Clarissa and Anna together suggests yet again that for him, feminine sexuality must be either for and by itself or for and with man.

Needless to say, this is where Lovelace comes in. In an attempt to steal the show, Lovelace stages and directs a scene that induces Clarissa to move from the actual into an imaginary realm. The stage is set when Lovelace appears at the garden gate brandishing a sword and proclaiming himself ready to free Clarissa from an all too familiar confinement. Taking her cue from Lovelace, Clarissa apprehensively imagines the presence of an armed man. However, that armed man is not Lovelace with his drawn sword but someone "more dreadful": "a father armed with terror in his countenance" (1:484). In turning away from the actuality of the armed Lovelace, Clarissa also turns away from another actuality: the unwitting and gouty old man who is her father. In the place of these two actualities, Clarissa installs an imaginary figure—part father, part lover—who appears to embody the sword Clarissa has so much wanted to keep out of play. But what Clarissa wants is transformed in the scene that she and Lovelace enact. That scene provokes an affective (mis)reading: an imaginary identification of power with the "opposite" sex. This displacement of the actual by the imaginary confuses Clarissa, so much so that she is open to appropriation by a loveless rake such as Lovelace. In figuring this imaginary appropriation as an elopement, Richardson suggests that what really interests him is not women per se but rather the problem of a feminine sexuality that is no longer bound by and to paternal authority as an actual fact. Apparently this is the problem that provoked Richardson into writing a novel whose titular character was to be an "Example to her Sex."

RAPE'S REASON

In my late teens I fled away from my father's house; it has taken me a long time to realize that I carried with me the Father from whom I could not escape by escaping childhood, from whom I have not yet escaped, and from whom I have had, and still have, to wrest my loves, my voice, my feminism and my freedom.
   —Sara Maitland, "Two for the Price of One"

The confusion that characterizes the elopement returns again and again in the second major scene of *Clarissa*, the seduction-rape scene. Although it is Clarissa who most often appears confused by events, Lovelace also has his confusing moments, times when he finds himself doing such things as explicitly proposing, emotionally responding, and inexplicably deferring. In general, this confusion implies that in the extra-familial relationships between men and women, the man's power is not necessarily sovereign. Since Lovelace initially desires Clarissa's desire and not just her obedience, he deploys power in a way that is other than sovereign: by means of various provocative strategies, he seeks to reveal Clarissa's sexuality and in so doing to turn a painfully imaginary elopement into a truly pleasurable liberation. The problem, however, is that this plan rests on the assumption that the truth of sex lies at the heart of pleasure. Consequently, it engenders a rationalization of pleasure according to the "laws" of sex, laws that Lovelace conceives in terms of the rake's code.

But even though Lovelace may indeed be a rake, what he wants to be is a "father." In the unfolding of the text this desire assumes three forms. After the rape, it appears in the mode of wish-fulfillment as Lovelace fantasizes that Clarissa is carrying his child (4:38, 164). Earlier, when Lovelace is busy prosecuting his schemes, it appears in a symbolic mode as Lovelace exultingly proclaims himself "the great name-father" (2:267). Initially, however, that desire takes a more familiar and romantic form: Lovelace's declared "resolution . . . to be a father, uncle, brother, and . . . husband to [Clarissa], all in one" (1:480).

Yet Lovelace would not be the cursing "unnatural" father that Mr. Harlowe seems to be; instead, he would be something "more," a father whose desire for the daughter brings her back to life—the life of desire:

> On my return I found her recovering from fits, again to fall into stronger fits; . . . Nor wonder at her being so affected; she, whose filial piety gave her dreadful faith in a father's curses; . . . What a miscreant had I been, not to have endeavoured to bring her back, by

all the endearments, by all the vows, by all the offers I could make her!

I *did* bring her back. More than a father to her; for I have given her a life her unnatural father had well-nigh taken away: shall I not cherish the fruits of my own benefaction? (2:183–84)

In displaying his desire for Clarissa, Lovelace can be said to feminize the father, for he exposes his power to be that of the seductive prick—the man who would forget the sovereign law of patriarchy in the interests of provoking a more lively and sensational display of sexuality.

Nevertheless, since Lovelace works according to the rake's code, he produces a veiled seduction that does nobody any good. In *Clarissa*, Richardson represents the rake's code as the attempt of a mother's son to identify himself through the formulation of the laws of sex. Rejecting Lord M as a model, Lovelace seeks aid and advice from the "masculine" Mother Sinclair, patterns his ideal love on the relationship between an indulgent mother and her wayward son (2:416), and finds himself in the dream figure of yet another madam—the candle-bearing Mother H (3:250). Indeed, even when Lovelace seems most intent on expressing the sovereign prerogative of the male, his language betrays something else— the sexual anxiety of a mother's son: "Knowst thou not, moreover, that man is the woman's sun . . . ?" (2:403).

Although the figure of the phallic mother haunts Lovelace, it is only by imagining a woman who is not yet castrated that the rake is able to give himself an *active* role in producing the laws of sex: "All that's excellent in her sex is this lady! Until by Matrimonial or Equal intimacies, I have found her *less than angel*, it is impossible to think of any other" (1:150). Rather than something to which he must submit, the law appears to be something Lovelace can produce by deploying his power to reveal the truth of (the) sex: the lack that makes woman a desiring body. In short, Lovelace-as-rake must show that Clarissa wants it, that she is asking for it: "But these high-souled and high-sensed girls, who had set up for shining lights and examples to the rest of the sex, are with such difficulty brought down to the common standard, that a wise man, who prefers his peace of mind to his glory in subduing one of that exalted class, would have nothing to say to them" (3:203). However, if Lovelace takes it upon himself to bring Clarissa down to the common standard, he does so not in the interests of sovereignty but rather in the interests of (his) pleasure—the sexual rationale of the libertine.

As Lovelace moves between desire and the law, so too does Clarissa. On the one hand she provokes seduction, if only because her desire for the father's desire grows increasingly desperate: "I should be glad to have a father who would own me!" (2:310). On the other hand she refuses to be seduced, if only because she suspects that Lovelace would deny her difference, her novel feminine sexuality:

> Am I not under a *necessity*, as it were, of quarrelling with him; at least every other time I see him? No prudery, no coquetry, no tyranny in my heart, or in my behaviour to him, that I know of. No affected procrastination. Aiming at nothing but decorum. . . . One plain path before us; yet such embarrasses, such difficulties, such subjects for doubt, for cavil, for uneasiness; as fast as one is obviated, another to be introduced, and not by myself—I know not how introduced. What pleasure can I propose to myself in meeting such a wretch? (2:377)

The problem is not that Clarissa represses her sexuality; nor is it that Lovelace oppresses her sexuality. Rather, the problem is that the very workings of sexuality engender a confusion both within and between bodies. In this regard, Lovelace and Clarissa are mirror images, nonidentical doubles doomed to endless confusion until something drastic happens—something like a rape.

In an attempt to dispel the confusion that had seduced some readers into desiring a marriage between Clarissa and Lovelace, Richardson noted that arguments against such a union "must continue in Force, till the eternal Difference of Vice and Virtue shall coalesce, and make one putrid Mass, a Chaos in the Moral and Intellectual World" (*"Clarissa"*: *Preface* 14). As this quotation suggests, Richardson seems to have considered seduction as a confusion fated to end in Chaos, a fate worse than rape or, for that matter, death. From the perspective of religion, Richardson's fear of chaos makes good sense. However, another perspective is needed to understand why Richardson would run the risk of confusing his readers in the first place. For what earthly reason would Richardson want to represent the confusion that overtakes Clarissa and Lovelace if that representation might seduce readers into chaos?

Recently, Terry Castle has explored the formal and psychological role that masquerade scenes play in the eighteenth-century novel ("Carnivalization"). In eighteenth-century life the masquerade was one of the most popular forms of public entertainment, an event that allowed people in disguise to place themselves under the sway of the pleasure principle and in so doing to transgress the traditional codes of behavior that governed their sex and class. Transposed into the novel, the masquerade becomes a carnivalesque moment, a moment that introduces something unfamiliar, fantastic, and scandalous yet absolutely necessary to the narrative's providential turn. Although Castle does not list *Clarissa* as one of the novels that includes a masquerade scene, I think it belongs on the list.[5] After all, the prolonged seduction scene proceeds by way of Lovelace's various disguises as well as by Clarissa's theatrical displays of emotion.

However, it also seems to me that something more than aesthetic form is at issue in Richardson's representation of a seductive chaos. While the masquerade may have been the most popular form of public entertainment, it was also part of a more general "reorientation of culture towards the pursuit of pleasure in this world" (Stone 159). As others besides Stone have noted, that reorientation produced an intense interest in sex (Boucé; Foucault; Hagstrum). Indeed, it seems that Georgian England not only tolerated but also promoted various forms of sexual libertinism. Prostitutes were plentiful, pleasure clubs popular, and copulation in public possible. In London, James Graham invited people to try out his "celestial bed," a bed guaranteed to cure all kinds of sexual dysfunctions; although his claim to a cure-all may have been spurious, it does give us the right to consider him one of the first paid sex therapists. In 1749 the first English pornographic novel appeared, followed in due time by the first English pornographic journal. Among the well-to-do, adultery was an accepted practice, as was the discreet engagement in a *ménage à trois*. And according to Francis Place, "the want of chastity" in girls of the tradesmen's class was neither uncommon nor socially stigmatized—an observation supported by the fact that a number of middle-class women were prostitutes and mistresses, often with the consent of their families (Roy Porter). Unlike the guilt-ridden libertinism of the Restoration, the enlightened libertinism of Georgian London was not an elite phenomenon; rather, it involved a large number of people in a social scene that was provocatively confusing, if not downright scandalous.

It is in the midst of just such a scene that the rape of Clarissa appears to clarify matters, for it introduces the possibility of distinguishing between the sexualized will of Clarissa and the sexualized body of the enlightened libertine. However, the distinction does not emerge in the act of rape (an act the novel refuses to represent); instead, it is engendered in the aftermath of the act. Having fulfilled the demands of the rake's code, Lovelace seems relieved, if not pleased. Clarissa, however, goes mad, if only temporarily. Although these immediate reactions to the rape differentiate Lovelace from Clarissa, the two are not yet distinct; there is something like relief in Clarissa's hysteria and something like hysteria in Lovelace's relief. Only after Clarissa's will returns does distinction become both possible and necessary.

When her will returns, Clarissa demands her freedom; citing her "birthright as an English subject," Clarissa reminds Lovelace that in "a country of liberty" even the "sovereign" dares not deny some rights to his subjects (3:267, 221–22). Since Lovelace is not operating according to sovereignty and its laws, Clarissa's demands for freedom have little or no effect. However, when Clarissa stages a scene that displays her sexualized will, it does have the desired effect. Holding a penknife to her bosom, Clarissa enforces a distinction between herself and the others, a distinction that nobody, not even Lovelace, dares to deny:

> "I offer not mischief to anybody but myself. You, sir, and ye women, are safe from every violence of mine. The LAW shall be all my resource: the LAW," and she spoke the word with emphasis, that to such people carries natural terror with it, and now struck a panic into them. . . .
> "The LAW only shall be my refuge!" (3:289)

What intimidates Lovelace and the whores about this display is not some specific English law whose enforcement might harm them but rather the figure of Clarissa, penknife to bosom, proclaiming her relationship to a LAW that the others do not and cannot enjoy. Unlike these others, Clarissa enjoys a sexuality whose resource and refuge is a law that entails the body's repression and if need be, its death. It is precisely Clarissa's willingness to accede to this law—her willingness to kill the body—that stuns the others and assures her triumph, a triumph she repeats in later declarations of the "I am nobody's" sort (4:416).

In turning to the law, Clarissa willingly represses her body. This repression of the body does not, however, entail the repression of Clarissa's feminine sexuality. On the contrary, it is only because Clarissa shows herself willing to kill the body that the others are forced to recognize her feminine sexuality as absolutely distinctive and essentially untouchable. Although Lovelace has manhandled Clarissa's body, he is unable to grasp the truth of her sex.[6] Here, as in the end, it is disembodiment rather than desexualization that distinguishes Clarissa from Lovelace and his band of prostitutes.

By the end of the seduction-rape scene, not only has Richardson effected a distinction between one kind of sexuality and another but he has also affirmed Clarissa's feminine sexuality at the expense of the libertine's feminized body. Two unresolved problems remain, however. First, there is Clarissa's invocation of the law, an invocation that might be confused with an appeal to the actual laws of England. To dispel this potential confusion, Richardson plots Clarissa's imprisonment by legal authorities. Although this turn in the plot exposes the limits of the actual laws of England, it also raises the need for an alternative conception of the law, a conception that can serve as both a resource and a refuge. That need is directly related to the second unresolved problem: although Clarissa's sexuality has been distinguished and affirmed, it remains nonaligned. Since no resolution to the problem of alliance has yet emerged, the basis of a viable community has still to be uncovered. At this point in the novel, Clarissa is a class of one; if Richardson is to enlarge that class, he will have to place Clarissa in some sort of circuit of exchange wherein she can be (re)productive.

THE RETURN TO THE (GRAND)FATHER

The Father inside my head runs a protection racket—the God Father. . . . For a very high price, he does provide protection. The price is behavior . . . : if you are good I will cherish you *and* if you are bad I will punish you. But I will never ignore you or leave you alone or let you go your own way.

—Sara Maitland, "Two for the Price of One"

By the time he was writing *Clarissa*, Richardson was quite familiar with at least one circuit of exchange: that of the literary marketplace. Not only had he been a commercially successful printer for some twenty years but more recently he had authored an extraordinarily popular novel. So pleased was Richardson by the public's warm reception of *Pamela* that he eventually let it be known that he had written the book. Nor did his pleasure diminish when critiques and parodies of *Pamela* began to appear, for he knew that more than one advocate stood ready to defend Pamela from each of her detractors.

However, when Richardson learned that a group of booksellers was planning to publish a sequel entitled *Pamela's Conduct in High Life*, he was anything but pleased. In a meeting with one of those booksellers, a man named Chandler, Richardson asked that plans to publish the "unauthorized" sequel be abandoned. In response, Chandler reminded Richardson that he had informed friends that he would not write a sequel to *Pamela*. Forced to recall his words, Richardson attempted to clarify their intention: although he had refused to write a sequel, he had done so only "upon a Supposition, no one would meddle with [*Pamela*], in which case [he] had resolved *to do it* [*himself*], rather than [his] Plan should be basely *ravished* out of [his] Hands" (Eaves and Kimpel 135; my italics). Since this clarification did not convince Chandler to abandon his plans, Richardson dutifully began work on an "authorized" sequel, thereby hoping to protect *Pamela* from circulating in a scandalously "debased" form.

When *Pamela's Conduct in High Life* was advertised for sale, Richardson responded with an advertisement that attacked this "Imposition on the Publick" while asserting the rights of *Pamela's* true author. In reply, the publishers of *Pamela's Conduct in High Life* not only referred to the "Original Papers" from which their continuation was printed but also attacked the vanity of the "*pretended* Author of Pamela or Virtue Rewarded" (Eaves and Kimpel 138). As this reply shows, Chandler and his cohorts stood ready and willing to capitalize on the fact that in his desire to sustain the illusion that both the letters and Pamela were real, Richardson had refused to name himself as the book's author. In consequence, there there was really no way that Richardson could put an end to "unauthorized" versions of Pamela's life; the most he could do was to put his own sequel into the literary market, where it would compete with others for the attention of the reading public.

Although Pamela's expropriation must have made Richardson less naive about the circulation of both women and letters, *Clarissa* also purports to be a collection of letters by real people engaged in "writing to the moment." Convinced that the illusion of reality was needed in order to provoke "debate" about the "Situations and Circumstances" of his characters (*Selected Letters* 296), Richardson once again denied himself the explicit role of author. Indeed, so eager was Richardson to provoke debate that he not only circulated drafts of *Clarissa* but also published the novel in installments, thereby leading some readers to presume that their advice and arguments might make a difference in the unfolding of Clarissa's destiny.

However, there was one argument that Richardson did not welcome: the debate about the story's ending. Having expressed his shock at those who questioned the appropriateness of his conclusion, Richardson informed Aaron Hill that he would no longer "trouble the World for its opinion" of his manuscript (*Selected Letters* 83). Later, after the first few volumes of *Clarissa* had been published, Richardson also voiced regret that he had decided to bring the novel out in installments, for as he saw it, this mode of publication encouraged debate about the story's conclusion (*Selected Letters* 103, 117). From Richardson's perspective, arguments about his "Management" of such "parts" as the family scene, Lovelace's character, and the relationship between Anna and Hickman were fine (*Selected Letters* 79–82, 112–16, 167–69); the story's conclusion, however, was beyond debate.

Clarissa concludes with a prolonged scene of death in which Richardson attempts to turn his text-in-process into a completed "whole" (*Selected Letters* 116). Since "all must die," Richardson hoped that the death scene would show people how to die well and in so doing "make [*Clarissa*] a much nobler and more useful Story than that of Pamela" (*Selected Letters* 83). There was, however, another, less didactic advantage to be gained by staging Clarissa's death: in turning a text-in-process into a completed whole, Richardson would also be able to protect Clarissa from the expropriation to which Pamela had been subjected. Indeed, the scene of death would seem to be a perfect solution to a number of "scandalous practices" of the age, a solution that did not require that Richardson dispel the illusion of reality he was so intent on sustaining.

Since Clarissa's death appears to be beyond debate, at least two contemporary readers have interpreted it as her "methodical self-expulsion from the realm of signification" (Castle, *Clarissa's Cyphers* 109).[7] But such is not the case: it is precisely the methodical expulsion of Clarissa's *body* that guarantees the inclusion of her sexuality in the realm of signification. Identifying writing as her sole "diversion" (4:10), Clarissa spends more and more of her time with pen in hand. Yet the more she writes, the more she encrypts herself in the realm of signification. Clarissa's dying is thus imaged as a process of encrypting, an agonizingly prolonged process that entails her accession to the symbolic order and her transformation into an exemplary sign or norm. In this way, Clarissa's death becomes a fortunate fall—a defeat of the body that signals the triumph of her sex.

The process that ends in Clarissa's triumphant death begins with a significant displacement of desire. Before the rape, Clarissa sought a reunion with her father and, by way of her father, reunion with the Harlowe family. But after the rape, Clarissa no longer seeks a reunion with Mr. Harlowe; believing that her "refuge must be death" (3:507), Clarissa asks only that her father recant his curse and utter a "last blessing." As these requests suggest, Clarissa is now explicitly concerned with the register of language, a register in which both the actual and imaginary fathers are displaced by the *name* of the father. Indeed, it is precisely because Clarissa has effected such a displacement that she is both willing and able to produce the (in)famous "father's house" pun. To keep Lovelace at a distance, Clarissa not only writes that she is "setting out with all diligence for [her] father's house" but adds that it is there that Lovelace "may possibly in time see [her]" (4:157). As Clarissa realizes, Lovelace is bound to read her message literally, if only because his interest in the body entails the desire for an actual reunion. But Clarissa has passed beyond such a desire; for her, *father* has become a disembodied name, a powerful and authoritative signifier that waylays at least one desire that it provokes—the desire for some body.

Yet Clarissa's turn to the name of the father does something more than block the actualization of Lovelace's desire; it also opens the possibility of an exemplary yet familiar structure of relations, a structure that will allow the daughter to transcend man's otherness through at-one-ment: "And I hope . . . my dear *earthly* father will set me the example my *heavenly* one has already set us all; and, by forgiving his fallen daughter, teach her to forgive the man, who then, I hope, will not have destroyed my eternal prospects, as he has my temporal!" (3:501). In this passage, Clarissa links transcendence with atonement and atonement with identification by and with the father. However, since an actual identification of daughter and father is difficult, if not impossible, Clarissa does what she also does in the "father's house" pun: at one level she divides the issue between earth and heaven, while at another she sutures the gap by calling on the name of the father. Rather than referring to some actual (male) body, the name of the father signifies a position of ethical authority, a position that may be assumed by one whose will is exemplary (i.e., "will set an example"). Thus, identification with and as the father has indeed become a real possibility, but only if one is willing to accede to the Lord's will.

Ideally, Clarissa would make the Lord's will her own: "I often say: Lord, it is Thy will; and it shall be mine." Literally, however, she models her last will and testament on her grandfather's will: "This deed may want *forms;* and it *does,* no doubt: but the less, as I have my grandfather's will almost by heart" (4:289). In the line of fathers, a line that sutures the gap between heaven and earth, it is Clarissa's grandfather who represents the position of ethical authority, for it is his will that is most clearly exemplary. While it may not be "strictly conformable to [man's] law," the grandfather's will obeys a higher law, the law that engenders the text of *Clarissa:* Richardson's deployment of sexuality in the interests of (re)producing a novel yet familiar cultural subject.

In the end, it is Clarissa's relation to the name of the father that makes her such a familiar sexual subject. Conceiving her death as a "weaning time" (4:258), Clarissa accedes to the name of the father, identifies her feminine sexuality with symbolic authority, and takes her place as the signified of the grandfather's will.[8] The image of Clarissa's crypt resting in the ancestral tomb at the feet of her grandfather epitomizes this relationship, a relationship in which Clarissa's passivity is represented as exemplary.

However, if Clarissa appears passive in relation to the name of the father, in relation to others she remains quite active. Her crypt is covered with writing for others to read, an image that suggests that even though Clarissa dies in body, she lives as and in signs. Yet such a mode of existence is not without its problems—problems implicitly recognized by Richardson and explicitly, although somewhat unwittingly, articulated by Clarissa's Uncle Anthony. In responding to Clarissa's pleas for understanding, Anthony Harlowe cites the passage from *Ecclesiasticus* (42:9–11) in which the father is reminded that a "shameless" daughter will make his name "a byword in the city" (4:105). To prevent such a scandal, the father is cautioned to take care that the daughter who circulates be both faithful and true.

In *Clarissa,* Richardson attempts to ensure Clarissa's fidelity and veracity by having her refuse to write her story *as a story:* "I had begun the particulars of my tragical story: but it is so painful a task, and I have so many more important things to do that . . . I would go no further in it" (4:61). If Clarissa were to go further and compose her story, not only would she have to accept "the pain of recollecting things" that would "vex" her "soul" (4:79) but she would also have to represent, if not assume, both her sexuality and her self as a story.[9] It is just such a possibility that Richardson would suppress by representing the exemplary daughter as real—someone who is faithful precisely because her letters are true to life.

Even though Clarissa is unwilling to compose *her story,* she is willing to have her letters published—but only on one condition: that they be published with Lovelace's letters. Having been assured that Lovelace's letters do her the "justice" of representing her as subject to but not complicit with "libertine power" (4:61), Clarissa feels confident that joint publication will further the truth—the truth of her feminine sexuality. Hence, she "dares" to "appeal with the same truth and fervour as he did, who says: *O that one would hear me! and that mine adversary had written a book! Surely I would take it upon my shoulders, and bind it to me as a crown! For I covered not my transgressions as Adam, by hiding mine iniquity in my bosom*" (4:61–62; Richardson's italics). If this appeal helps us to understand Clarissa's interest in Lovelace's letters, it also helps us to explain why so many women writers made so much of Milton.

Besides an adversary, Clarissa's will to publication requires an executor, someone whose job it is to collect and print the letters in the interests of liberating the truth of feminine sexuality from the perversions of power. In doing his job, this executor will promote the emergence of a new alliance, a class of people identified as much by the discourses and norms they share as by their position in the economy. In terms of discourses, this class of people will share an interest in producing a novel yet familiar discourse, one dedicated to the imaginary representation of the social, familial, and sexual relations of individuals. In terms of norms, however, this new class of people will share an interest in upholding the value of feminine sexuality—the valuable truth of an exemplary daughter whose heart belongs to (the name of the) daddy.

CAPITALIZING ON CLARISSA

Perhaps the English version of patriarchy is paternalism.
    —Olivia Harris, "Heavenly Father"

As my reading of *Clarissa* suggests, being the father's daughter is a symbolic position rather than an actual relationship. In order for women to assume this position, they must be inscribed in and by a discourse that structures a seemingly novel subject in familiar terms and relationships. *Clarissa,* I believe, is just such a discourse. By posing the question what Clarissa should do and be in a society governed by a market economy, it addresses women who needed—and still need—to represent their relationship to the real conditions of their existence. By imagining the possibility of a novel yet familiar sexual subject, it identifies a culturally valuable position for woman: being the father's daughter. In doing all this, however, *Clarissa* also tends to suppress the means by which this subject is really produced. Not only does Richardson efface his role in the production but his "new way of writing" encourages the reader to believe that Clarissa is real. Although these strategies are problematical, they are less dangerous than the other major strategy Richardson uses to produce Clarissa. Following Foucault, I have called this other strategy "the deployment of sexuality" and have analyzed it as a way of promoting the idea that there is a true sexuality—more specifically, a true feminine sexuality.

It seems to me that Richardson does indeed desire the daughter. However, as I read it, that desire is not grounded in the incest taboo— the rule that absolutely forbids the man to desire his mother. Rather, I believe that Richardson desires the daughter for more or less the same reasons that the Greek patriarchs desired Philomela, and the Roman patriarchs, Lucretia.[10] All three of these daughters are desired as valuable instruments for promoting the interests of one group of men over another. In short, all three women are caught up in a power play—the plot of male rivalry. In Richardson's novel, that plot takes the form of a class struggle, the struggle by the eighteenth-century bourgeosie to identify itself as a class. But even though the nature and function of male rivalry has changed, just as the classical myths covered up women's work—their weaving of stories (Joplin)—so too does *Clarissa* deny women's need to tell their stories as stories. Like all those (male) writers who preferred the image of Philomela as a bird with her breast pressed against a thorn, Richardson prefers the image of Clarissa with penknife to bosom.

Such images of the feminine suggest that women need someone to speak about, as, and for them. Hence, it is not particularly difficult to understand why men would find the imaginary figure of Clarissa appealing. It is more difficult, however, to understand why women would find this image appealing. One possibility is that *Clarissa* does indeed identify a significant sociocultural role for woman, and most especially for the woman writer. Furthermore, since that novel role is represented as familiar, *Clarissa* also protects the woman from feeling too much anxiety about her new place. This kind of protection may be of particular value to those women whose work requires that they leave their actual fathers behind.

Although *Clarissa* was not as immediately popular as *Pamela* had been, it did bring Richardson an admiring coterie, most of whose members were female. Referring to these female admirers as his "adopted daughters" (Eaves and Kimpel 335), Richardson delighted in the opportunity to play both "grandfather" and "executor" to such an amiable, kind, and tender group of women. Capitalizing on their interest in *Clarissa*, Richardson encouraged his adopted daughters to write confessional letters, not only about themselves but also about the characters and situations in what would eventually become his fourth and final novel, *Sir Charles Grandison*. And write they did. However, like Clarissa's letters, their writing was ruled by the will of a grandfather and collectively deployed by an executor intent on liberating the truth of sexuality. In short, Richardson not only assigned the topics but also managed the flow.

Over the past two hundred years, novelistic discourse has changed a lot. Nevertheless, an argument can be made that in some very important ways, Richardson has continued to assign the topics and manage the flow. As Stephen Heath has demonstrated, novelistic discourse of both the nineteenth and the twentieth century is in large part a discourse on sex, a discourse that wittingly or unwittingly (re)produces all too familiar sexual subjects. However, what makes these subjects familiar is not so much the novel's interest in representing familial relations; rather, it is the novel's involvement in an ideology of sexuality, an ideology that imagines that social and familial relations are more or less fixed, since one is either male or female, man or woman, mother's son or father's daughter. How much this "sexual fix" owes to Richardson has yet to be calculated, perhaps because Clarissa's novel yet familiar sexuality as well as her position as the father's daughter have been doubly appealing, seductive to both men and women.

But what is appealing in a novel may be less so in life, especially in the life of women who often live that double appeal as what Olivia Harris calls a "fatal" contradiction: the father's demand that the daughter be both an "obedient slave" and a "suffragette" (51). Although Richardson's *Clarissa* represents just such a contradiction, it does so in an imaginary way, a way that resolves on a symbolic level what in actuality is irresolvable. Yet we need not identify with Clarissa; instead, we can sympathize with her plight while reading the novel as a historical and ideological representation of the real conditions of our existence. In so doing, we may be better able to work the contradiction of being the father's daughter so that it becomes fatal not to women but to the patriarchal and paternalistic structures in which we have for too long been inscribed.

Notes

1. An aura of fatalism pervades the closing pages of Gilbert's essay. For an analysis of how Freud and Lévi-Strauss work to promote such a fatalistic view of

culture see Rubin. For an analysis of their ideological assumptions about the cultural subject see de Lauretis 18–36; and Silverman 126–237.

2. Amongst modern critics, Clarissa's value and status have been subject to debate. On the one hand, critics such as Van Ghent and William Warner deny Clarissa's true greatness; on the other hand, Castle and Eagleton present her as a true heroine for feminists, while Kinkead-Weekes and Eaves and Kimpel consider her to be a true heroine of humanity. Somewhere between these two extremes are Watt, Rita Goldberg, and Sale, all of whom consider Clarissa more interesting than heroic.

3. Although Foucault does not deny the reality of the sexual in the life of people, he does insist that sexuality is a production of the last few hundred years. As a thing to be discovered, experienced, and recognized as fundamentally true, sexuality is constructed by a set of discursive practices which represent the existence of such a thing and then refer people's experience to this supposed thing. For a more detailed account of the workings of sexuality in nineteenth- and twentieth-century culture see Heath.

4. Ever since *Clarissa's* publication in 1747, critics have noted and debated about Richardson's interest in sex. For his contemporaries' reaction see Eaves and Kimpel chap. 12. Modern critics have continued to argue about the nature, function, and propriety of Richardson's interest in sex. Those who see something perverse in that interest include Van Ghent, Wilt, Watt, Braudy, and Morris Golden—however, the last three of these critics praise rather than censure Richardson, for they appreciate his willingness to probe the depths of the preconscious or unconscious mind. Those who tend to consider Richardson's interest as sincerely ethical include Kinkead-Weekes, Sale, and Hagstrum. More neutral in their judgments are Dussinger and Gerald Levin.

5. Since Castle has written a book on *Clarissa*, this omission may seem especially strange. However, while Castle tends to read the masquerade scene as an instance of positive, life-giving confusion, she believes strongly that the seduction scene in *Clarissa* is a prolonged instance of violence against women. Given her interpretation of *Clarissa*, it makes sense that she would not list it as including a carnivalesque movement.

6. In *The Rape of Clarissa*, Eagleton identifies Clarissa's sexuality with her distinctive body, and both of these with the "real"—with the locus of a truth that we must recognize, protect, and celebrate as liberating. Given this position, it is not all that surprising to find Eagleton arguing that Lovelace never really touches Clarissa's body and that Clarissa's repudiation of the body constitutes "a radical refusal of any place within the 'symbolic order'" (60–63). As I see it, there are at least three problems with these arguments. First, by claiming that Lovelace never really touches Clarissa's body, Eagleton comes close to disavowing rape as an actuality. Second, by (mis)reading Clarissa's repudiation of the body as a refusal of the "symbolic order," Eagleton suppresses Clarissa's post-rape investment in writing. And finally, by identifying sexuality with the body, Eagleton comes close to projecting feminine sexuality as a reality rather than analyzing it as a cultural construction.

7. Eagleton writes along similar lines when he describes Clarissa's dying as

both "a ritual of deliberate disengagement from patriarchal and class society" and a "refus[al of] incorporation into social discourse" (*Rape* 73, 75).

8. Although I have used terms appropriate to *Clarissa*, I trust that the reader will recognize here the familiar (Freudian) account of how a normal female resolves the Oedipal crisis:

> The turning-away from her mother is an extremely important step in the course of a little girl's development. It is more than a mere change of object. . . . hand in hand with it there is to be observed a marked lowering of the active sexual impulses and a rise of the passive ones. . . . The transition to the father-object is accompanied with the help of the passive trends. . . . The path to the development of femininity now lies open to the girl, to the extent to which it is not restricted by the remains of the pre-Oedipus attachment to her mother which she has surmounted. (Freud, "Female Sexuality," 21:239)

9. In her stunning essay "Beyond Oedipus," Shoshana Felman explores the possibility that in representing and assuming the self as a story, one moves beyond Oedipus—beyond the confines of psychoanalytic *science* and into the more open spaces of an authentic practice of speech. Her essay helped me to understand why I was so ill-at-ease not only with Richardson's refusal to allow Clarissa to compose her story as a story but also with his representation of the scene of death.

10. For a brilliant analysis of the sociosexual politics of the Philomela myth see Joplin. To my knowledge, no similar analysis exists of the rape of Lucretia; however, Ian Donaldson's *The Rapes of Lucretia* does discuss the political implications of the myth.

EVAN CARTON

"A Daughter of the Puritans" and Her Old Master: Hawthorne, Una, and the Sexuality of Romance

TORTURED family relations and ambivalent representations of women are the heart of Hawthorne's fiction and have supplied the lifeblood of its critical history. Long before feminists began to focus critical attention on these elements of classic American literature, religious and psychological interpretations of Hawthorne regularly founded themselves on his apparent polarization of dark and fair women characters "along the axis of guilt and purity, or knowledge and innocence" (Baym, "Thwarted Nature" 59). For moralists, the triumphant fair ladies signaled Hawthorne's ultimate commitment to Christian virtues and social conservatism; for romantics and psychologists, the compelling dark ladies signaled his underlying radicalism or his Victorian prurience and sexual guilt. This debate anticipates, and to a degree informs, the more recent critical polarization of a misogynist and a feminist Hawthorne. The misogynist uses women as symbolic tokens, subordinating their humanity to the schematic demands of his fiction and punishing any female character who challenges these demands or threatens the social order that they reflect. He is also the man who, outside of his fiction, repeatedly and patronizingly commends women to their "proper sphere," as he vilifies the "damned mob of scribbling women" (Wagenknecht 150) who are his literary competitors and deplores the "false liberality, which mistakes the strong division-lines of Nature for arbitrary distinctions" (*Works* 12:218). The feminist, on the other hand, depicts more insistently and more sensitively than any male writer of Hawthorne's time the victimization of superior women by the myraid forms of patriarchy; in fact, as Nina Baym contends, women in his fiction may be seen to possess "desirable and valuable qualities lacking in the male protagonist" ("Thwarted Nature" 60).

Hawthorne sustains this controversy, for its partisans must identify him and locate his textual authority in order to establish their respective positions, and his elusiveness and equivocality tend to thwart such critical feats. "Your father kept his very existence a secret, as far as possible,"

Elizabeth Hawthorne told her nephew Julian after her brother's death, and the remark echoes Hawthorne's own repeated claim in letters, prefaces, and other ostensible vehicles of self-revelation (Young 6). The man who lengthily indulges "an autobiographical impulse" in "The Custom-House," his preface to *The Scarlet Letter*, nonetheless promises at the outset to keep "the inmost Me behind its veil" (1:4).[1] In fact, *The Scarlet Letter*, while it marks Hawthorne's emergence from the Salem customs house, from his mother's house, and from literary obscurity, conceals its author behind at least four veils. The intertwined authorial and filial roles that he assumes publicly in "The Custom-House" and privately in the act of composition associate Hawthorne with each of the four characters who make up the novel's disjoined and incestuous family—an association that his 1851 preface to *The Snow Image* acknowledges in principle. Casting that preface in the form of a letter to his friend Horatio Bridge, Hawthorne confides that an author's introductory statements and the "external habits" and details of his life "hide the man, instead of displaying him. You must make quite another kind of inquest, and look through the whole range of his fictitious characters, good and evil, in order to detect any of his essential traits" (11:4). Hawthorne writes "good and evil" here, but he implies, and might more revealingly have written, "male and female." In Hester and Pearl, no less than in Chillingworth and Dimmesdale, the author's identity is invested; indeed, Hawthorne's mysteriousness lies partly in the unexamined fact that female characters throughout his fiction embody many of his own "essential traits." This investment (or veiling) is crucial to an understanding of the relations between men and women in the "neutral territory" of Hawthorne's fiction, a territory in which "the strong division-lines of Nature" that separate male and female appear no more distinct or inevitable than the boundary between the actual and the imaginary that Hawthorne exuberantly and guiltily blurs.

The image of the veil, behind which Hawthorne resolves to keep "the inmost Me," itself connotes feminine modesty and innocence. It is prominent in *The Blithedale Romance* as the delicate barrier to the world that Priscilla removes only for her lover; ironically, it is also the emblem of her psychic enthrallment by Westervelt. The veil's moral ambivalence in this instance is significant, for while Coverdale may believe that Priscilla keeps her "virgin reserve and sanctity of soul" (3:203) despite her mesmeric violation, Hawthorne characteristically equates "the display of woman's natal mind" with the offering of her naked body (*Works* 12:218). In 1841, for example, shortly before his marriage, he entreats Sophia not to seek a mesmeric cure for her headaches: "There would be an intrusion into thy holy of holies," he writes, "and the intruder would not be thy husband" (*Love Letters* 2:62–63). But mesmerism, although it retains a figural power for Hawthorne that I shall want shortly to define, is not the medium of sexual transgression that most troubles him; writing is. Repeatedly he associates literature—and, as we shall see, not only literature written by women—with the illicit revelation or dispensation of female sexuality. Julia Ward Howe's *Passion Flowers* are "admirable poems," he remarks to William Ticknor in 1854, "but the devil must be in the woman to publish them. . . . What a strange propensity it is in these scribbling women to make a show of their hearts, as well as their heads, upon your counter, for anybody to pry into that chooses!" A new publication by another popular literary woman prompts him to write Sophia: "I wonder she did not think it necessary to be brought to bed in public, or, at least, in presence of a committee of the subscribers. My dearest, I cannot enough thank God that, with a higher and deeper intellect than any other woman, thou has never—forgive me the base idea!—prostituted thyself to the public, as that woman has, and as a thousand others do" (Wagenknecht 151–52).

This is not simply the voice of Victorian prudery or chauvinism; it is a more idiosyncratic and more threatened one. Hawthorne is unnerved, in fact, not because he thinks that writing exposes the sexuality of women but because he cannot help but feel that women expose the (female) sexuality of writing, his own chosen profession. Undoubtedly, this apprehension is heightened by the predominance of women as producers and consumers of literature in nineteenth-century America, but its sources lie deep in a personal history whose circumstances complicated Hawthorne's establishment of a sexual identity and gave a special urgency to the distinction between male and female spheres of activity.

As Gloria Erlich has suggested in her recent study *Family Themes and Hawthorne's Fiction,* Hawthorne's childhood was defined by the unfulfilled desire for a father and by the overbearing authority of a father *figure,* his uncle Robert Manning, whose presence for Hawthorne was at once exemplary, reproachful, and "tinged with eros" (118). The tension between the impulse to identify with this model of masculinity and the impulse to rebel, to escape, or to passively submit produced in Hawthorne a deep sense of sexual irresolution. Not only did the "strong division-lines of Nature" divide Hawthorne himself, but they found spatial expression in the distance between Salem, where the boy stayed and, until age seventeen, shared a bed with his uncle, and Raymond, Maine, where his mother and sisters lived in what the exiled Hawthorne once termed "a second garden of Eden" (Baym, "Hawthorne and His Mother" 12). Early on, for Hawthorne, reading and writing literature constituted a guilty—and often self-balked—rebellion against the obligations and constraints of masculine identity, an escape from the father and from the patriarchal province that he associated with the sphere of the daughter.

This association of writing, femininity, childhood, and homelessness or instability assumes various shapes but remains powerful throughout Hawthorne's career, as the self-castigating early tale "Passages From a Relinquished Work" may begin to demonstrate. There, the first-person narrator defies the patriarchal authority of his guardian Parson Thumpcushion—one of a number of fictional avatars of Robert Manning—by remaining resolutely "aloof from the regular business of life" (10:407) and, at last, setting off to be an itinerant storyteller.[2] From the first sentence, in which it is stipulated that the Parson made "no distinction" between the narrator and the three natural sons who became "respectable men, and well settled in life" (10:405), a hint of sexual deviance attends the narrator's account of his solitary rebellion. "He could neither change the nature that God gave me, nor adapt his own inflexible mind to my peculiar character," the narrator states, absolving his guardian of responsibility for the "misfortunes" of his life which he prepares to depict (10:406). No chronicle of misfortunes follows, though; rather, the "passages" of Hawthorne's tale outline the storyteller's rise to professional success. Yet this success is somehow shameful, and the nature of its shame is implicit in the narrator's explanation of his initial reluctance to commence his literary occupation: "A slight tremor seized me, whenever I thought of relinquishing the immunities of a private character, and giving every man, and for money, too, the right, which no man yet possessed, of treating me with open scorn" (10:415). This is the last tremulous resistance of a young *woman* on the point of not only sacrificing her virginity but initiating a career in prostitution. Appropriately, the narrator consummates his professional ambition several pages later in a tavern, where he is emboldened by a conversation with a "bewitching" young person "of doubtful sex" (10:419). To an audience that rolls on the floor with delight, he recites Hawthorne's "Mr. Higginbotham's Catastrophe," but as he leaves the stage, he is handed a letter from his guardian uncannily "directed to [his] assumed name" (10:420). The narrator cannot read this letter, which he imagines to be a missive of "paternal wisdom, and love, and reconciliation," but neither can he escape the specter that it evokes of "the puritanic figure of my guardian, standing among the fripperies of the theatre, and pointing to the players,—the fantastic and effeminate men, the painted women, the giddy girl in boy's clothes, merrier than modest,—pointing to these with solemn ridicule, and eyeing me with stern rebuke." Although unable to return home, he flees the scene of his triumph oppressed with a vision of "the guilt and madness of [his] life" (10:421). It is the association of his life with sexual ambiguity that prompts the storyteller's feelings of guilt and madness, and twenty years later it is this same association that the specter of a "mob of scribbling women" renews for Hawthorne. "Generally women write like emasculated men, and are only to be distinguished from male authors by greater feebleness and folly," observes the successful romancer, in a sentence whose comparative adjective strikes more insidiously at "male authors" than at women (Wagenknecht 153). All writers, the sentence implies, are feeble, foolish, and emasculated; the women who provide particularly vivid evidence of those traits only expose their male counterparts the more clearly.

Like his narrator in "Passages From a Relinquished Work," however, Hawthorne pursues his literary course despite the guilt and the sense of emasculation or sexual confusion that it generates in him. "It is one of my few sources of pride," the wandering storyteller notes wryly, "that, ridiculous as the object was, I followed it up with the firmness and energy of a man" (10:416). So Hawthorne follows up his college resolution to become an author—a commitment that he sealed in a wager with his closest friend, Jonathan Cilley, that he would not marry within twelve years of his graduation—by withdrawing for thirteen years to the Salem house of his cloistered mother and two retiring sisters. Writing thus becomes Hawthorne's veil, the sign and justification of his decision to remain "aloof from the regular business of life" and the symbol of his nunlike marriage to a strange and distant ideal whose pursuit requires and celebrates the "female" capacities for imagination, intuition, solitude, emotion, and mystery. It is in this context of Hawthorne's personal and professional identity that Nina Baym's argument for his feminism is most powerful. Throughout Hawthorne's fiction, "'woman' stands for a set of qualities which the male denies within himself and rejects in others," Baym insists, adding that "the ability to accept woman—either as the 'other' or as a part of the self—becomes in his writing a test of man's wholeness" ("Hawthorne's Women" 250–51). The truth of these judgments lies not in their representation of Hawthorne's women characters (Baym has to disqualify Phoebe, Priscilla, and Hilda as "creatures of the patriarchy" ["Hawthorne's Women" 259] in order to preserve her critical category) nor in their claim to define a consistent authorial intention but in their descriptiveness of Hawthorne's own predicament. Not only in many of his fictional women but in his fiction writing itself Hawthorne gives form and gives quarter to qualities that "the male" denies within himself and rejects in others, qualities that Hawthorne must indeed sustain in order to be whole but that he also finds threatening to his wholeness as a man or perhaps even symptomatic of his emasculation. Romance is the medium of these tensions, the veil that allows him at once to indulge and constrain, to reveal and disguise, "the inmost Me."

Mesmerism, to which we may now return, provides a striking figure of Hawthorne's art and suggests its double function as a veil. In *The Blithedale Romance* and in a crucial scene in *The House of the Seven Gables* the male mesmerist and his female subject are united and divided by the veil suspended between them. One face fronts the manipulative artistry, the cool control, the phallic power of the man; the other looks towards the natural receptiveness, the sympathetic intuition, the vulnerability of the woman. Each role in the production of the mesmeric effect is facilitated and obscured by the mediation of the veil, which also preserves the ambiguity of the mesmeric inspiration's principal agency. Throughout his prefaces and narratives, Hawthorne assumes both roles, the role of exhibitor and that of subject or veiled exhibit. He is, in the terms of the preface to *The House of the Seven Gables,* the artist who may "manage his atmospherical medium" as theatrically as he chooses but who "sins unpardonably" if he should "swerve aside from the truth of the human heart" (2:1). Or in the terms of "The Custom-House," he is the "poking," "prying," "burrowing" (1:29) uncoverer of Hester Prynne's story, who allows himself "nearly or altogether as much license" in its retelling "as if the facts had been entirely of [his] invention" (2:33), yet he is also the communicant who holds the "mystic symbol" to his breast and experiences "a sensation not altogether physical, yet almost so, as of burning heat; and as if the letter were not of red cloth, but red-hot iron" (1:31). In *The Blithedale Romance* mesmerism pervasively emblematizes the literary art of Hawthorne's narrator Miles Coverdale, who perceives himself again and again on both sides of the veil. Admitting a tendency to arrange the other characters "upon my mental stage, as actors in a drama" (3:157), Coverdale also claims—with equal authority, I believe—a "quality of the intellect and the heart, which impelled me (often against my own will, and to the detriment of my own comfort) to live in other lives, and to endeavor—by generous sympathies, by delicate intuitions, by taking note of things too slight for record, and by bringing my human spirit into manifold accordance with the companions whom God assigned me—to learn the secret which was hidden even from themselves" (3:160). The narrative of the sporadically effeminate Coverdale at once indulges these sympathies and counters or covers them with the most violative manipulations. Similarly, in other texts, Hawthorne counters his own association of his enterprise with the incorporation and exposure of the female by displaying its capacity for male sexual force.

A significant and revealing instance of romance's defensive alignment with phallic power is the scene in *The House of the Seven Gables* in which Holgrave reads to Phoebe his story of her ancestor Alice Pyncheon's sexual and mesmeric enthrallment by his own forefather, Matthew Maule. In this episode from the family history of both teller and listener, Maule avenges his grandfather's emasculation by the patriarch Colonel Pyncheon, who with "iron energy" and "stern rigidity of purpose" convicts the original Matthew Maule of witchcraft in order to take possession of his "garden-ground" (2:8), to "drive the plough" (2:7) over it and to "[lay] the deep foundations" (2:9) of the Pyncheon mansion in it. At the same time, Maule revenges himself against the "womanly" Alice for her frankly admiring glance at his physique, a look that "most other men" (2:201) would have taken to be a compliment, as the narrator remarks, but that Maule takes as a contemptuous challenge to his manhood. Holgrave, in his literary performance, discovers himself on the verge of repeating the patrimonial mesmeric feat, of violating Phoebe as Maule had violated Alice.

> With the lids drooping over her eyes,—now lifted for an instant, and drawn down again as with leaden weights,—she leaned slightly towards him, and seemed almost to regulate her breath by his. Holgrave gazed at her, as he rolled up his manuscript, and recognized an incipient stage of that curious psychological condition, which, as he had himself told Phoebe, he possessed more than an ordinary faculty of producing. A veil was beginning to be muffled about her, in which she could behold only him, and live only in his thoughts and emotions. His glance, as he fastened it on the young girl, grew involuntarily more concentrated; in his attitude there was the consciousness of power, investing his hardly mature figure with a dignity that did not belong to its physical manifestation. It was evident, that, with but one wave of his hand and a corresponding effort of his will, he could complete his mastery over Phoebe's yet free and virgin spirit. (2:211–12)

This is the novel's true climactic moment. Both his future with Phoebe and the power of their ancestral past depend on Holgrave's decision. That decision is the moral one and the one that dissolves the reciprocal curse of the Pyncheons and Maules, but it also betrays Holgrave's fathers and, in a way, arrests his own manly development by relinquishing the power that has begun to "[invest] his hardly mature figure with a dignity that did not belong to its physical manifestation." Holgrave gives up fiction and resolves to burn his manuscript of the Alice Pyncheon story; Hawthorne, who publishes the manuscript, sets it apart somewhat from the course of his narrative by representing it as Holgrave's composition and as a distant historical event, but his repudiation of the story as a model of his own enterprise is a far more equivocal one. *The House of the Seven Gables* proceeds from this point to a saccharine conclusion, facilitated by Hawthorne's dispersion of literal difficulties and thematic tensions in a manner so sentimental and serendipitous as to smack of self-mockery. Holgrave and Phoebe ultimately marry and jointly inherit the Pyncheon estate, but their convergence represents neither an adult sexual union nor a successful consummation of the novel's energies and concerns; rather, they are, as the narrator presents them near the end, "like two children who go hand in hand, pressing closely to one another's side, through a shadow-haunted passage" (2:305).

Roger Chillingworth, wielding his abstruse scientific skills to revenge himself and, implicitly, to restore the authority of an outraged patriarchy, is a purer representative of the veiled, vindictive, masculinist face of Hawthorne's fiction—although, ironically, it is Chillingworth's own impotence and absence that have precipitated his betrayal and the subsequent exposure and sexual empowerment of Hester Prynne. "Delving," "prying," and "probing," Chillingworth penetrates "deep into his patient's bosom . . . like a treasure-seeker in a dark cavern" (1:124), determined to ravish Dimmesdale's secret if only, as he puts it, "for the art's sake" (1:137). The physician is Hester's competitor for Dimmesdale's body and soul and her formal counterpart in the novel. But their relationship, their concealed yet undissolved marriage, is only one figure of the structural dialectic that comprises *The Scarlet Letter,* and manifests itself in a number of ways. Indeed, one could argue that *The Scarlet Letter* is Hawthorne's greatest work because it is the text in which his "female" authority, in the fullness of its sympathetic and antinomian powers, is simultaneously most liberated and most bound, most proudly revealed and most ashamedly covered—most invested. The letter itself is the emblem of this dialectic: in its "fertility and gorgeous luxuriance of fancy" (1:53), it is the token of Hester's subversive sexuality; as a label and a burning stigma imposed by the Puritan fathers, it is the mark of their authority to define, control, and neutralize her. This is the tension that informs *The Scarlet Letter* and that expresses the equivocal sexual politics of Hawthorne's identity and sense of authorship. It is a politics that is recognizable, in fact, in Hawthorne's famous description of the "neutral territory" of romance as it first appeared to him in his moonlit study:

> There is the little domestic scenery of the well-known apartment; the chairs with each its separate individuality; the centre-table, sustaining a work-basket, a volume or two, and an extinguished lamp; the sofa; the bookcase; the picture on the wall,—all these details, so completely seen, are so spiritualized by the unusual light, that they seem to lose their actual substance, and become things of intellect. Nothing is too small or too trifling to undergo this change, and acquire dignity thereby. A child's shoe; the doll, seated in her little wicker carriage; the hobby-horse,—whatever, in a word, has been used or played with, during the day, is now invested with a quality of

strangeness and remoteness, though still almost as vividly present as by daylight. (1:35–36)

Romance, here, is a distinctly female domain, but one whose "actual substance" is somewhat disguised, translated, spiritualized, intellectualized—in other words, veiled in masculine attributes and "invested" with remoteness and "dignity" thereby. It is surely not intentional, but neither is it accidental, that the key terms of this description are prominent again at the moment in *The House of the Seven Gables* when Holgrave recognizes his imperial power over the housewifely Phoebe, a recognition that has the effect of "*investing his hardly mature figure with a dignity that did not belong to its physical manifestation*" (my italics). In both romancer and romance, the male and the female "may meet, and each imbue itself [nourish itself, disguise itself] with the nature of the other" (1:36).

IN HIS MEMOIRS, Julian Hawthorne wrote: "My father was two men, one sympathetic and intuitional, the other critical and logical" (Wagenknecht 17). Almost without exception, Hawthorne's literary friends shared and expressed the perception of his "double sensibility" (Erlich 124), a sensibility that they described, however, as an amalgam of male and female qualities. James Russell Lowell's "A Fable for Critics" provides a public, verse rendition of this judgment:

> When Nature was shaping him, clay was not granted
> For making so full-sized a man as she wanted,
> So, to fill out her model, a little she spared
> From some finer-grained stuff for a woman prepared,
> And she could not have hit a more excellent plan
> For making him fully and perfectly man.

Margaret Fuller, to whom Hawthorne was less charitable, wrote in a similar vein on hearing of his engagement to Sophia Peabody: "I think there will be great happiness; for if ever I saw a man who combined delicate tenderness to understand the heart of a woman, with quiet depth and manliness enough to satisfy her, it is Mr. Hawthorne" (Wagenknecht 18).

As I have argued by implication to this point, Hawthorne also recognized the "feminine" elements of his own nature, elements that included not only a delicate sensibility but a tendency towards passive dependence and a simultaneous repulsion from and attraction to representatives—and activities associated with the exercise or gratification—of masculine force and appetites. Such ambivalence is pervasively exemplified in Hawthorne's private and public commentary on his own work. Imagining his tales and essays as "blossoms," in "The Old Manse" and elsewhere, he at once extols their fragile beauty and scorns their failure to yield manly fruit. Drawn to the myth of Pandora, which he retells as "a story of what nobody but myself ever dreamed of—a Paradise of children" (and we might note here how considerable a portion of Hawthorne's writing is for or about children), he also regularly condemns his implicitly effeminate childishness (7:63). Perhaps the most direct and suggestive confession of Hawthorne's double nature, though, is a passage from a letter to his mother in Maine written shortly before Hawthorne entered college. "Oh how I wish I was again with you, with nothing to do but go agunning. But the happiest days of my life are gone. Why was I not a girl that I might have been pinned all my life to my mother's apron" (Erlich 21). The gun had belonged to Hawthorne's father, and the attractions of going "agunning" and of being a girl, asserted in such contiguity, express a tension that would shape the relationships between brothers and sisters and between fathers and daughters in Hawthorne's fiction.

To recognize the sexual tension of Hawthorne's literary enterprise is to begin to see the family dynamics of his fiction in ways obscured by the Oedipal orientation of Hawthorne's psychological critics. It is, for instance, to perceive the centrality of the father-daughter relationship—a relationship typically marked by the father's abandonment of a daughter whom he continues to dominate through figurative sons and by the daughter's ambivalent representation of the filial desire to escape or smash the paternal mold and to submit to paternal affection and control. The young men in Hawthorne's fiction, in fact, often find themselves (or lose themselves) in the context of the father-daughter relationship as unwilling agents of the father's power or as resistant choosers of a child-like—a daughterlike—identity.

Two of Hawthorne's earliest and most personal tales revolve around daughters whose fathers both abandon them and continue, through filial surrogates, to enthrall them. In the undergraduate novel *Fanshawe,* the title character, who deems himself "unconnected with the world" (3:350), is connected to the plot only negatively, by certain sorts of self-effacement and certain moments of inaction. At the center of the story is Ellen Langton, the daughter of an ambitious father, who has left her to be raised by a friend while he extends his fortune in Europe. On the pretext that this father is in danger, and by the challenge to "prove if his daughter has a daughter's affection" (3:361), a strange "messenger from her father" (3:359) lures Ellen from the home of her guardian. The messenger, Butler, turns out to be a once devoted foundling and "protégé" of Mr. Langton who has been disowned by his benefactor for committing "certain youthful indiscretions" (3:453) and who has resolved, on hearing a mistaken account of Langton's death at sea, to seduce and marry his daughter in order to inherit the fortune to which he already makes a sort of filial claim. Fanshawe, a reclusive student who is dying of a vague physical and emotional "blight" that has "come over him ere his maturity" (3:346), foils Butler's plan literally by accident.

From the moment of Butler's appearance in this juvenile work, Fanshawe (who shares with him the want of a Christian name) is more compellingly seen as his inverse than as the pale counterpart of Edward Walcott, a manly fellow student who loves Ellen conventionally and marries her after the deaths of both Butler and Fanshawe. Butler sees in Ellen his opportunity for sexual domination and worldly success; Fanshawe uses her not to fulfill these desires, or even to gratify them in fantasy, but to help him confirm his repudiation of them. "Had Fanshawe . . . acknowledged to himself the possibility of gaining Ellen's affections," Hawthorne writes, "his generosity would have induced him to refrain from her society before it was too late. He had read her character with accuracy, and had seen how fit she was to love, and to be loved by a man who could find his happiness in the common occupation of the world" (3:443). Despite one vague reference to a "dream of undying fame" (3:351), Fanshawe does not forgo a man's common occupation in favor of an uncommon, presumably literary one. Rather, he rejects manhood and the world outright and pursues "habits, mental and physical," calculated to "[bring] himself to the grave" (3:459) "ere his maturity." Significantly, his purgation of his feeling for Ellen and his extinction of his life are described simultaneously: "He had exerted the whole might of his spirit over itself—and he was a conqueror" (3:459). This sentence also suggests the form of his triumph over Butler, who represents the lustful masculine spirit that Fanshawe conquers. Appearing on a precipice at the foot of which Ellen is about to be raped by her captor, Fanshawe makes his presence known. Butler wildly abandons his unthreatened design and tries to ascend the sheer rock but slips just before he reaches his statuesque enemy and thus meets "the fate that he intended for Fanshawe" (3:451). Fanshawe then takes Butler's place below, and after allowing himself a gaze of "perfect bliss" and a moment's sensation of "triumph—that rose almost to madness" (3:452), he revives the fainted Ellen. Shortly afterward, he is again in a position to enjoy the spoils of Butler's place and must eschew both Mr. Langton's money and his daughter. Ellen would inevitably be "sacrificed" (3:459) in a marriage to him, he tells her, but Fanshawe—who in a portentous early scene is imaged not as a fisherman, with Butler and Walcott, but, with Ellen, as a pierced fish—would be sacrificed, too. To accept Mr. Langton's largesse or his "daughter's affection," in the logic of the novel, would be to become Butler, a "protégé" of the father and an agent of his lusts;

instead, Fanshawe dies at age twenty and evades the patriarchal prerogatives.

Fanshawe's balked attraction to Ellen impossibly combines sexual desire and, less consciously, sexual identification. "It was," Hawthorne writes, "the yearning of a soul, formed by Nature in a peculiar mould [recall the narrator's self-description in "Passages From a Relinquished Work"], for communion with those to whom it bore a resemblance, yet of whom it was not" (3:443–44). Thus, both his sexual status and his part in the action place Fanshawe between Butler and Ellen. A similar configuration informs "Alice Doane's Appeal," the early unpublished tale about a young man who commits "fratricide in fact, parricide in fancy, and incest in his heart" (Young 70). In this tale, though, the father's representative and the daughter's defender and counterpart are more explicitly portrayed as twin halves of a single identity. Every psychological critic has recognized that in killing Walter Brome, his double and his sister's apparent seducer, Leonard Doane destroys the incarnate prosecutor of his own incestuous desire. But Walter Brome stands for more than this: he is the model of mature masculinity that is Leonard's inescapable patrimony and that promises, at the moment of its acceptance, to obliterate Leonard's lifelong identification with his sister and to turn "the consecrated fervor of their affection from childhood upwards" (II:21) into "that impure passion which alone engrosses all the heart" (II:272). Before Walter Brome appears, at the threshold of Leonard's manhood, Leonard's character has been shaped by "the closeness of the tie which united him and Alice"; specifically, it has been "softened and purified" by their "lonely sufficiency to each other" (II:271). Yet, although she instills "something of her own excellence into the wild heart of her brother, [it is] not enough to cure the deep taint of his nature" (II:270). That taint is his nature itself, the aggressive sexuality that his shared and insular orphanhood has retarded but not squelched. "The germ of . . . fierce and deep passions, and of all the many varieties of wickedness" had always lived in Leonard's soul; in Walter these passions are simply "brought to their full maturity" (II:271). Significantly, in the instant that Leonard is confronted with "indubitable proofs of the shame of Alice" and kills Walter "before the triumphant sneer could vanish from his face" (II:272), he recognizes that face as his father's and is himself transformed from "a weeping infant by [his] father's . . . bloodstained hearth" to "a man of blood, whose tears were falling fast over the face of his dead enemy" (II:273). The "triumphant" father lives not only in the actual or imagined seduction of the daughter but in the ultimate masculine identification of the resistant son. In the end, it is the father who dominates the action in "Alice Doane's Appeal," as is emphasized by his gratuitous authorial presence in the form of "a wizard; a small, gray withered man, with fiendish ingenuity in devising evil, and superhuman power to execute it" (11:270), whose "machinations" (11:277), we later learn, have precipitated the entire plot.

Although he is partly unwilling, and although he is imbued with "something of [Alice's] excellence," Leonard Doane takes his place in the patriarchal scheme and joins "the men of history" (11:276) whose guilty specters line Gallows Hill and frame the events of "Alice Doane's Appeal." On March 3, 1844, Hawthorne assumed his own place in the patriarchy with the birth of a daughter he called Una, after Spenser's heroine in *The Faerie Queene*. Una's name disconcerted family and friends, one of whom wrote to Hawthorne that it should be "rather kept and hallowed in the holy crypts of the mind, than brought into the garish light of common day" (*Works* 14:276). The remark was strangely prescient. Una would remain throughout her life rather a product and a prisoner of her father's imagination than an inhabitant of the common day. Even more eerie is Hawthorne's own prefiguration of Una's fate in the life of the fictional daughter and prisoner Beatrice Rappaccini, whom he seems to have created in the month of his daughter's birth.[3] Beatrice is the creation, agent, and victim of the father with whom she lives in an exotic and cloistered garden. This "Eden of the present world" (10:96) is an inversion of the Biblical paradise; its plants and its atmosphere are toxic, and its creator is a diabolical scientist, a profane "artist" (10:126). It is also an inversion of Hawthorne's lost paradise at Raymond, the "second garden of Eden," in which a benign mother might protect her son from the authority and the example of a suffocating and seductive father figure; in Rappaccini's garden, a patriarchal horticulturist and brilliant hybridizer, as Uncle Robert was, effectively rapes his daughter, injecting her body with his deadly fluids until they become "her element of life" (10:117). Beatrice, I am suggesting, like *The Scarlet Letter*'s similarly innocent and dangerous Pearl, may be identified both with Hawthorne's daughter and with Hawthorne himself, or at least with those of his "essential traits" that "the male denies within himself" but that remain necessary to the "man's wholeness." Like her two fictional sisters, moreover, Una is imagined to embody her father's hidden taint—a projection of which Hawthorne almost seems conscious when he has Chillingworth propose "to analyze [the] nature" of the oddly named elf-child he has modeled on Una and "from its make and mould, to give a shrewd guess at the father" (1:116).

Every member of the Hawthorne family recognized and remarked Una's "immense . . . force" (*Works* 14:306) and her physical and temperamental likeness to her father. Hawthorne's wife and son also testified to his special and intense affection for her, an affection that could be frank and spontaneous but seems from the beginning to have included a more obsessive quality and to have been mingled with resistance and feelings of guilt that were transferred onto Una's character. Hawthorne's complex attitude towards his daughter is suggestively imaged in the clinical, defensive, attracted, and endangered creator Giacomo Rappaccini, who first appears as a "distrustful gardener," a man who walks among his shrubs "looking into their inmost nature, [and] making observations in regard to their creative essence" while avoiding "their actual touch, or the direct inhaling of their odors" (10:95–96). His practical engagement with these "vegetable existences" is primarily a matter of "pruning [their] too luxuriant growth" (10:96)), although he finds the perfume of his most magnificent creation—the hybrid plant that Beatrice calls "sister"—too powerful for him even to risk approaching. Like Beatrice, Una comes to be associated with a luxuriant and tainted artistic enterprise that at once expresses and alienates its author.

The language of Hawthorne's journal entries on his daughter is the language of the imagination, while his son typically reassures him of the stable actual, the paternal sphere that he had sought to escape as a child and as a writer and that he now ambivalently occupies. "There is something that almost frightens me about the child," he writes of the five-year-old Una. "I now and then catch an aspect of her, in which I cannot believe her to be my own human child, but a spirit strangely mingled with good and evil, haunting the house where I dwell. The little boy is always the same child, and never varies in his relation to me." What frightens Hawthorne about the unpredictability of his daughter's relationship to him is its reflection of his own internal inconsistency. In his notes on Una he is repeatedly entranced and appalled by what he calls her "manifestations," her ability to pass "from one character to another, male and female, youth, age, or infancy . . . , like the little flames that quiver and dance at the top of a coal grate" (8:411). This description evokes an image of the romancer, who, inspired by the play of firelight, distributes the elements of his identity among his fictional personae. But, typically, a sharp reaction to such personal fluidity follows: it is useless to seek Una's "real soul," Hawthorne pronounces, "for, before the establishment of principles, what is character but the series and successions of moods?" (8:413). Written early in 1849, these lines about Una articulate the conflict between the play of identity and the establishment of principles that informs *The Scarlet Letter*, which Hawthorne composed later in the same year. In part, it is the emotional conjunction of Hawthorne and Una at a passionate and guilty moment (his mother's death) that generates this novel, which is partly about the consequences of mutual recognition for a father and a daughter.

Hawthorne's notebook entries for July 29 and 30, 1849, the last days of his mother's life, interlace observations on his mother's condition, his own emotions, and his daughter's "strong and strange interest" (8:430) in the drama of death. The familial bond between these three is epitomized in Hawthorne's description of a moment in which, standing at the window of the dying woman's room, he glimpsed Una frolicking in the yard, then turned back to the sick bed "and seemed to see the whole of human existence at once, standing in the dusky midst of it" (8:429). Baym sees in this image the "linked chain of three" that would become Pearl, Dimmesdale, and Hester on *The Scarlet Letter*'s scaffold, and she argues that Hawthorne's intense and thwarted feelings for his mother underlie the Oedipal dimension of Dimmesdale's illicit passion ("Hawthorne and His Mother" 20). Erlich, emphasizing the adolescent Hawthorne's "serious problems with gender identity" as well as his "too close . . . relationship with the mother," suggests that the figure of little Pearl, who is "always at her mother's side," represents the author's "never wholly satisfied longing for symbiosis with the mother" (71–72). Both of these readings are supportable; and they are reconcilable. The unacknowledged intimacy and guilty attenuation of Dimmesdale's bond to Hester and to Pearl reflects the pattern of Hawthorne's relationships with both his mother and daughter. Moreover, the association of Hawthorne with diverse sexual and familial roles in *The Scarlet Letter* is reinforced by the general sexual and familial inconsistency of the novel's characters. Pearl is the model of an ontological and behavioral indeterminacy, "a spell of infinite variety" (1:90), that often seems to exempt her from a strictly human existence, or from the Puritan conception of one. In the adult world, however, it is Dimmesdale who plays roles more various and contradictory even than Pearl's. He is a public representative of the Puritan patriarchy and the private father of Pearl; he is Hester's lover and, in the forest, her emotional dependent; he stands in a filial relationship to Chillingworth and, in the oddly sexual symbiosis between them that Leslie Fiedler and others have noted, also assumes a female role. Dimmesdale is not only an adulterer but the prime exemplar of what Michael Ragussis, in a stimulating essay on *The Scarlet Letter,* calls "the adulterous self—the self that is mixed with another, from the beginning" (880). Ragussis remarks that "the father cannot be himself until he acknowledges his child" (871), but Dimmesdale's double bind is that neither in acknowledgment nor in disacknowledgment can he sustain a coherent identity. The devout spiritual leader cannot accommodate the passionate and inadvertent procreator, and in a larger sense, the patriarchal authority of the Puritan theocracy cannot be reconciled with Dimmesdale's paternity of Pearl. These contradictions are not resolved by the equivocal ending of the novel, in which Dimmesdale's dramatic but incomplete unveiling at once aligns him with Hester and Pearl and marks his total abandonment of them. If his final performance constitutes a manly acceptance of responsibility, it is curious that Hawthorne images his steps towards the scaffold as "the wavering effort of an infant with its mother's arms in view, outstretched to tempt him forward" (1.251). Indeed, the figure of an infant or a child is appropriately applied to Dimmesdale on the scaffold, but it is a figure very different from Pearl, and one that turns from the mother to seek the exclusive mercy of a supreme Father. Frederick Crews notes that "for both Pearl and Dimmesdale the plot eventually fulfills a need for the benevolent father who remains absent until Dimmesdale's confession" (269), and his formulation points up the way in which Dimmesdale's ultimate self-commitment to Pearl and to Hester is the means by which he frees himself from them. As for Pearl, she is freed from her spell ("of infinite variety") to become a woman in the world, a subject of its laws and customs, and even—as the armorial seals on her letters and Hester's embroidery of baby garments imply—a vehicle of its patrilineage. At the end, no less than at the beginning, Ragussis's observation stands: "Pearl's life is specified far outside herself, and her name seems an ironic tease" (867). The same, as we shall see, might be said about Una.

IN 1853, HOPING to achieve security for his growing family, Hawthorne accepted the post of American consul at Liverpool, offered him by the new president, and his old college friend, Franklin Pierce. For his nine-year-old daughter, the move to England marked the beginning of a dramatic change in her relationship with her father, whose days were no longer spent at home and whose evenings were often devoted to the social obligations of an American ambassador and literary notable. Suddenly, too, what time Hawthorne had for his children was usually spent with Julian. As his daughter approached adolescence, it seems, the father began to withdraw from her. The "strong division-lines of Nature" increasingly governed the activities of the Hawthorne family, and the girl whom Hawthorne had called "wild as a colt" (*Works* 14:409) a few years earlier had begun to exhibit, in her brother's recollective phrase, "a queer maturity and hardness" (Hull, "Una" 94). Homesick and lonely, Una became, in her mother's words, "disgusted with everybody and thing that did not suit her taste and principles" (Hull, *Hawthorne* 247). Throughout this period of anger and rebellion, however, she continued to idolize her father, as she did in the period of resignation that appears to have followed. During the latter years of the Hawthornes' English residence "Una seems to have accepted whatever plans were made for her" (Hull, *Hawthorne* 128). When left to herself, she read, with a passion that she alone among the children shared with her father. "Like many sensitive people," Hawthorne had written of her years earlier, "her sensibility is more readily awakened by fiction than realities" (8:415). This observation of Una, like so many others, is largely self-reflective for Hawthorne; indeed, his own affection and guilt towards his daughter would reemerge most intensely in the fiction that marked Una's passage into sexual maturity and almost out of life, Hawthorne's last completed novel, *The Marble Faun*.

Early in 1858 the Hawthornes left England to make an extended tour of Italy before returning home. For Sophia, the opportunity to live in Rome fulfilled a lifelong dream; Hawthorne's feelings about the family's continued "exile" (as he termed it) were more complex. In his Italian notebooks and letters, Rome often represents an evasion of home and of "the reality of life" (Hull, *Hawthorne* 162) that waits there to be taken up again—an evasion that Hawthorne's characteristic ambivalence towards his native soil and long absence from a profession that he doubted his ability to resume prompted him to continue. In Rome, engaged neither in imaginative creation nor in "the regular business of life," Hawthorne seems to have been more uncertain than at any time since his marriage not only of his proper place in the world but of the very moorings of his identity. His sense of double alienation is often conveyed in the Italian notebooks, and it informs Hawthorne's language in the preface to his last romance. Dismissing the possibility of writing about or in his own country, he explains that Italy afforded him "a sort of poetic or fairy precinct, where actualities would not be so terribly insisted upon, as they are, *and must needs be,* in America" (4:3; my italics). The actual and the imaginary no longer meet on neutral territory, nor can either command the field. America's atmosphere of "common-place prosperity" (4:30) is pure but forbidding; Italy, and particularly Rome, is a lush aesthetic garden—as a repeated image in *The Marble Faun* has it—but its atmosphere is poisonous, malarial. The "Eternal City" (4:213) is a deadly paradise. Its allure for Hawthorne, as his notebooks and *The Marble Faun* suggest, partakes of the allure of death.

The dangerous allure of Rome was inevitably associated as well with Una. Even in England Hawthorne had worried about his daughter's sudden interest in religious "forms and ceremonies," an interest that he seems to have interpreted as the desire to get unnaturally close to a heavenly Father: "Shall the whole sky be the dome of her cathedral? or must she compress the Deity into a narrow space, for the purpose of getting at him more readily?" (Hull, "Una" 94). In Italy, Una was strongly attracted by the more elaborate forms of Catholicism and of the art that it had inspired, and Hawthorne recorded his concern. "U—— spoke with somewhat alarming fervor of her love for Rome," he remarked in his notebook, and added: "We shall have done the child no good office, in bringing her here, if the rest of her life is to be a dream of this 'city of the soul,' and an unsatisfied yearning to come back" (14:230).

Hawthorne was to have greater cause for guilt than this, however, in Rome's effect on Una. On a damp October evening in 1858, while sketching outdoors near the Palace of the Caesars, Una contracted malaria; with a moral logic that would inform *The Marble Faun,* her "alarming fervor" for Rome was transformed into a case of "Roman fever" that almost took her life. During the four months between the onset of the illness and Una's first false recovery, Hawthorne wrote nothing in his journal. He worked fitfully instead on a draft of a novel that is dominated by treacherously intimate daughter-father relations, or by the collapse of relationship into two stark alternatives: utter filial submission to—and perhaps incestuous incorporation by—the father's imperial identity and symbolic—perhaps actual—patricide. A few days after Una passed the crisis that no one had expected her to survive, Hawthorne wrote that her illness had "pierced into [his] very vitals" (14:518) as no previous trouble had. *The Marble Faun* is shaped, I think, by his feeling of responsibility for Una's tortures on the verge of womanhood, a feeling rooted not so much in the fact of his having brought her to Rome as in the sense of an intimacy abandoned or betrayed. The novel is shaped, too, by Hawthorne's corresponding sense of alienation (practical and moral) from imaginative enterprise and from the part of himself—always associated with the daughter—that had determined his professional identity. Hawthorne's "double sensibility" is most violently divided against itself in *The Marble Faun,* and this division is reflected in the polarization of his voice into filial and patriarchal roles: the role of the daughter who desperately seeks and desperately resists paternal authority; and that of the father who offers wisdom and corruption, security and violation, in "lurid intermixture."

The critical and affective center of *The Marble Faun* is not the story of a mythical creature's fortunate or unfortunate fall into humanity but the story of two women, both defined as artists and as daughters, who are radically divided and radically united by their modes of fulfilling these determinative roles. The character Hilda identifies herself on three occasions as "a daughter of the Puritans" (4:54, 362, 466). She is devout, simple, presexual, and unwaveringly submissive to a generalized and internalized ideal of paternal authority. Like Una's in Italy, her need for patriarchal support in a time of uncertainty brings out troubling "Catholic propensities" (4:368). Hilda's friend Miriam seems to be her inverse. Irreverent, complex, and dangerously sexual, she does not find her identity—as we shall see Hilda does—in the agency of the father but in reaction against him. Miriam's origins are unknown, but in each of the various speculations about her she has "fled from her paternal home" (4:23), usually to escape an unsavory father or to avoid sexual domination by his representative. Like the Una of Hawthorne's journals, she repeatedly betrays a "rich, ill-regulated nature" (4:280); in fact, the first sustained description of her almost recreates Hawthorne's portrayal of the fitfully luminous daughter who enticed and disconcerted him by her unstable relationship to himself: "She resembled one of those images of light, which conjurors evoke and cause to shine before us, in apparent tangibility, only an arm's length beyond our grasp; we make a step in advance, expecting to seize the illusion, but find it still precisely so far out of our reach" (4:21). If this passage depicts Miriam as an utterly ungovernable force, its effect is mitigated by the narrator's remark, on the same page, that "Miriam had great *apparent* freedom of intercourse" (4:21; my italics). As the reader discovers, Miriam is actually more thoroughly dominated by patriarchal power than is her counterpart. The initial difference between Hilda and Miriam lies in their responses to the exercise and the agents of such power, responses epitomized in a curious passage fom the novel's climactic chapter, "On the Edge of a Precipice."

On a walk among the ruins of the Palace of the Caesars, the sculptor Kenyon suggests to his artist friends that they are standing at the site of the legendary chasm that threatened to swallow up Rome before the hero Curtius sacrificed himself to save the city. This was the "fatal gulf," Kenyon speculates, into which flowed "all the blood that the Romans shed," including the blood of Virginia, the daughter of an ancient centurion, whose father killed her rather than see her seduced by the powerful consul, Appius Claudius. "Virginia, beyond all question, was stabbed by her father, precisely where we are standing," Kenyon concludes. "Then the spot is hallowed forever!" replies Hilda, but Miriam bitterly counters: "Is there such blessed potency in bloodshed?" (4:163). For Hilda, the sacrifice of the daughter to the father's protective authority is sublime, an ultimate guarantee against the stains of sexuality and disgrace. For Miriam—who is insistently identified with Beatrice Cenci and who assents to the retributive murder of a "model" of patriarchal authority before this chapter is out—the violative seducer and the violative protector are one, and the daughter must fight for her life. Yet, as the narrator early informs us in defining "the moral" of Miriam's passionate paintings, "woman must strike through her own heart to reach a human life, whatever were the motives that impelled her" (4:44). Ironically, the self-preserving alternative suggested by the story of Virginia is unavailable to Miriam. The pointed hints about her history and the force of the novel's symbolic logic combine to indicate that her revolt against a rapacious father neither keeps her from sexual and moral compromises nor protects her identity from external domination; on the contrary, the alliance with the model that liberates her from her persecutor only binds her—sexually as well as criminally, Hawthorne implies—with another and eventually leads to a third unholy relationship that fails, in turn, to break the bonds of the second. Miriam's model (a brother, it would seem) embodies the "evil spirit" of the original tormentor, whom he kills, and himself becomes the model for the devoted Donatello, who kills him. Images of the father and son and allusions to the two crimes that destroy them merge in Miriam's parting gaze at the corpse of the dead model (whose alias, at death, is that of a Capuchin monk, Brother Antonio): "this was the visage that she remembered from a far longer date than the most intimate of her friends suspected; this form of clay had held the evil spirit which blasted her sweet youth, and compelled her, as it were, to stain her womanhood with crime" (4:190).[4] Hilda, by contrast, remains stainless, deifying the sexual authority of the father and, after she has witnessed the model's murder, repelling Miriam's plea that they are "sisters of the same blood" (4:207) with the reply: "I am a poor, lonely girl, whom God has set here in an evil world, and given her only a white robe, and bid her wear it back to Him, as white as when she put it on" (4:208).

The artistry of the two women is a function of these opposed daughterly roles. Miriam's compositions are powerful, passionate, and undisciplined, striking in their originality yet somewhat lacking in "technical merit" and "trained skill" (4:20). Her studio is, in effect, the locus of romance, or at least of its "poetic . . . precinct": it is "one of those delightful spots that hardly seem to belong to the actual world, but rather to be the outward type of a poet's haunted imagination, where there are glimpses, sketches, and half-developed hints of beings and objects, grander and more beautiful than we can anywhere find in reality" (4:41). Every canvas that Miriam produces in this magical realm, however, contrives to announce its own failure. "Over and over again, there was the idea of woman, acting the part of a revengeful mischief towards man," yet these compositions, which begin in celebration, are invariably "given the last touches in utter scorn" (4:44). Jael and Judith do not overcome their enemies, even though they slay them, and Miriam does not win creative control over her material through artistic execution; the portraits, she tells Donatello, are "not things that I created, but things that haunt me" (4:45). Miriam's "sister," on the other hand, frankly abandons all ambitions of personal distinction and authorial control. A schooled and talented young artist, the orphan Hilda comes to Rome and is so enthralled by "the mighty Old Masters" (4:57) that she "cease[s] to consider herself as an original artist" (4:56).

> Reverencing these wonderful men so deeply, she was too grateful for all they bestowed upon her—too loyal—too humble, in their awful presence—to think of enrolling herself in their society. . . . All the youthful hopes and ambitions, the fanciful ideas which she

had brought from home, . . . were flung aside, and, so far as those most intimate with her could discern, relinquished without a sigh. (4:57)

Hilda's decision to become a copyist, an "exquisitely effective piece of mechanism" for the transmission and reproduction of "the spirit of some great departed Painter" (4:59), is significantly associated with her gratitude to an artistic patriarchy and her relinquishment of the hopes and "fanciful ideas" of youth. These associations oppose her not only to Miriam but to the youthful Hawthorne, who indulged rebellious fancies well into the autumn of his life. Indeed, by the end of *The Marble Faun* Hilda has abandoned art altogether, and by the end of this introductory chapter the narrator's initial claim that Hilda sacrificed "a decided genius for the pictorial art" (4:55) has itself been undercut. With "utter scorn" for the very idea of original creation, the last few paragraphs of the chapter commend Hilda's willingness to "[lay] her individual hopes . . . at the feet" (4:60) of the Old Masters. "Would it have been worth Hilda's while," Hawthorne concludes, in resonantly self-indicting terms, "to relinquish this office, for the sake of giving the world a picture or two which it would call original; pretty fancies of snow and moonlight; the counterpart, in picture, of so many feminine achievements in literature!" (4:61).

The two chapters that contrast the artistry of Miriam and Hilda are presented consecutively near the beginning of *The Marble Faun*. The next chapter, "Beatrice," links the women through the figure of Beatrice Cenci, the notorious sixteenth-century daughter (and subsequently popular artistic subject) who conspired with her brother to kill their physically and perhaps sexually abusive father and who was executed by papal authority. Hilda has copied Guido's portrait of Beatrice from memory and shows her work to Miriam, who entreats the copyist to expound the "subtle mystery" (4:67) of Beatrice's expression, the mystery of her conscience. Pressed, Hilda pronounces, "Her doom is just" (4:66), and she is "startled to observe that her friend's expression had become almost exactly that of the portrait" (4:67). Later, though, after she has seen Donatello effect and Miriam silently authorize the death of the model, it is Hilda whose features take on Beatrice's expression. "Am I, too, stained with guilt?" she wonders, to which a suddenly obtrusive narrator replies, "Not so, thank Heaven!" (4:205). If Hilda is unstained, she nonetheless resembles the ravished Beatrice in the almost explicitly sexual nature of her relationship to the Old Masters. Asked by Miriam whether Guido might not be jealous that her "Beatrice" so successfully rivals his, Hilda exclaims: "Jealous, indeed! . . . If Guido had not wrought through me, my pains would have been thrown away" (4:68). And after she has become disillusioned with art's essential impurity and with the great Italian painters' "tremendous jest" of "offering the features of some venal beauty to be enshrined in the holiest places" (4:338), she finds herself still bound to these men, not by warm affection but by a chilling torpor (4:334). A final elaborate instance of Hilda and Miriam's convergence in and division by the figure of Beatrice Cenci is a painting by a young Italian artist who observes the despondent Hilda in a gallery and grows "deeply interested in her expression" (4:330). Catching her absorbed in thoughts of Miriam, he surreptitiously paints a portrait that "many connoisseurs" take to be a variation on Guido's "Beatrice": "It represented Hilda as gazing, with sad and earnest horrour, at a blood-spot which she seemed just then to have discovered on her white robe" (4:330). The artist calls his picture "Innocence, dying of a blood-stain"; his dealer changes the title to "The Signorina's Vengeance." These polarized versions of Beatrice Cenci's history are the daughter's options in *The Marble Faun*. In both, art is ultimately repudiated, and in both— whether early or late, willingly or inescapably—the daughter's identity is consumed.

If the father's guilt more thoroughly permeates *The Marble Faun* than it does *The Scarlet Letter*, the drive to sustain patriarchal authority is also more intense. There is little in Hawthorne's last ending of the moral and aesthetic equivocality that attends the account of Dimmesdale's submission to his heavenly Father. Rome is finally not the "home of art" but the domain of "an irresponsible dynasty of Holy Fathers" (4:100). Yet, despite its unsatisfying patriarchal models, the novel bears out the dictum of Kenyon—Hawthorne's normative "man of Marble" (4:4)—that "the heart of mankind . . . craves a true ruler, under whatever title, as a child its father!" (4:166). To this observation, Miriam responds that if there were a "rightful King," she would "lay [her troubles] at his feet" (4:166); but, in fact, no such King is required to bring both Miriam and Hilda to their knees. Miriam accepts her guilt (for a crime committed by a man) and a life of penance under a bronze statue of Pope Julius III, in whom she sees "the likeness of a father" (4:316) and of whom, though despairing of "so vast a boon," she asks "pardon and paternal affection" (4:318). Hilda kneels at a confessional in St. Peter's and pours out an account of the crime she has witnessed to an English-speaking priest, who promptly reports the matter to the Roman authorities. Shortly afterward, when she fulfills a promise to deliver a parcel for Miriam at the Palazzo Cenci, Hilda is held hostage by these authorities. Mystified by her disappearance, an anxious Kenyon comforts himself with a thought that, given the novel's father-daughter motif and Hawthorne's helpless guilt over Una's illness, constitutes *The Marble Faun*'s most ironic line: "A miracle would be wrought on her behalf, as naturally as a father would stretch out his hand to save a best-beloved child" (4:413). That miracle is the bald exchange of Miriam for Hilda, an exchange that parallels the transformation of Una Hawthorne to which her brother testifies: "Her intellect was active and capacious, and at one period of her life took a radical turn, questioning and testing all things with a boldness and penetration, combined with a sound impartiality, rare in the feminine mind. But at length the lofty religious bias of her nature triumphed over all doubts" (*Works* 15:373).

The daughter's sacrifice in *The Marble Faun* is the sacrifice of art as well. In this repudiation Hilda and Miriam are joined by Kenyon and the narrator. As Miriam submits to Roman justice, Hilda agrees to return with Kenyon to America, where he intends to "imprison her in his heart, and make her sensible of a wider freedom, there, than in all the world besides" (4:395). In the "Postscript" that Hawthorne added for the novel's second printing, the narrator enters the scene in order to go home with "his friends, Hilda and the sculptor": "We three had climbed to the top of St. Peter's, and were looking down upon the Rome which we were soon to leave" (4:464). At this point, Hilda and Kenyon have both forsaken artistic labor, and it seems clear that they will not resume it in America. The crisis of their commitment to the imagination has occurred in their joint contemplation of Kenyon's unfinished bust of Donatello. It is a work that contains what Hilda acknowledges to be art's "highest merit" (4:379), the "suggestiveness" that invites imaginative engagement and forgoes "the establishment of principles," or of "the strong division-lines of Nature," in favor of the play of identity. But Hilda and Kenyon cannot accept its suggestion of the possibility of a fortunate fall, an act of filial disobedience that might produce something of value. "You have shocked me beyond words!" exclaims Hilda when Kenyon gingerly presents this reading of Donatello's history, whereupon he instantly renounces it: "I never did believe it. But the mind wanders wild and wide; . . . Oh, Hilda, guide me home!" (4:460–61).

The Marble Faun does not take its Americans home. Hawthorne and his family returned in 1860, and Hawthorne died within four years—years of steadily declining health and utter literary breakdown. After his death, Sophia and the children again left Concord for Europe. In Dresden, where Julian attended an engineering school, Una copied her father's fragmentary manuscripts. In England several years later she nursed her dying mother and wrote that their "positions seemed reversed" (*Works* 15:361). On the day before Sophia's burial, Una records, "We took off her wedding ring and I wore it" (*Works* 15:371). Poised geographically between America and Rome, Una also joined the Anglican church—a compromise between the faith of her forefathers and her own "Catholic propensities"—and established a short-lived "preventive home" to provide an alternative to prostitution for destitute young women, a charity that she sought to finance by public appeals to her father's English readers. "It was hard to me, at first, to use my father's name in this appeal," she concluded a letter printed in *The Times*, "but I rely on the sympathy of your readers, having taught myself to feel no daughter can pay a more sacred tribute to her father's memory than making it help in a good cause" (Marks 18). While visiting her married younger sister in New York in 1874–75 Una met a consumptive, unpublished writer who was about to sail to the Sandwich Islands in the hopes of material for art and improved health. Una and Albert Webster became engaged by correspondence in 1876, but he died at sea six months before the reunion they had planned. According to Julian, with whose family Una lived, his sister received the news of Webster's death with the words "Ah—yes!" and quietly "relinquish[ed] the world" (*Works* 15:373). Shortly afterward, suffering from the last of the frequent physical breakdowns that had plagued her since her illness in Rome, Una entered a Protestant convent and died on a pallet there. She was, Julian wrote, "in every way worthy of her parents. Whatever they had hoped and prayed for was fulfilled in her character . . . ; no occasion for the manifestation of truth, charity, generosity, self-sacrifice, ever found her wanting" (*Works* 15:372). But Hawthorne's own observation of his four-year-old daughter is the fitter epitaph: "she comes to the table and stands beside me—weary, it seems to me, from mere idleness, and the want of a purpose in life" (8:422). The remark prefigures a line written ten years later and spoken in *The Marble Faun* by Miriam about the "jointed figure" that she uses to model the poses of her murderous heroines, the mannequin that she recognizes as a model of herself: "she pretends to assume the most varied duties and perform many parts in life, while really the poor puppet has nothing on earth to do" (4:41). As if she had been a creature not of the earth but of her father's imagination, no birthdate appears on Una's tombstone to accompany the legend: "Una, Daughter of Nathaniel Hawthorne."

Notes

1. Quotations from Hawthorne's fiction and notebooks refer to *The Centenary Edition*. Unless otherwise indicated, all parenthetical references are to this edition.

2. I follow Erlich's lead here, both in associating Parson Thumpcushion with Robert Manning and in approaching this tale biographically.

3. The editors of *The Centenary Edition* date three of Hawthorne's major tales of the Old Manse period—"The Artist of the Beautiful," "Drowne's Wooden Image," and "Rappaccini's Daughter"—from the winter and early spring of 1844. A letter written to George Hillard on March 24 suggests that the "irksome"

task of fictional composition still engaged Hawthorne, despite his distraction by the "business on earth" to which, as a father, he now had to attend. On April 1 he seems to have finished his last story, remarking in a letter to Bridge that "the sight of a pen makes me sick" (10:509–10). During these months the need for money prompted Hawthorne to send his stories to magazine editors as soon as they were completed. The fact that "The Artist of the Beautiful" was published in the *Democratic Review* for June, "Drowne's Wooden Image" in *Godey's Lady's Book* for July, and "Rappaccini's Daughter" not until the *Democratic Review* for December suggests that it was "Rappaccini's Daughter" that occupied Hawthorne throughout March of 1844. The revisions of the tale in 1846 and 1854 also indicate, as the editors note, Hawthorne's "special interest" in and "continuing rapport" with the tale (10:549–50).

4. The nineteenth-century admirers of Beatrice's supposed portrait were most intrigued and titillated by the possibility of her forced incestuous relations with her father. Hawthorne clearly models Miriam on this Beatrice and suggests in imagery and innuendo throughout *The Marble Faun* that Beatrice's secret is both a criminal and a sexual matter. Hawthorne complicates her speculative history by suggesting the horrifying duplication of the original sin in the relationship that is established to redress it—a pattern that is made explicit in Miriam and Donatello's fatal union after the model's murder and one that, as I have shown, accords with the curious relationships in earlier works in which brothers at once protect sisters against fathers and violate them as patriarchal representatives.

ELIZABETH BUTLER CULLINGFORD

A Father's Prayer, A Daughter's Anger:
W. B. Yeats and Sylvia Plath

"A PRAYER for My Daughter" and "Daddy" approach their common theme, the relationship between fathers and daughters, from opposite sides of the Atlantic. Plath's father is symbolically located in "the waters off beautiful Nauset," while Yeats's daughter is menaced by an Atlantic gale blowing westward onto the shores of Ireland. The two poems are also emotionally an ocean apart. The father's verse is measured, stately, and controlled; the daughter's is vividly angry, in tone and vocabulary suggesting a nursery tantrum. Yet the connection between them is profound and depends upon more than a coincidence of subject. Yeats was one of Plath's poetic progenitors, and she admired him passionately. As his cultural daughter, however, she felt the weight of his paternalistic prescriptions for femininity. In two early poems, "On the Difficulty of Conjuring Up a Dryad" and "Virgin in a Tree," she offers a critique of the idea of female imprisonment presented in "A Prayer for My Daughter"; and in "Daddy" her deliberate shrillness, the venomous intensity of hatred that Yeats deplored in women, poses a direct challenge to his image of the ideal daughter.

Plath's love-hatred for the father she seeks to escape merely confirms her imprisonment, and the relationship between "Daddy" and "A Prayer for My Daughter" provides a model in miniature of the father-daughter dialectic. The father's love for and control over his daughter should not issue either in incest or in her perpetual enslavement. The resolution is embodied in a third person: the bridegroom who legitimately replaces the father. This dialectic is, however, firmly constituted within patriarchal rules and assumptions: the daughter is both loved and then given away as her father's possession. As a result of her enforced dependency the daughter may find it hard to establish a psychically distinct relationship with the bridegroom, who is, by definition, another possessor. She may therefore enact a symbolic return to the father either in choosing a husband who resembles him or in remaining celibate.

Anne Butler Yeats was her father's favorite from the beginning. When she was born, he wrote that despite the disappointed family ambitions of his relations (including his wife, who wept when the sex of the child was revealed), "a daughter pleases me better" (Yeats Papers, MS 18734). He had from the first, however, a conventional conception of her future. "A Prayer for My Son" assumes that the male child will be an actor in the drama of his life, that some "haughty deed" awaits him (Yeats, *Variorum Edition* 426). In contrast, the female child will be acted upon: her bridegroom will "bring" her to his house.

The opening of the poem establishes her need for protection: "Once more the storm is howling. . . ." While Yeats has "bred" a frail girl-child, nature, in the shape of the Atlantic, has "bred" a powerful gale. The drafts of the poem reveal that "the haystack- and roof-levelling wind" was originally conceived of as a metaphor for the Marxist political movements that Yeats saw as threatening Europe after World War I and the Bolshevik revolution: it is described as a "popular tempest," "some demagogue's song / To level all things" (Stallworthy 29, 31). Plath's political environment is no less disturbing: her imagination encompasses World War II, the Holocaust, and Hiroshima. Yet her attitude towards her children's entry into a violent and destructive world is different from Yeats's. Anne, like Wordsworth's Lucy "half hid" in her cradle, seems nevertheless cruelly exposed, protected from the wind only by "Gregory's wood and one bare hill." Plath's babies, on the other hand, are images of power and solidity. She greets her daughter as a "new statue" beside whose strange and concrete otherness she herself is displaced like "the cloud that distills a mirror to reflect its own slow / Effacement at the wind's hand" ("Morning Song," *Collected Poems* 157). Her son, whom she identifies with Christ, defies the "storm" of the nuclear age: despite the "mercuric / Atoms that cripple,"

> You are the one
> Solid the spaces lean on, envious.
> You are the baby in the barn.
> ("Nick and the Candlestick," *Collected Poems* 242)

In this reversal of the power relationship between parent and child Plath reveals her emotional fragility. Nevertheless, her poems evoke and celebrate the physical immediacy of the contact between mother and baby.

In contrast, while Yeats's imagination is stimulated by Anne's birth, he reaches beyond her to the past and to the future, converting mundane into philosophical and ethical anxieties. Though the future is hers, the past belongs to him. His daughter has entered his life at a time when

> My mind, because the minds that I have loved,
> The sort of beauty that I have approved,
> Prosper but little, has dried up . . .   (*Variorum Edition* 405)

The beauties that have failed to prosper are Maud Gonne and her daughter Iseult, to both of whom Yeats had proposed marriage during the summer of 1917. Both, first the mother and then the daughter, refused him; and in October of the same year he married Georgiana (George) Hyde-Lees. All three of these women inhabit the poem, which catalogs both the failures and the successes of Yeats's own affective life. The birth of a daughter naturally leads the poet to consider his models of femininity, but it is striking that he should concentrate so single-mindedly upon the future sexuality of one who at the poem's inception was, according to the drafts, a month-old child (Stallworthy 29). The poem leaps from the baby in the cradle of stanzas 1 and 2 to the girl in front of her looking-glass of stanza 3; the intervening years of childhood go unmentioned. In three canceled stanzas the poet addresses his daughter as a young woman of twenty-four or twenty-five and begs her to come alone to Coole for a rendezvous with his shade (Stallworthy 38–42).

George Yeats was twenty-seven when she married the poet; he was fifty-one. In imagining Anne at the age of twenty-five Yeats is reimagining her mother; indeed, George herself was a daughter figure for him. Phyllis Chesler considers this kind of union to be the rule rather than the exception in patriarchal society: "While most women do not commit incest with their biological fathers, patriarchal marriage, prostitution, and mass 'romantic' love are psychologically predicated on sexual union between Daughter and Father figures" (43). Had Yeats's earlier proposal to the twenty-two-year-old Iseult Gonne proved successful, the incestuous implications would have been even clearer. Iseult, the offspring of Lucien Millevoye, was widely reputed to be the child of Yeats and Maud Gonne (Clarke 350). In September 1917 Yeats wrote, "Last night Maud Gonne returned to that strange conviction of hers, that Iseult is my child because when Iseult was born she was full of my ideas. Perhaps at the time Maud Gonne was in love with me" (Yeats Papers, MS 18734). In the poem "Owen Aherne and His Dancers" Yeats shows himself well aware of the embarrassing incongruity of his desire for the daughter of his great love:

> The Heart behind its rib laughed out. "You have called me mad,"
>   it said,
> "Because I made you turn away and run from that young child;
> How could she mate with fifty years that was so wildly bred?"
>   (*Variorum Edition* 450)

Although his relations with Iseult remained cordial, she was a source of constant perplexity to him: when shortly after refusing him she married Francis Stuart, a young man of eighteen whom he then considered a "dunce" (*Variorum Edition* 626), he was deeply upset. Despite her loveliness, Iseult was passive, lazy, moody, and addicted to cigarettes—certainly not an appropriate model for Anne.

Yeats had made Maud Gonne's beauty a matter of legend, but in his eyes she too had failed to prosper. Her nationalist politics were unbecomingly extreme, she supported the Bolsheviks, and at the time of the composition of "A Prayer for My Daughter" his personal relations with her were strained. In 1918 she was detained in London as a suspect in a nationalist conspiracy; meanwhile, Yeats and George, then pregnant with Anne, had borrowed her Dublin house. Evading the authorities, Maud arrived on her own doorstep only to be turned away by Yeats, who feared the effect of military searches on the health of his wife. George was suffering from severe pneumonia, but Maud was understandably enraged, and the result was a spectacular public quarrel. Beauty, therefore, was temporarily at a discount with Yeats. Women who are too beautiful, he argues,

> Consider beauty a sufficient end,
> Lose natural kindness and maybe
> The heart-revealing intimacy
> That chooses right, and never find a friend.
>
> (*Variorum Edition* 403–4)

Yeats had spent the first half of his creative life celebrating Maud Gonne as the supremely beautiful and inaccessible beloved. Perhaps he had chosen to address her in the best courtly love tradition in order to mask, from himself and from others, his own inadequacies as a lover. His marriage to a much younger, much more compliant woman and the reassuring evidence of his potency offered by the birth of his daughter caused him to look skeptically at the inspiration provided by inaccessibility. He offers instead a new model: George, who though "not entirely beautiful" has "earned" his heart through her kindness and courtesy:

> Yet many, that have played the fool
> For beauty's very self, has charm made wise,
> And many a poor man that has roved,
> Loved and thought himself beloved,
> From a glad kindness cannot take his eyes.
>
> (*Variorum Edition* 404)

In pleading with Anne to reject the image of femininity embodied in the women who scorned him and to imitate instead the figure who accepted him, Yeats hints at one of the commonest of incestuous patterns: the father who desires his child because she reincarnates the youthful image of her mother.

The poem attempts to overcome this desire. The qualities that Yeats prays his daughter may acquire—kindness, courtesy, the capacity for intimate friendship, charm, and moderate good looks—are all worthy but unlikely to set the pulses racing. That traditional image of female narcissism, the lovely woman with a looking-glass, is presented as less appealing than the "glad kindness" of a more homely female friend. Lest this assertion strike the reader as not only doubtful but also somewhat dreary, Yeats offers cautionary tales of Helen and Aphrodite, the legendary symbols of beauty and sexuality:

> Helen being chosen found life flat and dull
> And later had much trouble from a fool,
> While that great Queen, that rose out of the spray,
> Being fatherless could have her way
> Yet chose a bandy-legged smith for a man.

> (*Variorum Edition* 404)

Both the passive and the active beauties—Helen, who was abducted, and Aphrodite, who was free to choose—find inappropriate mates. Thus "the Horn of Plenty is undone," women's natural fertility is perverted. In Helen and Aphrodite Yeats is thinking of Iseult and of Maud, who has passed on to her daughter the face that launched a thousand ships, while retaining the more powerful goddess persona herself. While Plath's "Daddy' is an attempted exorcism of the vampire-father, Yeats's poem is an attempted exorcism of the negative anima, the witch woman who destroys and is destroyed through her own sexuality. The perfect beauties, supercharged with the freight of desire, are dismissed from Anne's world, just as Prospero, in supervising and manipulating his daughter's marriage, banished Venus and Cupid from the courtly masque.

Yeats's emphasis on the circumstances of Aphrodite's birth (she "rose out of the spray") and on the fact that being "fatherless," she was free to act as she pleased, masks a profound sexual anxiety. The legend of Aphrodite's origin tells how the Titan Cronos castrated and killed the original Father, Ouranos, while he was copulating with Gaia (the Earth). Cronos threw his father's genitals into the ocean, and out of the blood and semen that spread over the surface of the water the goddess was born. Aphrodite is thus a perfect image of the Fatal Woman, the daughter who takes life from her father's castration and who exemplifies the union of blood and seed, sexuality and violent death. According to Gēza Róheim, "the myth evidently means that Aphrodite can only originate after the father has been killed, and also points to the phallic origin of the love goddess" (169). The birth of a daughter evoked castration anxiety in Yeats; Sylvia Plath, as we shall see later, was obsessed by the fantasy that she had killed and castrated her father (*Journals* 301). The

237

destructiveness of daughters who lack fathers may be a psychological truth inscribed in the myth of Aphrodite. (Helen, though technically the offspring of Zeus, was to all intents and purposes fatherless too.) Without the security conferred by early male validation of her sexuality, the fatherless daughter is forced to exact approval from every man she meets. Aphrodite must win the golden apple; Helen, whose abduction was the direct consequence of that first beauty contest, could not resist the wooing of Paris. The result of her need for male validation was the destruction of Troy. The connection between female sexuality and violence was, for Yeats, an immutable fact: "Aphrodite rises from a stormy sea. . . . Helen could not be Helen but for beleaguered Troy" (*A Vision* 267–68). The addition of a potential Helen to his own household caused him to consider the implications of his images of femininity. A man who has worshipped Fatal Women may prefer not to rear one. The birth of his daughter initiated no less a project than a reevaluation of his Muse.

In an earlier poem, "No Second Troy," Yeats had viewed Maud Gonne's destructiveness as an essential part of her nobility (*Variorum Edition* 256–57). In 1919, with Europe in ruins, the Anglo-Irish War about to begin, and his daughter in her cradle, violence could no longer evoke admiration:

> I have walked and prayed for this young child an hour
> And heard the sea-wind scream upon the tower,
> And under the arches of the bridge, and scream
> In the elms above the flooded stream;
> Imagining in excited reverie
> That the future years had come,
> Dancing to a frenzied drum,
> Out of the murderous innocence of the sea.
>
> (*Variorum Edition* 403)

Two kinds of innocence are implicitly juxtaposed: the child in her cradle and the "murderous" innocence of the sea. Yeats's sea is a feminine archetype, and whipped by the wind, it produces the "spray" out of which Aphrodite rose. Although she is "innocent" of the parricide from which she originated, the blood and seed that were the conditions of her birth mark her as a "murderous" sexual deity.

The combination of sea and storm and the repetition of the word *scream* initiate a pattern of image and sound that conveys a deeply unpleasant idea of femininity. As the castrating sea-wind assaults the phallic man-made tower, Yeats employs a familiar contrast between the female and the male. Sherry Ortner has argued that the universal devaluation of woman results from the fact that she is perceived as being closer to nature than to culture (Ortner 67–87). Women's participation in certain kinds of

culture, "systems of thought and technology" (72), is discouraged by
paternal authority. Genevieve Lloyd contends that from its inception the
Western philosophical tradition has conceived of Reason itself as "the
transcendence of the feminine" (104). Yeats, who continually exalted
passionate intuition, was particularly horrified by women who were
enslaved by "opinions" or by any system of abstract thought. In a memorable if wholly negative depiction of the animus-driven woman, Maud
Gonne, Yeats warns his daughter of the evil effects of female involvement
in politics:

> An intellectual hatred is the worst,
> So let her think opinions are accursed.
> Have I not seen the loveliest woman born
> Out of the mouth of Plenty's horn,
> Because of her opinionated mind
> Barter that horn and every good
> By quiet natures understood
> For an old bellows full of angry wind?   (*Variorum Edition* 405)

The horn of plenty, or cornucopia, torn by Zeus from the she-goat
Amalthea, who suckled him, is a feminine symbol of natural abundance.
A woman who chooses the wrong mate or abandons femininity for the
sake of opinions exchanges quiet nature and endless fertility for a barren
piece of industrial machinery, the "old bellows full of angry wind" that
fans the flames of intellectual hatred. Perhaps she also exchanges one
wind instrument for another—the melodious horn for the spiteful bellows (Rowland 288)—or, in an even cruder pun, the fruitful womb for
the windy anus.

The most striking natural image in the poem occurs in the sixth
stanza:

> May she become a flourishing hidden tree
> That all her thoughts may like the linnet be,
> And have no business but dispensing round
> Their magnanimities of sound,
> Nor but in merriment begin a chase,
> Nor but in merriment a quarrel.
> O may she live like some green laurel
> Rooted in one dear perpetual place.   (*Variorum Edition* 404–5)

The child in the cradle was only "half" hidden; his grown daughter is to
be hidden entirely, to dwell amidst untrodden ways. Something of Prospero's interest in the preservation of Miranda's chastity is evident in
Yeats's allusion to Apollo and Daphne. Daphne, fleeing from the lustful
Apollo, prayed to her father, the river god Peneus, that she might remain

239

forever a virgin rather than be forced by the god. Peneus responded by turning her into a laurel tree, thus preserving her chastity at the expense of her humanity. Daniel Harris has criticized Yeats for his use of this allusion: "Apollo seeking sexual and marital bliss with Daphne is one thing; Yeats-Apollo seeking Anne-Daphne for the same reasons is quite another. The incest motif is inappropriate; the allusion encompasses more than Yeats meant it should, or shows too blatantly what he felt" (142). If Yeats-Apollo, however, is conscious of the desire to pursue Anne-Daphne, Yeats-Peneus (surely a more appropriate identification) is ready with the remedy. To protect his daughter from rape, he must imaginatively sequester her from all human relations, "hide" her within the chaste bark of a tree. If he must not have her, no one will. Beryl Rowland is unable to believe that Yeats means what he says: "Since Daphne was doomed to perpetual virginity, the allusion can have only limited reference" (289). Yet the idea of a single life is reinforced in this stanza by a second, less obvious allusion. Through his choice of the linnet and his use of the adjective *green,* Yeats directs our attention to Wordsworth's "The Green Linnet," a solitary bird:

> While birds, and butterflies, and flowers,
> Make all one band of paramours,
> Thou, ranging up and down the bowers,
> Art sole in thy employment:
> A Life, a Presence like the Air,
> Scattering thy gladness without care,
> Too blest with any one to pair;
> Thyself thy own enjoyment.   (Wordsworth 140)

This "self-delighting" creature has no "business" but the generous, "natural" dispensation of its "magnanimities of sound."

Joyce Carol Oates is so enraged by the implications of the Daphne allusion that she ignores the linnet altogether: "This celebrated poet would have his daughter an object in nature for others'—which is to say male—delectation. She is not even an animal or a bird in his imagination, but a vegetable: immobile, unthinking, placid, 'hidden.' . . . The poet's daughter is to be brainless and voiceless, *rooted* " (17). Despite her inaccuracy, Oates, like Ortner, sees the problems that arise when a male writer chooses to embody a feminine ideal in images, whether animate or inanimate, taken from nature. However charming or desirable the image may appear to be (and the tree in Yeats is frequently a symbol of strength, harmony, and integrity), it implies a lack of full humanity and a subordinate relationship to male-dominated culture. Men like to think they own trees; fathers like to think they own daughters.

Sylvia Plath responded ironically to the implications of the sixth stanza of "A Prayer for My Daughter" in her poem "On the Difficulty of Conjuring Up a Dryad." A tree is a tree, she insists, and not a woman:

> "My trouble, doctor, is: I see a tree,
> And that damn scrupulous tree won't practice wiles
> To beguile sight:
> E.g., by cant of light
> Concoct a Daphne;
> My tree stays tree.
>
> "However I wrench obstinate bark and trunk
> To my sweet will, no luminous shape
> Steps out radiant in limb, eye, lip,
> To hoodwink the honest earth. . . ." *(Collected Poems* 66)

In the phrase "sweet will" Plath alludes directly to "A Prayer for My Daughter" and challenges its assumptions. The reality of the "scrupulous tree" and the "honest earth" is immune to a Daphne "concocted" by the male imagination. In "Virgin in a Tree" Plath uses sarcastic puns to expose the conspiracy that offers "respect" and praise to

> . . . chased girls who get them to a tree
> And put on bark's nun-black
>
> Habit which deflects
> All amorous arrows.

Plath herself sees the metamorphosis as a hideous imprisonment:

> . . . a fashion that constricts
> White bodies in a wooden girdle, root to top
> Unfaced, unformed, the nipple-flowers
> Shrouded to suckle darkness.

The virgin is "on her rack," twisted out of shape and soured by neglect. Plath translates Yeats's "rooted in one dear perpetual place" into an image of petrifaction:

> . . . her fingers
> Stiff as twigs, her body woodenly
> Askew. *(Collected Poems* 81–82)

Plath's objections are cogent, but in fact Yeats does not remain paralyzed between the polar opposites of the screaming witch and the silent virgin, nor does he consistently imagine his daughter as an object. His penultimate stanza constitutes her as a subject whose soul knows that it is

241

> . . . self-delighting,
> Self-appeasing, self-affrighting,
> And that its own sweet will is Heaven's will.
>
> (*Variorum Edition* 405)

This creative autonomy belongs as much to a woman as to a man, as much to a daughter as to a father. Yeats offers Anne a recipe not only for "radical" innocence but also for spiritual independence. This independence, however, has limits. Yeats's prejudices are inevitably the prejudices of his time, and they are reinforced by his obsession with hierarchical and traditional values. In the social context of which he approves, a daughter can achieve freedom from paternal incest-wishes only when her father formally and publicly relinquishes her in the marriage ceremony.

How difficult it was for Yeats to imagine giving up his daughter is revealed by the drafts of the poem: as late in the process of composition as the typed fair copy he still had not found her a real man. He wrote: "And may she marry into some old house" (Stallworthy 43n), metaphorically joining her to sexless bricks and mortar rather than to the passions of the flesh. The hypothetical son-in-law who finally emerges is chosen because of his aristocratic social status and ownership of landed property rather than because of his sexuality. But in his emphasis on the "house" to which the bridegroom will bring her Yeats has clearly abandoned his image of his daughter as "rooted" solely in the natural world. The house, like the tower, is a cultural artifact: in order for her to enter it, the "rich horn" and the "spreading laurel tree" must be translated into the symbolic abstractions "custom" and "ceremony." Yet the authoritative weight of "custom" and "ceremony" establishes the "old house" as an image of the patriarchy. The bride, in recovering "radical innocence," remains linguistically "rooted" (in the original sense of *radical*) within a social and cultural milieu that endorses the passive rather than the active woman. Assaulted by wind and bellows, she is "happy still"—both continually happy and happy in abstention from movement. There may be ambiguity in her soul's discovery that "its own sweet will is Heaven's will": either Heaven endorses her own desires or she learns that her desires conform to the will of Heaven. In the latter case Heaven sanctifies the secular virtues of custom and ceremony and provides us with another version of "the angel in the house."

Implicit in the famous rhetorical question "How but in custom and in ceremony / Are innocence and beauty born?" is the idea of woman as the reproducer of the ideals and values of a patriarchal society. Only within the protective, paternal structures of tradition can the vulnerability of innocence and beauty be "borne," be endured; and out of the daughter's body are "born" the new generations who will sustain and continue those traditions. The baby in her cradle is imagined as a future wife and mother whose happy stillness and quiet nature act as a barrier against the destructive forces of arrogance and hatred unleashed by the "storm" of female revolt. Appropriately, therefore, the last lines of the poem return from abstractions to the "rich horn" of female fertility and to the rooted immobility of the pregnantly "spreading" laurel tree.

The laurel's privileged position as the poem's culminating image, however, also suggests a partial return to the Peneus-Daphne model of father-daughter relationships. The wedding "ceremony" implicit in the last stanza dissolves paternal ownership of the daughter, but in consigning her to a bridegroom who exists only as a reflection of his own prejudices and desires, Yeats has subverted the exogamous intention of the paternal gift. The dialectic is imperfectly sustained: its synthesis (daughter-bridegroom) turns back on itself to become a replica of the original father-daughter relationship. The "old house" of custom and ceremony represents Yeats himself: although publicly he releases his daughter to the bridegroom, covertly he invites her to return to him and to the imprisonment of the laurel tree.

Anne Yeats never married. Yeats's cultural daughter, Sylvia Plath, enacted a tragic return to the father by committing suicide in the house where Yeats had lived as a child. Plath attached enormous significance to the fact that her flat at 23 Fitzroy Road was in "*W. B. Yeats' house*—with a blue plaque over the door, saying he lived there!" (*Letters Home* 477–78). Abandoned by Ted Hughes, she wanted to reestablish her identity in London, away from the loneliness and overwhelming domesticity of her home in Devon. Finding Yeats's house meant finding a foothold in the world of literature, culture, and the intellect, a world she saw as dominated by Hughes. When she discovered that it was to let, she worked frantically to get it: "I am in an agony of suspense about *the* flat. . . . I had the uncanny feeling I had got in touch with Yeats' spirit (he was a sort of medium himself) when I went to his tower in Ireland. I opened a book of his plays in front of Susan as a joke for a 'message' and read, 'Get wine and food to give you strength and courage, and I will get the house ready'. Isn't that fantastic? . . . I will die if my references say I'm too poor! Living in Yeats' house would be an incredibly moving thing for me" (*Letters Home* 480–81).

Plath was replacing her absent poet-husband with a spiritual poet-father (Gilbert, "In Yeats's House" 163). Yeats's verse had been one of her most intense pleasures: "Worked on a couple of Yeats poems for class preparation and read and read in him: The scalp crawled, the hair stood up. He is genuine" (*Journals* 218). "My beloved Yeats," as she called him (*Letters Home* 223), was now to serve as the guarantor of her personal and poetic rebirth. But a poet who could write of his "rage / To end all

243

things" ("Nineteen Hundred and Nineteen," *Variorum Edition* 431) and of the "tragic joy" evoked by destruction ("The Gyres," *Variorum Edition* 564) was not the best protector for her to summon. When Plath paraphrases "The Wheel" as "the one about our restlessness: always longing for the next, the different season: our longing being the longing for the tomb" (*Journals* 225), she reveals that she is attracted by the nihilistic, death-obsessed side of Yeats. One of the epigraphs to her first journal notebook was his statement "We only begin to live when we conceive life as Tragedy" (*Journals* 2). Admiring both his tragic awareness and his formal restraint, she praised her own husband's work because it was "full of blood and discipline, like Yeats" (*Journals* 153). Yeats himself believed that the power of his verse came from its precarious control of violence or madness: "all depends on the completeness of the holding down, on the stirring of the beast underneath" (Yeats, *Letters to Dorothy Wellesley* 94). Poetically and personally this is a dangerous game to play. Yeats, despite occasional fears for his own sanity, had the emotional toughness and resilience to play it; Plath did not. As Jung said to James Joyce, parent of another disturbed child, the father was diving, but the daughter was drowning (Ellmann 679).

Both poets attempt to contain raw emotion within the framework of classical myth, but while Yeats's references are mostly overt, Plath reveals the mythical substructure of "Daddy" only in a note: "Here is a poem spoken by a girl with an Electra complex. Her father died while she thought he was God. Her case is complicated by the fact that her father was also a Nazi and her mother very possibly part Jewish. In the daughter the two strains marry and paralyse each other—she has to act out the awful little allegory once over before she is free of it" (*Collected Poems* 293). While a Freudian reading of "A Prayer for My Daughter" has to focus on the latent content of Yeats's images, "Daddy," by contrast, is programmatically explicit. As Hugh Kenner complains: "Parlor psychiatry is forestalled; she sketches the complex herself" (34).

Plath, who read Freud throughout her life, underwent two intensive courses of Freudian analysis with Dr. Ruth Beuscher. The first followed her suicide attempt in 1953; the second took place in 1958–59, during which time she also processed patients' records in a Boston mental hospital (*Journals* 262). As a result she concluded that the loss of her father, who died just after her eighth birthday, was the primary cause of her psychological difficulties. Her recorded expressions of agony about the death of Otto Plath began only after her first analysis. Indeed, in 1950 she wrote in her journal, "No-one I love has ever died" (*Journals* 19). Analysis provided her with a suitable narrative and mythic framework within which to organize and articulate her previously incoherent pain: "After an hour with Dr. B., digging, felt I'd been watching or participating in a

Greek play: a cleansing and an exhaustion" (*Journals* 285). On the common ground between myth and psychoanalysis Plath retroactively erected an elaborate incest fantasy, one that is blatantly expressed in poems like "The Beekeeper's Daughter," where she addresses Otto as "Father, bridegroom," and glories in "a queenship no mother can contest" (*Collected Poems* 118), and in melodramatic and antifeminist passages from her journal: "A woman, I fight all women for my men. . . . There is no loyalty, even between mother and daughter. Both fight for the father, for the son, for the bed of mind and body. . . . And I cry so to be held by a man; some man, who is a father" (*Journals* 100).

Plath's analyst was a woman, a circumstance that may obscure the fact that her relationship to Freud and to psychoanalysis is also that of a daughter to a father. While her hostility to Otto Plath eventually became overt and her loyalty to her literary father, Yeats, was tempered by considerable criticism, she seems never to have questioned the powerfully seductive and patriarchal claims of psychoanalysis itself. In her journals and poems she adopts Freud's language and assumptions with enthusiasm, although she frequently oversimplifies his insights. The belief that she suffered from what she called an Electra complex became her dominant obsession; it helped her to explain her origins and thus to structure her identity. According to Dianne Sadoff, "Freud's later formulations posit seduction as one of the primal fantasies inherited by each individual from a historically recurring set of fantasies [which] retroactively seeks to represent and solve a major enigma confronting the daughter: the origin or upsurge of her sexuality. The scene of seduction, then, dramatizes the moment of emergence of desire; when related as story, it represents the beginning of a woman's history" (68). Plath's father fixation sprang from her conviction that his death deprived her of the full working through, and out, of the father-daughter love relationship and thus arrested her development: "And this is how it stiffens, my vision of that seaside childhood. My father died, we moved inland. Whereon those nine first years of my life sealed themselves off like a ship in a bottle—beautiful, inaccessible, obsolete, a fine, white flying myth" ("Ocean 1212-W," *Johnny Panic* 124). In other words the beginning of her "history," or myth of herself, was incomplete and discontinuous. Schwartz and Bolas assert that the "gap" in Plath's psyche was "the unfulfilled confirmation of her identity by her father. A crucial component of this identity is erotic, the need for a preadolescent girl of nine to have her womanliness accepted and confirmed by the first male in her life" (186). This formulation is likely to have been the one offered by Dr. Beuscher, and it is Plath's overt longing for the paternal embrace that supports Alvarez's description of "Daddy" as a love poem (66). "I used to pray to recover you," she says, "Ach, du."

245

Plath's earliest poetic formulations of the Electra complex, such as "The Colossus" and "Electra on Azalea Path," focus primarily on the daughter's desire for the father, the filial fantasy of paternal seduction. She accepts Freud's notion that the seduction is only a fantasy, a product and expression of the child's emerging sexuality rather than of the power and desires of the father. There is no evidence whatever that Otto Plath's attitude towards his daughter was overtly sexual. Sylvia's first years, however, were passed in a quintessentially patriarchal family. Aurelia Plath, like George Yeats, was herself a daughter figure, twenty-one years younger than her husband and his former student. In her introduction to *Letters Home* Aurelia describes Otto's attitude of " 'rightful' dominance" and records her decision to become more "submissive" in order to preserve the family peace. Her submission went to considerable lengths, as she reveals in bitter vignettes of married life (13). Sylvia also presents her father as an autocrat: "You had one leg, and a Prussian mind," she writes in "Little Fugue" (*Collected Poems* 188), and in her journal she describes him as an "ogre" (*Journals* 268). Nevertheless, she was his favorite child, and she knew it. She used to dance for him as he lay on the sofa after dinner, and she won his approval by memorizing the Latin names of insects, on which he was an authority (Butscher 10). The family situation, an older man demanding homage from two competing daughter figures, bred in Plath an intense and paralyzing ambivalence about sexuality. In her journal she confesses her inability to love (*Journals* 34). Even where incest has not occurred, as in Plath's case, a patriarchal family structure (dominant father, submissive young mother, favorite daughter) may gravely damage the female child.

In her early work Plath employed the hypothesis of her desire for the father. By the time she wrote "Daddy" she had also come to recognize the effects of his power over her. Both dynamics, however, point to the one end: marriage with a "model" of the patriarch. In a passage from her journal, the exaggerated language of which may indicate a certain Freudian ventriloquism, Plath warns herself about the likely consequences of her obsession: "I would have loved him; and he is gone. . . . I lust for the knowing of him; I looked at Redpath [Theodore Redpath, a professor at Cambridge] at that wonderful coffee session at the Anchor, and practically ripped him up to beg him to be my father; to live with the rich, chastened, wise mind of an older man. I must beware, beware of marrying for that. Perhaps a young man with a brilliant father. I could wed both" (*Journals* 128). This strange mixture of sophistication and naiveté did not protect her when Ted Hughes appeared. She was unable to heed her own warning, despite her perception that Ted "fills somehow that huge, sad hole I felt in having no father" (*Letters Home* 289). Her letters and journals suggests that in marrying Hughes, Plath did indeed "make a model" of a regressive father-daughter relationship.

Plath felt that she had had the worst of both worlds: an intense relationship with a patriarchal figure and the loss of that figure before the Oedipal stage had been fully resolved. I say Oedipal because Plath's own formulation, the so-called Electra complex to which she often referred, was explicitly disavowed by Freud himself ("Female Sexuality," *SE* 21:228–29). Freud considered that the story of Electra, who loved her father and wanted to see her mother dead, suggested too great a symmetry between the male and female experiences of the Oedipus complex. In order to enter the Oedipal stage the little girl has to change her first object-choice from mother to father; the little boy does not. As a result, the girl's tie to her father is likely to be less strong than the boy's to his mother, and she seldom feels murderous impulses towards her female parent. In ignoring Freud's careful qualifications and identifying with Electra, Plath misreads her psychoanalytic father. Whether this misreading is an unconsciously rebellious "creative swerve" (Harold Bloom's term) or simply the product of ignorance, it directs us to examine her relationship with her mother, which is present in "Daddy" only by implication but which forms the subject of its equally venomous companion poem "Medusa" (*Collected Poems* 224–26), which she could well have entitled "Mummy." Although Plath's family myth gives overwhelming poetic importance to her father, the surviving evidence suggests that her relationship with her mother was equally significant. By appending her note about the Electra complex to "Daddy," was she reminding us that the parent whom Electra "had to kill" was not her father but her mother? Clearly one of the greatest problems Sylvia encountered on the death of Otto Plath was that his removal left her to the exclusive care of Aurelia. Reared in a house dominated by women (*Journals* 267), with an extremely anxious and protective female parent, she was unable to resolve the problems of separation and independence outlined by Nancy Chodorow as the negative legacy of the mother-daughter relationship (Chodorow, passim). Her letters and journals reveal a disturbing blend of intimacy, dependence, rage, and pure hatred in her attitude towards Aurelia: "My enemies are those who care about me most. First: my mother" (*Journals* 35). Freud was aware of the importance of the mother-daughter relationship, but he gave it little prominence in his writings. Later Freudians, including Dr. Buescher, who focused Plath's second course of analysis upon her mother, developed his preliminary ideas. Plath planned in her journal a story that would be "a ten-page diatribe against the Dark Mother. The Mummy. Mother of Shadows. An analysis of the Electra complex" (*Journals* 318). Here the essence of the Electra complex is not love for the father but hatred of the mother, a hatred of which Plath was quite conscious.

"Electra on Azalea Path" (a name that echoes "Aurelia Plath") chronicles a visit Plath made in 1959 to her father's grave. The visit is also described in *The Bell Jar*, where it is placed ten years earlier and made into one of the precipitating causes of the suicide attempt referred to in "Daddy": "At twenty I tried to die" (175–77). The sordid cemetery and the ugly artificial flowers on the next grave constitute a tacit reproach to the mother who could lay her husband in such a place, and the red dye dripping from the "ersatz petals" helps Sylvia to transform a neglectful wife into the murderous Clytemnestra:

> Another kind of redness bothers me:
> *The day your slack sail drank my sister's breath*
> *The flat sea purpled like that evil cloth*
> *My mother unrolled at your last homecoming.*

Plath evokes both Agamemnon's sacrifice of Iphigenia and Clytemnestra's deceitful welcome of her husband, prelude to his murder in the bath. Plath's Electra, however, alters the myth in order to play all three female parts—victim, lover, and murderess. Usurping her mother's role, she assumes both the guilt and the intimacy of parricide: "I brought my love to bear, and then you died." Plath told Nancy Hunter Steiner that she both "adored and despised" her father "and probably wished many times that he were dead. When he obliged me and died, I imagined that I had killed him" (Steiner 21).

> O pardon the one who knocks for pardon at
> Your gate, father—your hound-bitch, daughter, friend.
> It was my love that did us both to death.   (*Collected Poems* 117)

The masochistic and self-denigratory tone of these lines connects with her claim in "Daddy" that "every woman adores a Fascist": the "hound-bitch" invites "the boot in the face." "Daddy" demonstrates the interrelationship between masochism and sadism. Freud argues that "the death instinct which is operative in the organism—primal sadism— is identical with masochism" ("The Economic Problem of Masochism," *SE* 19:164). Plath begins by imagining herself as victim, trapped in her father's "black shoe," but her aggression is soon projected outward: because her father "died before [she] had time" to kill him in fact, she must now kill him in rhyme. Sandra Gilbert suggests that "Being enclosed—in plaster, in a bell jar, a cellar, or a wax house—and then being liberated from an enclosure by a maddened or suicidal or 'hairy and ugly' avatar of the self is . . . at the heart of the myth that we piece together from Plath's poetry, fiction and life" ("A Fine, White Flying Myth" 251).

Sensitive as she was to the implications of Yeats's laurel tree prison and to the metaphors of enclosure implied by the old house of patriarchal custom, Plath attempted in "Daddy" to escape from her literary as well as her biological father.

We have seen that in her emphasis on Electra she also diverges from her psychoanalytic father. When Electra becomes hostile to her supposedly beloved "Daddy," attacking her former love for him as the source of all her oppressions, Plath is proposing an idiosyncratic version of both the myth and the complex. Freud would certainly have rejected the idea that the role of the daughter is to murder the patriarch. Unable to replace the father, the daughter must realize instead that she will eventually be possessed by someone who resembles him. In abandoning traditional "feminine" passivity and usurping the boy's aggressive role in the Oedipal situation, does Plath recognize Freud himself as an object of her necessary anger, a father to be killed?

It appears that she does not. Her adoption of a "masculine" persona remains within the boundaries of psychoanalytic definition. According to Juliet Mitchell, both boys and girls originally "want to take the father's place, *and only the boy will one day be allowed to do so*" (404). By virtue of this desire, girls reveal themselves as "more bisexual" than boys. Linda Schierse Leonard, a Jungian analyst, suggests that when the father is emotionally or actually absent, the daughter may identify with the masculine role. If, as is likely, her mother has to adopt masculine qualities in order to survive, the daughter lacks a model of successful femininity (61). Indeed, as Sylvia wrote of Aurelia: "Life was hell. She had to work. Work, and be a mother, too, a man and woman in one sweet ulcerous ball" (*Journals* 267). Leonard uses Esther, the heroine of Plath's autobiographical novel *The Bell Jar*, as her example of one type of reaction to such a situation: the fatherless daughter becomes an Amazonic "super star," a workaholic overachiever cut off from her real feelings (63–66). Plath's early career of scholarships, prizes, and grants certainly indicates such a pattern, while her journals reveal her identification with masculinity and her impatience with the feminine role. Why should women, she asks, "be relegated to the position of custodian of emotions, watcher of the infants, feeder of soul, body and pride of man? Being born a woman is my awful tragedy. From the moment I was conceived I was doomed to sprout breasts and ovaries rather than penis and scrotum; to have my whole circle of action, thought and feeling rigidly circumscribed by my inescapable femininity" (*Journals* 30). Like Yeats, Plath conceives of feminity in terms of vegetation. Another Daphne, she "sprouts" breasts and ovaries. This version of "Anatomy is Destiny" was written during her time at Smith, and it is hard to avoid the conclusion that Plath had been reading Freud and thinking herself into a condition of acute penis envy: she asks herself, "Do I sound Freudian?" (*Journals* 35).

Envy of the penis leads her to imagine herself as a castrator, specifically a castrator of her father: "Facing dark and terrible things: those dreams of deformity and death. If I really think I killed and castrated my father may all my dreams of deformed and tortured people be my guilty visions of him or fears of punishment for me?" (*Journals* 301). This obsession finds its way into "Daddy": Plath presents her father as a "bag full of God," a scrotum full of patriarchal seed; similarly, she endows him with "one grey toe / Big as a Frisco seal." There are literal reasons for the "one grey toe," since Otto Plath's leg was amputated in the last stages of his illness, but the image nevertheless is as obdurately phallic as Yeats's tower. When Plath announces vindictively, "The black telephone's *off at the root*, / And the voices just can't *worm* through," the reference to castration is unmistakable. The threat contained in the image of the telephone "off at the root" is also aimed at her husband. Once, when Hughes's mistress telephoned their home, Sylvia ripped the instrument off the wall. Her repetition of the word *root* is also a response to Yeats's wish that his daughter remain "rooted in one dear perpetual place." Plath answers by "uprooting" both herself (like a "gypsy" she moves from America to Europe) and the father-husband who offers her authority but neither the custom nor the ceremony that might enable her to "bear" her subordinate position.

She also reverses Yeats's identification of the "murderous innocence of the sea" with destructive femininity. Plath's ocean is masculine, home of her "father-sea-god Muse" (*Journals* 244), with his "head in the freakish Atlantic." In "Full Fathom Five" she deliberately contradicts Yeats by applying his epithet "murderous" not to the sea but to the life-giving air:

> Father, this thick air is murderous.
> I would breathe water.   (*Collected Poems* 93)

This inversion suggests a rejection of her cultural father in favor of a self-destructive return to her natural father. The genesis of her association between Otto Plath and the sea is more complicated than she implies in "Ocean 1212-W": "My father died, we moved inland." It also springs from a dream of Aurelia's mentioned in "Electra on Azalea Path": "My mother dreamed you face down in the sea" (*Collected Poems* 117). Plath elaborates the dream in her journals: "It was her daughter's fault partly. She had a dream: her daughter was all gaudy-dressed about to go out and be a chorus girl, a prostitute too, probably. . . . The husband, brought alive in dream to relive the curse of his old angers, slammed out of the house in a rage that the daughter was going to be a chorus girl. The poor Mother runs along the sand beach. . . . The father had driven, in a fury, to spite her, off the road bridge and was floating dead, face down and bloated, in the slosh of ocean water by the pillars of the country club" (*Journals* 268–69). Plath referred to this dream several times, and it obviously held great importance for her. In assuming her role as a sexual female the daughter destroys the father, but in so doing she also destroys herself. As she concludes in "Electra on Azalea Path": "It was my love that did us both to death" (*Collected Poems* 117). Plath's own interpretation of the dream also highlights an intense sexual rivalry between mother and daughter: "I have lost a father and his love early; feel angry at her because of this and feel she feels I killed him (her dream about me being a chorus girl and his driving off and drowning himself)" (*Journals* 279).

The dream helps to explain why, in poems such as "Full Fathom Five" and "All the Dead Dears," Plath portrays Otto as drowned. Her fascination with death springs from her recognition that the source of her inspiration is the dead parent himself, the "father-sea-god Muse." The Muse is both desirable and deadly, creative and destructive: he embodies not only the fierce energy of her poetry but also parricidal and suicidal impulses. Plath conflates her dead father and the death drive posited by Freud with Yeats's "terrible beauty" to produce a romantically nihilistic vision of the relationship between creativity and self-obliteration. Describing an early poem, "Pursuit," she writes: "It is, of course, a symbol of the terrible beauty of death, and the paradox that the more intensely one lives the more one burns and consumes oneself; death, here, includes the concept of love, and is larger and richer than mere love, which is part of it. . . . Another epigraph could have been from my beloved Yeats: 'Whatever flames upon the night, Man's own resinous heart has fed.' The painter's brush consumes his dreams, and all that" (*Letters Home* 222–23). The Muse is Death-the-Father himself, and the female masochist embraces him with passionate intensity. But in "Daddy" the reemergence of her repressed sadism poses an agonizing question: What happens when the woman artist kills and castrates the father-Muse? Is she condemning herself to silence and infertility?

In "Daddy" the female persona is forced to confront the problem of male language and female silence through the medium of "the German tongue," the language of the father. Although Plath herself kept returning to the idea of mastering German, it constantly defeated her, and in the poem her inability to speak it suggests the impenetrable barriers between father and daughter (Butscher 98):

I never could talk to you.
The tongue stuck in my jaw.

It stuck in a barb wire snare.
Ich, ich, ich, ich,

> I could hardly speak.
> I thought every German was you.
> And the language obscene.

She can "hardly" define herself as a subject: the word *I*, translated into his language, sticks in her throat. Like her poetic progenitor Yeats, Otto Plath is a master of words, a teacher:

> You stand at the blackboard, daddy,
> In the picture I have of you. (*Collected Poems* 223)

The dead fathers control the transmission of poetic and scientific language. Since the daughter has no other tongue, both her rebellion and her poem are doomed to be defined by the patriarchal traditions that they seek to overturn. Her language is also "obscene" in its crudity and violence. To turn brutality back against its perpetrators is no escape from a situation constituted, as is the father-daughter relationship, in terms of power.

When Plath does find her utterance it is in the German language as spoken not by masters but by archetypal victims: "I began to talk like a Jew." If we reject the Nazi-Jew analogy as an appropriate model of father-daughter relationships, we are likely to regard the whole poem as a tasteless and pretentious failure. There is no doubt that on the personal level—Sylvia and Otto—the analogy is a gross overstatement. Plath's Jewish ancestry was imaginary, and her father was not a Nazi (Butscher 12). The frequently deployed argument that Plath's personal anguish is incommensurate with the horrors of the concentration camps is, therefore, difficult to refute. Ted Hughes, however, defends the sincerity of her identification with the suffering of others: "Her reactions to hurts in other people and animals, and even tiny desecrations of plant-life were extremely violent. The chemical poisoning of nature, the pile-up of atomic waste, were horrors that persecuted her like an illness—as her latest poems record. Auschwitz and the rest were . . . open wounds" (Hughes 190). Her letters also record her intense depression and fear about contemporary politics—the cold war, the growth of the military-industrial complex, and the threat of nuclear annihilation (*Letters Home* 437–38). In order to accept Plath's Jewish self-identification, it is essential to see it in these general and political terms. The relationship between Nazi and Jew is, metaphorically, the relationship between fathers and the whole female sex. "Daddy" in his various guises—God, devil, fascist leader, father, husband (we may add traditional Freudian psychoanalyst, although she did not)—epitomizes patriarchal authority.

Plath, however, also indicts women (and presumably Jews as well) as accomplices in the process of their oppression. She concludes that because daughters desire fathers, they actively seek violation. Her journals are disturbingly full of images of rape: "Love turns, lust turns, into the death urge. My love is gone, gone, and I would be raped" (*Journals* 132). Plath has obviously just been reading *Beyond the Pleasure Principle*. The desire for oblivion through sexual punishment underlies the lines

> Every woman adores a Fascist,
> The boot in the face, the brute
> Brute heart of a brute like you.   (*Collected Poems* 223)

Throughout the poem Plath explicitly associates sexuality with childishly pornographic violence: "the black man who / Bit my pretty red heart in two"; "a love of the rack and the screw"; "drank my blood for a year." This association, habitual with Plath, suggests a masochism that Freud defines as "feminine" ("The Economic Problem of Masochism," *SE* 19:161), a product of women's socialization within the father-dominated family. Its ramifications are political as well as sexual. In the depths of the suicidal depression that preceded her breakdown in 1953 Plath wrote: "My world falls apart, crumbles, 'the centre cannot hold.'" The allusion to Yeats's "The Second Coming" is crucial, for her response to collapse resembles his. The anarchy of things fallen apart is replaced by the beast of totalitarianism: "I long for a noble escape from freedom—I am weak, tired, in revolt from the strong constructive humanitarian faith which presupposes a healthy, active intellect and will. There is nowhere to go . . . I turn wearily to the totalitarian dictatorship where I am absolved of all personal responsibility. . . . I can begin to see the compulsion for admitting original sin, for adoring Hitler, for taking opium" (*Journals* 60–61). This absolute self-abasement, the yielding up of the will and submission to violence, is the emotional trap out of which the speaker of "Daddy" tries, unsuccessfully, to struggle.

Paradoxically, her first attempt at escape involves what appears to be a more extreme form of masochism: self-annihilation: "At twenty I tried to die." Plath, however, knows that suicide may actually be an act of sadistic rage: "Read Freud's *Mourning and Melancholia* this morning after Ted left for the library. An almost exact description of my feelings and reasons for suicide: a transferred murderous impulse from my mother onto myself: the 'vampire' metaphor Freud uses, 'draining the ego'" (*Journals* 280). In *The Bell Jar* Esther represses her desire to kill her mother (138), but in "Daddy" the "murderous impulse" is redirected to the father, himself a double for Ted Hughes. She frequently asserts Hughes's resemblance to "my own father, the buried male muse and god-creator risen to be my mate in Ted" (*Journals* 223), and writes: "Images of his faithlessness with women echo my fear of my father's relation with my mother and Lady Death" (*Journals* 280). The bitterness of betrayal intensified these feelings, and she argued that her marriage had been false from the start, her husband merely a projection of her fantasy of the absent father:

> I made a model of you,
> A man in black with a Meinkampf look
>
> And a love of the rack and the screw.
> And I said I do, I do. (*Collected Poems* 224)

This poetic strategy has the satisfying effect not only of abusing Hughes but also of belittling him. Once she has made her "model," she metaphorically drives a stake through its heart and thus destroys not only her husband but also the father of whom he is a copy:

> If I've killed one man, I've killed two—
> The vampire who said he was you
> And drank my blood for a year,
> Seven years, if you want to know. (*Collected Poems* 224)

Plath's use of the vampire metaphor at the end of "Daddy" epitomizes the pessimism and circularity of her analysis of the father-daughter relationship. Earlier she had wondered if the paradigm also applied to husband and wife: "Do we, vampire-like, feed on each other?" (*Journals* 260). In her journal entry about "Mourning and Melancholia" she linked the vampire analogy with Freud's insight that "The complex of melancholia behaves like an open wound . . . emptying the ego until it is totally impoverished" ("Mourning and Melancholia," *SE* 14:253). In Freud's terms, the "shadow" of the lost father has fallen upon the ego of the daughter ("Mourning and Melancholia," *SE* 14: 249), who keeps him alive by a process of narcissistic identification that drains away her own self-esteem. Plath must know that if the ego is identified with the lost object, any attack on the vampire must also be a suicidal attack on herself. Such is her rage, however, that she ignores her own danger, indulging in an unrestrainedly brutal and gleeful exorcism:

> Daddy you can lie back now.
>
> There's a stake in your fat black heart
> And the villagers never liked you. (*Collected Poems* 224)

Masochism, then, becomes sadism; victim becomes executioner. Yet the structure of the vampire myth itself reveals that Plath has not reached a solution. If the Dracula figure has drunk her blood for seven years, then she, too, is doomed to become a vampire. In her journals she so characterizes herself, swinging from desperate avowals of father-dependence to expressions of unbridled aggression: "Yet the vampire is there, too. The old, primal hate. That desire to go round castrating the arrogant ones who become such children at the moment of passion" (*Journals* 100). Thus the cycle of oppression and revenge is self-perpetuating, never ending. The persona begins as a willing victim and ends as a malevolent torturer, herself destined to belong to the Undead. The ambiguous final line, "Daddy, daddy, you bastard, I'm through," may suggest a successful conclusion to the ritual of exorcism, but in denying her father's legitimacy the daughter also undermines her own identity.

In her extremity, Plath becomes as shrill as Yeats's Atlantic gale, as loud as his old bellows full of angry wind. Yet her demonic energy, her utter absorption in the savage emotion of the moment, is what makes her poem memorable. If Yeats warns his daughter that "to be choked with hate / May well be of all evil chances chief," Plath retorts that for her, hatred of the fathers is a necessary, if also self-destructive, passion. Within the law of patriarchy there may be no more appropriate response, but it leads to a dead end. Plath's poem shows that to engage male structures of dominance on their own terms is inevitably to be reabsorbed into the destructive patriarchal system. Her exclamation "I'm through" expresses disgust and defeat more than success.

Note

I should like to acknowledge my debt to my editor Lynda Boose, whose article "The Father and the Bride in Shakespeare" first stimulated my interest in the subject of daughters and fathers. Her co-editor, Betty Sue Flowers, offered valuable interpretative corrections which I subsequently incorporated into the text. My greatest debt, however, is to my colleague Kurt Heinzelman, whose critical acumen identified numerous weaknesses in my original draft and whose excellent suggestions have, I hope, helped to focus my ideas about Plath.

SANDRA M. GILBERT

Life's Empty Pack: Notes toward a Literary Daughteronomy

If underneath the water
   You comb your golden hair
With a golden comb, my daughter,
   Oh would that I were there!
    —Christina Rossetti, "Father and Lover"

Sad and weary I go back to you, my cold father, my cold mad father,
my cold mad feary father . . . I rush, my only, into yur arms.
    —Anna Livia Plurabelle, in James Joyce, *Finnegans Wake*

FOR THE FIRST TIME all of us, men and women alike, can look back on almost two centuries of powerful literary ancestresses. Aside from the specifically literary-historical implications of such a phenomenon, an issue that Susan Gubar and I have addressed in essays on "Tradition and the Female Talent" and "The Complex Female Affiliation Complex," what effects has this unprecedented situation had? In particular, what paradigms of female sexuality have strong female precursors passed on to other women writers? These are questions I want to begin to address here—specifically, by exploring an aspect of female psychosexual development. A dark, indeed problematical, pattern emerges when we juxtapose the accounts of female maturation and obligation that are offered by such theorists as Sigmund Freud and Claude Lévi-Strauss with the meaning that George Eliot's frequently studied *Silas Marner* may have had for the women who are in a sense that powerful literary mother's aesthetic daughters.

I choose George Eliot as my paradigm of the female precursor because she was, as Virginia Woolf put it, "the first woman of the age," a thinker who became in one historian's words, a "Man of Ideas," her official importance sanctioned by the biography Woolf's own father dutifully produced for the English Men of Letters series. At the same time, however, I see Eliot as paradigmatic because her very power—the success that made her into what we call a precursor—evidently disquieted so many of her female contemporaries and descendants. As Elaine Showalter reminds us, "Most nineteenth-century women novel-

256

ists seem to have found [Eliot] a troublesome . . . competitor" (Showalter *A Literature of Their Own* 108). Moreover, even Eliot's most fervent
female admirers express ambivalence towards her in the rhetoric through
which they try to come to terms with her. Two of these notable Eliotian
heiresses are Emily Dickinson and Edith Wharton. Both offer commentaries curiously haunted by ambiguities, and though these commentaries
are ostensibly about the writer's life story, they provide a dramatic set of
metaphors that can help us interpret the messages these literary
daughters extracted from such an apparently legendary tale as *Silas
Marner*.

In 1883, after she had just finished reading the first Eliot biography,
Emily Dickinson wrote a letter in which she succinctly mythologizes the
career of her English precursor. "The life of Marian Evans had much I
never knew," she begins. "A Doom of Fruit without the Bloom, like the
Niger Fig," and a poem follows this strange introduction:

> Her Losses make our Gains ashamed—
> She bore Life's empty Pack
> As gallantly as if the East
> Were swinging at her Back.
> Life's empty Pack is heaviest,
> As every Porter knows—
> In vain to punish Honey—
> It only sweeter grows.   (*Letters* 769–70; *Poems* 650)

"A Doom of Fruit without the Bloom," "Life's empty Pack," "In
vain to punish Honey"—these are striking but mysterious phrases.
Where do they come from, and what do they mean? Several remarks by
Edith Wharton, though almost equally paradoxical, begin to provide
some clarification. Reviewing Leslie Stephen's English Men of Letters
series volume on Eliot, Wharton writes that "unconsciously, perhaps,
[the Victorian novelist] began to use her books as a vehicle of rehabilita-
tion, a means, not of defending her own course, but of proclaiming . . . her allegiance to the law she appeared to have violated." Earlier
in her essay, Wharton offers an almost Dickinsonian definition of what
she means by "the law": "The stern daughter of the voice of God," she
remarks, "stands ever at the side of [Eliot's major characters] and lifts
[many of them] to heights of momentary heroism" (Wharton, review
251–52).

Putting statements like these together with Woolf's sense of Eliot's
centrality, we can begin to see why the author of *Silas Marner* was both a
paradigmatic and a problematical female precursor. Metaphorically
speaking, such a conflation of reactions suggests that Eliot represents the
conundrum of the empty pack which until recently has confronted every

woman writer. Specifically, that conundrum is the riddle of daughter-hood, a figurative empty pack with which, it has seemed to many women artists, every powerful literary mother as well as every literal mother presents her daughter. For such artists, then, the terror of the female precursor is not that she is an emblem of power but rather that when she achieves her greatest power, her power becomes self-subverting: in the moment of psychic transformation that is the moment of creativity, the literary mother, even more than the literal one, becomes the "stern daughter of the voice of God" who paradoxically proclaims her allegiance to the law she herself appears to have violated.

As such a preceptor, the literary mother seems necessarily to speak both of and for the father, reminding her female child that she is not and cannot be his inheritor. For human culture, says the literary mother, is bound by linguistic and social rules of exchange, rules that make it possible for a woman to speak but oblige her to speak of her own powerlessness, since such rules appear to constitute what Jacques Lacan calls the "Law of the Father," the law that means culture is by definition both patriarchal and phallocentric and must therefore transmit the empty pack of disinheritance to every daughter ("On a Question" 199). Not surprisingly, then, even while the literary daughter, like the literal one, desires the matrilineal legitimation incarnated in her precursor/mother, she fears her literary mother: the more fully the mother represents culture, the more inexorably she tells the daughter that she cannot have a mother because she has been signed with and assigned to the Law of the Father. Like George Eliot, who aspired to be a "really cultured woman," this "culture mother" uses her knowledge, as Eliot in her scornful essay "Silly Novels by Lady Novelists" said she should, "to form a right estimate of herself," that is, to put herself (and by implication her daughters) in the "right" place (317). [1]

This speculation rests, of course, on syntheses of Freud and Lévi-Strauss that psychoanalytic thinkers such as Lacan and Juliet Mitchell have lately produced. Concentrating on the Oedipus complex, such writers have argued that every child enters the language-defined system of kinship exchange that we call culture by learning that he or she cannot remain permanently in the state of nature signified by the embrace of the mother; instead, the child must be assigned a social place denoted by the name (and the "Law") of the Father, the potent symbol of human order who disrupts the blissful mother-child dyad. What this means for the boy—a temporary frustration of desire coupled with the promise of an ultimate accession to power—has been elaborately explored by both Freud and Lacan (and also, in a different way, by Lévi-Strauss). What it means for the girl is less clearly understood, so that in meditating on the empty pack of daughterhood I am necessarily improvising both literary and psychoanalytic theory. But my task will, I hope, be made possible by George Eliot's status as paradigmatic female precursor or symbolic culture mother and be made plausible by the juxtaposition of one of Eliot's texts, *Silas Marner*, with what we might call a revisionary daughter text, Edith Wharton's *Summer*.

A DEFINITION of George Eliot as renunciatory culture mother may seem an odd preface to a discussion of *Silas Marner*, since of all Eliot's novels, this richly constructed work is the one in which the empty pack of daughterhood appears fullest, the honey of femininity most unpunished. I want to argue, however, that this "legendary tale," whose status as a schoolroom classic makes it almost as much a textbook as a novel, examines the relationship between woman's fate and the structure of society in order to explicate the meaning of the empty pack of daughterhood. More specifically, this story of an adoptive father, an orphan daughter, and a dead mother broods on events that are actually or symbolically situated on the margins of society, where culture must enter into a dialectical struggle with nature, in order to show how the young female human animal is converted into the human daughter, wife, and mother. Finally, then, this fictionalized "daughteronomy" becomes a female myth of origin narrated by a severe literary mother who uses the vehicle of a half-allegorical family romance to urge acquiescence in the Law of the Father.

If *Silas Marner* is not obviously a story about the empty pack of daughterhood, it is plainly, of course, a "legendary" tale about a wanderer with a heavy pack, and a pack of just the kind Dickinson must have meant when she insisted that "Life's empty pack is heaviest. . . ." In fact, it is through the image of the pack man that the story, in Eliot's own words, "came *across* my other plans by a sudden inspiration," and clearly her vision of this burdened outsider is a re-vision of the Romantic wanderer who haunts the borders of society.[2] I would argue further, though, that Eliot's depiction of Silas's alienation begins to explain Ruby Redinger's sense that the author of this "fluid" story "is" both Eppie, the redemptive daughter, and Silas Marner, the redeemed father. For in examining the outcast weaver's marginality this novelist of "the hidden life" examines also her own female disinheritance and marginality (Redinger 439).

Almost everything we learn about Silas tends to reinforce our sense that he belongs in what anthropologists call a "liminal zone." Pallid, undersized, alien-looking, he is one of the figures ordinary country people see at the edges of time and place. As a weaver, moreover, he is associated with those questionable (albeit necessary) transformations that mark the borders of culture and seem to partake "of the nature of conjuring." Again, he is liminal because, both short-sighted and cataleptic, he cannot participate meaningfully in the social world. That he dwells on the edge of Raveloe, near the disused Stone Pits, and never strolls "into the village to drink a pint at [the local pub called] 'The Rainbow'" further emphasizes his alienation, as does the story of his Job-like punishment when the casting of lots in Lantern Yard "convicted" him of a theft he had not committed (*SM* 1.1).[3] Finally, his obsessive hoarding, in which gold is drained of all economic signification, reduces the currency of society to absurdity, further emphasizing his alienation.

Considering all these deprivations of social meaning, it is no wonder that this wanderer's pack seems to be heavy with emptiness. Psychologically, moreover, it is no wonder that Eliot in some sense "is" the Silas whom we first encounter at the Stone Pits, if only because through him she examines the liminality experienced by Marian Evans in fact and Maggie Tulliver in fiction. Evans's own metaphors frequently remind us, furthermore, that just as he weaves textiles, she "weaves" texts—and at the time his story "thrust itself" into the loom of her art, her texts were turning to gold as surely (and as problematically) as his textiles did.[4] In addition, as a man without a place, Silas carries with him the dispossession that she herself had experienced as part of the empty pack of daughterhood. Perhaps, indeed, it is because he shares to some extent in what Sherry Ortner has seen as woman's liminal estate that Silas is often associated not only with the particulars of Marian Evans's femaleness but also with a number of socially defined female characteristics, including a domestic expertise that causes him, in the words of one Raveloer, to be "partly as handy as a woman" (*SM* 1.14).

Paradoxically, however, it is his handily maternal rearing of Eppie that redeems Silas as a *man* even while his transformation from outcast to parent reflects the similar but more troubled metamorphosis that Marian Evans was herself undergoing at the time she wrote the novel. Significantly, at the moment the plot of *Silas Marner* began to "unfold" in her mind, the unmarried George Eliot was becoming a "Mother" to George Henry Lewes's children. But where her ambiguous status as "Mother" of "a great boy of eighteen . . . as well as two other boys almost as tall" (Haight 336) isolated her further from the society that had cast her out when she eloped with Lewes, Silas's status as father of a golden-haired daughter definitively integrates him into a community that had previously thought him diabolical.[5] His transformations of role and rank, therefore, suggest at least one kind of redemption a fallen literary woman might want to imagine for herself: becoming a father.

Silas's redemptive fatherhood, which originates at Christmas time, is prepared for by Eliot's long meditation on the weaver's relationship to his gold, perhaps the most compelling passage of psychological analysis in the novel and the one that most brilliantly sets forth the terms of the submerged metaphor that is to govern the book's dramatic action. For the miser, as I noted earlier, what would ordinarily be a medium of economic exchange, a kind of language that links members of society, is empty of signification and therefore not only meaningless but dead-ended. Halted, even regressive, the currency does not flow: nothing goes out into the world, and therefore nothing returns. Silas's history is thus a history without a story because without characters—without, that is, both persons and signifiers. Yet its terror consists not merely in the absence of meaning but in the presence of empty matter: the shining heaps of coins which "had become too large for the iron pot to hold them" (*SM* 1.2). It is this mass of lifeless matter that must be imprinted with vital signification if the outcast weaver is to be redeemed. And ultimately, indeed, Silas's transformation from fall to fatherhood is symbolized, in a sort of upside-down myth of Midas, by the metamorphosis of his meaningless gold into a living and meaningful child, a child whose Christmas coming marks her as symbolically divine but whose function as divine daughter rather than sacred son is to signify, rather than to replace, the power of her newly created father.

To make way for Eppie, who is his gold made meaningful, Silas must first, of course, be separated from his meaningless gold. What is surely most important about this loss, however, is that the absence of the gold forces the miser to confront the absence that his gold represented. In addition, if we think of this blank, this empty pack, in relation to the Christmas myth for which Eliot is preparing us, we can see that Silas's dark night of the soul is the long dark night of the winter solstice, when dead matter must be kindled and dead flesh made Word if culture is to survive. That "the invisible wand of catalepsy" momentarily freezes the weaver in his open doorway on the crucial New Year's Eve that is to lead to his resurrection merely emphasizes this point. His posture is that of the helpless virgin who awaits annunciation "like a graven image . . . powerless to resist either the good or evil that might enter" (*SM* 1.12).

Because it depends on drastic role reversals, however, Eliot's parody of the Christmas story suggests that she is half consciously using the basic outlines of a central culture myth to meditate not on the traditionally sanctified relationship of Holy Mother and Divine Son but on the equally crucial bond of Holy Father and Divine Daughter. In doing so, she clarifies the key differences between sonship and daughterhood. For when the divine child is a son, he is, as the Christian story tells us, an active spiritual agent for his mother; to put the matter in a Freudian or Lacanian way, he is the "Phallus" for her, an image of sociocultural as well as sexual power. But when the divine child is a daughter, or so the story of Silas Marner tells us, she is a treasure, a gift the father is given so that he can give it to others, thus weaving himself into the texture of society. To put the matter in a Lévi-Straussian way, she is the currency whose exchange constitutes society, a point George Eliot stunningly anticipated in her submerged metaphor of the girl who is not only as good as but better than gold, because her very existence is a pot of gold, not at the end, but at the beginning of the Rainbow covenant between man and man.

This last allusion is, of course, a reference to the central notion of *The Elementary Structures of Kinship*, in which Lévi-Strauss argues that both the social order, which distinguishes culture from nature, and the incest taboo, which universally (if variously) constitutes and governs the social order, are based upon the exchange of women. In this anthropological view, a daughter is a "treasure" whose potential passage from man to man ensures psychological and social well-being: if the very structure of a patrilineage guarantees that a man's son will inexorably *take* his place and his name, it also promises that a daughter will never be such a usurper, since she is an instrument of culture rather than an agent. In fact, because she is the father's wealth, his treasure, she is what he *has*, for better or worse.

That Silas christens his Christmas child Hephzibah emphasizes this point even while it begins to weave him deeply into the common life of "Bible names" and to knit him back into his own past (*SM* 1.14). Hephzibah, or Eppie, was the name of both Silas's mother and his sister: in gaining her, he has regained the treasure of all his female kin. What is even more significant, the name itself, drawn from *Isaiah*, refers to the title Zion will be given after the coming of the Messiah. Literally translated as "My delight is in her," *Hephzibah* magically signifies both a promised land and a redeemed land (see Isa. 62:4, 5). Diffusely female— virginal sister, mother, bride, daughter—this delightful land incarnates the treasure that is possessed and exchanged by male citizens, and therefore it represents the culture that is created by the covenant between man and man as well as between God and man. A philological discovery upon which George Eliot herself once meditated further enriches such an association. According to an etymology given by the *Oxford English Dictionary* and based upon Grimm's law, the Anglo-Saxon word *daughter* can be traced back to the Indo-European root *dhugh*, "to milk." Hence this daughter named Hephzibah is both milkmaid and milk giver, she who nurtures as well as she who is nurtured—for as defined by both the Law and the lexicon of the Father, a daughter *is* the promised land of milk and honey, the gift of wealth that God the Father gives to every human father.[6]

Most of these ideas are made quite explicit in the concern with weddings that permeates *Silas Marner*, a concern that surfaces in the conversation that happens to be taking place at the appropriately named Rainbow Tavern just when Silas is discovering the loss of his gold. Old Mr. Macey, the town clerk, is recounting the ancient story of the Lammeter marriage ceremony, in which the minister got his phrases oddly turned around ("'Wilt thou have this man to thy wedded wife?' says he"). The tale asks the question, "Is't the meanin' or the words as makes folks fast i' wedlock?" and answers that "it's neither the meaning nor the words—it's the regester does it—that's the glue" (*SM* 1.16). But of course, as we learn by the end of *Silas Marner*, it is the very idea of the wedding itself, the having and giving of the daughter, that is the glue. For as Silas and Eppie, Aaron and Dollie, parade through Raveloe on their way back to Silas's enlarged cottage after the ceremony that marked Eppie's marriage to Aaron, the harmony of the bridal party contrasts strikingly with our memory of Silas's former isolation. In marrying Aaron, his daughter has married Silas—married him both to the world and to herself. What had been the "shrunken rivulet" of his love has flowed into a larger current and a dearer currency, a treasure he has given so that it can return to him. And it has returned: "O father," says Eppie, just as if she had married *him*, "what a pretty home ours is" (*SM*, "Conclusion"). Unlike that other Romantic wanderer, the Ancient Mariner, Silas Marner is a member of the wedding. But then the Ancient Mariner never got the Christian Christmas gift of a daughter.

How does the gift feel about herself, however? What does it mean to Eppie to mean all this for Silas? Certainly Eliot had long been concerned with the social significance of daughterhood. Both *The Mill on the Floss*, the novel that precedes *Silas Marner*, and *Romola*, the one that follows it, are elaborate examinations of the structural inadequacies of a daughter's estate. As for Marian Evans, moreover, her real life had persistently confronted her with the problematical nature of daughterhood and its corollary condition, sisterhood. As biographers have shown in detail, her feelings for her own father were ambivalent not only during his lifetime but throughout hers, yet his superegoistic legacy pervaded other relationships that she formed. When she was in her early twenties, for instance, she became a disciple to a Casaubonlike Dr. Brabant, who punningly baptized her "Deutera" "because she was to be a second daughter to him," and even when she was a middle-aged woman, she remembered her older brother Isaac as a kind of miniature father, observing wistfully that ". . . were another childhood world my share, / I would be born a little sister there" ("Brother and Sister," *Complete Poems* 397). Since Eppie was the name of Silas's little sister, it seems likely that in being "born" again to the mild weaver Marian Evans did in fact make "another childhood world" her share, recreating herself as both daughter and little sister.

Certainly Eppie's protestations of daughterly devotion suggest that she is in some sense a born-again daughter. "I should have no delight i' life any more if I was forced to go away from my father," she tells Nancy and Godfrey Cass (*SM* 2.19). Like the Marian Evans who became "Deutera," Eppie is not so much a second daughter as twice a daughter, that is, a doubly daughterly daughter. As such a "Deutera," she is the golden girl whose very being reiterates those cultural commandments Moses set forth for the second time in Deuteronomy. Thus, although scrupulous Nancy Lammeter Cass has often been seen as articulating George Eliot's moral position on the key events of this novel, it is really the more impulsive Eppie who is the conscience of the book.

This becomes clearest when Nancy argues that "there's a duty you owe to your lawful father," and Eppie instantly replies that "I can't feel as if I've got any father but one"—a more accurate understanding of the idea of fatherhood (*SM* 2.19). For in repudiating *God-free* Cass, who is only by chance (*Casus*) her natural father, and affirming Silas Marner, who is by choice her cultural father, Eppie rejects the lawless father in favor of the lawful one, indicating her awareness that fatherhood itself is both *a* social construct and *the* social construct that constructs society. For achieving this analysis and acting on it, she is rewarded with a domestic happiness that seems to prove Dickinson's contention that it is "vain to punish Honey, / It only sweeter grows." At the same time, in speaking such a law this creature of milk and honey begins the reeducation and redemption of Godfrey Cass: the cultural code of Deuteronomy speaks through her, suggesting that even if she is a Christmas child, she is as much a daughter of the Old Testament as of the New, of the first telling of the law as of its second telling.

Happy and dutiful as she is, however, Eppie is not perfectly contented, for she has a small fund of anxiety that is devoted to her other parent—her lost mother. This intermittent sadness, which manifests itself as a preoccupation with her mother's wedding ring, directs our attention to a strange disruption at the center of *Silas Marner*: the history of Eppie's dead mother. On the surface, of course, the ring that Silas has saved for his adopted daughter is an aptly ironic symbol of that repressed plot, for there never was any bond beyond an artificial one between Molly Farren and Godfrey Cass, the lawless father "of whom [the ring] was the symbol." But Eppie's frequent ruminations on "how her mother looked, whom she was like, and how [Silas] had found her against the furze bush" suggest that there is something more problematical than a traditional bad marriage at issue here (*SM* 2.16). As so often in this "legendary" tale, what seems like a moral point also offers an eerily accurate account of what Freud sees as the inexorable psychosexual growth of the daughter into a culture shaped by the codes of the father. "Our insight into [the pre-Oedipal] phase in the little girl comes to us as a surprise comparable . . . with . . . the discovery of the Minoan-Mycenaean civilization beyond that of Greece," remarks Freud, explaining that "everything connected with this first mother attachment has . . . seemed to me so elusive, lost in a past so dim and shadowy . . . that it seemed as if it had undergone some specially inexorable repression" ("Female Sexuality," trans. Riviere, 195).

Indeed, Molly Farren *has* undergone a "specially inexorable repression" in this novel. A few pages of a single chapter are devoted to her point of view, her life, and her death, though her damned and doomed wanderings in the snow strikingly recapitulate the lengthier wanderings of fallen women such as Hetty Sorel and Maggie Tulliver. I suggest that Eliot attempts this drastic condensation precisely because *Silas Marner*, in allowing her to speak symbolically about the meaning of daughterhood, allowed her also to speak in even more resonant symbols about the significance of motherhood. What she said was what she saw: that it is better to be a daughter than a mother, and better still to be a father than a daughter. For when the "Deuteronomy" of culture formulates the incest laws that lie at the center of human society, that severe code tells the son, in effect: You may not have your mother; you may not kill your father. But when it is translated into a "daughteronomy" preached for the growing girl, it says: You must bury your mother; you must give yourself to your father. Since the daughter has inherited an empty pack and cannot *be* a father, she has no choice but to be *for* the father—to be his treasure, his land, his voice.[7]

Yet as George Eliot shows, the growing girl is haunted by her own difficult passage from mother to father, haunted by the primal scene in the snow when she was forced to turn away from the body of the mother, the emblem of nature that can give only so much and no more, and seek the hearth of the father, the emblem of culture that must compensate for nature's inadequacies. This moment is frozen into the center of *Silas Marner* like the dead figure of Molly Farren Cass, whose final posture of self-abandonment brings about Eppie's "effort to regain the pillowing arm and bosom; but mammy's ear was deaf, and the pillow seemed to be slipping away backward" (*SM* 1.12). Indeed, for women the myth that governs personality may be based on such a moment, a confrontation of the dead mother that is as horrifying to daughters as Freud (in *Totem and Taboo*) claimed the nightmare of the dead father was to sons. Finally, the garden that Eppie and Silas plant at the end of the novel memorializes this moment. " 'Father,' " says the girl "in a tone of gentle gravity. . . . 'we shall take the furze bush into the garden,'"—for it was against the bush that Molly died (*SM* 2.16). Now, fenced in by the garden of the law, the once "straggling" bush will become a symbol of nature made meaningful, controlled and confined by culture.

In the end, then, it is Silas Marner, the meek weaver of Raveloe, who inherits the milk and honey of the earth, for he has affirmed the Law of the Father that weaves parents and children, kin and kindness, together. Not coincidentally, when Silas's adopted daughter's engagement to Aaron weaves him definitively into the world, Dunstan Cass's skeleton is uncovered, and the gold is restored: since Silas has been willing to give his treasure to another, his treasure is given back to him. The intricate web of nemesis and apotheosis that Eliot has woven around him reminds us, moreover, that the very name Raveloe preserves two conflicting meanings along with an allegorical pun on the word *law*. According to Webster, *to ravel* means both "to entangle" *and* "to disentangle." And indeed, in this "legendary" domain the "nots" and knots of the law are unraveled—untangled and clarified—in an exemplary manner, even while the *Ravel* or entanglement of the Law weaves people together with Rainbow threads of custom and ceremony.

Finally, too, all is for the best in this domain because this tale of ravelings and unravelings has been told both by and about a daughter of wisdom. Indeed, though Silas Marner as Job is of course no Jove, and the daughter of his single parenthood is no Minerva, the structure of the relationship between innocently wise Eppie and her lawful father repeats the structure of the relationship between the goddess of wisdom and her law-giving father, just as the frozen burial of Molly Farren Cass affirms the fateful judgment of the *Oresteia* that the mother "is not the true parent of the child / Which is called hers" (Aeschylus 169). In Hélène Cixous's wry words, there is "no need for mother—provided that there is something of the maternal: and it is the father then who acts as—is— the mother" (92). With no Eumenides in sight, the redeemed land of Raveloe belongs to fathers and daughters. It is no wonder that Edith Wharton begins her revisionary *Summer* with Charity Royall, an angry transformation of Eppie, trapped in a library ruled by a plaster bust of Minerva.

WRITING TO Edith Wharton in 1912 about *The Reef*, perhaps the most Jamesian of her novels, Henry James thought of George Eliot and suggested that his friend's revisionary clarification of Eliot's message was so radical that the American writer had made herself, metaphorically speaking, into her English culture mother's primordial precursor. "There used to be little notes in you that were like fine benevolent finger-marks of the good George Eliot—the echo of much reading of that excellent woman," he told Wharton. "But now you are like a lost and recovered 'ancient' whom *she* might have got a reading of (especially were he a Greek) and of whom in *her* texture some weaker reflection were to show" (Millicent Bell 274). In fact, James's remarks were more prophetic than analytical, for if the not altogether successful *Reef* was quasi-Jamesian rather than proto-Eliotian, the brilliantly coherent *Summer* does surface the Ur-myth, and specifically the dark "daughteronomy," on which *Silas Marner* is based.

It may seem odd to argue that *Summer*, a sexy story of an illicit love affair, has anything in common with Eliot's pedagogically "respectable" *Silas Marner*. Yet, like *Silas Marner*, *Summer* is a family romance that also incorporates a female *Bildungsroman*, the account of a daughter's growth to maturity. As in *Silas Marner*, too, both the covert symbolic romance and the overt educational *roman* are resolved through the relationship between an adopted daughter and a man who seems to act as both her father and her mother. Again, like *Silas Marner*, *Summer* broods on the winter of civilization's discontent and the summer of reproduction; in doing so, moreover, Wharton's romance, like Eliot's fable, explores events that are literally or figuratively situated on the margins of society, where culture must enter into a struggle with nature in order to transform "raw" female reality into "cooked" feminine sex roles. In addition, as a corollary of this exploration, *Summer*, like *Silas Marner*, traces the redemption that the father achieves through his possession of the daughter. Finally, therefore, the two novels illuminate each other with striking reciprocity: in the conciliatory cosiness with which it evades desire, *Silas Marner* is the story Edith Wharton might have liked to tell, while in the relentless rigor with which it renounces desire, *Summer* is the tale Eliot may have feared to confront.

As James's remark about her "ancient" quality implied, by the time she wrote this short novel, Wharton had begun to become a fierce mythologist. Thus, what Sylvia Plath once called "a blue sky out of the *Oresteia*" arches over *Summer*, illuminating every detail of a mythic narrative that revolves around a father who (to go on quoting Plath) "all by [himself is] pithy and historical as the Roman Forum" ("The Colossus," *Collected Poems* 129), a daughter who marries the "winter of [his] year" as helplessly as Aeschylus's Elektra or Plath's "Electra on Azalea Path" marries the shadow of Agamemnon (*Collected Poems*, 116–17), and a dead mother who must be as definitively consigned to barren ground as Clytemnestra or the Eumenides. Appropriately enough, in fact, the book begins as its heroine, teenage Charity Royall, walks down the featureless main street of the New England village of North Dormer to her dreary part-time job in a library presided over by a plaster cast of "sheep-nosed" Minerva, the divine daddy's girl who resolved the *Oresteia* by ruling in favor of "the father's claim / And male supremacy in all things." A representative of nature bewildered by culture, Charity is a sort of foundling who, we learn, was "brought down" from a nearby mountain when she was very little, an origin that places her among the "humblest . . . in North Dormer, where to come from the Mountain was the worst disgrace." At the same time, however, both her job as librarian and the odd fact that she keeps some lace she is making "wound about the buckram back of a disintegrated copy of '*The Lamplighter*'" significantly qualify her ignorance and humbleness (S 22, 14).[8] For, like Eliot's Eppie, and Gerty, the heroine of Maria Cummins's 1854 bestseller, Charity Royall is the ward of a solitary older man who dotes on and delights in her youth, her charm, her dependence.

While both Eliot's Silas Marner and Cummins's Trueman Flint are almost from the first sympathetic men, however, Charity's guardian is an equivocal figure, and his difference begins to reveal the secret dynamics that such apparently divergent works as Cummins's and Eliot's novels share with Wharton's. For Lawyer Royall, says the narrator of *Summer*, "ruled in North Dormer; and Charity ruled in Lawyer Royall's house. . . . But she knew her power, knew what it was made of, and hated it." *Lawyer* Royall—so far as we know, this "magnificent monument of a man" has no other name (S 23, 27). Indeed, as Charity's father/guardian/suitor and (eventually) husband he is, ultimately, no more than the role his professional title and allegorical surname together denote: a regal law giver, a mythologized superego whose occupation links him with the library and with culture, that is, with the complex realm of patriarchal history that both puzzles and imprisons the orphaned swarthy wild child he is trying to make into a desirable daughter/bride.

Even while he is a "towering" public man, however, Lawyer Royall is a notably pathetic private man, for from the first Wharton deconstructs the colossus of the father to make explicit the ways in which this paradigmatic patriarch is as dependent on his Charity as Silas Marner was on his Eppie, or indeed as Agamemnon was on Iphigenia or Elektra, Oedipus on Antigone and Ismene, or the biblical Jephthah on his (nameless) daughter. To begin with, we learn that Charity had long ago perceived Mr. Royall as "too lonesome" for her to go away to school; later, more dramatically, we discover that his "lonesomeness" manifested itself in an abortive attempt to rape her. Finally, and most significantly, we are told that it was this episode that drove the girl to try to establish her independence by taking her deathly job in the library. But, of course, we eventually discover also that this attempt at escape, as in some Sophoclean case history, simply impells her even more inexorably towards her fate.

For it is in "Minerva's" library that Charity meets her lover-to-be, a handsome architect named Lucius Harney and a far more glamorously equivocal representative of culture than the aging Lawyer Royall. Town-bred, easy with books, this dashing young man is culture's heir; at the same time, he is a golden boy whose "lusciousness," as Andrea Hammer has observed, links him to nature, even makes him into nature's emis-sary—and that is why *he* is an equivocal figure. Young, sensual, magnet-ic, he is frequently associated with the grass, the sky, the "flaming breath" of summer; indeed he and Charity conduct their affair while he is "camp-ing" halfway up the Mountain in a little abandoned house surrounded by rosebushes that have "run wild." That he is often connected in Charity's mind with her mysterious Mountain relative Liff Hyatt, whose initials echo his, seems at first to suggest, moreover, that like Liff, Lucius is a brother figure and his earliest advances *are* described as "more frater-nal than lover-like" (*S* 95). Yet just as Eppie Marner's marriage to the brother figure Aaron also marries her definitively to her father Silas, so Charity's apparently illegitimate romance with Lucius Harney moves her inexorably into the arms of Lawyer Royall, and this not just because it is Royall who marries her to "rescue" her from unwed motherhood but because it eventually becomes plain that even Lucius Harney's desire for her is inextricably entangled in his paradoxical but powerful feelings of rivalrous identification with the patriarchally "majestic" lawyer.

For Charity, in every sense of the word, must be given to the father, and as *Summer's* denouement finally makes clear, even while Harney has seemed to act against Royall, he has also acted *for* the lawyer, appearing as if by magic in the library to deflower Charity and impregnate her so that she is at last ready for the marriage she had earlier persistently refused. Indeed, it is arguable that throughout the affair in which he seems to have functioned as nature's emissary by drawing the girl into the wilder-ness of her own sexuality, Harney has really performed as culture's mes-senger, and specifically as a vivid and vital "phallus" whose glamor se-duces the daughter into the social architecture from which she would otherwise have tried to flee. For in patriarchal marriage, says Wharton's plot, the brother/equal inevitably turns into the father/ruler. Not sur-prisingly, therefore, when Charity and Lawyer Royall start on their journey towards the allegorically named town of *Nettle*ton, where the girl's sexual initiation began and where she is finally going to be married to her legal guardian, Charity briefly imagines that she is "sitting beside her lover with the leafy arch of summer bending over them." But "this illusion [is] faint and transitory," because it implies a deceptive liberty of desire (*S* 273). As Wharton reluctantly observed, the daughter's summer of erotic content blooms only to prepare her for what Dickinson called "a Doom of Fruit without the Bloom"—an autumn and winter of civilized discontent. As in Wharton's pornographic "Beatrice Palmato" fragment—a more melodramatic tale of father-daughter incest which makes overt some of the psychodynamics that are even in *Summer* only covert—the symbolic father will "reap [the] fruit" born from the son/lover's deflowering (Lewis 548).

Charity does, however, make one last frantic effort to flee the wintry prison house of culture that is closing around her, and that is in her wild pilgrimage up the Mountain in search of her mother. As the girl's affair with Harney has progressed, she has become increasingly concerned about her origins and begun to try, as Eppie did in *Silas Marner*, to explain to herself what it means both to have and to be a mother. Finally, when she realizes she is pregnant, she also understands that there is "something in her blood that [makes] the Mountain the only answer to her questioning," and in an astonishing episode, which includes some of the most fiercely imagined scenes in American fiction, she journeys towards the heart of darkness where she will find and lose her mother (*S* 236).

Appropriately enough, Charity's mother's name is *Mary* Hyatt, and just as appropriately, when Charity arrives in the outlaw community on the Mountain, the woman has just died, as if the very idea of the daughter's quest must necessarily kill her female progenitor, not only to emphasize the unavailability of female power but also to underscore the *Oresteian* dictum that "the mother is not the true parent of the child / Which is called hers." Worse still, this anti-virgin Mary is not only dead, she is horrifyingly dead, dead "like a dead dog in a ditch," one "swollen glistening leg" flung out, "bare to the knee," in a death paroxysm that parodies the paroxysm of birth and suggests the nausea of nakedness in which the flesh of the mother expels and repels the flesh of the child (*S* 250, 248). As Mr. Miles, the clergyman, who only ascends the Mountain for funerals, intones "Yet in my flesh shall I see God," Charity thinks of "the gaping mouth [and] glistening leg," and when he proposes that Jesus Christ shall change this "vile body," a last spadeful of earth falls heavily "on the vile body of Mary Hyatt" (*S* 251, 255).

Where such women poets as Elizabeth Barrett Browning and Emily Dickinson transformed mothers into "multitudinous mountains sitting in / [A] magic circle," and "sweet Mountains" into "Strong Madonnas," Wharton, like her culture mother George Eliot, mythologized the female parent as a blind, deaf, stony Medusa and the maternal Mountain as a place of mourning (Browning, bk. I, ll. 622–23, p. 57; Dickinson, *Complete Poems* 354). As if Eliot anticipated the French feminist psychoanalyst Christiane Olivier's contention that the mirror man holds towards woman "contains only the image of a dead woman" and, more specifically, a dead Jocasta, frozen into the center of *Silas Marner*—as we saw—is the morbid moment of Molly Farren Cass's death in the snow and her daughter Eppie's discovery that "mammy's ear was deaf" (Olivier 149); similarly, frozen into the center of *Summer* is the moment of Mary Hyatt's burial in the snow and her daughter Charity's mortifying discovery that there is no salvation from or for her mother's "vile body."

Neither is there salvation or even significant charity for Charity from other women in the novel. Like dead Mary Hyatt, she has nothing and is nothing but a vessel for her child: the annunciation of summer, she discovers, inexorably entails the renunciation that is winter, a divestment of desire that definitively prepares her for her final turn towards the rescuing father. Without alternatives, fated to move from father to library to lover to father, she goes to Nettleton and marries her guardian. And by now even the Romantic nature she had experienced with her lover has been transmuted into a set of cultural artifacts—an engraving of a couple in a boat that decorates her bridal chamber and a pin set with a lake-blue gem which implies that in the bloomless winter of her maturity the lake itself must turn to stone.

But if a stone is all Charity has, Charity is what Lawyer Royall has, an emblem of redemption that he needs as much as Silas Marner needs "his" Eppie. For if, as Freud argues, the girl arrives at "the ultimate normal feminine attitude in which she takes her father as love-object" only after "a lengthy process of [symbolically castrating] development" ("Female Sexuality," trans. Riviere, 199), then the daughter's desire for the father, like Charity's need for Lawyer Royall, must be understood to be coercively constructed by a social order that forces her to renounce more "natural" desires—for lover/brother, for mother, for self. But as the ambiguous allegory of Charity's name suggests, the father's desire for the daughter is natural and inevitable, a desire not only to give but to receive Charity. Standing outside the girl's room after proposing to her (and being rejected) for the second time, Royall seems to understand this: "his hand on the door knob[,] 'Charity!' he [pleads]" (*S* 119). For not only is the "daughter" a milk-giving creature, a suitably diminished, passive, and dependent mother, she is also, as a living manifestation of the father's wealth, the charity to which he is culturally entitled.

Finally, therefore, from Charity's point of view *Summer* is very much a novel about both renunciation and resignation. When her last hope for escape is buried with her mother, she must resign herself, or, rather, re-assign herself, to her symbolic Father.[9] After her marriage she will be Charity Royall Royall, a name whose redundancy emphasizes the proprietary power by which her guardian/husband commands her loyalty. But from Lawyer Royall's point of view *Summer* is a novel about assignment, that is, about both the roles of cultural authority to which men are assigned and the women who are assigned—marked out, given over—to them to signify that authority. "Of course, *he's* the book," said

Wharton enigmatically about Lawyer Royall (Wolff xv). Consciously, she no doubt meant that he is the novel's only Jamesian adult and therefore the only character whose redemption is worth tracing in detail. But less consciously she might have meant that, as law-giving patriarch, he is the "book" in which Charity's fate must be inscribed, for it is, after all, the text of his desire that determines the destiny of hers.

APART FROM such fictions as *Silas Marner* and *Summer*, what evidence have we that the father may need, even desire, the daughter at least as much as she needs him? Equally to the point, what proof is there that father-daughter incest is a culturally constructed paradigm of female desire? In May 1897, shortly before abandoning his theory that hysteria was caused by paternal seduction or rape, Sigmund Freud had a dream about "feeling over-affectionately towards" his oldest daughter, Mathilde, a dream that suggests that we do have some telling evidence about paternal desire, and evidence from the father of psychoanalysis himself. "The dream, of course, fulfills my wish to pin down a father as the originator of neurosis and put an end to my persistent doubts," Freud wrote to Fliess (Freud, *Origins* 206). Within four months, however, he had rejected that etiology, and subsequent writers on the subject, from O. Mannoni to Juliet Mitchell, have applauded the courage with which he did so. After all, says Mannoni, the "theory of trauma, of the seduction by the father . . . served as [Freud's] defense against the knowledge of the Oedipus complex" (45). Yet the Oedipus complex as it then, in Mannoni's phrase, "unfolded," as its name denoted, and as Freud himself eventually realized, transcribed a primordial human desire for the *mother*. Why, then, assume that Freud's dream of paternal desire "screens" a consciousness of *daughterly* eroticism towards the *father*? Is it not possible that paternal desire and the *son's* Oedipal wishes are inextricably linked, each a manifestation of the other? Certainly, admits Juliet Mitchell, "even Freud, as his dream [of Mathilde] revealed, found it more acceptable to be the father than the incest-desiring or rival-castrating son—*as do most men*" (75; my italics).

Certainly, too, as a number of writers have lately argued, not only Freud but many men express such desires for the daughter, and as Judith Herman and Lisa Hirschman's thoroughly documented study *Father-Daughter Incest* demonstrates, a surprising number enact their erotic paternal fantasies, fantasies that allow them both to have and to humble the mother. At the same time, Freud's own late perception of the significance of the little girl's first, pre-Oedipal mother attachment—the stage in female psychosexual growth that he compared to the "Minoan-Mycenaean" stage in human history—led him to the understanding that the girl's transference to her father is both the end result of an extraordinarily difficult procedure and, as he put it, a "positive" development, an implicit recognition, in other words, that the daughter's desire for the father *is* fundamentally a complex cultural construct: only by a "very circuitous path," he admits in his 1931 essay "Female Sexuality," does the girl "arrive at the ultimate normal feminine attitude in which she takes her father as love-object" ("Female Sexuality," trans. Riviere, 199).

That path, with its obstacles, its terrors, and its refusals, is the road studied in *Silas Marner* and *Summer*—in *Silas Marner*'s exploration of the powers the daughter gives the father and in *Summer*'s examination of the powers the father takes away from the daughter. But, of course, countless other literary texts—both male- and female-authored—focus on the submerged paradigm of father-daughter incest that shapes the possibilities inscribed in these novels. From the *Oresteia*'s repudiation and repression of the matriarchal Furies and its concomitant aggrandizement of Athena, the dutiful father's daughter, to *Oedipus at Colonus*'s praise of Antigone and Ismene, the two loyal daughters who have been their father's sole guardians in the blinded exile to which his incestuous marriage with his mother condemned him, Greek literature consistently valorizes such a paradigm. That Oedipus's daughters, in particular, functioned as their father's "eyes" reminds us, moreover, that "the word for daughter in Greek is *Kore*, the literal meaning of which is pupil of the eye" (Seidenberg and Papathomopoulos 150), while the violent obliteration of the mother in these works and many others recalls one version of the story of Athena's origin: after raping Metis the Titaness, the father-god *swallowed her*, having heard that she was now pregnant with a daughter but, if she had another child, she would bear a son who would depose him; then, "in due time" he himself gave birth to Athena, who "sprang fully armed" from his skull (Graves 1:46). In just the way that Antigone and Ismene properly replace Jocasta as Oedipus's helpmeets—indeed, as the "eyes" who, according to Freud, would signify his continuing sexual potency—so Athena supplants Metis as Zeus's true child/bride.

To be sure, these archaic texts enact the prescriptions of patriarchal culture with exceptional clarity; yet such imperatives also underlie a surprising number of other, later works, ranging from Shakespeare's *King Lear* to Percy Bysshe Shelley's *The Cenci*, from Mary Shelley's *Mathilda* to Christina Stead's *The Man Who Loved Children*, from some of Sylvia Plath's and Anne Sexton's most striking poems to Toni Morrison's *The Bluest Eye*. Where the stories of such heroines as Antigone and her later, more angelically Victorian avatar Eppie Marner had recounted the daughter's acquiescence in her filial destiny, however, these works, like Wharton's *Summer*, record her ambivalence towards a fate in which, as Beatrice Cenci cries, "all things" terrifyingly transform themselves into "my father's spirit, / His eye, his voice, his touch surrounding me" (Shelley, Cenci 5.4, p. 332). Specifically, in each of these works a father more or less explicitly desires a daughter. His incestuous demands may be literal or they may be figurative, but in either case the heroine experiences them as both inexorable and stifling. Thus, in each work the girl struggles with more or less passion to escape, arguing that "I love your Majesty according to my bond, no more, no less." And in almost all these works she discovers, finally, just what the nature of that bond is—no more, no less, than on the one hand, death, or on the other hand, a surrender to the boundless authority of paternal desire that governs the lives of mothers and daughters in what Adrienne Rich has called "the kingdom of the sons" and the fathers ("Sibling Mysteries," *Dream* 49). Indeed, in the few works where the daughter neither dies nor acquiesces (such as Plath's "Daddy" and Stead's *The Man Who Loved Children*), she becomes a murderess and an outlaw.

REDUCING the plot, as fairy tales so often do, to its most essential psychic outline, a narrative recorded by the brothers Grimm provides a resonant summary of the father-daughter "story" I have been exploring here. "Allerleirauh," meaning "All Kinds of Fur," introduces us to a king whose dying wife has made him promise not to remarry unless he can find a new bride who is as beautiful as she is and who has "just such golden hair as I have." Grief-stricken, the king keeps his word until one day he looks at his growing daughter, sees that she is "just as beautiful as her dead mother, and [has] the same golden hair[,] suddenly [feels] a violent love for her," and resolves to marry *her*. Shocked, the daughter tries to escape by setting him impossible tasks—she asks for three magical dresses and a "mantle of a thousand kinds of fur"—but when he, just as magically, fulfills her requests, she has no choice but to run away. Taking her three dresses and three tiny domestic treasures, she wraps herself in her fur mantle and escapes to a great forest. There she is asleep in a hollow tree when "the king to whom this forest belong[s]" passes through with some huntsmen, who capture her, thinking she is "a wondrous beast," and when she tells them she is simply a poor orphan child, they bring her to this king's palace, where they set her to work like Cinderella in the kitchen (Grimm and Grimm 327, 328).[10]

Of course, however, the king soon manages to discover her identity: he gives a series of three feasts, at each of which she appears in one of her magic dresses; he admires the soup she cooks in her furry Cinderella garb, and he finally manages to tear off her protective mantle, revealing her magic dress and her golden hair, so that, in the words of the story, "she [can] no longer hide herself," and the pair are wed soon after this epiphany (331). Like such texts as *Summer, Mathilda,* and *The Cenci,* then, this tale records the case history of a daughter who tries to escape paternal desire, and like the heroines of many such works (for instance, Charity journeying to the Mountain), the "fair princess" who becomes "Allerleirauh" flees from culture (her father's palace) to nature (the great wood) trying to transform herself into a creature of nature (a "Hairy Animal") rather than acquiesce in the extreme demands culture is making upon her. Like a number of the other protagonists of these stories, however, "Allerleirauh" cannot altogether abandon the imperatives her culture has impressed upon her: she brings with her the three magical dresses and the three domestic tokens which will eventually reveal her identity and knit her back into society. Like countless other heroines in such tales, moreover, she is motherless, a fact that has brought about the paternal persecution she is trying to evade. Finally, like that of so many of these heroines—perhaps most notably *Silas Marner's* Eppie—her function as a "treasure" to both kings is manifested by the golden hair that she is at last unable to conceal.

That there are in fact two kings in "Allerleirauh" may at first seem to controvert my argument that this tale offers us a paradigm of the prescription for father-daughter incest that lies at the heart of female psychosexual development in patriarchal society. Not just the princess but the first king's courtiers, for instance, express dismay at his desire to marry his daughter. In addition, the second king is distinguished from the first by a restrictive clause: he is not "the king, who owns this forest"—that is, the king from whose palace "Allerleirauh" has just fled—but rather the "king to whom this forest belong[s], that is, the king who owns this forest." Yet structurally and psychologically, if not grammatically, the two kings are one, paternal figures from both of whom the "fair princess" tries to escape, though not, perhaps, with equal vigor. In fact, for all practical purposes, the distinction between the two is best expressed by a single comma, the linguistic mark that marks the difference between illegitimate and legitimate incest, a difference "Allerleirauh" herself involuntarily acknowledges by the ambivalence with which she at one moment decks herself in glorious apparel and then, soon after, retreats into her old life as a wild child.

To be sure, given such ambivalence, some readers might see this tale simply as an account of the advances and retreats through which any adolescent girl comes to terms with her own mature desires. At the same time, however, what gives the story a good deal of its force is the fatality it shares with such subtler works as *Silas Marner* and *Summer*—specifically, a fatality provided by the *mother's* complicity in her daughter's destiny. For it is, after all, "Allerleirauh"'s mother who has set the girl's story going with her admonition to the father that he must only marry a bride as beautiful as she. Lost to the daughter like Molly Farren Cass and

Mary Hyatt, she nevertheless rules her daughter's life with the injunctions of the culture mother, saying in effect: You must bury your mother, you must give yourself to your father. In *Silas Marner* and *Summer* the authors themselves replace her, splitting the maternal function between the ignominy of the dead mother and the qualified triumph of the male-identified maternal authority. But in all these stories, as even in more apparently rebellious works, the text itself discovers no viable alternative to filial resignation. Certainly such paradigmatic culture mothers as Eliot and Wharton do not believe that the daughter has any choice but the choice of acquiescence. Though the "empty pack" of daughteronomy may be heavy, as Dickinson saw perhaps more clearly than they, it is vain to "punish" the cultural "honey" it manufactures: for the daughter who understands her duty and her destiny, such honey "only sweeter grows." Under what Sylvia Plath called "a blue sky out of the Oresteia," Eppie Marner, Charity Royall, and the fair princess "Allerleirauh," along with many others and each in her own way, obey the implicit command of society and marry the winter of the Father's year.

Notes

In essentially the form in which it appears here, this essay was first published in *Critical Inquiry* 11 (1985): 355–84; I am grateful to the editors for permission to reprint. As I wrote and rewrote the piece, I should add, I profited from criticisms and suggestions offered by many friends and colleagues, including (as always) Susan Gubar and Elliot Gilbert, as well as Andrea Hammer, Susan Lurie, Elyse Blankley, Peter Hays, Suzanne Graver, Judith Peck, and Michael Wolfe, all of whom I wish to thank.

1. In *Monsters of Affection,* Dianne Sadoff makes a point similar to this one, noting that Eliot seeks "to usurp [paternal authority] as the discourse of a male narrator, the authority of a male auther" (3).

2. Eliot's letter to Blackwood, dated 12 January 1861, is quoted in Redinger, p. 436. As Susan Gubar has suggested to me, the resonant image of the "pack man" may be associated with the figure of Bob Jakin in *The Mill on the Floss* (which Eliot had just completed), the itinerant pack-bearing peddler who brings Maggie Tulliver a number of books, the most crucial of which is Thomas à Kempis's treatise on Christian renunciation (so that its subject metaphorically associates it with Silas Marner's pack full of emptiness).

3. Throughout this essay *Silas Marner* is abbreviated as *SM* and keyed to the chapter and page in the Penguin edition.

4. Eliot consciously exploits the text-textile analogy in *Silas Marner,* referring to the "tale" of cloth Silas weaves and letting Silas accuse William Dane of having "woven a plot" against him (*SM* 1.2, 1). For discussions of her more general use of webs, weaving, and spinning as metaphors see Gilbert and Gubar, *Madwoman* 522–28; J. Hillis Miller; and Stump 172–214. On Eliot's own tendency to avarice—an inclination that, at least in the view of Blackwood, her publisher,

became problematical just at the time she was composing *Silas Marner*—see Dessner.

5. Knoepflmacher points out that Silas, like Shakespeare's Pericles, will become "another passive Job . . . redeemed through the miraculous gift of a daughter" (*Eliot's Early Novels* 229).

6. Eliot looks at Grimm's law in *A Writer's Notebook*. The theme of the daughter as treasure is, in addition, one that Eliot might have picked up from Balzac's *Eugenie Grandet* (1833), a novel that treats the relationship of a miserly father and a "treasured" only daughter far more cynically than *Silas Marner* does.

7. According to Freud, the Oedipus complex means for the girl an attachment to the father that parallels the boy's attachment to his mother; but for the girl, attachment to the father is a "positive" phenomenon that succeeds an earlier "negative" phase in which she experiences the same "first mother-attachment" that the boy feels. When the girl learns that her mother has not "given" her a penis, however—i.e., in Lacan's sense, that the mother has not given her the power represented by the "Phallus"—she turns in despair to the father, who may be able to give her some of its power (see Freud, "Female Sexuality," passim, and "Some Psychical Consequences." See also Sadoff, p. 69, on a "pattern of the displaced mother" in Eliot's novels).

8. Throughout this essay *Summer* is abbreviated as *S*.

9. Joseph Smith makes a similar case for the inevitability of "resignation" in women (see esp. 391 and 395). For a different formulation of the same point see Freud, "Analysis Terminable and Interminable," trans. Riviere, esp. 268–71. Freud's n. 14, a quotation from Sandor Ferenczi, is particularly telling in this regard: "In every male patient the sign that his castration-anxiety has been mastered . . . is a sense of equality of rights with the analyst; and every female patient . . . must have . . . become able to *submit without bitterness* to thinking in terms of her feminine role" (270 n. 14; my italics).

10. In a brief discussion of this tale, Herman argues that "Allerleirauh" is a version of "Cinderella" (2). Even more interestingly, the folklorist Alan Dundes argues a connection between the plot of this story ("tale type 923, Love Like Salt"), "Cinderella," and *King Lear*, although he claims that this basic plot functions as "*a projection of incestuous desires on the part of the daughter*" (Dundes 355, 360; my italics).

BETTY S. FLOWERS

Christina Rossetti: Dialogue with
the Father God

VIRGINIA WOOLF characterizes Christina Rossetti as having something "dark and hard, like a kernel" in the center of her being. "It was
religion, of course," says Woolf, adding that "everything in Christina's
life radiated from that knot of agony and intensity in the centre" ("'I Am
Christina Rossetti'" 55–56).

Rossetti's God is a harsh Father, one who calls his daughter to
sacrifice and to obey. What Gilbert and Gubar call "Rossetti's aesthetic of
renunciation" (*Madwoman* 587) is, from another point of view, an aesthetic of desire, for Rossetti is engaged in a passionate quest for love and
approval from this stern Father. To earthly lovers, the speaker in "'The
Heart Knoweth Its Own Bitterness'" says: "How should I spend my
heart on you, / My heart that so outweighs you all?"

> How can we say "enough" on earth—
>   "Enough" with such a craving heart?
> I have not found it since my birth,
>   But still have bartered part for part.
> I have not held and hugged the whole,
>   But paid the old to gain the new:
>   Much have I paid, yet much is due,
> Till I am beggared sense and soul.
> . . . .
> You scratch my surface with your pin,
>   You stroke me smooth with hushing breath:—
> Nay pierce, nay probe, nay dig within,
>   Probe my quick core and sound my depth.
> You call me with a puny call,
>   You talk, you smile, you nothing do:
>   How should I spend my heart on you,
> My heart that so outweighs you all?   (*PW* 192)[1]

The quest for the Heavenly Lover is seen most clearly in those
poems constructed on the model of a dialogue. Rossetti wrote dialogue
poems throughout her career. The dialogues of her early work often

278

occur between earthly lovers or sisters. But towards the end of her career, when she was spending a great deal of time in the composition of her six lengthy devotional works for the Society for Promoting Christian Knowledge, more and more the dialogue poems begin to take the form of conversations—and sometimes thinly veiled arguments—between the speaker and the Lord.

Explicit and implicit dialogues with God are to be found throughout English poetry, perhaps most notably in the work of George Herbert, whom Rossetti admired. However, even though Rossetti is working within a tradition, her position as a female within that tradition brings to light a significant aspect of all such dialogues: that no matter what the sex of the speaker, in a dialogue with the Christian Father God, the gender, or cultural identity of the aspiring Christian, is always female. The Christian speaks from the position of the female, of the daughter rather than the son, when speaking in dialogue with God.

At first, the assertion that the Christian in dialogue with God always speaks as a daughter may seem to be contradicted by the fact that most dialogue poems, including most of Rossetti's, refer to the speaker as "he." Our conventions of reading, in which "he" is the universal human, and "she" means a special case or specific instance, mask the family dynamics operating in the subtext of a dialogue with the Christian Father. The model of the divine family in Christianity is composed of God the Father, Mary the immaculately conceived Mother, and Christ the Son, a structure with its roots deep in the triads of ancient Egypt: Ptah, Sekhmet, and Nefertum; Amon, Mut, and Khonsu; Osiris, Isis, and Horus.

The fourth member of this family lies outside the iconography—it is liminal, other, and shifting. The number 3 is symbolically associated with heaven, while 4 is the number of the earth (Cirlot 232). In Christianity, the fourth, the earthly daughter, seeks to make herself worthy of membership in this family. In her institutional form, the daughter becomes the Church, united to the Son in a brother-sister union that Pharaonic Egypt made literal but Christianity makes symbolic and otherworldly. Yet since the central mystery of Christianity depends on the paradox that the Son is simultaneously the Father, this symbolic union of Bride and Bridegroom reunites the Bride with the Father as well and ultimately returns her to "dwell in the house of the Lord for ever" (Ps. 23:6).

The "Lord" whom the daughter/narrator/Christian of Rossetti's poetry addresses is both the Father and the Son. The word *Lord*, used for either Father or Son, emphasizes that the Son and the Father are one. When the daughter learns of the Father, she is learning to embrace the Son Who is One with the Father. A dialogue with the Lord, even if staged in the voice of the bride of Christ, is always a dialogue of daughter and Father that seems to exclude—and even reject—the Mother.

The absence of the Mother in the Protestant religion Rossetti embraced is in stark contrast to the presence of the Mother Mary in Roman Catholicism. Mary, as intercessor and acknowledged Queen of Heaven, posits the maturation of the "daughter" (male or female) through a model of return to both mother and father. In the spiritual journey mapped out for the Protestant, the "daughter" makes herself worthy of the holy family in the same way that children grow up within Protestant Christian society—by learning to separate themselves from the mother and identify with the world of the father. In terms of the spiritual family reflected in the structure of Rossetti's poetry, the daughter must give up the world of the archetypal Mother (Eros, the earth, the body, the elements, the processes of life, including death and time) in order to align herself with the Father (Logos, heaven, the mind, ideas, the processes of rational thought, monuments of culture, eternity).

Looked at from the daughter's position, Christina Rossetti's dialogue poems can be seen to enact strategies designed to help the daughter give up the Mother for the Father—or, as she depicts it, to give up the world for Paradise. Like Plato's dialogues—which Rossetti read "over and over again" (William Rossetti lxx)—Rossetti's poems reflect the way a neophyte is led by a wiser voice (almost always the Lord Himself) to see and embrace the truth, and thus to leave the world behind.

Leaving the world behind is made easier when the daughter is led to remember that while the world of the mother is beautiful and comforting and vivid, it is also, as a world of process, inescapably connected with suffering and death. Ancient cultures imaged this in their goddesses, who, like Kali with her necklace of skulls, were both benevolent and terrifying. Modern psychologists have retained and internalized the concept in the notion of the "good" and "bad" mother. While ancient cultures attempted to appease the terrifying goddess, modern Western cultures have attempted to reject the world of the mother altogether. This rejection is difficult to achieve, as the widespread devotion to the cult of the Virgin Mary makes clear. A powerful antidote to the lure of the world, however, is a reminder of the serpent of death who lurks in the center of the maternal garden. Rossetti's many poems on death attest, not to her morbid cast of mind, but to the Christian's fear of being lured by the good mother into forgetting her shadow side:

> Of all the downfalls in the world,
> The flutter of an Autumn leaf
> Grows grievous by suggesting grief:

Who thought, when Spring was first unfurled,
Of this? The wide world lay empearled;
Who thought of frost that nips the world?
(from " 'Vanity of Vanities' " [1858], CP 2:315)

In this context, "downfalls" reminds us of three falls: the original Fall in the Garden of Eden; the falling down of leaves in autumn; and the spiritual downfall in store for those who forget that death follows life. "Laughing Life cries at the feast,— / Craving Death cries at the door" (untitled, CP 2:308).

Many of Rossetti's poems proclaim that Eden—the world and its beauty, the comfort and joy associated with the natural realm and the archetypal Mother—is inferior to Paradise. But in almost every case this assertion is part of an argument, for the dynamic imagery of the natural world is difficult to depotentiate, especially when the alternative is the static imagery of the ceremonial world of palms and white robes and golden crowns that Rossetti often uses for the Fatherly realm. Paradise is the throne of the absent Father; it is abstract, a place predicated on rewards and punishments. While Rossetti's poetry outwardly concurs with culture in holding up Paradise as more desirable than Eden, the strength of her poetry comes in part from its inscription of the inward struggle necessary to train ourselves to desire it more than the sensuous world we naturally desire. In "Goblin Market," one sister's warnings about what happens to maidens who eat the goblins' fruit is met by the other sister's tantalizing catalog of the fruits themselves:

"Have done with sorrow;
I'll bring you plums tomorrow
Fresh on their mother twigs,
Cherries worth getting;
You cannot think what figs
My teeth have met in,
What melons icy-cold
Piled on a dish of gold
Too huge for me to hold,
What peaches with a velvet nap,
Pellucid grapes without one seed:
. . . . "
(CP 1:15)

The Father's call may be more powerful than the "puny call" of earthly lovers, but the heart yearns for the fruit that is "full in view":

O Lord, when Thou didst call me, didst Thou know
My heart disheartened thro' and thro'
Still hankering after Egypt full in view

281

> Where cucumbers and melons grow?
> —Yea, I knew.—   (untitled, *CP* 2:190)

The child of God in the dialogue expresses natural human desires for comfort, nurture, and happiness. "Lord, carry me," begins one untitled poem (*CP* 2:194). The response from the Father, unlike the response we might expect from the nurturing mother, begins with "Nay":

> Lord, carry me.—Nay, but I grant thee strength
> To walk and work thy way to Heaven at length.—

Each of the five stanzas that follow this one is set up in the same way, with an initial question or request from the daughter, interrupted halfway through the line with a strategic response from the Father as teacher. These responses—paradoxical affirmation, admonishment, appeal to omniscience, assertion of superiority in caring, and direct command—are common to many of Rossetti's daughter-Father dialogues. The Father's answers, often appearing more like peremptory interruptions than true responses, seem to reflect a character quite different from the loving Father the narrator overtly describes in many of Rossetti's poems. Rather than fulfill the daughter's request or answer her questions, the Father's responses often work to undercut the validity of the question itself, or to question the desire for change that underlies the daughter's request. For example, the question in the second stanza of the poem is met with the implicit command for the daughter to stay as she is:

> Lord, why then am I weak?—Because I give
> Power to the weak, and bid the dying live.—

The bargain in the daughter-Father relationship is based on a paradoxical affirmation: that once Paradise has been entered, weakness is empowered. The secular equivalent—"Someday my Prince will come"—highlights what the bargain involves for the daughter: waiting. Weakness is paradoxically affirmed as the condition necessary for blessedness. "Blessed are the meek: for they shall inherit the earth" (Matt. 5:5).

> Lord, I am tired.—He hath not much desired
> The goal, who at the starting-point is tired.—

The form of admonishment is subtle here, for it involves bringing into question the strength of the daughter's desire for the Father and therefore her worthiness to enter His House. If the Father interprets tiredness as lack of desire, then the daughter's feelings of tiredness (both physical and psychological) lead her to question the validity of her own desire. Thus, when weariness in "well-doing" is defined as lack of love, to complain of tiredness is to jeopardize the chance of being accepted into Paradise. Serving the Father is not enough: the daughter must serve Him without complaint if she really wants to be accepted into His realm.

> Lord, dost Thou know?—I know what is in man;
> What the flesh can, and what the spirit can.—

The Lord's assertion of His own omniscience suggests that the narrator, the daughter who complains, is not being asked to do more than she is capable of doing, no matter what she may think or feel. Again, the Father's response works to alienate the daughter from her own feelings. The daughter/pupil in Rossetti's poems very often asks whether the teacher cares, a question that arises only when one does not feel cared for or when one does not experience the caring of the other.

> Lord, dost Thou care?—Yea, for thy gain or loss
> So much I cared, it brought Me to the Cross.—

The caring here is very specific: the Father cares about the "gain" or "loss" of the daughter, not for her tiredness or weakness. This theme of not caring is a constant refrain in Rossetti's poetry. What the daughter asks for again and again is the kind of caring one might expect from a mother. When Rossetti does describe an instance of the Lord's caring, she conveys it as a form of mothering: "And years before, as one whom his mother comforteth, saintly Martha had been comforted by Christ Himself . . ." (*Face of the Deep* 17).

Paradise, the home of the Father, offers rewards for the soul's aspiration (palms and gold crowns) rather than nourishment for the body's hunger (fruit). Yet because comfort and *response* to the heart's yearning are associated with the Mother, when Rossetti writes a poem of desire for Paradise, she calls it the "Mother Country":

> Oh what is that country
> > And where can it be,
> Not mine own country,
> > But dearer far to me?   (*CP* 1:222)

In commenting on this poem, Gilbert and Gubar point out that the "ambiguities with which Rossetti describes her own relationship to this land ('Not mine own . . . But dearer far') reflect the uncertainty of the self-definition upon which her vision depends. Is a woman's *mother* country her 'own'?" (*Madwoman* 101). The second half of the stanza, however, which Gilbert and Gubar quote but do not comment upon, makes clearer what relation the daughter does have to her mother country:

> Yet mine own country,
>> If I one day may see
> Its spices and cedars,
>> Its gold and ivory.

This is a country that may someday be hers—if she earns it. It is already dearer to her than the home that is hers now and that she presumably must give up in order to become a citizen of this new country. While the "dearer" country may be called a "Mother Country" in this poem, it bears little relation to Mother Earth although a significant relation to the Heavenly Virgin ("tower of ivory" and "house of gold"). "Country" is a concept; spices, gold, and ivory—and in this context, cedars—are products that must be manufactured, chopped down, mined, and torn from elephants. This is a heavenly Solomon's Temple, the house of the Father, prepared for the Bride from the torn body of the Mother. The country is "dearer" indeed, having cost the body of the Mother and, in a different way, the body of the aspiring daughter as well.

Leaving Eden, the world of the Mother, to aspire to Paradise, the house of the Father, means leaving nourishment and comfort for a physical desert:

> "O Lord, how canst Thou say Thou lovest me?
>> Me whom Thou settest in a barren land,
>> Hungry and thirsty on the burning sand,
> Hungry and thirsty where no waters be
> Nor shadows of date-bearing tree:—
> O Lord, how canst Thou say Thou lovest me?"
>> ("When My Heart Is Vexed, I Will Complain" *CP* 1:227–28)

The Father sets the aspiring daughter in a "barren" desert presided over by the archetypally masculine light of the sun, which in this case is not so much a giver of life as something that burns. In this land desire is not met. Although the daughter is left "hungry and thirsty," she must act as if love exists in this desert, now, in order that she may be rewarded by feeling the love of God later, in Paradise, in the "Mother Country."

"When My Heart Is Vexed" justifies its complaint against the Father through its allusion to the children of Israel wandering in the desert en route to the Promised Land and complaining bitterly all the while. However, this authorized allusion covers over the unauthorized complaint of the daughter, whose authorship is muted in Rossetti's poems not only by frequent references to the narrator as "he" but also by the use of Biblical allusions and quotations as a mask.[2] What the Father does offer by the end of the poem is not shade, food, or water but a promise of sleep in place of death:

> ["]Peace, peace: I give to My beloved sleep,
> Not death but sleep, for love is strong as death:
> Take patience; sweet thy sleep shall be,
> Yea, thou shalt wake in Paradise with Me."

This is the trade-off then: by giving up hope of earthly fulfillment and by staying in the desert of the Father, the daughter avoids death, the central negative characteristic of the realm of the Mother. The world grows old, youth and beauty are lost; but the daughter aspiring to the house of the Father can escape the pain of this knowledge by accepting the Father's sleep while waiting for the resurrection. Her sleep will be "sweet," and when she wakes up the next morning, she will wake up with Him.

As with "When My Heart Is Vexed," the question "Do you care?" in "Lord, carry me," is a form of complaint. In the realm of the archetypal Mother, of Eros, the question is inconceivable. In the realm of the Father, of Logos, emotional life is subordinated to Reason. Thus, the response to "Do you care?" is not one of direct emotional affirmation or comfort but a fact given as proof: death on the Cross. The daughter can in no way match the love asserted by this historical fact. At this point in "Lord, carry me," the questioning ends, and the daughter receives the command to "rise":

> Lord, I believe; help Thou mine unbelief.—
> Good is the word; but rise, for life is brief.
>
> The follower is not greater than the Chief:
> Follow thou Me along My way of grief.   (*CP* 1:194)

Significantly, the final "The follower is not greater than the Chief" acknowledges openly the rebellion and perhaps even competition implicit in the questioning itself. The final argument is an appeal to hierarchical authority, a rhetorical move that effectively cuts off the dialogue.

This double move of opening a dialogue and quickly bringing it to closure is reflected not only in the appeals to superiority in knowledge, power, and love but also in the underlying emotional dynamic: the fear of death is primarily a fear of judgment from the very same Father to whom the daughter is pleading for help. In this regard, the Father assumes the same double-faced aspect that the terrible Mother did in ancient religions. When the only recourse for protection against the Father is the Father himself, the daughter must rely on reminding the Father of his merciful, Motherly side, and of the implicit bargain she has struck with him. Taking the lowest place now, under the promise of "the lowest shall be made highest," means that she will have the highest place later. "Give me the lowest place," says the narrator of "The Lowest Place" (*CP* 1:187); "Lord, give me grace / To take the lowest place," prays the narrator of "Sit down in the lowest room" (*CP* 2:259). "Blessed are the poor in spirit: for theirs is the kingdom of heaven" (Matt. 5:3). When the daughter asks the Father to "Give me the lowest place," she is asking him to give her what she has already received as an inheritance from Eve. Thus, Rossetti's narrator/daughter insists on the very hierarchy that would seem to denigrate her and shows how, by its own terms, it necessarily grants her eventual supremacy. The Son's words have already undone the Father's words in the Garden against the mother and all her daughters—or so the daughter reminds Him.

Rossetti again sets the text of the Father at odds with the text of the Son in "Despised and Rejected" (*CP* 1:178–80). In this poem the narrator hears a knock at the door and the voice of one who asks to be let in:

> "Friend, My Feet bleed.
> Open thy door to Me and comfort Me."

When the daughter refuses, the voice threatens:

> ["]Open, lest I should pass thee by, and thou
> One day entreat My Face
> And howl for grace,
> And I be deaf as thou art now.
> Open to Me."

That this threat will be made good is clear in the closing lines of the poem:

> On the morrow
> I saw upon the grass
> Each footprint marked in blood, and on my door
> The mark of blood for evermore.

Clearly, when the bridegroom knocks on the door of the soul, the call must be answered. But another allusion is at work in the poem, one from the Passover story, in which all the doors marked with blood were "passed over" by the angel of death. Furthermore, the passed-over door seems to suggest femininity, as a "door" (traditionally associated with the female) marked with "blood." Thus, the curse of the female blood-marking and of being literally passed over by being made subordinate to man is absorbed into the myth of Passover and transmuted into an elliptical myth of selection and salvation.

Rossetti's strategy of undercutting a threatening image with allusions to another, more comforting set of images is seen even more clearly in her prose. In *Time Flies* Rossetti offers a meditation on the "saddening" influence of mountain scenery. The passage is remarkable for its implicit response to the Father, symbolized by the "everlasting hills":

> Wherein lies the saddening influence of mountain scenery? For I suppose many besides myself have felt depressed when approaching the "everlasting hills."
>
> Their mass and loftiness dwarf all physical magnitudes familiar to most eyes, except the low-lying vastness of the ocean and the boundless overarching sky. They touch and pass through those clouds which limit our vision.
>
> Perhaps their sublimity impresses us like want of sympathy. (III)

Later, however, the narrator looks out a window, "And, lo! the evening flush had turned snow to a rose, 'and sorrow and sadness fled away'" (III). The going down of the sun (associated with the Father) has turned the cold purity of mountain snow into the color/emblem associated with the Virgin/Mother of many cultures—the rose. Suddenly comfort is found. The meditation ends with another quotation, this one from Psalms: "Yea, though I walk through the valley of the shadow of death, I will fear no evil: for Thou art with me; Thy rod and Thy staff comfort me" (III).

In "A Candlemas Dialogue" the Lord initiates the conversation by asking the daughter why her love for Him does not make her happy:

> "Love brought Me down: and cannot love make thee
> Carol for joy to Me?
> Hear cheerful robin carol from his tree,
> Who owes not half to Me
> I won for thee."
> (*CP* 2:176–77)

The daughter answers by saying that she has heard the robin's "wordless voice"; but then she points out that the robin knows nothing of death and that maybe she would sing, too, if she had "such a voice." The "wordless" voice of the robin, of course, belongs to the world of Eros rather than that of Logos, of Eden rather than of Paradise, for Paradise is predicated on the knowledge of death. The Lord concedes the daughter's point but continues to argue with her:

> "True, thou has compassed death: but hast not thou
> The tree of life's own bough?
> Am I not Life and Resurrection now?
> My Cross balm-bearing bough
> For such as thou."

The daughter's response emphasizes the difficulty of giving up the Mother's earthly realm for the Father's heavenly one: the joys of the earth are present now. Paradise is far in the future, and to reach it the daughter must find reality in an event that is far away in both time and space: "Ah me, Thy Cross!—but that seems far away. . . ." By the end of the poem the Father has extracted a promise from the daughter that she will " 'Give with both hands . . . / Thy pleasure to fulfil, / And work Thy Will' " (*CP* 2:177). To "work Thy Will" is not as straightforward as it sounds. As in the fairy tales in which in order to win their husbands the heroines have to perform seemingly impossible tasks—emptying a lake with a sieve, for example—the daughter of the Lord is also given tasks for which she feels ill-equipped. In the performance of these tasks the daughter, like the fairy-tale heroines, is subject to extreme fatigue. What makes the performance of the Father's will even more difficult, however, is that what the Father wills is, first of all, the breaking of the daughter's independent will:

> I would have gone; God bade me stay:
> > I would have worked; God bade me rest.
> He broke my will from day to day,
> > He read my yearnings unexpressed
> > > And said them nay.
>
> Now I would stay; God bids me go:
> > Now I would rest; God bids me work.
> He breaks my heart tossed to and fro,
> > My soul is wrung with doubts that lurk
> > > And vex it so.
>
> I go, Lord, where Thou sendest me;
> > Day after day I plod and moil:
> But, Christ my God, when will it be
> > That I may let alone my toil
> > > And rest with Thee?
>
> > > > ("Weary in Well-Doing," *CP* 1:182)

Not only does the Father not provide what the daughter is thirsty for but He orders her to do exactly the opposite of what she wills and in addition to breaking her will, breaks her heart.

But all this breaking of will and heart is done in the name of love. The model of love represented by a mother comforting her child is replaced by a love whose primary symbol is the voluntary sacrifice of a Son/self on the Cross. "Love is the law from kindled saint to saint," says the narrator of "Quinquagesima" (*CP* 2:220–21), in an image both beautiful (the kindling of the heart with love) and horrific (the saints burned at stakes for love of God). The love of mother and child comes through experiences of the body; the love of the Father comes through the mind and must be learned. "Quinquagesima," which begins with praise after praise of love, ends with a prayer to "teach me, Love, such knowledge as is meet / For one to know who is fain to love and learn." The praise of love is thus shown to be praise of something unknown; it is the lesson not yet learned, like the praise of something beautiful that she has not yet seen for herself.

The poem begins, "Love is alone the worthy law of love," and moves from a series of similar assertions to a kind of imagistic logic:

> Because Love is the fountain, I discern
> The stream as love: for what but love should flow
> From fountain Love? not bitter from the sweet!

The form of the poem shows the daughter to be learning her lesson well. She deduces the presence of love where she has not experienced it, thus proving herself a worthy student of Logos in its project of redefining Eros.

And what is the daughter as student being taught by Logos? First, she must learn to give up the earth and what is natural to her. She must learn to travel "up-hill all the way":

> Does the road wind up-hill all the way?
> Yes, to the very end
> Will the day's journey take the whole long day?
> From morn to night, my friend.   ("Up-Hill," *CP* 1:65–66)

As both Brzenk and Packer point out, Rossetti paired "Up-Hill" with "Amor Mundi" in the *Poems* of 1876. Both poems involve the image of the road; but in contrast to the pilgrim of "Up-Hill," the daughter of "Amor Mundi" is lured by a lover (with "love-locks flowing") to take the easy path:

> "The downhill path is easy, come with me an it please ye,
> We shall escape the uphill by never turning back."
>
> (*CP* 1:213)

"Never turning back" is echoed in the last line of the poem: "This downhill path is easy, but there's no turning back" (*CP* 1:214). As originally printed, "Amor Mundi" forms a kind of dialogue with "Up-Hill." Brzenk notes that in "Amor Mundi" the "tripping rhythm achieved through the use of anapests and feminine and internal rhymes conveys the ease with which the downhill path is negotiated" (369). In contrast to the expansiveness of "Amor Mundi" on the page, "Up-Hill" has the appearance and sound of a "catechism," and "the halting movement of the short lines made up largely of monosyllables reproduces the effort" of the up-hill journey (368–69).

One of the most illuminating dialogues about the nature of the up-hill journey takes place in "The Three Enemies" (*CP* 1:70–72), a poem in which the daughter talks to each of the enemies—the flesh, the world, and the devil—rather than to the Lord. The flesh speaks to her in comforting tones: "Sweet, thou art pale," and "Sweet, thou art sad," and "Sweet, thou art weary," revealing in its motherly concern that issues of personal discomfort and feeling belong in the world of temptation. To each of the solicitous comments the daughter replies that Christ was paler, sadder, and, significantly, *not* weary. Christ is paler and sadder, in fact, because he "bore His Father's wrath for me" and because he "trod / The winepress of the wrath of God." The world, in its solicitous comments, flatters: "Sweet, thou art young" and "fair" and "life is sweet." Again, the daughter proclaims, Christ was younger, fairer, and for Him life was *not* sweet—the model leading the daughter to overcome the temptation of the world. The last temptation, however, is the most difficult, for the Devil tempts using the very terms offered as reward for giving up Eden for Paradise: "Thou shalt win Glory" and "Thou shalt have Knowledge," for example. In every case the daughter asks Jesus to answer for her or to "cover up mine eyes" so that the glory and recognition should go to the One who has sacrificed most: the Lord Himself.

In giving up the earth and what is natural to her, and in putting behind her the flesh, the world, and the devil, the daughter gives up the realm of wholeness that includes death, passion, and imperfection and learns instead to seek her own perfection in the role of daughter. While the Father, too, has a role to play in the family, because He is Lord, He is the *whole* family: the family is His and carries His name. The daughter takes His name; she is a "Christian." The daughter, however, in order to earn her role as Bride in Paradise, must stay in her daughter role on earth and learn to *perfect* it through the spiritual dialogue with the Father and through the definition of herself inherited from her biological mother, whom culture trains to serve as a mouthpiece for Logos rather than Eros. Florence Nightingale saw clearly the relationship between doing the will of the Father and the self-alienation of Victorian mothers and daughters from the realm of Eros:

> And women, who are afraid, while in words they acknowledge that God's work is good, to say, Thy will be *not* done (declaring another order of society from that which He has made), go about maudling to each other and teaching to their daughters that "women have no passions." In the conventional society, which men have made for women, and women have accepted, they *must* have none,

they *must* act the farce of hypocrisy, the lie that they are without passion—and therefore what else can they say to their daughters, without giving the lie to themselves? (26)

In the earthly paradigm, the daughter of the father marries a son and bears children, becoming a mother herself. But in relation to the Heavenly Father, the daughter is faced with an impossible choice: either she can risk her place with her Jealous Lord by marrying an earthly husband, whom she must vow to obey; or rejecting the role of bride to an earthly spouse, she may choose to serve only her Father, thereby working for perfection in her daughter role. The Biblical precedent for this choice occurs in the story of Mary and Martha. Christ Himself made clear that He preferred the scholarly Mary, seated at His feet and listening to Him as teacher, over the more housewifely Martha, "careful and troubled about many things" (Luke 10:41). "Mary hath chosen that good part, which shall not be taken away from her," said the Lord (Luke 10:42), a sentiment that many of Rossetti's poems embody. The choice of Mary over Martha, the contemplative life over the active, mirrors Rossetti's choice of art over family life.[3] In aligning herself with the world of the Father, Rossetti creates a poetic persona in the image of Mary, a pupil sitting at the foot of the Master.

The ideal of wholeness, by definition, includes all—the domestic and physical as well as the spiritual, the realm of Martha as well as that of Mary. The world of perfection, however, excludes the imperfect and thus is based on an ideal that condemns the world of the physical, which is always flawed. In condemning the world of the physical, the ideal of perfection condemns the female and the life of the body she represents. The Son on the Cross must sacrifice the gift of the Mother (the body and life on earth) to ascend to the Father in Heaven. When the daughter aspires to perfection, she attempts to make herself as much like the Lord as she possibly can. If her sex is female, she must give up what is associated with the earthly female—the world itself—in order to become the perfect spiritual Bride. In "The World," the narrator is implicitly male, for the female is temptation itself. Only the male is in a position to resist her:

By day she wooes me, soft, exceeding fair:
    But all night as the moon so changeth she;
    Loathsome and foul with hideous leprosy
And subtle serpents gliding in her hair.
By day she wooes me to the outer air,
    Ripe fruits, sweet flowers, and full satiety:
    But thro' the night, a beast she grins at me
A very monster void of love and prayer.
By day she stands a lie: by night she stands

> In all the naked horror of the truth
> With pushing horns and clawed and clutching hands.
> Is this a friend indeed; that I should sell
> My soul to her, give her my life and youth,
> Till my feet, cloven too, take hold on hell?   (*CP* 1: 76–77)

Yet, while the daughter lives in danger from this world/woman/Satan, the Gospel tells her of a perfect Paradise in which the Father/Son dwells. Like heaven, hell, and purgatory in Dante's *Divine Comedy* (which Rossetti read fervently), Paradise and the world exist simultaneously. Why, then, the daughter asks, must she wait to go to Paradise? Why must she suffer? Why must she live on earth at all?

> Lord, if I love Thee and Thou lovest me,
> Why need I any more these toilsome days;
> Why should I not run singing up Thy ways
> Straight into heaven, to rest myself with Thee?
> What need remains of death-pang yet to be,
> If all my soul is quickened in Thy praise;
> If all my heart loves Thee, what need the amaze,
> Struggle and dimness of an agony?—   ("Why?" *CP* 2:163–64)

The Bridegroom's answer in "Why?" is clear:

> Bride whom I love, if thou too lovest Me,
> Thou needs must choose My Likeness for thy dower:
> So wilt thou toil in patience, and abide
> Hungering and thirsting for that blessed hour
> When I My Likeness shall behold in thee
> And thou therein shalt waken satisfied.

In order to be beloved of the Father, the Bride must mirror Him, so that when He looks at Her, He sees only Himself. In the realm of the Father, the daughter is loved not for who she is but for her potential to satisfy the Father's desire to propagate his likeness, to become the universal "him" to whom the Lord speaks.

While the daughter as student sits at the feel of the Master, the daughter as artist is putting her words into the Master's mouth. Of course, the presumption necessary to "speak for the Lord" is characteristic of all religious dialogues with God. In *Overheard by God,* Nuttall points out that George Herbert, "the character *within* the poem, displays the inept incomprehension of mere humanity, but Herbert the author undertakes to supply on God's behalf the answers only God can give" (3). In the numerous questions the daughter puts to the Father—questions with entirely predictable answers—lies the suggestion of catechetical instruction, in which, to quote Rossetti, the question is "propounded for the sake of the learner, not apparently of the asker" (*Face of the Deep* 233). If the learner is not the asker, the daughter who asks is doing so for the benefit of the Father, who, in a sense, is being reminded of the words He has spoken and the promises He has made.

When the narrator, whether Herbert's or Rossetti's, is seen as daughter/Christian, another irony emerges. While the daughter learns to be the perfect mirror of the Logos, the artist-daughter has already usurped the Creator's place, arranging her own resolution of the Oedipal triangle—the daughter marries the Father/Son, leaving the Mother/world behind. The daughter in training must give up the melons and cucumbers of Egypt ("A traditional symbol of the animal in man" [Cirlot 94]) in order to wander in the desert in search of the Promised Land. The daughter as artist, however, keeps the melons and cucumbers alive by naming them in the perpetual present of the poem, which preserves what she has been asked to give up.

Reading Rossetti's poems as creations of an artist-daughter detaches us from identification with the emotional stance of the daughter as narrator (one-sided, lyrical), situating us in the midst of a dialogue (two-sided, dramatic) in which we are made aware of the daughter as liminal or Other, who has created both sides. Put another way: the Creator/Father figure who traditionally authors the poem becomes a character created by the daughter. The daughter both fills her dramatic role and, as artist behind the scenes, designs the role her Father will play.

Unlike Emily Dickinson, Christina Rossetti gives her Father the traditional roles He is "used" to having. Even as artist she is an obedient daughter, modeling her character along Biblical lines and usually keeping separate the daughter as child in the scene and the daughter as creator behind the scene. In "'Rejoice with Me,'" however, the "adult" daughter, the daughter as designer, artist-lover of the Father, emerges in the drama of the poem itself. Perhaps this happens because the very form of the poem involves a rewriting of a literary father's production, Blake's "The Lamb." The daughter, who begins as "Little Lamb," asserts her own power even as she confesses guilt:

> Little Lamb, who lost thee?—
> I myself, none other.—   ("'Rejoice with Me,'" *CP* 2:196–97)

The act of assertion in confession is further strengthened not only by the reversal of Rossetti's normal pattern, in which the daughter is the questioner, but by the memory in the reader's mind of the first line of Blake's original, which forms a shadow question:

> Shadow: Little Lamb, who *made* thee?
> Answer: I myself, none other.—   (my italics)

Of course, this is not what the narrator is asserting, but the echo and response has a dynamic coloring that "bleeds" through the more orthodox surface.

To this implicit assertiveness, the Lord again responds with a question addressed to "Little Lamb":

Little Lamb, who found thee?—
    Jesus, Shepherd, Brother.
Ah, Lord, what I cost thee!
    Canst Thou still desire?—

The daughter's response, while orthodox, moves the dialogue from the Lamb-Shepherd model, which the Lord initiated, to the brother-sister archetype of desire and union. The pivot occurs in the movement from "Shepherd" to "Brother." Once the claim to structural equality has been made, the daughter alludes to her Bride price—in this case nothing less than the life of the Bridegroom Himself. In "Lord, carry me.—Nay, but I grant thee strength" (*CP* 2:194), this high cost is the very reason the Lord gives us proof that He cares: "Lord, dost Thou care?—Yea, for thy gain or loss / So much I cared, it brought me to the Cross." In "'Rejoice with Me,'" the positions are reversed, and the daughter's high price becomes emblematic of her worth; the daughter need not fear the answer to her question, "Canst Thou still desire?" The Father responds immediately, in words that describe the proof of His love in His actions:

Still Mine arms surround thee,
    Still I lift thee higher,
    Draw thee nigher.

The imagery moves from embrace ("surround thee") to ecstasy ("lift thee higher") to union ("draw thee nigher").

In nine lines the daughter has managed a metamorphosis from childlike, animal existence (with echoes of the child-language of Blake) to the adult Beloved of the Cosmic Lord. The dialogue form itself is one vehicle of this transformation, for it shows the Lord's response to the daughter's words, as He is "wooed" away from the image of the Shepherd to that of Brother/Lover. After the repeated "Little Lamb," the daughter says, "Ah, Lord"—an expression not at all in keeping with the childlike innocence predicated by "Little Lamb." The remainder of the line is similarly "adult": "Ah, Lord, what I cost Thee!" This line, which is the exact center of the poem, pivots the speaker from Little Lamb to Bride and from issues of losing and finding to those of cost and desire.

Characteristically, Rossetti has also fashioned an argument in her rhyme words. The "lost" is met by "cost," and "found" is followed by "surround," so that as the condition of rebellion is paid for by the Lover,

the result of being "found" is the embrace of "surround." Alternate lines
end with the address to the Lover or Beloved—"Thee" or "thee," a use of
the same word that erases all but the slightest difference between Lover
and Beloved. This pattern is broken only at the end, where the rhyme
word "desire" is met by ecstasy ("higher") and union ("nigher"). Even
here, "thee" is the word nearest to "higher" and "nigher" ("lift thee
higher / Draw thee nigher"), reminding us at the point of union of Bride
and Bridegroom that "Thee" and "thee" are the same word.

Most of Rossetti's poetry is similarly constructed, the daughter on
stage being taught by a Father whose lines are so carefully crafted that the
craft itself, like a hidden spotlight, reveals the daughter-artist behind the
scenes. Even where a narrative voice operates as an intermediary between the Father and the daughter, the poem moves to transform the
daughter in her role as servant to the daughter as the Father's Bride. For
example, in "'The Master Is Come, and Calleth for Thee'" (*CP* 1:226),
the Lord begins as a Father to a daughter:

> Who calleth?—Thy Father calleth,
>   Run, O Daughter, to wait on Him:

Each of the succeeding stanzas begins the same way: "Who calleth?"
However, the narrative intermediary between Father and daughter answers the question differently for each stanza, citing a role for the Lord
that requires a specific response from the daughter.

Stanza	Lord	Daughter	Command
1	Father	Daughter	Run to wait on Him
2	Master	Disciple	Sit and learn of Him
3	Monarch	Subject	Rise and follow
4	Lord God	Creature	Fall and adore
5	Bridegroom	Bride	Soar with the Seraphim

The sequence is significant, for it follows the course of training for
the daughter who is "waiting" (in both senses of the word) on the
Father. From servant to pupil to one capable of doing God's will, as a
subject would a monarch's—these stages, at least, the daughter in
Rossetti's poems is able to master, although sometimes complaining of
tiredness in the role of subject. It is the fourth stage, that of the "Lord
God" and His "Creature," that causes greatest difficulty for the daughter,
for this stage calls, not for willingness to serve or learn or work, but for an
emotional attitude of exclusive love for the Lord, accompanied by the
giving up of "life" and "limb," of the flesh and the world:

> Who calleth?—Thy Lord God calleth,
>   Fall, O Creature, adoring Him:

He is jealous, thy God Almighty,
  Count not dear to thee life or limb.

It is significant that of all the hierarchical pairings of the first four stanzas, this—Lord God/Creature—is the only one that is not symmetrical; the expected pair would be Creator/Creature. If the daughter-narrator bears any resemblance to the daughter-creator of the poem, then perhaps it can be said that the difficulty of this stage involves the problematical relationship between the Father-Creator and the daughter who also claims the role of creator. For one living so consciously in the shadow of the great "I AM," the assertion "I am Christina Rossetti" announces not simply identity but authorship. In her essay "'I Am Christina Rossetti,'" Virginia Woolf, referring to a tea party during which Rossetti made this assertion, says:

> [H]ad I been present when Mrs. Virtue Tebbs gave her party, and had a short elderly woman in black risen to her feet and advanced to the middle of the room, I should certainly have committed some indiscretion—have broken a paper-knife or smashed a tea-cup in the awkward ardour of my admiration when she said, "I am Christina Rossetti." (60)

If the narrator/creator can fall and, as Creature, learn to adore her Lord, she will attain the status of Bride, a queenly position in which the servant role is entirely superseded. The first line of one of Rossetti's untitled poems asks, "Who sits with the King in His Throne? Not a slave but a Bride" (*CP* 2:282). This reward, with its love of the Bridegroom for the Bride, awaits only those children who, in the position of the daughter, can learn to love the Father with a "filial" (from *filius*, "son") love.

> When all due weight has been conceded to secondary motives, the paramount motive for what we do or leave undone—if, that is, we aim at either acting or forbearing worthily—is love: not fear, or self-interest, or even hatred of sin, or sense of duty, but direct filial love to God. (*Letter and Spirit* 35)

The daughter's struggle with love for the Father—"direct filial love to God"—informs not only the drama within Rossetti's daughter-Father dialogues but the very writing of those dialogues:

> "Write"—not any ecstasy of thy love even in this moment of reunion. "Write"—little for the indulgence of thine own heart, unless it be meat and drink to thee to do the Will of Him that sendeth thee, and to finish His work. "Write" that which shall glorify God, edify the Church, bear witness against the world. John

the beloved and the true lover could endure this word: if it seems cold and disappointing to us, it seems so because we have not yet the mind of St. John; much less the mind of Christ." (From a commentary on Rev. 1:19 in *Face of the Deep* 45)

Notes

I am grateful to Lynda E. Boose and Elizabeth Butler Cullingford for reading an early draft of this essay and offering helpful advice.

1. So far only two volumes of Crump's three-volume edition of Rossetti's *Complete Poems* have been published. Where possible, I use Crump's edition (labeled *CP* in the text); otherwise, I use William Michael Rossetti's *Poetical Works* (labeled *PW* in the text). Many of Rossetti's poems are untitled and are referred to by first line (in lowercase letters).

2. I am grateful to Lynda E. Boose for this observation.

3. For further discussion of this point see Flowers, "The Kingly Self."

Enki and Inanna drank beer together.
They drank more beer together.
They drank more and more beer together.
With their bronze vessels filled to overflowing,
With the vessels of Urash, Mother of the Earth,
They toasted each other; they challenged each other.

Enki, swaying with drink, toasted Inanna:
"In the name of my power! In the name of my holy shrine!
To my daughter Inanna I shall give
The high priesthood! Godship!
The noble, enduring crown! The throne of kingship!"

Inanna replied:
"I take them!"

Enki raised his cup and toasted Inanna a second time:
"In the name of my power! In the name of my holy shrine!
To my daughter Inanna I shall give
Truth!
Descent into the underworld! Ascent from the underworld!
The art of lovemaking! The kissing of the phallus!"

Inanna replied:
"I take them!"

—*Inanna, Queen of Heaven and Earth: Her Stories and Hymns from Sumer*

Jan Steen, *The Drawing Lesson* (c. 1665)
Source: J. Paul Getty Museum, Malibu, California. Used by permission.

III

In Nomine Filiae: The Artist as
Her Father's Daughter

DIANNE F. SADOFF

The Clergyman's Daughters: Anne Bronte, Elizabeth Gaskell, and George Eliot

The clergyman's daughter, going to Mudie's for her three-decker novel by another clergyman's daughter, participated in a cultural exchange that had a special personal significance.
—Elaine Showalter, *A Literature of Their Own*

ELIZABETH GASKELL, George Eliot, and the Bronte sisters exchanged letters, novels, and in some cases visits. They read each other's work with care and in friendship; they shared similar families of origin, class backgrounds, and cultural gender ideologies. In their texts and their lives, these Victorian daughters were—or tried to be—good girls. They visited the poor, struggled to live religious young lives, and hoped to undertake a woman's "natural duties as wives & mothers" (Gaskell, *Letters* 117). Yet several transgressed Victorian femininity, each in her own way, and all dared write, despite a poet laureate's and fathers' warnings that the pen perverted woman's "proper duties," her "life's business" (Gérin, *Charlotte Bronte* 109–11). Whether real or symbolic, the Victorian patriarch prohibited, and his daughter—a good girl—denied herself to earn his approbation. The daughter's desire, often defined as egotism, got repressed; when that desire sought as its object a loving father but found instead an absent, rejecting, or withdrawn one, the daughter transferred her desire onto substitutes for fathers. Victorian religion, whether Methodist, Anglican, or Unitarian, added to the burden of daughterhood as Fathers, like fathers, demanded that daughters think not of themselves but of others. In their pastoral novels—rural and preaching—Anne Bronte, Gaskell, and the young George Eliot seek to expose their daughterly desire, the heroine's repressed but rebellious singularity, while at the same time teaching moralistic self-sacrifice. Dominant cultural ideologies about woman as sympathetic, self-sacrificing, and sexually ignorant paradoxically enable and threaten the tradition these women enact and write about.

These authors share their Victorian daughterhood. All lost their mothers in early childhood; Anne Bronte and Mary Ann Evans remained in their fathers' homes, and Elizabeth Gaskell would have liked to do so.

These present fathers, however, failed to gratify the needs of their desiring daughters: grief over his wife's death made Patrick Bronte distant, and, distraught about his house full of children, he withdrew to his own rooms and allowed his wife's Methodist sister to become Anne's virtual mother; Robert Evans disapproved of his ambitious, intellectual, and religiously outspoken daughter and nearly exiled her from the family home after she gave up Evangelicalism, questioned religion, and declined to attend church. Both Gaskell and Bronte were clergymen's daughters: Gaskell, the daughter of a Dissenting minister who had, by the time of her birth, rejected both the ministry and university lecturing in favor of experimental farming; and Bronte, of a father who officiated in the Church of England throughout his life. The young Mary Ann Evans, like Gaskell, the daughter of a farmer, found Anglicanism and her conventional, laconic father firmly wedded (Gérin, *Anne Bronte* 10–16 and *Gaskell* 6–44; Redinger 27–65).

Throughout their young lives, Bronte and Eliot, fixed by their culture at home with withholding fathers, and Gaskell, shipped off by her father to her dead mother's relatives, longed to transfer to a figure for the father the affection their own fathers had rejected or abused and so caused them to fixate and repress. Mary Ann Evans found figurative fathers among the clergy. Her early Evangelicalism and rigorous religious questioning earned her favor with Rev. John Sibree; she later asked Rev. Francis Watts to "foster father" her translation of Vinet, and when that failed, she became substitute translator of *Das Leben Jesu* under the fatherly tutelage of Dr. Robert Brabant. In both cases, the seductions of the doubly surrogate father-daughter relationship simultaneously enticed the young girl into these intellectual discipleships and also marred them. Brabant's wife understood why her husband called Mary Ann "Deutera, which *means* second and *sounds* a little like daughter," and demanded she leave Devise (Redinger 113, 129–33). Elizabeth Gaskell, like Eliot, found men upon whom to transfer her affection for a father: her uncle Dr. Peter Holland, grandfather Samuel Holland, and minister Rev. Henry Freen provided her training in devotion, love, and religion that supplemented her intimacy with Aunt Lumb, the crippled cousin who eventually became her virtual mother. Her courtship by William Gaskell provided her the love of a clergyman who resembled what her father had been but had, she felt, unrightly renounced. Only Anne Bronte, Methodized by Aunt Branwell, the youngest and most dutiful of the energetic Bronte children, missed out on the paternal surrogate's enticements; Charlotte, designated by the family system to enact that seduction for her sisters, fell under Branwell's spell as Anne prayed, wrote with Emily, and died.

These women married or wished to marry men to replace and

compensate for their fathers. George Henry Lewes encouraged Eliot's writing, hid the negative reviews of her novels, and acted as business manager, filling the intellectual and protective role she'd been denied. William Gaskell (overenthusiastically) committed himself to the Dissenting ministry Elizabeth's father had abandoned, leaving her to feel rejected but free to write, while providing her a culturally secure religious household. Willy Weightman, Patrick Brontë's curate, may well have loved Anne, but he, like Anne, died young and never declared his love for her; Anne's sister Charlotte would live out Anne's desire, detoured, and marry another father's curate, Arthur Bell Nicholls (Gérin, *Gaskell* 45–58 and *Anne Bronte* 136–49, 172–90; Showalter, *A Literature of Their Own* 54–72). These women, then, courting or married, remain desiring daughters, defining their womanhood in relation to figures of paternal support and care.

FREUD'S THEORY of the female Oedipus complex centers on the transfer of desire. The girl's sexual aim undergoes, for example, a "process of transition" from active to passive, and her sexual object a "change" from mother to father. Although the Oedipal boy must transfer his desire for the mother onto other women, his transition out of the Oedipal family bears few detours of aim and object; the girl, however, "enters the Oedipus situation as though into a haven of refuge . . . with the transference of the wish for a penis-baby on to her father." Late in his career Freud theorized that the girl's desire "has been transferred subsequently [from her mother] on to her father" ("Female Sexuality," *SE* 21:228). Having much sociological stake in giving up mother as love object and little in giving up father, the girl may remain in the Oedipal situation "an indeterminate length of time," may "demolish it late and, even so, incompletely" ("Femininity," *SE* 22:129, 119). Without fear of castration at the hands of the prohibiting father, then, the girl's Oedipus complex may never be completely resolved. The cultural lessons the girl learns from her Oedipal situation are that she may not grow up to be phallic and powerful like her father; that she may not have her mother, her first love object; but that she may marry someone like father and may transfer her Oedipal desire upon other figures of authority, such as teachers and clergymen (Chodorow 111–40; Herman 50–63).

It is not surprising, given his linguistic terms for "transfer" in the late essays on the female Oedipus complex, that Freud unintentionally stumbled on the psychoanalytic transference during his early clinical work with women. Not until his failed analysis with Dora did Freud realize that his patient had left treatment prematurely because he as analyst "did not succeed in mastering the transference in good time" and that, moreover, he had "neglected" to look for "the first signs of transference." In a "Postscript" to Dora, Freud realizes that he had "replaced her father in her imagination" and that he had also replaced Herr K., who had replaced Dora's father ("Fragment," *SE* 7:118, 112–22). This retrospective interpretation of transference does not appear in the earlier *Studies on Hysteria,* in which Freud and Breuer discover the "talking cure," as Anna O. described it, and argue that their patients' hysterical symptoms originate in psychical (usually sexual) trauma, banishment of the event from memory (repression into the unconscious), and conversion of the revived affect associated with such recollection into somatic pain, paralysis, or tremors, for example—a "physical reminiscence" (*SE* 2:127). Linked to this trauma, however, is the father. Freud and Breuer's text obscures this father's function, yet his daughter's hysterical text pictures him in the traumatic scene or defines him as complicit with it. Anne O. and Elisabeth von R. fall ill after nursing dying and beloved fathers; Elisabeth and Lucy R. transfer their intimacy with father onto figures surrogate for him (lovers, brothers-in-law, employers); Katharina and Rosalie H. suffer seduction by fathers, whom Freud disguises as "uncles." Elisabeth's recollections unconsciously reveal the absent father's presence inscribed on the female body: her thigh invariably hurts where each day her father had rested his leg while she changed his bandages. Breuer's own language betrays what he consciously wishes to avoid as interpretation: after being "separated from her father" by his death, Anna had "taken to her bed" (*SE* 2:32). This association of father, daughter, bed, and her "nursing" activities constructs a metaphorical incestuous story that competes with Freud and Breuer's textual efforts to ignore the father as a trope in the daughter's hysterical text, an inattention so profound that Freud felt himself forced, in footnotes dated 1924, to confess his "distortions," his representation of Katharina's paternal seduction as having been perpetrated by uncles (*SE* 2:134, 170).

Freud and Breuer's text also represents, while failing to interpret, the presence of the transference in the talking cure. Because of "discretion," Breuer neglects, for example, to mention Anna's confession of desire for him and her hysterical pregnancy by him. Strachey alludes delicately to the story that Ernest Jones finally told and admits to the reader in a footnote that in conversation Freud filled for the editor this "hiatus in the text" (*SE* 2:40). Freud likewise depicts but declines to interpret his role as father in the transference and his countertransference as well. His "deep human sympathy" for Elisabeth and his wish to keep her in treatment—"in touch"—with only himself masks his own (paternal) desire; his demand that Emmy give up her "open rebellion" or leave treatment and his welcome of her "submission and docility" disregards his role as punishing father (*SE* 2:82). By 1912 Freud had "discovered" and formulated the analyst's role as "father imago" in the dynamics of the transference; by 1914 the necessity that the patient not only remember but repeat and "act out" in the transference and so work through repressed stories of sexual trauma ("Dynamics of Transference," "Remembering, Repeating, and Working Through," "Transference-Love," (*SE* 12:100–108, 147–66; Laplanche and Pontalis, *Language* 455–61).

Hysterical daughters, moreover, suffer not only from reminiscences but from the failure to have told their stories. When his patients narrated their recollections of originary trauma in analysis, their hysterical symptoms disappeared. "Language," Freud learned, "serves as a substitute for action"; analytic language may well be "a lamentation, or giving utterance to a tormenting secret, e.g. a confession" (*SE* 2:8). The subject speaks; the subject of the unconscious speaks. When the patient creatively structures that utterance, that confession, as narrative, the talking cure relieves hysteria. In Freud's case histories—themselves, he apologizes, like stories—the speaking female subject tells a retrospective story about her sexuality, about her father as beloved and lost or as seducer. Her story replaces that desired or rejecting and repressed paternal figure with substitutes for him; storytelling and analytic interpretation end the symptoms and provide closure for the case, and for its case history as well.

The female narratives, then, of Anna, Emmy, Lucy, Katharina, and Elisabeth reveal the primacy of the father in a daughter's desiring life; her repression of this material into the unconscious; the transfer of desire from the lost father onto figures for him and, ultimately, transference onto the (paternal) analyst; and the necessity to tell stories in the "talking cure." The novels by Anne Bronte, Elizabeth Gaskell, and George Eliot that I shall examine reveal structural strategies and thematics analogous to the confessions of Freud's female storytellers. They, too, transfer desire for or repressed humiliation at the hands of fathers onto substitutes for him; they, too, create narrative in the wake of the father so as to attempt a daughterly cure in the womanly scene of writing. They remember and repeat but fail to work through conscious and unconscious material about fathers, desire, and paternity.

FATHER-DAUGHTER seduction forms two thematics in these novels by clergymen's daughters. The fictional daughter's desire for the father creates one of two patterns: either a pastoral romance of fulfilled family union or a sermon on debauchery. Anne Bronte's *Agnes Grey*, the clearest example, elaborates the pattern by narratively transferring the daughter's desire from father to clergyman. Agnes's aristocratic mother loved and married a vicar who had speculated away his patrimony, and Agnes helps her beloved father by becoming a governess. Yet she feels "degraded" by her life of humiliations at the hands of aristocratic and upper-middle-class families and needs the curate's simple, evangelical sermons to re-fresh and restore her. A poor man praises Mr. Weston's charity, and Agnes admits her loneliness to her reader; the fiction responds by having her mother call her home: her beloved father has died, and her mother becomes a daughter once more. The daughter's desire for the father displaces its needs onto the mother's filial relationship, and Agnes's grandfather not only magically restores her mother's maiden rank and fortune but promises to remember her daughters in his will. The now symbolically paired daughters, Agnes and her mother, open a school for girls; Mr. Weston moves nearby, and structurally positioned as a mother to daughters with a (grand)father who has financially redeemed the dead father's pecuniary irresponsibility, Agnes magically finds herself Mrs. Weston, happily married to a moral middle-class curate to whom she may transfer her love for father and Father. For when fictional daughters transfer their desire for father onto a clergyman, they choose a man close to the Father, a man outside the calculating world of economy yet dedi-cated to his profession and successful or upwardly mobile in it, a man whose allies and social contacts are primarily female. "The English Cler-gyman," after all, "is a gentleman, he is going to Heaven, he may make love. He has the attractions of both worlds" (Showalter, *A Literature of Their Own* 143). The incredible romance plot of *Agnes Grey* exposes the desiring fantasy at its heart: love for father and daughterly goodness earn modest worldly rewards.

Elizabeth Gaskell's *Wives and Daughters* embroiders this narrative sequence of father-daughter seduction, transference, and economic re-ward. Gaskell covers over and enhances her family romance of adoption by upper-class parents with metaphorical courtly love and fairy-tale motifs. In a series of scenes, the heroine falls asleep and awakes to find her prince: first her father and then the man onto whom she transfers her daughterly love. Molly Gibson visits the aristocratic Cumnors during an annual school festival; she falls asleep, and when awakened by Lord Cumnor, she wonders where her father is only to find that he has come for her (52–56). Cumnor jokes about Sleeping Beauty, Goldilocks and the Three Bears, and the Seven Sleepers. Later in the novel, Molly's father finds her sleeping in the afternoon sun; he wakes her, and they embrace: "she looked very soft, and young, and childlike; and a gush of love sprang into her father's heart as he gazed at her" (144). In this second scene, however, the gazing, desiring, Prince Charming declares his love, not for Sleeping Beauty, but for the Cumnors' governess. The fantasy the novel attributes to Molly—figurative adoption by Lord Cumnor or Squire Hamley, whose family "gives her the place of daughter in their hearts" (182)—collapses as she anticipates losing her real father to this lower-middle-class stepmother: "she had lost father's love; he was going to be married—away from her." This blockage of daughterly desire causes Molly to fall nearly unconscious; Roger Hamley, already constructed as Molly's metaphorical brother and now defined by the fictional structure as the paternal object of transference, hears Molly moan "Oh, papa, papa! If you would but come back?" (149). She awakens to find him her as-yet-unknown prince, her future "tutor," "mentor," and "Pope" (171–82).

Sleeping Beauty becomes Cinderella, however, after Dr. Gibson remarries. Molly and her father no longer enjoy their "unrestrained intercourse, which was the one thing they desired to have, free and open, without the constant dread of the stepmother's jealousy" (272). Both desire and the discourse that stands in for it get repressed. The wicked stepmother also has a pampered daughter with a wicked past as Gaskell's fiction conflates her own experience: the triad of Cinderella and her two stepsisters becomes "two stepsisters." For when her father remarried in 1814, Gaskell was not recalled home by him but stayed on with Aunt Lumb. Her visits to her father, stepmother, and (eventually) half sister made her, as she later wrote, "*very, very* unhappy"; in *Wives and Daughters* Gaskell writes out her contempt for the stepmother she imagines jealous and selfish and her anger against the father who withdrew from his daughter into the second marriage, which she covertly wished would be unhappy, as is Dr. Gibson's. When her brother disappeared at sea and her father died in 1829, Gaskell did not see her stepmother and half sister for twenty-five years; the visit occurred, significantly, when Gaskell wrote the life of Charlotte Bronte, another clergyman's daughter (Gérin, *Gaskell* 14–18, 33–38, 167). In *Wives and Daughters,* however, the author recompenses her own losses by granting them to Molly. Father and daughter have one wished-for reunion while the wicked stepmother cavorts in London: "'Somehow' all Molly's wishes came to pass; there was only one little drawback to this week of holiday and happy intercourse with her father. Everybody would ask them out to tea. They were quite like bride and bridegroom" (488). This Cinderella's ball happens at home.

In their other novels, however, Bronte and Gaskell do penance for the desire *Agnes Grey* and *Wives and Daughters* covertly attribute to daughters. Gaskell's *Ruth* and Bronte's *The Tenant of Wildfell Hall* imagine good girls undone by their transfer of desire for absent fathers onto "corrupted," "sinful" men—Bronte's and Gaskell's respective terms for sexual excess. Gaskell's narrative allows the orphaned Ruth, seduced while swooning, to retain her innocence through ignorance, as did her precursor, Clarissa. The victimized Helen Huntingdon, whose narratively absent father "shortened his days by intemperance" (*Tenant* 1:139), marries the perhaps more intemperate Arthur Huntingdon, himself son of a "bad, selfish, miserly father" (1:193); Bronte's narrative maintains Helen's virtue by keeping her naive: "a little daily talk with me," she tells her aunt before the marriage, will make the profligate "quite a saint" (1:118). These apparently innocent females, victims not of their desire but of the seductions of men who at least in one case resemble the father, call up the ghosts of fathers in their progeny. For as a consequence of seduction, both women bear sons, and both novels fear the patrilineage of profligacy. Helen has secretly forsaken her husband, changed her name, and run away with her son to save him from his father's instruction in drinking, swearing, and reviling women. She pets and pampers little Arthur because she believes that without devout maternal care, "he will be like his ———" (1:26). Although the reader does not yet know the mother-son history, the blank demands *father*. Ruth, seduced and abandoned by a citified rake, is metaphorically adopted by Thurstan Benson, a Dissenting minister, and his aptly named sister, Faith. Gaskell purges the seductive physicality implied in Bellingham from this figurative family, for Benson, the model of paternal virtue and wishful figure for Gaskell's own father, has a hunched back. This father replaces Ruth's dead father, restores her to health and so metaphorical sexual innocence, narratively eradicates a daughter's desire, and perhaps most important, expunges the fiction's covert fear that Leonard might repeat (the sins of) his father.

Both Arthur and Leonard replace in their mothers' affections the fathers whom they simultaneously allow their mothers to fantasize about and deny. Son is son but also feared and desired repetition of father. For both Helen and Ruth, however, the son paradoxically enhances the female purity that seduction has momentarily besmirched. Gaskell's ideal cleric and father figure undertakes to teach Ruth to "reverence her child"; "this reverence," he believes, "will shut out sin,—will be purification" (*Ruth* 118). For Bronte's heroine, child-rearing simply provides opportunity for and proof of her inherent goodness. In saving their sons, both mothers turn to God, to the idealized Symbolic Father and the Christian values associated with His Son. Through motherhood, these fallen and deceived women are purified, and the narratives therefore involve in the mother's reclamation the literal son and the clerical representative of the Father. The human family becomes metaphorically the Holy Family; the son is Son, the mother, Virgin Mother. Her earlier sexuality, then, is both validated and transformed; she has given birth, but through figurative immaculate conception, and her son will grow up to deny sin, corruption, and desire.

The turn to Father and the figurative identification with Virgin Mother functions differently for Bronte's and Gaskell's heroines and must be narratively tested. Helen Huntingdon's desire for brute masculinity undergoes repression, is purified and glorified as love of Son and Godhead. When Helen, enduring the trial that sends her, like Ruth, to nurse her ex-seducer through illness, sermonizes her husband to death, her metaphors transmute sexuality into religion. "God is infinite Wisdom, and Power, and Goodness—and LOVE," Huntingdon's "immaculate angel" preaches; "fix your mind on Him who condescended to take our nature upon Him, who was raised to heaven even in His glorified human body, in whom the fullness of the Godhead shines" (352–54). Such erotic language of rising, fullness, and distention applies to Father who becomes Son. Not surprisingly, the literal narrative son comes in for transfer of (repressed) desire, as does his heavenly incarnation; at the end of her interpolated journal-narration, Helen reports that she climbs into bed with her son, who "rouses" her with "gentle kisses" in the morning (307). Ruth, meanwhile, learns from her encounter with Son and Father "daily self-denial," the habit "to think of others before herself" (132). The truth of her seduction and her son's illegitimacy, when found out, tests her surrender of self; although her employer fires her and the town isolates her, she accepts with "patience" and "penance" her "holiest repentance" of "quiet and daily sacrifice" (364). Ruth submits fully to the Ideal Father's commands.

Their trials over and their virtues intact, our heroines undergo their authors' final glorifications. Helen has proved herself better preacher than any clerical representative of God. "Oh, Helen, if I had listened to you, it never would have come to this," Huntingdon moans as he dies when Helen refuses to "save" him (119). Gaskell decides that Ruth must choose to nurse the plague-ridden Bellingham, and the chapter heading "A Mother to be Proud Of" implies that she does so out of holy maternity. Now truly "purified" by suffering, her "former life" swept away by her goodness, Ruth dies of the plague that she catches from the recovering ex-seducer (Pollard 86–107). As the novel ends, Ruth becomes the subject of a sermon inadequate to express her goodness: having sacrificed herself to save her seducer, Ruth is worshiped by her repentant community and so, named for a Biblical female type of Christ, herself partially appropriates the narrative symbolism of the Son. Their heroines'—and their own—penances over, Gaskell and Bronte have atoned for, have purchased future expiation for, the sins of their other fictional and desiring daughters.

NOVELS by these clergymen's daughters often transfer repressed desire turned outward as aggression onto stern, phallocentric, or patriarchal fathers. Narrative punishments include various versions of castration: feminization, infantilization, vocational failure, unfortunate falls, death. Whether a high church vicar, an industrialist, or a farmer, these rejecting and arrogant fathers must be humbled or replaced by more charitable fathers. The new figure upon whom the daughter transfers her affection may be the now inauthoritative father, a sonly revision of him, a sympathetic clergyman, or a figurative preacher/minister (Showalter, *A Literature of Their Own* 143–47). Harsh curate, high churchman, or brutal and exploitative industrialist—bad daddies all—dispensed with, the benevolent clergyman or his figurative incarnation may take his place and speak volumes about love, charity, confession, and sympathy to eagerly listening heroines, while simultaneously the narrator speaks through him to avidly reading women just back from Mudie's. The clergyman himself, then, appears a partially castrated figure, a male with the feminine values so highly prized by these authors, their good-girl heroines, and their female readers (Showalter, *A Literature of Their Own* 149–52; Knoepflmacher, "Unveiling"). In league with good women, he, like them, preaches openness, honesty, and love to the already converted and unreformed alike. The moral lady novelist, herself a figurative preacher, seeks to teach her reader the virtues of fellow-feeling through the appropriated voice of the reformed clergyman.

In her early novels, George Eliot's narrative project undertakes to humble and humiliate sternly paternal figures of authority so as to teach sympathy. In *Scenes of Clerical Life*, Sir Christopher Cheverel must forgive his sister, who has married against his will, because his opposition, like his other behavior, has been "too proud and obstinate"; he must recognize his complicity in his adopted daughter's passion for her lover: his insistence that she marry the bumbling curate, Mr. Gilfil, is partial cause of her subsequent attempted murder and her self-despair. Amos Barton must lose Milly, his wife, and confess that he failed to love her sufficiently, and so in penance love his daughter in her place. Amos also loses his curacy; sexual scandal involves him with a visiting countess and contributes to his wife's demise. In *Mill on the Floss*, Mr. Tulliver must fall off his horse and into bankruptcy because he stubbornly insists on immediate payment of his debt to Mrs. Glegg, his sister-in-law, and therefore angers his brothers-in-law and neglects the needs of his wife and children. Savonarola, clerical Father to his spiritual "daughter" in *Romola*, must be executed for his "severity," his commitment to "law" over "mercy." *Romola*, moreover, kills off fathers and replaces them with a community of daughters and mothers. By the end of the novel, Lorenzo de Medici, Bardo, Baldassare, Savonarola, and Bernardo del Nero—fathers, patriarchs, and arrogant clerics—are all dead; one son remains, to be socialized into female values solely by women.

Elizabeth Gaskell's narratives punish severe fathers so as to teach them sympathy and pardon desiring daughters. In *North and South*, Mr. Thornton, the industrialist whose workers are structurally analogous to his children, loses his business and his mastery after a long strike, becomes a subordinate worker—a son—again, and sinks into his mother's arms. In a retrospective embedded narrative, *Cranford* rationalizes its fictional all-female community: Miss Jenkyns's overly harsh father once publicly flogged his son for a transvestite hoax, refused to acknowledge his own severity, alienated his wife's affections, caused his son to flee, and eventually lost his power as lawgiver. In the narrative present, men pay for the sins of this father by mysteriously dying off until the Cranford ladies once again approve male sexuality—but only when and if defined by women. In *Ruth*, the hypocritical moralist Mr. Bradshaw, whose "severe and arbitrary" treatment turns his son into a thief, loses his "iron will" when his son's literal and symbolic fall substitutes for his own; as in *Cranford*, this man's wife now turns her love towards the son and rejects her "cruel" and "hard" husband (402; see Auerbach 82–87). The son's centrality in this narrative structure means that he as figure enacts metaphorically the daughter's desire: he gets punished by the father but gains the exclusive affection of a parent—the mother—whom he desires. Peter Jenkyns's transvestite parody of his spinster sister suckling a child and Richard Bradshaw's "fall" as figure for Ruth's both exculpate the heroine's "sins" or desire by blaming their origins on paternal severity and rejection or displacing them onto the son/brother.

Eliot's Adam Bede may serve as paradigm for a son and figurative father whose fall teaches him sympathy. Based on Eliot's memories of her own father and therefore a figure for him, the tough and laconic Adam feels little remorse about the untimely death of the father he had rebuked for his laxness. In church, however, implicitly under the influence of the all-loving Father's message, Adam realizes that he humiliated his father. "I was always too hard," Adam chastises himself; he lacks patience with sinners, shuts his heart against and refuses to forgive transgressors (*Adam Bede*, pt. 1, 290). Adam must learn the lesson of sympathy, for he will later refuse to forgive Hetty Sorrel's love affair and her attempted infanticide. The secret of Adam's "hardness," the narrator preaches, is "too little fellow-feeling with the weakness that errs in spite of foreseen consequences." Adam must bind his "heart-strings" around the "weak and erring," must "share not only the outward consequences of their error, but their inward suffering" (pt. 1, 303). Eliot transforms the father's rejection and humiliation of the daughter, of herself as daughter, into a concealed replay that simultaneously takes revenge on the father; Adam as son gets blamed for rejecting the father—rejection is culpable—yet he, too, endures the revenge enacted on himself (as figure of the father) by the same paradigm. And Adam must learn this lesson from a woman, a Methodist preacher who gives rural sermons about sympathy, love, and the necessity for confession.

The idealized scene of sympathy in Gaskell's and Eliot's novels invokes confession, openness and honesty, moral transparency, and reciprocity. In *Wives and Daughters,* Molly implores her half sister Cynthia to confess her secret engagement with a scoundrel to Roger Hamley, to whom she is also secretly engaged; confession of fault, Cynthia agrees, provides such "comfort," creates reciprocity with an easily forgiving sister. Nonetheless, she confesses to no one but Molly. In *Adam Bede,* Dinah Morris twice implores Hetty Sorrel to speak openly about her troubles and the second time seeks Adam's forgiveness of his future bride after Hetty's confession of sexual transgression. Hetty, when dressed as woman preacher earlier in the novel, uncannily resembles Dinah as the two women, sinner and savior, mirror one another and provide a figure for reciprocity in the sympathetic exchange of words. The paradigmatic scene of sympathy, however, occurs not between two women but between a cleric and a woman, themselves resembling one another. Mr. Tryan, the perfectly sympathetic cleric in *Scenes of Clerical Life,* brings comfort to the alcoholic, abused, and abandoned wife Janet Dempster. Her confession of madness and temptation to murder her husband prompts Tryan's "sympathy," and he confesses to her his own past transgressions: seduction, abandonment of the woman, and implicit murder. One reciprocal confession recalls another, for Tryan, like Janet, had cured his despair only by confessing to a friend who preached to him Christ's loving salvation and nurture and the necessity for submission to Him. "It is because sympathy is but a living through our own past in a new form," the narrator moralizes, "that confession often prompts a response of confession" (355–62). Each person, then, has erred; transgression when confessed invokes the metaphor of resemblance, the ties that bind the reformed sinner to the still weak and erring other and so to a larger community. The confessor tells her story of sexual sin so as to unburden and prepare for change in herself, the teller; the listener recalls his or her own past story of transgression, retells it, and so confirms his own transformation from sinner to saved, while helping the other effect a similar change in her own present.

This scene of sympathy represents the idealized moment of reciprocal care that resembles the clinical exchanges Freud recounts in his studies of female hysterics. Eliot's and Gaskell's scenes of confession and sympathy represent the later-to-be-named "talking cure"; the telling of a sexual story in the presence of a listener—whether self-exposing, like Tryan, or silent, like Freud—creates a fictionalized transference. Central to both activities is the process of narrating: the confessor, the patient, must tell a retrospective story that at the same time stimulates introspection in the present; the subject's ability to fashion a narrative of her past that links key recollections with self-analysis about their symbolic meaning effects the psychoanalytic or confessional cure (Jay 21–32). The subject's story imaginatively reworks the past, both conscious and unconscious material; the analyst's or confesser's interpretations, narratives, and self-revelations contribute to the cure. Analyst and patient, clergyman and penitent—or by analogy, father and daughter—attempt to undo repression, liberate desire or transgression, and allow transference between the reciprocal subjects to facilitate healing. In the paradigmatic scene from *Scenes of Clerical Life,* Tryan's function as paternal imago—comforting, caring, curing clerical father—articulates Eliot's thematic wish for sympathy as compensation for deprivation, for the "self-despair" that the adult author condemns as narcissistic egoism

This desire for confession as cure, however, remains desire. Transference in these novels is symbolic and facilitates not so much therapeutic healing as fictional closure. The sudden change of heart serves the ends and limitations of fiction but not of psychoanalysis. As Freud gradually realized, analysis is in some manner interminable. In his essay on the problematical efficacy of psychoanalysis, Freud discusses an early hysterical patient whose recovery, under the pressure of continuing personal and familial disasters, collapsed and illness resumed; although analysis may temporarily "cure" the analysand, then, constitutional and environ mental factors may later "uncure" ("Analysis Terminable and Interminable," *SE* 23:222). The analytical transference opens up unconscious material that later may need reworking and retelling; the fictional transference symbolizes the beginning and end of that interminable process and may not rework the story sufficiently to fully unbind repressed desire. Eliot's and Gaskell's scenes of sympathy desire such unbinding and narrating, yet they contradict this wish thematically. For sympathy and confession, retrospection and introspection, force upon the penitent her daughterly limitations, discretions, and duties.

Gaskell's narratives, for example, endorse and enact repression at the same time that they preach confession. The fictional form of repression is secrecy. In *Wives and Daughters,* a plethora of engagements and marriages remains secret; Dr. Gibson represses knowledge of his second wife's faults and his love for his daughter and so makes Molly undemonstrative and laconic like himself. In *Ruth,* Thurstan Benson keeps secret Ruth's sin and past; Mr. Bradshaw, his complicity in bribery; his son, his profligacy. When Faith, Thurstan, and Ruth nearly whip little Leonard for telling lies, the servant figuratively reminds them that they are liars all: "It's for them without sin to throw stones at a poor child" (202). The secret sinners in these pastoral novels are severely punished for repression and secrecy, yet all imply that confession would not have alleviated the circumstance that demands it, would not have invoked sympathy, would simply have visited upon the confessing sinner earlier

DIANNE F. SADOFF

punishments of illness, death, or banishment that now close these novels. In the face of desired confession, then, Gaskell's characters and communities fail the test of sympathy.

Both Eliot and Gaskell also teach through the scene of sympathy not therapeutic healing but self-denial. In *Middlemarch,* Dorothea Brooke confesses to Rosamund Vincy that she knows Ladislaw loves her rival; in sympathy with Rosamund's perspective, she offers to forgo her own desire, supposing Rosamund to love Ladislaw as she herself does. That Dorothea is rewarded for her sympathetic sacrifice with Ladislaw's love is not without ambiguity, however: Dorothea gives up her plans to do social good, to build cottages, for the limitations of politician's wife and mother to future Teresas. In *Wives and Daughters,* in the scene of sympathy in which Molly confesses her love of father and Roger Hamley replaces him, Roger advises Molly in a figurative sermon to "think more of others than of oneself." With "grave, kind sympathy," Roger urges Molly to think of her father's happiness in his engagement rather than "clutch" the "gratification of her own wishes" (149–55). Repeated throughout the novel, this scene and its message indeed make Molly more self-denying, until she herself may teach the lesson of fellow-feeling to the shallow aristocrat Harriet Cumnor. Such self-sacrifice earns Molly Roger's love, but only through the intervention of Harriet, her narrative fairy godmother, who delivers Molly to the figurative brother in place of the father at the novel's close. The fairy-tale reward identifies itself as fantasy and the scene of sympathy as enacting a wishful transference.

Gaskell's and Eliot's pastoral romances of daughter and cleric/father, then, paradoxically enforce the paternal lesson of repression. Sympathy, so highly prized by these authors and so often invoked by Gaskell and Eliot, fails as transference and earns daughters not their desire but the false desire to pursue the "natural duty" of woman: selflessness. This fictional transference facilitates repression rather than undoes it; confession hardly heals the woman subject who enacts it; the talking cure talks into rather than out of repressed desire. Like Anne Bronte's paradigmatic *Agnes Grey,* Eliot's and Gaskell's humbling the patriarch and invoking the scene of sympathy paradoxically inculcate the morality of good daughterhood. The daughter who writes, attempting to break the rules of womanhood, ironically preaches to women readers her own sermons of self-denial and self-sacrifice in the transactional transference between writer and reader that reading represents.

THE DISCREPANCY between woman's life and text shapes the literary tradition of clergymen's daughters. "Lewes was describing Currer Bell to me yesterday," George Eliot writes Cara Bray, "as a little, plain, provincial, sickly-looking old maid. Yet what passion, what fire in her! Quite as much as in George Sand, only the clothing is less voluptuous" (*Letters* 2:91). Desire effaced yet implicit in the woman burns in her narrative, for Eliot's ambiguous reference to George Sand—whether the woman or her work—problematizes that woman writer's voluptuousness: is the clothing on the writer or her characters? Is the fire in Jane Eyre or Currer Bell? Elizabeth Gaskell finds this discrepancy not ironic but troubling. She writes Lady Kay-Shuttleworth: "The difference between Charlotte Bronte and me is that she puts all her naughtiness into her books, and I put all my goodness. I am sure she works off a great deal that is morbid *into* her writing, and *out* of her life; and my books are so far better than I am that I often feel ashamed of having written them and as if I were a hypocrite" (Gaskell, *Letters* 228). Gaskell's perceived gap between a writer's life and work, I would argue, means that writing inscribes the subject as other to herself, whether "better" or "naughtier"—Gaskell's terms for writing female sexuality.

We may also interpret Gaskell's "gap" as a trope for writing as self-analysis. The record of Freud's self-analysis exists as the text of his letters to Wilhelm Fliess about the seduction theory, about his Oedipal relations with mother, nursemaid, younger brother, and nephew, and in the dream texts about father, Hannibal, mentors, and burgher ministers in *The Interpretation of Dreams*. In this self-analysis the self is analyst and analysand, yet Fliess is "adopted analyst" as well as "transference object." Max Schur argues that the letter-writing relationship between Freud and Fliess appears "transferencelike": Freud overvalued Fliess's work; needed his praise and approbation when feeling insecure; denied his own ambivalent feelings about Fliess, which then appeared in dreams; acted alternately submissive and defiant towards his correspondent; and, he later realized, sexualized the relationship. Freud defined his transference figure as "the other, the *alter*." "I am so immensely happy that you bestow on me the gift of an Other," he wrote Fliess in 1898. "I cannot write entirely without an audience, but I do not at all mind writing only for you" (Schur 147). Schur implies that without this letter-writing transference, Freud might never have completed his self-analysis.

Freud's articulation of writing, self-analysis, and transference provides the terms for interpreting novel-writing as figurative self-analysis. In the writing cure, the subject's word is traced by and through the other, the writer as other to herself, and the Other, the discourse of the unconscious. The narratee and implied reader, receivers of the discourse, are also other, "*alter*," a kindly disposed but silent audience. As Freud's letter-writing enabled his uncovering of Oedipal material that determined his ambivalent adult relationships to mentors (including Fliess), these three Victorian authors uncovered in fiction writing their "naughty," "sinful," and "corrupt" other. As Freud attempted to arouse and garner Fliess's approbation and sympathy, so Anne Bronte, Elizabeth Gaskell, and the young George Eliot inscribe the scene of sympathy to arouse in their readers a countertransferential fellow-feeling for their heroines, figures for themselves; each occasionally hopes to garner that reciprocal care for herself as well, for the good girl, the daughter, that resides within the woman who writes. This self-analytical writing seeks to free the daughter from the ghost of her father by transferring to other figures daughter-father desire. Yet for each of these authors, the writing cure remains a wish. Each remembers and repeats her material with father in the trans-ferential relationship that narrative transmission establishes but fails fully to work through in fiction the transaction with his ghosts, his imago. Only George Eliot, in her later work, manages the confrontation with fathers as the male narrator endorses a wider life and grows virtually genderless. The fiction-writing transference, unlike Freud's letter-writing model, necessitates because of narrative form its own termination. As Freud's letters to Fliess came to an end, Freud too—as he only later realized—failed to resolve his transference with Fliess in writing.

Anne Bronte's fictional self-analysis and transference resolutely re-fuses to undo repression and, I would argue, uses its mechanism in the service of the Evangelical morality about womanhood that she learned from her Methodist Aunt Branwell. Bronte herself, virtually invisible in her own life's story—constructed by the letters and testimony of Char-lotte and others—repeats that self-effacement in her narrative voice, her inconsequential plotting, her refusal to assume narrative authority. Agnes Grey reports narrative events in indirect discourse and summary because her position as governess circumscribes her actions; neither her employer nor her author allows her to attend events—a ball, a poor-visit—necessary for plot to shape story. These absences and vicarious participations demonstrate not only the governess's lack of authority and social marginality but the powerlessness of her first-person female dis-course. Her life is circumscribed; her self, effaced. She may not talk back to those higher in class status than herself, nor may she flirt as aristocratic young women may. Only her goodness wins her action and voice, a discourse that self-reflexively celebrates her own womanly and eccentric moralism. She insists, for example, that her young charges kill several birds they have nastily removed from their nest (48–52); she silently accuses other women of jealousy while ignoring and denying her own. Agnes's self-righteous victimage atones for, covers over, yet represents her female self-effacement. The gaps in Agnes's life story effect an emp-tiness in her text and become the sign of repression that facilitates the fantasied daughterly seduction of the cleric who stands in for the father. In writing *Agnes Grey*, Anne Bronte fulfilled her desire to fill the gap left by the father but repressed its significance by refusing her autobiographical heroine narrative, discursive, and female authority. The daughter, indulged but contradicted, never frees herself from fathers through self-analysis but glorifies herself as good girl.

The incredible epistolary and diaristic form of *The Tenant of Wildfell Hall* accomplishes another repression of female desire. Gilbert Markham's letters to a long-absent friend early evaporate into fictional discourse complete with chapter numbers rather than invocations and signatures; these "letters" frame Helen Huntingdon's journal, which Markham fully records and reads as we, and supposedly his friend, do. Markham as fictional correspondent and autobiographer unconsciously betrays the repressed motivation of the novel's tandem narratives: revenge. After reading Helen's lengthy journal, Markham must "confess" that he feels "selfish gratification" as his rival, Arthur Huntingdon, declines towards death (2:169). He seems a perfect match for the mean-spirited woman who abuses her son so as to teach him morality and goodness, who to undo the sins of the father spikes her son's wine with nausea powder, which she threatens to make him drink if he is naughty (Eagleton, *Myths of Power* 122–38). Such unsavory self-revelation exposes the novel's moral sermonizing as a cover-up, a tool for narrative repression. Beside the exhortations to libidinal frugality, moderation, and calculation lies revenge on men—fathers, lovers, brothers—who dare desire. Early in the novel, for example, Markham sees Helen and her landlord embrace and thinks them lovers. He then meets Lawrence on a road one night, beats him, and leaves him to die, as did Oedipus to an unknown father. Markham justifies himself—he claims "no motives of revenge"—but the reader knows that this narrator speaks the silent motivation that competes with the text's message: through Markham, Bronte beats a figure of Branwell for daring desire. Markham's subsequent all-too-easy reconciliation with the forgiving Lawrence exposes both men as inauthoritative weaklings subservient at the novel's end to Helen. Anne Bronte's narrative closure represses while it enacts the fantasy of revenge on men while endorsing the female's self-satisfied moral superiority.

Elizabeth Gaskell's claim that her books are "better" than their author reveals, I would argue, her compromise with desire in the self-analytical writing transference. Her pose as "ashamed" and as "hypocrite" humbly enhances her own goodness and demands praise from her letter's female receptor. It also calls up for Gaskell's twentieth-century woman reader the ghost of her ambivalence about her desire to write. For the gadabout career woman and the dutiful clergyman's wife seem clearly at odds. The morality of Victorian daughterhood that structures Gaskell's texts—self-sacrifice, penitence, and submission—atones for the pleasures the writer earns, rewards normally denied women and accorded Gaskell primarily because of her much-publicized and self-glorified motherhood, her acceptance of woman's "natural" duty. Gaskell's "hypocrisy" betrays the desire she represses in her texts and uneasily accommodates in her life.

For Gaskell's narratives associate storytelling with lying, repression, and punishment. In *Ruth,* Faith Benson quips, "[I]f we are to tell a lie, we may as well do it thoroughly." She embroiders Ruth's "(fictitious) history," and enjoys doing so. She has "a talent for fiction," feels it "so pleasant to invent, and make the incidents dovetail together" (148–49). Richard Bradsaw, a forger, practices pretense with the "perfection of art"; Leonard tells childish stories, "fictions" about cows wearing bonnets (326, 201), and his near whipping for such "lies," like Peter Jenkyns's public whipping for his transvestite (fictional) parody in *Cranford,* discloses in Gaskell's work a buried fantasy about fictionalizing. In his essay "A Child Is Being Beaten" Freud discusses three phases of a daughter's fantasy of being beaten, each of which has a different story. In the first phase, the storyteller relates, "my father is beating the child"; in the second, uncovered by analysis, the child recognizes herself, and the storyteller says, "I am being beaten by my father"; in the third, which follows repression, the storyteller watches a (boy) child being beaten by someone unknown and reports that "a child is being beaten." Freud connects this constructed scene with "incestuous wishes" that persist "in the unconscious"; these narratives of paternal punishment signify to the teller of the story "deprivation of love and a humiliation" that has been—and still is—repressed (*SE* 17:179–204). In the two fictional whipping scenes, Gaskell tells the story "a child is being beaten"; in both cases, a boy who tells stories about desire (some version of "cross-dressing") is flogged by a stern father or clerical "uncle" (who stands for the father) and who inflicts punishment and demands repression. The whipping/beating fantasy covers over the scene Freud reconstructs by interpretation in which the daughter recognizes herself; Gaskell unconsciously exposes in these punishments for lying her own denied yearning for a father's affection and the humiliation and deprivation he caused her. She narratively represses desire by imagining the victim a boy (a brother) yet also transfers her longing for a father's affection onto brothers: she would in fantasy like to be him (his transvestism makes him herself) and have the father through him (his punishment signifies love in the unconscious).

Gaskell's plots focus on secrets about brothers that unconsciously trigger this complex of fantasies about fictionalizing, fathers, and daughters—fantasies that the moral and dutiful daughter as writer represses. Anne Bronte, however, originates this paradigm: in *The Tenant of Wildfell Hall,* the plot turns on Gilbert Markham's peeping at Helen Huntingdon at night only to find her in the arms of Mr. Lawrence, her (secret) brother; this pivotal scene betrays incestuous wishes that cause, through repression, the punishment and revenges that necessarily follow. In Gaskell's *Wives and Daughters,* Molly Gibson is seen in Heath Lane with Mr. Preston—her eventual stepbrother-in-law—and the Hollingford gossips accuse her of sexual transgression. In *North and South,* Mr. Thornton sees Margaret Hale in the arms of a man (her brother Frederick) who then accidentally commits murder; Margaret lies to the police to save Frederick from arrest for his present and past crimes. Peter's hoax in *Cranford* signifies that the brother and (as) a woman beget(s) a child; in *Ruth,* Thurstan and Faith Benson, brother (as well as clergyman in the place of the father) and sister, metaphorically beget Ruth. For Gaskell, the lost brother stands in for the father but returns the sister/daughter's affection; loss of him repeats paternal humiliation and rejection. The daughter lies—tells fictions—to recover the brother; he may then procreate with his (figurative) sister.

This daughter who lies is a figure for the writer. For narrating—structuring plot and secretly manipulating event—involves "plotting." Gaskell feels duplicitous about her plotting, so she conspires to manage her heroines' secrets about brothers by focusing plot on them yet condemning this secrecy; she likewise manages her own secret desire by inscribing while denying it. In her research for *The Life of Charlotte Bronte,* for example, Gaskell discovered her friend's secret love for M. Héger yet felt that to reveal it would sin against the good woman and dutiful daughter; she therefore antedated Branwell's affair with Mrs. Robinson to account for Bronte's despair and so falsified the "plot" of her biography (Gérin, *Gaskell* 159–78). Gaskell plots the brother guilty of secret desire, suppresses the daughter's desire for him, a brotherly/paternal figure, and clears herself as writer of seeking to expose it. In Freud's paradigm of paternity and the daughter's story, Gaskell narrates "a child is being beaten."

In *Cranford,* Gaskell links the social construction of gender to her guilt about plotting. When Peter returns to Cranford after fathers have been purged and desire accepted, he becomes a "favourite." He tells "more wonderful stories than Sinbad the Sailor" and is "quite as good as an Arabian Night any evening" (211). Mary Smith, the extradiagetic narrator, realizes that he embroiders the "truth": he shot a cherubim in the Himalayas! Peter's eye twinkles at Mary, and the reader understands that his gentle irony to and at the expense of the Cranford ladies resembles Mary's voice. As Mary demonstrates, the *Cranford* women tell stories badly: Miss Pole's disjointed diatribes against men and marriage; Miss Matty's horrors about men under beds; Mrs. Forrester's tales of faded aristocratic adventure; gossip in general. A female storyteller by definition digresses and tattles; a male storyteller may be less discreet yet may cross over into femininity and earn a female audience. Gaskell, like Mary Smith, must use her gender skills—delicacy, duty, gossip—to cover over the guilt of plotting, to atone for writing so as to go on telling stories.

Gaskell's ambivalence about writing and gender, her "hypocrisy," appears a moral inversion of George Eliot's. That an adulteress could write the highly moral *Scenes of Clerical Life* and *Adam Bede* threw Gaskell into a tizzy. Early in Eliot's career as storyteller, Gaskell addresses a witty note to "Gilbert Elliot," the then-current guess at the identity of the "clergyman" who had authored *Scenes of Clerical Life* and *Adam Bede*, signing herself "Gilbert Elliot"; she admires these fictions and so appropriates their unclaimed praise, their author's masculine identity. Not much later, of course, Gaskell's letters implore her correspondents to contradict that the transgressive "Miss Evans" wrote those "beautiful" books; "I wish you *were* Mrs. Lewes," she eventually writes Eliot (Gaskell, *Letters* 559, 575, 583–87, 592). Eliot responds enthusiastically to the author she admires—desperate for, yet publicly eschewing, admiration—and signs herself "Marian Evans Lewes." The adulteress claims solidarity and kinship with the Dissenting clergyman's wife; Gaskell's letter, she says, brought "an assurance of fellow-feeling. I shall always love to think that one woman wrote to another such sweet encouraging words—still more to think that you were the writer and I the receiver" (*Letters* 3:198–99). Gaskell's womanly sympathy failed this test: she did not write Marian Evans Lewes again (Hardy).

Anticipating such sentiment, Marian Evans Lewes became "George Eliot," who enjoyed being thought a clergyman, a Cambridge man, the "father of a family," a man who "might overhear his own praises at the club" (*Letters* 2:408). Eliot's male narrators acquire their authority through gender: memory of initiation into manhood and the knowledge of male community. In *Scenes of Clerical Life*, Eliot's narrator, who wears coattails for the first time at church, blushes when Miss Landor flirts with other young men and laughs at himself; during confirmation, he and the other "unimaginative boys" joke and feel "sheepish," wishing confirmation reserved for girls; afterward at home he imitates the sermon until his "yoaring" makes his little sister cry (256, 288, 292). This inappropriate boyish jollity, however, occurred in pre-Reform England; Evangelicalism later restored faith, and maturity endows the narrator in the present scene of writing with authority. Acquired through retrospection and achieved in introspection, this authority belongs to the maleness necessary for correct confirmation, for symbolic sermonizing, for accession to the powers of linguistic imitation and the place of authorship.

The anonymous Marian Evans Lewes, having not yet become the male author, slams "silly novels by lady novelists." Unlike the clerical narrator and male author, these ladies fail, among other things, to articulate faith with class-consciousness. The newly converted heroines of these "white neckcloth" novels invite to dinner not beaux but clergymen; their trivial conversation chats "gospel instead of gossip" ("Silly Novels" 317–18). Yet "the real drama of Evangelicalism," the (woman) reviewer claims, "lies among the middle and lower classes; and are not Evangelical opinions understood to give an especial interest in the weak things of the earth, rather than in the mighty? . . . Why can we not have pictures of religious life among the industrial classes in England?" (318–19). Eliot's narrator in *Scenes of Clerical Life* thus appropriately declares his adherence to a lowering gospel. He writes no "Evangelical travesty of the fashionable novel" but a moral tale of "ordinary fellow mortals" (97). His clerics, themselves ordinary men, demystify false clerical authority, discourse, and class aspiration. Amos Barton cannot bring his "geographical, chronological, exegetical mind" to the "pauper point of view" and lectures derelicts with "types and symbols"; Mr. Furness preaches only "metaphor and simile." The good cleric, however, eschews metaphor, type, and symbol. Mr. Cleves "preaches sermons which the wheelwright and the blacksmith can understand"; he calls a "spade a spade" without condescending to the members of his flock; he teaches poor men at night—a "conversational lecture on useful practical matters." He has "hereditary sympathies with the checkered life of the people" (63–65, 93–95). Felix Holt, like Cleves, preaches on the evils of drink, dirt, and lack of family life among the industrial working class; Dinah Morris speaks simply and from her own experience about God's eternal love, about Jesus' and Wesley's mission to help the poor. These admirable preachers sympathize with the lower classes, whether industrial or rural; their discourse is simple and moral; they refuse the goods gained by class-aspiring clergy.

Eliot's narrator of *Scenes of Clerical Life*, like Cleves and Tryan, lives among the poor. "I am on the level and in the press with [the ordinary man]," he avers, "as he struggles his way along the stony road, through the crowd of unloving fellow-men" (322). In allying himself with clerical morality, with sympathy for the working-class man, the narrator claims kinship with clergymen; he becomes a figurative cleric himself, mingling with the people of his story, as the clergyman moves with them on the stony road. His job, moreover, resembles the cleric's. When Mr. Cleves meets his parishioners on Mondays, he "tell[s] them stories, or reads some select passages from an agreeable book, and comment[s] on them" (94). Mr. Cleves's night school for working men teaches practical morality not only through lecture but through fiction and discursive interpretation of popular literature. The narrator, like Cleves, metaphorically gets together with his reader in a night school of fiction: "my only merit must lie in the truth with which I represent to you . . . my picture" (97). His representation teaches the moral lesson of class-lowering as proof of fellow-feeling; he grounds its claim to truth in his theory of sympathy with the weak and erring, here the poor.

The reader of *Scenes of Clerical Life*, then, like Cleves's parishioners or the confessing Janet Dempster, learns to care for weakness and acknowledge her own; listens to the narrator tell agreeable stories and comment upon them so as to preach practical morality. The novel becomes sermon; the narratee, the narrator's parishioners; the reading public, the writer's flock. Reading the novel as sermon, the middle-class lady reader—for our narrator creates his narratee female, as most real readers of fiction were (127–28)—learns sympathy with working-class people, the "real heroes" who know few "spiritual truths" but know them deeply "by long wrestling with their own sins," who have "earned faith and strength so far as they have done genuine work." This reader learns to replace religion and Evangelical fervor with "the idea of duty," the "recognition of something to be lived for beyond mere satisfaction of self": she learns the virtues of self-sacrifice (320–21). She learns them, moreover, from a figurative preacher, a male narrator who assumes clerical authority in an age when Evangelical enthusiasm no longer satisfies a secular-humanist reading public (Bedient 33–98; Ker; Knoepflmacher, *Eliot's Early Novels* 73–127; Steven Marcus, "Literature").

The male author of the novel-as-sermon becomes the final arbiter of morality in the wake of Evangelicalism. The creator of this metaphorical preachment, George Eliot, becomes Creator, a godly figure, a "father" who watches over his reading flock as the narrator does his narratee and the preacher his fictional parishioners. Having rejected the discourse of poetic sermonizing, of Biblical types and symbols of unsympathetic high churchmen, having humbled fictional fathers into sympathy, George Eliot, the author as Father, replaces those fathers and that discourse with his lexicon of sympathy and lowering. He usurps and supersedes paternal discourse and recreates it in his own image. His moral and fictional authority, claiming its origin in religion and its analogue as godly, appears impervious to challenge. Yet Eliot's paternal discourse, his narrator's clerical commentary, smacks of paternalism. He glorifies the working class and the lowering habits of the good clergy by himself knowing what is good for them, though he, like the narrator, is not of the working class but merely goes among its members. Felix Holt, Mr. Cleves, even Daniel Deronda, another figurative preacher reaching towards a religious "higher passion," know better than do their listener-parishioners a correct and dutiful morality. George Eliot appears a rhetorical step away from Elizabeth Gaskell's Unitarian charity and Anne Bronte's and Gaskell's glorified poor-visits in *Agnes Grey, Mary Barton,* and *North and South*. Such sympathy unconsciously enhances its giver's self-righteousness and invokes woman's "natural duty" to think of others before oneself.

Interpretation of the contradictions implied by paternal(istic) discourse raises the question of gender. For "George Eliot" is a woman and a transgressor of Victorian sexual morality. Here is *her* "hypocrisy": her books are "better" than she because in them a man preaches woman's duty, a middle-class man preaches the glory of lower-class work. When women preach the same duty and sympathy in Eliot's novels, they invariably fail. Dinah Morris's outdoor sermons seem efficacious, yet her early conversion of Bessie away from female vanity does not take. When Dinah hears Hetty's confession of sin and weakness, she cannot save Hetty from their consequence: transportation. No wonder George Eliot kept her male pen name despite widespread knowledge of her identity and eventual social acceptance, among lionizers, of her "marriage" to Lewes. Her "duty" and her womanhood conflicted.

George Eliot, Anne Bronte, and Elizabeth Gaskell share this equivocation about gender. "George Eliot" and "Acton Bell" declared themselves, however ambiguously, male authors; Mrs. Gaskell announced herself glorified wife and mother. These writers, taught the lessons of good daughterhood, broke the rules to risk the pen. All three, frustrated and deprived by the early death of mothers and the inadequacy of surviving fathers, transferred their desire onto fictional fathers and repeated but failed to work through in the fictional transference their paradoxical desire for and humiliations at the hands of fathers. Yet each, as I have argued, manages differently the contradiction between desire and repression as she inscribes female textuality/sexuality. Artistically and transferentially, Eliot succeeds better than does Gaskell or Bronte in coping with the contradictory forces of woman's desire and the cultural ideology of submissive self-sacrifice. All three authors, however, covertly preach the repressive morality of Victorian daughterhood that hindered their own personal and professional enterprise. This legacy of Victorian daughterhood, of the good girls, is created and facilitated by patriarchy; it defines these writing women as forebears of ourselves, contemporary reading daughters.

JOANNE FEIT DIEHL

Murderous Poetics: Dickinson, the Father, and the Text

> Rehearsal to Ourselves
> Of a Withdrawn Delight—
> Affords a Bliss like Murder—
> Omnipotent—Acute—
>
> We will not drop the Dirk—
> Because We love the Wound
> The Dirk Commemorate—Itself
> Remind Us that we died. (379)[1]

In this poem from her most productive year, 1862, Emily Dickinson engages the importance of absence as a prerequisite for joy. But the subtext is murder, a murder so joyous that to drop the weapon would vanquish the murderer. Who is this murderous "we," and wherein lies the bliss of violent death? The ambiguities that surround this brief poem are telling as well as absolutely characteristic of those encoded texts Dickinson creates, texts that treat subjects so potentially violative that they find their expression through deliberate figurative masking, indeterminacy of syntax, and the veil of the ellipsis. Yet the terms are present, and if the reader stays with the poem, the dynamic if not specific identity of the situation often becomes clear. Aggression, whether disguised or kept purposely vague, is this poem's subject, and it is an aggressive act that stands in for the withdrawal of an unnamed delight. The poem attempts to assume active control over a situation in which the self has been rendered passive, over which she has had little, if any, control. The delight has left. Yet the rehearsal continues as the self clutches the dirk that has symbolically killed the other while simultaneously stabbing the one who survives. It is the self who is killed through this murder. What is won, nevertheless, is the figurative reshaping of the situation so that she becomes agent rather than victim, even if the end be the same.

This issue of the active will, of exercising power rather than merely being its target, lies at the center of Dickinson's poetics and is linked not only to that desire on the part of all poets to triumph over time but

326

particularly to her identity as a woman poet whose own life is so circumscribed by choice or historical situation, or both, that language becomes
her means for the will's survival. Furthermore, the struggle Dickinson
engages is with another who does not remain wholly mysterious but
rather, when viewed through the entire body of the poems, is clearly
associated with a patriarchal presence. More specifically, one could argue
that Dickinson conceives of her chief adversary as the Father, a composite image whose power and dominance she continually confronts to
find a poetic freedom of her own. If such aggression towards the father is
hardly an orthodox or acceptable emotion to be voiced, it is a part of the
family romance all of us share. Yet, for Dickinson, this aggression assumes an especially strong force because it becomes a prerequisite for her
sense of mastery—the authority to write (David Porter 287–90).

Critics have noted Dickinson's aggression towards herself within
the context of the problematical aspects of the poetic vocation for wom-
en, but little attention has yet been paid to those poems that turn this
aggression outward and seek a solution, albeit a violent one, to the issues
of dominance and struggle for power at the center of Dickinson's poetics
(Cameron 56–90).[2] Dickinson's principal adversary, the Father, deserves
closer scrutiny because observing her war with him, we learn more about
what *she* valued and how she, as a daughter and as a poet, wins her war
over passivity and speaks beyond the silence of time. As various critics
have noted, Dickinson's image of the Father is a composite figure whose
qualities of austerity, denial, and unrelenting isolation conjoin aspects of
her biological father as well as a Calvinist God.[3] Chief among his powers
is the ability to bestow or take away life at the utterance of a word. This
link between the power of the word and the power of life itself, though it
may, in isolated instances, seem hyperbolic in Dickinson's poems, nonetheless diagnoses the Father's supremacy not only in Dickinson's eyes but
for the culture more generally.

Michel Foucault, in his study of patriarchal power, *The History of
Sexuality*, reaches back into history for the origins of patriarchal dominance in Western culture. Noting the evolution of the concept of the
patria potestas, the unlimited power of the Roman father over his household as it is modified by its more modern and less overt forms, Foucault
observes that "for a long time, one of the characteristic privileges of
sovereign power was the right to decide life and death. In a formal sense,
it derived no doubt from the ancient *patria potestas* that granted the
father of the Roman family the right to 'dispose' of the life of his children
and his slaves; just as he had given them life, so he could take it away"
(1:135). The issue of who retains the power to kill and who the power to
die—the issue of the *patria potestas*—emerges for Foucault as the crucial

327

holdover in modern history where patriarchal aggression is modified into a form of withholding power as evidence of its possession. Foucault continues:

> In any case, in its modern form—relative and limited—as in its ancient and absolute form, the right of life and death is a dissymmetrical one. The sovereign exercised his right of life only by exercising his right to kill, or by refraining from killing; he evidenced his power over life only through the death he was capable of requiring. The right which was formulated as the "power of life and death" was in reality the right to *take* life or *let* live. (1:136)

Although such feudal politics may seem initially remote from a discussion of Dickinson's poetics, the connection proves important, for what Dickinson's poems attest to, time after time, is her right to be her own master and the dissymmetry of her perceived relationship with the father to whom she consistently subjected herself in the abdication of that right. Dickinson testified to her ambition to be a poet, and it is this conflict between self-possession and the power to defy that she acknowledges as her own: "Mine—in Vision and in Veto—" (528). Possession cannot be shared but depends instead upon the aggressive, indeed murderous, impulses that emerge from her poems.

On the other hand, murderous impulses invite, as I have been suggesting, the need for an encoded poetics that allows the poet to retrieve those threatening impulses that in more overt form might be lost to her, rendered unacceptable by their violence and their object. Therefore, Dickinson adopts, among her many strategies, the mode of the child and the language of play, at times even the convention of female self-sacrifice, as ways to approach her aggression and so defuse while simultaneously investing her language with its own purgative, aggressive power.[4] Elsewhere, however, the bold assertiveness breaks through, and the reader may find herself contemplating a necrophiliac's version of ownership— the other made precious through its death.

> If I may have it, when it's dead,
> I'll be contented—so—
> If just as soon as Breath is out
> It shall belong to me—
>
> . . . .
> Forgive me, if to stroke thy frost
> Outvisions Paradise! (577)

The brief apologetic "forgive me" is directed, not towards excusing her wish for the other's death, but towards the heresy of her secular desire. Affection, then, becomes the means whereby Dickinson can express what she wants: the beloved, a cold corpse all her own. If the "it" remains unnamed, the psychodynamics of the poem are transparent. Thus, the pattern of recuperating from loss by assuming an intimacy with death preserves the poet as active agent and redeems her otherwise helpless presence before fate. Religious terms vie with the secular as the poet apologizes for not embracing an orthodox "paradise" rather than the corpse; but that other, be he "it," male lover, father, Christ, or Master, finally becomes the object of desire who must be subsumed.[5]

The "Other" is particularly dangerous for Dickinson because he recognizes no boundaries, extending his presence into and through herself, where the self's physical processes, such as breath and pain, may assume a male identity. At these moments, a part of the self splits from the female identified "me," the male at once intimate and intrinsic to her very being. This is not a balanced androgynous conception but rather a war of opposites that can be resolved by only one faction. And yet it is a war Dickinson judges worth fighting; she decides to take her

> . . . Chance with pain—
> Uncertain if myself, or He,
> Should prove the strongest One.   (574)

The context is internal and sexualized, the force identified with the male potentially destructive.[6] That she must strive with pain and that she is alone are the crucial facts determining her need to marshal inner forces and go against the inner adversary and the external world. In this dual confrontation, "all," as Dickinson knew, "is the price of All" (772).

Yet the consequences of such hard-won freedom may be a kind of purity that betrays at best a mutilated independence. If God the Father and His various avatars are one enemy, Mother nature only intermittently offers the consolations she had for the male Romantic imagination. Female images in nature can serve as a warning as much as they may console. Gazing upward into the night sky, Dickinson observes the female moon, who has gained her freedom at a price too high for the living woman to pay. Such astral sovereignty cannot be hers.

> . . . .
> But never Stranger justified
> The Curiosity
> Like Mine—for not a Foot—nor Hand—
> Nor Formula—had she—
> But like a Head—a Guillotine
> Slid carelessly away
> Did independent, Amber—
> Sustain her in the sky—   (629)

The poet chooses a simile that is revolutionary, bloody, and final. The moon, "engrossed to Absolute— / With shining—and the Sky," resolves life's concerns; but hers is a "superior Road" the speaker tells us she cannot follow. The price the moon pays for such stunning autonomy is, figuratively speaking, just the price of a beheading. The guillotine, moreover, did its work "carelessly," a carelessness characteristic of Dickinson's other descriptions of the processes of maiming. Within the serenity of the floating, free moon, Dickinson insinuates a description that presents a macabre scene of revolutionary dismemberment, a vision of independence achieved not simply through death but through a separation from the corporeal. The moon, in all its loveliness, is truly a bloodless orb, drained by the guillotine's blade. Once the guillotine image appears, moreover, the moon acquires a sudden partialness; it is incomplete through the fact of its beheading, and thus what sets it free simultaneously reminds the reader of the body sacrificed for this pallid serenity.

Just as these mutilations shadow the moon's autonomy, so other poems reveal a sense of indebtedness, of continued love for the other who takes away her life. "Most—I love the Cause that slew Me— / Often as I die / It's beloved Recognition / Hold a Sun on Me—" (925). She is willing to embrace the role of sacrificial victim: "Bind me—I still can sing— / Banish—my mandolin / Strikes true within— / Slay—and my Soul shall rise / Chanting to Paradise— / Still Thine" (1005). This self-sacrificial strain does not, I would argue, represent an alternative point of view so much as another degree of complexity in Dickinson's sense of injury, and beyond this, of emotional destitution. The "He," whether envisioned as sun or as "eclipse" (the masculine astral counterparts of the beheaded moon), remains as an essential adversary who represents a source of authorial power. The poetic dialogue with something beyond the perceived self must be maintained in order to exercise the power of language, in order to write. When she feels utterly beholden to the masculine power these images represent, Dickinson pleads for what she cannot have, complete sovereignty over self.

But what is perhaps more important, she yearns for freedom from a God who is not only distant but dangerous, who controls both entrapment and the possibility of escape.

> God of the Manacle
> As of the Free—
> Take not my Liberty
> Away from Me—   (728)

Her experience of total dependency must be met with a violence that can undo the double-bound knot of such patriarchal power. If, as I have been suggesting, we see the "father" as a composite presence, he is not only this God but Master, Stranger, and the father she once called "too intrinsic for renown." The patriarchal image is not limited to that of destruction but encompasses a vision of a force at once enticing, provocative, and deeply desired. These qualities reappear in her descriptions of the "Master," her preceptors, the "Other," and her elusive "Stranger." And these versions of the patriarchy offer the poet possible sources of salvation as well as attraction. But the renewed expectation of such salvation when followed by overwhelming rejection or loss in death comes to transcend individual occasions and is conceptualized into a poetic form equivalent to a repetition compulsion that does not erase but rather underscores Dickinson's need for the father, although always on her own terms, terms she knew were impossible for him or any other man to fulfill.

Haunted since childhood by a pervasive sense of loss, "a Mourner . . . among the children," the poet seeks to replace what she experiences as having missed, to give herself to new fathers only to be rejected, cast out, or self-propelled away from their sphere.[7] Enlisting the conventional romantic paradigm of the abandoned lover, Dickinson expresses her overwhelming resentment at her dependence upon him. The "savior," in whatever form, comes to rescue her from his absence, but his gifts are double; his bounty leaves her only more destitute, with a vision of what she cannot possess clear before her wounded sight. What gratitude can she feel towards him whose "riches—taught me Poverty" (299)? She learns of bounty from its distance, and so the poems assume the shape of an austere consolation, ways of bandaging psychic injury by making destitution bold.

The vastly self-contradictory poems that attest to Dickinson's abasement before the male other and her wish to sacrifice all for him derive their source from *his* dual legacy to her:

You left me—Sire—two Legacies—
A Legacy of Love
A Heavenly Father would suffice
Had He the offer of—

You left me Boundaries of Pain—
Capacious as the Sea—
Between Eternity and Time—
Your Consciousness—and Me—   (644)

The leaving itself conveys the doubleness of the gift; the Sire dowers only to depart. "Boundaries" conveys limits as well as distances—but here the limits themselves are as capacious as the sea, evi-

331

dently endless and unfathomably deep. They separate not two phenomena of the same kind but elements that are inherently exclusionary: the boundary between Eternity (measureless, unknowable) and the measured, limited sphere of temporality. If Dickinson's grammatical parallelism indicates analogy, then Eternity equals the Sire's Consciousness, and Time equals "Me." He is so far beyond her, so vast, that the boundaries are not limits but oceanic spaces unbridgeable by her imagination. Indeed, she feels insufficient for the supposedly joyous gift of love he bears, a gift that would have "suffice[d]" even the "Heavenly Father." Of course, legacies are gifts received after death, so that *she* remains alive (hence in time), while he has already entered Eternity. Could his death, then, have been willed by the text? Just how far is Dickinson willing to go to ensure the dual legacy that, no matter how problematical, she finds essential to make her own?

Does Dickinson sustain her poems' life by envisioning others', especially the father's, death? The necessity for such a death wish or murderous fantasy in the presence of the father is suggested by the fact that after Edward Dickinson's death in 1874 the rate of her poetic production slows somewhat.[8] Ironically, perhaps, the earlier fantasy of the biographical father's death may have provided Dickinson with one way to discharge her aggression and convert anger into poems. When, however, her father collapses on the floor of the state legislature, she attests that she is bereft of words. Wrested from her, the father leaves her, if not at a loss, then certainly searching for the words that once so freely and with a lethal intensity flooded the page. The control over life, or rather the control over *who* is to die, of which Foucault speaks is very much at issue here and becomes a means of asserting one's own verbal and thereby private power. Since, after 1874, Edward Dickinson is no longer present as object of fantasies but rather has carried them out on his own, his role changes to that of a forever absent presence. Earlier he had been, as Barbara Mossberg notes, an essential adversary for the creation of the poet's "daughter construct," enabling her to reenact the "recurring archetypal pattern of rebellion, duty, and quest. . . ." "There is," Mossberg continues, "a ceaseless moving away from and toward a daughter's needs for love and autonomy, and a constant effort to resolve the tensions caused by these opposing needs. In all the poems, the voice is that of the daughter in conflict between her need to be loved and her need to be 'great'" (102). Although Dickinson finds others, most notably Judge Otis Lord, to reenact her Oedipal fantasy, the death of the father carries its own ineradicable psychic meaning. Unable to bestow life and helpless in the face of another's death, she charts her territory as that of the "will" in both senses—the capacity to continue living beyond her life and the ability to cut off life at will.

Thus the "will" appears as the legacy of what she can leave behind, the legacy of language. The terribly dark side of such a deliberate experiment is how often it must be met with defeat. Bereft of all, she seeks only "the privilege to die" (536). Having constructed this scenario—and I think we must, as readers, recognize that what we are describing are strategies for poetic not physical survival—Dickinson invokes a different kind of freedom, one that explores the possible victory to be won through relinquishment, deprivation, and absence. In this way, she once again achieves control over that which cannot stay. Loss becomes a means of "procurement," of entitlement, a way of acquiring the attributes of the dead, of executing the skills for survival.

Dickinson will carry this strategy so far as to assert that death is a precondition of love, that only after one has experienced the loss of the beloved can one tear oneself away from that multifarious natural world and devote oneself exclusively to the beloved:

> But He whose loss procures you
> Such Destitution that
> Your Life too abject for itself
> Thenceforward imitate—
>
> Until—Resemblance perfect—
> Yourself, for His pursuit
> Delight of Nature—abdicate—
> Exhibit Love—somewhat—   (907)

The issue here is both poetic and personal entitlement. In an especially acute observation, Mossberg remarks that "Dickinson sets her poetry apart from the male literary tradition by emphasizing her problems in assuming her right to speak" (167). And it is the complex association of personal identity, allegiance, and poetic integrity that this poem addresses. The very category of compensation is troubling, and the poet's allegiance to it is not all that clear. Initially, "you" gain through "his" loss (a brand of compensation that would have made Emerson shudder), for what is won depends upon the survivor's life being so torn by her lover's death that she can only imitate the deceased. At the crux of the poem, Dickinson's syntax pulls in opposite directions: she imitates either her former life or his. The pronominal ambiguity and the ellipsis following "Until—Resemblance perfect—" pose characteristic obstructions to choosing any single interpretation at the expense of the other.

The poem's closing lines, however, clearly convey that in her grief over his loss, her life becomes so wasted that it sacrifices its integrity and falls back upon imitation as a mode of survival. Through imitation, she is completely devoted to the dead "other," so absorbed by his former

333

identity that nature no longer draws upon her affections. The natural world thus abdicates its authority over her, as her love is now reserved exclusively for him. How, then, does the final *somewhat* fit into the poem? Is the word's equivocal character an attempt to wrest some measure of control back into the self? If she sacrifices all for him, does the delight of nature only "somewhat" fade, or does she only "somewhat" exhibit love? Whatever the chosen interpretation, *somewhat* ironically reflects back upon the poem, introducing into the text's last moments a qualification that creates a distance and a degree of independent withholding from the absolute capitulation of self that the text has maintained up to this point. It may be, finally, that the fact of life itself keeps the speaker from showing complete devotion, that only *her* death can adequately suffice as a display of affection. But as poem after poem asserts, she does not hold that power in her hands.

The ambiguities of the closing stanzas of poem 907 do not "cloud" so much as they serve to clarify the tension between the competing pressures Dickinson faced from "him" and from nature, a conflict the ellipses graphically identify. She refuses to accept any solution that might abrogate her power of choice. If—and the tentativeness is all-important here—she can only assume the masculine other's authority after his death, and through an authority based not upon authenticity but upon imitation, then his demise proves a form of self-defeat for the "I." His death, therefore, neither mitigates her suffering nor makes her own life easier to bear. Power, if attained at the expense of another's death, is also won through the obliteration of the self. Nature provides no saving ground, becoming instead, as we have already seen, an adversarial presence that, despite its immediate temptations, denies the speaker any lasting consolation.

RETURNING to the issue of who it is that stops life and the power that accrues to the agent if not to the angel of death, we again approach the issue of murder and the negative powers historically associated with the *patria potestas*. Fundamental to the hegemonic tyranny of the father is that he retains, in Foucault's analysis, the final word. Killing, the original right granted to the Roman patriarchy, is thus converted into a passive exercise of power, that of allowing others to die. Thus, in Dickinson's metaphysics, control over one's life or another's death becomes an exercise of language to prove its authority as a means of establishing power. In this context, the final stanza of that much interpreted poem, "My Life had stood—a Loaded Gun—," assumes a slightly different guise.[9] To stress, as I have been doing here, the importance of the question of agency, of who has the power to *end* life, is both crucial and vexing. Despite recent feminist readings of the poem that side with victory for the female self, what transpires, I would suggest, is the transfer of power to the male. The crucial power—what counts—is the ability to end, and this capacity the poem identifies with the Master, whether internalized or not, who has what the speaker most covets: the power to control life through closure. "He" must live longer than she because she is alive (implying, of course, the fact that she will die) by and through him. Despite her role early in the poem as protector, as ally, he is sovereign because he retains the *patria potestas* and so retains mortal control.

> Though I than He—may longer live
> He longer must—than I—
> For I have but the power to kill,
> Without—the power to die—　　　　　　　　　　　　(754)

What counts most here is the capacity to cease, a power not given to the self as instrument but reserved instead for another who wields the will of mastery as well as the strength to destroy.

And it is just this question of control, whether cast in terms of hunting or in other less overtly aggressive forms, that continues to engage Dickinson's imagination and form a vision of literary activity based upon competition, specifically a contest against a masculine power judged negatively greater than herself—negatively because power arises from the capacity to destroy. Put in ultimate terms, what the heart asks is "the will of it's Inquisitor / The privilege to die—" (536). She conceives of herself as "a Being—impotent to end— / When once it has begun—" (565).

Even physical, ordinarily unconscious processes, such as breathing, are not under her own control, as we have already seen, but rather yield to a masculine identification which cannot be relied upon to do her bidding. In a poem that takes a drowning as its ostensible subject, the struggle between death and breath assumes dialectical intimacy. Characterizing her parting breath as other, Dickinson experiences it as possessing a will of its own that will determine her fate: "Three times　we parted—Breath and I— / Three times—He would not go—" (598). As if fighting against her own desire to dismiss him and thereby give up her life, he/breath insists he stay, thereby ensuring her survival. His obstinacy saves her life as the drowning self, passive, is torn between two apparently external forces—the male-identified breath and the waves whose subsiding strength determines her ability to withstand their undertow. That the wind and waves subside leaving breath triumphant not only saves the apparently reluctant self but seems to prepare the way for a different kind of salvation, as the poem's language echoes the resurrection: "Then Sunrise kissed my Chrysalis— / And I stood up—and lived—" (598). Bound, apparently immobilized in her cocoon, the self is

335

witness to a resurrection over which she has exercised no control; yet the altered form, the erect posture, the "Christ" echoing in "chrysalis," make this no simple rescue.[10] This may be a resurrection she herself would have preferred to forego.

Certainly, this poem's description of the self's dependency, the apparent lack of control over one's destiny, does not convey her acquiescence or her assent. Instead the contest is close and depends upon her capacity to convert defeat into victory. If Emerson would write in his journal, "I am *Defeated* all the time; yet to Victory I am born," Dickinson's poems attest to a similarly pervasive sense of defeat that might lead her to conclude, "Yet to repetition I am born." The Emersonian consolation falls before the more austere poignancy of an all-too-prophetic Freudian realism (Emerson 8:228 [April 1842]). Difficult as such a conclusion may be for us to accept about so victorious a poet, we need only observe a few poems wherein Dickinson repeatedly wrestles with her enemy, caresses a corpse, or in a cunningly revisionary lullaby sings him to his final rest. First the lullaby:

> Now I lay thee down to Sleep—
> I pray the Lord thy Dust to keep—
> And if thou live before thou wake—
> I pray the Lord thy Soul to make—   (1539)

Although Thomas Johnson remarks in his notes that the occasion of this "mock-elegy," as he calls it, is not known, its spirit is certainly consistent with that of those poems that assume and even flaunt the power she wields over her deadly beloved adversary. She controls him as he acknowledges her need.

Against the experience of powerlessness she demands a victory: "Mine Enemy is growing old— / I have at last Revenge—" (1509). What strategy can a victimized self best employ to attain a compensatory power so that the battle between self and other might continue, so that the poems might live? How is Dickinson able to keep the fight so close that she can characterize her relationship with the other as one of complete dependency on her part yet of an equal, or almost equal, and intimate dependency on his?

> But since We hold a Mutual Disc—
> And front a Mutual Day—
> Which is the Despot, neither knows—
> Nor Whose—the Tyranny—   (909)

The war with the Father is more than a war with the world because it is an internal struggle between an introjected patriarchal force and that aspect of consciousness Dickinson experiences as self. This is why the terms of her language are so extreme, why the violence of murder meshes with the desire for suicide. Resentment against the Father becomes a self-inflicted hatred that derives its source in exile and a knowledge of rejection.

"A mourner . . . among the children," Dickinson from the first feels cheated, starved to the point of extinction, and this hunger feeds upon the self. With both God the Father and Mother nature casting her out, she perceives herself as outnumbered and outclassed. When nature appears as an independent entity, it may side not with the experiential consciousness but rather with a God whose piercing, aggressive knowledge of the poet permits no reply. Nature pairs with Him only to increase, to intensify, Dickinson's sense of haunted isolation. Mother nature and God the Father overpower her, and the child is rendered defenseless, with only a partially repressed, barely stifled wish for the parents' death.

> Nature and God—I neither knew
> Yet Both so well knew me
> They startled, like Executors
> Of My identity.
>
> Yet neither told—that I could learn—
> My Secret as secure
> As Herschel's private interest
> Or Mercury's affair—   (835)

The alliance between nature and God becomes collusion in the face of the child, the parents withholding knowledge or a secret about her that they alone possess. They both execute (or kill) her identity and act it out by executing her will after her death (Diehl 161–62).[11] This threatening alliance is based upon their inscrutable, impenetrable knowledge of her. Her secret is "secure," but from whom—herself or the world? The elliptical closing stanza encourages an interpretative indeterminacy that leaves the reader as much in the dark as the speaker is herself. The poem thus recreates in its reader the sense of intrusion and withheld knowledge that is its overt subject.

What can break down the barriers and give Dickinson the strength to "go against" such a world? In my estimation, she derives the impetus for poetry from her ability to sustain intense conflict, the practice of a Keatsian negative capability *in extremis*. She draws energy from the intimate war with the father, at moments even imagining her victory. Though any Dickinsonian victory must be a vanquishment as well, victory nonetheless there is. Her triumphs, like her murders, are dramatic—both intimately staged and never final. Dickinson knows all too well the importance of the literary form: "But we—are dying in Drama," she writes, "And Drama—is never dead" (531). At times the drama assumes the language of the Church as her struggles take on the aura and the diction we associate with Christ's Passion. She would be the "Christa" of language if she were not fated to be Eve. Sacrificing her own life for God's word remains her constant offering. Yet denied the possibility of a role as sacrificial daughter, she has no place in the Trinity and no way to save herself or her world, to redeem it for belief, to save it for hope. Recalling her early feelings of exclusion, Dickinson writes,

> Who were 'the Father and the Son'
> We pondered when a child,
> And what had they to do with us
> And when portentous told
>
> With inference appalling
> By Childhood fortified
> We thought, at least they are no worse
> Than they have been described.   (1258)

No longer "fortified" by childhood innocence, her only retaliation becomes a tortured self-reliance. This is not, however, the Emersonian brand wherein each of us can share the confidence that the self will triumph, nor is it the Whitmanian faith that what he assumes we also shall assume. As a result, Dickinson's at times antagonistic but always ambivalent attitude towards her audience derives from her extenuating philosophical isolation as well as from a pervasive skepticism towards all experience not witnessed or controlled by the self (including the reading of her poems).

Where her triumph, then, and at what price? To illustrate this fundamental issue, I turn to a poem that speaks of victory, the father, and power. Although murder is not mentioned outright, the tension within the text can be traced, I would suggest, to the terms of a distinctly muderous poetics. The poem is the familiar "I'm ceded—I've stopped being Their's—" (508), which announces a break with family, religion, and history. Here Dickinson compares an orthodox and a defiant baptism. The lines of particular interest for our purposes are those that describe the physical positions of the speaker when first baptized and at the time of her second, self-appointed identification. Here is the final stanza:

> My second Rank—too small the first—
> Crowned—Crowing—on my Father's breast
> A half unconscious Queen—

But this time—Adequate—Erect,
With Will to choose, or to reject,
and I choose, just a Crown—

The infant is held against the Father's breast; in this vision of the family romance it is he who is the nurturer, who floods her with an overwhelming power or leaves her to starve. Note that as an infant she is not the princess but Queen, potentially the King's equal, an Oedipal identification in which the child replaces the mother and becomes the bride of Christ. That the infant cries at her own baptism is unexceptional; what is interesting is the "crowing," with its associations of the cock crow of morning, the predatory bird eating its carrion, the New Testament crowing that marks the betrayal of Christ.

The sense of insufficiency, of hunger for authority, the failure of orthodoxy to bestow identity, may indeed suggest submerged thoughts of murder, death of the father, the Church, and the representatives of patriarchal orthodox culture. To rename oneself may only prove possible by murdering the body of the Father to feed upon his power and create a separate self. In the poet's second transformation the father is indeed absent; and in full possession of her own will, she accepts a crown with a gesture full of conscious authority:

Baptized before, without the choice,
But this time, consciously, of Grace—
Unto supremest name—

But even though the name is her own, there remains a quality of responsiveness; she is "called" to her full, achieving royal/divine status or imperial selfhood by responding to a summons. Though the choice is all hers, she understands the demand or call as emanating from outside, as external to her. She wears the crown, and the religious emblem acquires, through its identification with royalty, not only the choice of independent authority but a slightly orthodox cast which modifies the otherwise radical quality of her self-bestowed status. She can select among alternatives, but she does not perceive herself as being the origin of these choices.

Despite her frequent rejection of the possibility of true usurpation, on other occasions Dickinson *does* envision her transformation, not into the bride of God, but into a true "Christa," or female Christ. Although the possibility is at times encoded in language that suggests the dangerously subversive cast of her thinking, Dickinson nevertheless makes the radical transformation plain. In poem 553 the speaker universalizes Christ's suffering only to defuse the full impact of her closing lines, which identify her specifically as the imminent Christ.

> Our Lord—indeed—made Compound Witness—
> And yet—
> There's newer—nearer Crucifixion
> Than that—

Our commonality depends upon our passion, and yet even in this knowledge she remains the outsider. Denied the legacy of the Father, she can save neither us nor herself. She is excluded from his generosity as well as denied the very thing she most requires—the self-sufficiency of the Spirit that would validate her own suffering.

Eager to please, desperate to attract God's attention and attain his good will, she asks that he not rebuke her for her efforts. "Whatever it is—she has tried it— / Awful Father of Love— / Is not Our's the chastising— / Do not chastise the Dove—" (1204). As the Dove of the Holy Spirit or the dove that flew from Noah's Ark in search of the first sign of dry land, of hope, she fears she will be banished. Excluded from God's house yet remaining throughout her life in the house of her father, Dickinson strives to assume the Father's power and to win his love. Having experienced the failure of both requirements, Dickinson makes of her exile a provisional home by converting her defeat into a victory that embodies the vanquished. The symbolic language of nature palls beside her quest, and the tie between nature and language, the possibilities for the natural world's serving as a symbolic counter for Dickinson's inner life, prove insufficient. Even the powerful promise of the sublime American West cannot match the audacity of Dickinson's interior pioneering.

> The Stars are old, that stood for me—
> The West a little worn—
> Yet newer glows the only Gold
> I ever cared to earn—
>
> Presuming on that lone result
> Her infinite disdain
> But vanquished her with my defeat
> 'Twas Victory was slain.   (1249)

The struggle with the Father continues, as does the expression of the inadequacy of nature to convey its intensity. Confronting the infinite disdain of her beloved Susan or her preceptor Higginson or the bird she had seen that morning (the precipitating occasion for the poem, according to Johnson), Dickinson renders the experiences interchangeable. Disdained by all around her, she vanquishes the adversary by her very defeat and thus slays victory.

Her power resides in her defeat, as Christ's power lies in his sacri-

fices. Imperfect as the analogy seems and almost too grim, perhaps, to
contemplate, there can be for Dickinson no other power except—and
the exception is all here—the power of the word. The world that excludes her is enemy, and she wants revenge.

> I took my Power in my Hand—
> And went against the world—   (540)

When the weapon is a pebble, as in this poem, the injury is to
herself; when the weapon is the word, with its attribute of power, the
result is different.

One asks, What other options were there? The choice of passive
aggression based upon waiting, upon watching, becomes instead an
encoded death sentence that provides her with renewed life, wiping out
the very passivity it would seem to protect.

> Mine Enemy—is growing old—
> I have at last Revenge—
> The Palate of the Hate departs—
> If any would avenge
>
> Let him be quick—the Viand flits—   (1509)

Even revenge may lose its savor when attained because it arrives
belatedly. Nevertheless, Dickinson survives to keep writing those austere
poems of the isolated imagination; she writes to survive. The symbiosis is
clear when she herself speaks: "I work to drive the Awe away / Yet Awe
impels the work." The issue comes down to the power of life and death
and who wields it. Though a "loaded gun," her life misses the "power to
die." Yet she repeatedly relies upon that death-dealer, just as she remains
firmly convinced that he will injure or, worse, reject her. Here is the
absolute God in all his kindness:

> Far from Love the Heavenly Father
> Leads the Chosen Child,
> Oftener through Realm of Briar
> Than the Meadow mild.
>
> Oftener by the Claw of Dragon
> Than the Head of friend
> Guides the Little One predestined
> To the Native Land.   (1021)

If salvation rests in the dragon's claw, Dickinson's pen must be
equally ready to wound. When she deals her pretty words like blades,
however, she finds that she may be their closest victim.

IN A LETTER to Higginson in March of 1876 Dickinson recalls her father: "When I think of my Father's lonely life and his lonelier Death, there is this redress—

> Take all away—
> The only thing worth larceny
> Is left—the Immortality. (*Letters* 3:551)

That "flood" subject "immortality" is alone worth the striving and alone offers tentative consolation. What can rescue the individual from such radical disenfranchisement is the word, the possibility of writing a poem that will withstand any assault on the self.

The transformation from a self defeated because it cannot will its own death into a triumphant poet able to claim victory over Father/God/Lover/Precursor depends upon the authority of language and the woman poet's assertion of her authority. The dirk still dripping, it metaphorically becomes for Dickinson the instrument of renewed life. Rejecting her role as vanquished woman, she converts her victimization into a life sentence. And, if only intermittently, she asserts for herself the *patria potestas,* sentencing her adversary to death. She writes from the blood of self-inflicted wounds, made in order to set her self free. If some of Dickinson's poems are encoded "little murders," they are acts of aggression towards the Father who would stifle her, who would silence her words for all time. In those poems where she achieves victory, her word becomes the Word. Speaking with the authority of a female Passion, they offer an alternative language to the hegemonic orthodoxy of Calvinist Amherst and Christian America. At their strongest, Dickinson's poems embody the Christa of language she would will for us and for herself.

Notes

1. All references to Dickinson's poems appear in the text identified by poem number according to the Johnson variorum edition.

2. Sharon Cameron discusses what she perceives as Dickinson's "dialectic of rage" (56–90). Although Cameron deals with the subject of the relationship between the "power to kill, / Without—the power to die," her approach and mine are vastly different.

3. Several critics have commented upon Dickinson's creation of a composite father; see, for example, Baym, "God, Father, and Lover" 198.

4. For a deeply informed discussion of Dickinson's adoption of the daughter persona as poetic strategy see Mossberg.

5. Of her attitude towards this composite figure, Mossberg notes, "It is curious, given her ambivalence to her father's dominant role, that each male is sought as a Master, Tutor, Preceptor, or Monarch. In each relationship, she

promises to be both obedient and remarkable; her father's daughter" (83). I suggest that the poems themselves are instances of defiance that challenge her obedience as they test the limits of her rhetorical audacity.

6. As Cameron has remarked, "Yet the poems themselves are not stark, are, in fact, loaded with energy that is, as I have been suggesting, close to explosive. And it is the energy that needs accounting for, fed as it is by the fuel of sexuality on the one hand, and death on the other, by that combustible that ignites rage" (87).

7. See, for example, poem 959.

8. See Mossberg's discussion of Dickinson's response to her father's death (81).

9. I mention only the most recent readings of the poem: those of Cameron (65 74), Mossberg, (19 23), Pollak (150 55), and David Porter (209 18). The critical discussion of this poem mirrors the changes in Dickinson interpretation over the years. Despite their differences, these readings share an interest in issues related to power and to gender.

10. This pattern of dependency and awakening to life provoked by another assumes a different guise in Dickinson's image of the Memnon stone (see poem 261).

11. My essay " 'Ransom in a Voice' " provides a more detailed reading of this poem, with particular attention to the double work of the word *executor*.

ELIZABETH ABEL

Cam the Wicked: Woolf's Portrait of the Artist as Her Father's Daughter

But the centre is father's character, sitting in a boat, reciting, We perished, each alone, while he crushes a dying mackerel. However, I must refrain. I must write a few little stories first and let the *Lighthouse* simmer, adding to it between tea and dinner till it is complete for writing out.
    —*Diary,* 14 May 1925

But I wrote the book [*To the Lighthouse*] very quickly; and when it was written, I ceased to be obsessed by my mother. I no longer hear her voice; I do not see her. . . .
    Certainly, there she was, in the very centre of that great Cathedral space which was childhood; there she was from the very first.
    —"A Sketch of the Past," 1939

TO THE LIGHTHOUSE is in doubt about its center. The novel dramatizes the contradictions between Woolf's prospective and retrospective definitions of its center, between "father's character, sitting in a boat," and mother "there . . . in the very centre." In this autobiographical fiction Woolf explores the complexities of narrating family history. The lacuna that "Time Passes" offers as a textual center is only the most striking manifestation of a discontinuity sustained more discreetly through the multiple histories she hoped would counteract the sentimentality threatened by her theme: "The word 'sentimental' sticks in my gizzard. . . . But this theme may be sentimental; father and mother and child in the garden; the death; the sail to the Lighthouse. I think, though, that when I begin it I shall enrich it in all sorts of ways; thicken it; give it branches—roots—which I do not perceive now" (*Diary* 3:36). Woolf's metaphors of textual enrichment have changed since *Mrs. Dalloway:* the "beautiful caves" that were to deepen private history have been exchanged for metaphors drawn from the interdependent parts of a tree— a family tree whose "branches" and "roots" will ironize the family romance by refracting a plural subject through a plural narrative (*Diary* 2:30).
    This heterogeneity has been neglected in Woolf criticism. Interested primarily in specific aspects of Woolf's "theme," critics usually focus

344

either on the variations on androgyny played by the Ramsays (Bazin; DiBattista; Fleishman; Freedman; Kelley) or on the dilemma of the woman artist dramatized by Lily Briscoe (Gubar; Lilienfeld; Phyllis Rose; Ruddick; Spivak, "Unmaking and Making"). (Both critical focuses are drawn in part from issues Woolf articulates in *A Room of One's Own*.) Analyses of genre often take as their starting point Woolf's own uncertainty about the appropriate label for her text: "I am making up *To the Lighthouse*—the sea is to be heard all through it. I have an idea that I will invent a new name for my books to supplant 'novel.' A new ——— by Virginia Woolf. But what? Elegy?" (*Diary* 3:34). But most of these analyses translate Woolf's indecision into an assertion, ignoring her question mark (Beer; DiBattista). Circumscribing genre in this way unifies a text whose origins and broadest patterns may be elegiac but whose fractured exploration of elegiac subjects resists consolidation as a single genre or theme.

A reading of the novel's "thickening" also anticipates *A Room of One's Own,* where Woolf's metaphors conflate the family with narrative: "we think back through our mothers if we are women" (79). In *To the Lighthouse* the familial context, accentuated by the island setting, is likewise an arena of self-conscious narrative, though here the claims of patrilinearity compete with those of matrilinearity. *To the Lighthouse* is shot through with scenes of reading, writing, and painting, inconspicuous yet germinal incidents from which memory spins its tale, textual moments (in Lily Briscoe's words) "ringed round, lit up, visible to the last detail, with all before it blank, for miles and miles" (254). The links among family, narrative, and gender constitute the psychoanalytic substance of this text, which distributes its author's narrative concerns among disparate characters. Thus, Woolf's two most explicit textual representatives—Lily and Cam—inherit her competing narrative loyalties. Lily is her vehicle for thinking back through her mother. Heir to and remnant of Woolf's original plan of centering her story on "father's character, sitting in a boat, reciting, We perished, each alone, while he crushes a dying mackerel," Cam enables Woolf to dramatize the plight of the daughter who thinks back through her father.

Because critics have systematically neglected Cam in favor of Lily and James, who are accented and counterpointed in the text, this essay plucks her from the web of narrative to illuminate, and account for, her obscurity. By her name and her position as the youngest Ramsay daughter, Cam is Woolf's most literal narrative counterpart, her self-portrait as her father's daughter, yet she is powerfully, though erratically, submerged.[1] Minimally outlined in part 1, Cam nevertheless joins the finale in part 3—and yet, as such a shadowy, attenuated presence that it is not clear why she is included. The arrival at the lighthouse caps James's drama exclusively. Cam, who has never longed for this journey, drifts suspended between the text's dual resolutions: the arrival at the lighthouse and the completion of Lily's painting. Yet rather than a sign of aesthetic incoherence, her plight brilliantly discloses one intersection of psychoanalysis and narrative: the imaginative field delimited by the daughter's shift from pre-Oedipal mother to Oedipal father (Abel, "Narrative Structure(s)"; Freud, "Female Sexuality," "Femininity," and "Some Psychical Consequences," all in *SE*).

Cam is an enigma throughout the text. Less central than James, she is also less programmatic: no psychoanalytic clichés (such as the axes, knives, and pokers with which James fantasizes murdering his father) allegorize her consciousness. As a child, Cam is fiercely independent: "She would not 'give a flower to the gentleman' as the nursemaid told her. No! no! no! she would not!" (36). Hence her appellation by Mr. Bankes: "Cam the Wicked" (83). Indecipherable even to her mother, Cam seems wholly present to herself as she dashes through part 1 like a projectile guided by some urgent private desire: "She was off like a bird, bullet, or arrow, impelled by what desire, shot by whom, at what directed, who could say? What, what? Mrs. Ramsay pondered, watching her" (84). This defiant energy has dissipated by part 3: Cam sits passively in the boat while her brother navigates, her father reads and chats with Macalister, and Macalister's boy catches fish. Like the boat that bobs up and down in place, Cam's thoughts circle back on themselves as she aimlessly dabbles her hand in the water and watches the fish that objectify her feeling of entrapment. Whereas the narrative holds James psychically responsible for the interrupted progress of the boat by linking his drama of memory and repression to the rise and fall of the wind (section 8), thereby according him the task of reshaping the past to enable the future, Cam's internal drama (section 10) is severed from this narrative teleology. James faces the lighthouse and navigates towards it; Cam sits in the bow and gazes back towards the island. Though brother and sister share the task of reconstructing memory, Cam's efforts in no way impinge on the action. Her project is purely historical.

At the beginning of "The Lighthouse," the cowed and angry siblings share a single will, though Cam's syntactic subordination—"He would be impatient in a moment, James thought, and Cam thought" (242); "So James could tell, so Cam could tell" (245)—indicates the brother's dominance. Woolf chooses the occasion of an interpolated story to introduce Cam as an independent consciousness. Macalister's tale of maritime rescue and disaster, prompted by Mr. Ramsay's questions about the great storm at Christmas, weaves an alliance between the two old men, overcoming class and ethnic differences to constitute a homogeneous narrative voice as Mr. Ramsay adjusts his gaze and speech to Macalister's and mimics his Scottish accent. Shared pleasure in the sexual division of labor and its representation in narrative outweighs other differences: Mr. Ramsay "liked that men should labour and sweat on the windy beach at night. . . . he liked men to work like that, and women to keep house and sit beside sleeping children indoors, while men were drowned, out there in a storm" (245).

Woolf dramatizes the impact of this story not on James, who can aspire to a future role in it, but on its more problematical female auditor, whose access to this explicitly masculine discourse requires mediation. The imaginative arena the story opens frees the carefully guarded love Cam feels for her father, but this release is qualified by the mental act it presupposes. Cam can enter this discourse only by displacing herself as its potential subject, transferring her childhood love of adventure to an idealized image of her (elderly) father, with some consequent mystification of her own emotion. "Cam thought, feeling proud of him *without knowing quite why,* had he been there he would have launched the lifeboat, he would have reached the wreck. . . . He was so brave, he was so adventurous" (246; my italics). Woolf marks Cam's emergence in the third part of the novel as a reaction to a masculine "text" that grants her the gendered relationship to narrative explored two years later in *A Room of One's Own:* "It is useless to go to the great male writers for help. . . . The ape is too distant to be sedulous" (12).

Cam's idealization of Mr. Ramsay, moreover, provokes a return of what it has repressed: the knowledge of his tyranny. This knowledge is Cam's as well as James's, and the "compact" that declares it and that suddenly checks her surge of affection for her father has presumably been forged by both siblings, who had "vowed, in silence, as they walked, to stand by each other and carry out the great compact—to resist tyranny to the death" (243). Yet Cam perceives the agreement as a text she can neither revise, revoke, nor fully endorse, a coercive force that evolves into the "tablets of eternal wisdom" lying on "James the lawgiver"'s knee, silencing her (251). Cam is complicit in this silencing. Though the compact *does* represent James's perspective more fully than her own, and *does* reflect his greater authority, Cam's desire to evade her own anger obscures her part in the creation of an unwritten text that records a strand of her relation to her father. As she projects her former adventurousness onto her father, she projects onto her brother her former defiance, the voice that had said "No! no! no!" to the gentleman, and divides her salient childhood traits between two men and two texts in which participation leads to alienation. Denying herself the roles of both protagonist and author, she colludes with the assumptions of patriarchal textuality.[2] The scene on the boat reflects some prior learning.

Paralyzed by the stand-off between her father and her brother, Cam recovers her own memories only after this drama is resolved in section 8 and the boat is speeding towards the lighthouse once again. In section 10 the motion sparks Cam's imagination, which converts the growing distance into time and reverts to a single privileged scene, her counterpart to James's epiphanic vision of his mother "saying simply whatever came into her head. She alone spoke the truth; to her alone could he speak it" (278). Cam, however, remembers her father, not her mother; scenes of reading and writing rather than of speech; and a study rather than a garden. Eden to her is the garden's aftermath, though the narrative suggests that this revision is delusion. Her memory focuses on her father's study. "Sometimes she strayed in from the garden purposely to catch them at it. There they were (it might be Mr. Carmichael or Mr. Bankes who was sitting with her father) sitting opposite each other in their low armchairs. . . . Just to please herself she would take a book from the shelf and stand there, watching her father write" (281). In Cam's imagination, fathers know best, and they speak the knowledge of the printed text. "They were crackling in front of them the pages of *The Times,* when she came in from the garden, all in a muddle about something some one had said about Christ, or hearing that a mammoth had been dug up in a London street, or wondering what Napoleon was like" (281). "Straying" from garden to study, from nature to culture, from the private muddle to the public text, Cam concludes one developmental era.

In Cam's memory, closure is gentle, a gradual transition from one sphere to another, a gradual translation of experience to thought that unfolds organically like a leaf that has gained, not lost, its natural environment. As a child in the study Cam had felt that "one could let whatever one thought expand here like a leaf in water; and if it did well here, among the old gentlemen smoking and *The Times* crackling then it was right" (282). Yet the tension between her metaphor and her literal description undercuts her evolutionary model, reasserting a distinction she would blur. Throughout the text Cam associates the leaf with Mrs. Ramsay. In "The Window" Cam carries a leaf when she responds to her mother's call; in "The Lighthouse" the leaf is her recurrent image for the island that incarnates the receding past. "It lay like that on the sea, did it, with a dent in the middle and two sharp crags, and the sea swept in there, and spread away for miles and miles on either side of the island. It was very small; shaped something like a leaf stood on end" (280). Cam's simile revises but does not conceal a prior, less overt metaphorization of the island as a female body from which she is drawn slowly away. With a sea-swept dent in the middle of two crags, the island hovering behind the leaf is a figure of the mother. As a child Cam hoped to extend, articulate, and assess the past identified with the garden and the mother by translating the leaf into the language of the father—and in so doing to imitate her father's own translations of hedges into periods, of geranium leaves into "scraps of paper on which one scribbles notes in the rush of reading" (66), of nature's leaves into the pages of a book. When she repeats this gesture in the present, a fissure surfaces. It is the image of the leaf-shaped island that triggers her adolescent memory: "Small as it was, and shaped something like a leaf stood on its end with the gold-sprinkled waters flowing in and about it, it had, she supposed, a place in the universe— even that little island? The old gentlemen in the study she thought could have told her. Sometimes she strayed in from the garden . . ." (281). The rift between the gold-sprinkled island and the old men in the study reveals what has been lost in the translation and what now is lost more emphatically in Cam's attempt to situate one domain of experience within the discourse of another.

Only these repercussions of the past in the present lend credibility to the hints of a Fall. If the young Cam "strays" from the garden in search of information, this knowledge is not forbidden, nor is she expelled. The garden, moreover, is no unfallen natural paradise, for voices within it have produced the muddle that sends her in search of clarification. If there is a Fall, it does not pertain to the search for knowledge, or even to its source (the study is a logical, perhaps inevitable, resource to enlist), but to its consequences. The historical questions that arise in the garden—about Christ, Napoleon, and a prehistoric mammoth—are appropriately carried to the study, but they differ from the issue the older Cam mentally refers to the same place: a question of personal history, of the private past, of the mother's place "in the universe." However passionately motivated her search for knowledge, and however legitimate her indebtedness to her father, Cam's apprenticeship in the study ensnares her as well as liberates her, sanctioning certain modes of thought, discouraging others, creating an intellectual framework that becomes her single frame of reference. The old gentlemen in the study reinforce Cam's interest in history, priming her for the position she assumes in the boat.[3] Studying the past, she also learns to privilege it. By "The Lighthouse" Cam is expert at gazing backward, at translating images of a shifting present into the framework of the past, at repeating in adolescence patterns learned as a child.

The scene in the study both mirrors and prepares the scene in the boat. Cam's psychological position in the present, as well as her literal one, moreover, finds a precedent in her father's study. In both situations Cam's curiosity and responsiveness draw her imaginatively into a conversation between men, with a consequent erosion of her own subjectivity. As the two scenes blur in her mind, similarities emerge between her relation to the story spun by Mr. Ramsay and an old gentleman "who might be Mr. Carmichael or Mr. Bankes," whose identity matters less than his structural position opposite her father, Macalister's position. (We are told this location obliquely through stage directions: when James fears his father's admonition about a slackening sail, he imagines that Mr. Ramsay "would say sharply, 'Look out! Look out!' and old Macalister would turn slowly on his seat"—presumably to look at the drooping sail; when Mr. Ramsay listens to Macalister's story, he leans forward—presumably to catch every word [244].)

In the study ambiguity obscures who talks with whom. Cam wants to believe that her questions received answers, but the text suggests that the gentlemen conversed primarily with one another. Whom did they address when they turned their papers, crossed their knees, "and said something now and then very brief" (281)? An almost identical phrase in the next sentence records a conversation between the two old men: Mr. Ramsay said something "briefly to the other old gentlemen opposite" (281). Only in Cam's final recapitulation of the scene does someone explicitly answer her question: "The old gentleman, lowering the paper suddenly, said something very brief over the top of it about the character of Napoleon" (283). Is this a wishful secondary revision, part of her project of rescuing her father from James's hostile fantasy? The substance of the interaction reinforces its structural ambiguity. Cam's only question to be answered, and the only specified content of any verbal exchange, concerns the character of Napoleon, ominous since Woolf elsewhere depicts him as the paradigmatic figure who excludes women from history.[4] That his character should be the climax of a scene in which Cam struggles to learn history reveals the pathos of her eagerness for access to a discourse whose terms diminish her and for a place in an exchange that calls into question her status as interlocutor.

The apprenticeship in the study is not the only source of Cam's attenuation in language. It may be her fate as youngest daughter to serve as a vehicle of messages rather than their sender or recipient, and her willing metamorphosis into a blank page encourages her use as a transparent medium. The significant variable is the sex of the speakers. In "The Window" Woolf briefly sketches an alternative semiotic context for Cam. When sent by Mrs. Ramsay to ask the cook whether Andrew, Paul, and Minta have returned from the beach, Cam mimics for her mother the cook's exact response. But between the question and the answer, she inserts her own story, and "it was only by waiting patiently, and hearing that there was an old woman in the kitchen with very red cheeks, drinking soup out of a basin, that Mrs. Ramsay at last prompted that parrot-like instinct which had picked up Mildred's words quite accurately and could now produce them, if one waited, in a colourless singsong" (85). A diminutive female Hermes shuttling between two female speakers, Cam nevertheless succeeds in imposing her own embryonic narrative. Its subject, "an old woman in the kitchen," resonates against Woolf's first description of the vision to which Cam is heir: the father in a boat.

The text associates the red-cheeked old woman with the bibulous elderly cleaning woman, Mrs. McNab, who in "Time Passes" remembers being "always welcome in the kitchen," where the cook, at Mrs. Ramsay's request, kept a plate of milk soup for her (206). Though stripped of Mrs. Ramsay's arabesquing consciousness, Mrs. McNab serves in "Time Passes" as a bare corporeal remainder and reminder of her mistress, an incarnation of memory who tears the "veil of silence" that has fallen on the Ramsay home (196). As the lowest common denominator of female artistry, the work of preservation whose psychological correlate Mrs. Ramsay calls "the effort of merging and flowing and creating" (126), Mrs. McNab is the figure who by sheer determination rescues the Ramsays' home from "the sands of oblivion" and connects the first part of the novel to the third (209). As Cam's kitchen muse, she fleetingly inspires a story that refuses to be squelched. In the same way that her position in the novel inscribes the traces of female labor in a bleakly inhuman textual center, her position in Cam's circuit as messenger raises the prospect of a third rendition of the novel's three-part form.

Cam's vision of the island as a sea-swept dent between two crags hints at this rendition. The configuration of mass and space shows a family resemblance with Lily Briscoe's "question . . . how to connect this mass on the right hand with that on the left" (83) and with James's "night's darkness" between two days (9), but Cam represents the center as a place of origin. Her glimpse of the island shares with her miniature narrative a buried notion of female engendering. These echoing accounts could evolve into Cam's counterpart to the narrative formulas offered by Lily and James; they could become Cam's story, her metanarrative, her version of history. But this nascent narrative design never emerges, and can not. Cam's muted presence in the text is no accident, for it is precisely when she first perceives the island as a body ("She had never seen it from out at sea before" [280]) that she turns to the memory of the study.

Cam's poignancy derives from a narrative perspective that blends sympathy with irony. It is less that we see options to which Cam is blind (to whom should she refer her questions about history?) than that we can gauge the cost of choices she has made, interpret metaphors opaque to her, and register her pleasure as an index of her innocence. Though Cam's course may look easier than James's, since the death of their mother appears less devastating to her and her father less peremptory with her, we can also observe that if her suffering is less sharply focused and articulate, it is also less empowering. If James renounces a privileged bond with his mother and the truth her language signifies to him and accepts in their place the poverty and power of linguistic signs, Cam never fully accedes to this symbolic register. The sole loss culturally acknowledged as prerequisite to language is that which the son undergoes. Cam's own metaphors betray that her father's study, in which she takes such pleasure, offers her the material of language more readily than its significance. Within this sanctuary, Cam relishes the tangible signs of language with no expectation that their content is available. She represents the old gentlemen's clarification of her muddle as a tactile, rather than a verbal, intervention: "Then they took all this [muddle] with their clean hands (they wore grey coloured clothes; they smelt of heather) and they brushed the scraps together" (281). Instead of reading the book she takes from the shelf "just to please herself," she watches her father write and admires the evenness of his lines without attempting to decipher their meaning.

The scene on the boat mirrors this relation to paternal texts. Cam is both thoroughly familiar with and ignorant of the book in which her father is engrossed, "the little book whose yellowish pages she knew, without knowing what was written on them. It was small; it was closely printed. . . . But what might be written in the book which had rounded its edges off in his pocket, she did not know. What he thought they none of them knew" (283). The father as text, like the father's texts, remains hermetic to her, and her attempt to generalize this condition cracks against James's conviction that he and his father "alone knew each other" (275). Cam's image of the tiller's transformation into tablets marks her only conscious recognition of their father's differing legacies. These differences crystallize in the children's final interactions with Mr. Ramsay. Cam's relationship with her father culminates in a silent gesture of paternal courtship, as Mr. Ramsay hands her "a gingerbread nut, as if he were a great Spanish gentleman, she thought, handing a flower to a lady at a window (so courteous his manner was)" (305). The father-son relationship concludes with the breaking of silence in the long-withheld "Well done!" that answers James's unspoken desire for paternal recognition and praise (306). Despite (or because of) Cam's delight in her father's courtly gesture, this resolution of their relationship implies that her apprenticeship did not fulfill its promise. Revising a Keatsian model of treacherous seduction as the failure of a (feminine) imagination to sustain its offer of transcendence, the father-daughter narrative outlines a seduction by a (masculine) tradition that reneges on its equation of knowledge and authority.

The "most touching" of the "life-giving affinities" between Leslie Stephen and his youngest daughter, according to Leon Edel, was Sir Leslie's gift on Virginia's twenty-first birthday of a ring and a declaration: she was, he averred, "a very good daughter." Oblivious to the dissonance of his metaphors, Edel explains: "It was as if there were a marriage and also a laying on of hands, a literary succession. The father . . . performed a marriage between Virginia and the world of letters" (90). Woolf herself, however, was well aware that being wed to a tradition was not being its heir, and she dramatized this difference in the Ramsay children's destinies. The personal inclinations of daughter and of father have little relevance to the course of events. Cam's education in the study prepares her to inherit her mother's position rather than her father's. Whether overtly enacted as dialogue or mediating more subtly between a masculine authorship and readership, the textual tradition transmitted by the study returns its female initiate to the original female position between two gentlemen: between Ramsay and Macalister, between Ramsay and the generic old gentleman, between Ramsay and his son—the nuclear masculine pair. The daughter's position thus slides imperceptibly into the mother's. Though the father-mother-son triad that prevailed in "The Window" gives way in "The Lighthouse" to a father-daughter-son triad, the median feminine position is unchanged. As the scene on the boat gradually recreates its predecessor at the window, the characters psychically alter their positions. Having explicitly established that Mr. Ramsay sits "in the middle of the boat between them (James steered; Cam sat alone in the bow)" (242), Woolf inconsistently rearranges the protagonists to conform with emotional topography. Cam's "brother was most god-like, her father most suppliant. And to which did she yield, she thought, sitting between them, gazing at the shore" (251). As Cam inherits her mother's median position, for which her training in the study paradoxically has groomed her, Woolf dissects the configuration that silences the daughter.

Ostensibly, Mr. Ramsay tries during the boat trip to engage his daughter in conversation, but Woolf portrays the scene as an unvoiced dialogue between Mr. Ramsay and his son. After Mr. Ramsay's opening question, we shift directly to James's response: "Who was looking after the puppy today? he [Mr. Ramsay] asked. Yes, thought James pitilessly, seeing his sister's head against the sail, now she'll give way. I shall be left to fight the tyrant alone" (250). Mr. Ramsay's second question similarly returns us to James's consciousness, and to the trauma at the window. Sliding pronouns (*she, her, they, somebody*) replace Cam with Mrs. Ramsay as the pressure of the struggle recalls its prototype: "She'll give way, James thought, as he watched a look come upon her face, a look he remembered. They look down, he thought, at their knitting or something. Then suddenly they look up. There was a flash of blue, he remembered, and then somebody sitting with him laughed, surrendered, and he was very angry. It must have been his mother, he thought, sitting on a low chair, with his father standing over her. . . . a man had marched up and down and stopped dead, upright, over them" (251–52). Having blurred his sister with his mother, James succeeds in adolescence where he failed as a child and prevents his father's victory. Torn between the irreconcilable demands of her father and his son, Cam succumbs to silence, unable to find a language for her own split desire.

In the prototype of this scene, Mr. Ramsay played ventriloquist; here he is humble, not apparently engaged in any struggle, eager only to converse with his daughter. His motivation, however, mirrors his son's: like James, he uses Cam to replay and repair the past, though he tries to compensate to his wife through his daughter rather than exact compensation from her. When Cam's uncertainty about the points of the compass recalls Mrs. Ramsay's imprecision about the weather, Mr. Ramsay merges daughter and mother: "He thought, women are always like that; the vagueness of their minds is hopeless. . . . It had been so with her—his wife" (249). Grieving for his wife and feeling remorse over his anger at her, Mr. Ramsay craves the solace of his daughter's approval. The scene on the boat thus becomes a scene of seduction that locates Cam between two men struggling to redo their relation to her mother: "I will make her smile at me, Mr. Ramsay thought" (250). His manner is courteous, but his project is coercive, and his instrument again is language. From his daughter he wants a literal echo, or at least this is how Cam interprets his desire. Though he struggles to suppress his longing for confirmation, Cam reads it clearly: "And what was she going to call him [the puppy]? her father persisted. He had had a dog when he was a little boy, called Frisk. . . . she wished, passionately, to move some obstacle that lay upon her tongue and to say, Oh, yes, Frisk. I'll call him Frisk" (252). In this competition for her tongue, Cam can be silenced by Mosaic tablets or echo a paternal language that suggests an Adamic ritual of naming: "So she said nothing, but looked doggedly and sadly at the shore. . . . They have no suffering there, she thought" (253).

Ironically, Cam's education in the tradition that situates her in a silent center enables her to gloss the ramifications of this situation. Assuming her mother's place between Mr. Ramsay's "entreaty—forgive me, care for me" and James's exhortation, "Resist him. Fight him," Cam feels herself divided not only between father and son but also between the claims of pity and justice, the binary opposition that conventionally distinguishes the Christian from the Judaic tradition. The terms are transposed (the son demands justice, the father pity), but their reversibility does not alter the female position as a pivot between two dispensations, a place where centrality amounts to mediation. Cam's allusive language also echoes classical tragedy, especially the Sophoclean trilogy that has been a reservoir of cultural paradigms. The "god-like" brother and the "suppliant" father between whom Cam imagines herself seated suggest incarnations of the same individual: Oedipus the king, regal lawmaker, godlike in his splendor, who becomes the blind old man, the homeless suppliant of *Oedipus at Colonus,* an aged hero guided by his daughter. Woman again is pivot of this transformation. Mother and daughter to both father and son, Cam also assumes these overlapping female roles within the implied Oedipal drama. As stand-in for her mother, she holds the place of Jocasta to both Mr. Ramsay and James. As daughter she must also be Antigone (both daughter and half sister to Jocasta) and forgive, nurture, and protect her father in his frail old age. As sister, however, she must be Antigone to James and select her role from the last play of the trilogy, where sororal loyalty to brother over "father" (both her father's brother and her prospective father-in-law) is the principled, heroic choice of living death over ethical compromise.[5] Cam wants to play both Antigone's roles, to be the loyal sister and the loving daughter, but James forbids her to play Antigone to her father, and Mr. Ramsay tries to lure her from the compact with her brother. Paralyzed between father and son, between two manifestations of a patriarchal God and two incarnations of Oedipus, Cam is the ambiguous mother and maid whose body is a fulcrum in the sequences of history and a page on which the tests and texts of masculinity are inscribed. The only escape is out of the body, the desire motivating the suicidal fantasy (another echo of Jocasta and Antigone) latent in Cam's envious gaze at the island, where people, it seems, "had fallen asleep . . . were free like smoke, were free to come and go like ghosts" (253).

Cam is released from these fantasies only after James resolves the conflict with his father that places her between the two men. Section 10 opens with a sense of liberation; to describe it, Cam tentatively adopts, and then rejects, a narrative model drawn from Macalister, a story about escaping from a sinking ship. Her search for images more appropriate to her sense of adventure towards an unknown future begins by echoing the language of her mother in Mrs. Ramsay's only solitary scene, the moment of visionary eroticism elicited by the lighthouse beam ("The Window," section 11).

> What then came next? Where were they going? From her hand, ice cold, held deep in the sea, there spurted up a fountain of joy at the change, at the escape, at the adventure (that she should be alive, that she should be there). And the drops falling from this sudden and unthinking fountain of joy fell here and there on the dark, the slumbrous shapes in her mind; shapes of a world not realised but

> turning in their darkness, catching here and there, a spark of light;
> Greece, Rome, Constantinople. (280–81)

Gazing at the past illumined by this anticipation of the future, at the leaf-shaped island transformed by "gold-sprinkled waters," Cam identifies her distinctive narrative task: to hinge the maternal shape of the past with the fleetingly illumined shapes of the future by articulating the central place she occupies, turning her historical aptitude to an unwritten history. It is here that she remembers her father. The section ends with the disappearance of the island: "the leaf was losing its sharpness. . . . The sea was more important now than the shore" (283–84). The final words return to Macalister's story and to Mr. Ramsay's refrain, as Cam "murmured, dreamily, half asleep, how we perished, each alone" (284).

Unable to assume an adversarial stance towards a masculine tradition, Cam only gestures towards a story she cannot tell. Through a different "daughter" to Mrs. Ramsay, Woolf glosses Cam's dilemma by indicating the strategies that must be employed to record the "slumbrous shapes . . . of a world not realised" but fleetingly revealed in a moment of release. Minta Doyle, an enigmatic figure revealed primarily through other female characters, shares Cam's role as a vehicle for Woolf's meditation on female narrative. The most overtly erotic figure in the novel, a vibrantly attractive "golden-reddish" girl who sparks Mr. Ramsay's gallantry and Mrs. Ramsay's jealousy (149), Minta is also the most opaque. Like the hole in her stocking that signifies her unruliness to the proper Mr. Bankes, Minta's subjectivity is a hole in the text, a sign of a story that resists direct narration.[6] Hinted at through images similar to Cam's, Minta's experience is filtered primarily through the consciousness of Cam's older sister Nancy, who grasps just enough to articulate the limits of conventional narrative.

Woolf chooses the most traditional strand of her text, the story of Minta Doyle and Paul Rayley's courtship, as an occasion for revealing how fictional conventions can serve the unconventional female narrator. It is not simply that the Rayley marriage eventually fails; courtship, more significantly, offers a reservoir of tropes and sequences for Woolf to problematize. The climax of this plot, and the only traditional scene of passion in the novel, is ingeniously located behind a rock. We see the event that celebrates Paul and Minta's engagement exclusively through Nancy Ramsay's shocked, indignant eyes, and even this eyewitness report is uncertain. Nancy is "carried by her own impetuosity and her desire for rapid movement right behind a rock and there—oh, heavens! in each other's arms, were Paul and Minta kissing *probably*" (115; my italics). Minta's own reaction to the engagement remains yet more ambiguous. Woolf represents it exclusively through the most conventional trope for female sexual initiation, Minta's loss at the beach of "the sole ornament she possessed" (116). Yet Minta's loss is undecodable, for her grandmother's brooch, a weeping willow set in pearls, suggests not only the conventional virginity but also a female heritage, disrupted equally by marriage. If the allegorical value of the metaphor directs us to one loss, its quotidian particulars—"the brooch which her grandmother had fastened her cap with till the last day of her life"—direct us to another (116). When the loss is scrutinized obliquely through Nancy's consciousness, uncertainty is all that can be ascertained: "Nancy felt, it might be true that she [Minta] minded losing her brooch, but she [Minta] wasn't crying only for that. She was crying for something else. We might all sit down and cry, she felt. But she did not know what for" (117). Finally, Minta's experience can only be represented as an unspecifiable "something else" (117).

This is true of Minta's future as well as of her past. Woolf's framing of the unseen scene behind the rock, enclosed by matching processions to and from the beach, differentiates between male and female relationships to narrative. The procession home at nightfall is presented through the consciousness of Paul, who effortlessly translates an immediate temporal sequence into the signifiers of a future one: "And as they came out on the hill and saw the light of the town beneath them, the lights coming out suddenly one by one seemed like things that were going to happen to him—his marriage, his children, his house" (118). No gap divides the unrepresented scene from the traditional significance Paul attaches to the neutral chain of lights. His desire finds expression in a list that designates the (con)sequences of patriarchal courtship: though things will happen *to* him, they will nevertheless be *his*. Paul imagines conducting a silent Minta, psychically as well as physically effaced by him, through the links of this chain: "they would retreat into solitude together, and walk on and on, he always leading her, and she pressing close to his side (as she did now)" (118).

The movement towards the scene behind the rock, by contrast, points to Minta's future only obliquely through a Morse code transmitted by her intermittent pressure on her companion Nancy's hand. Nancy poses the central question for her: "What is it that she wants?" (112). (What does a woman want? And, we might add, from whom?) The difficulty of formulating an answer is represented as a gap dividing female desire and language. Standing on the site from which Paul sees "his marriage, his children, his house," Nancy tries to decipher Minta's future. Her images prefigure Cam's:

> When Minta took her hand and held it, Nancy, reluctantly, saw the whole world spread out beneath her, as if it were Constantinople seen through a mist, and then, however heavy-eyed one might be, one must needs ask, 'Is that Santa Sofia?' 'Is that the Golden Horn?' So Nancy asked, when Minta took her hand, 'What is it that she wants? Is it that? And what was that?' Here and there emerged from the mist (as Nancy looked down upon life spread beneath her) a pinnacle, a dome; prominent things without names. (112–13)

In contrast to Paul, who unproblematically attaches word to image, Nancy can visualize, but not designate, the novel shapes of Minta's desire. To record in language these "things without names" requires an antithetical strategy of playing figures against themselves. Cam, more than Nancy, lacks this strategy. When she swerves away from a story that would link the "shapes of a world not realised" with the shapes of a feminine past beyond the study, Cam reveals her enclosure in the textual tradition she would need to contest to write a different history.

"If we continue to speak the same language to each other, we will reproduce the same story," Luce Irigaray insists. "If we continue to speak this sameness, if we speak to each other as men have spoken for centuries, as they taught us to speak, we will fail each other. Again. . . . Words will pass through our bodies, above our heads, disappear, make us disappear" ("When Our Lips" 69). A certain circularity marks Cam's narrative activity, for the story she tells is the story of how she came to tell that story. It is a paradigmatic story of the daughter who thinks back through her father, a story of narrative imprisonment. Woolf's feat in this text is to read the Oedipal narrative as an account of the daughter's shift to her father's dialogue with his son(s), a discourse that situates her (like her mother) in a median position between two men. The Oedipal narrative now accounts for an attenuated female language as well as sexuality, for a language that itself attenuates women's sexuality.

As Woolf's conception of the center of her text shifted from father to mother, her narrative attention gravitated to the figure of Lily Briscoe, a peripheral character in the holograph manuscript.[7] Mr. Ramsay in a boat reciting "We perished, each alone" became a focus of the third part of a text whose longest, richest, opening portion is dominated by his wife, psychically and aesthetically resurrected in part 3 by her surrogate daughter Lily rather than by Cam. Though Cam is overshadowed by this more successfully articulate "sister," she nevertheless performs a vital function in disclosing the narrative costs of paternal filiation. Through Cam's narrative failures, as well as through Lily's success, then, Woolf adumbrates the claim from which much of her preeminence in feminist literary history derives: "we think back through our mothers if we are women."

Notes

This essay is a revised version of my essay by the same title that appeared in *Virginia Woolf and Bloomsbury*, ed. Jane Marcus (Bloomington: Indiana UP; London: Macmillan, 1987).

1. Cam's full name is undoubtedly Camilla, the name of Virginia's counterpart in Leonard Woolf's novel *The Wise Virgins*. Camilla is also the name of a legendary maiden in the *Aeneid* (7.803, 11.539–828). A huntress brought up by her father, who to protect her from their tribal enemies tied her to a javelin, dedicated her to Diana, and threw her across the Amasenus river, she has a clear affiliation with patrilineage. This affiliation and its discontents are also suggested by the nickname of Woolf's character, the name of the river identified with the university attended by generations of Stephen males. I am grateful to Jane Marcus for pointing these associations out to me.

2. On the distinctive problems of this (inevitable) collusion, generated by women's "(ambiguously) nonhegemonic" relation to the dominant discourse, see Homans; and DuPlessis, and members of Workshop 9. On the question of Woolf's own evasion of anger in her literary theory and practice see Showalter, "Virginia Woolf." Woolf's account in "A Sketch of the Past" of her acquiescence to Thoby's tyranny provides an explicitly autobiographical parallel to Cam's relationship to James.

3. For the autobiographical roots of Woolf's portrait of Cam's relationship to Mr. Ramsay see Quentin Bell (26); DeSalvo; Katherine Hill; and Virginia Woolf, *Diary* 3:208 and "Leslie Stephen."

4. In *A Room of One's Own* Woolf explains that "mirrors are essential to all violent and heroic action. This is why Napoleon and Mussolini both insist so emphatically upon the inferiority of women, for if they were not inferior, they would cease to enlarge" (36). By *The Years* "the character of Napoleon" has evolved onto "the psychology of great men," exemplified explicitly by Napoleon, which obstructs the knowledge of "ourselves, ordinary people" (women, homosexuals, foreigners, in this context), which would enable us to make "laws and religions that fit"—in contrast, presumably, to such homogenizing codes as the tablets of eternal wisdom transmitted from father to son (281–82).

5. As the political struggles of the 1930s intensified, Antigone became Woolf's recurrent figure for the silenced female hero who resists masculine dictatorship; see, for example, *Three Guineas* 81, 141, 169–70; and *The Years* 135–37. For a discussion of Antigone's place in Woolf's politics and aesthetics see the essays in the Winter 1977 *Bulletin of the New York Library*, a special issue on Virginia Woolf.

6. The hole in Minta's stocking bears a clear resemblance to the metaphors Margaret Homans cites of women's "nonrepresentational alternatives" to a linguistic tradition understood as male. For example, the cry that concludes Toni Morrison's *Sula*, "a fine cry—loud and long— . . . just circles and circles of sorrow," and the photograph of the concentric circles of The Sojourner's stump

that concludes Alice Walker's *Meridian* (191–95). In *To the Lighthouse* the hole in the "golden-reddish" Minta's stocking contrasts with the reddish-brown stocking Mrs. Ramsay knits for the lighthouse keeper's son.

7. In this version of the manuscript, transcribed and edited by Susan Dick, Lily first appears as "Miss Sophie Briscoe," a fifty-five-year-old dilettante painter with middle-class tastes. Only as Woolf determined to make Mrs. Ramsay central did she transform and elaborate Lily into an adequate vehicle of a mother-daughter narrative. For an extended account of the contrast between Lily's role as Mrs. Ramsay's "daughter" and Cam's role as Mr. Ramsay's daughter see Abel, *Fictions*.

"The Skies and Trees of the Past":
Anne Thackeray Ritchie and
William Makepeace Thackeray

WHEN ANNE THACKERAY was a small child, she was convinced her father was Jesus Christ (Gérin, *Anne Thackeray Ritchie* 21). Thackeray's homecomings to his two daughters in Paris were nothing short of miraculous: he appeared at the door loaded with gifts and books, he gathered the girls into his protective embrace, he showered them with kisses and tender affection. But Anne Thackeray also associated her father with paternal figures of a rather different sort. At the age of ten she clapped her hands over her ears in a theater to shut out the sound of Lear cursing his daughters (32); at the age of fifteen she wrote Thackeray that he reminded her of Agamemnon in *Iphigénie* (Ritchie, *Thackeray and His Daughter* 47). As a smaller child, Anne Thackeray had screamed in fear upon seeing pictures of Abraham and Isaac and tried to pull the son to safety, away from the father's grasp (Thackeray, *Letters* 1:424). It seems that Anne Thackeray considered herself the amply protected child of a deity. Yet she also identified deeply when fathers threatened their daughters—or their sons.

Anne Thackeray indeed saw herself as both her father's son and her father's daughter, a bifocal vision that shaped her particular talents and the trajectory of her writing career. Anne Thackeray is only one of many women writers who picture themselves in relation to an eminent father in this dual manner. Maria Edgeworth, Mary Shelley, and Virginia Woolf also spring immediately to mind. The dual sense of self as simultaneous daughter and son lies at the heart of the achievement of many women writers, and of professional women in general. It often creates the conditions for remarkable successes in both the world of work and domestic life; equally often, it engenders a blurred self-image that blocks a woman's full use of her talents. The dual sense of self as daughter and son grows from a recurrent set of family circumstances, takes root in a daughter's strong attachment to her father, and is cultivated by a father's twofold—and often contradictory—expectations for his daughter.

Elaine Showalter has remarked upon a recurrent family pattern in the lives of women writers: the surprising frequency with which they identify with and depend upon their fathers and either lose or feel alienated from their mothers (Showalter, *A Literature of Their Own* 61). Psychologists such as Erik Erikson, Nancy Chodorow, and Marjorie Leonard articulate the psychological theory that explains this pattern. They all indicate, in various ways, that it is the father who is the crucial figure in developing a daughter's work identity. More recently, Carolyn Heilbrun, drawing on the work of Margaret Hennig and others, has noted the extent to which fathers can affirm and prepare their daughters for the world of work and serve as beloved role models (50, 93–124). These fathers generally make their daughters their spiritual heirs and treat them as sons—often because there is no actual or appropriate son in the family.

To be treated as a son though one is biologically a daughter has vast advantages: the father is apt to give his daughter special training; likely to encourage her in a profession; apt to give her aspirations that are wide and unconventional for a woman. But there are also inherent dangers: as the daughter grows older, her father might not allow her to inherit the prerogatives of his power, though he has encouraged her to expect them; or bound by convention and other pressures, among them the need for a female companion to take the place of a missing wife, he might belatedly insist that she assume the traditional role of the dutiful daughter. In the latter eventuality, how will the father's ambivalent attitude affect his daughter's sense of herself and her capacity to work? The case of Anne Thackeray Ritchie provides us with one answer.

Anne Thackeray Ritchie was a *grande dame* of the Victorian literary aristocracy. Daughter of William Makepeace Thackeray, sister-in-law to Leslie Stephen, aunt to Virginia Woolf, Lady Ritchie lived with her family at the center of three generations of English literary output. Her circle of friends was equally distinguished. As a child she went to birthday parties with the Dickens children and drank cocoa in the kitchen of Jane Carlyle; in later years she dined with the Tennysons, Thomas Hardy, and John Ruskin. Henry James called her "that dear fantastic lady"; during her long life she amazed the British literary world with her extraordinary energy, unflagging good humor, and wild imagination.

Yet, for all of Anne Thackeray Ritchie's immense personal attraction, she presents us with a curious dilemma: a woman with the makings of her own distinctive genius, she is remembered today primarily as her father's daughter and biographer. Anne Thackeray published one widely acclaimed novel before her father died in 1863 and four more popular works before her own marriage in 1877. After an eight-year hiatus she produced one more novel but then gave up fiction completely to devote the last thirty-four years of her life to reminiscences of her friendships with Victorian writers and biographical introductions to her father's works. In her early years Anne Thackeray showed all the energy and aspiration of a first-born son determined to follow in his father's footsteps; as her life wore on, she became more and more the dutiful daughter, devoted to recapturing her happy youth in her father's home.

ANNE THACKERAY was not by constitution or nature a retiring child. At the age of seven she ran away from her grandmother's home in Paris three times in one day. She refused to dress, she insisted on eating from the floor, she argued with her grandmother about religion constantly. She had a quick wit: her grandfather remarked when she was nine that "she can receive a great deal of useful information with much advantage, and she has a mind thirsting for knowledge" (Thackeray, *Letters* 2:250). The robust quality of Anny's personality was matched by the robust character of her physique: she was tall and wide; her father teasingly referred to her as "Old Fat" (3:368).

From a very early date Thackeray relished his eldest daughter's unfeminine bearing and rebellious pride. Before she reached her twelfth birthday he gleefully described her to Arthur Shawe as "a great sensible clever girl, with a very homely face, and a very good heart and a very good head and an uncommonly good opinion of herself as such clever people will sometimes have" (Thackeray, *Letters* 2:545). Two years later he remarked to Jane Brookfield that "Anny is a fat lump of pure gold—the kindest dearest creature as well as a wag of the first order" (2:796). And if Thackeray delighted in Anny's sense of humor and lack of femininity, he delighted even more in her obvious intelligence. When she was ten years old he commended one governess because "she seems to understand and appreciate our dear Anny's great noble heart and genius" (2:292); he dismissed another because she was "not clever enough for Anny," who had a "particular bent and strong critical faculty; she will learn for herself more than most people can teach" (2:379, 382). Thackeray teasingly told his mother, who thought his intellectual talents made him one of the great writers of his generation, that "I have almost as much veneration for Anny's brains as you have for your own prodigy of a son" (2:288).

Partly in recognition of what Thackeray saw as Anny's masculine intelligence and partly because he had no sons, Thackeray apprenticed his first-born daughter to his own profession as a writer. Thackeray had numerous reasons for pointing her in this professional direction. Writing was one of the few professions open to Victorian women, and Thackeray, who had lived through all the strains of poverty as a young man, felt the urgent need of providing his eldest daughter with the skills to earn an income to support herself and her younger sister, Minny. Further, Thackeray, like any father, cherished the idea that his older child took

363

after him. He told his friends that Anny had "all my better parts & none of my worse" (Ray, *Thackeray: Age of Wisdom* 400) and was delighted when she imitated him in writing mannerisms and small writing exercises. Finally, Thackeray wanted someone to carry on his work—a literary and intellectual heir. In the hope that "when my weary old quill is worn to the stump, please God she'll be able to use that honest pen of her's" (Thackeray, *Letters* 3:248), Thackeray shepherded his daughter into a literary career. In doing so, he offered Anny all the prerogatives and expectations normally reserved for a first-born son.

Yet, even before Anny reached adolescence, Thackeray felt ambivalent about some of the very qualities he admired and encouraged in her. He told her directly: "I would sooner have you gentle and humble-minded than ever so clever" (Thackeray, *Letters* 2:223). And when Thackeray's mother bemoaned the fact that Anny, at nine years old, was "so clever: so selfish: so generous: so tender-hearted yet so careless of giving pain," Thackeray summed up his agreement: "I am afraid very much she is going to be a man of genius: I would far sooner have had her an amiable and affectionate woman" (2:240). If Thackeray wanted Anny to be a brilliant son, he also needed her to be a supportive daughter and began to prepare her for this role, too, at an early age.

It is not unusual for a father to want a dutiful and supportive daughter, but Thackeray's desire was intensified by the inclinations of his personality and the events of his marriage. He was by nature a man who craved female support and feared its abrupt removal. This tendency developed early in Thackeray's childhood when he was removed from the arms of an adoring mother at age five and sent home from colonial India to England to face alone all the horrors of British boarding-school life. Thackeray felt the pain of separation acutely; before going to bed at night in England he habitually thought "Pray God, I may dream of my mother!" (Ray, *Thackeray: Uses of Adversity* 70). Thackeray idolized the warmth of maternal affection when reunited with his mother four years later; he spent much of his subsequent life striving to assure himself that he would not be deprived of such affection again. As Gordon Ray puts it, "Thackeray came to see life permanently in terms of a dichotomy between the warmth and trust of a happy home circle and the brutality or indifference of the outside world" (*The Buried Life* 14).

Because Thackeray cherished the emotional supports of the happy home circle, he grew to prefer a certain female type: the humble, affectionate woman whose self-sacrifice and sweet temper held the family together. This was precisely the kind of woman he married: Isabella Shawe, who was frail, childlike, and completely devoted to her husband and children. Thackeray married Isabella when he was only twenty-five; in later years he loved to remind his daughters how beautiful and "how humble-minded their mother was" (Thackeray, *Letters* 2:789). But Isab ella was also prone to extreme depression; the strains of three rapid pregnancies, the devastating death of an infant daughter, and other emotional pressures proved too much: four years after their wedding she slipped into melancholy, then fits of distraction, and soon failed to recognize her husband or children. In 1840, on a trip to Margate, Isabella tried to drown three-year-old Anny in the surf; on a boat trip to Cork a few months later she tried to drown herself. Isabella was eventually committed to institutional care in the autumn of 1840, and Thackeray was shattered. He feared he had contributed to Isabella's collapse by being too absorbed in his work and too much absent from home. He felt robbed of the domestic stability on which he so much relied. Bereft, he turned to his fragment of a family—Anny and Minny—and hoped they could fill up the "great vacuum" in his emotional life (2:382). In doing so, Thackeray did what widowed fathers have done for centuries: he invited his daughter to play the role of wife and to become the emotional anchor of his home.

Accordingly, while Thackeray prepared his elder daughter to become his literary heir, he also prepared her to become the female companion who would take Isabella's place. His letters are packed with comments that express this intention. Just before Anny's tenth birthday Thackeray wrote: "[Anny] will be a young woman directly, and please God a she-friend to me" (Thackeray, *Letters* 2:292). A few days before Anny's eleventh birthday, in a letter that seems to target age fourteen as Anny's entry into womanhood, Thackeray wrote his mother again about Anny: "My dear old girl. She is wise as an old man. In three years she will be a charming companion to me: and fill up a part of a great vacuum which exists inside me" (2:382). Eighteen months later Thackeray remarked approvingly on Anny's progress towards womanhood: "Anny is grown to be almost a young woman, & will soon be a capital companion for me" (2:609).

Anny, for her part, absorbed the contradictory currents of her fa ther's expectations by the time she reached adolescence. On the one hand, she responded with all the force of her robust nature to the intellectual and professional horizons he opened for her, striving to make herself into his literary son. She modeled herself after her father: she signed letters "A. Thanakins Titmarsh" in imitation of Thackeray's own pseudonym Michael Angelo Titmarsh; she copied his habit of drawing faces at the bottom of letters; she mimicked his manner in small writing exercises (Ritchie, *Thackeray and His Daughter* 28–29; Thackeray, *Letters* 2:668). By the time Anny was fifteen she had written, according to her own count, several novels and a tragedy. She took Harriet Martineau, the popular writer and advocate of social reform, as her model for female achievement and vowed to "earn very much & become celebrated like the aforesaid Harriet who is one of the only sensible women living" (Ray, *Thackeray: Age of Wisdom* 205). Anny was, in short, intent upon accomplishing something concrete in the world of work. In May of 1852, as she approached her fifteenth birthday, she wrote, "I should like a profession so much not to spend my life crochetting mending my clothes & reading novels—w^h seems the employment of English ladies" (205).

But intent as Anny was upon finding a profession, she was equally intent upon remaining at her father's side. Bereft of a mother, encouraged by Thackeray's loving protectiveness, Anny fastened all her emotional energy upon him. She came to idolize him: she deified him in his absences, thought of him as Jesus Christ, and saw him as the source of all her power and authority (Gérin, *Anne Thackeray Ritchie* 21). She cherished her father's every tenderness and sign of affection and felt amply safe in the blanket of his protective love. Even as a child Anny made her father's concerns her concerns. George Smith remembers that he once saw Anny burst into tears when Thackeray could not find his glasses (259); she herself admitted that "I care more if my father's finger aches than if the whole Imperial family be extinguished" (Ritchie, *Thackeray and His Daughter* 69). Wrapped in the cocoon of her father's devotion, Anny warmed to the role of dutiful daughter and future female companion. As Anny's biographer puts it, her love for her father became "the essence of her life" (Gérin, *Anne Thackeray Ritchie* 268). By the time she reached adolescence Anne Thackeray's devotion to her father was complete; it was a devotion weighted with heavy consequences for her career as a writer.

THE MERE FACT of Anny's age, coupled with other family circumstances, made it possible for Thackeray to treat her as simultaneous son and daughter until she was fourteen or fifteen. The two roles existed for both father and daughter in an uncertain but unusually achievable equilibrium. But as Anny passed her fourteenth birthday in June of 1851 and approached young womanhood, the uneasy balance of roles shifted and became sexually polarized. It became harder for Thackeray to treat his blossoming daughter like a son; simultaneously, a developing train of emotional events led him to rely on Anny even more as a pillar of daughterly support.

From 1848 until 1851 Thackeray had carried on an intimate though sexually unconsummated affair with Jane Brookfield, wife of William Henry Brookfield. Jane, an amiable, humble-minded, and attractive woman, was desperately unhappy in her marriage; Thackeray, who needed womanly solace, was lonely and unresigned to the privations of living without a wife. In 1848 Thackeray and Jane made a pact: they would relate to each other as brother and sister, relying on each other for solace and support (Ray, *Thackeray: Age of Wisdom* 69). They corresponded frequently; Thackeray visited Jane in her home as often as he could, sometimes daily. Jane became Thackeray's confidante and emotional center; he fulfilled the same function for her. Though their relationship was always conducted by the strictest standards of Victorian decorum, Thackeray saw it as his physical and emotional anchor—the closest thing he could expect to domestic happiness. His attachment to Jane Brookfield was, as Thackeray put it, the "one good thing" that reconciled him to life in London (157).

But the good thing was not to last for long. In the summer of 1851 William Brookfield became infuriated over the situation and demanded that his wife sever her ties to Thackeray. Thackeray himself admitted to a friend much later that he had "got so fond of her that it was no longer safe to continue the intimacy" (Ray, *Thackeray: Age of Wisdom* 167). But he felt set adrift, desperate, and poured out his anguish to his mother:

> As a man's leg hurts just as much after it's off they say: so you suffer after certain amputations; & though I go about and grin from party to party & dinner to dinner, and work a good deal and put a tolerably good face upon things I have a natural hang dog melancholy within—Very likely it's *a* woman I want more than any particular one: and some day may be investing a trull in the street with that priceless jewel my heart—It is written that a man should have a mate above all things The want of this natural outlet plays the deuce with me. . . . I think that's my grievance: and could I be suited I should get happy and easy presently." (Thackeray, *Letters* 2:813)

In his disappointment, and in the absence of adult female companionship, Thackeray turned to his daughters for emotional support. Thackeray had already prepared Anny to become his female companion when she reached the age of fourteen; now, when she was just past her fifteenth birthday, he took advantage of this preparation to claim the allegiance of her attentions. Following the pattern enacted by countless fictional and historical fathers—Lear, Oedipus, Leslie Stephen—Thackeray began to make his care over to his daughter, who would assume the emotional duties of a wife. In doing so, Thackeray implicitly withdrew the prerogatives of sonship he had offered Anny earlier. Further, Thackeray behaved in a manner that bears a striking resemblance to what Judith Herman has described as the behavior of the "seductive father."

According to Herman (109–25), the "seductive father" behaves in a way extremely typical in a society that values the qualities of male dominance and female submission. He dominates his daughter, though he often has her genuine good interests in mind. He does not force her to play the role of wife in any literal sexual sense, but he does treat her as a wife and expect her to respond as a wife, in more subtle, emotional ways. The "seductive father" might court a daughter almost as would a lover, with gifts, flowers, and verbal protestations of affection. He might confide the details of his own love affairs to his daughter and question her closely about the details of hers. And the "seductive father" usually turns to his daughter when he is upset or angry, to obtain her solace and comfort.

The daughter of a "seductive father" typically reaps benefits and difficulties from her relationship to her father. On the one hand, she experiences this relationship as privileged and special and basks in the glow of his flirtatious and protective love. On the other hand, she often senses that her father's interest is not necessarily a response to her own need for paternal nurturing—it often expresses that father's emotional neediness. Further, the daughter of a "seductive father" might find that her special relationship with her father interferes with her own strivings for independence and autonomy. He might attempt to monopolize her time and control her activities; he will certainly become jealous of her young suitors. Most important for our purposes, the daughter of a "seductive father" often has difficulty separating from her own father as she grows older, even after she marries. She might continue to return home to serve and care for her father; she might seek out a powerful, charming protector, rather than a real partner for a husband.

Thackeray's behavior towards Anny after 1851 and her emotional response fit this pattern in several crucial ways. To begin with, after Jane Brookfield's withdrawal Thackeray increasingly turned to Anny for solace and comfort. Before this time he encouraged her to play the role of son in addition to the role of daughter; after this time he increasingly stressed the role of daughter, and the aspects of the daughterly role that verged on wifeliness. The equilibrium in Thackeray's expectations for Anny shifted; he increasingly let her know that her chief role should be comforting and caring for him. He wrote her when she was fifteen in a typical letter: "What is the use of humbugging . . . I intend when I am dismal that you shall console me if you can and I must tell you musn't I?" (Thackeray, *Letters* 3:56–57). Even Thackeray's admonitions to Anny to study hard became weighted with reminders that the purpose of her lessons was learning to care for him. He wrote both his daughters that "my darling women must work hard in my absence and be able to play polkas and waltzes to set me asleep doucement after dinner" (3:61); and to Anny specifically he said, "So now please to learn French very well and to play the piano if you can. It will be a comfort to me in future days"

(3:93). Thackeray took the ceremonious occasion of Anny's sixteenth birthday to sum up the specific ways in which she could look forward to caring for him:

> You see every year now as you grow older we shall grow more intimate, at least I hope and think so: and as it is an ascertained fact that I can't live without female friends I shall have a pair at home, in my own women, who'll understand my ways, laugh at my jokes, console me when I'm dismal &c, as is the wont and duty of women in life. (3:275–76)

In addition to stressing his own need for solace and comfort, Thackeray behaved like the "seductive father" in other significant ways. He repeatedly characterized himself as Anny's lover; in one typical comment, made in a letter to a friend when Anny was almost sixteen, he described himself as her "faithful swain and admirer, who loves her quite as much as a girl need desire" (Thackeray, *Letters* 3:215). Before Anny had any suitors, he feared their appearance. "What shall I do," he wondered in the summer of 1853, "if any scoundrel of a husband takes away Anny's kind cheerfulness from me?" (Ritchie, *Thackeray and His Daughter* 57). A year later, pleased that no suitors had yet materialized, he recognized that his possessiveness was in some sense "brutal" and selfish: "My dearest Old Fat," he wrote, "is the best girl I see anywhere: and I am brutally happy that she is not handsome enough to fall in love with: so that I hope she'll stay by me for many a year yet" (Thackeray, *Letters* 3.368). After a real suitor appeared, Thackeray cautioned her against involvement. When Anny was eighteen she became attracted to Robert Creyke, a young man she met in Paris. Recognizing that Creyke had no means of support, fearing lest Anny throw herself away on a one-sided attachment—and fearing the loss of his own emotional comfort—Thackeray advised her to withdraw: "[E]very time a girl permits herself to *think* an advance of this sort she hurts herself—loses somewhat of her dignity, rubs off a little of her maiden-bloom. Keep yours on your cheeks till 50 if necessary" (3:524).

Generally, however, Thackeray delighted that his daughter played her wifely role so thoroughly and felt that with her he "at last" had the domestic comfort for which he so much hungered. He wrote of both Anny and Minny in 1855:

> How kind they are to me! What daily increasing comforts and blessings many and many a night as I lie awake or when I walk off moping and melancholy, I think of them with the keenest pleasure and thank God for giving them to me. Why, perhaps it is better than the wife whose want has made me so uncomfortable these many

years past. I have 2 little wives not jealous of each other; and am at last most comfortable in my *harem*. (Thackeray, *Letters* 3:415)

Thackeray's choice of the word *harem* might be somewhat disconcerting to the modern reader steeped in Freud. But Thackeray certainly knew he needed wifely attentions and was utterly candid about the extent to which his daughter fit his emotional needs.

Anny, for her part, strove to become her father's domestic partner in the absence of his wife. Thackeray hated to be parted from his daughters for more than a few days at a time, and Anny returned the attachment, thinking she "cd not bear two days to pass without seeing him more often" (Thackeray, *Letters* 4:299). She lifted his spirits when he was melancholy, delighting in her ability to drive his "blue devils" away with her cheerfulness. She played music for him and became his hostess, presiding at his dinners and parties with spirited determination if not utter grace. When she stood by him on one of these occasions, she felt she had reached the very pinnacle of human happiness. "I suppose this is the *summit*," she thought to herself. "I shall never feel so jubilant so grand so wildly important and happy again—It [is] a sort of feeling like Fate knocking at the door" (Gérin, *Anne Thackeray Ritchie* 125). Though Anny constantly lamented the absence of suitors, she jettisoned Creyke. She did not wait for another involvement until she was fifty, as her father had asked, but she did wait until she was thirty-nine—fourteen years after her father's death.

But as Anny endeavored to make herself into her father's female companion, strains developed. Though she wanted to fit herself to his expectations, her robust constitution did not naturally incline her to all the accomplishments of conventional femininity. She practiced the piano dutifully for hours, but to her dismay, she could never send her father off to sleep—she only sent him out of the room. She was incapable of handling money; and she was so prone to lateness that her sister once said that if the angel Gabriel came to fetch her, Anny would say, "Just wait a minute till I have finished this note" (Ritchie, *Thackeray and His Daughter* 119). Anne Thackeray, in short, lacked the natural equipment necessary to be the graceful, humble, domestically oriented feminine type. This role was played more easily by her younger sister, Minny, who nursed sick kittens and fed injured flies on rose leaves until they recovered (Gérin, *Anne Thackeray Ritchie* 156).

Further, Anny felt strains because of her father's attitude towards her writing. As Anny moved past her fourteenth and fifteenth years Thackeray did not stop encouraging her to become a writer. Indeed, as she approached her sixteenth birthday he still hoped that "in 5 or 6 years, she will be able to do the writing business; and I can sit on the sofa as easy as the Professor of Deportment in *Bleak House*" (Thackeray, *Letters* 3:238). But Thackeray's emphasis changed subtly; the methods he chose to prepare her for a writer's career did little to stimulate her confidence or autonomy. Thackeray took two chief tacks. First, he made Anny into his secretary and part-time amanuensis for his novels. She answered his letters for him and kept track of his appointments; beginning with *Esmond*, she wrote her father's novels down from dictation. Anny began working with her father on his novels in June 1851, just as his affair with Jane Brookfield was ending. She finished *Esmond* with him in May of 1852; they finished *The Newcomes* in June of 1855. Anny's handwriting appears in all succeeding manuscripts of her father's novels; as her biographer puts it, their work together "became a close partnership that ended only with his death" (Gérin, *Anne Thackeray Ritchie* 60).

Thackeray took a second step to prepare his daughter for a writer's career at about this same time: he advised her to stop writing altogether. George Smith once asked Anny at what stage she began to write; her reply is remarkable, among other things, for the number of lengthy works it suggests she had completed by age fifteen:

> I feel much flattered you should ask such a question. I had written several novels and a tragedy by the age of fifteen, but then my father forbade me to waste my time any more scribbling, and desired me to read *other* people's books.
>
> I never wrote any more except one short fairy tale, until one day my father said he had got a very nice subject for me, and that he thought I might now begin to write again. That was "Little Scholars" which he christened for me, and of which he corrected the stops and spelling, and which you published to my still pride and rapture. (Ritchie, *Thackeray and His Daughter* 124)

Anny's reply is also remarkable for its indication of her absolute adherence to her father's desire. As her contemporary diaries confirm, Anne Thackeray refrained from sustained literary practice for eight years, from age fifteen to nearly twenty-three. She did, of course, produce informal literary work during that period—her diaries contain many self-conscious literary exercises, and she vowed, after reading Fanny Burney, to produce her own "Pepysina" (76). But Anny otherwise took her father's advice utterly literally. She stopped writing for a good number of years in what became a very difficult period of her life. When she began again, it was at her father's suggestion, with a topic he selected, and at the time he had envisioned for her writing debut several years before (Thackeray, *Letters* 3:238).

The point, of course, is that Thackeray's specific attention to his daughter's writing career, though thoroughly well-intentioned and motivated by deep love, was nevertheless domineering, and apt to stifle her personal and professional autonomy. Thackeray made Anny his amanuensis for good reasons: he needed her help, he wanted her to share his literary life, and he wanted her to see how a novelist worked and how novels were written. In short, he gave Anny all the advantages of seeing at first hand the fits and starts of literary composition. But when he simultaneously told her to stop writing her own novels, he deprived her of her independent expressive voice and her chief means of testing out, for herself, her talents and limits. As a result, Anny became utterly reliant on her father's direction and, at the same time, lost the clarity of purpose that had earlier marked her attitude towards writing as a career.

It is not surprising, therefore, that Anny lived through a troubled adolescence, marked chiefly by her growing dependence on her father and her inability to take firm hold of writing as a profession. Anny wrote of her dependence on her father herself. She admitted that she and her sister "never liked anything much until we knew he approved" (Ray, *Thackeray: Age of Wisdom* 15), and at the age of twenty-six she never felt "happy or easy until I had gone to him about everything" (Thackeray, *Letters* 4:303). Anny shuddered to think that she and Minny had not displayed enough initiative for Thackeray (Ritchie, *Chapters from Some Unwritten Memoirs* 89); she was so attached to her father's guidance that she was consumed by guilt if her efforts to please him failed. Anny was painfully aware of the excessiveness of her dependence on her father; the difficulties engendered by dependence on a protective male figure subsequently became, in fact, one of the central preoccupations of her novels.

Anny cataloged her professional aimlessness—and her resultant depressions—in her journals of the period. Beginning in 1855 her diaries are packed with comments that attest to her unhappiness; by 1857 she looked back, summed up, and pronounced upon the "enormous quantity of melancholy these last two years in my journal" (Ritchie, *Thackeray and His Daughter* 106). Anny berated herself for "wasting my time in the Castle of Indolence" (117); she bemoaned the fact that she had too many interests to pursue a single one thoroughly. She pledged to be cheerful over and over again; she resolved to make herself happy and less sentimental. Nevertheless, she stood on the verge of nervous collapse just after her nineteenth birthday and attributed her "nerves" to having no work:

Minnie has been telling me how cross I am getting sometimes. Twenty isn't a great deal, but things seem to pierce through and through my brain somehow, to get inside my head and remain there jangling. I wonder if it is having nothing to do all day pottering about with no particular object? It is no use writing novels, they are so stupid, it's no use drawing little pictures, what's the good of them? Reading Algebra is no use, I can't understand it. It's the same with Astronomy, and I mingle them all up together. I often think how pleasant it would be to have no brains, only good honest well defined bodily labor.

I had one of my nightmares last night, sleeping and then presently waking up in a wretchedness impossible to describe. All my nerves in a state of tension; any fancy gripping hold of me and getting perfect dominion, i.e. that I can't turn in bed—that my heart is going to beat too quickly, tap, tap. It is only by determining to lie still with all my might and to go to sleep again, that this sort of state of annoyance with a tremendous jangling goes off. (103–4)

Encouraged to be more of a daughter and less of a son, left to potter about all day "with no particular object" in sight, the formerly determined Anny felt her emotional balance shaken.

Anny eventually took up her pen again at age twenty-two, when her father "thought I might now begin to write again." Her first published piece was "Little Scholars"—an essay describing charity schools for destitute children—for which Thackeray selected the subject, chose the title, and did the final editing. "Little Scholars" appeared in the May 1860 issue of *Cornhill* magazine, the monthly founded by Thackeray and George Smith several months previously. Shortly afterward, Anny finished a novel begun much earlier, *The Story of Elizabeth* (1863). George Smith reports that as he was leaving Thackeray's house one day he was stopped by Anny, who waited for him and pushed a small parcel into his hands. "Do you mind looking at that?" she whispered. It was the manuscript of *The Story of Elizabeth* (Gérin, *Anne Thackeray Ritchie* 126). The novel dealt with a subject entirely of Anny's choosing and was presented in her own impressionistic and idiosyncratic narrative voice. Smith was delighted with the book and quickly agreed to publish it. *The Story of Elizabeth* was serialized in *Cornhill* magazine from September 1862 to January 1863; it appeared in book form a few months later, in April 1863. Anny's first published novel met with instant critical acclaim; people began to say that Anny possessed every bit of her father's literary talent. The novel earned its author "quite a little fortune and more" (Ritchie, *Thackeray and His Daughter* 128).

It is not clear whether Thackeray ever read his daughter's first published book—one account says that he "broke down so thoroughly" over the proofs that he could not finish them; another account says that he made Anny change the ending to a happy one.[1] But it is clear that Thackeray was ambivalent—and threatened—by his daughter's quick success with an independent writing project. Just before the novel appeared in print, he said somewhat ambiguously, "[Anny] is very modest and I am mistrustful too. I am sure I shan't love her a bit better for being successful" (Thackeray, *Letters* 4:272). Later, after the book's publication, when Fanny Kemble remarked to Thackeray that people were beginning to say that Anny stood next to him as a writer, he replied with emotion, "Yes, it tears my guts out!" (Ritchie, *Thackeray and His Daughter* 128). Anny, for her part, was thrilled at her success and simultaneously felt guilty about it, no doubt in response to her father's ambivalence. "*Elizabeth* continues to be a success. . . . My good fortune, I don't know why, makes me feel ashamed" (128).

The *Story of Elizabeth* was published one year before Thackeray's death. In the last months of his life Thackeray worked on *Denis Duval*, the novel left unfinished at his death, and worried continually that he was losing his creative powers. In the meantime, he and Anny grew even more attached to each other. After their vacation together in the summer of 1863 she felt that a new level of intimacy and harmony had been established between them, and she wrote that "we had never been so happy in our lives" (Thackeray, *Letters* 4:299). Her father's death at the age of fifty-three came as a shock. Charles Dickens, who wrote Thackeray's obituary for *Cornhill* magazine, summed up Thackeray's relationship to his daughters thus: "In those twenty years of companionship with him they had learned much from him; and one of them has a literary course before her worthy of her famous father" (Gérin, *Anne Thackeray Ritchie* 142).

WILLIAM MAKEPEACE THACKERAY died on Christmas Eve 1863. Anny was devastated by the loss and nearly collapsed under the weight of her grief, spending long hours in tears and hating the birds for singing outside her window. Though one of Anny's comforts during this period was feeling that "the dead are dearer than the living and more alive at times" (Thackeray, *Letters* 4:298–99), she immediately began to grapple with the long shadow of her father's influence, using *The Village on the Cliff* as her initial weapon. *The Village on the Cliff* is typical of all Anne Thackeray's novels in the way it deploys two obsessive themes: the need for women to fight clear of their dependence on protective male figures and the conflict between the conventional and the unconventional woman.

Anny began *The Village on the Cliff* early in 1865. She worked on it through that year and into 1866, as she tried to come to terms with her father's absence and, later, her grandmother's death. Anny remembered saying to a friend at this time "how *terrible* this pain of parting was and would it ever cease?" (Ritchie, *Thackeray and His Daughter* 137). In October of 1866, as Anny was finishing *The Village on the Cliff,* Leslie

Stephen proposed marriage to Minny, Anny's remaining emotional mainstay. Anny was so upset that she could not finish the novel; with her father gone, Anny relied on Tennyson, another paternal figure, to help her with the closing paragraphs.

The plot of *The Village on the Cliff* reenacts the emotional struggle facing Anne Thackeray after her father's death: the necessity of working out of dependence on a protective male figure and learning to stand alone. The novel's heroine, Catherine George, bears a striking resemblance to her creator. She is, like Anne Thackeray, single and directionless, and she fears the attitude of her society towards unmarried women, what the narrator calls "the just dislike of the world for the persons who could not conduce to its amusement or comfort" (49). Both Catherine and Anny are emotional orphans and cling, in fear, "to every support and outstretched hand which came in her road" (51). During 1865, as Anny was beginning her novel, she was forced to cling to every outstretched hand in a very literal way: since her father died before he signed his will, their house had to be sold before she and her sister could receive any assets. For six months, with no home of their own, she and Minny were forced to live with friends and rely on their generosity. Both Catherine and Anny even have a motherly younger sister who tries to protect and soothe the elder sister, thereby helping her to overcome her sorrow. Rosy George, Catherine's little sister, is described in the same maternal—and sweetly sentimental—terms that many contemporary descriptions use to portray Minny Thackeray: "Some girls have the motherly element strongly developed in them from their veriest babyhood, when they nurse their dolls to sleep upon their soft little arms, and carefully put away the little broken toy, because it must be in pain" (121).

When Catherine is separated from Dick Butler, the first male figure she idealizes as a protector, she grieves as if Dick has died. Her desperation—exaggerated as a response to a lost lover—expresses Anne Thackeray's own grief over her father's death:

> Catherine George somehow expected that the sun would never rise, that the land would always be dark and strange, and desolate to her; that she would find herself utterly alone, and wandering here and there in the gloom. . . . She forgot in how great a measure one's future is made up of one's past—how we see and understand things by all those which have preceded them—how it is yesterday which makes tomorrow. . . . It is all one's whole past life which claims the future and draws it into itself. The lesson given long, long ago by the love which foresaw, teaches in after-years when the occasion has come. (126–27)

But Catherine George and Anne Thackeray are most alike in their habit of dependence on a strong male for support and guidance. Catherine's chief struggle in the novel is conquering her crippling dependence on an idealized male figure and learning to stand alone; her struggle reflects the emotional conflict facing Anne Thackeray as she wrote *The Village on the Cliff.* Catherine is thrust into the disappointing life of a governess by her parent's death, where her chief release from despair becomes retreat into an imagined world of protecting men and protected ladies: King Arthur, gallant knights, ladies such as herself courted and saved. During one of her romantic reveries, Dick Butler walks into the room and assumes for her all the proportions of a sheltering chevalier, a figure on whom she can rely for "full and entire sympathy" as well as protection and support (52–53). For half the novel, Catherine courts Dick Butler mentally and convinces herself that he returns her affection, desiring to defend and guide her.

When Catherine discovers that Dick loves another woman—Reine Chretien—she becomes terrified of losing her emotional refuge. Rather than have her central character take some steps towards independence, Anne Thackeray has her sink herself yet more deeply in dependence: Catherine quickly finds a new sanctuary in marriage to the mayor of Petitport, M. Fontaine, a paternal figure whom she does not love but who will protect her and be "a friend in her sore necessity" (210). Subsequently, however, M. Fontaine dies suddenly; his death finally catapults Catherine into her first steps towards autonomy. Catherine recognizes and castigates her "foolish, wicked longing for a fancied security" (197) and realizes, in the narrator's words, that "to no one—neither to governesses nor pupils nor parents—is that full and entire sympathy given, for which so many people—women especially—go seeking all their lives long" (52–53). Catherine accepts her lonely life, determines to rely on her own resources, and when it seems that Dick Butler might finally propose, renounces his affection so that Reine, whose love for Dick is not tainted by a desire for protection, may claim him. At the end of the novel Catherine is independent and autonomous. The narrator applauds Catherine's new self-knowledge: "Her chief troubles in life had come from her timidity and want of courage and trust in herself" (280). And in a passage that could describe Anne Thackeray's own hard-won struggle for awareness and self-possession, the narrator goes further: "It is only as women grow older and know more of life that they escape from the Rhadamanthine adoration which haunts their inexperience. . . . They discover when it is too late sometimes, that the tall, superior beings who are to take the calm direction of their poor little flustered souls are myths and impossibilities" (314).

Certainly, Catherine George takes an important step when she realizes that perfectly protective men, capable of guiding flustered women in the calm manner of a father, are "myths and impossibilities." Catherine's self-sufficiency reflects an autonomy that Anne Thackeray won in her own life at this same time; it is likely, in fact, that the very act of writing *The Village on the Cliff* gave Anny a powerful tool for grappling imaginatively with the issues of paternal influence, dependence, and daughterly autonomy. Deprived of her father's "tender care and domination" (*Miss Angel* 291), Anne Thackeray was able to imagine autonomy for Catherine George; through imagining autonomy for Catherine George, she was able to imagine and shape her own autonomy, thus freeing herself temporarily from some of the negative effects of her father's influence. It was during the next ten years, in fact—until her marriage to Richmond Ritchie in 1877—that Anne Thackeray produced the great bulk of her highly successful fictional work.

But in the final analysis, Catherine George's autonomy—at least in the terms in which Anne Thackeray presents it—is not entirely satisfying. Catherine is husbandless, having renounced Dick Butler's protection; she is lonely and chastened. She is left with three children not her own—her two younger sisters and her husband's son—and will gain emotional sustenance for the rest of her days from the maternal act of caring for them. On one level, this fictional solution reflects the author's autobiographical circumstances yet again: in October 1865, halfway through her writing of *The Village on the Cliff*, Anne Thackeray took over the care of Edward Thackeray's two infant daughters when his wife, Amy, died shortly after childbirth.[2] But on another level, Catherine's situation at the close of *The Village on the Cliff* reflects its author's ambivalence and fear about autonomy itself. Anne Thackeray can imagine a dutiful daughter who wins her emotional independence, but she cannot imagine the same woman in a balanced relationship to a man. Perhaps for Anne Thackeray, trained as she was to paternal tenderness and guidance, autonomy seemed a necessary but incurably lonely state.

The Village on the Cliff orchestrates another of Anne Thackeray's recurrent themes: the conflict between the conventional and the unconventional woman. And here again the novel draws on the legacy of Anne's relationship to her father. In *The Village on the Cliff*, Catherine George is not only a young woman who struggles for autonomy; she is also the representative of a Victorian female type: the self-effacing, childlike, ultimately domestic woman. Coventry Patmore, or Virginia Woolf after him, might have described Catherine George's tendencies as belonging to the "Angel in the House"; Anne Thackeray's father might have approvingly noted her similarities to Amelia Sedley in *Vanity Fair*. As the plot of *The Village on the Cliff* unfolds, Catherine George is pitted against a very different and unconventional sort of woman: Reine Chretien, who is resolutely independent, who owns and works at her own business, who refuses to accept the hand of the man she loves because her pride has been wounded. Catherine George embodies all the attributes of the good wife and dutiful daughter that Thackeray prepared Anny to be; Reine Chretien is the questing, determined son and daughter that Anny wanted to be and temporarily became. The trajectory of the novel's plot poses an emotionally charged question: which type of woman will prevail?

Reine Chretien is enormously important both as a key to *The Village on the Cliff* and as a hallmark in Anne Thackeray's fiction—Anne Thackeray never again created a female character as strong, as attractive, as fully rounded and complex. Reine Chretien possesses all the strength and determination of a male, yet her resolute masculine qualities are balanced and softened by the best virtues of femininity. She is described in this way when she first appears:

> Here was a striking and heroic type of physiognomy. She interested me then, as she has done ever since that day. There was something fierce, bright, good-humoured about her. There was a heart and strength and sentiment in her face. . . . It is a rare combination, for women are not often both gentle and strong. (12)

Later in the novel, the narrator is not so unquestioningly flattering but still paints Reine as a tantalizing complex of traditional male and female traits:

> Reine was one of those people whose inner life works upon their outer life, and battles with it. She had inherited her mother's emotional nature, and her father's strong and vigorous constitution. She was strong where her mother had been weak. She had thoughts and intuitions undreamt of by those among whom she lived. But things went crossways with her, and she suffered from it. She was hard and rough at times, and had not that gentleness and openness which belong to education and culture. . . . She was a woman with love in her heart, but she was not tender, as some are, or long-suffering; she was not unselfish, as others who abnegate and submit until nothing remains but a soulless body, a cataleptic subject mesmerized by a stronger will. She was not humble, easily entreated, unsuspicious of evil. The devil and his angels had sown tares enough in her heart to spring up in the good soil thick and rank and abundant; only it was good soil in which they were growing, and in which the grain of mustard-seed would spring up too, and become a great tree in time, with wide-spreading branches, although the thick weeds and poisonous grasses were tangling in a wilderness at its root. (138–39)

In this passage, Anne again depicts Reine as a powerful and attractive woman with masculine traits. But the passage is revealing for the narrative ambivalence it betrays. In the first half the narrator's attitude towards Reine's self-possession is unquestionably positive, especially when she commends her for refusing to "abnegate and submit until nothing remains but a soulless body, a cataleptic subject mesmerized by a stronger will." But in the latter half of the passage, Reine's pride and other unfeminine traits become her weakness, "tares" sown by the devil, "poisonous grasses" that threaten to choke the "mustard tree" of Reine's otherwise magnificent personality.

The narrative ambivalence of this passage, as it turns out, predicts the fate of Reine's unconventionality in the plot of the novel. As *The Village on the Cliff* unfolds, Reine's chief obstacles become the same masculine aspects of her nature that initially made her so singular and attractive. When Dick Butler shows concern for Catherine George, Reine's jealousy makes her "hard and rough" (317); when Catherine's husband dies, Reine is utterly unsympathetic and practical, remarking that "widows recover and marry again" (320). When Dick Butler's aunt hints that Reine is not good enough for her nephew, Reine's powerful pride and independence make her scorn marriage to Dick and leave town (324–26). The narrator remarks that Reine's "pride, her waywardness" make her life difficult and that she (the narrator) has "no excuse to make for Reine Chretien, nor do I want to make one for her" (320). Reine retreats to a convent, where she suffers a transforming illness. When she recovers, her masculine traits have given way to more traditionally female ones. She has become submissive and has learned renunciation. She heartily regrets having lost Dick Butler; she feels "peace, resignation, regret, remembrances more or less aching" (334–35). As the novel closes, the fiery Reine Chretien has been subdued. Reine is able to marry Dick Butler, but only because two things have happened: because she has overcome her masculine pride and independence and because Catherine George has practiced the female virtue of renunciation.

The point, of course, is that Anne Thackeray felt imaginatively stirred by—but also ambivalent about—the possibilities of unconventional womanhood she embodied in Reine Chretien. Reine Chretien incarnates all the best male and female traits, all the strengths of the simultaneous son and daughter, and represents, in fact, exactly what Anne Thackeray became when she worked as a writer. One senses Anne Thackeray pouring her own natural robustness, all her own appetite for the power and authority of the male, into her portrait of her unconventional heroine. But Anne Thackeray also felt ambivalent about Reine's unconventionality and its masculine aspects and finally found it necessary to curb and feminize her. If Catherine George, the woman who grows to autonomy, must pay the price in loneliness, then Reine Chretien, who begins autonomous, must learn femininity before she can live with a man. In the world of *The Village on the Cliff,* in Anne Thackeray's own mind, in the real world of the Victorian era, unconventional femininity does not have much of a future.

Anne Thackeray explores these same two themes—the necessity of breaking free of dependence on a paternal figure and the conflict between the conventional and the unconventional woman—in all her subsequent fiction, but with differences. In subsequent novels Anne's heroines love or marry out of dependency, succeed in escaping their need for paternal male protection, and eventually remarry for love. But the second lover or husband usually possesses many fatherly characteristics, though of a more positive sort than the first lover, so that in the heroine's love-match she accepts the "tender care and domination" (*Miss Angel* 291) of a male. This plot arrangement appears in *Old Kensington* (1873), *Miss Angel* (1875), and *Mrs. Dymond* (1885).

Finally, Anne Thackeray's heroines have one even more striking similarity: all are orphans or half-orphans, and most have been deprived of fathers. For all the tenderness of Anne Thackeray's relationship to William Makepeace Thackeray, her fictional works are filled with truncated relationships between parent and child. This recurrent situation certainly represents Anne Thackeray's literal family situation after 1863. But one wonders if it does not also present her sense of the emotional legacy she received from her father. Though Anne Thackeray adored William Makepeace Thackeray, she must have felt in some sense "orphaned" by the man who promised her sonship but gave her the duties of daughterhood instead. Ironically, her growth to stature as a writer was both because of and in spite of her father's influence. It is not surprising, therefore, that Anne Thackeray identified with both the cries of Isaac and the grief of Iphigenia.

FROM 1863 UNTIL 1877, the period bracketed by her father's death and her marriage to Richmond Ritchie, Anne Thackeray made herself into a remarkably productive writer of fiction. Including *The Village on the Cliff,* she published three highly successful novels, eight novellas, several fairy tales, and numerous short stories and essays. Rhoda Broughton reacted to Anny's work with "astonished delight" (Ritchie, *Thackeray and His Daughter* 127); George Eliot said that though she generally fasted from fiction, she could not resist Miss Thackeray's stories when they came near her. Anne Thackeray developed a consuming attachment to her fiction and threw herself into it with a vengeance that often exhausted her. She cautioned herself in her diary in 1874, as she began to write *Miss*

Angel: "I must give myself four or five hours off every day or I shall break down and be utterly useless" (166).

But notwithstanding all her professional success and hard-won autonomy during these years, Anne Thackeray was inevitably drawn back under the spell of paternal protection. Like the typical daughter of a "seductive father," she encountered real difficulty in separating emotionally from William Makepeace Thackeray after he died; she never succeeded totally. In 1877, fourteen years after her father's death, she married Richmond Ritchie. This event and other pressures soon brought to a close her career as a writer of fiction.

When Anny married Richmond Ritchie, she made a deliberate return to the protection of a paternal figure, a man who was eager to guide and support her and whom she even associated in her mind with her father. Outwardly, there was nothing in the least paternal about Richmond Ritchie; he seemed, in fact, a shocking choice for a husband because of his youth and family connections to the Thackerays. Richmond was sixteen years younger than Anny; he was both her cousin and godchild; she remembered dandling him on her knee when he was a baby (Ticknor 320). But for all his youth, Richmond Ritchie was a charmingly dominant figure who recreated for Anny crucial aspects of her relationship to her father. Richmond guided and advised Anny in a paternal manner: he wrote in December of 1875, "It is rather funny . . . to find myself giving you good advice but I do feel quite capable now of taking care of you and putting a little finger to your burdens" (Gérin, *Anne Thackeray Ritchie* 181). Richmond provided Anny with emotional stability. Howard Sturgis, describing the emotional buttressing Richmond gave Anny, remarked that "Richmond's nature supplied the prop on which [Anny's nature] could spread itself most happily in the sun" (193). Anny even conflated Richmond and her father in her mind and to some extent cherished her husband because he continued her access to her earlier life with her father. She wrote Richmond in 1875: "Do you know, the last time I saw his [Thackeray's] dear face he sent me away. I just remember going back and standing by his bedside . . . looking at him, and you see after eleven years I find you my dear to talk to about him and to be yourself too" (181).

Anny's marriage to such a dominant and protective figure constituted both a return to her father and her ultimate embracing of the daughterly role—with all its wifely aspects—for which she had been so carefully prepared. In the end, Anne Thackeray's attachment to her father was so strong, and the comforts of paternal affection so seductive, that she could not resist being drawn back into the web of dependency. After assuming the privileges of the son for a period of time, Anne

Thackeray found she preferred the safe limits of a daughter. And it is likely in any case that she saw little room in her Victorian world for the kind of unconventional woman she became for a time. That woman would flower more audaciously in the next generation—and in Anny's own family, with her nieces Virginia Woolf and Vanessa Bell.

Whatever Anne Thackeray's reasons for opting for her dependent role, one thing is certain: her writing changed after her marriage. In 1885, eight years after her wedding, she published one last novel, *Mrs. Dymond;* then, at the age of forty-eight, she abandoned the novelist's career entirely. Anne Thackeray Ritchie remained a productive writer for the rest of her life, but she shifted into other genres. She wrote biographies of women writers, portraying them as good, dutiful women and stressing their happy relationships with their fathers (see *A Book of Sibyls* [1883]); she wrote memoirs, which tend to depict the literary figures of her father's world and thus recapture for her the texture of her childhood. Anne Thackeray Ritchie certainly had numerous practical reasons for giving up fiction: with children and family responsibilities, she lost the concentration necessary for fiction; she became heavily involved in philanthropic work; and she had a hectic social life. But one suspects more fundamental forces at work, too. Perhaps, having given up the autonomy associated with her fiction, she could not write novels as easily. Perhaps, having opted for the conventionally feminine role of wife and daughter, her old recurrent themes—the struggle for autonomy and the possibilities of unconventional womanhood—either did not interest her or were no longer available to her. Perhaps, having discovered herself inescapably devoted to her father, she finally preferred autobiographical works, which evoked him, rather than fictional works, which competed with him.

In any event, as Anne Thackeray Ritchie's life drew on, her greatest joy became returning more and more to her life with her father. When George Smith suggested in 1891 that she write biographical introductions to Thackeray's novels, she jumped at the chance. The project allowed her to set the record straight on recent, unauthorized speculation about his private life. But what was more important, the project allowed Anny to research and reconstruct her father's life, thus resurrecting his ghost and reinhabiting her idyllic days in her father's home. She worked on the *Biographical Introductions* for three years, from 1894 through 1897. The project obsessed her; she often relived her past so vividly that she lost contact with the present and lectured herself about retaining her balance and controlling her feelings (Gérin, *Anne Thackeray Ritchie* 244, 265).

It is to this period that Virginia Woolf's portrait of Anne Thackeray Ritchie as Mrs. Hilberry in the novel *Night and Day* dates. Woolf's depiction of her aunt is accurate and touching: it is both a celebration of a life generously lived and a eulogy to lost chances. Mrs. Hilberry is the daughter of an eminent Victorian poet and a friend to all of London's literary aristocracy. She is the figure in the novel who links the generations together with her optimism. Yet she is a lost woman, too, who lingers in the happy memory of her father's affection and prefers her childhood recollections to her adult life. Mrs. Hilberry's life's work is her father's biography, a work she cannot possibly complete because it calls up memories too joyful to let go. Mrs. Hilberry cannot escape her past; she dwells happily in it, "raising round her the skies and trees of the past with every stroke of her pen."

Notes

I am indebted to Carolyn Heilbrun for first suggesting that I work on Anne Thackeray Ritchie. I am also grateful to Judith Jordan Oppenheimer's excellent unpublished essay, "Victorian Daughter: Anne Thackeray Ritchie" (Columbia University Masters Essay, 1966).

1. Desmond MacCarthy, who was a close friend of Anne Thackeray Ritchie and presumably got his information from her, writes in his introduction to Hester Fuller and Violet Hammersley's *Thackeray's Daughter:* "By the bye, it was Anne Thackeray's father who made her change the end of *The Story of Elizabeth* into a happy one" (9). Gordon Ray reports, in a different context, that Thackeray told George Smith that he broke down so thoroughly when he began reading the proofs of Anny's novel that he "could not face the rest" (Ray, *Thackeray: Age of Wisdom* 400) and that Thackeray told Fanny Kemble that he could not bear to finish his daughter's novel because "it would *tear my guts out!*" (Ray, *Thackeray: Age of Wisdom* 400; Thackeray, *Letters* 4:272). It is possible, of course, that in his comment to Kemble Thackeray referred to his experience with the first of the proofs and that he later read the novel in its entirety and suggested that Anny change the ending to a happy one. This latter interpretation casts interesting light on the arrangement of the novel's plot: by novel's end the spirited and independent heroine learns to behave humbly and submissively; she then rejects the proposal of the man she loves because she does not deserve him; in the last chapter she is united to him in blissful matrimony after all. Did Thackeray suggest to his daughter that Elizabeth's new humility and meekness should be rewarded with a good husband, thus intimating in one more way that conventional womanhood had more rewards than sorrows? In another version of Fanny Kemble's story, Thackeray again refers to having his "guts torn out." But in this second version, the cause of his pain is Anny's growing reputation as a writer (see text, below). Whichever version we accept, it is clear that Thackeray reacted ambiguously and intensely emotionally to his daughter's first novel.

2. Anne Thackery cared for the two girls—Margie and Anny Thackeray— until they became young adults and gained a good portion of emotional satisfaction from this quasi-maternal relationship.

JUDITH KEGAN GARDINER

Male Narcissism, Capitalism, and the Daughter of *The Man Who Loved Children*

SNAKEMAN

To celebrate her father's fortieth birthday, Louisa Pollit writes him a play which her younger siblings perform. It is called "Tragos. Herpes. Rom," that is, "The Tragedy of the Snakeman, or Father," and it is written in a pseudoclassical gibberish that Louie invents because her French grammar is not good enough for her to write in French. In this tedious brief piece, the adolescent daughter first claims that a stranger, hatred, is strangling her, then that the stranger is her father. Hissing, her father demands an embrace from her. The play ends, "Mother, father is strangling me. Murderer! (She dies.)" (Stead, *The Man Who Loved Children* 377).[1]

Samuel Pollit, Louie's father and the title character of Christina Stead's brilliant novel, fails to understand this remarkable drama. "Why can't it be in English?" he querulously asks, undeterred by Louie's proud rejoinder that Euripides did not write in English either (375). Her cheeks burning with pride, perhaps as she thinks of Euripedes' strong, angry women, Louie provides her father with a translation of the play, but his angry disgust shortly reduces her to self-pity: "I am so miserable and poor and rotten and so vile and melodramatic, I don't know what to do" (379). Sam knows what to do: he restores himself and his other children to good humor by chanting the names of Maryland's waterways.

The Snakeman play dramatizes the chief conflict in the novel, that between father and daughter. This conflict has psychological, political, and aesthetic dimensions that reach far beyond the confines of this auto-biographical fiction. Stead identifies the daughter's maturity with a project of liberation and her father's domestic narcissism with the capitalist patriarchy that dominates the undeveloped world. She analyzes some political origins of psychological repression, satirizes the oppressor's delusions, and champions the female rebel who subverts socially dominant discourses and the literary canon for her own ends. By her attention to the father-daughter conflict at the center of a global maelstrom, Stead shapes this novel, uniquely among her prolific fiction, into a fully coherent masterpiece. In doing so, she alters traditional literary paradigms

384

in order to accommodate them to a girl's experience. She describes a polarized marriage in which male and female war perpetually. But unlike many other novels of female development, hers does not stop with this polarity between the sexes or with the father's dominance. The daughter Louisa grows beyond her parents, and Stead transforms the legacy of the *Bildungsroman* to portray the artist as a young woman who is empowered rather than destroyed by the "monstrous tempers and ego-tisms" of adults (464).

"Herpes"' murder inversely recalls the beginning of the novel, digests its central conflict, and ironically forecasts its conclusion. The most striking incident of the novel's opening chapters reverberates in the play's climax. Late one night, Sam's bitter wife Henrietta attempts to strangle her stepdaughter: "Henny rushed at her with hands outstretched and thrust her bony fingers round the girl's neck. . . . Louisa looked up into her stepmother's face, squirming, but not trying to get away, questioning her silently, needing to understand, in an affinity of misfortune" (23). Coming home from his Washington office and from a "frippery flirtation" with his young secretary, Sam observes this frightening scene from an outside window. When Louie tells him nothing about the incident, he cheerfully decides that there is "nothing morbid" about his daughter (25). However, he is wrong in concluding that she reflects his outlook. As she approaches puberty, she begins to shift her loyalties from her bombastic father to her miserable stepmother, who, like her, "was guilty, rebellious, and got chastised" (37). Henny loathes the big, clumsy girl, but it is a compassionate loathing based on their common lot as women in a man's world: "Henny was one of those women who secretly sympathize with all woman against all men" (38). Therefore, "Louie had not been wrong in seeing a distorted sympathy for her in Henny's pretense of strangling her" (39).

Familial violence haunts the novel. Henny threatens to murder Sam, the children, and herself. When she is desperately in debt, Henny steals her oldest son's small savings, and he promptly hangs himself in effigy. However, the Pollit melodrama ends more like a fairy tale than a tragedy. Louie decides that the only way to "save the children" from "those two selfish passionate people, terrible as gods in their eternal married hate," is to kill the parents (468). Bolstered by Sam's own platitudes about moral relativity and sacrificial murder, she steals Sam's cyanide. But she is so nervous that she pours all the poison into one teacup. Understanding that the cup is death, Henny drinks it and exonerates Louie, who watches with sympathy and horror as the murder she has planned takes place. Her stepmother crashes to the concrete floor like a felled witch, her death bringing her family peace and happiness. By killing Henny, Louie asserts her independence from Henny's role as degraded female. She will not become what her stepmother was (Gardiner, "Wake"). But as the Snakeman play shows, Sam, not Henny, is her chief antagonist. In "Herpes," the daughter futilely calls to an off-stage mother who cannot help her; then she dies in her father's embrace. Unlike her conventional little sister Eve, Louisa wants not to marry her father but to flee him; by acting out the murder of her mother, she can. Her story thus revises both Freudian and Christian models of female development, since she abjures the destiny of marriage and motherhood to which God sentences the Biblical Eve, and Freud the normal woman.

The Snakeman play represents Sam's incestuous and hostile attitudes towards Louisa; it also projects Louie's hostility and incestuous adolescent sexual desires onto him. Herpes' daughter accuses her father, "Every day with rascally wiles you ravish my only joy, my peace of mind" (377). She conflates familial love and hatred as one intrusive and destructive emotion that she must resist. In order to mature, Louie must reject this romantic tradition of stifling incestuous love, that is, of women "ravished" into perpetual daughterhood. Louisa is right in thinking Sam does not want her to grow up. He does not value women, and he does not want her to be an independent person. The novel shows the dangers of such a fix in Henny's disastrous dependence on her pretty playboy father. Henny's "gay kindhearted father . . . had ruined her life by spoiling her so" (287). She was her father's "Pet," a daddy's girl, "waiting for the silly toys her father would buy her," such as "marriage to a great name" (15). Daddy did not marry her off quickly enough, leaving her susceptible to recently widowed Sam with his infant daughter. Sam, too, calls Henny "Pet," but he needs too much petting himself for the needy, greedy couple to be happy together. Even after her marriage, Henny continues to rely on her father's financial and emotional support. When he dies in debt, her ruin follows.

Sam's excessive involvement in Louie's life is less simple than Henny's father's in hers. Sam loves little girls but fears female sexuality. Louie's adolescent body disgusts both her parents, but for different reasons. Her menarche repulses Henny, for whom subjection to reproduction is women's damned lot, and she becomes repugnant to Sam, who "wanted a slim, recessive girl whose sex was ashamed" (309). However, when he learns of Louie's menarche, her father "goggled like some insignificant wretch crept in secretly on the Eleusinian mysteries, frightened but licking his lips" (411). Sam's fascination with his daughter's sexuality and his denial of this interest are so strong that when he reads about a man accused of incest, he wants to set up a posse, not to attack the incestuous father but to attack the newspaperman who wrote about him—a "miserable cowardly yellow devil who dares attack a father in his own home, on top of the sorrow he must be feeling at finding his daughter in trouble, a little girl with a baby to come" (356).

Although the snake symbolism of her play reveals Louisa's adolescent sexual fears, her main struggle with her father centers on his efforts to control her mind and to prevent her from growing up. Sometimes he wants to incorporate her into himself, claiming that they are identical. Sometimes he imitates a maternal role. Sam likes baby girls better than school-age children, and he flirts with numerous "office virgins," whom he teaches devotion to Mother Nature. He wants to keep everyone around him children so that he will always be their Peter Pan: "I want my children forever children" (293). He wants Louie to be like her mother, his dead and idealized first wife, of whom he comments, "I would not have minded if her mind had not developed" (128).

UNCLE SAM

Sam wants to control his wife and children completely. He believes they are his property by natural right. When they show any signs of rebellion, he teases and humiliates them. Moreover, he constantly intrudes on their privacy in a way that suggests incestuous violation: Sam "poked and pried into [Louie's] life, always with a scientific, moral purpose, stealing into her room when she was absent" (309). He grabs her diary and reads her poems aloud to the other children, ridiculing as he reads. He thinks Louie should relate to others only through him: "It is the father who should be the key to the adult world, for his daughters, for boys can find it out for themselves" (355). High school gives Louie her first inkling of a world broader than her own family. Sam resents this new perspective intently, claiming that he is going to take her out of school and keep her at home until she "recovers" her docility: "I am going to watch every book you read, every thought you have," he warns (488). Because he sees his children entirely as extensions of himself, he threatens his daughter's existence by ignoring it as well as by trying to control it. "We are one nature," he tells her (331). "You are myself; I know you cannot go astray" (129). He wants her to remain as his mirror and reflector, the ancillary role he assigns all women, not to become an independent person: "You see why you must stay by me forever? I have had too many burdens" (450).

Sam sees his children as his dependent babies, as his property, and as himself. He recognizes no boundaries between himself and them and intrudes into every aspect of their lives. He fears and devalues adult sexuality, being both prudish and hypocritical. In all these respects, Sam's attributes resemble those that contemporary feminist psychoanalytic object-relations theorists assign to mothers, not fathers, in their intense and ambivalent bonds with their daughters (Chodorow; Eichenbaum and Orbach). According to these theorists, mothers merge in symbiotic unions with their infant daughters, confusing their identities, so that the boundaries between their bodies, and later their egos, blur. For the mother, the stage is a healthful regression to her own infancy in the service of empathically nurturing her child. For the child, this early symbiosis is a necessary stage, out of which the infant's self will gradually differentiate (Mahler). However, the social and psychological identification between mother and daughter makes such separation difficult for girls and later makes it difficult for women to achieve autonomy. Thus daughters often perceive their mothers as intrusive and controlling, even though they may continue to depend on their mothers profoundly and to demand their unquestioning love.

Sam acts according to these descriptions of maternal behavior in that he sees his children as extensions of himself. He believes he understands them perfectly and intuitively. To Louie, his first-born, he shows the most consistently "maternal" behavior. He says that when he was widowed, he "had to be a mother and father too, to little Looloo. . . . We were very close then . . . and communicated by thought alone" (58). In one particularly grotesque scene he tries to spit chewed-up banana into Louie's mouth as a mother bird would, saying that he did so when she was a baby. For Sam, the ideal roles of baby, daughter, and wife are identical; he wanted to mother her but also to be mothered by her: "I thought a little girl would be easy to bring up and would have such belief in me" (410).

Sam's incursion into the maternal role extends even to childbirth. When Henny is screaming with labor pains, Sam gathers the children around him as though the birth is his, and when the new baby cries, Sam is "red with delight and success" (272). Thus Sam the patriarch defines himself as total parent, father and mother in one, and his children as miniature versions of himself. Unless he has this control, he feels his fatherhood is barren and meaningless: "Wasn't his life empty, always amusing the kids, thinking up projects for them, teaching them to be good men and women when they ran off upon their own bents and a woman was always twisting them, snatching them away from him?" (442–43).

Sam fights Henny for control of the children, and Louie eventually kills Henny, but she fears and fights Sam only. Why is her father so frightening to her? Why does she not hate her hostile and neglectful stepmother? The answers are both psychological and political. Psychologically, Henny both nurtures and endangers Louie less than Sam does. Stepmother and child never bonded in infancy, and Henny respects Louie's differences from herself even though she scorns their common lot as women. By playing a fairy-tale stepmother or wicked witch, Henny embodies all the negative aspects of maternal personality and womanly role that Louie must kill in order to become her mature self. In contrast, Sam has taken over the intensity and ambivalence usually associated with the mother-daughter bond, and as we have seen, Louie's growth depends on escaping his incestuous engulfment.

However, Sam is not merely a psychological portrait. Throughout the novel he represents the political powers of patriarchy. Even though Pollit father and mother seem deadlocked in their perpetual warfare, the patriarch always wins; society sanctions his power to oppress, and this power forbids a girl from becoming an independent and creative person. Sam's character reflects his politics, and his politics reflect his character. He is a brilliant caricature, but that does not mean he is atypical. Far from it. Like many of Dickens's characters, he both typifies and symbolizes the dominant social relationships of his culture. Only someone with Sam's ego could treat people as Sam does, and only someone with Sam's ideology could so self-righteously enjoy his domination. Stead, an Australian, connects Sam's narcissism not only with patriarchy in the sense of adult male rule over women and children but also more generally: she shows that Sam's inflated self-esteem depends on a cultural as well as a personal ideology of male superiority over women; of "masculine" technology, science, and reason over "feminine" nature, religion, and emotion; and of capitalist U.S. imperialism over the "childlike" rest of the world.

One of the reasons why Sam seems so ambivalently "maternal" is that his own psyche is still embroiled in the developmental tasks of infancy—separating the self from others, forming a coherent sense of self, and justly valuing both self and others as whole beings of mixed good and bad traits. His development in these areas derailed, Sam has become what contemporary psychoanalysts call a "narcissistic personality," an arrogant egotist who sees other people only in terms of his voracious needs for admiration and approval (Kernberg, *Borderline Conditions;* Kohut, *Analysis of the Self.* See also Gardiner, "Self Psychology").

Freud thought that narcissism, which he defined as perverse self-regard, was natural to women. Because of their early development, men wished to love; women, to be beloved. Hence, according to Freud, women are less capable than men of true love for other people, just as they are less capable of justice ("On Narcissism," *SE* 14). Sam Pollit shares this sexist view. On the other hand, many women contemporary with Freud believed the reverse. They thought men were selfish, and women moral and loving. In *A Room of One's Own* Virginia Woolf claims that a giant phallic "I" obscures everything men write and that this male egotism is in part women's responsibility: "women have served all these centuries as looking-glasses possessing the magic and delicious power of reflecting the figure of man at twice its natural size" and so of inciting men to "violent and heroic action." Like Woolf, Stead links "the rule of a patriarchy" with the masculine "self confidence, that self-assurance, which have had such profound consequences in public life and lead to such curious notes in the margins of the private mind" (Woolf, *Room* 35–36, 33, 37). Stead paints clinically accurate narcissists who are also socially representative types. She does not claim that only men are such egotists, but she does show how society reinforces male narcissism and how male narcissism fuels patriarchal sexual and political attitudes.

Sam's egotism overwhelms everyone around him. Henny calls him the "Great I-Am" and "that Big-Me" who needs "public women to admire him and hold his hand" (88, 132). Although he loves only himself, he vows that he loves everyone. There is no room in his busy world for any ego but his own; in fact, there are no other people in his world. Sam projects his own devouring greed onto others. He is both a voyeur and an exhibitionist, prying into the rooms of his children and constantly demanding their allegiance, angry, even sadistically vengeful, when they stray into inattention or independence.

Like other male narcissists, Sam both envies and hates women (Kernberg, *Object-Relations Theory* 195). He holds a highly polarized male supremacist view of the sexes, believing that men can do everything women do better than women can, thus obliterating the need for women altogether. Thus he claims, in his idiosyncratic dialect, that "all the improvements in household technique have been made by men, becaze women got no brains" (349). His gender stereotypes oppress his sons as well: "Men must fight, Tomahawk (but only for the right)," he tells his boys while forcing them to hit one another (83). Yet most of the pleasure, variety, and opportunity of life goes to men, and Sam hopes that his boys will grow up to be great scientists. He expects his girls merely to marry, do housework, and have babies. His image of women, too, is highly polarized between an impossible ideal, like his dead wife, and an evil reality, like his living one: "Womenfolk ain't no good, en yore pore little Dad . . . was brought up to worship women as sweet pure beings" (454). With breathtaking comic hypocrisy he instructs his children, "Now, you know I'm always frank and honest myself. But women have been brought up much like slaves, that is to lie. I don't want to teach you to criticize your mother" (62).

Sam's ego puffs itself by denigrating women, and it also requires that he control female sexuality. He would prefer women to be without desire, reproducing annually in the legitimate patriarchal line. Henny rebels against Sam through a furtive affair with a Washington bounder bachelor. When Sam learns of the affair, he doubts the paternity of his youngest son and threatens to take the children away from Henny, precipitating her final despair. Sam calls Henny a "termite" destroying his house; his house is his castle, and his self-esteem depends on controlling everyone in it. Sam disguises his domestic domination with Dickensian sentiments, sentiments shared by all "Pollitry." At Sam's fortieth-birthday party, his vain old father dramatizes Dickens, playing both Mr. Wemmick and his "Aged Parent" (244). The allusion to *Great Expectations* illustrates the dichotomy of public and private life that bolsters competitive capitalism by providing a snug refuge from it: Wemmick's miniature castle home represents "all the innocent cheerful playful ways" with which he "refresh[es his] business life" (418). Stead's portrait of Sam questions the innocence of such "innocent" domestic playfulness.

The women in Sam's household are exploited workers, though Sam does not acknowledge their work. He confines women to the house and therefore excludes them from public life as unworthy to be citizens: "En if I had my way no crazy shemales would so must as git the vote! Becaze way? . . . Becaze they know nuffin! Becaze if they ain't got childer, they need childer to keep 'em from goin' crazy; en if they have childer the childer drive 'em crazy" (108).

The Pollit children understand the political structure of their difficult household, even though, like other families, they believe their family represents the natural order. They perceive their parents as rather like mythological deities, implacably powerful, not necessarily good, and continually warring with one another. The children believe "their father was the tables of the law, but their mother was natural law; Sam was household czar by divine right, but Henny was the czar's everlasting adversary, household anarchist by divine right" (36). The roles in the Pollit family also have their class connotations. To self-made, bourgeois Sam, Henny is a fallen aristocrat, a "worthless, degenerate society girl" expecting to live on inherited money and resourceless on her own (37). To married Henny, Sam is a slavemaster. Sam is a boss; his wife and children, his workers. "I wish I had a hundred sons and daughters . . . then I wouldn't have a stroke of work to do, see. All you kids could work for me. I'd have a CCC camp for the boys and an SSS, spick-and-span settlement for the girls" (49).

Sam is the family boss and also its high priest, preaching his religion of science and technology. He believes that scientists like himself should rule society and that they already rule nature. "You will know your dad was always right," he rags the children. "I make it rain, don't I kids" (262). Sam is an atheist who poses as a scientific Christ. He rejects his sister's attempts to teach the children about God, saying, "Now they believe in their poor little dad: and when they grow up they'll believe in Faraday, Clerk Maxwell, and Einstein" (108). As he walks past a creek, "it seemed to Sam that nature was licking at his feet like a slave, like a woman, that he had read of somewhere, that washed the feet of the man

391

she loved and dried them with her hair" (443). In his fantasies, "a council of scientists" would run the world, and if he were "autocrat of all nations," he "might arrange the killing off of nine-tenths of mankind in order to make room for the fit" by gassing them in eugenic concentration camps—an alarmingly prescient tirade for a novel set in 1936–39 and published in 1940 (349). Sam calls his solipsistic utopia "Manunity" or "Monoman," but Louie knows enough to relabel it her father's "Monomania" (51).

Although at his most extreme Sam sounds like a fascist, he usually upholds a bourgeois liberal ideology and therefore is opposed to the concept of class conflict. He does not even want his children to learn history, because the past might teach them to fight for change: "There is no need of revolution, but only of guidance," Sam says. "Wise men" will administer "good laws," so that "through evolution . . . we will reach the good world" (339). With marvelous zest, Stead shows how Sam's egotistical hypocrisies parallel the bourgeois myths necessary to those who self-righteously dominate other races and nations and the other sex. Infuriated by Sam's posturing, Henny rails: "He talks about human equality, the rights of man, nothing but that. How about the rights of woman, I'd like to scream at him. It's fine to be a great democrat when you've a slave to rub your boots on" (89).

Sam's trip to Malaya with the Smithsonian scientific expedition dramatizes the extent to which his domestic patriarchy parallels Western imperialism in the Third World. Throughout the expedition, Sam claims scientific objectivity, while he treats the residents of the world as he does the residents of his own household: they are all his children, whom he misunderstands, bullies, patronizes, and says he loves. "What a gift he had been given, he thought, to love and understand so many races of man!" (203). He wants to be the "great White Father" to a whole family of races, including black, tan, and Chinese babies: "I am sorry that the kind of father I can be is limited" (204). Behind his back, Sam's native subordinates reverse his view of them. They view *him* as the silly child, suspecting that the home office sent him abroad to get rid of him. Sam's hard-working Chinese secretary Wan Ho simultaneously escapes the moneylenders to whom he is indebted and Sam's patronage by fleeing to the mainland, where he joins the revolution for China's independence. Just as Sam's idea of the family is to make his children extensions of himself in the name of love, so his idea of the world is to remake it as the United States in the name of interracial and international concord; he looks forward to "the United States of Mankind" (202).

As the novel draws to a close, Stead connects Sam's egotism more and more closely to U.S. imperialism. He tells his brood about American children of varying ethnic backgrounds "whose only dream in life is to come and see the Great White Father—whoever he may happen to be: while my tadpoles can see not only him but me, every day that is" (71). Henny says Sam thinks he lives at the White House. He sings patriotic songs and rhapsodizes on the beauties of the nation. After he has been fired from his job at the fisheries, he takes on a new project, doing a radio show. With his deferential love of the powerful, he easily gets advertisers to promote his vision of the democratic republic. He promises that his show will talk of "our forefathers" and praise "the freedom we have, such freedom that, thank Heaven, there is no need to go through again the turmoil that now confronts poor bonded Europe" (483). In his medium as well as his message, Sam is the agent of modern capitalism. He believes that "the radio was the great new medium of spreading enlightenment" and that "if a real savior ever came, he would come over the radio. Perhaps, he, Samuel Clemens Pollit, was a forerunner of the truly great man" (483–84). His officemates call him "Softsoap Sam" because of his verbal lather, and of course he is named for humorist Mark Twain. However, he achieves his apotheosis under another, more famous name that conflates his domestic and political roles: he becomes the nation's uncle with his radio "Uncle Sam Hour."

THE DAUGHTER

Louie grows up under the law of the father—her father as representative of capitalist patriarchy. In Henny's lost-gambler terms, "life's a rotten deal with men holding all the aces" (38). Sam treats his children as technology treats nature and as U.S. imperialism treats the Third World. Narcissistic controller that he is, Sam does not want his children to grow up, and he denies that females can grow up. Louie is right to cast Sam as her embracing strangler, the enemy of her development. How can she win when the deck is so stacked? To put this question another way, how can Stead plausibly portray a nascent artist who is also a young woman? Stead directs Louie out of her familial impasse: she does not follow her mother to clear-sighted despair, nor her father to self deluded control. Her maturity is a psychological achievement with significant political dimensions, involving her rejection of paternal seduction and of indoctrination into female social roles. It is also a literary achievement. Louie appropriates patriarchal language and literary tradition to her own needs as Stead refashions the female novel of development. Stead creates a monstrous family that is also a typical one and then demonstrates that this environment can be psychologically empowering as well as damaging to its adolescent daughter.

Like the fathers of many successful women, Sam favors his firstborn daughter (Gedo 63–65; Heilbrun 50). He makes Louie his confidante and expects her to follow in his footsteps, though his encouragement is always ambivalent, unconsciously undermining her and so trying to trap her into dependence on him. For example, he writes her from Malaya, "Work at your schoolwork. I expect great things of you later on, even if you do seem a little dopey now" (229). He cannot help thinking that a woman's future is no future: "Certainly Louie would grow up to be like her own sweet, womanly mother, a blessing to some man. Thus he dismissed Louie" (219).

His sexism is at odds with the democratic individualism he spouts, and Louie learns to ignore his pronouncements on women and to identify instead with the male heroes whose words Sam makes her memorize. Theodore Roosevelt tells her to "win in spite of a thousand repulses or defeats," and David Starr Jordan assures her that "the world stands aside to let the man pass who knows whither he is going" (44). She takes the motto Throw Not Away the Hero in Thy Soul and practices her stoicism by holding her hand in a candle flame (293). Such efforts help her repel her humiliating and intrusive father. "What is fun to you is death to me," she tells him when he bullies her. "That is what the frog said to the boys, you know" (455). She imagines her own life in terms of saving myths and fairy tales as well as in terms of male heroes. She "knew she was the ugly duckling. But when a swan she would never come sailing back into their village pond; she would be somewhere away, unheard of, on the lily-rimmed oceans of the world" (60). Like many another adolescent, she sustains herself with fantasies of future triumph. Although she is "the legend of the family, whom everyone had a right to correct . . . she felt a growing, sullen power in herself which was merely darkness to the splendid sunrise that she felt certain would flash in her in a few years" (59). Her most consoling fantasy is that she is a genius: "If I did not know I was a genius, I would die" (53). To some extent she becomes like her father—not in accordance with his wishes as an extension of himself but like a son who successfully completes his Oedipal development, as a new center of ambition and self-interest that competes with him.

When Louie starts high school, she suddenly blossoms, discovering "dazzling aptitudes within a few days in the new school" (315). She joins a set of shabbily dressed girls and begins "to bounce about in her new sphere with stolid self-confidence" (315). At school she establishes two crucial relationships, both with women. One is an idealizing crush on a pretty teacher, Miss Aiden, and the other is a friendship with a buddy of her own age. For the first time, Louie has an appreciative and understanding audience. The teacher encourages her schoolwork and mothers her, sewing her bedraggled clothes and protecting her from ridicule. Like her haranguing parents, Louie is astonishingly fluent; but unlike them, she produces written art rather than wastes her volubility in family quarrels. She suddenly begins to write comic prose and rhapsodic poetry in reams. Her friend Clare can hardly believe that her awkward chum authors these romantic raptures and vows that she would "give the top of my head to have the madness of [Louie's] little finger" (408). These encouraging women help Louie separate from the locked polarities of her family.

She also escapes her family by a withdrawal into her own thoughts. She "had a real genius for solitude and could manage to have the solace of loneliness even in this community" (312). Her teacher's visit helps her to see her household through an outsider's eyes, dispelling the myths "of her mother's rich family, and of her father's superiority in intellect and feeling to the rest of mankind" (395). She learns alternative values to Sam's. Her brother notices that "Louie had her own right and wrong. She was already entering the world of power," and she braves her father with the information, "I know there are people not like us, not muddleheaded like us, better than us" (106, 283). To achieve autonomy, however, Louie needs more than self-confidence; she also needs to reject the stereotyped female roles that destroy so many promising girls.

THE STEPMOTHER

Like many a Cinderella, Louie lost her loving mother in infancy and acquired a wicked stepmother instead—this is Sam's myth about his two wives. However, Louie is not willing to abide by the myth of her motherlessness, not willing to split women's roles like a fairy tale. When a Dickensian servant tries to convince her that she, too, is a bastard and "norphan," Louie objects. When Sam tries to enlist her against Henny, calling her a poor motherless child, she disputes his view: "Mother is my mother (meaning Henny)" (309). Moreover, she refuses his sentimental pieties about her dead mother: "What do you know about my mother? She was a woman. . . . Well, I'm my own mother . . . and I can look after myself. I want you to let me go away" (488). Paradoxically, both accepting and rejecting her stepmother aid her flight to freedom by undercutting her father's sentimental sexism. Henny despises traditional female roles, although she sees no possible alternatives to them: "About the girls she only thought of marriage, and about marriage she thought as an ignorant, dissatisfied, but helpless slave did of slavery" (426). In her weak way, Henny, too, strives for autonomy, taking a lover and resisting Sam, though eventually she is swallowed by the black hole of her husband's egotism. She teaches Louie this resistance: whenever Louie's "irritations got too deep, she mooched in to see her mother. Here she had learned . . . was a brackish well of hate to drink from . . . something that put iron in her soul and made her strong to resist the depraved healthiness and idle jollity of the Pollit clan" (243).

If Sam treats Louie as a mother might, engulfing and devouring her, Louie sometimes joins with her stepmother in an even odder alliance, an unholy parthenogenesis in which they bear a strange new Frankensteinian monster child: "Against him, the intuitions of stepmother and stepdaughter came together and procreated, began to put on carnality, feel blood and form bone, and a heart and brain were coming to the offspring. This creature that was forming against the gay-hearted, generous eloquent goodfellow was bristly, foul, a hyena, hate of woman the house-jailed and child-chained against the keycarrier, childnamer, and riot-haver" (38). Stepdaughter and mother unite in the "natural outlawry of womanhood" (244).

This female outlawry has its political implications in the novel. To be free, Louie must reject the confining traditional roles of dutiful daughter and of prospective wife and mother. When she strikes out on her own, she consigns her siblings to their aunt: "I suppose, if I had any decency . . . I'd think of my little sister and brothers" (490). Thus Louie's way out of the family is the way of the rebel, even of the revolutionary. As the idle daughter of a rich father, Henny is a sort of feudal remnant; as the drudge of Sam's family, she is an exploited worker, no match for Pollitry's self-made, domineering, hard-working capitalist pomposity. The deeply indebted Henny cannot escape to another society, unlike Sam's indebted Chinese secretary in Malaya, who became a revolutionary. Louie is encouraged by models of rebellion that Henny lacks. Her buddy Clare is a "Wobbly," and when Louie leaves home on a "walk around the world," her immediate and appropriate destination is her mother's family in Harper's Ferry, site of the American revolt against slavery. Her father insists that Louie thinks of him all the time. She replies, "When I was in Harper's Ferry, I only thought about John Brown" (488).

Thus Louie achieves autonomy, the precondition for her goal of becoming an artist, by rejecting the stereotyped female roles of passive wife and stepmother witch. She also rejects her father's patriarchal views and his power to control her. She kills the mother she fears to become and escapes the father, sustaining herself with the vision of herself as rebel genius.

LANGUAGE AND LITERATURE

Although rejecting both father and mother, Louie learns from them her mastery of language, a mastery that renders her fantasies of artistic eminence plausible and proves her independence in our eyes. She both opposes and appropriates patriarchal control of language and of the literary canon, and she produces her own literary works. Unctuous and unceasing, Sam's speech dominates his household like the smell of the marlin he boils for oil. Louie counters this linguistic domination in four ways: she learns Henny's language; she ceases to listen to Sam; she makes up her own language; and finally, she revises the literary canon to serve her own purposes.

Louie's two parents speak separate languages (Lidoff). Sam platitudinizes about love, virtue, and patriotism; Henny spits vile, vivid epithets: "He called a spade the predecessor of modern agriculture, she called it a muck dig: they had no words between them intelligible" (132). Although her parents cannot understand one another, Louie understands them both and can speak like either. However, Sam's language is the dominant one, the voice of society. Henny's muck slides under it without confronting it, and Louie lapses into Henny's language mostly when reproaching her own vile and "rotten" nature. To resist Sam, she needs stronger stuff. In one key scene, she shows that she has learned to shut out Sam's gab if not to silence it. He sits her down for a long conference, yearning to confide his woes; loving humanity but beset by troubles, he craves his daughter's unending support. As he rants, he notices Louie's "drained, martyred face." "Are you making notes of what your dad is telling you?" he asks (340). Then he snatches her scribblings and reads, "I can't stand your gassing, oh, what a windbag, what will shut you up, shut up, shut up" (341).

Like Adam in his garden, Sam names and nicknames everything he owns, including his children and his house. He also makes up a dialect composed of baby talk, scientific tags, and an obnoxious running Artemus Ward imitation, which implies that his nasty badgering of "shemales" and others is all in fun. When Sam was widowed and left · with the infant Louie, his "first true joy" was teaching her; "as a reward, he one day heard her say his name, 'Tamma, Tamma!' " (116). Baby Louie thus returned the childnamer his name, gratifying his pride and ownership of children and of language, although as a baby she innocently did what she later learns to do willfully as an adolescent, that is, to distort Sam's names for her own uses.

Sam makes up his own humorous language and insists that the rest of the family speak it. In the Snakeman tragedy, Louie too invents a new language, dares her father through it, and then provides her own translation. The Snakeman play also shows her ability to wrest the Western patriarchal literary canon to subversive purposes. Lynda Boose suggests that Louie revises the Biblical Garden/Fall myth by making God the Father into the serpent and by validating the daughter Eve's quest for knowledge and independence. Louie takes her theme of father-daughter incest and her imagery of vipers and devils from Milton's *Paradise Lost,* in which Satan consorts with his daughter Sin, and from Shelley's *Cenci,* which sympathetically portrays a daughter's murder of her incestuous father. Louie wants to marry a man like Shelley, and she thinks, "(eliminating the gloomy and gorgeous scene) Beatrice was in a case like hers" (358). She declaims from the play:

> I, alas!
> Have lived but on this earth a few sad years,
> And so my lot was ordered, that a father
> First turned the moments of awakening life
> To drops, each poisoning youth's sweet hope. . . .
>
> (*Cenci* 5.2, p. 325)

Louisa casts her father as the Satan of *Paradise Lost,* who inhabits a snake and is then doomed, hissing, to become one. Most shockingly, her play daughter champions Western literature's wickedest daughters, whose ingratitude bites "sharper than a serpent's tooth": "If I could, I would hunt you out like the daughters of King Lear" (377). Thus Stead, as "mother" of her fiction, selects, uses, and rewrites some key Western, male-authored texts in order to free her fictional daughter from both the father in the text and the patriarchal tradition of the text.

Outside of the Snakeman play, Stead alludes to another canonical literary work to show Louisa's growth diverging from the pattern set by the traditional male *Bildungsroman.* When Henny is playing solitaire, her perennial game with fate against herself, she exclaims, "Anything rather than lose my expectations!" (132). Her great expectations of inherited wealth lock her into debt and passivity. Stead claimed that *Great Expectations* was part of her own family's private myth: inspired by its rich, transported convict Magwitch, her grandfather Samuel emigrated from England to Australia, where he belonged to the Dickens Lodge ("Waker" 482). *Great Expectations* softens its exposition of adult hypocrisy with sentimental allegiance to the kind heart, the good woman, the happy hearth, the noble tear, and the redeeming empire, but whereas Dickens centripetally reassembles severed families, Stead flings her characters centrifugally and unsentimentally out of them. Louisa's great expectations point to artistic growth and solitary flight: "There was a book called *Great Expectations,* which she had never read: she supposed, though, that it referred to something like her own great expectations, which were that at a certain moment, like a giant Fourth of July Rocket, she would rise and obscure all other constellations with hers" (395).[2]

Even when given the translation, Sam cannot read his daughter's "Herpes" play, just as later he cannot hear her direct confession that she murdered Henny and wanted to kill him. He dismisses this revelation as just another childish lie. Thus it is not enough that Louie learns to use the patriarchal canon for her own subversive purposes; she must also develop a new audience, one that can hear her and appreciate her. At home she builds on the surreal lore of women and children, telling her younger siblings scary stories. At school she finds a new audience, along with new subject matter, developments that foreshadow her future as a woman writer: her audience is female, and her subject is love and friendship between women. She writes a sonnet cycle to her teacher and memorizes *Paradise Lost* in her honor. At the end of *The Man Who Loved Children*, Louie rejects the garden of domesticity in which the father is a seducing and punishing snake. Instead, she leaves the non-paradise of home with no one's hand in her hand, feeling fresh as "the morning of the world" (489).

Notes

For their comments and suggestions, I thank Elizabeth Abel, Jonathan Arac, and Lynda Boose.

1. *Herpes* does not seem to reverberate with its current connotations of venereal disease in this novel.

2. The dominating and American connotations of this image may bode ill for Louie's attempt to escape her father's narcissism completely.

LEAH S. MARCUS

Erasing the Stigma of Daughterhood: Mary I, Elizabeth I, and Henry VIII

ON WEDNESDAY, SEPTEMBER 10, 1533, Elizabeth Tudor, daughter of Henry VIII and Anne Boleyn, was christened. The church was decked with tapestry and fine cloth, the princess herself adorned richly with pearls, presented with gifts of fretted pearl and gold. Great nobles attended the ceremony. Her father, however, was not present. All Europe had watched the protracted scandal of his repudiation of Catherine of Aragon, who had not provided him with male issue, his break with the Church of Rome, his sudden display of Anne Boleyn, already six months pregnant, as his new wife and queen only shortly after the annulment of his first marriage. Henry's vanity and public credibility required that Anne's child be a boy: that was the prize that would redeem the unseemly spectacle of his divorce and remarriage. Instead, to the "great regret" of the king and queen and the "great reproach of the physicians, astrologers, sorcerers, and sorceresses," all of whom had promised a male, the child was a daughter—perhaps the most conspicuously unwanted daughter in history (*Letters and Papers of the Reign of Henry VIII* 6:464–71).

According to modern notions of personality development, Elizabeth should have turned out broken or delinquent. Quite aside from the glaring disadvantage of her sex, she endured a childhood of disruption and massive inconsistency. Her father ordered her mother beheaded for adultery when she was only two and a half and at the same time declared her illegitimate. Although Henry showed signs of fondness for Elizabeth when she was in his presence, she saw him infrequently until almost the end of his life and never achieved anything like intimacy with him. Always, the extent and quality of their relationship was defined by Henry's shifting maneuvers to secure a male succession. He died when Elizabeth was thirteen, leaving her legitimacy and her claim to the English throne in question. Until her coronation she lived in a dangerous political limbo. She was more than once imprisoned, several times threatened with execution. Yet she emerged one of England's most brilliantly successful monarchs, showing occasional vulnerabilities that we could perhaps trace to her early experience but much more characteristically displaying strength, poise, and ironclad self-confidence.

How did Elizabeth negotiate the perilous distance between her early childhood and her emergence as England's Eliza, the object of more worship and veneration than ever her father received? That question has been answered in political terms: she possessed both adroitness and charisma and was able from a very early age to fend off damaging associations, make important alliances, and attract the devotion of those around her. But there is a missing chapter to this story: how did she deal with the overpowering image of her father? We cannot assume that the disruption of parent-child relationships in what Lawrence Stone has termed the "open lineage family" necessarily had the same traumatic impact it tends to have in the modern nuclear family. Elizabeth, like most children of the sixteenth century aristocracy, had her own household establishment and developed stronger emotional bonds with her day-to-day caretakers than with her less available parents. When she was fifteen and suddenly separated from a lady-in-waiting who had been with her nearly all her life, she cried all night. An observer noted, "She fully hopes to recover her old mistress again. The love she beareth her is to be wondered at" (Plowden 113). And she did get her back—the threat of losing Mistress Ashley seems to have moved her more than the loss of either of her parents. In the Tudor aristocracy, affectionate intimacy could develop between a father and a daughter, but the roles of fatherhood and daughterhood were defined in clearly public terms relating to the welfare of the house and lineage. To such a larger concern intimacy might well be sacrificed.[1] Both for Elizabeth and for her elder half sister Mary, daughterhood, like Tudor fatherhood, was essentially public and political, a relationship enacted upon the stage of public life and never separable from it.

But there were many shapes such daughterhood could take. Mary was Henry's daughter by his first wife, Catherine of Aragon, and was bastardized by the divorce that allowed him to marry Anne. The half sisters suffered much the same dislocation and effacement but dealt with them in markedly different ways. Mary, predictably and understandably, devoted most of her energies to defiance and rejection of her father. Elizabeth, much more inscrutably, appeared submissive, professed devotion, subtly emphasized continuities between her father and herself, and used the relationship in remarkably creative ways to buttress her own power.

We shall discover some of these tactics by examining Elizabeth's strategies with the language of public life—the rhetoric of her speeches, letters, proclamations. She grew to effectiveness as a ruler by taking on aspects of her father's royal identity, fashioning for herself a persona that incorporated her father's idealized "body politic" so that she could be perceived as a composite of male and female attributes, "king and queen both" (Johnson III). That does not mean that she sacrificed her identity as a woman, at least not in her own terms: she seems never to have subscribed to the contemporary expectation that if she was female she would perforce marry and bear children. Rather, she gained authority as a woman. Her assimilation of her father's identity allowed her finally to become free of it, to discard his effacement of her sex, his overbearing concern for the Tudor succession, his notion that royal authority had to be validated through the production of a masculine heir. Mary provides an illuminating contrast. For all her show of defiance, she ended up trapped within some of her father's chief obsessions, considering herself valueless unless she could produce a male heir and going to frantic lengths to convince herself and her people that she was capable of doing so.

By any measure, Henry VIII would not have been an easy father to deal with. He was an impressive man possessing abundant charm and talent. But his style of life and government was markedly narcissistic, even if judged against the standards of sixteenth-century monarchy. He was driven to demand absolutes, to perceive the slightest deviation from his wishes as an affront to his own power. In the words of a later contemporary, he was "opinionate and wilfull, inasmuch as the impressions privately given him by any court whisperer were hardly or never effaced. . . . Besides, this wilfullness had a most dangerous quality annexed to it (especially towards his later end), being an intense jealousy of all persons and affairs, which predisposed him to think the worst" (Cherbury). A more modern name for this "jealousy" might be paranoia. Henry perceived his wives and offspring, like his chief ministers, not as separate individuals but as extensions of himself and his sacred authority. His close relationships tended to follow a pattern of initial idealization, inevitable disappointment, then a sudden, ferocious casting off through execution, divorce, or some other spectacular assertion of power. He could not bear to look foolish, yet at one time or another everyone close to him was bound to do something that revealed him as less than all-powerful. The names of his chief victims are well known: Anne Boleyn, Catherine of Aragon, Catherine Howard, St. Thomas More, Thomas Cromwell, Cardinal Wolsey.[2]

Although a woman had never held the English throne in her own right, there was in theory no legal impediment to a female succession. For Henry, however, the idea was inconceivable. The chief Biblical text by which he justified his divorce from Catherine was Leviticus 20:21: "If a man shall take his brother's wife, it is an unclean thing: he hath uncovered his brother's nakedness; they shall be childless." Catherine had been his elder brother Arthur's wife before she was passed on to Henry after Arthur's death. Henry and Catherine could scarcely be termed childless, since they had a living daughter, Mary. But when it came to the succession, in Henry's eyes daughters did not count as children. Indeed, he seems to have viewed his daughters as by definition "illegitimate" if considered as heirs to the throne. Even after the succession was secured, he left his daughters' status in doubt.[3]

Given Henry VIII's markedly narcissistic style, having girls was not just the political misfortune it would have appeared to any sixteenth-century monarch: it was a deep injury to the king's self-esteem and hence to the glory of the monarchy. He was capable of fathering sons: Catherine of Aragon had produced three infant boys, all of whom were stillborn or died shortly after birth.[4] He had also fathered a bastard son by his mistress Elizabeth Blunt. It would therefore have been reasonable for him to blame his wives for the fact that there was no male heir, particularly since some sixteenth-century opinion about the determination of sexual identity held that the woman alone was responsible for the sex of the child.[5] Sometimes Henry did seem to lay the blame on his wives: Anne in particular was said to suffer from a "defective constitution"; she miscarried of a boy when Elizabeth was about two years old (Plowden 49). But such weakness could not account for the fact that the same pattern kept repeating itself with different women. On a deeper level, Henry seems genuinely to have regarded his "childlessness"— since daughters did not count—as evidence of divine wrath. In marrying Catherine he had violated ecclesiastical law, based on the text in Leviticus, and God had punished him. When it became clear that Catherine was past childbearing, Henry briefly considered grooming his bastard son for the throne: he had him created duke of Richmond and saw that he was properly educated. But there was taint there too, because the child was the product of an immoral union. His marriage to Anne, like the marriage to Catherine, was incestuous because Anne's sister had been his mistress before Anne became his wife. As Lacey Smith has noticed, nearly all of Henry's marriages violated canonical restrictions in one way or another (65n). If he felt himself a victim of God's wrath, he also repeatedly placed himself in a situation that provoked that wrath, as though to create in advance conditions that would account for his failure. For on the most fundamental level, sadly familiar to us across the centuries, he viewed the fathering of girls as evidence of defective masculinity. On one occasion, when the imperial ambassador suggested that perhaps it was God's judgment that the English succession remain in the female line, Henry shouted three times in anguish, "Am I not a man like others?" Despite his appearance of robust virility, he suffered at least at times from sexual dysfunction. One of Anne's unforgivable crimes was that she had gossiped about Henry's impotence (Bowle 202; Lacey Smith 65). Eventually, of course, Henry did father a male heir, Prince Edward, by his third wife, Jane Seymour. But even this welcome event was not quite the triumphant vindication of manhood he had hoped for. This time it was not the child but the wife who died, a grievous loss to the king because he was still very fond of her. Never could the production of a royal heir be managed simply, in the manner of a "man like others." Henry's acute vulnerability on the matter of the sex of his offspring was too obvious to be overlooked even by the young daughters who were themselves visible signs of his inadequacy.

Mary was seventeen when her father finally succeeded in divorcing her mother—old enough to bitterly resent her sudden loss of status. Despite strong pressure from her father and his chief ministers, she continued, in Henry's irate language, to "arrogantly usurp the title of Princess" and deny that she was a disinherited bastard (Plowden 42). Mary did many of the psychologically comprehensible things we might have expected Elizabeth to do. She took up her mother's cause against her father, clinging to Catherine's Catholicism despite the king's demands that she become Protestant. At one point, Henry tried to force Catherine into accepting the divorce by threatening to "withdraw his fatherly love" from her daughter. But Catherine still would not give in, and Mary was just as obdurate, holding out courageously through several years of constant intimidation and even after her mother's death. During the brief two and a half years of Henry's marriage to Anne Boleyn, Mary refused to pay the required deference to her younger half sister and, except for brief periods of rapprochement, never forgot Elizabeth's usurpation of her own legitimate daughterhood. Finally, after Anne's execution, she capitulated, reportedly on the advice of Emperor Charles V but perhaps also because the usurper Elizabeth was now no more privileged than she. She signed articles acknowledging the "King's Highness" head of the Church of England and his marriage to Catherine "by God's law and Man's law incestuous and unlawful" (Neale, *Queen Elizabeth* 10; Plowden 37–60). By this declaration of her bastardy, ironically, Mary was publicly and joyously reconciled to her father, whom she had not seen for five years. But secretly she felt remorse, sending to the pope for absolution from her betrayal of her faith and continuing to identify with her mother's Spanish heritage rather than the English culture of her father. Her feelings towards Henry were not unremittingly hostile, particularly with the passage of the years; but she never abandoned her close ties to her mother's Spanish and papal allies.

After the early death of Edward VI, the unthinkable female succession became reality, and Mary was crowned queen. She quickly began to translate her allegiances into political action, undoing England's rupture with the Church of Rome and other key Henrician policies. Her proclamations only rarely referred to Henry, symbolically effacing him as he had once effaced her.[6] She occasionally made statements linking herself with her father, but like the actual measures she took, they pointed at disjunction rather than continuity. For example, when she was attempting to prosecute Elizabeth for treason and her council had the temerity to bring a letter from Elizabeth protesting her innocence, Mary railed that they would never have dared such defiance in her father's time. She wished, illogically, "that he were alive again, if only for a month," to impose obedience upon her ministers (Plowden 163). The outburst is significant: despite her campaign to undo her father's policies, she perceived him as having been strong, herself as weak and in need of a powerful figure to control the machinery of government. Within a year she had negotiated a marriage with Prince Philip of Spain, who took over many of her administrative duties, while she, although somewhat advanced in years, set herself the task of conceiving a male heir who would ensure England's continuing safety from the heresy of her father. Within weeks of the marriage she thought herself pregnant. When the first papal legate since pre-Reformation times arrived with a revocation of the pope's excommunion of England, she felt her child quicken in her womb, leaping in acknowledgement of her country's restoration to the faith (Plowden 180). In the same way, according to familiar Biblical tradition, John the Baptist had leaped in the womb of Elizabeth to salute the unborn Savior (Luke 1:41; Voragine 323). It is a revealing episode: the Biblical Elizabeth, barren and past childbearing, was granted a son by God as a reward for her faith and steadfast devotion. Queen Mary, at the age of thirty-eight, seems to have perceived her pregnancy in similar terms, as a miraculous reward for her fidelity to the cause of Catholicism.

The sad aftermath is well known. Mary's pregnancy advanced in seemingly normal fashion, and as the expected child came due, she prepared for her lying in. Nursemaids, midwives, and court ladies were at hand, and all was breathless expectancy. Rumors went out that a son had been born to her "with little pain and no danger." But the celebratory bonfires fizzled when the news proved false. Months passed, but the queen was not delivered: the long wait became first an embarrassment, then a joke. Mary had all the appearances of pregnancy, including swollen and lactating breasts, according to one report, but suffered from pseudocyesis—either some physical disease that triggered the signs of imminent parturition or, more probably, hysterical pregnancy, which in better documented cases has been known to take such extreme forms.[7] When it became obvious that no heir was forthcoming, Philip suddenly discovered that he had pressing business in Spain and left Mary to endure the excruciating humiliation alone. He finally returned some two

405

years later, and her symptoms immediately recurred. Pathetically, she kept her condition a secret for seven months, to ensure that this time the pregnancy was real, but again she was mistaken. Even though Queen Mary reversed so many of her father's policies, trying to fashion her reign into a showcase for triumphant Catholicism, she reenacted his desperation over producing an heir and shared his belief that failure to do so was a demonstration of deep inadequacy. There is a strong family resemblance between Henry VIII's flamboyant pageant of the pregnancy of Anne Boleyn, confidently predicted to produce a healthy male, and the drawn-out spectacle of Queen Mary's pseudocyesis. Both were played out before the eyes of all Europe; both ended in shame and confusion.

There was perhaps a lesson to be learned from such fiascos: not to arouse expectations of a succession. Elizabeth Tudor may never have married in any case—her mother's execution, her father's parade of wives, and the tragic farce of her sister's marriage in themselves would have generated skepticism about the value and endurance of wedlock. Nevertheless, her lifelong refusal even to place herself in a situation that would make a Tudor succession possible was the only sure way of avoiding the circumstances that had brought her father and sister so much anguish and political embarrassment. Unlike Mary, Elizabeth was far too young to comprehend her plight when her mother was put to death and she herself was declared illegitimate. Her household continued to operate in much the same fashion (although at one point her governess had to send a plea for money), and she was to an extent sheltered from the trauma of Anne's trial and execution. Her supposed reaction at the age of two and a half to the declaration of her illegitimacy—"How haps it, Governor, yesterday my lady Princess, today but my lady Elizabeth?" (Plowden 61)—is almost certainly apocryphal. Indeed, most of the stories attributing to Elizabeth anxieties replicating her father's or her sister's are very slenderly documented—not because she could not experience such emotions, but because from a very early age she conducted herself with such inscrutable aplomb that no one could be sure whether or not she did. If Mary reenacted Henry's vulnerabilities, Elizabeth resurrected his strengths. Not only did she resemble him in appearance, in her personal charm, and in the range of her talents, but she spoke of him frequently in ways that caused observers to associate father and daughter. During Mary's reign court observers noted of Elizabeth by contrast with Mary, "She prides herself on her father and glories in him; everybody saying that she also resembles him more than the Queen does" (*Calendar of State Papers Venetian* 6.2:1059). While Mary was immersing herself in things Spanish, Elizabeth emphasized her English blood, her connection with the Tudor line (Neale, *Queen Elizabeth* 69–70). Even years before there was any assurance that she would become queen, she was closely associated in people's minds with positive, regal aspects of her father.

Almost to the end, Mary resisted acknowledging Elizabeth heir to the English throne. The uncertainty of her status had its good points: it was easier for Elizabeth to dodge the various plots to marry her off than if Mary had publicly proclaimed her heir apparent. Finally, when Mary was only a few weeks from death and it was clear that she would not be able to carry out her plans for England, she was pressed into naming Elizabeth as her successor, though she also requested that Elizabeth maintain English Catholicism. At the age of twenty-five Elizabeth was crowned queen. Her coronation pageant underscored what for years had been a major element of her self-presentation and the public's perception of her: she was her father's daughter. The first show was a three-tiered arch displaying Unity and Concord. On the bottom tier were represented Henry VII and his queen; on the next, Henry VIII and Anne Boleyn (redeemed after so many years of obloquy); and on the top, Elizabeth I (Neale, *Queen Elizabeth* 60).

Few would have predicted, however, that the Tudor succession would stop there, with Elizabeth on the summit alone, supported by her father and grandfather. Everyone expected her to marry. Philip was certain that Elizabeth, like his deceased wife Mary, would wish to be relieved "of those labours which are only fit for men" (Neale, *Queen Elizabeth* 67), and he laid plans to marry her himself. But Elizabeth instinctively recognized that her identification with Tudor strength would be fatally compromised by any participation in the institution that had revealed Tudor weakness. Her steadfast refusal to marry and create a succession had its own political costs: until she was past childbearing, counselors and parliamentarians kept pressuring her to take a husband, and her biographers are divided over whether she might genuinely have been willing to give up her single state if circumstances had favored her marriage.[8] But what is important for our purposes is that nobody knew with certainty. She conducted her flirtations, her courtships, in a way that kept contemporaries guessing, as uncertain as we remain today about the level of her interest in any given attachment. She used such traditionally womanly strategies to obscure her intentions and tease her public into thinking that she would eventually play the woman's part and marry, but simultaneously she cultivated another set of public identities that enhanced her authority as her father's daughter.

There has been tremendous interest lately in the mythicized self-representations that Queen Elizabeth either created or allowed her subjects to confer upon her. She was the divine Astraea returned or, in place of the Holy Virgin banished from Protestant spirituality, a secularized Virgin Mother to the nation. She was a Queen of Shepherds, a new

Deborah, a Cynthia or Diana, the unreachable object of male desire and worship. All of these images of the queen are familiar to us from the language of sixteenth-century poets and courtiers. But alongside such womanly identifications, which she certainly did nothing to discourage, the queen developed a set of symbolic male identities that are much less familiar to us, in part because they surface most frequently in her speeches and public pronouncements, in part because her rhetoric confounds our own preconceived notions about gender. Queen Elizabeth presented herself to the nation as both man and woman, queen and king, mother and first-born son. Especially in times of particular crisis, she emphasized the male component of her identity, her participation in the kingship of her father. As a virgin queen she was anomalous, set apart from the usual sexual divisions. Her virginity exempted her from most of the recognized categories of female experience, allowing her to preserve her independence while simultaneously tapping into the emotional power behind the images of wife and mother through fictionalized versions of herself. But the identity that lay behind all the others and lent them much of their authority was her identity as ruler. Elizabeth envisioned this primary public identity in clearly male terms, at first as a continuation of the public identity of her father but eventually as a "kingship" in her own right.

Even years before she was crowned or had any assurance that she would be, Elizabeth seems to have believed that women in power needed to appropriate the language of kingship. Her letters to Queen Mary are almost startling in the ways they associate her sister with the language of male rule. One famous appeal begins, "If any ever did try this old saying that a King's word was more than another man's oath, I most humbly beseech your Majesty to verify it in me, and to remember your last promise" (Plowden 161). In another, protesting her innocence of treason towards her sister's reign, Elizabeth again surrounds Mary with the aura of male monarchy, vowing that she does not share the "rebellious hearts and devilish intents" of those who showed malice towards "their anointed king" (Plowden 195). The rhetorical effect is subtle, but striking. Was she flattering Mary in order to win her pardon? Or was she, perhaps unconsciously, offering advice, suggesting a public identity that would enhance Mary's capacity to rule? Elizabeth's language parallels an attempt by Mary's advisers early in her reign to associate her with the discourse of male authority (Heisch, "Rhetoric"). But Mary herself ceded such language and the power it evoked to Philip, partaking only through him in the glory of a king. Elizabeth as queen had the task of making the language of monarchy her own as a woman, but without creating the subversion that appropriation of male discourse could easily imply.[9]

There was a concept in English law that made the appropriation not only possible but necessary—the medieval concept of the King's Two Bodies, which the early Tudors had brought to new significance as part of their expansion of the power of the monarchy. According to the traditional formulation, the monarch is at once a frail earthly being, subject to death and disease, and an immortal being, the incarnation of a sacred principle of kingship that exists along with the merely mortal body from the monarch's first anointment as king.[10] Henry VIII's narcissism had caused him to deemphasize the mere mortal component of his identity. If anything, the doctrine of the King's Two Bodies made it harder for him to envision a woman as heir than it might otherwise have been: how could one of his daughters, a visible sign of his inadequacy, possibly embody the perfection of his regal identity? But the concept had clear utility for monarchs with more obvious liabilities than he had. It was crucial to advisers of the boy king Edward VI, who insisted that the transcendent powers of his office resided in him despite the childish weakness of his person. The same strategy was used at the beginning of Mary's reign to counter anxieties about the presence of a "weak" woman on the throne, although her marriage and open dependence on Philip undermined its credibility. It was left to Elizabeth to explore the doctrine's rhetorical potential: she frequently appealed to her composite nature as queen. Her "body natural" was the body of a frail woman; her "body politic" was the body of a king, carrying the strength and masculine spirit of the best of her male forebears, especially of the late king Henry VIII, whom she was said to resemble so strongly.

Let us take a fairly late example first because of its particular clarity. By 1588 Philip was no longer a potential suitor to Elizabeth but an enemy threatening England with his formidable Spanish Armada. Elizabeth rode out to inspect the English troops massed at Tilbury in 1588 and, in her famous Armada speech, offered herself as a model of kingly courage: "I have the body of a weak and feeble woman, but I have the heart and stomach of a king, and of a king of England too." On this martial occasion, her costume gave visual embodiment to her verbal appeal. She carried a truncheon as she rode between the ranks and wore upon her breast a "silver cuirass"—appropriate covering for the heart and stomach of a king. Poets commemorating the occasion drew the conclusions her language and attire had been designed to suggest, praising her "tough manliness," her "*mascula vis*," her likeness to her father Henry VIII, "Whose valour wanne this *Island* great renowne."[11]

The urgency of the Spanish threat and the queen's Amazonian attire made her Tilbury performance atypical, the only documented occasion on which she donned male clothing. On other occasions she was more subtle, asserting her "male" prerogative through language rather than dress. In marked contrast to Mary, who had been uncomfortable with such discourse, Elizabeth appealed very frequently to her male authority as the embodiment of sacred monarchy and gave the ideal special emphasis when she needed to enforce her will upon a group of recalcitrant men. Mary had never spoken to Parliament. Elizabeth did. As early as 1563, for example, when she first encountered significant parliamentary opposition, she argued before that body, "The weight and greatness of this matter might cause in me, being a woman wanting both wit and memory, some fear to speak and bashfulness besides, a thing appropriate to my sex. But yet, the princely seat and kingly throne wherein God (though unworthy) hath constituted me, maketh these two causes to seem little in mine eyes, though grievous perhaps to your ears" (Neale, *Parliaments* 1:107–8).[12] Or to take a more elaborate example from 1566, in response to a petition that she marry and declare a successor:

> As for my own part, I care not for death; for all men are mortal. And though I be a woman, yet I have as good a courage, answerable to my place, as ever my father had. I am your anointed Queen. I will never be by violence constrained to do anything. I thank God I am endued with such qualities that if I were turned out of the realm in my petticoat, I were able to live in any place in Christendom.
>
> Your petition is to deal in the limitation of the succession. At this present it is not convenient; . . . But as soon as there may be a convenient time, and that it may be done with least peril unto you—although never without great danger unto me—I will deal therein for your safety, and offer it unto you as your Prince and head, without request; for it is monstrous that the feet should direct the head. (Neale, *Parliaments* 1:149–50)[13]

These passages adapt the theory of the King's Two Bodies to a rhetorical formula that Elizabeth I was to use successfully throughout her reign. She concedes to male discomfort at being commanded by a woman through her open acknowledgment of her weakness. But that disarming confession of the visible truth disables her audience's resistance to the invisible truth that follows. As monarch she exceeds them all; her participation in the undying principle of kingship outranks their masculinity. Small chance that she would be turned out of the nation in her petticoat! That belated reference to her femininity in the 1566 speech, appearing after the appeal to her father's authority and her continuation of his "place," takes on almost the quality of self-inflicted sacrilege. Her self-demeaning corners the market on that potential strategy and renders it unavailable to her subjects. Henry VIII had insisted on his absolute strength and thereby made himself vulnerable to any revelation of weakness. Elizabeth I adopted precisely the opposite strategy, setting forth the "defect" of her womanhood from the outset, using that to mask her hidden strength, a strength she portrayed in terms of her participation in the "immortal body" or monarchy.

We could argue that such appeals to kingship do not amount to the construction of a second, male identity. But Elizabeth I used a number of other strategies that reinforced the sense of her "body politic" as a continuation of her father's. For one thing, she took great care with the vocabulary used to describe her position on the throne. She had no objection to the term *queen* and used it herself throughout her reign. But much more habitually, she referred to herself as *prince*. The word's most basic sixteenth-century meaning was ruler, especially male ruler; it was also applied to the eldest son of a reigning monarch. The equivalent female term was *princess*. But although Queen Elizabeth was frequently called princess in the early years of her reign and used the word of herself, with the passing of time that feminine epithet tended to disappear in favor of the more masculine *prince*. *Princess* was, in the queen's own later usage, a term of disparagement applied to discredited female monarchs such as Mary, Queen of Scots. While she and Mary Stuart were on friendly terms, her letters acknowledged Mary's authority by conferring upon her the language of male monarchy. But after the Scottish queen had fallen in her esteem, Elizabeth subtly tipped the balance of power by abandoning that discourse. In her policy statements weighing the fate of the Scottish "princess" Mary, Elizabeth calls herself "prince."[14]

We can trace the gradual masculinization of Queen Elizabeth's epithets quite clearly in the formulaic openings to her proclamations. Mary Tudor's proclamations had, as often as not, begun "The Queen our sovereign Lady," with explicit reference to her sex. That formula is also quite common at the beginning of Elizabeth's reign, sometimes tied to elaborate formulaic tributes to her father, "the noble King of famous memory, King Henry VIII, father to our sovereign lady the Queen's majesty" (Hughes and Larkin 2:257). But gradually in Elizabeth's proclamations, at least some of which she wrote herself, *lady* tends to be replaced by more sexually ambiguous formulas: first "The Queen's majesty," then more elaborate formulas such as "the Queen's most excellent majesty in her princely nature considering" or "Monarch and prince sovereign" substituting for the earlier "sovereign lady." In very late proclamations *lady* disappears even in formulaic references to Elizabeth's father, who becomes "the Queen's majesty's dearly beloved father of famous memory, King Henry VIII." Early proclamations frequently refer to Queen Elizabeth as "princess," but late ones almost never. The formula "The Queen our sovereign Lady" lingers on in contexts for which an evocation of her feminine nature is particularly appropriate—in time of plague, when the measures she has taken assume the aura of maternal concern for her stricken people, or famine, in connection with feeding the hungry.[15] But otherwise she was always a "prince." In parliamentary speeches or court audiences it was quite common for the queen to be addressed as "princess"; in her response she would deftly underline her own authority by referring to herself as "prince." Subtly, perhaps not always consciously, she constructed a vocabulary of rule that was predominantly male-identified. Gradually, perhaps not consciously, her subjects yielded to the symbolic truths she sought to convey through her precision with vocabulary and modeled their language upon her own.

At the very end of her life, as her "mortal body" became older and frailer, the queen insisted more strongly upon the male component of her regal identity and began to refer to herself with increasing frequency as "king." In her famous Golden Speech of 1601, which was printed and disseminated throughout England, she protested, in a variation of the rhetorical formula that had served her well for forty years:

> I know the title of a King is a glorious title; but assure yourself that the shining glory of princely authority hath not so dazzled the eyes of our understanding, but that we well know and remember that we also are to yield an account of our actions before the great Judge. To be a King and wear a crown is a thing more glorious to them that see it, than it is pleasant to them that bear it. For myself, I was never so much enticed with the glorious name of a King or royal authority of a Queen, as delighted that God hath made me His instrument to maintain His truth and glory. . . . Shall I ascribe anything to myself and my sexly weakness? I were not worthy to live then; and, of all, must unworthy of the mercies I have had from God, who hath given me a heart that yet never feared any foreign or home enemy. (Neale, *Parliaments* 2:388–91)

In a message to Parliament that same year, the Speaker noted, "She said her kingly prerogative (for so she termed it) was tender" (Neale, *Parliaments* 2:385). "For so she termed it": the queen's contemporaries were aware of something distinctly anomalous in her adoption of male epithets for her "body politic." But they also grasped what she was trying to convey, commenting that in her "Stately and Majestick comportment" she carried "more of her Father than Mother" and that she had "too stately a stomach to suffer a commander"; she was "king and queen both" (Johnson 111; Naunton 15).[16] Even foreign monarchs made similar observations, Henry IV of France exclaiming of her by contrast with other European monarchs, "She only is a king! She only knows how to rule!" (Neale, *Queen Elizabeth* 377).

As king and queen both, how could she accommodate a husband? It is almost comical to note how during the early years of her reign, when Elizabeth at least appeared to entertain the possibility of marriage, she used her chosen epithet "prince" to cool potential suitors. We might suppose that being wooed would bring out her feminine side, as it did in the symbolic, half-playful courtship of admirers such as Sir Walter Raleigh. But when she was wooed in earnest, she tended to insist on her status as a prince: the subtle masculine identification of her language repulsed the potential lover even as she seemed in other ways to encourage him (Elizabeth I 145). One of her usual ploys when Parliament or her advisers pleaded with her to marry was to insist that she was already married to her kingdom. On one such occasion early in her reign she held up the hand bearing her coronation ring, seeming to portray herself symbolically as the nation's wife. But as time went on, she more and more frequently placed herself in the role of husband. In 1596, for example, she claimed, "Between Princes and their Subjects there is a most straight tye of affections. As chaste women ought not to cast their eye upon any other than their husbands, so neither ought subjects to cast their eyes upon any other Prince, than him whom *God* hath given them. I would not have my sheepe branded with another mans marke; I would not they should follow the whistle of a strange Shepheard" (Camden 469).

One of Queen Elizabeth's most clearly womanly self-portrayals was as Virgin Mother to her people. She used this role throughout her reign, particularly when the matter of the succession reared its ugly head: how, she would protest, could her people demand that she marry and produce an heir when she was already mother to them all? In an interesting recent paper, Carole Levin has shown how versions of the unsolved problem of the succession would surface to plague her at moments of political vulnerability. There were persistent rumors that the boy king Edward VI was still alive and ready to claim his throne; several imposters claimed to be the long-lost king; there were rumors that she had given birth to illegitimate children; a particularly impudent rebel protested "that the land had been happy if Her Majesty had been cut off twenty years since, so that some noble prince might have reigned in her stead"— that prince, of course, being male (57–61).

The longing for a male successor to Elizabeth was unquestionably intense, even among the queen's most adoring subjects. One of the ways she tried to assuage that longing was by depicting herself, on a subliminal, symbolic level, as a son, her own son—the son her father and sister had spent such anxiety trying to produce. Her favored term *prince* conveys this to some degree: even though it was a generic term for monarch, its more specific use was for a male heir apparent. Her perpetual status as young virgin or "virgin Prince" even as she passed beyond the childbearing years may have fostered the idea of her sonship, since in the sixteenth century women, like boys, were commonly regarded as immature men (Dusinberre 95).[17] Costume emphasized the connection. As anyone who has viewed the portrait of the Sidney children at Penshurst has noted, just like their mother and sisters, young Tudor boys wore skirts, with only a sword at their side to suggest their sexual differentiation. So long as Elizabeth I's identity continued to allow the symbolic potential of growth into manhood, however irrational that hope was given the fact of her womanhood, she was able to alleviate at least some of the longing for an heir.

Occasionally, her political rhetoric seems to deploy language in ways that foster the fantasy. When Mary, Queen of Scots, gave birth to a prince, Prince James, the English still hoped for the like from Elizabeth. According to one report, she took the news of Mary's success very hard, halting the evening's merriment and bursting out to some of her court ladies, "The Queen of Scotland is lighter of a fair son, and I am but a barren stock!" (Neale, *Queen Elizabeth* 137). This story, like others attributing such spontaneous sentiment to the queen, is almost certainly apocryphal, recorded only by Mary's Scottish emissary years after the event. But Mary Stuart's production of an heir did fuel English unrest over the succession. Matters became particularly delicate when James was hailed by the Scots as "Prince of Scotland, England, France and Ireland." Queen Elizabeth issued a proclamation denying rumors that Prince James was to "be delivered into her majesty's hands, to be nourished in England as she should think good," and that Elizabeth meant to control the Scottish succession if the "young Prince" should die "without bairns." In this context, the word *prince* is used to mean male heir to the throne. But the language that follows seems subtly to suggest that the English have no need of such a prince and such rumors. Elizabeth herself is their prince: she "is (and by God's grace intendeth during her life to be) a prince of honor and a maintainer of truth" (Hughes and Larkin 2:308). Her gradual substitution of *king* for *prince* towards the end of her rule suggests that she had achieved autonomy in her use of the discourse of monarchy. She no longer needed to present herself symbolically as her father's son, but had grown to political "manhood" in her own right, eclipsing Henry VIII's glory in her own life and rule. Like the emblematic phoenix, a device closely associated with the queen, she embodied her own succession—she was queen, king, and prince—encompassing within her own nature the separate beings required for an actual generational transfer of the crown. Non-Western cultures offer frequent analogues: a woman, either a young virgin or an aging woman past menopause, who is set apart from the usual female functions and allowed access to otherwise exclusively male activities, who is perceived as embodying both male and female attributes and given hieratic status, her mysterious containment of opposites seeming to exempt her from the impermanence of ordinary life.[18]

There is more than a touch of her father's narcissism in some of Queen Elizabeth's strategies for deflecting public anxiety about the succession. She, like her father, resisted giving up the reins of power even when the time came to do so and died without making clear and public her plans for an orderly succession—as though she actually believed on some level that she could live out the immortality of her "body politic."[19] But unlike Henry VIII, Elizabeth knew how to present herself as disinterested. She made use of some of her father's devious and unsettling tactics and was reportedly capable of her father's intense rage, but without the element of drivenness that made her father's public policy look so personal. She was able to convince her public, or at least a significant segment of it, that even her unsettling adoption of male epithets was a strategy born out of genuine love for her people and concern for the welfare of England.

To what extent might Queen Elizabeth have believed her own public mythology? It would be easy for us to interpret her insistence on her male identity as monarch as compensation for feelings of deep inadequacy at having been born female, at having been rejected by her father. But there is precious little evidence that Elizabeth needed to think of herself as male in order to consider herself able enough for the formidable tasks of government. Her frequent protests about her "sexly weakness" never ring true—they are too open, too patently designed to placate a potentially hostile auditorship, to be convincing evidence as to her own feelings about her womanhood. We are left at the end with the implacable cultural otherness we had to face at the beginning. Tudor daughterhood, like Tudor fatherhood, was a public phenomenon, played out through political strategies and in the language of public life. She needed to assert her participation in the "body politic" of her father in order to be perceived as a genuine successor to her father, for as contemporary jurists put it, "King is a Name of Continuance" (Kantorowicz 23, 407). Elizabeth fashioned her identity as a legitimate monarch who was her father's daughter, not by establishing her separateness from him, but by incorporating the "immortal body" of his kingship, neutralizing its specificity to him, melding it into a distinctive and effective instrument for rule. Her private view of these tactics, if she had one, was left in baffling indeterminacy.

Notes

Parts of this essay are reprinted with permission from *Women in the Middle Ages and the Renaissance: Literary and Historical Perspectives*, ed. Mary Beth Rose (Syracuse: Syracuse UP, 1986).

1. See Stone pts. 1–2. I am, however, dissenting from Stone's bleak evaluation of the possibilities for affective bonding in an open-lineage family. For correctives of Stone see Fraser; Leah Marcus, *Childhood* chap. 1; and Ozment. I am also indebted to Greenblatt's (*Self-Fashioning* and *Ralegh*) and Jonathan Goldberg's (*James I*) studies of the public nature of monarchy and self-formation in the Renaissance.

2. Of the major biographers of Henry VIII, Lacey Smith has offered the most penetrating analysis of the king's more psychologically aberrant public strategies. My own brief interpretation is indebted to the new theories of narcissism and self-psychology offered by Kernberg and especially Kohut, whose work is particularly valuable for its capacity to shed light on the relationships between general historical circumstances and personality formation. As Kohut has noted in his essay "Creativeness, Charisma, Group Psychology," charismatic leaders such as Henry tend to suffer from grandiose overestimation of their own powers. While they may be said to be suffering from a personality disorder, their conviction as to their own omnipotence can make them remarkably effective political leaders, particularly in wartime or periods of extreme volatility such as the 1530s in England.

3. I am indebted for this suggestion to Lynda Boose, personal communication, 17 November 1984. Although Henry established Mary and Elizabeth as heirs to the throne in his will, the document did not restore their legitimacy and was apparently unsigned at the time of his death (see Johnson 21–22; and Lacey Smith 267–73).

4. The precise number of Catherine's pregnancies is uncertain, but this is the count that gained acceptance by historians (see Neale, *Queen Elizabeth* 4).

5. See Fraser 119 and n. There were, however, competing theories attributing infertility and perhaps also the determination of sex to the father. Cecil noted much later on of Leicester that he and his brothers had never fathered children, although their wives had children by other marriages (Neale, *Queen Elizabeth* 142).

6. The only noteworthy mentions of Henry that I have found are in Hughes and Larkin 2: 10, 42, 49, 71, each in connection with a continuation of Henrician policy. It is unlikely, however, that Mary herself was responsible for the wording of her proclamations. The effacement of her father may have been less a matter of deliberate intention than of Philip and Mary's break with Henrician precedents. Nevertheless, as we shall note below, Elizabeth's practice was quite different.

7. See Plowden 187; Prescott; and for studies of Mary's "case history" by modern psychoanalysts, Aldrich 88 and Brown and Barglow. I am indebted to Peter Barglow, M.D., for kindly providing me with the final two references.

8. See, for example, Neale, *Queen Elizabeth,* which argues (76–82) that Elizabeth genuinely wanted to marry Robert Dudley; and Johnson's rebuttal (121).

9. On the rhetoric of subversion see Spivak, "Displacement." I discuss this aspect of Elizabeth's political rhetoric in *Puzzling Shakespeare.*

10. For two differing accounts of the doctrine see Axton; and Kantorowicz. In general, Elizabeth's use of the doctrine is more clearly explicable in terms of Kantorowicz's interpretation than in terms of Axton's.

11. See Schleiner's important article. For other references to the queen's androgynous image and related strategies see Jonathan Goldberg, *Endlesse Worke* 150–53; and Montrose. I am also indebted to Tennenhouse 17–71.

12. I am also indebted to Heisch, "Rhetoric," which gives excerpts from many of Elizabeth's speeches in their original manuscript form. When it comes to interpreting her strategies, however, I differ with Heisch: she presents Elizabeth as disclaiming responsibility for her show of strength and "pointing at heaven"; I see her rather as deploying the formula of the King's Two Bodies in order to emphasize that she herself is the conduit of such divine authority. See also Heisch, "Patriarchy."

13. At least some of her contemporaries noted the skill with which she used the strategy (See Neale, *Parliaments* 2: 248–49).

14. For examples of the use of *princess* to imply demeaned status see Elizabeth I 180, 219; Neale, *Parliaments* 2:127; and Rice 89–91.

15. For illustrations of the masculinization of epithets see, for example, Hughes and Larkin 2:100, 103, 144, 210, 258, 273; 3:119, 121, 125, 185, 193, 198, 236, 242, 245, 256. For proclamations issued in time of plague see 2:236, 317, 321, 345, 420, 430, and for the later more masculine plague-time proclamations 3:121; for feeding the hungry see 3:193–94. I have not made a thorough study of the changes in formulaic references to Henry; however, at least one set of proclamations on the same subject and repeating the same formulaic language does show a shift away from *lady* (see 2:257, 273, 364; 3:31, 97).

16. There are many other examples of such language, too many to be mere chance or idle flattery.

17. See also the early chapters of Ariès.

18. See Ortner and Whitehead, esp. the essays by Poole (116–65) and Ortner (359–409); and Ardener, intro., esp. 41, 47, and 49–65. I am indebted to Judith Kegan Gardiner for suggesting both these references. Of course, a familiar if partial Western analogue is the Virgin Mary (Ashe). But there was also a Renaissance tradition of portraying monarchs as hermaphroditic (Wind 214), and Elizabeth was frequently associated with male images of rule (Bevington 6; Strong, *Cult* 122–24 and *Portraits* 68, 156–57; Yates 42–51).

19. On Henry's attempts to extend his authority beyond his death see esp. Lacey Smith 262–70; and for Elizabeth see Elton 474 and Johnson 436.

CAROLYN G. HEILBRUN

Afterword

THE FIRST VOLUME of *No Man's Land,* Sandra Gilbert and Susan Gubar's three-volume sequel to *The Madwoman in the Attic,* is dedicated "to the memory of our fathers . . . the two men who first taught us to love men" (xvi). It is a dedication that speaks volumes about the relations between daughters and fathers. One has only to imagine a book by men similarly dedicated to their mothers to discover how anomalous, almost pitiful, is this loving memory. Where fathers have "taught" daughters to love men, they have accomplished, we may suppose, two aims: the daughters do not fear men as tyrants or sexual aggressors and do not require them as social ratifiers of the female position. Any book on daughters and fathers must, therefore, conclude with a harsh question: if marriage or significant attachment to a man were not of social value to a woman, how often would her father's lesson be enacted?

Lynda Boose mentions "the amorphous threat to patriarchal construction inherent in the daughter's independent, unassigned status." Elsewhere in her essay she notes that "the fathers who seemed least inclined to become incestuous were those whose relations with their daughters had been from birth defined by active participation in a physical and maternally nurturing role." These sentences, juxtaposed, suggest that it is only in a world freed from the organization of the Freudian or Biblical nuclear family that a non–power-driven relationship between women and men is possible. As Boose writes, "In both Freudian and Lacanian theory, the psychosocial dynamics of the family resemble something akin to an all-determining game of who's-got-the-phallus. By these terms, the daughter is clearly the one person who *does not.* To become an offical player, the daughter must eradicate the one kinship status that is contained within, yet liminal to, the family institution. She enters the cultural story, we might say, only by relinquishing her structural isolation/independence from its male-authored script and becoming an agent to ensure its duplication. Yet, as psychoanalytic theory makes clear, what allows her even this entree is the receipt of a signal passed on to her not *from* the mother but from the phallus that is the sign of the father."

If one reads many biographies of women, as I have done in recent years, one discovers that the fathers are as crucial to the lives of their

Note: This afterword is copyrighted by Carolyn G. Heilbrun.

daughters as they were to the ceremony of marriage in Shakespeare's plays. They are the pivot on which turns the life of the daughter seeking a destiny beyond her mother's or that "normally" ascribed to women. This occurs in one of three ways. The engine of the daughter's ambition is driven either by her father's preference for sons and his evident disappointment at her sex (Elizabeth Cady Stanton, Emma Goldman); or by the evident fact of his more challenging, worldly, and exciting life compared with that of any woman within her sights: as Isak Dinesen's biographer Judith Thurman puts it, where Dinesen "uses the word 'life' it is often synonymous with the word 'father'" (7); or by the fact that the father, supportive of his daughter's intelligence and talents, propels her into a world for which she is not fit, or in which she can find no place (Adrienne Rich, Margaret Fuller).

As Christine Froula makes clear, the daughter may be driven by the father's sexual violation of her, but this story does not as yet appear widely in biographies. It is, of course, the more remarkable that in abandoning the seduction theory and adopting the phallocentric Oedipus complex, Freud not only escaped the accusation he feared most—that of the father's seduction of the daughter—but successfully reinforced the game of "who's-got-the-phallus." Father-daughter incest has been confined, for the most part, to fictional renditions or versions until the recent women's movement, and often even then. (I have heard Freudian psychoanalysts, however, mention their belief in Freud's incest with his daughter Anna. Considering his analysis of her, it is a possibility, or fantasy, worth contemplating.) Similarly, the father's brutality to the mother may inspire the daughter's independence (Agnes Smedley), but it is significant that the defense of battered women, rather than of the battering husbands (or the rapist), is a recent development, also attributable to the women's movement.

If one looks at the "Dinesen" father-daughter pattern, one discovers that, inevitably, the father stands for "life," while the mother represents lack of autonomy and confinement within a routine that is brutal or, as in the upper classes, insipid, and that all the attraction and risk of a lived life is embodied in the father. The girl wishes to be like him but where that is not possible, comforts herself for her own deficiency by caring for him. (Dickens presents this situation persuasively in fiction.) The daughters who will not settle for father-care may well end up ill-disposed towards men, or unlikely to "love" them.

The ironies inherent in the fathers' ordering of their daughters' destinies is continuously made palpable to me by students each year who announce: "My mother was the dominant (powerful) person in our family." Fathers are remarkably often portrayed as quiet, patient, long-suffering, sweet, and so on. That the mother's manipulation and domination may well arise from her essential powerlessness has rarely if ever been perceived by the children, at least before the rise of feminism in the early seventies. Adrienne Rich first stated boldly that "it is a painful fact that a nurturing father, who replaces rather than complements a mother, *must be loved at the mother's expense*" (*Of Woman Born* 245). Certainly all novels since their earliest times have portrayed women not so much as the victims of the patriarchal system but as the ones who must, given the rules of the game, victimize the victims. So Samuel Butler in *The Way of All Flesh* has the sisters play at cards for Theobald; yet if he has not really chosen her, Theobald nevertheless ultimately dominates his wife. (In this book as in the works of male authors generally, it is the father's domination of the sons, not the daughters, that most absorbs the storytellers.)

The editors of this volume ask a profound question in the preface: "As the daughter-father representations are re-presented . . . though the reader will no doubt hear an anger that speaks out, perhaps especially in the voices of women critics, beneath even the anger what is the desire that speaks?"

I want to try to characterize that desire. It is for affection for the father that does not deprive the mother, or scorn or fear her; for a love from the father that desires neither the daughter herself nor the use of her to relate to other men; for a fatherly devotion that does not, as in Shakespeare, serve only to redeem the father morally and socially, without the daughter's undergoing any moral change. Above all, it is for a fondness between the daughter and father that allows for the interplay of other affections, that threatens her neither with control nor desertion, and that in no way reflects the father's unique power.

When the father is an outsider—black, Jewish, ill, what the society deems unmanly—he often suggests to the daughter the position she can inhabit if she is sufficiently ambitious. His powerlessness or fear of exclusion matches her own; he must *seek*, as she wishes to do. Fathers who are either brutal or inept and self-serving, like Louisa May Alcott's, force their daughters wholly into a position of countering the paternal example, of seeking, as a woman, "paternal" responsibility. Clearly, then, if we look forward to a time when all women as well as men aspire to lifelong work, when not to work will be as shocking and shaming for a woman as not to marry has been, the father will earn his devotion, not at the expense of the mother or women generally, but because his interaction, his dialogue, with the daughter is pleasing and lasting. But this can scarcely happen in the nuclear family as we know it now. No doubt the family will have to be redefined, enlarged, extended, totally undone in those aspects that make it Oedipal.

It is remarkable to read accounts by black men of their mothers. During the Iran-Contra hearings, Congressman Stokes spoke of how his mother scrubbed floors so that he might achieve what he has, in fact, achieved; his brother reached a similar position of influence. William Julius Wilson, a professor of sociology at the University of Chicago, is described, in an interview published in the *New York Times Book Review* in connection with the review of his book *The Truly Disadvantaged*, as having "grown up in rural poverty. His father worked in steel mills and coal mines, but died when William was 12. His mother supported the family of six children by working as a maid" (47). Few, if any, of these men remark on the difference in the achievements of black men and women or on the overwhelming debt of achieving black men to their mothers; they continue to search for the reasons for dereliction in black fathers and other black males but never question that the father, as a fact in the black family, may simply not fit in with the usual picture of the Oedipal family. The father's absence, in short, is never seen as productive, benign, or even advantageous to accomplished black men. That it may be all of these things to accomplished black women has long been suspected. What has happened in these black families is that the father's failure to perform his nuclear or Freudian role has aided the daughters, and where the mother had sufficient strength and support, even the sons. That is not a conclusion likely to be granted by many.

Nor are the reasons far to seek. As Leslie Rabine remarks in an article on the writings of Maxine Hong Kingston: "The privileged members of patriarchy can afford to give themselves a certain freedom from their own phallocentric symbolic order, but they cannot afford to give it to the oppressed who might use it to overthrow that order" (491). Rabine also observes: "In *China Men*, the grandfathers and great-grandfathers, admitted to the United States as agricultural and railroad workers, long to go home because the cruel treatment they receive deprives them of a worthwhile life. But in *The Woman Warrior*, the place Maxine's family calls 'home' is the country where families sell their daughters into slavery and where daughters-in-law are tortured. 'Home' is a place she does not want to go" (480). The ways in which this brilliant observation applies to immigrant groups but not to blacks—men or women—is worth pondering.

"Home" in *The Woman Warrior* is a place where the mother is without power to change the daughter's life to something different from her own. At home the mother's only role is to educate the daughter to ensure that role's duplication so that the daughter may safely enter the cultural story in the service of the patriarchy. Clearly, if the mother erupts from this role, as she has done in the past two decades in middle-class white marriages, as she has long done in black marriages, the father is displaced as the only family member representing "life," as the only possible mentor for a daughterly role beyond conventional womanhood.

Daughter-father relationships then cease to be power relationships, or events in the cycle of circulation where the father exchanges the daughter for his own additional social scope, and become solely relationships of parenting and mentoring. As things now stand, few women born before the second half of this century have found a woman mentor, mother or not, and have been professionally mentored, where they have been mentored at all, wholly by men: fathers or father surrogates. When this situation changes, the position of the father changes, as does his dominance in the game of "who's-got-the-phallus." In all the literary and psychological cases and situations analyzed in this collection, the positioning of the mother within the power structure, or the discontinuation of the phallus as the mark of power, would create new possibilities for the daughter-father relationship. The father's regular care and nuture of his children from birth, which does not mean constant, daily care, but regular care provided by him and the mother, as part of each day, further alters the daughter-father relationship. It is possible that in some cases, in some immigrant and some black families, to speak only of this country, these factors have already been altered. But the failure to recognize these changes doubles the burden of the mother and places the non-Oedipal father in a wholly anomalous position that he might, under other circumstances, occupy with less tension and resentment.

There is a powerful irony in the fact that the final essay in this collection, "Erasing the Stigma of Daughterhood: Mary I, Elizabeth I, and Henry VIII," is not only the only essay that recounts the daughter's "erasure of the stigma of daughterhood" (of course, in the person of Elizabeth I) but also the one that deals with the earliest historical person in the book. True, Elizabeth was a queen, forced into a "male" role through the absence of a male heir, but she managed both to learn techniques of ruling from her father and to counter or ignore his brutal and destructive lessons. Dorothy Sayers found it extraordinarily entertaining to watch historians inventing "the most complicated and astonishing reasons both for [Elizabeth I's] success as a sovereign and for her tortuous matrimonial policy. . . . Only recently has it occurred to a few enlightened people . . . that she might be one of the rare people who were born into the right job and put that job first" (111). Had she been a man, Sayers concludes, no one "would have thought either her statesmanship or her humanity in any way mysterious" (112). Surely it is worth observing also that Elizabeth did *not* grow up in an Oedipal or nuclear family position; she achieved power and esteem in her job because the usual daughter-father relationship did not, in her case, apply.

No doubt the present solution to the problem of daughter-father relationships lies there. We cannot, of course, arrive at a solution unless we wholly understand, and carefully analyze, the historical daughter-father connection. The value of the essays in this collection, particularly in the originality of their analysis, is therefore inestimable. But we must also ask where the solution to the daughter-father problem lies. Adrienne Rich has written: "I believe large numbers of men could, in fact, undertake child care on a large scale, without radically altering the balance of male power in a male-identified society." She is probably right. Rich describes the major goal for women, the one she identifies as what men, certainly fathers, most fear: "that women could be indifferent to [men] altogether, that men could be allowed sexual and emotional—therefore economic—access to women *only* on women's terms" ("Compulsory Heterosexuality" 36, 43). Yet until this major goal is achieved, we must, I think, try to involve fathers more in the daily care of their children. This may not revolutionize the patriarchy or make evident to everyone the terrible dangers to women in what Rich calls "compulsory heterosexuality." It will at the least, however, reduce incest and the daughter's seduction. At the most, it may lead to quite other concepts of the family, moving further and further from the Oedipal or nuclear family and the system that family construct inevitably reproduces.

Notes on Illustrations

John Singer Sargent, *The Sitwell Family* (1900)

If the twentieth century may be said to mark the disintegration of the nuclear family, then it seems prophetically appropriate that John Singer Sargent's portrait of the Sitwell family made its debut in 1900. Rather than connection or coherence, what emerges as the image on Sargent's canvas are three unrelated groups of people who seem only coincidentally to occupy the same space. In the right hand, closest plane, two little boys play toy soldiers on the floor, watched over by their dog; in the middle, a lone woman, dressed for the ball, waits self-consciously; and on the left side, emerging from the deepest plane is the painting's only coupled relationship and its dominant image: the self-assertively sultry young woman in red with the moustached man in riding boots, his arm draped possessively around her shoulder. While the painting alludes to conventions of the family portrait genre, against that tradition it has deployed a series of dispersals and incongruities that collectively serve to fragment the iconography of the family. Of all such devices, the most prominent are those that effect the composition of the daughter, whose image has been manipulated so that she seems considerably older than her actual age of eleven and likewise more than three years senior to Osbert, the elder of the two Sitwell sons.

To memorialize the Sitwell family on the eve of the new century, the painter finally selected by Sir George Reresby Sitwell, fourth Baronet of Renishaw Hall, was unquestionably the most sought after, highly paid contemporary portrait artist on either side of the Atlantic. And yet, while Sargent's profession itself would insure his familiarity with the codes of the aristocratic family, Sargent was nonetheless an American—or, from Sir George's perspective, simply not one of us. And in the juxtaposition of social philosophies signalled by an American artist memorializing a titled British family, there is an inherent irony. Sargent's Americanism meant identity with a nation that had outlawed inherited titles and reconstituted its own unacknowledged class structure on the wider franchise of self-fashioning entrepreneurialism. It meant that his relationship to the titled families he painted was by definition that of an outsider—but moreover, an outsider probably much like the condescendingly perceived American in Europe that Sargent's friend Henry James so often wrote about. In short, an outsider probably too acutely aware of that status not to have noticed what Osbert's remembrance of the portrait sitting in *Left Hand, Right Hand!* imagines him oblivious to; of having been treated by Sir George as if he were a servant. This strangely orchestrated portrait that hangs in Renishaw Hall is suggestively a product of such tensions; as such, perhaps it is a portrait that could only have been constructed by someone who stood far enough outside the aristocratic family tradition he painted to feel the need to dismantle it—and in doing so, to end up disassembling the image of the nuclear family itself.

As a genre, family portraiture is inseparable from both aristocracy and patriarchy precisely because family portraits are a representational apparatus for reproducing those privileges. What family portraits are really all about is sons, and about visually confirming the heirs apparent as authoritative transmitters of the family line. Accordingly, the portrait of the Sitwell children done a century earlier in 1787 by John Singleton Copley—for which Sargent's painting was intended as a companion piece—foregrounds the family's three lively boys romping in energetic competition, the eldest son symbolically asserting his priority as he playfully knocks down the house of cards that the two younger, unentitled brothers have built. Meanwhile, the sister in white hat and gown sits demurely in the window behind them, holding a music book as she watches over her brothers in maternal affection, institutional harmony preserved as her claim of seniority silently yields to the preemptive authority of gender. In Sargent's 1900 version of the Sitwell heirs, Sacheverell and Osbert may occupy the so-called strong side of the canvas and be bathed in the light that also illuminates their mother, but by the enormity of the mother's stature and her utter detachment from them, the sons end up diminished into virtual inconsequentiality. The mother in this portrait— nominally at its center and the largest figure in it—does not emblematically bond the family together, but seems instead to stand uneasily inside it, incongruously formal in her white ballgown and hat and looking if anything like a displaced Reynolds lady who has arrived past a century late for the family portrait sitting. Rather than linking father to sons and thus visually confirming the legal fiction upon which paternity and hereditary entitlement depend, the centralized mother in this group visually mediates nothing except the sense of family dissolution.

In Sargent's vision, what emerges as the most memorable image is the one figure who does *not* extend the family, yet the one who is here aligned with its patriarch. The vivid red suit once worn by the centermost son in the Copley painting has been reconstituted into the defiantly red dress that compositionally imbalances the Sargent portrait and empowers the daughter to decenter it from the margins where she stands, her arm akimbo, her uncoiffed hair and emphatically modern style boldly discrediting the passive centrality of the mother, usurping attention from the young male heirs, and authorized such usurpations by her partnered symmetry with the father. The father, imaged in opposition to the mother and lacking any implied relationship to his sons, stands with his riding boot thrust forward in an almost defiant alliance with his daughter, the physical connection between the two working to unsettle the sexual taboos as well as the lineal privileges that define the nuclear family. As the mother's hand reaches toward the red flowers on the table that spatially barricades daughter and father into a space of their own, her gesture reemphasizes rather than bridges the opposition. Even the center of the painting seems to shift into the gap that her hand points us to as it, too, is drawn there by the allure of the bright red flower— the object that, as a visual metaphor for the daughter on the other side, symbolically both creates the gap and is synonymous with it.

426

Sargent's emphasis on the Sitwell daughter proved, of course, to be somewhat prophetic: although first Osbert and then Sacheverell inherited the Sitwell estate and title, it was Edith Sitwell, through her own talent as a writer, who became the best known bearer of the Sitwell name. But by making the daughter into a defiant emblem of the claims of excludedness, Sargent has projected the exclusions of class onto the exclusions of gender and thereby inscribed his portrait with meanings he no doubt never intended. For the vision of the daughter in red not only redraws the internal lines of family but challenges privileges and entitlements far beyond those of merely the aristocratic institution. Ultimately, what Sargent's image of Edith Sitwell challenges is the hierarchy of gender that serves as the foundation upon which the patriarchal nuclear institution is built.

Sofonisba Anguisciola, *Father Amilcare and His Children* (c. 1558/59)

Sixteenth-century Italian painter Sofonisba Anguisciola's portrait of her own father, her sister Minerva, and her brother Asdrubàle, seems to be one of the few daughter-father images drawn from a daughter's perspective; since Berthe Morisot used her own husband and child as models for her idyllic images of a father and daughter, Morisot's vision comes less from the imagination of a daughter than of a mother. Apparently, Sofonisba's is also one of the few portraits of a father painted by his own daughter (the only view Mary Cassatt would paint of her father was the back of his head). In Sofonisba's family grouping, the significance of son to father is spatialized as the absolute bond that preemptively displaces any potential connection between father and daughter. As the father confidently returns the viewer's gaze, his arms, knees, and shoulders thoughtlessly block out the excluded daughter while they protect and encircle the cherished son. The young boy, whom the painter has dressed in bright orange, looks adoringly up at his father, his future participation in the outside world confirmed by the window positioned behind him and the mountain above his head that reaches upward into open sky. Meanwhile, behind the father and unnoticed by him, dressed in a more sober blue and framed by the hallway back into the house, an inhibiting canopy directly above her and only a small sliver of the window outward available inside her space, the daughter stands with demurely downcast eyes, clutching something to her chest and shyly twisting her skirt in the apparently timeless gesture of little girls. At the same time that Sofonisba's portrait confirms the traditional centrality of the father-son bond, it insists that the privileging of sons be seen in relation to the exclusion of daughters that is here imaged as its context. But if the daughter/artist has painted a somewhat painful picture of the preferences of lineage within the family frame, she also seems to have left us with a slyly mocking comment about them. In the parodically close resemblance she constructs between the father and the family dog, not only has the dog apparently inherited the father's nose and the father's bearded face, it even gazes out at us—and thus literally views the world—from precisely the same angle.

Edgar Degas, *The Bellilli Family* (1858–62)

A daughter occupies the central space of Degas's portrait of the Bellilli family. She perches on a chair, turning toward her father as if to enter the masculine space of the right half of the picture with its chair, desk, clock, and candle. Her black dress and pinafore, however, link her to the left or female side of the portrait in which her mother and sister stand. The mother, pregnant and in mourning, looks withdrawn and isolated. Her eyes turn away from the father's penetrating stare. She lays a claiming hand on the sister, who primly stands beside her mother. The three female figures occupy two-thirds of the canvas, but when the gaze is shifted to the plane of the sitting father, the daughter in the chair pulls the masculine space further over into the center against the self-contained standing figures on the left. The space between mother and father in this formally rendered family portrait is one of alienation. It is this space that the daughter occupies, in ambivalent relation to both sides of the canvas.

When Degas began this portrait, he was living with his aunt, Laura Bellilli, and her family. Laura Bellilli, the pregnant woman in black, was in mourning for the death of her own father, whose picture hangs on the wall behind her, a reigning presence over his creation (he arranged the marriage which here appears so strained). While working on *The Bellilli Family,* Degas was also painting *The Daughter of Jephthah,* another tale of the father's sacrifice of a daughter.

Jan Steen, *The Drawing Lesson* (c. 1665)

This painting by seventeenth-century Dutch artist Jan Steen features his own family: his daughter, his son, and possibly even himself. Yet while Steen's paintings are quite typically narrative, just how we are to read the story implied by this one is not only unclear but disturbingly problematic. The painter has painted his own daughter (who was frequently his model) as the pupil in a drawing studio that seems suggestively his own because filled with items that appear as props in several of his other paintings. The father—or the drawing master—is here wholly involved with instructing the daughter, while the excluded younger son looks on, his face conspicuously distraught. Given the contemporary disrepute of drawing studios, however, plus the odd tone conveyed by the detached bodies, body parts, and male faces that dangle about this space, the iconography implied by this curious arrangement makes the narrative problematically ambivalent. While the drawing master apparently sketches a demonstration or corrects his pupil's drawing of the male nude statue that is set before her as the object of the lesson, a "putti" (a baby? a cupid? an angel?) dangles apparently unseen over the concentrating daughter while she, in innocent suggestiveness, sharpens a pencil. Meanwhile, a huge foot threatens to descend upon the head of the little boy as he watches this lesson, his anguished face merging with a series of impassive, plaster-cast male faces that voyeuristically occupy the space. Two radically opposed readings suggest themselves. In the first one, Steen has used his daughter and a projected drawing master/double in this anatomy lesson in the service of depicting a father's liberating desire both to educate his daughter from the sexual ignorance society imposes on young women and, simultaneously, to designate her, rather than the son, as legitimate heir to the father's artistic authority. It is equally possible, however, to infer that Steen's painting instead depicts the leeringly comic prelude to an unsuspecting young woman's initiation into another kind of male anatomy lesson—and that in the service of a lewd joke that the male painter shares with the male viewer, Steen has even used his own daughter in a jocular commentary that mocks the mere notion of a woman artist and inscribes even her daughterly relationship with educational mentors into a scene that is in reality only a disguise for sexual appropriation, both visual and physical.

Works Cited

Abel, Elizabeth. "Narrative Structure(s) and Female Development: The Case of *Mrs. Dalloway.*" *The Voyage In: Fictions of Female Development.* Ed. Elizabeth Abel, Marianne Hirsch, and Elizabeth Langland. Hanover, N.H.: UP of New England, 1983. 161–85.

———. *Virginia Woolf and the Fictions of Psychoanalysis.* Chicago: U of Chicago P, forthcoming.

Aeschylus. *The Eumenides, The Oresteian Trilogy.* Trans. Philip Vellacott. Harmondsworth: Penguin, 1959.

Aldrich, C. K. *An Introduction to Dynamic Psychiatry.* New York: McGraw, 1966.

Althusser, Louis. "Freud and Lacan." *"Lenin and Philosophy"* 189–219.

———. "Ideology and Ideological State Apparatuses." *"Lenin and Philosophy"* 123–73.

———. *"Lenin and Philosophy" and Other Essays.* Trans. Ben Brewster. London: New Left, 1971.

———. "The 'Piccolo Teatro': Bertolozzi and Brecht." *For Marx.* Trans. Ben Brewster. New York: Pantheon, 1969. 129–51.

Alvarez, Al. "Sylvia Plath." *The Art of Sylvia Plath.* Ed. Charles Newman. London: Faber, 1970. 58–68.

"Amniocentesis Leads to Abortion of Female Fetuses in India." *Valley News* [Lebanon, N.H.] 18 July 1986: 10.

Anaya, Rudolfo. *Bless Me, Ultima.* Berkeley: Quinto Sol, 1972.

———. *The Legend of La Llorona.* Berkeley: Tonatiuh, 1984.

Angelou, Maya. *I Know Why the Caged Bird Sings.* 1969. New York: Bantam, 1970.

Ardener, Shirley, ed. *Defining Females: The Nature of Women in Society.* New York: Wiley, 1978.

Arens, W. *The Original Sin: Incest and Its Meanings.* New York: Oxford UP, 1986.

Ariès, Philippe. *Centuries of Childhood: A Social History of Family Life.* Trans. Robert Baldick. New York: Knopf, 1962.

Armstrong, Louise. *Kiss Daddy Goodnight.* New York: Hawthorn, 1978.

Ashe, Geoffrey. *The Virgin.* London: Routledge, 1977.

Auerbach, Nina. *Communities of Women: An Idea in Fiction.* Cambridge: Harvard UP, 1976.

Axton, Marie. *The Queen's Two Bodies: Drama and the Elizabethan Succession.* London: Royal Historical Society, 1977.

Baker, Houston. *Blues, Ideology, and Afro-American Literature: A Vernacular Theory.* Chicago: U of Chicago P, 1984.

Bal, Mieke. "Sexuality, Sin, and Sorrow: The Emergence of the Female Character (A Reading of *Genesis* 1–3)." *Poetics Today* 6.1–2 (1985): 21–42.

Baldwin, James. *Just Above My Head*. New York: Dell, 1979.

Balmary, Marie. *Psychoanalyzing Psychoanalysis: Freud and the Hidden Fault of the Father*. 1979. Trans. Ned Lukacher. Baltimore: Johns Hopkins UP, 1982.

Balzac, Honoré de. *Eugénie Grandet*. 1833. New York: New American Library, 1964.

Barnett, Rosalind D., and Grace K. Baruch. *The Competent Woman: Perspectives on Development*. New York: Wiley, 1978.

Barth, Fredrik. "Descent and Marriage Reconsidered." Goody 3–19.

Baym, Nina. "God, Father, and Lover in Emily Dickinson's Poetry." *Puritan Influences in American Literature*. Ed. Emory Elliot. Urbana: U of Illinois P, 1979. 193–209.

———. "Hawthorne and His Mother: A Biographical Speculation." *American Literature* 54 (1982): 1–27.

———. "Hawthorne's Women: The Tyranny of Social Myths." *Centennial Review* 15 (1971): 50–72.

———. "Thwarted Nature: Nathaniel Hawthorne as Feminist." *American Novelists Revisited*. Ed. Fritz Fleishmann. Boston: Hall, 1982. 58–77.

Bazin, Nancy Topping. *Virginia Woolf and the Androgynous Vision*. New Brunswick: Rutgers UP, 1973.

Beauvoir, Simone de. *The Second Sex*. 1949. Trans. and ed. H. M. Parshley. New York: Vintage, 1953.

Bedient, Calvin. *Architects of the Self: George Eliot, D. H. Lawrence, and E. M. Forster*. Berkeley: U of California P, 1972.

Beer, Gillian. "Hume, Stephen, and Elegy in *To the Lighthouse*." *Essays in Criticism* 34 (1984): 33–55.

Bell, Millicent. *Edith Wharton and Henry James: The Story of Their Friendship*. New York: Braziller, 1965.

Bell, Quentin. *Virginia Woolf: A Biography*. New York: Harcourt, 1972.

Beowulf. Trans. Howell D. Chickering, Jr. Dual Language Edition. New York: Anchor, 1977.

Bergren, Ann L. T. "Language and the Female in Early Greek Thought." *Arethusa* 16 (1983): 69–95.

Bernheimer, Charles, and Claire Kahane, eds. *In Dora's Case: Freud—Hysteria—Feminism*. New York: Columbia UP, 1985.

Bevington, David. *Tudor Drama and Politics: A Critical Approach to Topical Meaning*. Cambridge: Harvard UP, 1968.

Blake, William. *The Poetical Works of William Blake*. Ed. John Sampson. London: Oxford UP, 1913.

The Book of Common Prayer. Ed. John E. Booty. Charlottesville: U of Virginia P, 1967.

Boose, Lynda E. "The Father and the Bride in Shakespeare." *PMLA* 97 (1982): 325–47.

Boucé, Paul-Gabriel, ed. *Sexuality in Eighteenth-Century Britain*. Totowa, N.J.: Barnes, 1982.

Bowle, John. *Henry VIII: A Biography*. London: Allen, 1964.

Braudy, Leo. "Penetration and Impenetrability in *Clarissa.*" *New Approaches to Eighteenth-Century Literature: Selected Papers from the English Institute.* Ed. Phillip Harth. New York: Columbia UP, 1976. 177–206.

Bronte, Anne. [Acton Bell]. *Agnes Grey.* 1847. Oxford: Shakespeare Head, 1931.

———. *The Tenant of Wildfell Hall.* 1848. 2 vols. Oxford: Shakespeare Head, 1931.

Brooks, Peter. *Reading for the Plot: Design and Intention in Narrative.* New York: Knopf, 1976.

Brown, Edward, and Peter Barglow. "Pseudocyesis: A Paradigm for Psychophysiological Interactions." *Archives of General Psychiatry* 24 (1971): 221–29.

Browning, Elizabeth Barrett. *Aurora Leigh.* "*Aurora Leigh*" *and Other Poems.* 1856. Rpt. London: Women's Press, 1978.

Brownmiller, Susan. *Against Our Wills: Men, Women, and Rape.* New York: Simon, 1975.

Brzenk, Eugene J. "'Up Hill' and 'Down' by Christina Rossetti." *VP* 10 (1972). 367–71.

Bulletin of the New York Public Library 80 (1977).

Butler, Sandra. *Conspiracy of Silence: The Trauma of Incest.* San Francisco: New Glide, 1978.

Butscher, Edward. *Sylvia Plath: Method and Madness.* New York: Seabury, 1976.

Calendar of State Papers Venetian, 1534–1603. Ed. Rawdon Brown et al. 38 vols. 1873–97. London: Longmans, 1864–1947. Vols. 5–9.

Camden, William. *Annales.* Trans. R. N[orton]. 3rd ed. London, 1635.

Cameron, Sharon. *Lyric Time.* Baltimore: Johns Hopkins UP, 1979.

Campa, Arthur L. *Spanish Folk-Poetry in New Mexico.* Albuquerque: U of New Mexico P, 1946.

Carby, Hazel V. "'On the Threshold of Woman's Era': Lynching, Empire, and Sexuality in Black Feminist Theory." *Critical Inquiry* 12 (1985): 262–78.

Castle, Terry. "The Carnivalization of Eighteenth-Century English Narrative." *PMLA* 99 (1984): 903–16.

———. *Clarissa's Ciphers: Meaning and Disruption in Richardson's "Clarissa."* Ithaca: Cornell UP, 1982.

"Cenci, Beatrice." *The Reader's Encyclopedia.* 1955 ed.

Chambers, Marjorie Bell. "A Political Diary of an Assertive Woman." Murray 233–41.

Cherbury, Edward, Lord Herbert of. *The Life and Reign of Henry VIII.* London, 1649.

Chesler, Phyllis. *Women and Madness.* New York: Avon, 1973.

Chestnutt, Charles W. *The Marrow of Tradition.* Ann Arbor: U of Michigan P, 1969.

———. *The Short Fiction of Charles W. Chestnutt.* Ed. Sylvia Lyons Render. Washington: Howard UP, 1974.

"China: Population Control Policy Eased in Countryside after Protests." *Los Angeles Times* 12 May 1985, sec. 1: 8+.

Chodorow, Nancy. *The Reproduction of Mothering: Psychoanalysis and the Sociology of Gender.* Berkeley: U of California P, 1978.

Christian, Barbara. "The Rise and Fall of the Proper Mulatta." *Black Women*

Novelists: The Development of a Tradition, 1892–1976. Westport: Greenwood, 1980. 35–62.

Cirlot, J. E. *A Dictionary of Symbols*. Trans. Jack Sage. 2nd ed. New York: Vail-Ballou, 1971.

Cisneros, Sandra. *The House on Mango Street*. Houston: Arte Publico, 1983.

Cixous, Hélène. "Sorties." *New French Feminisms: An Anthology*. Trans. Ann Liddle. Ed. Elaine Marks and Isabelle de Courtivron. New York: Schocken, 1981. 90–98.

Cixous, Hélène, and Catherine Clément. *La jeune née*. Paris: UGE, 1975. Trans. as *The Newly Born Woman*. Trans. Betsy Wing. Minneapolis: U of Minnesota P, 1986.

Clarke, Austin, "Glimpses of W. B. Yeats." *W. B. Yeats: Interviews and Recollections*. Ed. E. H. Mikhail. 2 vols. London: Macmillan, 1977. 2: 349–53.

Cosby, Bill. *Fatherhood*. New York: Dolphin/Doubleday, 1986.

Crews, Frederick C. *The Sins of the Fathers: Hawthorne's Psychological Themes*. New York: Oxford UP, 1966.

Davis, Angela Y. *Women, Race, and Class*. New York: Random, 1981.

DeHuff, Elizabeth W. "The Metamorphosis of a Folk Tale." *Puro Mexicano*. Ed. J. Frank Dobie. Dallas: Southern Methodist UP, 1935. 122–34.

de Lauretis, Teresa. *Alice Doesn't: Feminism, Semiotics, Cinema*. Bloomington: Indiana UP, 1984.

DeSalvo, Louise A. "1897: Virginia Woolf at Fifteen." *Virginia Woolf: A Feminist Slant*. Ed. Jane Marcus. Lincoln: U of Nebraska P, 1983. 78–108.

Dessner, Lawrence Jay. "The Autobiographical Matrix of *Silas Marner*." *Studies in the Novel* 11 (1979): 251–82.

Diaz-Guerrero, R. *Psychology of the Mexican*. Austin: U of Texas P, 1975.

DiBattista, Maria. *Virginia Woolf's Major Novels: The Fables of Anon*. New Haven: Yale UP, 1980.

Dickens, Charles. *Great Expectations*. 1861. New York: Holt, 1962.

Dickinson, Emily. *The Complete Poems of Emily Dickinson*. Ed. Thomas H. Johnson. Boston: Little, 1960.

———. *The Letters of Emily Dickinson*. Ed. Thomas H. Johnson and Theodora ward. 3 vols. Cambridge: Belknap-Harvard UP, 1958.

———. *The Poems of Emily Dickinson*. Ed. Thomas H. Johnson. Cambridge: Belknap-Harvard UP, 1955.

Diehl, Joanne Feit. "'Ransom in a Voice': Language as Defense in Dickinson's Poetry." *Feminist Critics Read Emily Dickinson*. Ed. Suzanne Juhasz. Bloomington: Indiana UP, 1983. 156–75.

Dinnerstein, Dorothy. *The Mermaid and the Minotaur: Sexual Arrangements and Human Malaise*. New York: Harper, 1976.

Donaldson, Ian. *The Rapes of Lucretia: A Myth and Its Transformations*. Oxford: Clarendon, 1982.

Doolittle, Hilda [H.D.]. Letter to Bryher. 25 April 1933. Unpublished ms., Beinecke Rare Book Room and Manuscript Library, Yale University.

———. "The Master." *Feminist Studies* 7 (1981): 407–16.

———. *Tribute to Freud*. London: Pantheon, 1956.

Dorson, Richard M. Foreword. Paredes, *Folktales.*

Douglas, Mary. *Purity and Danger: An Analysis of the Concepts of Pollution and Taboo.* New York: Praeger, 1966.

Dreher, Diane Elizabeth. *Domination and Defiance: Fathers and Daughters in Shakespeare.* Lexington: U of Kentucky P, 1986.

duBois, Page. *Centaurs and Amazons: Women and the Pre-History of the Great Chain of Being.* Ann Arbor: U of Michigan P, 1982.

DuBois, W. E. B. *The Souls of Black Folk: Essays and Sketches.* 1903. New York: Fawcett, 1961.

Dundes, Alan. "'To Love My Father All': A Psychoanalytic Study of the Folktale Source of *King Lear.*" *Southern Folklore Quarterly* 40 (1976): 353–66.

DuPlessis, Rachel Blau, and Susan Stanford Friedman. "'Woman Is Perfect': H.D.'s Debate with Freud." *Feminist Studies* 7 (1981): 416–30.

DuPlessis, Rachel Blau, and Members of Workshop 9. "For the Etruscans: Sexual Difference and Artistic Production—the Debate over a Female Aesthetic." *The Future of Difference.* Ed. Hester Eisenstein and Alice Jardine. Boston: Hall, 1980. 128–56.

Dusinberre, Juliet. *Shakespeare and the Nature of Woman.* New York: Barnes, 1975.

Dussinger, John. *The Discourse of the Mind in Eighteenth-Century Fiction.* The Hague: Mouton, 1974.

Eagleton, Terry. *Literary Theory: An Introduction.* Minneapolis: U of Minnesota P, 1983.

———. *Myths of Power: A Marxist Study of the Brontës.* New York: Barnes, 1975.

———. *The Rape of Clarissa: Writing, Sexuality, and Class Struggle in Samuel Richardson.* Minneapolis: U of Minnesota P, 1982.

Eaves, T. C. Duncan, and Ben D. Kimpel. *Samuel Richardson: A Biography.* Oxford: Clarendon, 1971.

Edel, Leon. *Bloomsbury: A House of Lions.* New York: Avon, 1979.

Eichenbaum, Luise, and Susie Orbach. *Understanding Women.* New York: Basic, 1983.

Eliot, George. *Adam Bede.* 1859. *Writings* 3–4.

———. *The Complete Poems of George Eliot.* Boston: Estes and Laureat, 1887.

———. *The George Eliot Letters.* Ed. Gordon S. Haight. 9 vols. New Haven: Yale UP, 1954–78.

———. *Middlemarch: A Novel of Provincial Life.* 1847. Ed. David Carroll. Oxford: Clarendon, 1986.

———. *Scenes of Clerical Life.* 1858. Ed. David Lodge. Harmondsworth: Penguin, 1973.

———. *Silas Marner: The Weaver of Raveloe.* Ed. Q. D. Leavis. Harmondsworth: Penguin, 1967.

———. "Silly Novels by Lady Novelists." *The Writings of George Eliot.* Ed. Thomas Pinney. London: Routledge, 1963. 300–324.

———. *A Writer's Notebook, 1854–1879, and Uncollected Writings.* Ed. Joseph Wiesenfarth. Charlottesville: U of Virginia P, 1981.

———. *The Writings of George Eliot.* 25 vols. Boston: Houghton, 1907–8.

Elizabeth I. *The Letters of Queen Elizabeth I.* Ed. G. B. Harrison. 1935. New York: Funk, 1968.

Ellison, Ralph. *Invisible Man.* New York: Random, 1952.

Ellmann, Richard. *James Joyce.* 2nd ed. New York: Oxford UP, 1982.

Elsasser, Nan, Kyle Mackenzie, and Yvonne Tixier y Vigil. *Las Mujeres: Conversations from a Hispanic Community.* Old Westbury: Feminist, 1980.

Elton, G. R. *England under the Tudors.* 2nd ed. London: Methuen, 1974.

Emerson, Ralph Waldo. *The Journals and Miscellaneous Notebooks of Ralph Waldo Emerson.* Ed. William H. Gilman and J. E. Parsons. 16 vols. Cambridge: Belknap-Harvard UP, 1970.

Erickson, Peter. *Patriarchal Structures in Shakespeare's Drama.* Berkeley: U of California P, 1983.

Erikson, Erik. *Identity: Youth and Crisis.* New York: Norton, 1968.

Erlich, Gloria. *Family Themes and Hawthorne's Fiction.* New Brunswick: Rutgers UP, 1984.

Fairweather, Eileen. "The Man in the Orange Box." Owen 194–202.

Fanon, Frantz. *The Wretched of the Earth.* Trans. Constance Farrington. New York: Grove, 1968.

Faulkner, William. *Absalom, Absalom!* 1936. New York: Vintage, 1972.

Felman, Shoshana. "Beyond Oedipus: The Specimen Story of Psychoanalysis." *Lacan and Narration.* Ed. Robert Con Davis. Baltimore: Johns Hopkins UP, 1983. 1021–53.

Fiedler, Leslie. *Love and Death in the American Novel.* New York: Criterion, 1960.

Flandrin, Jean-Louis. *Families in Former Times: Kinship, Household, and Sexuality.* Trans. Richard Southern. New York: Cambridge UP, 1979.

Fleishman, Avrom. *Virginia Woolf: A Critical Reading.* Baltimore: Johns Hopkins UP, 1975.

Flowers, Betty S. "The Kingly Self: Rossetti as Woman Artist." *The Achievement of Christina Rossetti.* Ed. David Kent. Ithaca: Cornell UP, 1987. 159–74.

Foucault, Michel. *An Introduction.* New York: Pantheon, 1980. Vol. 1 of *The History of Sexuality.* Trans. Robert Hurley. 3 vols. 1980–87.

Fraser, Antonia. *The Weaker Vessel.* New York: Knopf, 1984.

Frazier, E. Franklin. *The Negro Family in the United States.* Chicago: U of Chicago P, 1966.

Freedman, Ralph. *The Lyrical Novel: Studies in Hermann Hesse, André Gide, and Virginia Woolf.* Princeton: Princeton UP, 1973.

Freeman, Lucy, and Herbert Strean. *Freud and Women.* New York: Ungar, 1981.

Freud, Martin. *Glory Reflected.* London: Angus, 1957.

Freud, Sigmund. "The Aetiology of Hysteria." 1896. *Standard Edition* 3: 191–221.

———. "Analysis Terminable and Interminable." 1937. *Standard Edition* 23: 216–53.

———. "Analysis Terminable and Interminable." 1937. Trans. Joan Riviere. *Therapy and Technique.* Ed. Philip Rieff. New York: Macmillan, 1963.

———. "'A Child Is Being Beaten': A Contribution to the Study of the Origin of Sexual Perversions." 1919. *Standard Edition* 17: 177–204.

———. *Civilization and Its Discontents.* 1930. *Standard Edition* 21:57–145

———. *The Complete Letters of Sigmund Freud to Wilhelm Fliess.* Ed. Jeffrey Moussaieff Masson. Cambridge: Harvard UP, 1985.

———. "The Economic Problem of Masochism." 1924. *Standard Edition* 19: 157–70.

———. "Female Sexuality." 1931. *Standard Edition* 21: 233–43.

———. "Female Sexuality." 1931. Trans. Joan Riviere. *Sexuality and the Psychology of Love.* Ed. Philip Rieff. New York: Macmillan, 1963.

———. "Femininity." 1933. *Standard Edition* 22: 112–35.

———. "Fragment of an Analysis of a Case of Hysteria [Dora]." 1905. *Standard Edition* 7: 1–122.

———. "Hysterical Phantasies and Their Relation to Bisexuality." 1908. *Standard Edition* 9: 155–66.

———. "The Infantile Genital Organization." 1923. *Standard Edition* 19: 141–45.

———. *The Letters of Sigmund Freud, 1873–1939.* Ed. Ernst Freud. Trans. Tania Stern and James Stern. London: Hogarth, 1961.

———. "Mourning and Melancholia." 1917. *Standard Edition* 14: 237–60.

———. *New Introductory Lectures on Psychoanalysis.* 1933. *Standard Edition* 22: 5–182.

———. "On Narcissism: An Introduction." 1914. *Standard Edition* 14: 69–102.

———. "On Transformations of Instinct as Exemplified in Anal Erotism." 1917. *Standard Edition* 17: 127–33.

———. *The Origins of Psychoanalysis: Letters to Wilhelm Fliess, Drafts and Notes: 1887–1902.* Ed. Marie Bonaparte, Anna Freud, and Ernst Kris. Trans. Eric Mosbacher and James Strachey. New York: Basic, 1977.

———. "Some Psychical Consequences of the Anatomical Distinction between the Sexes." 1925. *Standard Edition* 19: 241–60.

———. *The Standard Edition of the Complete Psychological Works of Sigmund Freud.* 24 vols. Trans. and ed. James Strachey et al. London: Hogarth and The Institute for Psycho-Analysis, 1953–74.

———. *Three Essays on the Theory of Sexuality.* 1905. *Standard Edition* 7: 123–245.

———. *Totem and Taboo.* 1913. *Standard Edition* 13: vii–162.

———. "Wild Psycho-analysis." 1910. *Standard Edition* 11: 221–27.

Freud, Sigmund, and Joseph Breuer. *Studies on Hysteria.* 1893–95. *Standard Edition* 2: 1–311.

Froula, Christine. "When Eve Reads Milton: Undoing the Canonical Economy." *Critical Inquiry* 10 (1983): 321–48.

Frye, Northrop. *The Great Code: The Bible and Literature.* New York: Harcourt, 1982.

Fuller, Hester Thackeray, and Violet Hammersley, comps. *Thackeray's Daughter: Some Recollections of Anne Thackeray Ritchie.* Dublin: Euphorion, 1951.

Gallop, Jane. *The Daughter's Seduction: Feminism and Psychoanalysis.* Ithaca: Cornell UP, 1982.

Gardiner, Judith Kegan. "Self Psychology as Feminist Theory." *Signs* 12 (1987): 761–80.

———. "A Wake for Mother: The Maternal Deathbed in Women's Fiction." *Feminist Studies* 4 (1978): 146–65.

Gaskell, Elizabeth. *Cranford*. 1853. Ed. Peter Keating. Harmondsworth: Penguin, 1976.

———. *The Letters of Mrs. Gaskell*. Ed. J. A. V. Chapple and Arthur Pollard. Manchester: Manchester UP, 1966.

———. *The Life of Charlotte Bronte*. 1857. Harmondsworth: Penguin, 1975.

———. *North and South*. 1855. London: Dent, 1971.

———. *Ruth*. 1853. London: Dent, 1967.

———. *Wives and Daughters*. 1866. Ed. Frank Glover Smith. Harmondsworth: Penguin, 1969.

Gedo, John. *Portraits of the Artist*. New York: Guilford, 1983.

Geertz, Clifford. *Culture and Communication: The Logic By Which Symbols Are Connected*. Cambridge: Cambridge UP, 1976.

———. *The Interpretation of Cultures*. New York: Basic, 1973.

Gérin, Winifred. *Anne Bronte*. London: Lane, 1976.

———. *Anne Thackeray Ritchie*. New York: Oxford UP, 1981.

———. *Charlotte Bronte: The Evolution of Genius*. London: Oxford UP, 1967.

———. *Elizabeth Gaskell: A Biography*. Oxford: Clarendon, 1976.

Gilbert, Sandra M. "A Fine, White Flying Myth: The Life/Work of Sylvia Plath." *Shakespeare's Sisters*. Ed. Sandra M. Gilbert and Susan Gubar. Bloomington: Indiana UP, 1979. 245–60.

———. "In Yeats's House." *Coming to Light*. Ed. Diane Middlebrook and Marilyn Yalom. Ann Arbor: U of Michigan P, 1985. 145–66.

———. "Life's Empty Pack: Notes toward a Literary Daughteronomy." *Critical Inquiry* 11 (1985): 355–84. Published as chapter 10 in this volume.

Gilbert, Sandra M., and Susan Gubar. "'Forward into the Past': The Complex Female Affiliation Complex." *Historical Studies in Literary Criticism*. Ed. Jerome J. McGann. Madison: U of Wisconsin P, 1985.

———. *The Madwoman in the Attic: The Woman Writer and the Nineteenth-Century Literary Imagination*. New Haven: Yale UP, 1979.

———. "Tradition and the Female Talent: Modernism and Masculinism." *The War of the Words* 125–62.

———. *The War of the Words*. New Haven: Yale UP, 1988. Vol. 1 of *No Man's Land: The Place of the Woman Writer in the Twentieth Century*. 1 vol. to date. 1988– .

Girard, René. *Deceit, Desire, and the Novel: Self and Other in Literary Stucture*. Trans. Yvonne Freccero. Baltimore: Johns Hopkins UP, 1965.

Goldberg, Jonathan. *Endlesse Worke: Spenser and the Structures of Discourse*. Baltimore: Johns Hopkins UP, 1981.

———. *James I and the Politics of Literature*. Baltimore: Johns Hopkins UP, 1983.

Goldberg, Rita. *Sex and Enlightenment: Women in Richardson and Diderot*. London: Cambridge UP, 1984.

Golden, Daniel. "What Makes Mommy Run?" *Boston Globe Magazine*. 24 Apr. 1988: 13–31.

Golden, Morris. *Richardson's Characters*. Ann Arbor: U of Michigan P, 1963.

Goodell, William. *The American Slave Code in Theory and Practice, etc*. 1853. New York: Arno, 1969.

Goody, Jack, ed. *The Character of Kinship*. Cambridge: Cambridge UP, 1973.

Graves, Robert. *The Greek Myths.* 1955. Rev. ed. 2 vols. New York: Penguin, 1978.

Greenblatt, Stephen. *Renaissance Self-Fashioning: From More to Shakespeare.* Chicago: U of Chicago P, 1980.

———. *Sir Walter Ralegh: The Renaissance Man and His Roles.* New Haven: Yale UP, 1973.

Grimm, Jakob, and Wilhelm Grimm. "Allerleirauh." Trans. Margaret Hunt and James Stern. *The Complete Grimm's Fairy Tales.* Rev. ed. New York: Pantheon, 1972. 326–27.

Griswold del Castillo, Richard. *La Familia: Chicano Families in the Urban Southwest, 1848 to the Present.* Notre Dame: U of Notre Dame P, 1984.

Gubar, Susan. "The Birth of the Artist as Heroine: (Re)production, the *Kunstlerroman* Tradition, and the Fiction of Katherine Mansfield." *The Representation of Women in Fiction.* Ed. Carolyn G. Heilbrun and Margaret R. Higgonet. Baltimore: Johns Hopkins UP, 1983. 19–59.

Gutiérrez, Ramón A. "Marriage, Sex, and the Family: Social Change in Colonial New Mexico, 1660–1848." Diss. U of Wisconsin, Madison, 1980.

Gutiérrez-Christensen, Rita. "Eulogy for a Man from Jalostitlan." *Grito del Sol* 1.4 (1976): 59–68.

Hagstrum, Jean. *Sex and Sensibility: Ideal and Erotic Love from Milton to Mozart.* Chicago: U of Chicago P, 1980.

Haight, Gordon S. *George Eliot: A Biography.* New York: Oxford UP, 1968.

Hanawalt, Barbara. *The Ties That Bound: Peasant Families in Medieval England.* New York: Oxford UP, 1986.

Hardy, Barbara. "Mrs. Gaskell and George Eliot." *The Victorians.* Ed. Arthur Pollard. London: Barrie, 1970. 169–95.

Harper, Frances E. W. *Iola Leroy, or Shadows Uplifted.* 1892. New York: AMS, 1971.

Harris, Daniel. *Yeats: Coole Park and Ballylee.* Baltimore: Johns Hopkins UP, 1974.

Harris, Olivia. "Heavenly Father." Owen 46–60.

Havelock, Eric. *Preface to Plato.* New York: Oxford UP, 1963.

Hawthorne, Nathaniel. *The Centenary Edition of the Works of Nathaniel Hawthorne.* Ed. Roy Harvey Pearce et al. 16 vols. to date. Columbus: Ohio State UP, 1962– .

———. *Love Letters of Nathaniel Hawthorne.* 2 vols. Chicago: Society of the Dofobs, 1907.

———. *The Works of Nathaniel Hawthorne.* Introd. George Parsons Lathrop and including *Nathaniel Hawthorne and His Wife* by Julian Hawthorne. 15 vols. Boston: Houghton, 1881–84.

Heath, Stephen. *The Sexual Fix.* New York: Schocken, 1982.

Heilbrun, Carolyn. *Reinventing Womanhood.* New York: Norton, 1979.

Heisch, Allison. "Queen Elizabeth I: Parliamentary Rhetoric and the Exercise of Power." *Signs* 1 (1975): 31–55.

———. "Queen Elizabeth and the Persistence of Patriarchy." *Feminist Review* 4 (1980): 45–56.

Hellbom, Anna-Britta. *La participación cultural de las mujeres, indias y mestizas en el México precortesiano y postrevolucionario.* Ethnographical Museum Monograph Series 10. Stockholm, 1967.

Hennig, Margaret. *The Managerial Woman*. Garden City: Doubleday, 1977.

Herman, Judith Lewis, with Lisa Hirschman. *Father-Daughter Incest*. Cambridge: Harvard UP, 1981.

Hill, Christopher. "Clarissa Harlowe and Her Times." *Essays in Criticism* 5 (1955): 315–40.

———. "Sex, Marriage, and the Family in England." *Economic History Review* 2nd ser. 31 (1978): 450–63.

Hill, Katherine C. "Virginia Woolf and Leslie Stephen: History and Literary Revolution." *PMLA* 96 (1981): 351–62.

Hirsch, Marianne. "Ideology, Form, and *Allerleirauh:* Reflections on *Reading for the Plot*." *Children's Literature* 14 (1986): 163–68.

Holland, Norman. "Freud and H.D." *International Journal of Psycho-Analysis* 50 (1969). Rpt. in Ruitenbeek 449–62.

———. "H.D. and the 'Blameless Physician.'" *Contemporary Literature* 10 (1969): 474–506. Rpt. in Ruitenbeek 463–94.

Homans, Margaret. "'Her Very Own Howl': The Ambiguities of Representation in Recent Women's Fiction." *Signs* 9 (1983): 186–205.

Homer. *The Iliad*. Trans. Robert Fitzgerald. Garden City: Doubleday, 1974.

Hopkins, Pauline. *Contending Forces*. Lost American Fiction Series. Ed. Matthew J. Bruccoli. Carbondale: Southern Illinois UP, 1978.

Hughes, Paul L., and James F. Larkin, eds. *Tudor Royal Proclamations*. 3 vols. New Haven: Yale UP, 1964–69.

Hughes, Ted. "Notes on the Chronological Order of Sylvia Plath's Poems." *The Art of Sylvia Plath*. Ed. Charles Newman. London: Faber, 1970. 187–95.

Hull, Raymona E. *Nathaniel Hawthorne: The English Experience, 1853–1864*. Pittsburgh: U of Pittsburgh P, 1980.

———. "Una Hawthorne: A Biographical Sketch." *Nathaniel Hawthorne Journal* 6 (1976): 87–119.

Hunter, Dianne. "Hysteria, Psychoanalysis, and Feminism: The Case of Anna O." *The (M)other Tongue: Essays in Feminist Psychoanalytic Interpretation*. Ed. Shirley Garner, Claire Kahane, and Madelon Sprengnether. Ithaca: Cornell UP, 1985. 89–115.

Irigaray, Luce. *Ce Sexe qui n'en est pas un*. Paris: Minuit, 1977. Trans. as *This Sex Which Is Not One*. Trans. Catherine Porter and Carolyn Burke. Ithaca: Cornell UP, 1985.

———. "Psychoanalytic Theory: Another Look." *This Sex* 34–67.

———. *Speculum de l'autre femme*. Paris: Minuit, 1974. Trans. as *Speculum of the Other Woman*. Trans. Gillian C. Gill. Ithaca: Cornell UP, 1985.

———. "When Our Lips Speak Together." Trans. Carolyn Burke. *Signs* 6 (1980): 69–79.

Janeway, Elizabeth. "On 'Female Sexuality.'" *Women & Analysis: Dialogues on Psychoanalytic Views of Femininity*. Ed. Jean Strouse. New York: Grossman, 1974. 73–88.

Jay, Paul. *Being in the Text: Self-Representation from Wordsworth to Roland Barthes*. Ithaca: Cornell UP, 1984.

The Jerusalem Bible. Ed. Alexander Jones. Garden City: Doubleday, 1966.

Johnson, Paul. *Elizabeth I: A Study in Power and Intellect*. London: Weidenfeld, 1974.

Jones, Ernest. *The Life and Work of Sigmund Freud*. 3 vols. New York: Basic, 1953–57.

Jones, Gayle. *Corregidora*. New York: Random, 1975.

Joplin, Patricia Klindienst. "The Voice of the Shuttle Is Ours." *Stanford Literature Review* 1 (1984): 25–53.

Jordan, Rosan A. "The Vaginal Serpent and Other Themes from Mexican American Women's Lore." *Women's Folklore, Women's Culture*. Ed. Rosan A. Jordan and Susan J. Kalcik. Philadelphia: U of Pennsylvania P, 1985. 26–44.

Joyce, James. *Finnegans Wake*. New York: Viking, 1958.

Kahn, Coppélia. "The Rape in Shakespeare's *Lucrece*." *Shakespeare Studies* 9 (1976): 45–72.

Kantorowicz, Ernst. *The King's Two Bodies: A Study in Mediaeval Political Theology*. Princeton: Princeton UP, 1957.

Kaplan, Cora. "Wicked Fathers: A Family Romance." Owen 115–33.

Kelley, Alice van Buren. *The Novels of Virginia Woolf: Fact and Vision*. Chicago: U of Chicago P, 1973.

Kenner, Hugh. "Sincerity Kills." Lane 33–44.

Ker, I. T. "George Eliot's Rhetoric of Enthusiasm." *Essays in Criticism* 26 (1976): 39–52.

Kernberg, Otto F. *Borderline Conditions and Pathological Narcissism*. New York: Aronson, 1975.

———. *Object-Relations Theory and Clinical Psychoanalysis*. New York: Aronson, 1976.

Kingston, Maxine Hong. *The Woman Warrior: Memoirs of a Girlhood among Ghosts*. New York: Knopf, 1976.

Kinkead-Weekes, Mark. *Samuel Richardson: Dramatic Novelist*. Ithaca: Cornell UP, 1973.

Knoepflmacher, U. C. *George Eliot's Early Novels: The Limits of Realism*. Berkeley: U of California P, 1968.

———. "Unveiling Men: Power and Masculinity in George Eliot's Fiction." *Men and Women*. Ed. Janet Todd. Spec. issue of *Women and Literature* n.s. 2 (1981): 130–46.

Kohut, Heinz. *The Analysis of the Self: A Systematic Approach to the Psychoanalytic Treatment of Narcissistic Personality Disorders*. New York: International Universities, 1971.

———. "Creativeness, Charisma, Group Psychology: Reflections on the Self-Analysis of Freud." *Search* 2: 793–843.

———. *How Does Analysis Cure?* Ed. Arnold Goldberg. Chicago: U of Chicago P, 1984.

———. *The Restoration of the Self*. New York: International Universities, 1977.

———. *The Search for the Self: Selected Writings of Heinz Kohut, 1950–1978*. Ed. Paul H. Ornstein. 2 vols. New York: International Universities, 1978.

Kolodny, Annette. *The Lay of the Land: Metaphor as Experience and History in American Life and Letters*. Chapel Hill: U of North Carolina P, 1975.

Lacan, Jacques. *Écrits: A Selection*. Trans. Alan Sheridan. New York: Norton, 1977.

——. *Feminine Sexuality: Jacques Lacan and the école freudienne*. Trans. Jacqueline Rose. Ed. Juliet Mitchell and Jacqueline Rose. New York: Norton, 1982.

——. *The Language of the Self: The Function of Language in Psychoanalysis*. Trans. Anthony Wilden. New York: Dell, 1968.

——. "On a Question Preliminary to Any Possible Treatment of Psychosis." *Écrits* 179–225.

LaFaye, Jacques. *Quetzalcóatl and Guadalupe: The Formation of Mexican National Consciousness, 1531–1813*. Chicago: U of Chicago P, 1976.

Lane, Gary, ed. *Sylvia Plath: New Views on the Poetry*. Baltimore: Johns Hopkins UP, 1979.

Laplanche, Jean, and J. B. Pontalis. "Fantasy and the Origins of Sexuality." *International Journal of Psychoanalysis* 49 (1968): 1–18.

——. *The Language of Psycho-Analysis*. Trans. Donald Nicholson-Smith. New York: Norton, 1973.

Leach, Edmund. *Claude Lévi-Strauss*. 1970. Rev. ed. Penguin Modern Masters Series. Ed. Frank Kermode. Middlesex: Penguin, 1976.

——. "Complementary Filiation and Bilateral Kinship." Goody 53–58.

——. *Culture and Communication: The Logic By Which Symbols Are Connected*. Ed. Jack Goody and Geoffrey Hawthorn. Themes in Social Sciences 1. Cambridge: Cambridge UP, 1983.

——. "Genesis as Myth." *Structuralist Interpretations of Bible Myth*. Ed. Edmund Leach and D. Alan Aycock. New York: Cambridge UP, 1983. 1–13.

Leonard, Linda S. *The Wounded Woman: Healing the Father-Daughter Relationship*. Boulder: Shambhala, 1983.

Leonard, Marjorie. "Fathers and Daughters: The Significance of 'Fathering' in the Psychosexual Development of the Girl." *International Journal of Psycho-Analysis* 47 (1966): 325–34.

Letters and Papers, Foreign and Domestic, of the Reign of Henry VIII. Ed. J. S. Brewer, J. Gairdner and R. H. Brodie. 21 vols. London, 1862–1910.

Levin, Carole. "Queens and Claimants: Political Insecurity in Sixteenth-Century England." *Gender, Ideology, and Action: Historical Perspectives on Women's Public Lives*. Ed. Janet Sharistanian. New York: Greenwood, 1986. 41–66.

Levin, Gerald. *Richardson the Novelist: The Psychological Patterns*. Amsterdam: Rodopi, 1978.

Lévi-Strauss, Claude. *The Elementary Structures of Kinship*. 1949. Trans. James Harle Bell, John Richard von Sturmer, and Rodney Needham. Ed. Rodney Needham. Rev. ed. Boston: Beacon, 1969.

Lewis, R. W. B. *Edith Wharton: A Biography*. New York: Harper, 1975.

Lidoff, Joan. *Christina Stead*. New York: Ungar, 1982.

Lilienfeld, Jane. " 'The Deceptiveness of Beauty': Mother Love and Mother Hate in *To the Lighthouse*." *Twentieth Century Literature* 23 (1977): 345–76.

Lloyd, Genevieve. *The Man of Reason: "Male" and "Female" in Western Philosophy*. London: Methuen, 1984.

Lowell, James Russell. "A Fable for Critics." *The New Oxford Book of American Verse*. Ed. Richard Ellmann. New York: Oxford UP, 1976. 182–89.

MacC[arthy], D[esmond]. Foreword. Fuller and Hammersley 5–15.

McKendrick, Melveena. "Woman against Wedlock: The Reluctant Brides of Golden Age Drama." Beth Miller 115–46.

Madsen, William. *The Mexican-Americans of South Texas*. New York: Holt, 1964.

Mahler, Margaret. *Separation-Individuation*. New York: Aronson, 1979.

Maitland, Sara. "Two for the Price of One." Owen 18–28.

Mannoni, O. *Freud*. Trans. Renaud Bruce. New York: Pantheon, 1971.

Marcus, Leah S. *Childhood and Cultural Despair: A Theme and Variations in Seventeenth-Century Literature*. Pittsburgh: U of Pittsburgh P, 1978.

———. *Puzzling Shakespeare: Local Reading and Its Discontents*. U of California P, forthcoming.

Marcus, Steven. *Freud and the Culture of Psychoanalysis*. New York: Columbia UP, 1984.

———. "Literature and Social Theory: Starting In with George Eliot." *Representations: Essays on Literature and Society*. New York: Random, 1975. 183–213.

Marks, Patricia. "Una Hawthorne's 'House for Orphans Tiny.'" *ESQ* 25 (1979): 17–19.

Masson, Jeffrey Moussaieff. *The Assault on Truth: Freud's Suppression of the Seduction Theory*. New York: Farrar, 1983.

Mauss, Marcel. "Essai sur le don: Forme et raison de l'échange dans les sociétés archaïques." *Année sociologique* ns 1 (1925): 30–186.

Miller, Alice. *Thou Shalt Not Be Aware: Society's Betrayal of the Child*. 1981. Trans. Hildegarde Hannum and Hunter Hannum. New York: Farrar, 1984.

Miller, Beth, ed. *Women in Hispanic Literature: Icons and Fallen Idols*. Berkeley: U of California P, 1983.

Miller, Elaine K. *Mexican Folk Narrative from the Los Angeles Area*. Austin: U of Texas P, 1973.

Miller, J. Hillis. "Optic and Semiotic in *Middlemarch*." *The Worlds of Victorian Fiction*. Ed. Jerome H. Buckley. Cambridge: Harvard UP, 1975. 125–45.

Mirandé, Alfredo, and Evangelina Enríquez. *La Chicana: The Mexican-American Woman*. Chicago: U of Chicago P, 1979.

Mirandé, Alfredo, and Evangelina Enríquez. *La Chicana: The Mexican-American Woman*. Chicago: U of Chicago P, 1979.

Mitchell, Juliet. *Psychoanalysis and Feminism*. 1974. New York: Random, 1975.

Moi, Toril. "Representation of Patriarchy: Sexuality and Epistemology in Freud's Dora." *Feminist Review* 9 (1981): 60–74.

Montrose, Louis Adrian. "'Shaping Fantasies': Figurations of Gender and Power in Elizabethan Culture." *Representations* 1 (1983): 61–94.

Moraga, Cherríe. *Loving in the War Years*. Boston: South End, 1983.

Mossberg, Barbara. *Emily Dickinson: When a Writer Is a Daughter*. Bloomington: Indiana UP, 1982.

Mullen, Harryette. "Daughters in Search of Mothers." *Catalyst* 1 (1986): 45–49.

Murray, Meg McGavran, ed. *Face to Face: Fathers, Mothers, Masters, Monsters—Essays for a Nonsexist Future*. Contributions to Women's Studies 16. Westport: Greenwood, 1983.

Myers, Robert Manson, ed. *The Children of Pride: A True Story of Georgia and the Civil War*. New Haven: Yale UP, 1971.

Naunton, Sir Robert. *Fragmenta Regalia*. 1870. Ed. Edward Arber. New York: AMS, 1966.

Neale, J. E. *Elizabeth I and Her Parliaments*. 2 vols. London: Cape, 1953–57.

———. *Queen Elizabeth*. New York: Harcourt, 1934.

Nightingale, Florence. *Cassandra*. 1852. Westbury: Feminist, 1979.

Nuttall, A. D. *Overheard by God: Fiction and Prayer in Herbert, Milton, Dante and St. John*. London: Methuen, 1980.

Oates, Joyce Carol. "'At Least I Have Made a Woman of Her': Images of Women in Twentieth-Century Literature." *Georgia Review* 37 (1983): 7–30.

Okin, Susan Moller. "Patriarchy and Married Women's Property in England: Questions on Some Current Views." *Eighteenth-Century Studies* 17 (1983): 121–38.

Olivier, Christiane. *Les Enfants de Jocaste: L'Empreinte de la mère*. Paris: Denoel/Gonthier, 1980.

Ortner, Sherry B. "Is Female to Male as Nature Is to Culture?" *Woman, Culture, and Society*. Ed. Michelle Zimbalist Rosaldo and Louise Lamphere. Stanford: Stanford UP, 1974. 67–87.

Ortner, Sherry B., and Harriet Whitehead, eds. *Sexual Meanings: The Cultural Construction of Gender and Sexuality*. Cambridge: Cambridge UP, 1981.

Ovid. *Metamorphoses*. Trans. Rolfe Humphries. Bloomington: Indiana UP, 1955.

Owen, Ursula, ed. *Fathers: Reflections by Daughters*. New York: Pantheon, 1985.

Ozment, Steven. *When Fathers Ruled: Family Life in Reformation Europe*. Cambridge: Harvard UP, 1983.

Packer, Lona Mosk. *Christina Rossetti*. Berkeley: U of California P, 1963.

Paley, Grace. "A Conversation with My Father." 1972. Owen 233–39.

Paredes, Américo. *The Folktales of Mexico*. Chicago: U of Chicago P, 1970.

———. *A Texas-Mexican Cancionero*. Urbana: U of Illinois P, 1976.

Paz, Octavio. "The Flight of Quetzalcóatl and the Quest for Legitimacy." Foreword. LaFaye ix–xxii.

———. *The Labyrinth of Solitude*. Trans. Lysander Kemp. New York: Grove, 1961.

Pear, Robert. "His Heroes Are Social Democrats." *New York Times Book Review* 25 Oct. 1987.

Pembroke, Simon. "Women in Charge: The Function of Alternatives in Early Greek Tradition and the Ancient Idea of Matriarchy." *Journal of the Warburg and Courtauld Institutes* 30 (1967): 1–35.

Perry, Ruth. *Women, Letters, and the Novel*. New York: AMS, 1980.

Peters, Uwe. *Anna Freud: A Life Dedicated to Children*. New York: Schocken, 1985.

Phillips, John A. *Eve: The History of an Idea*. San Francisco: Harper, 1984.

Phillips, Rachel. "Marina/Malinche: Masks and Shadows." Beth Miller 97–114.

Pitt-Rivers, Julian. *The Fate of Shechem: Or, The Politics of Sex*. Essays in the Anthropology of the Mediterranean. Cambridge Studies in Social Anthropology Series. Cambridge: Cambridge UP, 1977.

Plath, Sylvia. *The Bell Jar*. 2nd ed. London: Faber, 1966.

———. *Collected Poems.* Ed. Ted Hughes. New York: Harper, 1981.

———. *Johnny Panic and the Bible of Dreams.* London: Faber, 1977.

———. *Journals.* Ed. Ted Hughes and Frances McCullough. New York: Dial, 1982.

———. *Letters Home.* Ed. Aurelia Plath. London: Faber, 1978.

Plowden, Alison. *The Young Elizabeth.* London: Macmillan, 1971.

Pollak, Vivian. *Dickinson: The Anxiety of Gender.* Ithaca: Cornell UP, 1984.

Pollard, Arthur. *Mrs. Gaskell: Novelist and Biographer.* Cambridge: Harvard UP, 1965.

Porter, David. *Dickinson: The Modern Idiom.* Cambridge: Harvard UP, 1981.

Porter, Roy. "Mixed Feelings: The Enlightenment and Sexuality in Eighteenth-Century Britain." Boucé 1–27.

Portillo Trambley, Estela. "The Paris Gown." *Rain of Scorpions.* Berkeley: Tonatiuh, 1975.

Prescott, H. F. M. *Mary Tudor.* 1952. Rev. ed. New York: Macmillan, 1962.

Price, Martin. "Clarissa and Lovelace." *To the Palace of Wisdom.* Carbondale: Southern Illinois UP, 1964. 277–85.

Rabine, Leslie W. "No Lost Paradise: Social Gender and Symbolic Gender in the Writings of Maxine Hong Kingston." *Signs* 12 (1987): 471–92.

Rackin, Phyllis. "Anti-Historians: Women's Roles in Shakespeare's Histories." *Theatre Journal* 87 (1985): 329–44.

Ragussis, Michael. "Family Discourse and Fiction in *The Scarlet Letter.*" *ELH* 49 (1982): 863–88.

Rainwater, Lee, and William L. Yancey, eds. *The Moynihan Report and the Politics of Controversy: A Transaction. Social Science and Public Policy Report.* Cambridge: MIT P, 1967. 47–94.

Ramos, Samuel. *Profile of Man and Culture in Mexico.* Austin: U of Texas P, 1962.

Ray, Gordon. *The Buried Life: A Study of the Relation between Thackeray's Fiction and His Personal History.* London: Oxford UP, 1952.

———. *Thackeray: The Age of Wisdom (1847–1863).* New York: McGraw, 1958.

———. *Thackeray: The Uses of Adversity (1811–1846).* New York: McGraw, 1955.

Redinger, Ruby V. *George Eliot: The Emergent Self.* New York: Knopf, 1975.

Rice, George P., Jr. *The Public Speaking of Queen Elizabeth.* 1951. New York: AMS, 1966.

Rich, Adrienne. "Compulsory Heterosexuality and Lesbian Existence." *Blood, Bread, and Poetry: Selected Prose, 1979–1985.* New York: Norton, 1986. 23–75.

———. *The Dream of a Common Language: Poems, 1974–1977.* New York: Norton, 1978.

———. *Of Woman Born: Motherhood as Experience and Institution.* New York: Norton, 1976.

Richardson, Samuel. *Clarissa.* 1747–48. Ed. Ernest Rhys. 4 vols. London: Dent, 1932.

———. *"Clarissa": Preface, Hints of Prefaces, and Postscript.* Ed. R. F. Brissenden. Augustan Reprint Society 103. Los Angeles: William Andrews Clark Memorial Library, 1964.

———. *Pamela or Virtue Rewarded.* 1740. New York: Norton, 1958.

———. *Selected Letters*. Ed. John Carroll. Oxford: Clarendon, 1964.

Ritchie, Anne Thackeray. *Biographical Introductions to the Works of William Makepeace Thackeray*. 13 vols. New York: Harper, 1894–98.

———. *A Book of Sibyls: Mrs. Barbauld, Mrs. Opie, Miss Edgeworth, Miss Austen*. 1883. *Works* 13.

———. *Biographical Introductions. The Complete Works of William Makepeace Thackeray*. (The Centenary Biographical Edition) 26 vols. London: Smith, 1910–11.

———. *Chapters from Some Unwritten Memoirs*. New York: Harper, 1895.

———. "Little Scholars." *Cornhill*, May 1860.

———. *Miss Angel*. 1875. *Works* 7.

———. *Mrs. Dymond*. 1885. *Works* 14–15.

———. *Old Kensington*. 1873. *Works* 3–4.

———. *Records of Tennyson, Ruskin and Robert and Elizabeth Browning*. London: Macmillan, 1892.

———. *The Story of Elizabeth*. 1863. *Works* 1.

———. *Thackeray and His Daughter: The Letters and Journals of Anne Thackeray Ritchie*. Ed. Hester Thackeray Ritchie, with Unpublished Drawings by Thackeray and Lady Ritchie. New York: Harper, 1924. Published in Britain under the title *Letters of Anne Thackeray Ritchie*.

———. *The Village on the Cliff*. 1867. *Works* 2.

———. *The Works of Miss Thackeray*. 15 vols. Leipzig: Tauchnitz, 1863–86.

Roazen, Paul. *Freud and His Followers*. New York: Knopf, 1975.

Robbins, Kittye Delle. "Tiamat and Her Children: An Inquiry into the Persistence of Mythic Archetypes of Woman as Monster/Villainess/Victim." Murray 47–69.

Roberts, Michele. "Outside My Father's House." Owen 89–98.

Róheim, Géza. *The Panic of the Gods*. New York: Harper, 1972.

Rose, Jacqueline. " 'Dora'—fragment of an analysis." *m/f* 2 (1978): 5–21.

Rose, Phyllis. *Woman of Letters: A Life of Virginia Woolf*. New York: Oxford UP, 1978.

Rossetti, Christina. *The Complete Poems*. 2 vols. Ed. R. W. Crump. Baton Rouge: Louisiana State UP, 1979–86.

———. *The Face of the Deep: A Devotional Commentary on the Apocalypse*. London: Society for Promoting Christian Knowledge, 1892.

———. *Letter and Spirit: Notes on the Commandments*. London: Society for Promoting Christian Knowledge, 1883.

———. *The Poetical Works*. 1904. Ed. William Michael Rossetti. London: Macmillan, 1911.

———. *Time Flies: A Reading Diary*. London: Society for Promoting Christian Knowledge, 1885.

Rossetti, William Michael. "Memoir." Christina Rossetti, *Poetical Works* xlv–lxxi.

Roustang, François. "Uncertainty." *October* 28 (1984): 91–105.

Rowland, Beryl. "The Other Father in Yeats's 'A Prayer for My Daughter.' " *Orbis Litterarum* 26 (1971): 285–89.

Rubel, Arthur J. *Across the Tracks: Mexican-Americans in a Texas City*. Austin: U of Texas P, 1966.

Rubin, Gayle. "The Traffic in Women: Notes on the 'Political Economy' of Sex." *Toward an Anthropology of Women*. Ed. Rayna Reiter. New York: Monthly Review, 1975. 157–210.

Ruddick, Sara. "Learning to Live with the Angel in the House." *Women's Studies* 4 (1977): 181–200.

Ruitenbeek, Henry, ed. *Freud as We Knew Him*. Detroit: Wayne State UP, 1973.

Rush, Florence. *The Best-Kept Secret: Sexual Abuse of Children*. Englewood Cliffs: Prentice, 1980.

Russell, Diana E. H. *The Secret Trauma: Incest in the Lives of Girls and Women*. New York: Basic, 1986.

Saccio, Peter. *Shakespeare's English Kings: History, Chronicle, and Drama*. New York: Oxford UP, 1977.

Sadoff, Dianne. *Monsters of Affection: Dickens, Eliot, and Bronte on Fatherhood*. Baltimore: Johns Hopkins UP, 1982.

Sale, William. "From Pamela to Clarissa." *The Age of Johnson*. Ed. F. W. Hilles. New Haven: Yale UP, 1949. 127–38.

Sayers, Dorothy L. "Are Women Human?" *Unpopular Opinions*. London: Gollancz, 1946. 106–15.

Scarry, Elaine. *The Body in Pain: The Making and Unmaking of the World*. New York: Oxford UP, 1985.

Schleiner, Winfrid. "*Divina Virago:* Queen Elizabeth as an Amazon." *SP* 75 (1978): 163–80.

Schoenbaum, Samuel. *William Shakespeare: A Compact Documentary Life*. Oxford: Oxford UP, 1975.

Schur, Max. *Freud: Living and Dying*. New York: International Universities, 1972.

Schwartz, Murray M., and Christopher Bolas. "The Absence at the Center: Sylvia Plath and Suicide." Lane 179–201.

Seidenberg, Robert, and Evangelos Papathomopoulos. "Daughters Who Tend Their Fathers: A Literary Survey." *Psychoanalytic Study of Society* 2 (1962): 135–60.

Shakespeare, William. *The Complete Works of Shakespeare*. Ed. David Bevington. London: Scott, 1980.

Shelley, Percy Bysshe. *The Complete Poetical Works*. Ed. Thomas Hutchinson. 1905. Rpt. London: Oxford UP, 1960.

Showalter, Elaine. *A Literature of Their Own: British Women Novelists from Bronte to Lessing*. Princeton: Princeton UP, 1977.

———. "Virginia Woolf and the Flight into Androgyny." *A Literature of Their Own* 263–97.

Silverman, Kaja. *The Subject of Semiotics*. New York: Oxford UP, 1983.

Slater, Philip. *The Glory of Hera*. Boston: Beacon, 1971.

Smith, Joseph H. "Fathers and Daughters." *Man and World: An International Philosophical Review* 13 (1980): 385–402.

Smith, Lacey Baldwin. *Henry VIII: The Mask of Royalty*. London: Cape, 1971.

Sophocles. *Oedipus at Colonus: The Theban Plays*. Trans. E. F. Watling. Baltimore: Penguin, 1947.

———. *The Theban Plays*. Trans. Robert Fagles. New York: Penguin, 1982.

Spiegel, Gabrielle M. "Genealogy: Form and Function in Medieval Historical Narrative." *History and Theory: Studies in the Philosophy of History* 22 (1983): 43–53.

Spivak, Gayatri Chakravorty. "Displacement and the Discourse of Woman." *The Politics of Displacement*. Ed. Peter Eisinger. New York: Academic, 1980. 169–95.

———. "Unmaking and Making in *To the Lighthouse*." *Woman and Language in Literature and Society*. Ed. Sally McConnell-Ginet, Ruth Borker, and Nelly Furman. New York: Praeger, 1980. 311–27.

Stallworthy, Jon. *Between the Lines*. Oxford: Clarendon, 1963.

Stead, Christina. *The Man Who Loved Children*. New York: Avon, 1966.

———. "A Waker and Dreamer." *Ocean of Story*. Ed. R. G. Geering. New York: Viking, 1985. 481–93.

Steiner, Nancy H. *A Closer Look at Ariel*. London: Faber, 1974.

Stevens, Evelyn P. "Marianismo: The Other Face of Machismo in Latin America." *Female and Male in Latin America*. Ed. Ann Pescartello. Pittsburgh: U of Pittsburgh P, 1973. 89–101.

Stone, Lawrence. *The Family, Sex and Marriage in England 1500–1800*. New York: Harper, 1977.

Strathern, Andrew. "Kinship, Descent, and Locality: Some New Guinea Examples." Goody 21–33.

Strathern, Marilyn. *Women in Between: Female Roles in a Male World: Mount Hagen, New Guinea*. 1972. Seminar Studies in Anthropology 2. London: Seminar, 1975.

Strong, Roy. *The Cult of Elizabeth*. Wallop, Hampshire: Thames, 1977.

———. *Portraits of Queen Elizabeth I*. Oxford: Clarendon, 1963.

"Study: Abused Children Unprotected, Unbelieved." *Valley News* [Lebanon, NH] 2 Nov. 1987: 11.

Stump, Reva. *Movement and Vision in George Eliot's Novels*. Seattle: U of Washington P, 1959.

Suleiman, Susan, ed. *The Female Body in Western Culture: Contemporary Perspectives*. Cambridge: Harvard UP, 1986.

Tate, Claudia. "Pauline Hopkins: Our Literary Foremother." *Conjuring: Black Women, Fiction, and Literary Tradition*. Ed. Marjorie Pryse and Hortense J. Spillers. Bloomington: Indiana UP, 1985. 53–67.

Taylor, Barbara. "Freud: Father." Owen 100–104.

Tennenhouse, Leonard. *Power on Display: The Politics of Shakespeare's Genres*. London: Methuen, 1986.

Thackeray, William Makepeace. *The Letters and Private Papers of William Makepeace Thackeray*. Ed. Gordon Ray. 4 vols. New York: McGraw, 1945–46.

———. *The Works of William Makepeace Thackeray*. With biographical introductions by his daughter, Lady Ritchie. (The Centenary Biographical Edition) 26 vols. London: Smith, 1910–11.

Thurman, Judith. *Isak Dinesen: The Life of a Storyteller*. New York: St. Martin's, 1982.

Ticknor, Caroline. *Glimpses of Authors*. Boston: Houghton, 1922.

Traugott, John. "*Clarissa*'s Richardson: An Essay to Find the Reader." *English Literature in the Age of Disguise*. Ed. Maximillian Novak. Berkeley: U of California P, 1977. 157–208.

Trible, Phyllis. *God and the Rhetoric of Sexuality*. 1978. Overtures to Biblical Theology 20. Philadelphia: Fortress, 1983.

Turner, Victor. *The Ritual Process: Structure and Anti-Structure*. Ithaca: Cornell UP, 1977.

Tyrrell, Wm. Blake. *Amazons: A Study in Athenian Mythmaking*. Baltimore: Johns Hopkins UP, 1984.

Van Ghent, Dorothy. "On Clarissa Harlowe." *The English Novel: Form and Function*. New York: Harper, 1961. 45–63.

Vásquez, Richard. *Chicano*. Garden City: Doubleday, 1970.

Villamontes, Helena M. "Growing." *Cuentos: Stories by Latinas*. Ed. Alma Gómez, Cherríe Moraga, and Mariana Romo Cardona. New York: Kitchen Table, 1983. 65–73.

Villanueva, Alma. "I Sing to Myself." *Third Chicano Literary Prize, 1976–77*. Irvine: Dept. of Spanish, U of California, 1977.

Villarreal, José A. *Pocho*. Garden City: Anchor-Doubleday, 1970.

Voragine, Jacobus de. *The Golden Legend*. Trans. Granger Ryan and Helmut Ripperger. New York: Longmans, 1941.

Wadlington, Warwick P. Letter to Lynda E. Boose. 22 July 1985.

Wagenknecht, Edward. *Nathaniel Hawthorne: Man and Writer*. New York: Oxford UP, 1961.

Walker, Alice. "The Child Who Favored Daughter." *In Love and Trouble*. New York: Harcourt, 1973. 35–47.

——. *The Color Purple*. New York: Harcourt, 1982.

——. "Writing *The Color Purple*." *In Search of Our Mothers' Gardens: Womanist Prose*. New York: Harcourt, 1983. 355–60.

Ward, Elizabeth. *Father-Daughter Rape*. London: Women's Press, 1984.

Warner, Marina. *Alone of All Her Sex: The Myth and Cult of the Virgin Mary*. New York: Knopf, 1976.

Warner, William Beatty. *Reading "Clarissa": The Struggles of Interpretation*. New Haven: Yale UP, 1979.

——. "Reading Rape: Marxist-Feminist Figurations of the Literal." *Diacritics* 13 (1983): 12–32.

Watt, Ian. *The Rise of the Novel*. Berkeley: U of California P, 1957.

Wharton, Edith. Rev. of *George Eliot*, by Leslie Stephen. *Bookman* 15 (May 1902): 247–51.

——. *Summer*. 1917. New York: Perennial, 1980.

Wilden, Anthony. Commentary, *Lacan: Language of the Self*.

Wilt, Judith. "He Could Go No Farther: A Modest Proposal about Lovelace." *PMLA* 92 (1977): 19–32.

Wind, Edgar. *Pagan Mysteries in the Renaissance*. 2nd ed. London: Faber, 1968.

Winnicott, D. W. "Mirror-Role of Mother and Family in Child Development." *Playing and Reality*. London: Tavistock, 1971. 111–18.

Wolff, Cynthia Griffin. Introd. Wharton, *Summer* v–xxvii.

Wolkstein, Diane, and Samuel Noah Kramer. *Inanna, Queen of Heaven and Earth: Her Stories and Hymns from Sumer.* New York: Harper, 1983.

Woolf, Leonard. *The Wise Virgins, A Story of Words, Opinions, and a Few Emotions.* London: Arnold, 1914.

Woolf, Virginia. *The Diary of Virginia Woolf.* Ed. Anne Olivier Bell. 5 vols. New York: Harcourt, 1977–84.

———. "'I Am Christina Rossetti.'" 1930. *Collected Essays.* Ed. Leonard Woolf. 4 vols. London: Chatto, 1966–67. 4: 54–60.

———. *Jacob's Room.* 1922. New York: Harcourt, 1978.

———. "Leslie Stephen." *The Captain's Death Bed and Other Essays.* New York: Harcourt, 1950. 69–75.

———. *Night and Day.* 1919. London: Hogarth, 1971.

———. *The Pargiters: The Novel-Essay Portion of "The Years."* Ed. Mitchell A. Leaska. New York: Harcourt, 1978.

———. "Professions for Women." 1932. *The Death of the Moth and Other Essays.* New York: Harcourt, 1942.

———. *A Room of One's Own.* 1929. New York: Harcourt, 1957.

———. "A Sketch of the Past." *Moments of Being: Unpublished Autobiographical Writings.* Ed. Jeanne Schulkind. New York: Harcourt, 1976.

———. *Three Guineas.* New York: Harcourt, 1938.

———. *To the Lighthouse.* New York: Harcourt, 1927.

———. *To the Lighthouse: The original holograph draft.* Transcr. and ed. Susan Dick. Toronto: U of Toronto P, 1982.

———. *The Years.* New York: Harcourt, 1937.

Wordsworth, William. *The Poetical Works.* Ed. E. de Selincourt. 2nd ed. Oxford: Clarendon, 1952.

Wright, Richard. *Native Son.* New York: Harper, 1966.

Yates, Frances A. *Astraea.* London: Routledge, 1975.

Yeager, Patricia, and Beth Kowalski-Wallace, eds. *Feminist Readings of the Father.* Carbondale: U of Southern Illinois P, forthcoming.

Yeats, W. B. *Collected Poems of W. B. Yeats.* London: Macmillan, 1950.

———. *Letters on Poetry from W. B. Yeats to Dorothy Wellesley.* London: Oxford UP, 1940.

———. *The Variorum Edition of the Poems.* Ed. Peter Allt and Russell K. Alspach. New York: Macmillan, 1957.

———. *A Vision.* 2nd ed. London: Macmillan, 1962.

———. Yeats Papers, National Library of Ireland, Dublin.

Young, Philip. *Hawthorne's Secret.* Boston: Godine, 1984.

Notes on Contributors

ELIZABETH ABEL is an associate professor of English at the University of California at Berkeley. She is the author of *Virginia Woolf and the Fictions of Psychoanalysis*, forthcoming from the University of Chicago Press, editor of *Writing and Sexual Difference*, and coeditor of *The Voyage In: Fictions of Female Development* and *The Signs Reader* and has published articles on Woolf, Lessing, and Rhys.

LYNDA E. BOOSE is an associate professor of English at Dartmouth College. Her publications include "The Father and the Bride in Shakespeare" in *PMLA*, plus articles in *English Literary Renaissance, Philological Quarterly, Modern Philology, Hamlet Studies, Shakespeare Studies, Renaissance Quarterly, Teaching Approaches to "King Lear,"* and *Vietnam in Remission*. She is currently writing a book on *Othello*.

EVAN CARTON is an associate professor of English at the University of Texas at Austin. His publications include *The Rhetoric of American Romance* (Johns Hopkins), "Henry James the Critic" (*Raritan*), "The Politics of Selfhood: Bob Slocum, T. S. Garp, and Auto-American Biography" (*Novel*), "Hawthorne and the Province of Romance" (*ELH*), and "Complicity and Responsibility in Pandarus' Bed and Chaucer's Art" (*PMLA*).

ELIZABETH BUTLER CULLINGFORD was educated at Oxford, taught for eight years at the University of Lancaster, England, and is currently an associate professor of English at the University of Texas at Austin. Her publications include *Yeats, Ireland and Fascism* (1981) and a casebook on the middle poetry of Yeats. She is the director of the Yeats Summer School in Sligo, Ireland.

JOANNE FEIT DIEHL is an associate professor of English at Bowdoin College. She has published essays on American women poets and nineteenth-century American literature, as well as a book on Emily Dickinson, *Dickinson and the Romantic Imagination* (Princeton, 1981). Currently she is completing a book on women poets and the American Sublime (forthcoming from Indiana University Press).

BETTY S. FLOWERS is an associate professor of English and director of the Plan II liberal arts honors program at the University of Texas at Austin. She is the author of *Browning and the Modern Tradition*, coauthor of *Four Shields of Power*, and editor of *The Power of Myth*. She has also published poetry, fiction, and articles on Barthelme, Rich, Christina Rossetti, novel writing, and poetry therapy.

CHRISTINE FROULA is an associate professor of English and of comparative literature and theory at Northwestern University. She has published books and essays on modern literature, contemporary theory, and feminist criticism. Her new book, *Joyce and Woolf: Gender, Culture, and Literary Authority,* is forthcoming from Columbia University Press.

JANE GALLOP, Herbert S. Autrey Professor of Humanities at Rice University, is the author of *The Daughter's Seduction: Feminism and Psychoanalysis* (1982), *Reading Lacan* (1985), and *Thinking through the Body* (1988).

JUDITH KEGAN GARDINER is an associate professor of English and women's studies at the University of Illinois at Chicago and writes about Renaissance English literature, feminist and psychoanalytic theory, and modern women writers. Her book *Rhys, Stead, Lessing and the Politics of Empathy* is forthcoming from Indiana University Press.

SANDRA M. GILBERT, a professor of English at Princeton University, is coauthor of *The Madwoman in the Attic: The Woman Writer and the Nineteenth-Century Literary Imagination* (Yale, 1979) and *The War of the Words,* vol. 1 of *No Man's Land: The Place of the Woman Writer in the Twentieth Century* (Yale, 1987), and coeditor of *The Norton Anthology of Literature by Women* (Norton, 1985), all with Susan Gubar; and author of other critical studies and collections, as well as four volumes of poetry, most recently *Blood Pressure* (Norton, 1988).

JANICE HANEY-PERITZ is an associate professor and chair of the Department of English at Beaver College. Her articles have appeared in *JEGP, Studies in Romanticism, ELH,* and *Women's Studies.*

CAROLYN G. HEILBRUN, also known to readers as award-winning mystery writer Amanda Cross, is Avalon Foundation Professor for the Humanities at Columbia University, past president of the Modern Language Association, and winner of the Guggenheim, Rockefeller, and NEH fellowships. In addition to numerous journal articles and chapters in books, her academic publications include *Towards a Recognition of Androgyny, Reinventing Womanhood,* and, most recently, *Writing a Woman's Life* (Norton, 1988).

KATHERINE C. HILL-MILLER, most recently a Fulbright fellow at the Universität zu Köln, has taught at the College of William and Mary and is an associate professor at the C. W. Post Center of Long Island University. She has published articles on Virginia Woolf, Jane Austen, James Joyce, and Thomas Hardy and is currently working on *The Double Bind of Love and Power: Some Literary Fathers and Daughters* (University of North Carolina Press).

LEAH S. MARCUS has taught at the University of Illinois at Chicago and the University of Wisconsin and is presently a professor of English at the University of Texas at Austin. She is the author of articles on Jonson, Herrick, Vaughan, Herbert, medieval drama, rape and the political milieu of Milton's *Comus,* and Shakespeare's androgynous heroines. Her books include *Childhood and Cultural Despair: A Theme and Variations in Seventeenth-Century Literature* (1978), *The Politics of Mirth: Jonson, Herrick, Milton, Marvell, and the Defense of Old Holiday*

Pastimes (1986), and *Puzzling Shakespeare: Local Reading and Its Discontents*, forthcoming from the University of California Press.

RAYMUND A. PAREDES is a professor of English and associate dean of the graduate division at UCLA. He has published extensively on Mexican-American subjects.

DIANNE F. SADOFF is professor of English at Colby College. She is the author of *Monsters of Affection: Dickens, Eliot, and Bronte on Fatherhood* (Johns Hopkins) and of essays in journals such as *PMLA, Signs, Genre, Papers on Language and Literature, Dickens Studies Annual, Massachusetts Review, Victorian Poetry*, and *Victorian Newsletter* on nineteenth- and twentieth-century literature, psychoanalysis, and feminist criticism. She is currently at work on a book about Freud's case histories and nineteenth-century narrative.

HORTENSE J. SPILLERS, winner of the National Magazine Award for Excellence in Fiction in 1976, is a professor of English at Cornell University. She is coeditor with Marjorie Pryse of *Conjuring: Black Women, Fiction, and Literary Tradition* (Indiana University Press, 1985). Her *In the Flesh: A Situation for Feminist Inquiry* is forthcoming from the University of Chicago Press.

DAVID WILLBERN is an associate professor of English, associate dean of arts and letters, and director of the Center for the Psychological Study of the Arts at SUNY-Buffalo. He has published essays on Shakespeare, Renaissance drama, D. H. Lawrence, Robert Duncan, Freud, and psychoanalytic criticism. He is currently completing a book titled *Poetic Will: Shakespeare and the Play of Language*.